Principles of Microeconomics

Principles of Microeconomics

Dirk Mateer
Pennsylvania State University

Lee Coppock
University of Virginia

W. W. NORTON & COMPANY
NEW YORK • LONDON

W. W. Norton & Company has been independent since its founding in 1923, when William Warder Norton and Mary D. Herter Norton first published lectures delivered at the People's Institute, the adult education division of New York City's Cooper Union. The firm soon expanded its program beyond the Institute, publishing books by celebrated academics from America and abroad. By midcentury, the two major pillars of Norton's publishing program—trade books and college texts—were firmly established. In the 1950s, the Norton family transferred control of the company to its employees, and today—with a staff of four hundred and a comparable number of trade, college, and professional titles published each year—W. W. Norton & Company stands as the largest and oldest publishing house owned wholly by its employees.

ISBN 978-0-393-92141-0

W. W. Norton & Company, Inc., 500 Fifth Avenue, New York, NY 10110-0017
wwnorton.com

W. W. Norton & Company Ltd., Castle House, 75/76 Wells Street, London W1T 3QT

1 2 3 4 5 6 7 8 9 0

CONTENTS

Principles of Microeconomics

Photo to come

Introductory
MATERIAL

CHAPTER 1

The Five Foundations of Economics

Economics is the dismal science.

Perhaps you have heard of the "dismal science"? This derogatory term was first used by historian and essayist Thomas Carlyle in the 19th century. He called economics the dismal science after he read a prediction from economist Thomas Malthus stating that because our planet had limited resources, continued population growth would ultimately lead to widespread starvation.

Malthus was a respected thinker, but he was unduly pessimistic. The world population was one billion in 1800 and it is seven billion today. One of the things that Malthus did not take into account was increases in technology and productivity. Today, the efficiency of agricultural production enables seven billion people to live on this planet. Economists, like meteorologists, often get a bad rap; when we are right, no one notices, but when we are wrong, people demand answers. This textbook will provide the tools you need to be able to make your own assessments about the economy. What other discipline helps you discover how the world works, how to be an informed citizen, and how to live your life to the fullest? Economics can improve your understanding of the stock market and help you make better personal finance decisions. If you are concerned about Social Security, this textbook explains how it works. If you are interested in learning more about health care, the answers are here. Economics provides answers to all of these questions and much more.

In this chapter, you will learn about the five foundations of economics—incentives, trade-offs, opportunity cost, marginal thinking, and how trade creates value. You will find that many of the more

Predicting the future is a tough business.

complex problems presented later in the text are derived from one of these foundations. Once you have these five concepts mastered, the most involved processes can be reduced to many smaller, more easily understood parts. Think of this chapter as a road map that provides a broad overview of your journey into economics. Let's get started!

BIG QUESTIONS

* What is economics?
* What are the five foundations of economics?

Scarcity
refers to the limited nature of society's resources.

Economics
is the study of how people allocate their limited resources to satisfy their nearly unlimited wants.

Microeconomics
is the study of the individual units that comprise the economy.

Macroeconomics
is the study of the broader economy.

What Is Economics?

Economists study how decisions are made. Examples of economic decisions include whether or not you should buy or lease a car, sublet your apartment, and buy that Gibson guitar you've been eyeing. And, just as individuals must choose what to buy within the limits of the income they possess, society as a whole must determine what to produce from its limited set of resources.

Of course, life would be a lot easier if we could have whatever we wanted whenever we wanted it. Unfortunately, life does not work that way. Our wants and needs are nearly unlimited, but the resources available to satisfy these wants and needs are limited. The term used to describe the limited nature of society's resources is **scarcity**. Even the most abundant resources, like the water we drink and the air we breathe, are not always abundant enough everywhere to meet the wants and needs of every person. So how do individuals and societies make decisions about scarce resources? This is the basic question economists seek to answer. **Economics** is the study of how people allocate their limited resources to satisfy their nearly unlimited wants.

Microeconomics and Macroeconomics

The study of economics is divided into two subfields: *microeconomics* and *macroeconomics*. **Microeconomics** is primarily concerned with the decisions of individuals, households, and businesses. **Macroeconomics** looks at the broader

Water is scarce . . .

economy, including phenomena such as inflation, growth, employment, interest rates, and the productivity of the economy as a whole. To see if you understand the difference, consider a worker who gets laid off and becomes unemployed. Is this an issue that would be addressed in microeconomics or macroeconomics? The question seems to fit parts of both definitions. The worker is an individual, which is micro, but employment is one of the broad areas of concern for economists, which is macro. Don't let this confuse you. Since only one worker is laid off, this is a micro issue. If many workers had been laid off and this led to a higher unemployment rate across the entire economy, it would be an issue broad enough to be studied by macroeconomists.

. . . and so are diamonds!

PRACTICE WHAT YOU KNOW

Microeconomics and Macroeconomics: The Big Picture

Identify whether each of the following statements is a microeconomic or macroeconomic issue.

This mosaic of the flag illustrates the difference between micro and macro.

The national savings rate is less than 2% of disposable income.

Answer: The national savings rate is a statistic based on the average amount each household saves as a percentage of income. As such, this is a broad measure of savings and something that is discussed in macroeconomics.

Jim was laid off from his last job and is currently unemployed.

Answer: Jim's personal financial circumstances are discussed in microeconomics.

Apple decides to open up 100 new stores.

Answer: Even though Apple is a very large corporation and 100 new stores will create many new jobs, Apple's decision is discussed in microeconomics because the basis for Apple's decision is best understood as part of the firm's competitive strategy.

> **The government passes a jobs bill designed to stabilize the economy during a recession.**
>
> **Answer:** You might be tempted to ask how many jobs are being created before deciding, but that is not relevant to this question. The key part of the statement refers to "stabilizing the economy during a recession." This is an example of a *fiscal policy*, in which the government takes an active role in managing the economy. Therefore, this is discussed in macroeconomics.

The Five Foundations of Economics

To help break the study of economics into smaller chunks, we've created a road map for you to follow. If you keep these concepts in mind, you'll find that understanding economics is rewarding and fun. The rest of the chapter introduces the five principles that collectively form a solid foundation for thinking like an economist.

Incentives Matter

Incentives Matter

When you are faced with a decision, you usually make the choice that you think will most improve your situation. In making your decision, you respond to **incentives**—factors that motivate you to act or to exert effort. For example, the choice to study for an exam you have tomorrow instead of spending the evening with your friends is based on the belief that doing well on the exam will provide a greater benefit. You are incentivized to study because you know that an A in the course will raise your grade-point average and make you a more attractive candidate on the job market when you are finished with school. We can further divide incentives into two paired categories: *positive and negative*, and *direct and indirect*.

Incentives
are factors that motivate a person to act or exert effort.

Positive and Negative Incentives

Positive incentives are those that encourage action. For example, end-of-the year bonuses motivate employees to work hard throughout the year, higher oil prices cause suppliers to extract more oil, and tax rebates encourage citizens to spend more money. Negative incentives also encourage action. For instance, the fear of receiving a speeding ticket keeps motorists from driving too fast, and the dread of a trip to the dentist causes people to brush their teeth regularly. In each case, a potential negative consequence spurs individuals to action.

Grades: carrot or stick?

Conventional wisdom tells us that "learning is its own reward," but try telling that to most students. Teachers are aware that incentives, both positive and negative, create additional interest among their students to learn the course material. Positive incentives include bonus points, gold stars, public praise, and extra credit. Many students respond to these encouragements by studying more. However, positive incentives are not enough. Suppose that your instructor never gave any grade lower than an A. Your incentive to participate actively in the course, do assignments, or earn bonus points would be small. For positive incentives to work, they generally need to be coupled with negative incentives. This is why instructors require students to complete assignments, take exams, and write papers. Students know that if they do not complete these requirements they will get a lower grade, perhaps even fail the class.

Direct and Indirect Incentives

In addition to having positive and negative consequences, incentives can also be direct or indirect. For instance, if one gas station lowers its prices, it will get business from customers who would not usually stop there. This is a direct incentive. Cheap gasoline prices also work as an indirect incentive, since lower prices might encourage consumers to use more gas.

Direct incentives are easy to recognize. "Cut my grass and I'll pay you $30" is an example of a direct incentive. Indirect incentives are much harder to recognize. But learning to recognize them is one of the keys to mastering economics. For instance, consider the indirect incentives at work in welfare programs. Almost everyone agrees that societies should provide a safety net for those without employment or whose income isn't enough to meet basic needs. Thus, a society has a direct incentive to alleviate suffering caused by poverty. But how does a society provide this safety net without taking away the incentive to work? In other words, if the amount of welfare a person receives is higher than the amount that person can hope to make from a job, the welfare recipient might decide to stay on welfare rather than work. The indirect incentive to stay on welfare creates an *unintended consequence*—people who were supposed to use government assistance as a safety net until they can find a job use it as a permanent source of income.

Policymakers have the tough task of deciding how to balance such conflicting incentives. To decrease the likelihood that a person will stay on welfare, policymakers could cut benefits. But this might

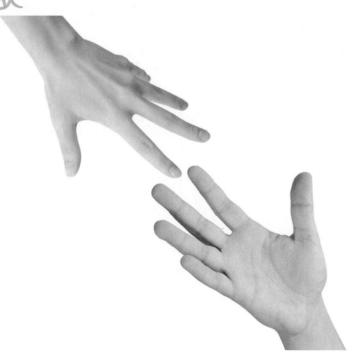

Public assistance: a hand in time of need or an incentive not to work?

leave some people without enough to live on. For this reason, many government programs specify limits on the amount of time people can receive benefits. Ideally, this allows the welfare programs to continue to meet basic needs while creating incentives that encourage recipients to search for jobs and learn skills that will enable them to do better in the workforce. We'll learn more about the issues of welfare in Chapter 15.

ECONOMICS IN THE REAL WORLD

How Incentives Create Unintended Consequences

Let's look at an example of how incentives operate in the real world, and how they can lead to consequences no one envisioned when implementing them. Two Australian researchers[1] noted a large spike in births on July 1, 2004. The sudden spike was not an accident. Australia, like many other developed countries, has seen the fertility rate fall below replacement levels, which is the birthrate necessary to keep the population from declining. In response to falling birthrates, the Australian government decided to enact a "baby bonus" of $3,000 for all babies born on or after July 1, 2004.

The policy was designed to provide a direct incentive for couples to have children and, in part, to compensate them for lost pay and the added costs of raising a newborn. However, this direct incentive had an indirect incentive attached to it too—the couples found a way to delay the birth of their children until after July 1, perhaps jeopardizing the health of the child and mother. This was clearly an unintended consequence. Despite reassurances from the government that would-be parents would not put financial gain over the welfare of their newborn child, over 1,000 births were switched from late June to early July through a combination of additional bed rest and pushing scheduled caesarian sections back a few days. This behavior is testament to the power of incentives. ✳

On a much smaller scale, the same dynamic exists in the United States around January 1 each year. Parents can claim a tax credit for the entire year, whether the child is born in January or in December. This gives parents an incentive to ask for labor to be induced or for a caesarian section late in December so they can have their child before January 1 and thereby capitalize on the tax advantages. Ironically, hospitals and newspapers often celebrate the arrival of the first baby of the new year even though his or her parents are actually financially worse off.

Incentives and Innovation

Incentives also play a vital role in innovation, the engine of economic growth. There is no better example than Steve Jobs and Apple: between them, he and the company he founded held over 300 patents at the time of his death in 2011.

---

[1] See Joshua S. Gans and Andrew Leigh, "Born on the First of July: An (un)natural experiment in birth timing," *Journal of Public Economics* 93 (2009): 246–263.

The Five Foundations of Economics / **11**

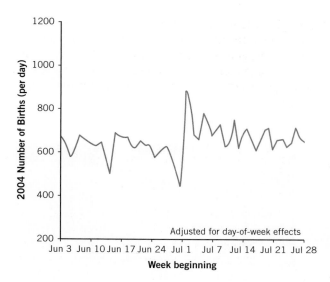

The plunge and spike in births are evidence of an unintended consequence.

In the United States, the patent system and copyright laws guarantee inventors a specific period of time in which they can exclusively sell their work. This system encourages innovation by creating a powerful financial reward for creativity. Without patents and copyright laws inventors would bear all the costs, and almost none of the rewards, for their efforts. Why would firms invest in research and development or artists create new music if their work could be immediately copied and sold by others? To reward the perspiration and inspiration required for innovation, society needs patents and copyrights to create the right incentives for economic growth.

In recent years, new forms of technology have made the illegal sharing of copyrighted material quite easy. As a result, illegal downloads of music and movies are widespread. When musicians, actors, and studios cannot effectively protect what they have created, they earn less. So, illegal downloads reduce the incentive to produce new content. Will the next John Lennon or Jay-Z work so hard? Will the next Dan Brown or J. K. Rowling hone their writing craft so diligently, if there is so much less financial reward for success? Is the "I want it for free" culture causing the truly gifted to be less committed to their craft, thus depriving society of excellence? Maintaining the right rewards, or incentives, for hard work and innovation is essential for advancing our society.

Incentives Are Everywhere

There are many sides to incentives. However, financial gain almost always plays a prominent role. In the film *All the President's Men*, the story of the Watergate scandal that led to the unraveling of the Nixon Administration in the early 1970s, a secret source called "Deep Throat" tells Bob Woodward, an investigative reporter at the *Washington Post*, to "follow the money." Woodward responds, "What do you mean? Where?" Deep Throat responds, "Just . . . follow the money." That is exactly what Woodward did. He eventually pieced

Incentives

Ferris Bueller

Many people believe that the study of economics is boring. In *Ferris Bueller's Day Off* (1986), Ben Stein plays a high school economics teacher who sedates his class with a monotone voice while referring to many abstract economic theories and uttering the unforgettable, "Anyone, anyone?" while trying to engage his students. The scene is iconic because it is a boring economics lecture that inspires Ferris and his friends to skip school, which leads to his wild adventures. In fact, the movie is really about incentives and trade-offs.

Was this your first impression of economics?

everything together and followed the "money" trail all the way to President Nixon.

Understanding the incentives that led the participants in the Watergate scandal to do what they did led Bob Woodward to the truth. Economists use the same process to explain how people make decisions, how firms operate, and how the economy functions. In fact, understanding incentives, from positive to negative and direct to indirect, is the key to understanding economics. If you remember only one concept from this course, it should be that incentives matter!

Trade-Offs

Life Is About Trade-offs

In a world of scarcity, each and every decision incurs a cost. Even time is a scarce resource; after all, there are only twenty-four hours in a day. So, deciding to read *Harry Potter* now means that you won't be able to read *Twilight* until later. More generally, doing one thing often means that you will not have the time, resources, or energy to do something else. Casting a ballot in an election is another good example, since you can only vote for one person at a time. Similarly, paying for a college education can require spending tens of thousands of dollars that might be used elsewhere.

Trade-offs are an important part of policy decisions. For instance, one decision that some modern governments face is the trade-off between a clean environment and a higher level of income for its citizens. Transportation and industry cause air pollution. Developed nations can afford expensive technology that reduces pollution-causing emissions. But developing nations, like China, generally have to focus their resources elsewhere. In the months leading up to the 2008 Olympics, China temporarily shut down many factories and discouraged the use of automobiles in order to reduce smog in Beijing. The air improved and the Olympics showcased China's remarkable growth into a global economic powerhouse. However, the cost of keeping the air clean—shutting down factories and restricting transportation—is not a trade-off China is willing to make for longer than a few weeks. The Chinese people, like the rest of us, want clean air *and* a high standard of living, but for the time being most Chinese seem willing to accept increased pollution if it means a higher income. In more developed countries, higher standards of living already exist and the cost of pollution control will not cause the economy's growth to slow down to unacceptable levels. People in these countries are much less likely to accept more pollution in order to raise the level of income even further.

Clean air or economic prosperity?

Opportunity Cost

The existence of trade-offs requires making hard decisions. Choosing one thing means giving up something else. Suppose that you receive two invitations, the first to spend the day hiking, and the second to go to a concert. Since both events occur at the same time, accepting one invitation means that you cannot accept the other. No matter which event you choose, you will have to sacrifice the other option. In this example you can think of the cost of going to the concert as the lost opportunity to be on the hike. Likewise, the cost of going hiking is the lost opportunity to go to the concert. No matter what choice you make, there is an **opportunity cost**, or next-best alternative, that must be sacrificed.

Opportunity Cost

Every time we make a choice, we experience an opportunity cost. The key to making the best possible decision is to minimize your opportunity cost by selecting the option that gives you the largest benefit. If you prefer going to a concert, you should go to the concert. What you give up, the hike, has less value to you than the concert; so it has a lower opportunity cost.

The hiking/concert choice is a simple and clear example of opportunity cost. Usually it takes deliberate effort to see the world through the opportunity-cost prism. But it is a worthwhile practice because it will help you make better decisions. For example, imagine you are a small-business owner. Your financial officer informs you that you have had a successful year and earned a sizable profit. So everything is good, right? Not so fast. An economist will tell you to ask yourself, "Could I have made *more* profit doing something differently?" Good economic thinkers ask this question of themselves all the time. Could I be using my time, talents, or energy on another activity that would be more profitable for me?

Opportunity cost is the highest-valued alternative that must be sacrificed in order to get something else.

Do you have the "moves like Jagger?"

Profits on a balance sheet are only part of the story, because they only measure how well a business does relative to the bottom line. Accountants cannot measure what *might* have been better. For example, suppose that your business had decided against an opportunity to open a new store. A few months later a rival opened a very successful store in the same location you had considered. Your profits were good for the year, but if you had made the investment in the new store, your profits could have been even better. So when economists mention opportunity cost, they are assessing whether the alternatives are better than what you are doing, which considers a larger set of possible outcomes.

Mick Jagger did just that. Before joining the Rolling Stones, he attended the London School of Economics. For Mick, the opportunity cost of becoming a musician was a degree in economics. Given the success of the Rolling Stones, it is hard to fault his decision!

ECONOMICS IN THE REAL WORLD

Breaking the Curse of the Bambino: How Opportunity Cost Causes a Drop in Hospital Visits While the Red Sox Play

If you are injured or severely ill, you head straight to the emergency room, right? Not so fast! A study published in the *Annals of Emergency Medicine* found that visits to the ER in the Boston area fall as much as 80% when the Red Sox are playing. Part of the decline is attributable to more people sitting inside at home—presumably watching the ballgame—instead of engaging in activities that might get them hurt. But the study was able to determine that this did not explain the entire decline in emergency room visits. It turns out that a surprising number of people are willing to put off seeking medical attention for a few hours. Apparently, for some people the opportunity cost of seeking medical attention is high enough to postpone care until after the Red Sox game. ✳

Economic thinking requires a purposeful evaluation of the available opportunities to make the best decision possible.

Marginal Thinking

Marginal Thinking

The process of systematically evaluating a course of action is referred to as **economic thinking**. By weighing the costs and benefits of any action, a rational decision-maker can determine the best choice from the opportunities available. Economic thinkers use a process called *marginal analysis* to break down decisions into smaller parts. Often the choice is not between doing and not doing something, but between doing more or less of something. For instance, if you work a part-time job while in school, you probably wrestle with the question of how many hours you should work. If you work a little more, you can earn additional income. If you work a little less, you have more time to study. Working more has a tangible benefit—more money, and a tangible cost—poorer grades. All of this should sound familiar from our earlier discussion about trade-offs. The work-study trade-off affects how much money you have and what kind of grades you make. An economist would say that your decision—weighing how much money you want against the grades you want—is a decision at the *margin*. What exactly

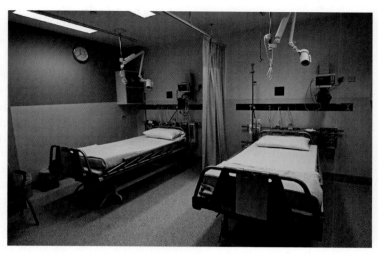

What is wrong with this picture?

MB/mc

does the word "margin" mean? There are many different definitions. To a reader, the margin is the blank space bordering a page. "Margin" can also be thought of as the size of a victory. In economics, **marginal thinking** requires decision-makers to evaluate whether the benefit of one more unit of something is greater than its cost. This can be quite challenging, but understanding how to analyze decisions at the margin is essential to becoming a good economist.

> **Marginal thinking** requires decision-makers to evaluate whether the benefit of one more unit of something is greater than its cost.

For example, have you ever wondered why people straighten their places, vacuum, dust, scrub the bathrooms, clean out their garages, and wash their windows, but leave the dust bunnies under the refrigerator? The answer lies in thinking at the margin. Moving the refrigerator out from the wall to clean requires a significant effort for a small benefit. Guests who enter the kitchen can't see behind your refrigerator. So most of us ignore the dust bunnies and clean the visible areas of our homes. In other words, when economists say that you should think at the margin, what we really mean is that people weigh the costs and benefits of their actions and choose to do the things with the greatest payoff. For most of us, that means we are willing to live with dust bunnies. The *marginal cost* of cleaning under the refrigerator, or on top of the cabinets, or even behind the seat cushions is too high and the added value of making the effort, or the *marginal benefit*, is too low to justify the additional cleaning.

Economics helps us understand why dust bunnies are safe when they are hidden from view.

ECONOMICS IN THE REAL WORLD

Why Buying *This* Textbook Is Such a Good Decision

New textbooks are expensive. The typical textbook purchasing pattern works as follows: you buy a textbook at the start of the term, often at full price, and sell it back at the end of the term for half the price you paid. Ouch. Nobody likes to make a bad investment, and textbooks depreciate the moment that they are bought. Even non-economists know not to buy high and sell low— but that is the textbook cycle for most students.

One solution would be to avoid buying textbooks in the first place. But that is not practical, nor is it a good decision. To understand why, let's use marginal analysis to break the decision into two separate components: the decision to buy and the decision to resell.

Let's start with the decision to buy. A rational buyer will only purchase a textbook if the expected value of the information included in the book is greater than the cost. For instance, say the book contains mandatory assignments or information that is useful for your major and you decide that it is worth $200 to you. If you are able to purchase the book for $100, the gain from buying the textbook would be $100. But what if the book is supplemental reading and you think it is worth only $50? If you valued the book at $50 and it costs $100, purchasing the book would entail a $50 loss. If students only buy the books from which they receive gains, every textbook bought will increase the welfare of someone.

A similar logic applies to the resale of textbooks. At the end of the course, once you have learned the information inside the book, the value of hanging on to it is low. You might think it is worth $20 to keep it for future reference, but if you can sell it for $50, the difference represents a gain of $30. In this case, you would decide to sell.

We have seen that buying and selling are two separate decisions made at the margin. If you combine these two decisions and argue that the purchase price ($100) and resale price ($50) are related, as most students typically think they are, you will arrive at a faulty conclusion that you have made a poor decision. That is simply not true.

Textbooks may not be cheap, but they create value twice, once when bought and again when sold. This is a win-win outcome. Since we assume that decision-makers will not make choices that leave them worse off, the only way to explain why students buy textbooks and sell them again later is because they benefit at the margin from both sides of the transaction. ✳

Why do students buy and sell textbooks?

Trade Creates Value

Imagine trying to find food in a world without grocery stores. The task of getting what you need to eat each day would require visiting many separate locations. Traditionally, this need to bring buyers and sellers together was met by weekly markets, or bazaars, in central locations like town squares. **Markets** bring trading partners together and help to create order out of chaos. As commerce spread throughout the ancient world, trade routes developed. Markets grew from infrequent gatherings, where exchange was done by trading goods and services for other goods and services, into more sophisticated systems that use cash, credit, and other financial instruments. Today when we think of markets we often think of eBay or craigslist, where goods can be transferred from one person to another with the click of a mouse. For instance, if you want to find a rare DVD of season 1 of *Entourage*, there is no better place to look than eBay, which allows users to search for just about any product, bid on it, and then have it sent directly to their homes.

Trade is the voluntary exchange of goods and services between two or more parties. Voluntary trade among rational individuals is beneficial to everyone involved. Imagine you are on your way home from class and you want to pick up a gallon of milk. You know that milk will be more expensive at a convenience store than it will be at the grocery store five miles away, but you are in a hurry to study for your economics exam and are willing to pay up to $5.00 for the convenience of getting it quickly. At the store, you find that the price is $4.00 and you happily purchase the milk. This ability to buy for less than the price you are willing to pay provides a positive incentive to make the purchase. But what about the seller? If the store owner paid $3.00 to buy the milk from a supplier, and you are willing to pay the $4.00 price that he has set in order to make a profit, the store owner has an incentive to sell. This simple voluntary transaction has made both sides better off.

By fostering the exchange of goods, trade helps to create additional growth through specialization. **Comparative advantage** refers to the situation in which an individual, business, or country can produce at a lower opportunity cost than a competitor. Comparative advantage harnesses the power of specialization. As a result, it is possible to be a physician, teacher, or plumber and not worry about how to do everything yourself. The physician becomes proficient at dispensing medical advice, the teacher at helping students, and the plumber at fixing leaks. The physician and teacher call the plumber when they need work on their plumbing. The teacher and plumber see the doctor when they are sick. The physician and the plumber send their children to school to learn from the teacher. This trading of services increases the welfare of everyone in society. Trade creates gains for everyone involved.

Trade Creates Value

Markets
bring buyers and sellers together to exchange goods and services.

Trade
is the voluntary exchange of goods and services between two or more parties.

Comparative advantage
refers to the situation where an individual, business, or country can produce at a lower opportunity cost than a competitor.

Our economy depends on specialization.

The same process is at work among businesses. For instance, Starbucks specializes in making coffee and Honda makes automobiles. You would not want to get your morning cup of joe at Honda any more than you would want to buy a car from Starbucks!

ex specialization

Specialization exists at the country level as well. Some countries have highly developed workforces capable of managing and solving complex processes. Other countries have large pools of relatively unskilled labor. As a result, businesses that need skilled labor gravitate to countries where they can easily find the workers they need. Likewise, firms with production processes that rely on unskilled labor look for employees in less-developed countries. By harnessing the power of increased specialization, global companies and economies are able to increase production and growth.

However, globalized trade is not without controversy. When goods and jobs are free to move across borders, not everyone benefits equally. Consider the case of an American worker who loses her job when her position is outsourced to a call center in India. The worker who loses her job has to find new employment—a process that will require significant time and energy. On the other hand, the new position in the call center in India provides a job and an income that improve the life of another worker. Also, the American firm enjoys the advantage of being able to hire lower-cost labor elsewhere. The firm's lower costs often translate into lower prices for domestic consumers. None of those advantages make the outsourcing of jobs any less painful for affected workers, but it is nevertheless important for the health of the economy in the long run.

The Benefits of Trade

ECONOMICS IN THE MEDIA

Trade Makes Us Better Off

What would happen if you could trade something you had, and get something better in return? This is exactly what happens in this short classroom demonstration filmed in one of your textbook author's classes.

Check out this video on YouTube: http://www .youtube.com/watch?v=Bdl6UamG6BI. It shows the incentives behind trade. (The impact of incentives on deadweight loss shown in the video will be discussed in greater detail in Chapter 6.)

Ever wondered what your textbook author's class looks like?

PRACTICE WHAT YOU KNOW

The Opportunity Cost of Attending College

Question: What is the opportunity cost of attending college?

Answer: When people think about the cost of attending college, they usually think of tuition, room and board, textbooks, and travel-related expenses. While those expenses are part of going to college, they are not the full opportunity cost of attending college. The opportunity cost is the next-best alternative that is sacrificed. This means that the opportunity cost—or what you potentially could have done if you were not in college—includes the lost income you could have earned working a full-time job. If you take the cost of attending college plus the forgone income lost while in college, it is a very expensive proposition. Setting aside the question of how much more you might have to pay for room and board at college than elsewhere, consider the costs of tuition and books. Those fees can be $30,000 or more at many of the nation's most expensive colleges. Add those out-of-pocket expenses to the forgone income from a full-time job that might pay $30,000, and your four years in college can easily cost a quarter of a million dollars.

In college? You could be working instead!

Conclusion

Is economics the dismal science?

We began this chapter with this misconception. Now that you have begun your exploration of economics, you know that this is not true. Economists ask, and answer, big questions about life. This is what makes the study of economics so fascinating. Understanding how an entire economy operates and functions may seem like a daunting task. It is not nearly as hard as it sounds. If you remember the first time you drove a car, the process is similar. When you are learning to drive, everything seems difficult and unfamiliar. Learning economics is the same way. However, once you learn a few key principles, and practice them, you can become a good driver quite quickly. In the next chapter we will use the ideas developed here to explore the issue of trade in greater depth.

Midcareer Earnings by Selected Majors

A 2008 study by PayScale surveyed 1.2 million full-time employees across the United States who possessed a bachelor's degree but no advanced degree. Twenty popular subjects are listed in the graph below.

Not all majors are created equal. However, the majors that produce more income initially do not necessarily keep their advantage a decade or two later. That means that today's newly minted economics majors, with a median starting salary of $48,000, will likely surpass those who majored in computer science in earnings by the time they reach midcareer. The same can said about political science majors, who have a lower starting salary than accounting majors but eventually surpass them. In the long run, pay growth matters to income level as much as, if not more than, starting salary. In terms of salary, any decision about what to major in that only looks at starting pay is misleading. How much you make over your whole career is what matters!

Will you make more majoring in economics or finance?

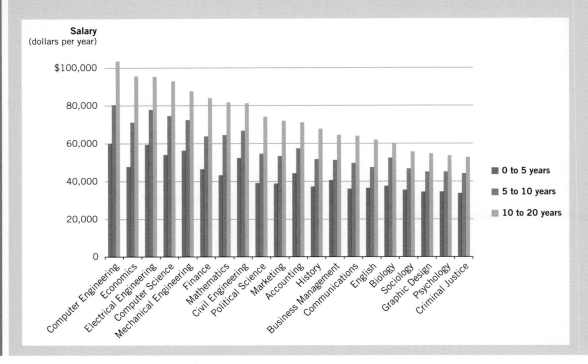

Salary
(dollars per year)

Legend:
- 0 to 5 years
- 5 to 10 years
- 10 to 20 years

Majors (left to right): Computer Engineering, Economics, Electrical Engineering, Computer Science, Mechanical Engineering, Finance, Mathematics, Civil Engineering, Political Science, Marketing, Accounting, History, Business Management, Communications, English, Biology, Sociology, Graphic Design, Psychology, Criminal Justice

ANSWERING THE BIG QUESTIONS

1. What is economics?

✳ Economics is the study of how people allocate their limited resources to satisfy their nearly unlimited wants. Because of the limited nature of society's resources, even the most abundant resources are not always abundant enough everywhere to meet the wants and needs of every person. So how do individuals and societies make decisions about how to use the scarce resources at our disposal? This is the basic question economists seek to answer.

2. What are the five foundations of economics?

The five foundations of economics are: incentives matter; life is about trade-offs; opportunity cost; marginal thinking; and trade creates value.

✳ Incentives matter because they help economists explain how decisions are made.

✳ Trade-offs exist when a decision-maker has to choose a course of action.

✳ Each time we make a choice we experience an opportunity cost, or a lost chance to do something else.

✳ Marginal thinking requires a decision-maker to weigh the extra benefits against the extra costs.

✳ Trade creates value because participants in markets are able to specialize in the production of goods and services that they have a comparative advantage in making.

Each of the five foundation concepts developed in this chapter will reappear throughout the book and enable you to solve complex problems.

Every time we encounter one of the five concepts you will see an icon of a house to remind you of what you have learned. As you become more adept at economic analysis, it will not be uncommon to use two or more of these central ideas to explain the economic world around us.

Incentives Matter
Life Is about Trade-offs
Opportunity Cost
Marginal Thinking
Trade Creates Value

CONCEPTS YOU SHOULD KNOW

Comparative advantage (p. 17) Macroeconomics (p. 6) Opportunity cost (p. 13)
Economics (p. 6) Marginal thinking (p. 15) Scarcity (p. 6)
Economic thinking (p. 14) Market (p. 17) Trade (p. 17)
Incentives (p. 8) Microeconomics (p. 6)

QUESTIONS

1. How would you respond if your instructor gave daily quizzes on the course readings? Is this a positive or a negative incentive?

2. Explain why many seniors often earn lower grades in their last semester before graduation. Hint: this is an incentive problem.

3. What is the opportunity cost of reading this textbook?

4. Comment on the following statement: "Trade is like football: one team wins and the other loses."

5. Give a personal example of how pursuing your self-interest has made society better off.

STUDY PROBLEMS

∗ 1. What role do incentives play in each of the following situations?
   a. You learn that you can resell a ticket to next week's homecoming game for twice what you paid.
   b. A state government announces a "sales tax holiday" for back-to-school shopping during one week each August.

2. Compare your standard of living with that of your parents when they were the same age as you are now. Ask them or somebody you know around their age to recall where they were living and what they owned. What has happened to the average standard of living over the last 25 years? Explain your answer.

3. By referencing events in the news or something from your personal experiences, describe one example of each of the five foundations of economics.

∗ 4. Suppose that Colombia is really good at growing coffee but not very good at making computer software, and that Canada is good at making computer software but not very good at growing coffee. If Colombia decided to grow only coffee and Canada only made computer software, would both countries be better or worse off? Can you think of a similar example from your life?

5. After some consideration you decide to hire someone to help you move. Wouldn't it be cheaper to move yourself? Do you think this is a rational choice?

∗ 6. The website www.ultrinsic.com has developed an "*ult*erior motive that causes the person to have an int*rinsic* love of knowledge." At Ultrinsic, students pay a small entry fee to compete in grades-based contests for cash prizes. Suppose that 20 students from your economics class each pay $20 to enter a grades-based contest. This would create a $400 prize pool. An equal share of the $400 pot is awarded at the end of the term to each contestant who earns an A in the course. If four students earn A's, they each receive $100. If only one student earns an A, that person gets the entire $400 pot. What economic concept is Ultrinsic harnessing in order to encourage participants to learn more?

SOLVED PROBLEMS

1.a. Since your tickets are worth more than you paid for them, you have a direct positive incentive to resell them.

b. The "tax holiday" is a direct positive incentive to buy more clothes during the back-to-school period. An unintended consequence of this policy is that fewer purchases are likely to be made both before and after the tax holiday.

4. If Columbia decided to specialize in the production of coffee, it could trade coffee to Canada in exchange for computer software. This process illustrates gains from specialization and trade. Both countries have a comparative advantage in producing one particular good. Columbia has ideal coffee growing conditions and Canada has a workforce that is more adept at writing software. Since each country specializes in what it does best, they are able to produce more than what they could produce by trying to make both products on their own.

6. Ultrinsic is using the power of incentives to motivate learning. Earning a letter grade is a positive motivation to do well, or a penalty—or negative incentive—when you do poorly. Ultrinsic takes this one step further and the student who earns an A also receives a small cash payment—a positive incentive. This provides extra motivation to study hard and achieve an A, since it pays, as opposed to earning a B or lower.

CHAPTER 2

Model Building and Gains from Trade

Trade always results in winners and losers.

When most people think of trade, they think of it as a zero-sum game. For instance, suppose that you and your friends are playing Magic.

Players collect cards with special powers in order to assemble decks to play the game. Magic players love to trade their cards and it is often the case that novice players do not know which cards are the most powerful or rare. When someone swaps one of the desirable cards, the other player is probably getting a much better deal. In other words, there is a winner and a loser. Now think of international trade. Many people believe that the rich nations exploit the natural resources of poor countries and even steal their most talented workers. The rich countries are winners and the poor countries lose. Still others think of trade as the redistribution of goods. If you trade your kayak for a friend's bicycle, no new goods are created; how can this possibly create value? After all, someone must have come out ahead in the trade.

In this chapter we will see that trade is not an imbalanced equation of winners and losers. Trade generally results in only winners. We will begin by looking at how economists use the scientific method to help explain the world we live in. These foundations will give us the tools we need to explore the more nuanced reasons why trade creates value.

Photo to come

BIG QUESTIONS

* **How do economists study the economy?**
* **What is a production possibilities frontier?**
* **What are the benefits of specialization and trade?**
* **What is the trade-off between having more now or later?**

How Do Economists Study the Economy?

Economics is a social science that uses the scientific method. Economists build models, analyze how well those models work, and refine our understanding of the economy based on the information we collect. In order to understand how the economy functions, economists make many simplifying assumptions. This approach helps identify the key relationships that drive decisions and focuses our attention on the relationships that matter most. In this section you will begin to learn about how economists approach their discipline and the tools they use.

The Scientific Method in Economics

On the television show *MythBusters*, popular myths are put to the test by Jamie Hyneman and Adam Savage. In Savage's words, "We replicate the circumstances, then duplicate the results." The entire show is dedicated to scientifically testing the myths. At the end of each episode, the myth is confirmed, labeled plausible, or busted. For instance, during a memorable episode Hyneman and Savage explored the reasons behind the *Hindenburg* disaster. The *Hindenburg* was a German passenger airship that caught fire and was destroyed as it attempted to dock in New Jersey on May 6, 1937. Thirty-six people died during the disaster.

Some people have hypothesized that the painted cotton fabric used to wrap the zeppelin sparked the fire. Others believed that the hydrogen used to give the airship lift was the primary cause of the disaster. To test the hypothesis that the fabric and paint were to blame, Hyneman and Savage built two small-scale models. The first model was filled with hydrogen and had a non-flammable skin; the second model used a replica of the original fabric for the skin, but did not contain any hydrogen. They then compared the burn times of their models with the original footage of the disaster.

After examining the results, they determined that the myth of the incendiary paint was "busted"; the model containing the hydrogen burned twice as fast as the one with just the painted cotton fabric skin.

Economists work in much the same way; they use the scientific method to answer questions about observable phenomena and to explain how the world works. The scientific method consists of several steps. First, researchers observe a phenomenon that interests them. Based on these observations, they develop a hypothesis, which is an explanation for the phenomenon. Then, they construct a model to test the hypothesis. Finally, they design experiments to test how well the model (which is based on the hypothesis) works. After collecting the data from the experiments, they can verify, revise, or refute the hypothesis. After many tests, they may agree that the hypothesis is well supported enough to qualify as a theory.

The scientific method was used to discover why the *Hindenburg* caught fire.

The economist's laboratory is the world around us and ranges from the economy as a whole to the decisions made by firms and individuals. As a result, economists cannot always design experiments to test their hypotheses. Often they must gather historical data or wait for real-world events to take place—for example, the Great Recession of 2008–2009—in order to better understand the economy.

Positive and Normative Analysis

As scientists, economists strive to approach their subject with objectivity. This means that they rigorously avoid letting personal beliefs and values influence the outcome of their analysis. In order to be as objective as possible, economists deploy *positive analysis*. A **positive statement** can be tested and validated. Each positive statement can be thought of as a description of "what is." For instance, the statement "the unemployment rate is 7.0%" is a positive statement because it can be tested by gathering data. In contrast, a **normative statement** cannot be tested or validated; it is about "what ought to be." For instance, the statement "an unemployed worker should receive financial assistance to help make ends meet" is a matter of opinion. One can reasonably argue that financial assistance to the unemployed is beneficial for society as a whole because it helps eliminate poverty. On the other hand, many would argue that financial assistance to the unemployed provides the wrong incentives. If the financial assistance provides enough to meet basic needs, workers may end up spending more time unemployed than they otherwise would. Neither opinion is right or wrong; they are differing viewpoints based on values, beliefs, and opinions.

Economists are concerned with positive analysis. Normative questions are the realm of policy-makers, voters, and philosophers. For example, if the unemployment rate rises, economists try to understand the conditions that

A positive statement can be tested and validated.

Normative statements are opinions that cannot be tested or validated.

created the situation. Economics does not attempt to determine who should receive unemployment assistance, which is a normative question. Economics, done properly, is confined to positive analysis.

Economic Models

Thinking like an economist means learning how to analyze complex issues and problems. Many economic topics, such as international trade, Social Security, job loss, and inflation are complicated. To analyze these phenomena and to determine the effect of various policy options related to them, economists use models, or simplified versions of reality. Models help us analyze the component parts of the economy.

A good model should be simple to understand, flexible in design, and able to make powerful predictions. Let's consider one of the most famous models in history, designed by Wilbur and Orville Wright. Before the Wright brothers made their famous first flight in 1903, they built a small wind tunnel out of a six-foot-long wooden box. Inside the box they placed an aerodynamic measuring device and used a small fan to supply the wind. The brothers then tested over two hundred different wing configurations to determine the lifting properties of each design. Using the data on aerodynamics they collected, the Wright brothers were able to determine the best type of wing to use on their aircraft.

Similarly, economic models provide frameworks that allow us to predict the effect that changes in prices, production processes, and government policies have on real-life behavior. Economists do this by building models that are simple to understand, flexible, and powerful.

Ceteris Paribus

Ceteris paribus is the process of examining a change in one variable in a model, while assuming that all the other variables remain constant.

Using a controlled setting that holds many other variables constant allowed the Wright brothers to experiment with different wing designs. By altering only a single element, they could test whether or not the change in design was advantageous. The process of examining a change in one variable while holding everything else constant is known as *ceteris paribus*, from the Latin meaning "other things being equal." This idea is central to model building. If the Wright brothers had changed many variables simultaneously and found that the wing worked better, they would have no way of knowing which change was responsible for the improved performance. For this reason, engineers generally modify only one element at a time and test it to see which design is most successful.

Like the Wright brothers, economists start with a simplified version of reality. Economists build models, change one variable at a time, and ask whether the change in the variable had a positive or negative impact on performance. Perhaps the best-known economic model is supply and demand, which economists use to explain how markets function. We'll get to supply and demand in Chapter 3.

Endogenous versus Exogenous Factors

Endogenous factors are the variables controlled for inside a model.

Models must account for things that we can control and things that we can't. The Wright brothers' wind tunnel was critical to their success because it allowed them to control for as many *endogenous* factors as possible before attempting to fly. Factors that we know about and can control are **endogenous factors**. For example, the wind tunnel allowed the Wright brothers to see how well each wing design—an important part of the model—performed under controlled conditions.

Once the Wright brothers had determined the best wing design, they built the full-scale airplane that took flight at Kitty Hawk, North Carolina. That plane, known as the "Flyer," was no longer in a controlled environment. It was subject to the gusting wind and other *exogenous* factors that made the first flight so challenging. Factors beyond our control—outside the model—are known as **exogenous factors**.

Building an economic model is very similar to the process Wilbur and

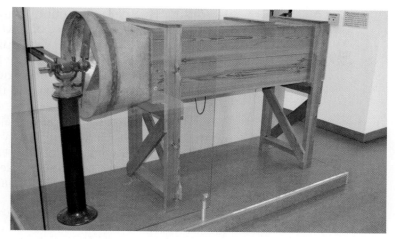

The Wright brothers' wind tunnel

Orville used. We need to be mindful of three factors. First, we need to consider what we include in the model. Second, we need to be aware of the assumptions we make when choosing what to include in the model. Third, we need to recognize the outside conditions that can affect our model's performance. In the case of the first airplane, the design was an endogenous factor because it was within the Wright brothers' control. The weather (wind, air pressure, and other atmospheric conditions) was an exogenous factor because it was something that the Wright brothers could not control. Because the world is a complex place, an airplane model that flies perfectly in a wind tunnel may not fly reliably once it is exposed to the elements. Therefore, if we add more exogenous variables, or factors—for example wind and rain—to test our model's performance, the test becomes more realistic.

Exogenous factors are the variables that are not accounted for in a model.

The Danger of Faulty Assumptions

In every model we make certain choices about which variables to include and how to model them. Ideally, we would like to include all the important variables inside the model and exclude all of the variables that should be ignored.

However, no matter what we include, using a model that contains faulty assumptions can lead to spectacular policy failures. There is no better example than the financial crisis and Great Recession that began in 2008. We will go into this in much greater detail in later chapters, so don't sweat the details here. Instead, focus on the big picture.

In the years leading up to the crisis, banks sold and repackaged mortgage-backed securities under the faulty assumption that real estate prices would always rise. In fact, the computer models used by many of the banks did not even have a variable for declining real estate prices. Investors around the globe bought these securities because they thought they were safe. This sounds perfectly reasonable in a world where real estate prices rise on an annual basis.

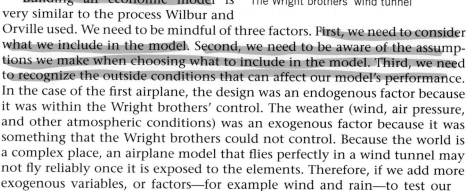

Some investors believed that real estate prices could only rise.

Unfortunately, that assumption turned out to be false. From 2006 to 2008, real estate prices fell. Because of one faulty assumption, the entire financial market teetered on the edge of collapse. This is the danger of poor modeling.

Models can be useful, but as the current financial crisis shows, they are also potentially dangerous. Models necessarily simplify the world by using a set of assumptions. It is critical that the assumptions be correct. But because a model is always a simplification, decision-makers must be careful about assuming that a model can present a solution for complex problems. As you go through this book, we will slowly increase the complexity of the models we build. The material you learn in early chapters is only a small part of the much bigger picture. Economics, like life, is complex. The more you understand and know, the easier it is to make fully informed decisions.

PRACTICE WHAT YOU KNOW

Positive versus Normative Statements

Question: Which of the following statements are positive?

1. Winters in Arkansas are too cold.
2. Everyone should work at a bank to see the true value of money.
3. The current exchange rate is .7 pounds per dollar.
4. On average, people save 15% when they switch to Geico.
5. Everyone ought to have a life insurance policy.
6. University of Virginia graduates earn more than Duke University graduates.
7. Harvard University is the top education institution in the country.
8. The average temperature in Fargo, N.D., in January is 56 degrees.

You should eat five servings of fruit or vegetables a day. Is that a positive or normative statement?

Answers

1. *Winters in Arkansas are too cold.* **Answer:** The word "too" is a matter of opinion. This is a normative statement.
2. *Everyone should work at a bank to see the true value of money.* **Answer:** While working at a bank might give someone an appreciation for the value of money, the word "should" is an opinion. This is a normative statement.
3. *The current exchange rate is .7 pounds per dollar.* **Answer:** You can look up the current exchange rate and verify if this statement is true or false. This is a positive statement.
4. *On average, people save 15% when they switch to Geico.* **Answer:** This was a claim made by the insurance company Geico in one of its commercials. Don't let that fool you. It is still a testable claim. If you had the data from

Geico, you could see if the statement was correct or not. This is a positive statement.

5. *Everyone ought to have a life insurance policy.* **Answer:** It sounds like a true statement, or at least a very sensible one. However, the word "ought" makes it an opinion. This is a normative statement.

6. *University of Virginia graduates earn more than Duke University graduates.* **Answer:** You can look up the data and see which university's graduates earn more. This is a positive statement.

7. *Harvard University is the top education institution in the country.* **Answer:** Many national rankings indicate that this is true, but others do not. Since different rankings are based on different assumptions, it is not possible to identify a definitive "top" school. This is a normative statement.

8. *The average temperature in Fargo, N.D., in January is 56 degrees.* **Answer:** The statement is wrong. North Dakota is much colder than that. However, the statement can be verified by looking at the climatology data. This is a positive statement.

What Is a Production Possibilities Frontier?

Now it's time for our first economic model. However, before you go on, you might want to review the appendix on graphing at the end of this chapter. It includes graph-reading skills and related concepts, such as the slope of a line, that are used in this section. Graphs are one of the key tools in economics because they provide a visual display of the relationship between two variables over time. Your ability to read a graph and understand the model it represents is crucial to learning economics.

In Chapter 1 we learned that economics is about the trade-offs individuals and societies face every day. For instance, you may frequently have to decide between spending more time studying to get better grades or going to a party with your friends. The more time you study, the less time you have for your friends. Similarly, a society has to determine how to allocate its resources. The decision to build new roads will mean there is less money available for new schools and vice versa.

A **production possibilities frontier** is a model that illustrates the combinations of outputs that a society can produce if all of its resources are being used efficiently. In order to preserve *ceteris paribus*, we assume that the technology available for production and the quantity of resources remain constant. These assumptions allow us to model trade-offs more clearly.

Let's begin by imagining a society that produces only two goods—pizzas and chicken wings. This may not seem very realistic, since a real economy is comprised of millions of different goods and services, but the benefit of this approach is that it allows us to understand the trade-offs in the production process without making the analysis too complicated.

Figure 2.1 shows the production possibilities frontier for our two-product society. Remember that the number of people and the total resources in this

Trade-Offs

A **production possibilities frontier** illustrates the various combinations of output that a society can produce if all of its resources are being used efficiently.

two-product society are fixed. Later we will relax these assumptions and make our model more realistic. If the economy uses all of its resources to produce pizzas, it can produce 100 pizzas and zero wings. If it uses all of its resources to produce wings, it can make 300 wings and zero pizzas. These outcomes can be found by locating points A and B on the production possibilities frontier. It is unlikely that the society will choose either of these extreme outcomes because it is human nature to enjoy variety.

If society decides to spend some of its resources producing pizzas and some of its resources making wings, its economy will end up with a combination of pizzas and wings that can be placed somewhere along the production possibilities frontier (PPF) between points A and B. At point C, for example, society would deploy its resources to produce 70 pizzas and 90 wings. At point D, the combination would be 50 pizzas and 150 wings. Each point along the production possibilities frontier represents a possible set of outcomes that society can choose if it uses all of its resources efficiently.

Notice that some combinations of pizza and wings cannot be produced. This is because resources within society are scarce. A society would enjoy point E, but given the available resources, it cannot produce at that output level. Points beyond the production possibilities frontier are desirable but not feasible, given the resources and technology society has available.

At any combination of wings and pizzas along the production possibilities frontier, the society is using all of its resources in the most productive way possible. These points are considered efficient because society is producing the largest possible output from its resources. But what about point F, and all the other points located in the blue-shaded region? These points represent outcomes inside the production possibilities frontier, which are an inefficient use of society's resources. Consider, for example, the resource of labor. If

FIGURE 2.1

The Production Possibilities Frontier for Pizza and Wings

The production possibilities frontier shows the trade-off between producing pizzas and wings. Any combination of pizzas and wings is possible along, or inside, the curve. Combinations of pizza and wings beyond the production possibilities frontier, for example at point E, are not possible with the current set of resources. Point F and the other points located in the blue-shaded region are inefficient.

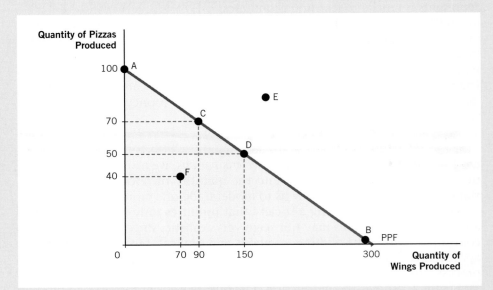

employees spend many hours at work surfing the web instead of doing their jobs, the output of pizzas and wings will drop and output will no longer be efficient. If the workers had used all of their time efficiently, they would have been able to produce the maximum amount of pizza and wings.

Whenever society is producing on the production possibilities frontier, the only way to get more of one good is to accept less of the other. Since an economy operating along the frontier will be efficient at any point, economists do not favor one point over another. But a society may favor one particular point over another because it prefers that combination of goods. For example, if wings suddenly become more popular, the movement from point C to point D will represent a desirable trade-off. Society will have 20 fewer pizzas (from 70 to 50) but 60 additional wings (from 90 to 150).

The Production Possibilities Frontier and Opportunity Cost

Since our two-good society produces only pizzas and wings, the trade-offs that occur along the production possibilities frontier represent the opportunity cost of producing one good instead of the other. As we noted in Chapter 1, an opportunity cost is the highest-valued alternative given up to pursue another course of action. In Figure 2.2, when society moves from point C to point D, it gives up 20 pizzas; this is the opportunity cost of producing more wings. The movement from D to C has an opportunity cost of 60 wings.

We have assumed that there would be a constant trade-off between the number of pizzas and the number of wings produced. However, that is not

Trade-Offs

Opportunity cost

FIGURE 2.2

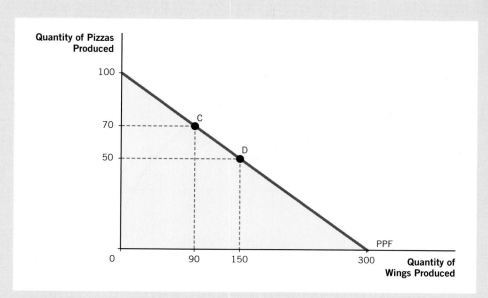

Opportunity Costs and the Production Possibilities Frontier

In moving from point C to point D, society gains 60 wings but loses 20 pizzas. The 20 pizzas are the opportunity cost. If society moves from point D to point C, society gains 20 pizzas but gives up 60 wings. The opportunity cost is the 60 wings.

most
bester
least
worst

typically the case. Not all resources in society are perfectly adaptable for use in making pizzas and wings. Some workers are good at making pizzas and others are not so good. When society tries to make as many pizzas as possible, it will be using both. That is, to get more pizzas society will have to use workers who are increasingly less skilled at making them. This means that pizza production does not expand at a constant rate. You can see this in the new production possibilities frontier in Figure 2.3; it is bowed outward rather than a straight line.

Since resources are not perfectly adaptable, production does not expand at a constant rate. For example, in order to produce 20 extra pizzas, society can move from point E (30 pizzas) to point D (50 pizzas). But moving from point E (280 wings) to point D (250 wings) means giving up 30 wings. So, moving from E to D has an opportunity cost of 30 wings. Suppose that the society decides it wants more pizza and moves from point D (50 pizzas) to point C (70 pizzas). Now the opportunity cost of more pizza is 50 wings, since wing production declines from 250 to 200. If society decides that 70 pizzas are not enough, it can expand pizza production from point C (70 pizzas) to point B (90 pizzas). Now society gives up 80 wings. Notice that as we move up along the PPF, the opportunity cost of producing an extra 20 pizzas has risen from 30 wings to 80 wings. This reflects the increased trade-off necessary to produce more pizzas.

A bowed-out production possibilities frontier reflects the increasing opportunity cost of production. This is described by the **law of increasing relative cost**, which states that as you move along the production possibilities frontier toward a greater quantity of one good, the costs of producing it increase relative to the costs of producing the other good. Changes in relative cost mean that society faces a significant trade-off if it tries to produce an extremely large amount of a single good.

The **law of increasing relative cost** states that the opportunity cost of producing a good rises as you produce more of it.

The Law of Increasing Relative Cost

To make more pizzas, society will have to use workers who are increasingly less skilled at making them. As a result, as we move up along the PPF, the opportunity cost of producing an extra 20 pizzas rises from 30 wings between points E and D to 80 wings between points C and B.

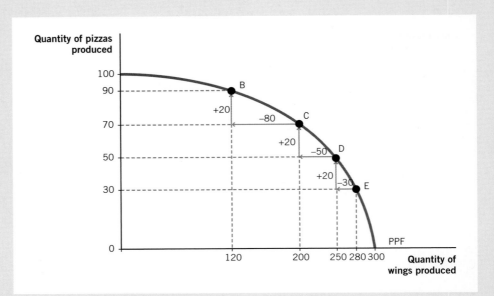

The Production Possibilities Curve and Economic Growth

So far we have modeled the location of the frontier as a function of the resources available to society at a particular moment in time. However, most societies hope to create economic growth. Economic growth is the process that allows society to produce more output in the future. Without economic growth in the past we'd all be a lot poorer.

We can use the production possibilities frontier to explore economic growth. For example, we can ask what would happen to the PPF if the society developed a new technology that increases efficiency and therefore productivity. Suppose that a new pizza assembly line improves the pizza production process and that the development of the new assembly line does not require the use of more of society's resources—it is simply a redeployment of the resources that already exist. This development would allow society to make more pizza with the same number of workers. Or it would allow the same amount of pizza to be made with fewer workers than previously. Either way, society has expanded its resource base. The change is shown in Figure 2.4.

With the new technology it becomes possible to produce 120 pizzas using the same number of workers and in the same amount of time that it previously took to produce 100 pizzas. Although the ability to produce wings has not changed, the new pizza technology makes the production possibilities frontier expand outward from PPF_1 to PPF_2. It is now possible for society to move from point C to point G, where it can produce more of both (80 pizzas and 210 wings). Why can society produce more of both? Because the improvement in pizza-making technology—the assembly line—allows the labor force to be deployed in a way that also increases the production of wings. Improvements in technology make point G possible.

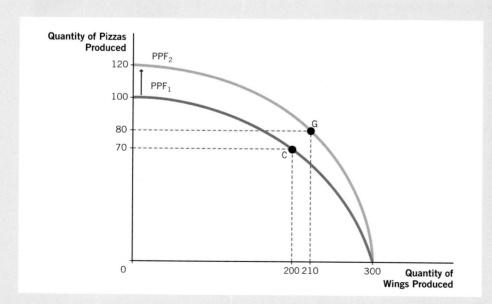

FIGURE 2.4

A Shift in the Production Possibilities Frontier

A new technology that improves the productive capacity of pizza-makers shifts the PPF upward from PPF_1 to PPF_2. Not surprisingly, more pizzas can be produced. Comparing points C and G, you can see that the enhanced pizza-making capacity also makes it possible to enjoy more wings at the same time.

PRACTICE WHAT YOU KNOW

The Production Possibilities Frontier

Question: Are the following statements true or false?

1. Point A represents the amount of cars and bicycles that will be sold.

2. The movement along the curve from point C to point A shows the opportunity cost of producing more bicycles.

3. If we have high unemployment, the PPF shifts in.

4. If an improved process for manufacturing cars is introduced, the entire PPF will shift out.

Answers

1. Point A represents the number of cars and bicycles produced, not sold. False.

2. Moving from point C to point A shows the opportunity cost of producing more cars, not more bicycles. False.

3. Unemployment does not shift the curve inward, since the PPF is the maximum that can be produced when all resources are being used. More unemployment would locate society at a point inside the PPF, since some people who could help produce more cars or bicycles are not working. False.

4. The PPF shifts out along the car axis, but it does not shift upward along the bicycle axis. False.

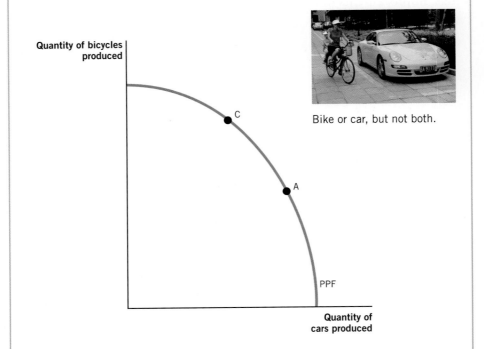

Bike or car, but not both.

The production possibilities frontier will also expand if the population grows. A larger population means more workers to help make pizza and wings. Figure 2.5 illustrates what happens when society adds a worker to help produce pizza and wings. With more workers the society is able to produce more pizzas and wings than before. This causes the curve to move from PPF_1 to PPF_2, expanding up along the y-axis and out along the x-axis. Like improvements in technology, additional resources expand the frontier and allow society to reach a point—in this case, H—that was not possible before. The extra worker has pushed the entire frontier out, not just one end, as the pizza assembly line did.

What Are the Benefits of Specialization and Trade?

We have seen that improving technology and adding resources make an economy more productive. A third way to create gains for society is through specialization and trade. Determining what to specialize in is an important part of this process. Every worker, business, or country is relatively good at producing certain products or services. Suppose that you decide to attend music school. You earn a certificate or degree and find an employer who hires you for your specialized skills. Your skills as a musician determine your salary. You can use your salary to purchase other goods and services that you desire and that you are not so good at making yourself.

In the next section we will explore why specializing and exchanging your expertise with others makes gains from trade possible.

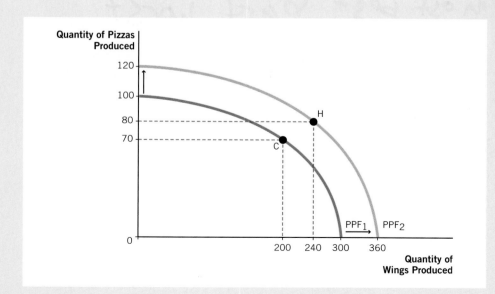

FIGURE 2.5

More Resources and the Production Possibilities Frontier

When more resources are available for the production of either pizza or wings, the entire PPF shifts up and out. This makes a point like H, along PPF_2, possible.

Gains from Trade

Let's return to our two-good economy. Now make the further assumption that this economy has only two people. One person is good at making pizzas and the other is better at making wings. When this is the case, the potential gains from trade are clear. Each person will specialize in what he or she is good at producing and then trade in order to acquire some of the good that the other person produces.

Figure 2.6 shows the production potential of the two people in our economy, Debra Winger and Mike Piazza. From the table we see that if Debra Winger devotes all of her work time to making pizzas, she can produce 60 pizzas. If she does not spend any time on pizzas, she can make 120 wings. On the other hand, Mike Piazza can spend all his time on pizzas and produce 24 pizzas, or all his time on wings and produce 72 wings.

The graphs show a side-by-side illustration of the amount of pizza and wings that each person produces daily. Wing production is plotted on the x-axis and pizza production is on the y-axis. Each of the production possibilities frontiers is drawn from data in the table.

Debra and Mike each faces a constant trade-off between producing pizza and wings. Debra produces 60 pizzas for every 120 wings; this means her trade-off between producing pizza and wings is fixed at 1:2. Mike produces 24 pizzas for every 72 wings. His trade-off between producing pizzas and wings is fixed at 1:3. Since Debra and Mike can choose to produce at any point along their production possibilities frontiers, let's assume that they each want to produce an equal number of pizzas and wings. When this is the case, Debra produces 40 pizzas and 40 wings, while Mike produces 18 pizzas and 18 wings. Since Debra is more productive in general, she produces more of each food. We say that Debra has an **absolute advantage**, meaning that she has the ability to produce more with the same quantity of resources than Mike.

Absolute advantage refers to the ability of one producer to make more than another producer with the same quantity of resources.

FIGURE 2.6

The Production Possibilities Frontier with No Trade

Debra Winger (a) can produce more pizza and more wings than Mike Piazza (b). Since Debra is more productive in general, she produces more of each food. When Debra and Mike both produce each item, Debra makes 40 units of each and Mike makes 18 units of each.

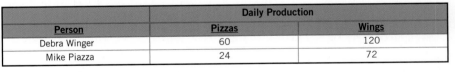

Person	Daily Production	
	Pizzas	Wings
Debra Winger	60	120
Mike Piazza	24	72

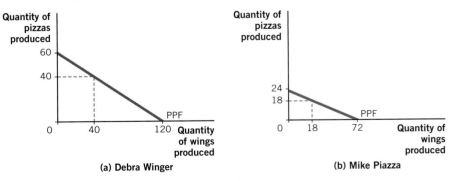

(a) Debra Winger

(b) Mike Piazza

TABLE 2.1

The Gains from Trade

Person	Good	Without Trade		With Specialization and Trade		Gains from Trade
		Production	Consumption	Production	Consumption	
Debra	Pizza	40	40	60	41 (keeps)	+ 1
	Wings	40	40	0	47 (from Mike)	+ 7
Mike	Pizza	18	18	0	19 (from Debra)	+ 1
	Wings	18	18	72	25 (keeps)	+ 7

At first glance, it would appear that Debra should continue to work alone. But consider what happens if they each specialize and then trade. Table 2.1 compares production with and without specialization and trade. Without trade, Debra and Mike have a combined production of 58 units of pizza and wings (Debra's 40 + Mike's 18). But when Debra specializes and produces only pizza, her production is 60 units. In this case, her individual pizza output is greater than the combined output of 58 pizzas (Debra's 40 + Mike's 18). Similarly, if Mike specializes in wings he is able to make 72 units. His individual wing output is greater than their combined output of 58 wings (Debra's 40 + Mike's 18). Specialization has resulted in the creation of two additional pizzas and 14 additional wings.

Specialization leads to greater productivity. But Debra and Mike would like to eat both pizza and wings. So if they specialize and then trade with each other, they will benefit. If Debra gives Mike 19 pizzas in exchange for 47 wings, they are each better off by one pizza and 7 wings. This result is shown in the final column of Table 2.1 and in Figure 2.7.

FIGURE 2.7

The Production Possibilities Frontier with Trade

(a) If Debra produces only pizza, she will have 60 pizzas, shown at point A. If she does not specialize, she will produce 40 pizzas and 40 wings (B). If she specializes and trades with Mike, she will have 41 pizzas and 47 wings (C). (b) If Mike produces only wings, he will have 72 wings (A). If he does not specialize, he will produce 18 pizzas and 18 wings (B). If he specializes and trades with Debra, he can have 19 pizzas and 25 wings (C).

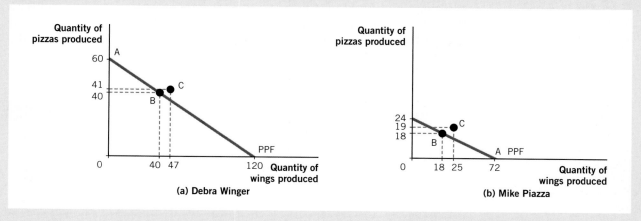

(a) Debra Winger

(b) Mike Piazza

In Figure 2.7a we see that at point A Debra produces 60 pizzas and 0 wings. If she does not specialize, she produces 40 pizzas and 40 wings, represented at B. If she specializes and then trades with Mike, she can have 41 pizzas and 47 wings, shown at C. Her gains from trade are 1 pizza and 7 wings. In Figure 2.7b we see a similar benefit for Mike. If he produces only wings, he will have 72 wings, shown at A. If he does not specialize, he produces 18 pizzas and 18 wings. If he specializes and trades with Debra, he can have 19 pizzas and 25 wings, shown at C. His gains from trade are 1 pizza and 7 wings. In spite of Debra's absolute advantage in making both pizzas and wings, she is still better off trading with Mike. This amazing result occurs because of specialization. When they spend their time on what they do best, they are able to produce more collectively and then divide the gain.

Comparative Advantage

We have seen that specialization allows workers to enjoy gains from trade. The concept of opportunity cost provides us with a second way of validating that trade produces gain. Recall that opportunity cost is the highest-valued alternative that is sacrificed to pursue something else. Looking at Table 2.2, you can see that in order to produce one more pizza Debra must give up producing two wings. We can say that the opportunity cost of one pizza is two wings. We can also reverse the observation and say that the opportunity cost of one wing is half a pizza. In Mike's case, each pizza he produces means giving up the production of three wings. In other words, the opportunity cost for him to produce one pizza is three wings. In reverse we can say that when he produces one wing he gives up one-third of a pizza.

Recall from Chapter 1 that comparative advantage is the ability to make a good at a lower cost than another producer. Looking at Table 2.2 you can see that Debra has a lower opportunity cost of producing pizzas than Mike—she gives up two wings for each pizza she produces, while he gives up three wings for each pizza he produces. In other words, Debra has a comparative advantage in producing pizzas. However, Debra does not have a comparative advantage in producing wings. For Debra to produce one wing she would have to give up production of half a pizza. Mike, on the other hand, gives up one-third of a pizza each time he produces one wing. So Debra's opportunity cost for producing wings is higher than Mike's. Because Mike is the low-opportunity-cost producer of wings, he has a comparative advantage in producing them. Recall that Debra has an absolute advantage in the production of both pizzas and wings; she is better at making both. However, from this example we see that she cannot have a comparative advantage in making both goods.

TABLE 2.2

The Opportunity Cost of Pizza and Wings

	Opportunity Cost	
Person	1 Pizza	1 Wing
Debra Winger	2 wings	1/2 of a pizza
Mike Piazza	3 wings	1/3 of a pizza

Applying the concept of opportunity cost helps us to see why specialization allows people to produce more. Debra's opportunity cost of producing pizzas (she gives up making 2 wings for every pizza) is less than Mike's opportunity cost of producing pizzas (he gives up 3 wings for every pizza). Therefore, Debra should specialize in producing pizzas. If you want to double-check this result, consider who should produce wings. Debra's opportunity cost of producing wings (she gives up half a pizza for every wing she makes) is more than Mike's opportunity cost of producing wings (he gives up one-third of a pizza for every wing he makes). Therefore, Mike should specialize in producing wings. When Debra produces only pizzas and Mike produces only wings, their combined output is 60 pizzas and 72 wings.

Finding the Right Price to Facilitate Trade

We have seen that Debra and Mike will do better if they specialize and then trade. But how many wings should it cost to buy a pizza? How many pizzas for a wing? In other words, what trading price will benefit both parties? To answer this question we need to return to opportunity cost. This process is similar to the trading of lunch food that you might recall from grade school. Perhaps you wanted a friend's apple and he wanted a few of your Oreos. If you agreed to trade three Oreos for the apple, the exchange benefitted both parties because you valued your three cookies less than your friend's apple and your friend valued your three cookies more than his apple.

In our example, Debra and Mike will benefit from exchanging a good at a price that is lower than the opportunity cost of producing it. Recall that Debra's opportunity cost is 1 pizza per 2 wings. We can express this as a ratio of 1:2. This means that any exchange with a value lower than 1:2 (0.50) will be beneficial to her since she ends up with more pizza and wings than she had without trade. Mike's opportunity cost is 1 pizza per 3 wings, or a ratio of 1:3 (0.33). For trade to be beneficial, the ratio of the amount exchanged must fall between the ratio of Debra's opportunity cost of 1:2 and the ratio of Mike's opportunity cost of 1:3. If the ratio falls outside of that range, Debra and Mike will be better off without trade, since the price of trading, which is the ratio in this case, will not be attractive to both parties. In the example, Debra trades 19 pizzas for 47 wings. The ratio of 19:47 (0.40) falls between Debra's and Mike's opportunity costs, as shown in Table 2.3.

As long as the terms of trade fall between the opportunity costs of the trading partners, the trade benefits both sides. But if Mike insists on a trading ratio of one wing for one pizza, which would be a good deal for him, Debra

TABLE 2.3

Gaining from Trade

Person	Opportunity Cost	Ratio
Debra Winger	1 pizza equals 2 wings	1:2 = 0.50
Terms of trade	19 pizzas for 47 wings	19:47 = 0.40
Mike Piazza	1 pizza equals 3 wings	1:3 = 0.33

Opportunity Cost

Saving Private Ryan

In most war movies the calculus of battle is quite apparent. One side wins if it loses fewer airplanes, tanks, or soldiers during the course of the conflict. These casualties of war are the trade-off that is necessary to achieve victory. *Saving Private Ryan* (1998) is different because the calculus of war does not add up; the mission is to save a single man. Private Ryan is one of four brothers who are all fighting on D-Day—June 6, 1944—the day the Allies landed in Normandy, France, to liberate Europe from Nazi occupation. In a twist of fate, all three of Ryan's brothers are killed. The general believes that the family has sacrificed enough and sends orders to find Ryan and return him home.

The catch is that in order to save Private Ryan the army needs to send a small group of soldiers to find him. A patrol led by Captain Miller loses many good men in the process, and those who remain begin to doubt the mission. Captain Miller says to the sergeant, "This Ryan better be worth it. He better go home and cure a disease, or invent a longer-lasting light bulb." The catch is that there is

Saving one life means sacrificing another.

no way of knowing what will happen in the future. Captain Miller hopes that saving Private Ryan will be worth the sacrifices they are making. That is how he rationalizes the decision to try to save him.

The opportunity cost of saving Private Ryan ends up being the lives that the patrol loses, lives that otherwise could have been pursuing a strategic military objective. In that sense, the entire film is about opportunity cost.

will refuse to trade because she will be better off producing both goods on her own. Likewise, if Debra insisted on receiving 4 wings for every pizza she gives to Mike, he would refuse to trade with her because he would be better off producing both goods on his own.

ECONOMICS IN THE REAL WORLD

Why Shaquille O'Neal Has Someone Else Help Him Move

Shaquille O'Neal is a mountain of a man—7'1" tall and over 300 pounds. At times during his Hall-of-Fame basketball career he was traded from one team to another. Whenever he was traded he had to relocate to a new city. Given his size and strength, you might think that Shaquille would have moved his household himself. But despite the fact that he could replace two or more ordinary movers, he kept playing basketball and hired movers. Let's examine the situation to see if this was a wise decision.

During his career, Shaquille had an absolute advantage in both playing basketball and in moving furniture. But, as we have seen, an absolute advantage doesn't mean that Shaquille should do both tasks himself. When he was traded to a new team, he could have asked for a few days to pack up and move, but each day spent moving would have been one less day he was able to work with his new team. When you are paid millions of dollars to play a game, the time spent moving is time lost practicing or playing basketball, which incurs a substantial opportunity cost.

Experienced movers can make about $50 an hour. If Shaquille was able to replace two movers, his value as a mover would have been only $100 an hour. If he put in a ten-hour day he could have saved the cost of two movers, or $1,000 a day. In this situation many people might have chosen to do their own moving. But $1,000 is not a lot of money to Shaquille. He could have been making more by playing basketball or filming a commercial. However, since Shaquille is now retired, the value of his time is lower. If the opportunity cost of his time becomes low enough, it is conceivable that he will move himself rather than pay movers. ✳

Shaq would be a big help when moving.

PRACTICE WHAT YOU KNOW

Opportunity Cost

Question: Imagine that you are traveling to visit your family in Chicago. You can take a train or a plane. The plane ticket costs $300 and it takes 2 hours each way. The train ticket costs $200 and it takes 12 hours each way. Which form of transportation should you take?

Answer: The key to answering the question is learning to value time. The simplest way to do this is to calculate the financial cost savings of taking the train and compare that to the value of the time you would save if you took the plane.

Plane or train, but not both!

Cost savings with train	Round trip time saved with plane
$300 − $200 = $100	24 hours − 4 hours = 20 hours
(plane) − (train)	(train) − (plane)

A person who takes the train can save $100, but it will cost 20 hours to do so. At an hourly rate, the savings would be $100/20 hours = $5/hour. If you value your time at $5 an hour, you will be indifferent between plane and train travel. If your time is worth more than $5 an hour, you should take the plane, and if your time is worth less than $5 an hour, you should take the train.

It is important to note that this approach gives us a more realistic answer than simply observing ticket prices. The train has a lower ticket price but very few people ride the train instead of flying because the opportunity cost of their time is worth more to them than the difference in the ticket prices. This is why most business travelers fly—it saves valuable time. Good economists learn to examine the full opportunity cost of their decisions, which must include both the financials and the cost of time.

We have examined this question by holding everything else constant, or *ceteris paribus*. At no point did we discuss possible side issues such as the fear of flying, sleeping arrangements on the train, or anything else that might be relevant to someone making the decision.

What Is the Trade-off Between Having More Now or Later?

So far we have examined short-run trade-offs. In looking at our wings-pizza trade-off, we were essentially living in the moment. But both individuals and society as a whole must weigh the benefits available today with those available tomorrow.

Study now . . .

. . . enjoy life later.

Many of life's important decisions are about the long run. We must decide where to live, whom to marry, where to go to college, and what type of career to pursue. Getting these decisions right is far more important than simply deciding how many wings and pizzas to produce. For instance, the decision to save money requires giving up something you want to buy today for the benefit of having more money available in the future. Similarly, if you decide to go to a party tonight, you benefit today, while staying home to study creates a larger benefit at exam time. We are constantly making decisions that reflect this tension between today and tomorrow—eating a large piece of cake versus a healthy snack, taking a nap or exercising at the gym, buying a jet ski or investing in the stock market. Each of these decisions is a trade-off between the present and the future.

Consumer Goods, Capital Goods, and Investment

We have seen that the trade-off between the present and the future is illustrated by the tension between what we consume now and what we plan to consume later. Any good that is produced for present consumption is a **consumer good**. These goods help to satisfy our wants now. Food, entertainment, and clothing are all examples of consumer goods. **Capital goods** help produce other valuable goods and services in the future. Capital goods are everywhere. Roads, factories, trucks, and computers are all capital goods.

For households, education is also a form of capital. The time you spend earning a college degree stays with you for many years to come and makes you more attractive to future employers. Even though education is not a durable good, like a house, it can be utilized in the future to earn more income. When you decide to go to college instead of working, you are making an *investment* in your human capital. **Investment** is the process of using resources to create or buy new capital.

Since we live in a world with scarce resources, every investment in capital goods has an opportunity cost of forgone consumer goods. For example, if you decide to buy a new laptop to take notes in class, you cannot use the money you spent to travel over spring break. Similarly, a firm that decides to invest in a new factory to expand future production is unable to use that money to hire more workers now.

The decision between whether to consume or to invest has a significant impact on economic growth in the future, or the long run. What happens when society makes a choice to produce many more consumer goods than capital goods? Figure 2.8a shows the result. When relatively few resources are invested in producing capital goods, not very much new capital is created. Since new capital is a necessary ingredient for economic growth in the future, the long-run production possibilities curve only expands a small amount.

What happens when society makes a choice to plan for the future by producing more capital goods than consumer goods? Figure 2.8b shows the result. With investment in new capital, the long-run production possibilities curve expands outward much more.

All societies face the trade-off between spending today and investing for tomorrow. Emerging global economic powers like China and India are

Consumer goods
are produced for current consumption.

Capital goods
help produce other valuable goods and services in the future.

Investment
is the process of using resources to create or buy *new* capital.

good examples of the benefit of investing in the future. Over the last twenty years the citizens of these countries have invested significantly more on the formation of capital goods than have the citizens in wealthier nations in North America and Europe. Not surprisingly, growth rates in China and India are much higher than in more developed countries. Part of the difference in investment rates can be explained by the fact that the United States and Europe already have larger capital stocks per capita and have less to gain than developing countries from operating at point B in Figure 2.8b. The Chinese government clearly prefers point B at this stage of its economic development, but point B is not necessarily better than point A. Developing nations, like China, are sacrificing the present for a better future, while many developed countries, like the United States, take a more balanced approached to weighing current needs against future growth. For Chinese workers this trade-off typically means longer work hours and higher savings rates than their American counterparts, despite far lower average salaries. In contrast, American workers have far more leisure time and also more disposable income, a combination that leads to far greater rates of consumption.

FIGURE 2.8

Investing in Capital Goods and Promoting Growth

(a) When a society chooses point A in the short run, very few capital goods are created. Since capital goods are needed to enhance future growth in the long run, PPF expands, but only slightly. (b) When a society chooses point B in the short run, many capital goods are created. Since capital goods are needed to enhance future growth, the long-run PPF expands significantly.

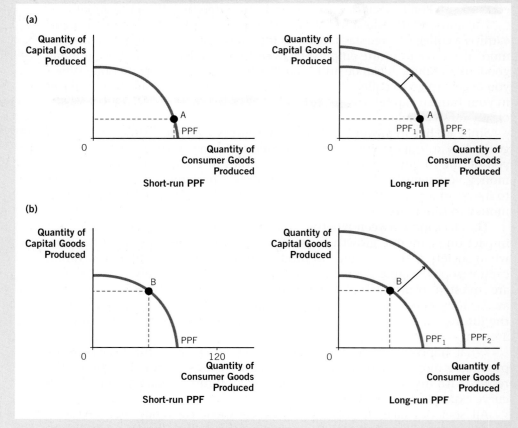

The Trade-off Between the Present and the Future

A Knight's Tale

Before the late Heath Ledger played the Joker in *The Dark Knight*, or starred in *Brokeback Mountain*, he played an entrepreneurial peasant in *A Knight's Tale* (2001).

In the movie, three peasants unexpectedly win a jousting tournament and earn 15 silver coins. They face a choice about what to do next. Two of the three want to return to England and live the high life for while, but the third (played by Ledger) suggests that they take 13 of the coins and reinvest them in training for the next tournament. He offers to put in all five of his coins and asks the other two for four coins each. His partners are skeptical about the plan because Ledger's character is good with the sword and not very good with the lance. For them to win additional tournaments they will have to invest considerable resources in training and preparation.

The movie illustrates the trade-off between enjoying consumer goods in the short run and investing in capital goods in the long run. The peasants' choice to forgo spending their winnings to enjoy themselves now in order to prepare for the next

Learning to joust is a long-term skill.

tournament is not easy. None of the three has ever had any money. Five silver coins represent an opportunity, at least for a few days, to live the good life. However, the plan will elevate the three out of poverty in the long term if they can learn to compete at the highest level. Therefore, investing the 13 coins is like choosing point B in Figure 2.8b. Investing now will allow their production possibilities frontier to grow over time, affording each of them a better life in the long run.

PRACTICE WHAT YOU KNOW

Trade-offs

Question: Your friend is fond of saying he will study later. He eventually does study, but he often doesn't get quite the grade he had hoped for because he doesn't study enough. Every time this happens he says, "It's only one exam." What advice would you give?

No pain, no gain.

Answer: Your friend doesn't understand long-term trade-offs. You could start by reminding your friend that each decision has a consequence at the margin and also later in life. The marginal cost of not studying enough is a lower exam grade. To some extent your friend's reasoning is correct. How well you do on one exam over four years of college is almost irrelevant. The problem is that many poor exam scores have a cumulative effect over the semesters. If you graduate with a 2.5 GPA instead of a 3.5 GPA because you did not study enough, your employment prospects are significantly diminished.

ECONOMICS FOR LIFE

Failing to Account for Exogenous Factors When Making Predictions

Predictions are often based on past experiences and current observations. Many of the least accurate predictions fail to take into account how much technological change influences the economy. Here we repeat a few predictions as a cautionary reminder that technology doesn't remain constant.

PREDICTION: "There is no reason anyone would want a computer in their home." Said in 1977 by Ken Olson, founder of Digital Equipment Corp. (DEC), a maker of mainframe computers.

FAIL: Over 80% of all American households have a computer.

PREDICTION: "There will never be a bigger plane built." Said in 1933 by a Boeing engineer referring to the 247, a twin-engine plane that holds ten people.

FAIL: The Airbus A380 can hold more than 800 people.

PREDICTION: "The wireless music box has no imaginable commercial value. Who would pay for a message sent to no one in particular?" Said by people in the communications industry when David Sarnoff (founder of NBC) wanted to invest in the radio.

FAIL: Radio programs quickly captured the public's imagination.

PREDICTION: "The world potential market for copying machines is five thousand at most." Said in 1959 by executives of IBM to the people who founded Xerox.

Source: Listverse, http://listverse.com/2007/10/28/top-30-failed-technology-predictions/

FAIL: Today a combination printer, fax machine, and copier costs less than $100. There are tens of millions of copiers in use throughout the United States.

PREDICTION: "The Americans have need of the telephone, but we do not. We have plenty of messenger boys." Said in 1878 by Sir William Preece, chief engineer, British Post Office.

FAIL: Today, almost everyone in Britain has a telephone.

These predictions may seem funny to us today, but note the common feature: they did not account for how the new technology would affect consumer demand and behavior. Nor do these predictions anticipate how improvements in technology through time make future versions of new products substantially better. The lesson: don't count on the status quo. Adapt with the times to take advantage of opportunities.

Epic fail: planes have continued to get larger despite predictions to the contrary.

Conclusion

Does trade create winners and losers? After reading this chapter you should know the answer: trade creates value. We dispelled the misconception that many first-time learners of economics begin with—that every trade results in a winner and a loser. The simple, yet powerful idea that trade creates value has far-reaching consequences for how we should organize our society. Voluntary trades will maximize society's wealth by redistributing goods and services to people who value them the most.

We also developed our first model, the production possibilities frontier. This model illustrates the benefits of trade and also allows us to describe ways to grow the economy. Trade and growth rest on a more fundamental idea—specialization. When producers specialize, they focus their efforts on those goods and services for which they have the lowest opportunity cost and trade with others who are good at making something else. In order to have something valuable to trade, each producer, in effect, must find its comparative advantage. As a result, trade creates value and raises the standard of living in society. The popular belief that trade creates winners and losers is simply not true in many circumstances.

In the next chapter we examine the supply-and-demand model to illustrate how markets work. While the model is different, the fundamental result we learned here—that trade creates value—still holds.

ANSWERING THE BIG QUESTIONS

1. How do economists study the economy?

* Economists design theories and then test them by collecting real data. The economist's laboratory is the world around us and ranges from the economy as a whole to the decisions that firms and individuals make. A good model should be simple to understand, flexible in design, and able to make powerful predictions. A model is both more realistic and harder to understand when it involves many variables. Maintaining a positive framework is crucial for economic analysis because it allows decision-makers to observe the facts objectively.

2. What is a production possibilities frontier?

* A production possibilities frontier is a model that illustrates the combinations of outputs that a society can produce if all of its resources are being used efficiently. Economists use this model to illustrate trade-offs and to explain opportunity costs and the role of additional resources and technology in creating economic growth.

3. What are the benefits of specialization and trade?

* Society is better off if individuals and firms specialize and trade based on the principle of comparative advantage.
* Parties that are better at producing goods and services than their potential trading partners, or hold an absolute advantage, still benefit from trade because this allows them to specialize and trade what they produce for other goods and services that they are not as good at making.
* As long as the terms of trade fall between the opportunity costs of the trading partners, the trade benefits both sides.

4. What is the trade-off between having more now or later?

* All societies face a critical trade-off between consumption in the short run and greater productivity in the long run. Investments in capital goods today help to spur economic growth in the future. However, since capital goods are not consumed in the short run, this means that society must be willing to sacrifice how well it lives today in order to have more later.

CONCEPTS YOU SHOULD KNOW

Absolute advantage (p. 38)
Capital goods (p. 45)
Ceteris paribus (p. 28)
Consumer goods (p. 45)
Endogenous factors (p. 28)

Exogenous factors (p. 29)
Investment (p. 45)
Law of increasing relative
  cost (p. 34)
Normative statement (p. 27)

Positive statement (p. 27)
Production possibilities
  frontier (p. 31)

QUESTIONS

1. What is a positive economic statement? What is a normative economic statement? Provide an example of each.

2. Is it important to build completely realistic economic models?

3. Draw a production possibilities frontier curve. Illustrate the set of points that is not possible, the set of points that is efficient, and the set of points that is not feasible.

4. Why does the production possibilities curve bow outward from the origin? Give an example of two goods for which this would be the case.

5. Does having an absolute advantage mean that you should undertake everything on your own? Why or why not?

6. What criteria do you use to determine which of two workers has a comparative advantage in performing a task?

7. Why does comparative advantage matter more than absolute advantage for trade?

8. What factors are most important for economic growth?

STUDY PROBLEMS

* 1. Michael and Angelo live in a small town in Italy. They work as artists. Michael is the more productive artist. He can produce 10 small sculptures each day but only 5 paintings. Angelo can produce 6 sculptures each day but only 2 paintings.

	OUTPUT PER DAY	
	Sculptures	Paintings
Michael	10	5
Angelo	6	2

  a. What is the opportunity cost of a painting for each artist?
  b. Based on your answer in part a, who has a comparative advantage in producing paintings?
  c. If they decide to specialize, who should produce the sculptures and who should produce the paintings?

* 2. The following table shows scores that a student can earn on two upcoming exams according to the amount of time devoted to study:

Hours Spent Studying for Economics	Economics Score	Hours Spent Studying for History	History Score
10	100	0	40
8	96	2	60
6	88	4	76
4	76	6	88
2	60	8	96
0	40	10	100

  a. Plot the production possibilities frontier.
  b. Does the production possibilities frontier exhibit the law of increasing relative cost?
  c. If the student wishes to move from a grade of 60 to a grade of 88 in economics, what is the opportunity cost?

3. Think about comparative advantage when answering this question. Should your professor, who has highly specialized training in economics, take time out of his teaching schedule to mow his lawn? Defend your answer.

✳ 4. Are the following statements positive or normative?
   a. My dog weighs 75 pounds.
   b. Dogs are required by law to have rabies shots.
   c. You should take your dog to the veterinarian once a year for a check-up.
   d. Chihuahuas are cuter than bulldogs.
   e. Leash laws for dogs are a good idea because they reduce injuries.

5. How does your decision to invest in a college degree add to your capital stock? Show this on your projected production possibilities frontier for ten years from now compared to your production possibilities curve without a college degree.

✳ 6. Suppose that an amazing new fertilizer doubles the production of potatoes. How would this discovery affect the production possibilities frontier between potatoes and carrots? Would it now be possible to produce more potatoes *and* more carrots, or only more potatoes?

7. Suppose that a politician tells you about a plan to create two expensive but necessary programs to build more production facilities for solar power and wind power. At the same time the politician is unwilling to cut any other programs. Use the production possibilities frontier graph below to explain if this is possible.

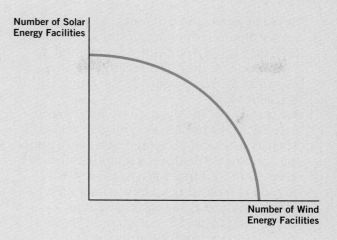

✳ 8. Two friends, Rachel and Joey, enjoy baking bread and making apple pies. Rachel takes 2 hours to bake a loaf of bread and 1 hour to make a pie. Joey takes 4 hours to bake a loaf and 4 hours to make a pie.
   a. What are Joey's and Rachel's opportunity costs of baking bread?
   b. Who has the absolute advantage in making bread?
   c. Who has a comparative advantage in making bread?
   d. If Joey and Rachel each decides to specialize in order to increase their joint production, what should Joey produce? What should Rachel produce?
   e. The price of a loaf of bread can be expressed in terms of an apple pie. If Joey and Rachel are specializing in production and decide to trade with each other, what range of ratios of bread and apple pie would allow both parties to benefit from trade?

9. Where would you plot unemployment on a production possibilities frontier? Where would you plot full employment on a production possibilities frontier? Now suppose that in a time of crisis everyone pitches in and works much harder than usual. What happens to the production possibilities frontier?

SOLVED PROBLEMS

1.a. Michael gives up 2 sculptures for each painting he produces. How do we know this? If he devotes all of his time to sculptures, he can produce 10. If he devotes all of his time to paintings, he can produce 5. The ratio of 10:5 is the same as 2:1. Michael is therefore twice as fast at producing sculptures. Angelo gives up 3 sculptures for each painting he produces. If he devotes all of his time to sculptures, he can produce 6. If he devotes all of his time to paintings, he can produce 2. The ratio of 6:2 is the same as 3:1.

b. For this part of the question we need to compare Michael's and Angelo's relative strengths. Michael produces 2 sculptures for every painting and Angelo produces 3 sculptures for every painting. Since Michael is only twice as good at producing sculptures, his opportunity cost of producing each painting is 2 sculptures instead 3. Therefore Michael is the low-opportunity-cost producer of paintings.

c. If they specialize, Michael should paint and Angelo should do the sculptures. You might be tempted to argue that Michael should just work alone, but if Angelo does the sculptures, it frees up Michael to concentrate on the paintings. This is what comparative advantage is all about.

b. Yes.

c. The opportunity cost is that the student's grade falls from 96 to 76 in history.

4.a. Positive.
b. Positive.
c. Normative.
d. Normative.
e. Normative.

6. A new fertilizer that doubles potato production will shift the entire PPF out along the potato axis but not along the carrot axis. Nevertheless, the added ability to produce more potatoes means that less acreage needs to be planted in potatoes and more land can be used to produce carrots. This makes it possible to produce more potatoes and carrots at many points along the production possibilities frontier. Figure 2.3 has a nice illustration if you are unsure how this works.

8.a. Rachel gives up 2 pies for every loaf she makes. Joey gives up 1 pie for every loaf he makes.
b. Rachel.
c. Joey.
d. Joey should make the bread and Rachel the pies.
e. Rachel makes 2 pies per loaf and Joey makes 1 pie per loaf. So any trade between 2:1 and 1:1 would benefit them both.

2.a.
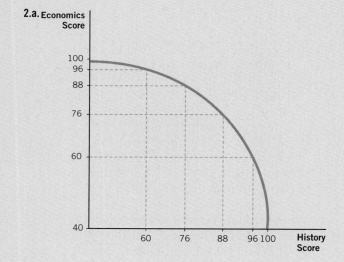

Graphs in Economics

Many beginning students try to understand economics without taking the time to learn the meaning and importance of graphs. This is shortsighted. You can "think" your way to a correct answer in many cases, but the models we build and illustrate with graphs are designed help analyze the tough questions, where your intuition can lead you astray.

Economics is by nature a quantitative science. In many cases, economists solve problems by finding a numerical answer. For instance, economists determine the unemployment rate, the rate of inflation, the growth rate of the economy, prices, costs, and much more. Economists also like to compare present-day numbers to numbers from the immediate past and historical data. Throughout your study of economics you will find that many data-driven subjects—for example, financial trends, transactions, the stock market, and other business-related variables—naturally lend themselves to graphic display. You will also find that many theoretical concepts are easier to understand when depicted visually in graphs and charts.

Economists also find that graphing can be a powerful tool when attempting to find relationships between different sets of observations. For example, the production possibilities frontier model we presented earlier in this chapter involved the relationship between the production of pizzas and wings. The graphical presentations made this relationship, the trade-off between pizzas and wings, much more vivid.

In this appendix we begin with simple graphs, or visuals, involving a single variable and then move to graphs that consist of two variables. Taking a few moments to read this material will help you learn economics with less effort and with greater understanding.

Graphs That Consist of One Variable

There are two common ways to display data with one variable: bar graphs and pie charts. A **variable** is a quantity that can take on more than one value. Let's look at the market share of the largest carbonated beverage companies. Figure 2A.1 shows the data in a bar graph. On the vertical axis is the market share held by each firm. On the horizontal axis are the three largest firms (Coca-Cola, Pepsi, and Dr. Pepper Snapple) and the separate category for the remaining firms called "Others." Coca-Cola Co. has the largest market share at 42%, followed by Pepsi Co. at 30%, and Dr. Pepper Snapple at 16%. The

A **variable** is a quantity that can take on more than one value.

height of each firm's bar represents its market share. The combined market share of the other firms in the market is 12%.

We illustrate the same data from the beverage industry on a pie chart in Figure 2A.2. Now the market share is expressed as the size of the pie slice for each firm.

FIGURE 2A.1

Bar Graphs

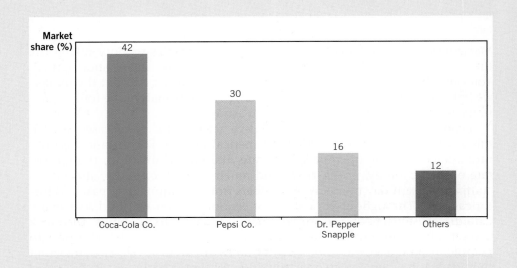

FIGURE 2A.2

Pie Chart
Each firm's market share in the beverage industry is represented by the size of the pie slice.

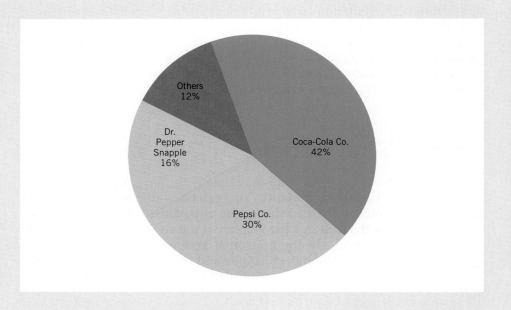

Advice on When to Use a Bar Graph or Pie Chart

The information in a bar graph and pie chart is the same, so does it matter which visualization you use? Bar graphs are particularly good at illustrating which piece of information is the largest. Pie charts are generally better at showing the proportion each variable holds. However, there is an episode from *How I Met Your Mother* where Marshall says, "Here's a pie chart that shows the bars I like to go to, and here's a bar chart that shows my favorite pies." His point is that it doesn't really matter which visualization you use; what matters is how the audience sees your graph or chart.

Photo to come

Marshall knows his pie charts and bar graphs!

Time-Series Graphs

Information about a single variable can also be displayed across time. For instance, if you want to show how the rate of inflation has varied through time, you could list the annual inflation rates in a lengthy table, or you could illustrate each point as part of a time series in a graph. Graphing the points makes it possible to quickly determine when inflation was at its highest and lowest without having to scan through the entire table. Figure 2A.3 illustrates this point.

FIGURE 2A.3

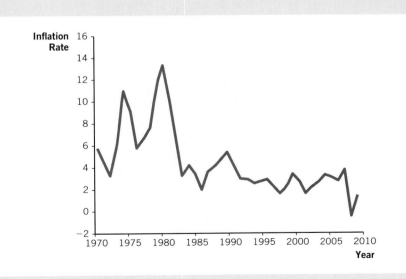

Time-Series Graph
A time-series graph displays the data found in the table. You immediately get a sense of when the inflation rate was highest, lowest, the trend through time, and the amount of volatility in the data.

Graphs That Consist of Two Variables

Sometimes understanding graphs requires you to visualize relationships between two economic variables. Each variable is plotted on a coordinate system, or two-dimensional grid. The coordinate system allows us to map a series of ordered pairs that show how the two variables relate to one another. For instance, suppose that we examine the relationship between the amount of lemonade sold and the air temperature in Figure 2A.4.

The air temperature is graphed on the x-axis (horizontal) and cups of lemonade sold on the y-axis (vertical). Within each ordered pair (x,y), the first value, x, represent the value along the x-axis and the second value, y, represents the value along the y-axis. For example, at point A, the value of x, or the temperature, is 0 and the value of y, or the amount of lemonade sold, is also 0. No one would want to buy lemonade when it is that cold. At point B the value of x, the air temperature, is 50 degrees and y, the number of cups of lemonade sold, is 10. By the time we reach point C, the temperature is 70 degrees and the amount of lemonade sold is 30 cups. Finally, at point D, the temperature has reached 90 degrees and 60 cups of lemonade are sold.

The type of graph you see in Figure 2A.4 is known as a **scatterplot** because the points are scattered across the coordinate system. Note that in this example the amount of lemonade sold rises as the temperature increases. When the two variables move together in the same direction, we say that there is a **positive correlation** between them. Conversely, if we graph the relationship between hot chocolate sales and temperature, we find that they move in opposite directions; as the temperature goes down, hot chocolate consumption goes up. This data reveals a **negative correlation** between the two variables, hot chocolate and temperature. Since

A scatterplot
is a type of graph that shows individual (x,y) points.

Positive correlation
occurs when two variables move in the same direction.

Negative correlation
occurs when two variables move in the opposite direction.

FIGURE 2A.4

Plotting Points in a Coordinate System

Within each ordered pair (x,y), the first value, x, represents the value along the x-axis and the second value, y, represents the value along the y-axis. The combination of all the (x,y) pairs is known as a scatterplot.

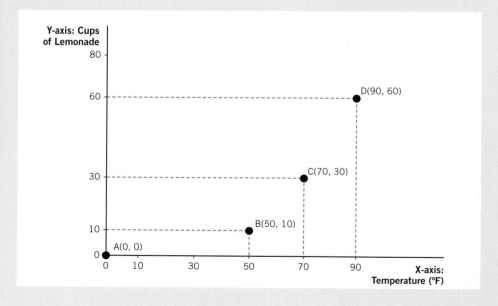

economists are ultimately interested in using models and graphs to make predictions and test theories, the coordinate system makes both positive and negative correlations easy to observe.

Figure 2A.5 illustrates the difference between a positive correlation and a negative correlation. Figure 2A.5a uses the same information as Figure 2A.4. When the temperature increases, the quantity of lemonade demanded increases as well. However, in 2A.5b we have a very different set of ordered pairs. Now, as the temperature increases, the quantity of hot chocolate falls. This can be seen by starting with point E, where the temperature is 32 degrees and hot chocolate consumption is 60 cups. At point F, the temperature rises to 50 degrees, but hot chocolate consumption falls to 30 cups. Finally, at point G the temperature is 70 degrees and hot chocolate consumption is down to 10. The green line connecting points E–G illustrates the negative relationship between hot chocolate and temperature, since the line is downward sloping. This contrasts with the positive relationship in Figure 2A.5a, where lemonade consumption rises from point B to point D and it is upward sloping.

The Slope of a Curve

A key element in any graph is the **slope**, or the rise between two points on a curve divided by the run between those two points. The *rise* is the amount that the vertical distance changes. The *run* is the amount that the horizontal distance changes.

$$slope = \frac{change\ in\ y}{change\ in\ x}$$

Slope
refers to the change in the rise along the y-axis (vertical) divided by the change in the run along the x-axis (horizontal).

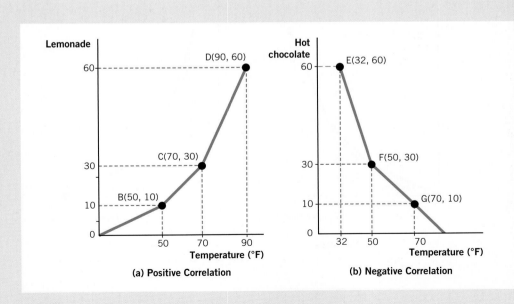

(a) Positive Correlation

(b) Negative Correlation

Positive and Negative Correlations

Panel (a) displays the positive relationship between lemonade consumption and higher temperatures. Panel (b) displays the negative relationship between hot chocolate consumption and higher temperatures.

A slope can take on a positive, negative, or zero value. A slope of zero—a straight line—indicates that there is no change in y for a given change in x. However, that result is not very interesting. The slope can be positive, as it is was in Figure 2A.5a, or negative, as it was in 2A.5b. Figure 2A.6 highlights the changes in x and y between the points on Figure 2A.5.

In Figure 2A.6a the slope from point B to point C is

$$slope = \frac{change\ in\ y}{change\ in\ x} = \frac{(30 - 10)\ or\ 20}{(70 - 50)\ or\ 20} = 1$$

All of the slopes in Figure 2A.6 are tabulated in Table 2A.1.

Each of the slopes in (a) is positive and the values slowly increase from 0.2 to 1.7 as you move along the curve from point A to point D. However, in (b) the slopes are negative as you move along the curve from E to H. An upward, or positive, slope indicates a positive correlation, while a negative slope indicates a negative correlation.

Notice that in both panels of Figure 2A.6 the slope changes values from point to point. Because of this we say that the relationships are *nonlinear*. The slope tells us something about how responsive consumers are to changes in temperature. Consider the movement from point A to point B in Figure 2A.6a. The change in y is 10, while the change in x is 50 and the slope (10/50) is 0.2. Since zero indicates no change and 0.2 is close to zero, we can say that lemonade customers are not very responsive as the temperature rises

FIGURE 2A.6

Positive and Negative Slopes

Notice that in both panels the slope changes values from point to point. Because of this we say that the relationships are nonlinear. As you move along the curve from point A to point D, the slopes are positive. However, in (b) the slopes are negative as you move along the curve from E to H. An upward, or positive, slope indicates a positive correlation, while a negative slope indicates a negative correlation.

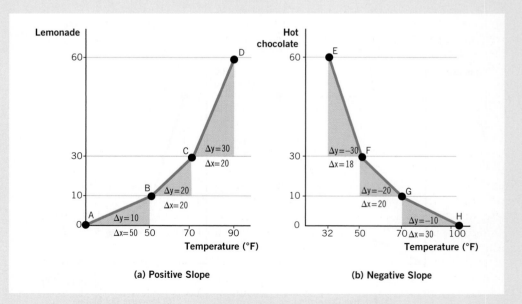

(a) Positive Slope

(b) Negative Slope

TABLE 2A.1

Positive and Negative Slopes

(a)		(b)	
Points	Slope	Points	Slope
A to B	0.2	E to F	−1.7
B to C	1.0	F to G	−1.0
C to D	1.5	G to H	−0.3

from 0 to 50 degrees. However, lemonade customers are much more sensitive from point C to point D, when the temperature rises from 70 to 90 degrees. At this point, lemonade consumption—the change in y—rises from 30 to 60 cups and the slope is now 1.5. The strength of the positive relationship is much stronger and, as a result, the line is much steeper, or more vertical. This contrasts with the movement from point A to point B, where the curve is flatter, or more horizontal.

The same analysis can be applied to Figure 2A.6b. Consider the movement from point E to point F. The change in y is −30, the change in x is 18, and the slope is −1.7. This value represents a strong negative relationship, so we would say that hot chocolate customers were quite responsive; as the temperature rose from 32 to 50 degrees, they cut their consumption of hot chocolate by 30 cups. However, hot chocolate customers are not very sensitive from point G to point H, where the temperature rises from 70 to 100 degrees. In this case, consumption falls from 10 to 0 cups and the slope is −0.3. The strength of the negative relationship is much weaker (closer to zero) and, as a result, the line is much flatter, or more horizontal. This contrasts with the movement from point E to point F, where the curve was steeper, or more vertical.

Formulas for the Area of a Rectangle and Triangle

Sometimes economists interpret graphs by examining the area of different sections below a curve. Consider the demand for Bruegger's bagels shown in Figure 2A.7. The demand curve has a downward slope, which tells us that when the price of bagels falls, consumers will buy more bagels. But this curve also can tell us about the revenue the seller receives, shown by the green rectangle. One of the most important considerations for the firm is how much money it receives from sales of its product. In this case, the sale price of each bagel is $0.60 and Bruegger's sells 4,000 bagels each week. We can illustrate the total amount Bruegger's takes in by shading the area bounded by the number of sales and the price. In addition, we can identify the benefit consumers receive from purchasing bagels. This is shown by the blue triangle. Since many buyers are willing to pay more than $0.60 per bagel, we can visualize the "surplus" that consumers get from Bruegger's Bagels by highlighting the blue triangular area under the blue line and above $0.60.

To calculate the area of a rectangle we use the formula:

$$\text{Area of a rectangle} = \text{height} \times \text{base}$$

In Figure 2A.7 the green rectangle is the amount of revenue that Bruegger's Bagels receives when it charges $.60. The total revenue is $0.60 x 4,000, or $2,400.

To calculate the area of a triangle we use the formula:

$$\text{Area of a triangle} = 1/2 \times \text{height} \times \text{base}$$

In Figure 2A.7 the pink triangle represents the amount of surplus consumers get from buying bagels. The amount of consumer surplus is $1/2 \times \$0.60 \times \$4,000$, or $1,200.

Cautions in Interpreting Numerical Graphs

In Chapter 2 we utilized *ceteris paribus*, or the condition of holding everything else around us constant while analyzing a specific relationship. Suppose that you omitted an important part of the relationship. What effect would this have on our ability to use graphs as an illustrative tool? Consider the relationship between lemonade consumption and bottles of suntan lotion. The graph of the two variables would look something like Figure 2A.8.

Looking at Figure 2A.8, you would not necessarily know that something was wrong. However, when you stop to think about the relationship, you quickly recognize that the result is deceptive. Since the slope is positive, the

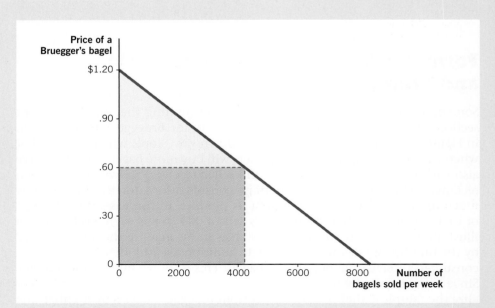

FIGURE 2A.7

Working with Rectangles and Triangles

We can determine the area of the green rectangle by multiplying the height by the base. This gives us $0.60 × 4,000, or $2,400 for the total revenue earned by Bruegger's Bagels. We can determine the area of a triangle by using the formula 1/2 × height × base. This gives us 1/2 × $0.60 × 4,000, or $1,200 for the area of consumer surplus.

graph indicates that there is a positive correlation between the number of bottles of suntan lotion used and the amount of lemonade people drink. At first glance this seems reasonable, since we associate suntan lotion and lemonade with summer activities. But the association is not **causal**, where one action implies the other or causes it to happen. Using more suntan lotion does not

Causality
occurs when one variable influences the other.

FIGURE 2A.8

Graph with an Omitted Variable

What looks like a strongly positive correlation is misleading. The demand for lemonade and suntan lotion rises because the temperature rises, so the correlation between lemonade and suntan lotion use is deceptive, not informative.

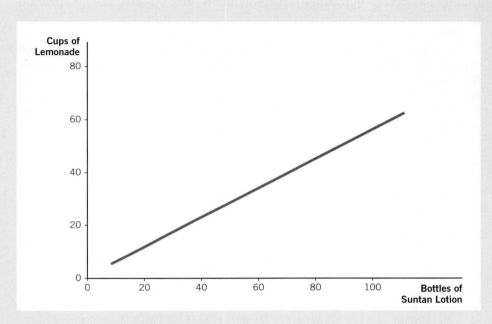

FIGURE 2A.9

Reverse Causality and an Omitted Variable

At a quick glance, this figure should strike you as odd. AIDS deaths are associated with having more doctors in the area. The doctors are there to help and treat people, not harm them. This is an example of reverse causation.

cause people to drink more lemonade. It just so happens that when it is hot outside, more suntan lotion is used and more lemonade is consumed. The graph makes it look like the number of people using suntan lotion affects the amount of lemonade consumed, when in fact they are not directly related.

Reverse causation occurs when causation is incorrectly assigned among associated events.

Another possible mistake is known as **reverse causation**, which occurs when causation is incorrectly assigned among associated events. Suppose that in an effort to fight the AIDS epidemic in Africa, a research organization notes the correlation shown in Figure 2A.9.

After looking at the data, it is clear that as the number of doctors per 1,000 people goes up, so do rates of death from the AIDS virus. The research organization puts out a press release claiming that doctors are responsible for increasing AIDS deaths and the media hypes the discovery. But hold on! Maybe there happen to be more doctors in areas with high incidences of AIDS because that's where they are most needed. Coming to the correct conclusion about the data requires that we do more than simply look at the correlation.

CONCEPTS YOU SHOULD KNOW

Causality (p. 61)
Negative correlation (p. 56)
Positive correlation (p. 56)

Reverse causation (p. 62)
Scatterplot (p. 56)
Slope (p. 57)

Variable (p. 53)

STUDY PROBLEMS

1. The following table provides the price and the quantity demanded of apples (per week)

Price per apple	Quantity demanded
$0.25	10
0.50	7
0.75	4
1.00	2
1.25	1
1.50	0

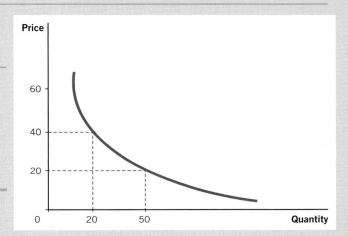

   a. Plot the data provided in the table into a graph.
   b. Is the relationship between the price of apples and quantity demanded negative or positive?

✳ 2. In the following graph, calculate the value of the slope if the price rises from $20 to $40.

3. Explain the logical error in the following sentence: "As ice cream sales increase, the number of people who drown increases sharply. Therefore, ice cream causes drowning."

SOLVED PROBLEMS

2. The slope is calculated by using the formula:

$$slope = \frac{change\ in\ y}{change\ in\ x}$$

$$= 20\ /-30$$

$$= -0.6667$$

Photo to come

PART 2

The Role of
MARKETS

The Market at Work: Supply and Demand

Demand matters more than supply.

What do Starbucks, Nordstrom, and Microsoft have in common? If you guessed that they are all headquartered in Seattle, that's true. But even

more interesting is that each company supplies a product much in demand by consumers. Starbucks supplies coffee from coast to coast and seems to be everywhere someone

wants a cup of coffee. Nordstrom, a giant retailer with hundreds of department stores, supplies fashion apparel to meet a broad spectrum of individual demand, from the basics to designer collections. Microsoft supplies software for customers all over the world. Demand for Microsoft products has made large fortunes for founder Bill Gates and the other investors in the company.

Notice the two recurring words in the previous paragraph: *supply* and *demand*. These words are consistently used by economists when describing how an economy like ours functions. Students often think that demand matters more than supply. Since we have much more experience as buyers than sellers, our first instinct is to wonder how much something costs to buy rather than how much it costs to produce. This one-sided impression of the market undermines our ability to fully appreciate how prices are determined. To help correct this misconception, this chapter describes how markets work and the nature of competition. To shed light on this process, we will introduce the formal model of demand and supply. We will begin by looking at demand and supply separately. Then we will combine them to see how they interact to establish the market price and determine how much is produced.

Black Friday crush at Target.

BIG QUESTIONS

❋ **What are the different types of markets?**

❋ **How is demand determined?**

❋ **What determines supply?**

❋ **What happens when supply and demand shift?**

Markets and the Nature of Competition

We have seen that markets bring trading partners together to create order out of chaos. Companies supply goods and services. Customers want to obtain the goods and services that companies supply. In a **market economy**, businesses compete with little or no government interference to supply customers with what they demand. Adam Smith, the founder of modern economics, described the dynamic best: "It is not from the benevolence of the butcher, the brewer, or the baker, that we expect our dinner, but from their regard to their own self-interest." In other words, producers earn a living by selling the products that consumers want. Consumers are also motivated by self-interest; they must decide how to use their money to select the goods that they need or want the most. This process, which Adam Smith called the *invisible hand*, guides resources to their highest-valued use.

A **market economy** allocates resources among households and firms with little or no government interference.

The exchange of goods and services in a market economy happens through prices that are established in markets. Those prices change, depending on the level of demand for a product and how much is supplied. For instance, hotel rates near Disney World are reduced in the fall when demand is low, and peak in March when demand is high. If spring break takes you to a ski resort, you will find lots of company and high prices. But if you are looking for an outdoor adventure during the summer, ski resorts have plenty of lodging available at great rates.

Similarly, many parents know how hard it is to find a reasonably priced hotel room in a college town on graduation weekend. Likewise, a pipeline break or unsettled political conditions in the Middle East can disrupt the supply of oil and cause the price of gasoline to spike overnight. When higher gas prices continue over a period of time,

Peak season is expensive . . .

consumers respond by changing their driving habits or buying more fuel-efficient cars.

Why does all of this happen? Supply and demand tell the story. We will begin our exploration of supply and demand by looking at where they interact—in markets. The degree of control over the market price is the distinguishing feature between *competitive markets* and *imperfect markets*.

Competitive Markets

Buyers and sellers of a specific good or service come together to form a market. Formally, a market is a collection

. . . but off-season is a bargain.

of buyers and sellers of a particular product or service. The buyers create the demand for the product, while the sellers produce the supply. It is the interaction of the buyers and sellers in a market that establishes the price and the quantity produced of a particular good or the amount of a service offered.

Markets exist whenever goods and services are exchanged. Some markets are online, and others can be found in traditional "brick and mortar" stores. Pike Place in Seattle is a market spread across nine acres. For over a hundred years it has brought together buyers and sellers of fresh, organic, and specialty foods. Since there are a number of buyers and sellers for each type of product, we say that the markets at Pike Place are *competitive*. A **competitive market** is one in which there are so many buyers and sellers that each has only a small impact on the market price and output. In fact, the impact is so small that it is negligible.

At Pike Place Market, like other local produce markets, the goods sold are similar from vendor to vendor. Because each buyer and seller is small relative to the whole market, no one individual has any influence over the market price. These two characteristics— similar goods and many participants— create a highly competitive market where the price and quantity sold are determined by the market rather than any one person or business.

To understand how this works, let's take a look at sales of salmon at Pike Place. On any given day, dozens of vendors sell salmon at this market. So, if a single vendor is absent or runs out of salmon, the quantity supplied that day will not be significantly altered—the remaining sellers will have no trouble filling the void. The same is true for those buying salmon.

A **competitive market** exists when there are so many buyers and sellers that each has only a small impact on the market price and output.

Pike Place Market

Whether a particular salmon buyer decides to show up on a given day makes little difference when hundreds of buyers visit the market each day. No single buyer or seller has any appreciable influence over the price that prevails in the salmon market. As a result, the market for salmon at Pike Place is an almost perfectly competitive market.

Imperfect Markets

An **imperfect market**
is one in which either the buyer or the seller has the ability to influence the market price.

A **monopoly**
exists when a single company supplies the entire market for a particular good or service.

Markets, like life, are not always perfect. An **imperfect market** is a market in which either the buyer or the seller has an influence on the market price. For example, the Empire State Building affords a unique view of Manhattan. Not surprisingly, the cost of taking the elevator to the top of the building is not cheap. But many customers buy the tickets anyway because they have decided that the view is worth the price. The managers of the Empire State Building can set a high price for tickets because there is no other place in New York City with such a great view. From this we see that when sellers produce goods and services that are different from their competitors, they gain some control, or leverage, over the price that they charge. The more unusual the product being sold, the more control the seller has over the price. When a seller has some control over the price, we say that market is imperfect. Specialized products, such as popular video games, front-row concert tickets, or dinner at a trendy restaurant, give the seller substantial pricing power.

In between the highly competitive environment at the Pike Place Market and markets characterized by a lack of competition, such as the unique view from the top of the Empire State Building, there are many other varieties of markets. Some, like the market for fast-food restaurants, are highly competitive but sell products that are not identical. Other businesses, for example Microsoft, function like *monopolies*. A **monopoly** exists when a single company supplies the entire market for a particular good or service. We'll talk a lot more about different market structures such as monopoly in later chapters. But even in imperfect markets, the forces of supply and demand have a significant influence on producer and consumer behavior. For the time being we'll keep our analysis focused on supply and demand in competitive markets.

The Empire State Building has the best view in New York City.

Demand

Demand exists when an individual or group wants something badly enough to pay or trade

PRACTICE WHAT YOU KNOW

Competition: Markets and the Nature of Competition

Question: Which of the following are competitive markets?

1. Gas stations at a busy interstate exit
2. A furniture store in an isolated small town
3. A fresh produce stand

Answers

How many buyers and sellers are there?

1. Since all gas stations sell the same product, they have very little pricing power. Most buyers will search for the lowest price. You may have noticed that there are usually many gas stations at a crowded highway exit. Because each station sells the same product and competes for the same customers, they will probably offer the same price. This is a competitive market.

2. Residents would have to travel a significant distance to find another store. This allows the small-town store to charge more than other furniture stores. The furniture store has some monopoly power. This is not a competitive market.

3. Since consumers can buy fresh produce in season at many local stands, individual growers have very little market pricing power. They must charge the same price as other growers in order to attract customers. This is a competitive market.

for it. How much an individual or group actually buys will depend on the price. In economics, the amount of a good or service purchased at the current price is known as the **quantity demanded**.

When the price of a good increases, consumers often respond by purchasing less of the good or buying something else. For instance, many consumers who would buy a salmon fillet at $5 would buy something else if the price rose to $20. Therefore, as price goes up, quantity demanded goes down. Similarly, as price goes down, quantity demanded goes up. This inverse relationship between the price and the quantity demanded is referred to as the *law of demand*. The **law of demand** states that, *all other things being equal, the quantity demanded falls when the price rises, and the quantity demanded rises when the price falls*. This holds true over a wide range of goods and settings.

The **quantity demanded** is the amount of the good or service that buyers are willing and able to purchase at the current price.

The **law of demand** states that, all other things being equal, quantity demanded falls when prices rise, and rises when prices fall.

The Demand Curve

We can create a table that lists various prices of a good and the number of people willing to purchase that good at any given price. A table that shows the relationship between the price of the good and the quantity demanded is known as a **demand schedule**. Table 3.1 shows Meredith Grey's hypothetical demand schedule for salmon fillets. When the price is $20 or more, Meredith will not purchase any salmon. However, below $20 the amount that Meredith purchases is inversely related to the price. For instance, at a price of $10, Meredith's quantity demanded is 4 fillets per month. If the price rises to $12.50 per serving, she demands 3 fillets. Every time the price increases, Meredith buys less salmon. In contrast, every time the price falls, she buys more. If the price falls to zero, Meredith would demand 8 fillets. That is, even if the fillets are free, there is a limit to her demand because she would grow tired of eating the same thing.

The numbers in Meredith's demand schedule from Table 3.1 are plotted on a graph in Figure 3.1, known as a *demand curve*. The **demand curve** is a graph of the relationship between the prices in the demand schedule and the quantity demanded at those prices. For simplicity, the demand "curve" is often drawn as a straight line. Economists always place the independent variable, which is the price, on the y-axis, and the dependent variable, which is the quantity demanded, on the x-axis. The relationship between the price and the quantity demanded produces a downward-sloping curve. As the price rises from $0 to $20 along the y-axis, the quantity demanded decreases from 8 to 0 fillets along the x-axis.

A **demand schedule**
is a table that shows the relationship between the price of a good and the quantity demanded.

The **demand curve**
is a graph of the relationship between the prices on the demand schedule and the quantity demanded at those prices.

Market demand
is the sum of all the individual quantities demanded by each buyer in the market at each price.

Photo to come

Market Demand

So far we have studied individual demand, but markets are comprised of many different buyers. In this section we will examine the collective demand of all of the buyers in the market. The **market demand** is the sum of all the individual quantities demanded by each buyer in the market at each price. During a typical day at Pike Place, over one hundred individuals buy salmon. However, to make our analysis simpler, assume that our market consists of only two buyers, Derek and Meredith, each of whom enjoys eating salmon. Figure 3.2 shows individual demand schedules for the people in this market, a combined market demand schedule, and the corresponding graphs. At a price of $10, Derek, who is Meredith's coworker, buys 2 salmon fillets a month, while Meredith buys 4 fillets. To determine the market demand curve,

TABLE 3.1

Meredith's Demand Schedule for Salmon

Price of Salmon (dollars per fillet)	Salmon Fillets Demanded
$20.00	0
17.50	1
15.00	2
12.50	3
10.00	4
7.50	5
5.00	6
2.50	7
0.00	8

Demand Schedule

we add Derek's 2 fillets to Meredith's 4 for a total of 6. As you can see in Figure 3.2, by adding Derek and Meredith's demand we arrive at the total market demand.

FIGURE 3.1

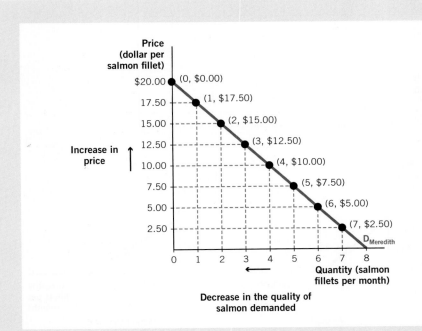

Meredith's Demand Curve for Salmon

Meredith's demand curve for salmon plots the data from Table 3.1. When the price of salmon is $10.00 per pound, she buys 4 fillets. If the price rises to $12.50 per pound, Meredith reduces the quantity that she buys to 3 fillets. The figure illustrates the law of demand by showing a negative relationship between price and the quantity demanded.

Demand Curve

Shifts in the Demand Curve

We have examined the relationship between price and quantity demanded. This relationship, described by the law of demand, shows us that when price changes, consumers respond by altering the amount they purchase. But in addition to price, many other variables influence how much of a good or service is purchased. For instance, news about the possible risks or benefits associated with the consumption of a good or service can change overall demand. Suppose that the government issues a nationwide safety warning that cautions against eating cantaloupe because of a recent discovery of the bacteria listeria in some melons. The government warning would cause consumers to buy less cantaloupe at any given price and overall demand will decline. Looking at Figure 3.3, we see that an overall decline in demand will cause the entire demand curve to shift to the left of the original curve, from D_1 to D_2. Note that though the price remains at $5 per cantaloupe, demand has moved from 6 melons to 3. Figure 3.3 also shows what does *not* cause a shift in demand curve: the price. The orange arrow along D_1 indicates that the quantity demanded will rise or fall in response to a price change. A price change causes a movement along a given demand curve, but it cannot cause a shift in the demand curve.

A decrease in overall demand causes the demand curve to shift to the left. What about when a variable causes overall demand to increase? Sup-

FIGURE 3.2

Calculating Market Demand

To calculate market demand for salmon, we add Derek's demand and Meredith's demand.

Price of Salmon (dollars per fillet)	Derek's Demand	Meredith's Demand	Market Demand
$20.00	0	0	0
$17.50	0	1	1
$15.00	1	2	3
$12.50	1	3	4
$10.00	2	4	6
$7.50	2	5	7
$5.00	3	6	9
$2.50	3	7	10
$0.00	4	8	12

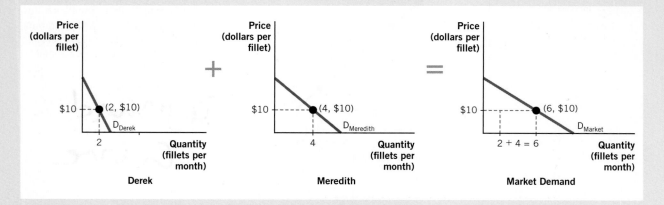

pose that the press has just announced the results of a medical study indicating that cantaloupe contains a natural substance that lowers cholesterol. Because of the newly discovered health benefits of cantaloupe, overall demand for it would increase. This increase in demand would shift the demand curve to the right, from D_1 to D_3.

In the example above we saw that demand shifted because of changes in tastes and preferences. However, there are many different variables that can shift demand. These include changes in income, the price of related goods, changes in tastes and preferences, expectations regarding the future price, and the number of buyers. Let's look at each.

The average American eats about 8.5 pounds of cantaloupe a year.

Changes in Income

When your income goes up, you have more to spend. Assuming that prices don't change, individuals with more purchasing power are able to buy more of what they want. Similarly, when your income declines, your purchasing power falls. In either case, the amount of income you make affects overall demand.

When economists look at how consumers spend, they often differentiate between two types of goods: *normal* and *inferior*. A consumer will buy more of a **normal good** if the consumer's income goes up. For example, because people with higher incomes often purchase more restaurant meals, they are a normal good. When income goes up and demand for restaurant meals increases, the demand curve shifts to the right. Similarly, if income falls and demand for restaurant meals goes down, the demand curve shifts to the left.

Consumers buy more of a **normal good** as income rises, holding other things constant.

FIGURE 3.3

A Shift in the Demand Curve

When the price changes, the quantity demanded changes along the existing demand curve in the direction of the orange arrow. A shift in the demand curve, indicated by the black arrows, occurs when something other than price changes.

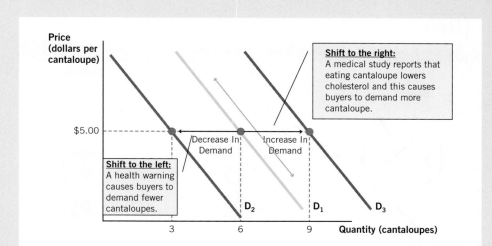

Price (dollars per cantaloupe)

Shift to the right: A medical study reports that eating cantaloupe lowers cholesterol and this causes buyers to demand more cantaloupe.

$5.00

Decrease In Demand | Increase In Demand

Shift to the left: A health warning causes buyers to demand fewer cantaloupes.

D_2 D_1 D_3

3   6   9   Quantity (cantaloupes)

Bill Gates does not have to worry about the relationship between income and demand!

Consumers buy less of an **inferior good** as income rises, holding other things constant.

Complements
are two goods used together. When the price of a complementary good rises, the demand for the related good goes down.

Substitutes
are two goods that are used in place of one another. When the price of a substitute good rises, the demand for it and the related good goes up.

While a consumer with an increase in income may purchase more of some things, the additional purchasing power will mean the consumer purchases less of other things. An **inferior good** is a product that consumers consider to be of lesser quality. Examples include used cars as opposed to new cars, rooms in boarding houses as opposed to your own apartment or house, and hamburger as opposed to filet mignon. As income goes up, consumers buy less of an inferior good because they can afford something better.

Within a specific product market, you can often find examples of inferior and normal goods in the form of different brands. Table 3.2 shows an example from the coffee market. Diehard coffee drinkers with a lower income will buy Folgers. But if their income rises, instead of buying a higher quantity of Folgers, many will switch to the more expensive Starbucks.

The Price of Related Goods

Another thing that can shift the demand curve is the price of related goods. Certain goods directly influence the demand for other goods. These goods are known as *complements* and *substitutes*. **Complements** are used together. **Substitutes** are used in place of one another.

Consider this pair of complements: color ink cartridges and photo paper. You need both to print a photo in color. What happens when the price of one, say color ink cartridges, rises? As you would expect, the quantity demanded of ink cartridges goes down. But demand for its complement, photo paper, also goes down. This is because people are not likely to use one without the other.

Substitute goods work the opposite way. When the price of a substitute good increases, the demand for the alternative good increases. For example,

TABLE 3.2

Inferior versus Normal Goods: A Coffee Example

Brands	Inferior	Normal
	Folgers	Starbucks
	Maxwell House	Caribou Coffee
	Many store brands	Expensive imports

if the price of the Nintendo Wii goes up and the price of Microsoft's Xbox remains unchanged, the demand for Xbox will increase.

Changes in Tastes and Preferences

In fashion, types of apparel go in and out of style quickly. Walk into Nordstrom or another clothing retailer, and you will see that fashion changes from season to season and year to year. For instance, what do you think of Madras shorts? They were popular twenty years ago and they may be popular again now, but it is safe to assume that in a few years Madras shorts will once again go out of style. While something is popular, demand increases. As soon as it falls out of favor, you can expect demand for it to return to its former level. Tastes and preferences can change quickly and this alters the demand for a particular good.

Fashion faux pas, or *c'est magnifique*?

Tastes and preferences can change because we gain better information about the goods and services that we buy. Recall our example of shifting demand for cantaloupe as the result of either the listeria infection or new positive medical findings. This is one example of how information can influence preferences. Contamination caused a decrease in demand because people no longer cared to eat the cantaloupe. On the other hand, if people learn that eating cantaloupe lowers cholesterol, their preference for the melon will go up.

Expectations Regarding the Future Price

Have you ever waited to purchase a sweater because spring was right around the corner and you expected the price to come down? Conversely, have you ever purchased an airline ticket sooner because you figured that the price would rise as the flight filled up? In both cases, expectations about the future influenced your current demand. If we expect a price to be higher tomorrow, we are likely to buy more today to beat the price increase. This leads to an increase in current demand. Likewise, if you expect a price to decline soon, you might delay your purchases to try to capitalize on a lower price in the future. An expectation of a lower price in the future will therefore decrease current demand.

The Number of Buyers

Recall that the market demand curve is the sum of all individual demand curves. Therefore, another way for the market demand to increase is for more individual buyers to enter the market. In the United States we add 3 million people each year to our population through immigration and births. All of those new people have needs and wants like the rest of us. Collectively, they add about 1% to the overall size of many existing markets on an annual basis.

The number of buyers also varies by age. Consider two markets, one for baby equipment, such as diapers, high chairs, and strollers, and the other for health care, including medicine, cancer treatments, hip replacement surgery, and nursing facilities. In countries with aging populations, for example in Italy where the birthrate has continued to plummet over several generations, the demand for baby equipment will decline and the demand for health care will expand. Therefore, demographic changes in society are another source of shifts in demand. In many markets, from movie theater attendance to home ownership, population trends play an important role in determining whether the market is expanding or contracting.

Figure 3.4 provides an overview of the variables that shift demand. The easiest way to keep all of these elements straight is to ask yourself a simple question: *Would this change cause me to buy more or less of the good?* If the change lowers your demand for the good, you shift the demand curve to the left. If the change increases your demand for the good, you shift the curve to the right.

Supply

Even though we have learned a great deal about demand, our understanding of markets is incomplete without also analyzing supply. Let's start by focusing on the behavior of vendors interested in selling fresh salmon at Pike Place.

We have seen that with demand, price and output are negatively related. With supply, however, the price level and quantity supplied are positively related. For instance, vendors would not bother to sell salmon if the market price was $2.50 per fillet, but many vendors would sell it if the price was $20.00. The **quantity supplied** is the amount of the good or service that producers are willing and able to sell at the current price. Higher prices cause the quantity supplied to increase. Conversely, lower prices cause the quantity supplied to decrease.

The **quantity supplied** is the amount of the good or service that producers are willing and able to sell at the current price.

Factors that Shift the Demand Curve

The demand curve shifts left when a factor adversely affect demand. The demand curve shifts right when a factor positively influences demand.

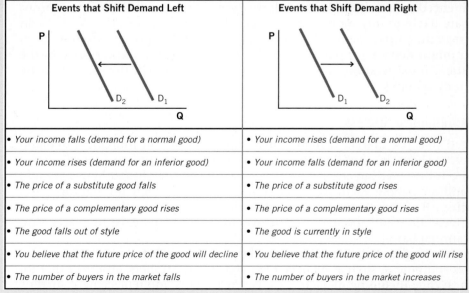

Events that Shift Demand Left	Events that Shift Demand Right
• *Your income falls (demand for a normal good)*	• *Your income rises (demand for a normal good)*
• *Your income rises (demand for an inferior good)*	• *Your income falls (demand for an inferior good)*
• *The price of a substitute good falls*	• *The price of a substitute good rises*
• *The price of a complementary good rises*	• *The price of a complementary good rises*
• *The good falls out of style*	• *The good is currently in style*
• *You believe that the future price of the good will decline*	• *You believe that the future price of the good will rise*
• *The number of buyers in the market falls*	• *The number of buyers in the market increases*

Shifting the Demand Curve

The Hudsucker Proxy

This 1994 film chronicles the introduction of the hula hoop, a toy that set off one of the greatest fads in United States history. According to Wham-O, the manufacturer of the hoop, when the toy was first introduced in the late 1950s over 25 million were sold in four months.

One scene from the movie clearly illustrates the difference between movements along the demand curve and a shift of the entire demand curve.

The Hudsucker Corporation has decided to sell the hula hoop for $1.79. We see the toy-store owner leaning next to the front door waiting for customers to enter. But business is slow. The movie cuts to the president of the company, played by Tim Robbins, sitting behind a big desk waiting to hear about sales of the new toy. It is not doing well. The store lowers the price, first to $1.59, then to $1.49, and so on, until finally the hula hoop is "free with any purchase." Even this is not enough to attract consumers. The toy-store owner throws the hula hoops into the alley behind the store.

One of the unwanted toys rolls across the street and around the block before landing at the foot of a boy who is skipping school. He picks up the hula hoop and tries it out. He is a natural. When school lets out, a throng of students rounds the corner and sees him playing with the hula hoop. Suddenly everyone wants a hula hoop and there is a run on the toy store. Preferences have changed, and the overall demand has increased. The hula hoop craze is born. In economic terms, we can say that the increased demand has shifted the entire demand curve to the right. The toy store responds by ordering new hula hoops and raising the price to $3.99, which happens to be the new market price after the increase, or shift, in demand.

How did the hula hoop craze start?

The scene reminds us that changes in price cannot shift the demand curve. Shifts in demand can only happen when an outside event influences human behavior. The graph below uses demand curves to show us the effect.

First Part of the Scene: The price drops from $1.79 to "free with any purchase." There is no change in demand. As a result, we slide along the demand curve.

Second Part of the Scene: The hula hoop craze begins and kids run to the toy store. The sudden change in behavior is evidence of a change in tastes, which shifts the demand curve to the right.

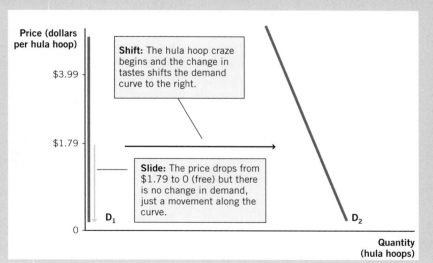

Price (dollars per hula hoop)

Shift: The hula hoop craze begins and the change in tastes shifts the demand curve to the right.

$3.99

$1.79

Slide: The price drops from $1.79 to 0 (free) but there is no change in demand, just a movement along the curve.

D_1

D_2

0

Quantity (hula hoops)

PRACTICE WHAT YOU KNOW

Shifts in the Demand Curve

Cheap pizza or . . .   cheap drinks?

Suppose that a local pizza place likes to run a "late-night special" after 11 p.m. The owners have contacted you for some advice. One of the owners tells you, "We want to increase the demand for our pizza." They have two marketing ideas to accomplish this.

1. Reduce the price of large pizzas
2. Reduce the price of a complementary good—for example, offer two half-priced bottles or cans of soda with every large pizza ordered

Question: What will you recommend?

Answer: First consider why "late-night specials" exist in the first place. Since most people prefer to eat dinner early in the evening, the store has to encourage late-night patrons to buy pizzas by stimulating demand. "Specials" of all sorts are used during periods of low demand when regular prices would leave the establishment largely empty.

Next, look at what the question asks. The owners want to know which option would "increase demand" more." The question is very specific; it is looking for something that will increase (or shift) demand.

Consider the first option, a reduction in the price of pizzas. Let's look at this graphically.

A reduction in the price of a large pizza causes a movement along the demand curve, or what is known as a change in the quantity demanded. Price changes are part of the definition of the demand curve, so they do not cause the curve to shift.

Now consider the second option, a reduction in the price of a complementary good. Let's look at this graphically.

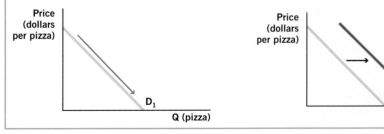

A reduction in the price of a complementary good (like soda) causes the entire demand curve to shift. This is the correct answer, since the question asks which of the following would increase (or shift) demand more.

As you can see, only one of the two options will shift (or increase) the demand curve. Recall that a reduction in the price of a complementary good shifts the demand curve to the right. This is the correct answer by definition! The other answer, cutting the price of pizzas, will cause an increase in the quantity demanded, or a movement along the existing demand curve.

You must be careful to differentiate between changes in the quantity demanded, which happen only when the price of the good changes, and a change in overall demand, which happens as the result of any positive or negative event that shifts the location of the entire demand curve. If you move along a curve instead of shifting it, you will analyze the problem incorrectly.

When price increases, suppliers often respond by selling more. As price goes down, quantity supplied also goes down. This direct relationship between price and quantity supplied is referred to as the *law of supply*. The **law of supply** states that, all other things being equal, the quantity supplied increases when the price rises, and the quantity supplied falls when the price falls. This holds true over a wide range of goods and settings.

The Supply Curve

A **supply schedule** is a table that shows the relationship between the price of a good and the quantity supplied. The supply schedule for salmon in Table 3.3 shows how many salmon fillets that Sol Amon, owner of Pure Food Fish, would sell each month at different prices. When the market price is $20.00,

The **law of supply** states that, all other things being equal, the quantity supplied of a good rises when the price of the good rises.

A **supply schedule** is a table that shows the relationship between the price of the good and the quantity supplied.

TABLE 3.3

Pure Food Fish's Supply Schedule for Salmon

Price of Salmon (dollars per fillet)	Salmon Fillets Supplied
$20.00	800
17.50	700
15.00	600
12.50	500
10.00	400
7.50	300
5.00	200
2.50	100
0.00	0

Photo to come

Sol Amon has been selling fish at the Pike Place Market for over fifty years.

Sol is willing to sell 800 salmon fillets. At $12.50 Sol's quantity supplied is 500. If the price falls to $10.00, he supplies 100 fewer fillets, or 400. Every time the price falls, Sol supplies less salmon. This means he is constantly adjusting the amount of salmon he offers. As the salmon prices fall, so do Sol's profits. Since Sol's livelihood depends on selling seafood, he has to find a way to compensate for the lost income. So he might offer more cod instead.

Sol and the other seafood vendors must respond to price changes by adjusting what they offer for sale in the market. This is why Sol offers more salmon when the price of salmon rises, and less salmon when the price declines.

When we plot the supply schedule in Table 3.3, we get the *supply curve* shown in Figure 3.5. A **supply curve** is a graph of the relationship between the prices in the supply schedule and the quantity supplied at those prices. As you can see in Figure 3.5, this relationship produces an upward-sloping curve. Sellers are more willing to supply the market when prices are high, since this generates more profits for the business. The upward-sloping curve means that the slope of the supply curve is positive, which illustrates a direct, or positive, relationship. For instance, when the price of salmon increases from $10.00 to $12.50 per fillet, Pure Food Fish will increase the quantity it supplies to the market from 400 to 500 fillets.

Market Supply

Sol Amon is not the only vendor selling fish at the Pike Place Market. The **market supply** is the sum of the quantities supplied by each seller in the market at each price. However, to make our analysis sim-

---

Pure Food Fish's Supply Curve for Salmon

Pure Food Fish's supply curve for salmon plots the data from Table 3.3. When the price of salmon is $10.00 per pound, Pure Food Fish supplies 400 fillets. If the price rises to $12.50 per pound, Pure Food Fish increases the quantity that it supplies to 500 fillets. The figure illustrates the law of supply by showing a positive relationship between price and the quantity supplied.

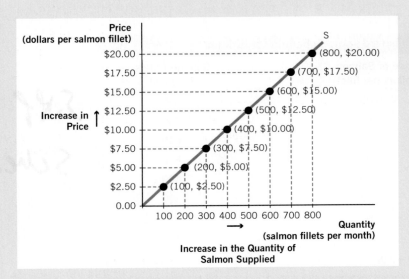

pler, let's assume that our market consists of just two sellers, City Fish and Pure Food Fish, each of which sells salmon. Figure 3.6 shows supply schedules for our two fish sellers and the combined, total-market supply schedule and the corresponding graphs.

Looking at the supply schedule, you can see that at a price of $10.00 City Fish supplies 100 salmon fillets, while Pure Food Fish supplies 400. To determine the market supply we add City Fish's 100 fillets to Pure Food Fish's 400 for a total market supply of 500.

Shifts in the Supply Curve

We have seen that the relationship between price and quantity supplied follows the law of supply; whenever the price changes, producers respond by altering the amount they supply. Yet in life many variables influence how much is supplied. When a variable other than the price changes, the entire supply curve shifts. For instance, suppose that food scientists at Starbucks discover a new way to brew a richer coffee at half the cost. The new process would increase the profits of Starbucks because the costs of supplying a cup of coffee would go down. The increased profits as a result of lower costs motivate Starbucks to sell more coffee and open new stores. Therefore, overall supply increases. Looking at Figure 3.7, we see that the supply curve shifts to the right of the original curve, from S_1 to S_2. Note that the retail price of

A supply curve is a graph of the relationship between the prices on the supply schedule and the quantity supplied at those prices.

Market supply is the sum of all the individual quantities supplied by each seller in the market at each price.

FIGURE 3.6

Calculating Market Supply

Market supply is calculated by adding together the amount supplied by individual vendors. Each vendor's supply, listed in the second and third columns of the table, is illustrated graphically. The total supply, shown in the last column of the table, is illustrated in the market supply graph.

Price of Salmon (dollars per fillet)	City Fish's Supply (salmon fillets)	Pure Food Fish's Supply (salmon fillets)	Market Supply (salmon fillets)
$20.00	200	800	1000
17.50	175	700	875
15.00	150	600	750
12.50	125	500	625
10.00	100	400	500
7.50	75	300	375
5.00	50	200	250
2.50	25	100	125
0.00	0	0	0

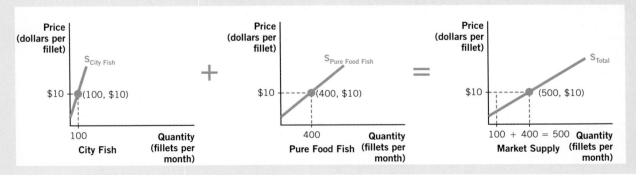

The first Starbucks opened in 1971 in Pike Place Market.

coffee ($3.00 per cup) has not changed. When we shift the curve, we assume that price is constant and that something else has changed. In this case, the new brewing process, which has made it less expensive to produce coffee, has stimulated additional supply.

An increase in supply causes the supply curve to shift to the right. What happens when a variable causes supply to decrease? Suppose that a hurricane devastates the coffee crop in Colombia and reduces world supply by 10% for that year. There is no way to make up for the destroyed coffee crop, and for the rest of the year at least, the quantity of coffee supplied will be less than the previous year. This decrease in supply shifts the supply curve to the left, from S_1 to S_3.

There are many variables that can shift supply, but Figure 3.7 also reminds us of what does *not* cause a shift in supply: the price. Recall that price is the variable that causes the supply curve to slope upward. The orange arrow along S_1 indicates that the quantity supplied will rise or fall in response to a price change. A price change causes a movement along the supply curve, not a shift in the curve.

FIGURE 3.7

A Shift in the Supply Curve

When price changes, the quantity supplied changes along the existing supply curve, illustrated by the orange arrow. A shift in supply occurs when something other than price changes, illustrated by the black arrows.

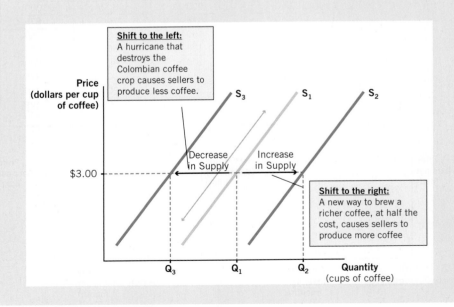

Factors that shift the supply curve include the cost of inputs, changes in technology and the production process, taxes and subsidies, the number of firms in the industry, and price expectations. Let's take a closer look at each.

The Cost of Inputs

Inputs are resources used in the production process. Inputs can take a number of forms and may include workers, equipment, raw materials, buildings, and capital. Each of these resources is critical to the production process. When the prices of inputs change, so does the seller's profit margin. If the cost of inputs declines, profit margins improve. Improved profit margins make the firm more willing to supply the good. So, for example, if Starbucks is able to purchase coffee beans at a significantly reduced price, it will want to supply more coffee. Conversely, higher input costs reduce profits. For instance, at Starbucks, the salaries of store employees, or baristas as they are commonly called, are a large part of the production cost. An increase in the minimum wage would require Starbucks to pay its workers more. This would raise the cost of making coffee, cut into Starbucks' profits, and make Starbucks less willing to supply coffee at the same price.

In addition, Starbucks must account for the opportunity cost of using one input at the expense of another. If the new minimum wage raises the cost to produce a cup of coffee more than using new equipment raises the price, Starbucks has to make the decision that is most beneficial for its profits. This means that an increase in the minimum wage would encourage Starbucks to invest more in automated equipment in order to use less labor.

Inputs
are the resources that firms use in the production of final goods and services.

Changes in Technology or the Production Process

Technology refers to knowledge that producers use to make their products. An improvement in technology allows a producer to increase output with the same resources or to produce a given level of output with fewer resources. For example, if a new espresso machine works twice as fast as the old technology, Starbucks could serve its customers more quickly, reduce long lines, and increase the number of sales it makes. As a result, Starbucks would be willing to produce and sell more espressos at each price. In other words, if the producers of a good discover a new and improved technology or a better production process, there will be an increase in supply; the supply curve for the good will shift to the right.

Baristas' wages make up a large share of the cost of selling coffee.

Taxes and Subsidies

Taxes placed on suppliers are an added cost of doing business. The firm may attempt to pass along the tax to consumers through higher prices, but this will discourage sales. In other cases, the firm will simply have to accept the taxes as an added cost of doing business. Either way, a tax makes the firm less profitable. Lower profits make the firm less willing to supply the product and shift the supply curve to the left. For example, if property taxes are increased, this raises the cost of doing business. As a result, the overall supply declines.

The reverse is true for a subsidy, which is a payment made by the government to encourage consumption or production of a good or service. For example, a large portion of the cost of flu shots is subsidized. The subsidized price causes an increase in the quantity demanded and increases the immunization rates among high-risk persons, exactly as we hope. However, subsidies often have unintended consequences. Subsidies for flu shots don't work perfectly. Some people receive the shots even though they are not in the highest-risk groups. Other subsidies are designed to increase the available supply of the good and act to reduce a firm's costs. For example, the government provides subsidies to farmers to plant certain crops and to companies that produce renewable energy. Supply-side subsidies encourage production, but an unintended consequence is that this often encourages wasteful spending.

The Number of Firms in the Industry

We saw that when there were more total buyers, the demand curve shifted to the right. A similar response happens with an increase in supply. Each additional firm that enters the market increases the available supply of a good. In graphic form, the supply curve shifts to the right to reflect the increased production. By the same reasoning, if the number of firms in the industry decreases, the supply curve will shift to the left. Changes in the number of firms in a market are a regular part of business. If a new pizza joint opens up nearby, more pizzas can be produced and supply expands. Conversely, if a pizza shop closes, the number of pizzas produced falls, and supply contracts.

Price Expectations

A seller who expects a higher price for the product in the future may wish to delay sales until a time when it will bring a higher price. For instance, florists know that the demand for roses spikes on Valentine's Day and Mother's Day. Because of higher demand, they can charge higher prices. In order to be able to sell more flowers during the times of peak demand, many florists work longer hours and hire temporary employees. This allows them to make more deliveries and therefore increase their ability to supply flowers while the price is high. Likewise, the expectation of lower prices in the future will cause sellers to offer more while prices are still relatively high. This is particularly noticeable in the electronics sector where newer—and much better—products are constantly being developed and released. Sellers know that their current offerings will soon be replaced by something better and consumer demand for the existing technology will plummet. This means that prices typically fall when a product has been on the market for a time. Since producers know that the price will fall, they supply as many of the new models as possible before the next wave of innovation cuts the price that they can charge.

We have seen that a number of variables can influence supply. Each of these variables can shift the entire supply curve to the right or left. A shift to the right will occur when the change in the variable results in an additional supply of the good or service. A shift to the left will occur when a change in the variable results in a smaller supply of the good or service.

Figure 3.8 provides an overview of the variables that shift the supply curve. The easiest way to keep all of these elements straight is to ask yourself a simple question: *Would the change cause a business to produce more or less of the good?* If the change lowers the willingness to supply the good or service, you shift the supply curve to the left. If the change increases the willingness to supply the good or service, you shift the curve to the right.

Bringing Supply and Demand Together

We have examined supply and demand separately. Now it is time to see how the two interact. The real power and potential of supply and demand analysis is how it predicts prices and output in the entire market. We'll even go one step further and allow demand and supply to shift at the same time—as often happens in the real world—to see how far we can take the model.

FIGURE 3.8

Factors that Shift the Supply Curve

The supply curve shifts left when a factor adversely affects supply. The supply curve shifts right when a factor positively influences supply.

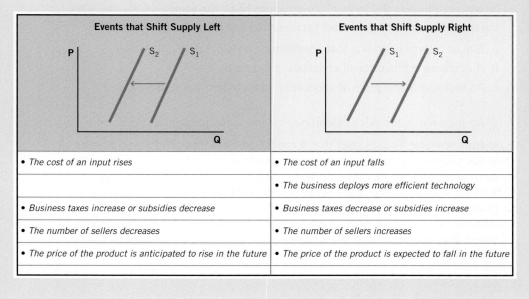

Events that Shift Supply Left	Events that Shift Supply Right
• The cost of an input rises	• The cost of an input falls
	• The business deploys more efficient technology
• Business taxes increase or subsidies decrease	• Business taxes decrease or subsidies increase
• The number of sellers decreases	• The number of sellers increases
• The price of the product is anticipated to rise in the future	• The price of the product is expected to fall in the future

PRACTICE WHAT YOU KNOW

Supply and Demand: The Supply and Demand of Ice Cream

Try these two questions:

Question: Which of the following will increase the demand for ice cream?

a. A decrease in the price of the butter used to make ice cream.

b. A decrease in the price of ice cream.

c. An increase in the price of the milk used to make ice cream.

d. An increase in the price of frozen yogurt, a substitute for ice cream.

I scream, you scream, we all scream for ice cream.

Answer: If you answered b, you made a common mistake. A change in the price of the good cannot change overall market demand; it can only cause a movement along an existing curve. So, as important as price changes are, they are not the right answer. First, you need to look for an event that shifts the entire curve.

Answers a and c refer to the prices of butter and milk. Since these are the inputs of production for ice cream, a change in prices will shift the supply curve. That leaves answer d as the only possibility. D is correct since the increase in the price of frozen yogurt will cause the consumer to look elsewhere. Consumers substitute away from frozen yogurt and toward ice cream. This shift in consumer behavior results in an increase in the demand for ice cream even though the price of ice cream remains the same.

Question: Which of the following will decrease the supply of chocolate ice cream?

a. A medical report finding that consuming chocolate prevents cancer.

b. A decrease in the price of chocolate ice cream.

c. An increase in the price of chocolate, an ingredient used to make ice cream.

d. An increase in the price of whipped cream, a complementary good.

Answer: We have already seen that b cannot be the answer because a change in the price of the good cannot change supply; it can only cause a movement along an existing curve. Answers a and d would both cause a change in demand without affecting the supply curve. That leaves answer c as the only possibility. The price of chocolate is an ingredient used in the production process. Whenever the price of an input rises, it squeezes profit margins and makes the supplier less willing to produce the good at the existing price.

Supply, Demand, and Equilibrium

Let's consider the market for salmon again. This example meets the conditions for a competitive market because salmon sold by one vendor is essentially the same as the salmon sold by another.

In Figure 3.9 we see that when the price of salmon fillets is $10, consumers demand 500 fillets and producers supply 500 fillets. This is represented graphically at point E, known as the **equilibrium** point, where the demand curve and the supply curve intersect. At this point, the two opposing forces of supply and demand are perfectly balanced.

Notice that at $10 per fillet, the quantity demanded equals the quantity supplied. At this price, and only this price, the entire supply of fillets in the market is sold. Moreover, every buyer who wants a fillet is able to find one and every producer is able to sell his entire stock of fillets. We say that $10 is the **equilibrium price**, because the quantity supplied equals the quantity demanded. The equilibrium price is also called the *market-clearing price*, since this is the only price where no surplus or shortage of the good exists. Similarly, there is also an **equilibrium quantity**, of 500 fillets, where the quantity supplied equals the quantity demanded. When the market is in equilibrium, we sometimes say that *the market clears*, or that *the price clears the market*. The equilibrium has a special place in economics because movements away from that point throw the market out of balance. The equilibrium process is so powerful that it is often referred to as the *law of supply and demand*. According to the **law of supply and demand**, *market prices adjust to bring the quantity supplied and the quantity demanded into balance*.

Equilibrium
occurs when the price causes the quantity supplied to be equal to the quantity demanded.

The **equilibrium price**
is the price at which the quantity supplied is equal to the quantity demanded. This is also known as the *market-clearing price.*

The **equilibrium quantity**
is the amount where the quantity supplied is equal to the quantity demanded.

The **law of supply and demand**
states that the price of any good will adjust to bring the quantity supplied and the quantity demanded into balance.

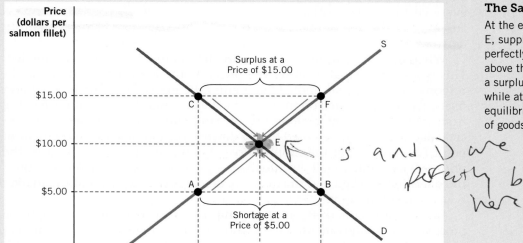

FIGURE 3.9

The Salmon Market
At the equilibrium point, E, supply and demand are perfectly balanced. At prices above the equilibrium price, a surplus of goods exists, while at prices below the equilibrium price, a shortage of goods exists.

Price (dollars per salmon fillet)

Surplus at a Price of $15.00

$15.00

$10.00

$5.00

Shortage at a Price of $5.00

Quantity (salmon fillets per month)

S and D are perfectly balanced here

Shortages and Surpluses

How does the market respond when it is away from equilibrium? Let's look at two other prices for salmon fillets shown on the y-axis in Figure 3.9: $5 and $15.

At a price of $5, salmon fillets are quite attractive to buyers but not very profitable to sellers—the quantity demanded is 750 fillets, represented by point B on the demand curve. However, the quantity supplied, which is represented by point A on the supply curve, is only 250. So, at $5 per fillet there is an excess quantity of 500 fillets demanded. This excess demand creates disequilibrium in the market.

A shortage occurs whenever the quantity supplied is less than the quantity demanded.

When there is more demand for a product than sellers are willing or able to supply, we say there is a **shortage**. In our case, at a price of $5 there are three buyers for each fillet. New shipments of salmon fly out the door. This is a strong signal for sellers to raise the price. As the market price increases in response to the shortage, sellers continue to increase the quantity that they supply. You can see this on the graph in Figure 3.9 by following the upward-sloping arrow from point A to point E. At the same time, as the price rises, buyers will demand an increasingly smaller quantity, represented by the upward-sloping arrow from point B to point E along the demand curve. Eventually, when the price reaches $10, the quantity supplied and the quantity demanded are equal. The market is in equilibrium.

What happens when the price is set above the equilibrium point, at $15? At a price of $15, salmon fillets are quite profitable for sellers but not very attractive to buyers. The quantity demanded, represented by point C on the demand curve, is 250 fillets. However, the quantity supplied, represented by point F on the supply curve, is 750. In other words, sellers provide 500 fillets more than buyers wish to purchase. This excess supply creates disequilibrium in the market. When the price is $15, there are more fillets available than buyers wish to purchase. As a result, any buyer who is willing to pay $15 for a salmon fillet can find one since there are three fillets available for every customer. This situation is known as a *surplus*. A **surplus**, or excess supply, exists whenever the quantity supplied is greater than the quantity demanded.

A surplus occurs whenever the quantity supplied is greater than the quantity demanded.

When there is a surplus, sellers realize that salmon fillets are oversupplied. This is a strong signal to lower the price. As the market price decreases in response to the surplus, more buyers enter the market and purchase salmon fillets. This is represented on the graph by the downward-sloping arrow moving from point C to point E along the demand curve. At the same time, sellers reduce output, represented by the downward-sloping arrow moving from point F to point E on the supply curve. As long as the surplus persists, the price will continue to fall. Eventually the price will reach $10. At this point, the quantity supplied and the quantity demanded are equal and the market is again in equilibrium.

In competitive markets, surpluses and shortages are resolved through the process of price adjustment. Buyers who are unable to find enough salmon at $5 compete to find the available fillets; this drives the price up. Likewise, businesses that cannot sell their product at $15 must lower their prices to reduce inventories; this drives the price down.

Every seller and buyer has a vital role to play in the market. Venues like the Pike Place Market bring buyers and sellers together. Amazingly, all of this

happens spontaneously, without the need for government planning to ensure an adequate supply of the goods that consumers need. You might think that a decentralized system would create chaos. Nothing could be further from the truth. Markets work because buyers and sellers can rapidly adjust to changes in prices. These adjustments bring balance. When markets were suppressed in Communist command economies during the 20th century, shortages were commonplace, in part because there was no market price system to signal that additional production was needed. This led to the creation of many black markets, discussed in Chapter 5.

How do markets respond to additional demand? In the case of the bowling cartoon above, the increase in demand comes from an unseen customer who wants to use a bowling lane already favored by another patron. An increase in the number of buyers causes an increase in demand. The lane is valued by two buyers, instead of just one, so the owner is contemplating a price increase! This is how markets work. Price is a mechanism to determine which buyer wants the good or service the most.

Changes in Both Demand and Supply

We have considered what would happen if supply *or* demand changed. But life is often more complex than that. To provide a more realistic analysis, we need to be able to shift supply and demand at the same time. Doing this adds considerable uncertainty to the analysis.

Suppose that a major drought hits the United States. The water shortage reduces both the amount of farmed salmon and the ability of wild salmon to spawn in streams and rivers. Figure 3.10a shows the ensuing decline in the salmon supply, from point S progressively leftward, represented by the dotted supply curves. At the same time, a medical journal reports that people who consume at least four salmon fillets a month live five years longer than those who consume an equal amount of cod. Figure 3.10b shows the ensuing rise in the demand for salmon, from point D progressively rightward, represented by the dotted demand curves. This scenario leads to a twofold change. Because of the water shortage, the supply of salmon shrinks. At the same time, new information about the health benefits of eating salmon causes demand for salmon to increase. There is less salmon available, yet more people want it. When something is in high demand and suppliers cannot provide enough of it, the market-clearing price must rise.

However, the effect on the equilibrium quantity is not certain. In this situation, we have a simultaneous decrease in supply and an increase in demand. Since we do not know the size of the supply reduction or the demand increase, the overall effect on the equilibrium quantity cannot be determined. This result can be seen in Figure 3.10c, where the shaded areas overlap in the purple region. The points where supply and demand cross within this area represent the set of possible new market equilibriums. Since each of the possible points of intersection in the purple region occurs at prices greater than

FIGURE 3.10

A Shift in Supply and Demand

When supply and demand both shift, the resulting equilibrium can no longer be identified as an exact point. This is seen in (c), which combines the supply shift in (a) with the demand shift in (b). When supply decreases and demand increases, the result is that the price must rise, but the equilibrium quantity is unknown.

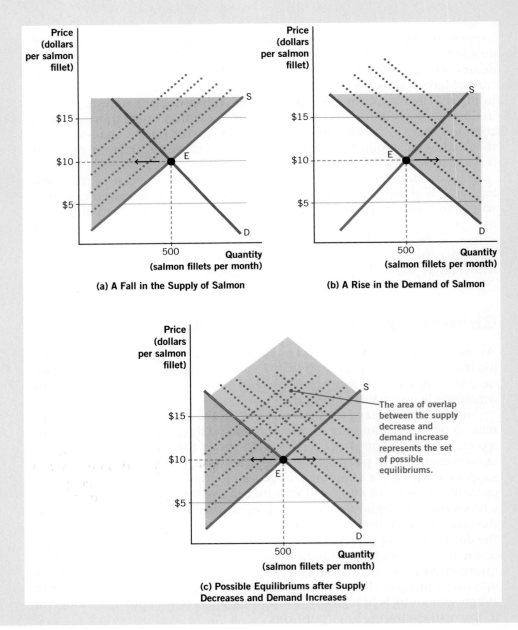

(a) A Fall in the Supply of Salmon

(b) A Rise in the Demand of Salmon

The area of overlap between the supply decrease and demand increase represents the set of possible equilibriums.

(c) Possible Equilibriums after Supply Decreases and Demand Increases

$10, we know that the price must rise. However, the left half of the purple region produces equilibrium quantities less than 500, while the right half of the purple region results in equilibrium quantities greater than 500. Therefore, the equilibrium quantity may rise or fall.

Figure 3.11 provides eight examples of what happens when supply and demand curves shift. As you study these, you should develop a sense for how the price and quantity are affected by changes in supply and demand. When one curve shifts, we can make a definitive statement about how price and quantity change. However, when supply and demand both change, it is only possible to determine the price *or* the quantity, not both. The world we live in is complex and often more than one variable will change simultaneously. When more than one variable changes, it is not possible to be as definitive. The new equilibrium, E_1, is no longer a single point but a range of outcomes represented by the shaded pink area. Therefore, we cannot be exactly sure where the new price *and* quantity will settle.

ECONOMICS IN THE REAL WORLD

Why Do the Prices of New Electronics Always Drop?

Why did consumers pay $5,000 for this?

The first personal computers released in the 1980s cost as much as $10,000. Today a laptop computer can be purchased for less than $500. When a new technology emerges, prices are initially very high and then tend to fall rapidly. The first PCs created a profound change in the way people could work with information. Prior to the advent of the PC, complex programming could be done only on large mainframe computers that could take up as much space as a whole room. But at first only a few people could afford a PC. What makes emerging technology so expensive when it is first introduced and so cheap later in its life cycle? Supply and demand tell the story.

In the case of PCs and other recent technologies, both demand and supply increase through time. Demand increases as consumers find more uses for the new technology. An increase in demand, by itself, would ordinarily drive the price up. However, producers are eager to supply this new market and ramp up production quickly. Since the supply expands more rapidly than the demand, there is both an increase in the quantity sold and a lower price.

Differences in expectations account for some of the difference between the increase in supply and demand. Both parties expect the price to fall and they react accordingly. Suppliers try to get their new products to market as quickly as possible—before the price starts to fall appreciably. Therefore, the willingness to supply the product expands quickly. Consumer demand is slower to pick up. Consumers expect the price to fall. This expectation tempers their desire to buy the new technology immediately. The longer they wait, the lower the price. Therefore, demand does not increase as fast as the supply. ✳

FIGURE 3.11

**Price and Quantity
When Supply and
Demand Change**

[handwritten: ex of shift in D and S]

Change	Illustration	Impact on Price and Quantity
1. Demand increases, supply does not change	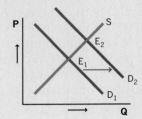	The demand curve shifts to the right. As a result, the equilibrium price and equilibrium quantity increase.
2. Supply increases, demand does not change	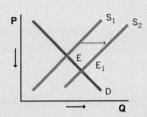	The supply curve shifts to the right. As a result, equilibrium price declines and the equilibrium quantity increases.
3. Demand decreases, supply does not change	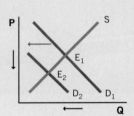	The demand curve shifts to the left. As a result, the equilibrium price and equilibrium quantity decrease.
4. Supply decreases, demand does not change	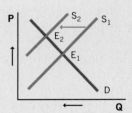	The supply curve shifts to the right. As a result, the equilibrium price rises and the equilibrium quantity decreases.

5. Demand and supply both increase

Curves

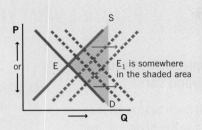

E₁ is somewhere in the shaded area

The demand and supply curves shift to the right. The shifts reinforce each other with respect to quantity, but act as countervailing forces along the prices axis. Price will be indeterminate.

6. Demand and supply both decrease

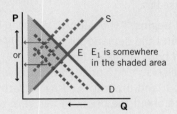

E₁ is somewhere in the shaded area

The demand and supply curves shift to the left. The shifts reinforce each other with respect to quantity, but act as countervailing forces along the price axis. Price will be indeterminate.

7. Demand increases and supply decreases

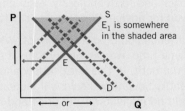

E₁ is somewhere in the shaded area

The demand curve shifts to the right and the supply curve shifts to the left. The shifts reinforce each other with respect to price, but act as countervailing forces along the quantity axis. Quantity will be indeterminate.

8. Demand decreases and supply increases

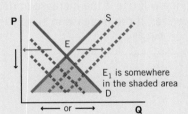

E₁ is somewhere in the shaded area

The demand curve shifts to the left and the supply curve shifts to the right. The shifts reinforce each other with respect to price, but act as countervailing forces along the quantity axis. Quantity will be indeterminate.

PRACTICE WHAT YOU KNOW

When Supply and Demand Both Change: Hybrid Cars

Question: At lunch two friends are engaged in a heated argument. Their exchange goes like this:

Hybrid cars are becoming increasingly common.

The first friend begins, "The supply of hybrid cars and the demand for hybrid cars will both increase, I'm sure of it. I'm also sure the price of hybrids will go down."

The second friend interrupts, "I agree with the first part of your statement, but I'm not sure about the price. In fact, I'm pretty sure that hybrid prices will rise."

They go back and forth endlessly, each unable to convince the other, so they turn to you for advice. What do you say to them?

Answer: Your friends could both be correct. When supply and demand both shift at the same time, we can be sure about how price or quantity will respond, but not both. In this case supply and demand both shift out, so we know the quantity bought and sold will increase. However, since an increase in supply would normally lower the price and an increase in demand would typically raise the price, we can't we sure whether the price will rise or fall. The overall price will rise if the increase in demand is larger than the increase in supply. However, if the increase in supply is larger than the increase in demand, prices will fall.

Conclusion

Does demand matter more than supply? As you have learned in this chapter, the answer is no. Demand and supply contribute equally to the functioning of markets. Five years from now, if someone asks you what you remember about your first course in economics, you will probably respond with two words, "supply" and "demand." These two opposing forces enable economists to model market behavior through prices. Prices help establish the market equilibrium, or the price where supply and demand are in balance. At the equilibrium, every good and service produced has a corresponding buyer who wants to purchase it. When the market is out of equilibrium, it causes a shortage or surplus. These conditions persist until buyers and sellers have a chance to adjust the quantity they demand and the quantity they supply. This refutes the misconception we noted at the beginning of the chapter.

Bringing Supply and Demand Together
Advice for Buying Your First Place

There is an old adage in real estate, "location, location, location." Why does location matter so much? Simple. Supply and demand. There are only so many places to live in any given location—there is your supply. The most desirable locations have many buyers who'd like to purchase in that area—there is your demand. Consider for a moment all of the variables that can influence where you want to live. As you're shopping for your new home, you may want to consider proximity to where you work, your favorite restaurants, public transportation, and the best schools. You'll also want to pay attention to the crime rate, differences in local tax rates, traffic concerns, noise issues, and nearby zoning restrictions. In addition, many communities have restrictive covenants that limit how you can use your property. Smart buyers determine how the covenants work and whether they would be happy to give up some freedom in order to maintain an attractive neighborhood. Finally, it is always a good idea to visit the neighborhood in the evening or the weekend to meet your future neighbors before you buy. All of these variables determine the demand for any given property.

Once you've done your homework and settled on a neighborhood, you will find that property values can vary tremendously across very short distances. A home along a busy street may sell for half the price of a similar property that backs up to a quiet park a few blocks away. Properties near the subway line command a premium, as do properties with views or close access to major employers and amenities (such as parks, shopping centers, and places to eat). Here is the main point to remember, even if some of these things aren't important to you: when it comes time to sell, the location of the home will always matter. The number of potential buyers depends on the characteristics of your neighborhood and the size and condition of your property. If you want to be able to sell your place easily, you'll have to consider not only where you want to live now but who might want to live there later.

All of this brings us back to supply and demand. The best locations are in short supply and high demand. The combination of low supply and high demand raises property values in those areas. Likewise, less desirable locations have lower property values because demand is relatively low and the supply is relatively high. Since first-time buyers often have wish lists that far exceed their budgets, considering the costs and benefits will help you find the best available property.

There is a popular HGTV show called *Property Virgins* that follows first-time buyers through the process of buying their first home. If you have never seen the show, watching an episode is one of the best lessons in economics you'll ever get. Check it out, and remember you may be new to buying property, but you can get a good deal if you use some basic economics to guide your decision.

Where you buy is more important than *what* you buy.

In the next chapter we will extend our understanding of supply and demand by examining how sensitive, or elastic, consumers and producers are to price changes. This will allow us to determine whether price changes have a big effect on behavior or not.

ANSWERING THE BIG QUESTIONS

1. What are the different types of markets?

* A market consists of a group of buyers and sellers for a particular product or service.
* When competition is present, markets produce low prices.
* Not all markets are competitive. When suppliers have market power, markets are imperfect and prices are higher.

2. How is demand determined?

* The law of demand states that there is an inverse relationship between the price and the amount that the consumer wishes to purchase.
* As a result of the law of demand, the demand curve is downward sloping.
* A price change causes a movement along the demand curve, not a shift in the curve.
* Changes other than price cause the demand curve to shift.

3. What determines supply?

* The law of supply states that there is a direct relationship between the price and the amount that is offered for sale.
* The supply curve is upward sloping.
* A price change causes a movement along the supply curve, not a shift in the curve.
* When the price changes, it causes a change in the quantity supplied.
* Changes in the prices of inputs, new technologies, taxes, subsidies, the number of sellers, and expectations about the future price all influence the location of the new supply curve, and cause the supply curve to shift.

4. What happens when supply and demand shift?

* Supply and demand interact through the process of market coordination.
* Together, supply and demand create a process that leads to equilibrium, the balancing point between the two opposing forces. The market-clearing price and output are determined at the equilibrium point.

* When the price is above the equilibrium, a surplus exists and inventories build up. This will cause suppliers to lower their price in an effort to sell the unwanted goods. This process continues until the equilibrium price is reached.

* When the price is below the equilibrium, a shortage exists and inventories are depleted. This will cause suppliers to raise their price in order to ration the good. The price rises until the equilibrium price is reached.

CONCEPTS YOU SHOULD KNOW

Competitive market (p. 69)
Complement (p. 76)
Demand curve (p. 72)
Demand schedule (p. 72)
Equilibrium (p. 89)
Equilibrium price (p. 89)
Equilibrium quantity (p. 89)
Imperfect market (p. 70)
Inferior good (p. 76)

Inputs (p. 85)
Law of demand (p. 71)
Law of supply (p. 81)
Law of supply and demand (p. 89)
Market demand (p. 72)
Market economy (p. 68)
Market supply (p. 83)
Monopoly (p. 70)
Normal good (p. 75)

Quantity demanded (p. 71)
Quantity supplied (p. 78)
Shortage (p. 90)
Substitutes (p. 76)
Supply curve (p. 83)
Supply schedule (p. 81)
Surplus (p. 90)

QUESTIONS

1. What is a competitive market and how does a competitive market depend on the existence of many buyers and sellers?

2. Why does the demand curve slope downward?

3. Does a price change cause a movement along a demand curve or a shift of the entire curve? What factors will cause the entire demand curve to shift?

4. Describe the difference between inferior and normal goods.

5. Why does the supply curve slope upward?

6. Does a price change cause a movement along a supply curve or a shift of the entire curve? What factors will cause the entire supply curve to shift?

7. Describe the process that leads the market toward equilibrium.

8. What happens in a competitive market when the price is above or below the equilibrium?

9. What roles do shortages and surpluses play in the market?

10. What happens to price and quantity when supply and demand change at the same time?

STUDY PROBLEMS

1. In the song "Money, Money, Money" by ABBA, the lead singer, Anni-Frid Lyngstad, is tired of the hard work life requires and plans to marry a wealthy man. If successful, how would this marriage change the artist's demand for goods? How would it change her supply of labor? Illustrate both changes with supply and demand curves. Be sure to explain what is happening in the diagrams. (Note: the full lyrics for the song can be found by googling the song title and ABBA. For inspiration, try listening to the song while you solve the problem!)

2. Check out this short video from www.forbes.com on the oil market: http://video.forbes.com/fvn/business/pm_non022208?partner=truveo. Using your understanding of the market forces of supply and demand, explain how the market works. In your explanation be sure to illustrate how increasing global demand for oil has impacted the equilibrium price.

3. For each of the following, determine if there is an increase or decrease in demand for the good in *italics*.
   a. The price of *oranges* increases.
   b. The cost of producing *tires* increases.
   c. Samantha Brown, who is crazy about *air travel*, gets fired from her job.
   d. A local community has a mosquito problem because of an unusually wet spring. What happens to the demand for *citronella,* a mosquito deterrent?

e. Many motorcycle enthusiasts enjoy riding without a helmet (in states where this is permitted by law). The price of new motorcycles rises. What happens to the demand for *helmets*?

4. For each of the following, determine if there is an increase or a decrease in supply for the good in *italics*.
a. The price of *silver* increases.
b. Growers of *tomatoes* experience an unusually good growing season.
c. New medical evidence reports that consumption of *organic products* reduces the incidence of cancer.
d. The wages of low-skill workers, a resource used to help produce *clothing*, increase.
e. The price of movie tickets, a substitute for *video rentals*, goes up.

5. Are laser pointers and cats complements or substitutes? (Not sure? Search for videos of cats and laser pointers online.) Discuss.

﹡ 6. The market for ice cream has the following demand and supply schedules:

Price	Quantity Demanded	Quantity Supplied
$2	100	30
$3	80	45
$4	60	60
$5	40	75
$6	20	90

What are the equilibrium price and quantity in the ice cream market? Confirm your answer by graphing the demand and supply curves. If the actual price was $3, what would drive the market toward the equilibrium?

7. Starbucks Entertainment announced in a 2007 news release that Dave Matthews Band's *Live Trax* CD was available only at the company's coffee shops in the United States and Canada. The compilation features recordings of the band's performances dating back to 1995. Why would Starbucks and Dave Matthews agree to partner in this way? To come up with your answer, think about the nature of complementary goods and how both sides can benefit from this arrangement.

8. The Seattle Mariners wish to determine the equilibrium price for each of the next two seasons. The supply of seats at the ballpark is fixed at 45,000.

Price	Quantity Demanded in Year 1	Quantity Demanded in Year 2	Quantity Supplied
$25	75,000	60,000	45,000
$30	60,000	55,000	45,000
$35	45,000	50,000	45,000
$40	30,000	45,000	45,000
$45	15,000	40,000	45,000

Draw the supply curve and each of the demand curves for years 1 and 2.

﹡ 9. The demand and supply curves that we use can also be represented with equations. Suppose that the quantity demanded, Q_d, is represented by the following equation:

$$Q_d = 90 - 2P$$

The quantity supplied, Q_s, is represented by the equation:

$$Q_s = P$$

a. Find the equilibrium price and quantity. **Hint:** Set $Q_d = Q_s$ and solve for the price, P, and then plug your result back into either of the original equations to find Q.
b. Suppose that the price is $20. Determine the Q_d and the Q_s.
c. At a price of $20, is there is a surplus or a shortage in the market?
d. Given your answer in part c, will the price rise or fall in order to find the equilibrium?

SOLVED PROBLEMS

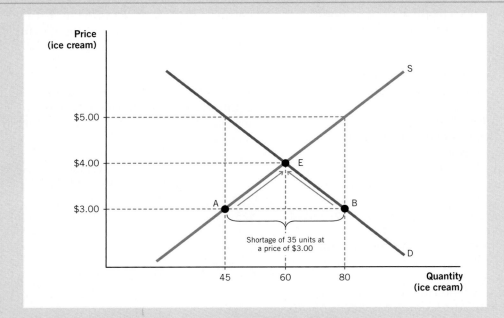

6. What are the equilibrium price and quantity in the ice cream market? The answer is 60 units at $4, which is the price where supply and demand are equal. The next step is to graph the curves. This is done above.

A shortage of 35 units of ice cream exists at $3, therefore there is excess demand. Ice cream sellers will raise their price as long as excess demand exists. That is, as long as the price is below $4, a shortage continues to exist. It is not until $4 that the equilibrium is reached and the shortage is resolved.

9.a. The first step is to set $Q_d = Q_s$. Doing so gives us $90 - 2P = P$. If we collect terms, we find that $90 = 3P$, or $P = 30$. Once we know that

$P = 30$, we can plug this value back into either of the original equations, $Q_d = 90 - 2P$ or $Q_s = P$. Beginning with Q_d, we get $90 - 2(30) = 90 - 60 = 30$, or we can plug it into $Q_s = P$, so $Q_s = 30$. Since we get a quantity of 30 for both Q_d and Q_s, we know that the price of $30 is correct.

b. In this part we plug $20 into Q_d. This yields $90 - 2(20) = 50$. Now plug $20 into Q_s. This yields 20.

c. Since $Q_d = 50$ and $Q_s = 20$, there is a shortage of 30 units.

d. Whenever there is a shortage of a good, the price will rise.

Elasticity

Producers charge the highest price possible.

In the previous chapter, we learned that demand and supply help regulate economic activity by balancing the interests of consumers and producers. We also observed how that balance is achieved through prices. Higher prices encourage producers to supply more and discourage consumers from buying more. Lower prices cause producers to supply less and create higher demand among potential buyers. In this chapter we will examine how decision-makers respond to differences in price and income.

The concept of *elasticity*, or responsiveness to a change in market conditions, is a tool that we need to master in order to fully under-stand supply and demand. By utilizing elasticity in our analysis, our understanding will become much more precise. This will allow us to determine the impact of policy measures on the economy, to vote more intelligently, and even to make wiser day-to-day decisions, like whether or not to eat out. Elasticity will also help us understand the faulty logic behind the common misconception that producers charge the highest possible price.

Photo to come

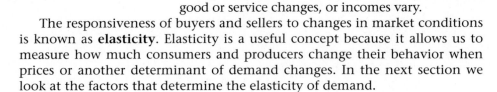

BIG QUESTIONS

* What is the price elasticity of demand and what are its determinants?
* How do changes in income and the prices of other goods affect elasticity?
* What is the price elasticity of supply?

The Price Elasticity of Demand

Many things in life are replaceable, or have substitutes: boyfriends come and go, people rent DVDs instead of going out to a movie, and students ride their bikes to class instead of taking the bus. Pasta fans may prefer linguini to spaghetti or angel hair, but they all taste about the same and can be substituted for each other in a pinch. In cases such as pasta, where consumers can easily purchase a substitute, we think of demand as being *responsive*. That is, a small change in price will cause many people to switch from one good to another.

Your "average"-looking boyfriend is replaceable.

Elasticity is a measure of the responsiveness of demand and supply to changes in market conditions.

On the other hand, many things in life are irreplaceable, or have few good substitutes. Examples include electricity, a hospital emergency room visit, or water for a shower. A significant rise in price for any of these items would probably not cause you to consume a smaller quantity. If the price of electricity goes up, you might try to cut your usage somewhat, but you will probably not start generating your own power. Likewise, you could try to treat a serious medical condition without a visit to the ER—but the consequences of making a mistake are enormous. Even something as simple as taking a shower has few good alternatives. In cases such as these, we say that consumers are *unresponsive*, or unwilling to change their behavior, even when the price of the good or service changes, or incomes vary.

The responsiveness of buyers and sellers to changes in market conditions is known as **elasticity**. Elasticity is a useful concept because it allows us to measure how much consumers and producers change their behavior when prices or another determinant of demand changes. In the next section we look at the factors that determine the elasticity of demand.

The Determinants of the Price Elasticity of Demand

The law of demand tells us that as price goes up, quantity demanded goes down, and as price goes down, quantity demanded goes up. In other words, there is an inverse relationship between the price of a good and the quantity demanded. Elasticity allows us to measure how much the quantity demanded changes in response to a change in price. If the quantity demanded changes significantly as a result of a price change, then demand is *elastic*. If the quantity demanded changes a small amount as a result of a price change, then demand is *inelastic*. For instance, if the price of a sweatshirt with a college logo rises by $10 and the quantity demanded falls by half, we'd say that the price elasticity of demand is elastic. But if the $10 rise in price results in very little or no change in the quantity demanded, the price elasticity of demand is inelastic. The **price elasticity of demand** measures the responsiveness of quantity demanded to a change in price.

> The **price elasticity of demand** is the measure of the responsiveness of quantity demanded to a change in price.

Three determinants play a crucial role in influencing whether demand will be elastic or inelastic. These are the existence of substitutes, the share of a budget spent on a good, and time and the adjustment process.

The Existence of Substitutes

The most important determinant of price elasticity is the number of substitutes available. When substitutes are plentiful, market forces tilt in favor of the consumer. For example, an unexpected freeze in Florida reduces the supply of oranges. As a result, the supply of orange juice shifts to the left, and since demand remains unchanged, the price of orange juice rises. However, the consumer of orange juice has many good substitutes. Since cranberries, grapes, and apple crops are unaffected by the Florida freeze, prices for juices made with those fruits remain constant. This leads to a choice. A consumer could continue to buy orange juice at a higher price or choose to pay a lower price for juice by switching to something he doesn't like as much. Faced with higher orange juice prices, some consumers will switch. How quickly this switch takes place, and to what extent consumers are willing to replace one product for another, determines whether demand is elastic or inelastic. Since many substitutes exist for orange juice, the price elasticity of demand for orange juice is elastic, or responsive, to price changes.

Beyoncé is irreplaceable.

What if there are no good substitutes? Let's return to the Empire State Building example from the previous chapter. Where else in New York City can you get such an amazing view? Nowhere! Since the view cannot be beat, the number of close substitutes is small and this makes demand more inelastic, or less responsive, to price changes.

To some degree, the price elasticity of demand depends on consumer preferences. For instance, sports fans are often willing to shell out big bucks to follow their passions. Amateur golfers can play the same courses as professional golfers. But the opportunity to golf where the professionals play does not come cheaply. A round of golf at the Tournament Players Club at Sawgrass, a famous course in Florida, costs close to $300. Why are some golfers willing to pay that much? For an avid golfer with the financial means, the experience of living out the same shots seen on television is worth $300. In this case, demand is inelastic—the avid golfer does not view other golf courses as good substitutes. However, less enthusiastic golfers, or those without the

Would you pay $300 to play this golf course?

In the **immediate run** there is no time to adjust your behavior.

Saving 10% on this purchase adds up to hundreds of dollars.

financial resources, are happy to golf on a less expensive course even if the pros don't play it on TV. When less expensive courses are viewed as good substitutes, the price tag makes demand elastic, or price responsive. Ultimately, whether demand is inelastic or elastic depends on the preferences and the resources of the buyer.

The Share of the Budget Spent on the Good

Despite the example above of an avid and affluent golfer willing to pay a premium price to play at a famous golf course, in most cases price is a critical element in determining what we can afford and what we will choose to buy. If you plan to purchase a 72-inch-screen TV, which can cost as much as $3,000, you will probably be willing to take the time to find the best deal. Because of the high cost, even a small-percentage discount in the price can cause a relatively large change in consumer demand. A "10% off sale" may not sound like much, but when purchasing a big-ticket item like a TV, it can mean hundreds of dollars in savings. The willingness to shop for the best deal indicates that the price matters, so demand is responsive, or elastic.

The price elasticity of demand is much more inelastic for inexpensive items on sale. For example, if a candy bar is discounted 10%, the price falls by pennies. The savings from switching candy bars is not enough to make a difference in what you can afford elsewhere. Therefore, the incentive to switch is small. Most consumers go ahead and buy their favorite candy since the price difference is so insignificant. In this case, demand is inelastic because the amount of money in the consumer's budget is large compared to the savings gained by purchasing a less desirable candy bar.

Time and the Adjustment Process

When the market price changes, consumers and producers respond. But that response does not remain the same over time. As time passes, they are able to find substitutes. To understand these different market responses, economists consider time in three distinct periods: the *immediate run*, the *short run*, and the *long run*.

In the **immediate run**, there is no time to adjust your behavior. Consider the demand for gasoline. When the gas tank is empty, you are forced to stop at the nearest gas station and pay the posted price. Filling up as soon as possible is more important than the price you have to pay. Inelastic demand exists whenever price is secondary to the desire to

Saving 10% on this purchase amounts to a few pennies.

attain a certain amount of the good. So in the case of an empty tank, the demand for gasoline is inelastic.

But what if your tank is not empty? In the **short run**, you have some time to adjust your behavior, and therefore can search for a good deal on gas. When consumers have some time to make a purchase, they gain flexibility. This allows them to shop for lower prices at the pump, carpool to save gas, or even to change how often they drive. In the short run, flexibility reduces the demand for expensive gasoline and makes consumer demand more elastic.

Finally, if we relax the time constraint completely, it is possible to use even less gasoline. In the **long run** a decision-maker has the luxury of time to make a full adjustment to market conditions. If gasoline prices are high in the long run, consumers can relocate closer to work and purchase fuel-efficient cars. These changes further reduce the demand for gasoline. As a result of the flexibility that additional time gives the consumer, the demand for gasoline becomes more elastic.

We have looked at three determinants of elasticity—substitutes, the share of the budget spent on the good, and time. Each is significant, but the number of substitutes tends to be the most influential factor and dominates the others. Table 4.1 will help you develop your intuition about how different market situations influence the overall elasticity of demand.

This is NOT the time to try and find cheap gas.

The **short run** occurs when you can adjust, but only partially.

The **long run** exists when the decision-maker has time to fully adjust.

Computing the Price Elasticity of Demand

Until this point our discussion of elasticity has been descriptive. To apply the concept of elasticity in decision-making, we need to be able to view it in a more quantitative way. For example, if the owner of a business is trying to decide whether to put a good on sale, he needs to be able to estimate how many new customers would purchase it at the sale price. Or if a government is considering a new tax, it needs to know how much revenue that tax would generate. These are questions about elasticity that we can evaluate using a mathematical formula.

Photo to come

TABLE 4.1

Developing Intuition for the Price Elasticity of Demand

Example	Discussion	Overall Elasticity
Football tickets for a true fan	Being able to watch a game live and go to pre- and post-game tailgates is a unique experience. For many fans, the experience of going to the game has few good substitutes.	Tends to be relatively inelastic
Assigned textbooks for a class	The information inside a textbook is valuable. Substitutes such as older editions and free online resources are not exactly the same. As a result, most students buy the required course materials. Acquiring the textbook is more important than the price paid, therefore demand is inelastic. The fact that a textbook is needed in the short run (for a few months while taking a class) also tends to make demand inelastic.	Tends to be inelastic
A slice of pizza from Domino's	In most locations, many pizza competitors exist, so there are many close substitutes. This tends to make the demand for a particular brand of pizza elastic.	Tends to be elastic
A Red Pontiac Torrent	There are many styles, makes, and colors of cars to choose from. With large purchases, consumers are sensitive to smaller percentages of savings. Moreover, people typically plan car purchases many months or years in advance. The combination of all of these factors makes the demand for any particular model and color relatively elastic.	Tends to be relatively elastic

Price Elasticity of Demand

Jingle All the Way

This amusing comedy from 1996 features two fathers who procrastinate until Christmas Eve to try to buy a Turbo Man action figure for their children for Christmas morning. It's the only present that their kids truly want from Santa. The problem is that almost every child in America feels the same way. Thus, the Turbo Man toys are in short supply because of strong demand. However, related items, like Turbo Man's pet, Booster, are readily available.

Based on this description, what can we say about the price elasticity of demand for Turbo Man and Booster?

Turbo Man—Since the toy is needed immediately, no good substitutes exist. Also, because the amount this toy costs (the share of the budget) is relatively small, people are not as concerned about getting a good deal and demand is, therefore, relatively inelastic. We see this in the movie when a toy store receives a last-minute shipment of the action figure and a crowd of shoppers shows up.

Booster—If you cannot find a Turbo Man action figure, you are not likely to want his pet. Therefore, the demand for Booster is much more elastic than for Turbo Man, since there are many good substitutes for Booster. We see this in the movie when a toy store sales associate informs the crowd of would-be Turbo Man buyers that the store has plenty of Boosters available, and the throng yells back, "We don't want it."

Is the demand for Turbo Man elastic or inelastic?

The Price Elasticity of Demand Formula

Let's begin with an example of a pizza shop. Consider an owner who tries to attract customers. For one month he lowers the price by 10% and is pleased to find that sales jump by 30%.

Here is the formula for the price elasticity of demand (E_d):

Price Elasticity of Demand $= E_d$

$$= \frac{\text{Percentage change in the quantity demanded}}{\text{Percentage change in price}} \quad (4.1)$$

Using the data from the example, we can calculate the price elasticity of demand as follows:

$$\text{Price Elasticity of Demand} = E_d = \frac{30 \text{ percent}}{-10 \text{ percent}} = -3$$

What does that mean? The price elasticity of demand, -3 in this case, is expressed as a coefficient (3) with a specific sign (it has a minus in front of it). The coefficient, 3, tells us how much the quantity demanded changed (30%) compared to the price change (10%). In this case, the percentage change in the quantity demanded is three times the percentage change in the price. Whenever the percentage change in the quantity demanded is larger than the percentage change in price, we say that demand was responsive, or elastic, to the price change. In other words, the price drop made a big difference in how much pizza consumers purchased from the pizza shop. If the opposite occurs and a price drop makes a small difference in the quantity that consumers purchase, we say that demand was unresponsive, or inelastic.

The negative sign in front of the coefficient is equally important. Recall that the law of demand describes an inverse relationship between the price of a good and the quantity demanded; when prices rise, the quantity demanded falls. The E_d coefficient reflects this inverse relationship with a negative sign. In other words, the pizza shop drops its price and consumers buy more pizza. Since pizza prices and consumer purchases of pizza generally move in opposite directions, the sign of the price elasticity of demand is usually negative. Note that not all textbooks use the negative sign in front of the price elasticity of demand. Some books use absolute values, meaning they drop the negative sign, to simplify the discussion. Don't let this confuse you!

The Midpoint Method

The above calculation was straightforward because of the way we set up the calculation. But when calculating elasticity there is a complication. Consider the following demand schedule:

Price	Quantity Demanded
$12	20
$6	30

Let's calculate the elasticity of demand. If the price drops from $12 to $6—a fall of 50%—the quantity demanded increases from 20 to 30—a rise of 50%. Plugging in the percentage changes into E_d yields

$$\text{Price Elasticity of Demand} = E_d = \frac{50 \text{ percent}}{-50 \text{ percent}} = -1$$

But if the price rises from $6 to $12—an increase of 100%—the quantity demanded falls from 30 to 20, or decreases 33%. Plugging the percentage changes into E_d yields

$$\text{Price Elasticity of Demand} = E_d = \frac{-33 \text{ percent}}{100 \text{ percent}} = -0.33$$

This result occurs because percentage changes are usually calculated by using the initial value as the base, or reference point. In this example we worked the problem two ways: using $12 as the starting point and dropping the price to $6, and using $6 as the starting point and increasing the price to $12. Even though we are measuring elasticity over the same range of values, the percentage changes are different.

To avoid this problem, economists use the *midpoint method*, which gives the same answer for the elasticity no matter what point you begin with. Equation 4.2 uses the midpoint method to express the price elasticity of demand. While this equation looks more complicated than Equation 4.1, it is not. The midpoint method merely specifies how to plug in the initial and ending values for price and the quantity to determine the percentage changes. Q_1 and P_1 are the initial values and Q_2 and P_2 are the ending values.

$$E_d = \frac{\text{Change in Q} \div \text{average value of Q}}{\text{Change in P} \div \text{average value of P}}$$

$$= \frac{(Q_2 - Q_1) \div [(Q_1 + Q_2) \div 2]}{(P_2 - P_1) \div [(P_1 + P_2) \div 2]} \tag{4.2}$$

The change in the quantity demanded, $(Q_2 - Q_1)$, and the change in price, $P_2 - P_1$, are each divided by the average of the initial and ending values or $[(Q_1 + Q_2) \div 2]$ and $[(P_1 + P_2) \div 2]$ to provide a way of calculating elasticity.

The midpoint method is the preferred method for solving elasticity problems. To see why this is the case, let's return to our pizza demand example.

If the price rises from $6 to $12, quantity falls from 20 to 30. Here the initial values are $P_1 = \$6$ and $Q_1 = 20$. The ending values are $P_2 = \$12$ and $Q_2 = 30$. Using the midpoint method:

$$E_d = \frac{(20 - 30) \div [(30 + 20) \div 2]}{(\$12 - \$6) \div [(\$12 + \$6) \div 2]} = \frac{-10 \div 25}{\$6 \div \$9} = -0.58$$

If the price falls from $12 to $6, quantity rises from 20 to 30. This time the initial values are $P_1 = \$12$ and $Q_1 = 30$. The ending values are $P_2 = \$6$ and $Q_2 = 20$. Using the midpoint method:

$$E_d = \frac{(30 - 20) \div [(20 + 30) \div 2]}{(\$6 - \$12) \div [(\$6 + \$12) \div 2]} = \frac{10 \div 25}{-\$6 \div \$9} = -0.58$$

When we calculated the price elasticity of demand from $6 to $12 using $6 as the initial point, $E_d = -0.33$. Moving in the opposite direction, from $12 to $6, made $12 the initial reference point and $E_d = -1.0$. The midpoint method shown above splits the difference and uses $9 and 25 pizzas as the midpoints. This makes the calculation of the elasticity coefficient the same, -0.58, no matter what direction the price moves. Therefore, economists use the midpoint method to standardize the results. So, using the midpoint method, we arrived at an elasticity coefficient of $-.58$, which is between 0 and -1. What

For many pet owners, the demand for veterinary care is perfectly inelastic.

does that mean? In this case the percentage change in the quantity demanded is less than the percentage change in the price. Whenever the percentage change in the quantity demanded is smaller than the percentage change in price, we say that demand was relatively unresponsive, or inelastic, to the price change. In other words, the price drop does not make a big difference in how much pizza consumers purchased from the pizza shop.

Graphing the Price Elasticity of Demand

Visualizing elasticity graphically helps us understand the relationship between elastic and inelastic demand. Figure 4.1 shows elasticity graphically. As demand becomes increasingly elastic, or responsive to price changes, the demand curve flattens.

Figure 4.1a depicts the price elasticity for pet care. Many pet owners report that they would pay any amount of money to help their pet get better. For these pet owners, the demand curve is a vertical line. If you look along the quantity axis you will see that the quantity of pet care demanded remains constant no matter what it costs. At the same time we see that the price increases from P_0 to P_1. We can calculate the price elasticity coefficient as follows:

$$E_{\text{pet care}} = \frac{\text{percentage change in } Q_d}{\text{percentage change in P}} = \frac{0}{\text{percentage change in P}} = 0$$

When zero is in the numerator, we know that the answer will be zero no matter what we find in the denominator. This makes sense. Many pet owners will try to help their pet feel better no matter what the cost, so we can say that their demand is *perfectly inelastic*. This means that value of E_d will always be zero.

Moving on to Figure 4.1b, we consider the demand for electricity. Whereas many pet owners will not change their consumption of healthcare for their pet no matter what the cost, consumers of electricity will modify their use of electricity in response to price changes. When the price of electricity goes up, they will use less, and when it is relatively cheap, they will use more. But since living without electricity is not practical, using less is a matter of relatively small lifestyle adjustments—buying energy-efficient light bulbs or turning down the thermostat a few degrees. As a result, the demand curve in 4.1b is relatively steep, but not completely vertical as it was in 4.1a.

When the variation on the quantity axis is small compared to the variation on the price axis, the price elasticity is *relatively inelastic*. Plugging these changes into the elasticity formula, we get

$$E_{\text{electricity}} = \frac{\text{percentage change in } Q_d}{\text{percentage change in P}} = \frac{\text{small change}}{\text{large change}}$$

Recall that the law of demand describes an inverse relationship between price and output. Therefore, the changes along the price and quantity axes will always be in the opposite direction. A price elasticity of zero tells us there is no change in the quantity demanded when price changes. So when demand is relatively inelastic, the price elasticity of demand must be relatively close to zero. The easiest way to think about this is to consider how a 10% increase in electric rates works for most households. How much less electricity will you use? The answer for most is a little less, but not 10% less. You can adjust your thermostat, but you still need electricity to run your appliances and lights. When the price changes more than quantity used changes, there is a larger change in the numerator than the denominator. Therefore the price elasticity of demand is between 0 and −1.

In Figure 4.1c we consider an apple. Since there are many good substitutes for an apple, the demand for an apple is *relatively elastic*. The flexibility of consumer demand for apples is illustrated by the degree of responsiveness we see along the quantity axis relative to the change exhibited along the price axis. We can observe this by noting that a relatively elastic demand curve is flatter than an inelastic demand curve. So, whereas perfectly inelastic demand shows no change in demand with an increase in price, and relatively inelastic demand shows a small change in demand with an increase in price, relatively elastic demand shows a large change. Placing this information into the elasticity formula gives us

$$E_{apples} = \frac{\text{percentage change in } Q_d}{\text{percentage change in } P} = \frac{\text{large change}}{\text{small change}}$$

FIGURE 4.1

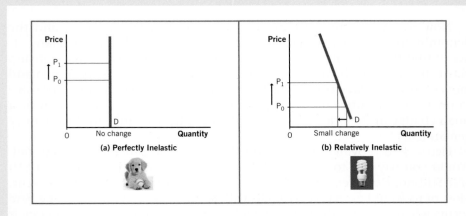
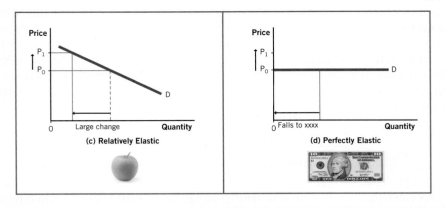

Elasticity and the Demand Curve

For any given price change across two demand curves, demand will be more elastic on the flatter demand curve than on the steeper demand curve. In (a) demand is perfectly inelastic, so the price does not matter. In (b) demand is relatively inelastic, so the price is less important than the quantity purchased. In (c) demand is relatively elastic, so the price matters more than quantity. In (d) demand is perfectly elastic, so price is all that matters.

The demand for electricity
is relatively inelastic.

The demand for an apple is relatively elastic.

Now the numerator—the percentage change in Q_d—is large, and the denominator—the percentage change in P—is small. E_d is less than -1. Recall that the sign must be negative, since there is an inverse relationship between price and the quantity demand. As the price elasticity of demand moves farther away from zero, the consumer becomes more responsive to price change. Since many other fruits are good substitutes for apples, a small change in the price of apples will have a large change in the quantity demanded.

Figure 4.1d provides an interesting example: the demand for a $10 bill. Would you pay $11 to get a $10 bill? No. Would you pay $10.01 for a $10 bill? Still no. However, when the price drops to $10, we become indifferent. Most of us would exchange $10 bills with someone else. The real magic here occurs when the price drops to $9.99. How many $10 bills would you buy if you could buy them for $9.99 or less? The answer: as many as possible! This is exactly what happens in currency markets, where small differences among currency prices around the globe allow traders to buy and sell large quantities of currency and clear a small profit on the difference in exchange rates. This extreme form of price sensitivity is illustrated by a perfectly horizontal demand curve. This means that demand is *perfectly elastic*. Solving for the elasticity yields

$$E_{\$10\,\text{bill}} = \frac{\text{percentage change in } Q_d}{\text{percentage change in P}} = \frac{\text{nearly infinite change}}{\text{very small (\$0.01) change}}$$

We can think of this very small price change, from $10.00 to $9.99, as having essentially an unlimited effect on the quantity of $10 bills demanded. Traders go from being uninterested in trading at $10 to seeking to buy as many $10 bills as possible when the price drops to $9.99. As a result, the price elasticity of demand approaches infinity (∞).

The demand for a $10 bill is perfectly elastic.

There is a fifth type of elasticity, not depicted in Figure 4.1. *Unitary elasticity* is the special name given to describe the situation where elasticity is neither elastic nor inelastic. This occurs when the E_d is exactly -1, and it happens when the percentage change in price is exactly equal to the percentage change in quantity. This characteristic of unitary elasticity will be important when we come to discuss the connection between elasticity and total revenue later in this chapter. You're probably wondering what an example of a unitary good would be. Relax. It is impossible to find a good that has a price elasticity of exactly -1 at all price points. It is enough to know that unitary demand represents the crossover from elastic to inelastic demand.

Now that you have had a chance to look at all four panels in Figure 4.1, here is a handy mnemonic that you can use to keep the difference between inelastic and elastic demand straight.

$$I = \text{inelastic and } E = \text{elastic}$$

The "I" in the word inelastic is vertical, just like the inelastic relationships we examined in Figure 4.1. Likewise, the letter "E" has three horizontal lines to remind us that elastic demand is flat.

Finally, it is possible to pair the elasticity coefficients with an interpretation of how much price matters. You can see this in Table 4.2. When price does not matter, demand is perfectly inelastic; conversely, when price is the only thing that matters, demand becomes perfectly elastic. In between these two extremes, the extent to which price matters determines whether demand is relatively inelastic, unitary, or relatively elastic.

Time, Elasticity, and the Demand Curve

We have already seen that increased time makes demand more elastic. Figure 4.2 shows this graphically. When the price rises from P_1 to P_2, consumers cannot immediately avoid the price increase. For example, if your gas tank is almost empty, you must purchase gas at the new price. Over a slightly longer time horizon—the short run—consumers are more flexible and are able drive less in order to avoid higher-priced gasoline. This means that in the short run consumption declines to Q_2. In the long run, when consumers have time to purchase a more fuel-efficient vehicle, or move closer to work, purchases fall even further. As a result, the demand curve continues to flatten and the quantity demanded falls to Q_3.

Slope and Elasticity

In this section we pause to make sure that you understand what you are observing in the figures. The demand curves shown in Figures 4.1 and 4.2

TABLE 4.2			
The Relationship Between Price Elasticity of Demand and Price			
Elasticity	E_d Coefficient	Interpretation	Example in Figure 4.1
Perfectly inelastic	$E_d = 0$	Price does not matter.	Saving your pet
Relatively inelastic	$0 > E_d > -1$	Price is less important than the quantity you purchase.	Electricity
Unitary	$E_d = -1$	Price and quantity are equally important.	
Relatively elastic	$-1 > E_d > -\infty$	Price is more important than the quantity you purchase.	An apple
Perfectly elastic	$E_d \rightarrow -\infty$	Price is everything.	A $10 bill

FIGURE 4.2

Elasticity and the Demand Curve Over Time

Increased time acts to make demand more elastic. When the price rises from P_1 to P_2, consumers are unable to avoid the price increase in the immediate run. In the short run (D_2), consumers become more flexible and consumption declines to Q_2. Eventually, in the long run (D_3) there is time to make lifestyle changes that further reduce consumption. As a result, the demand curve continues to flatten and the quantity demanded falls to Q_3 in response to higher prices.

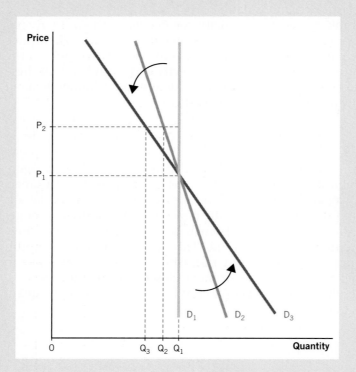

are straight lines, and therefore they have a constant slope, or steepness. (A refresher on slope is part of the appendix to Chapter 2.) So, looking at Figures 4.1 and 4.2, you might think that slope is the same as the price elasticity. But slope does not equal elasticity.

Consider, for example, a trip to Starbucks. Would you buy a tall skinny latte if it was $10? How about $7? What about $5? Say you decide to buy the skinny latte because the price drops from $5 to $4. In this case, a small price change, a drop from $5 to $4, causes you to make the purchase. You can say the demand for skinny lattes is relatively elastic. Now turn to Figure 4.3, which shows a demand curve for skinny lattes. At $5 the consumer purchases 0 lattes, at $4 she purchases 1 latte, at $3 she purchases 2, and she continues to buy one additional latte with each $1 drop in price. As you progress downward along the demand curve, price becomes less of an inhibiting factor and, as a result, the price elasticity of demand slowly becomes more inelastic. Eventually the price falls to zero. At that point, price no longer matters because the lattes are free. Whenever price is irrelevant we say that the price elasticity is perfectly inelastic. Notice that the slope of a linear demand curve is constant. However, when we calculate the price elasticity of demand between the various points in Figure 4.3, it becomes clear that demand is

FIGURE 4.3

The Difference Between Slope and Elasticity

Along any straight demand curve, the price elasticity of demand is not constant. You can see this by noting how the price elasticity of demand changes from highly elastic near the top of the demand curve to highly inelastic near the bottom of the curve.

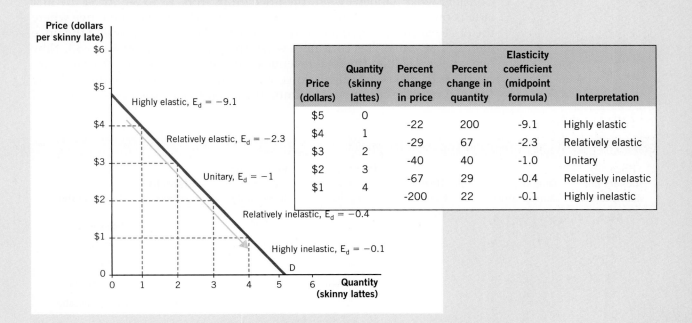

Price (dollars)	Quantity (skinny lattes)	Percent change in price	Percent change in quantity	Elasticity coefficient (midpoint formula)	Interpretation
$5	0				
$4	1	-22	200	-9.1	Highly elastic
$3	2	-29	67	-2.3	Relatively elastic
$2	3	-40	40	-1.0	Unitary
$1	4	-67	29	-0.4	Relatively inelastic
		-200	22	-0.1	Highly inelastic

increasingly inelastic as you move down the demand curve. You can see this in the change in E_d from −9.1 to −0.1.

Perfectly inelastic demand would exist if the elasticity coefficient reached zero. Recall that a value of zero means that there is no change in the quantity demanded as a result of a price change. Therefore, values close to zero reflect inelastic demand, while those farther away reflect more elastic, or price-responsive, demand.

The Relationship Between the Price Elasticity of Demand and Total Revenues

Understanding the price elasticity of demand for the product you sell is important when running a business. The responsiveness of consumers to price changes determines whether a firm would be better off raising or lowering its price. In this section we explore the relationship between the price elasticity of demand and a firm's total revenue.

Total revenue is the amount consumers pay and producers receive for a good.

But first we need to understand the concept of *total revenue*. **Total revenue** is the amount that consumers pay and producers receive for a good. It is calculated by multiplying the price of the good by the quantity of the good that is sold. Table 4.3 reproduces the table from Figure 4.3 and adds a column for the total revenue. We find the total revenue by multiplying the price of a tall skinny latte by the quantity purchased.

After calculating total revenue at each price, we can look at the column of elasticity coefficients for a possible relationship. When we link revenues with the price elasticity of demand, a trade-off emerges. Total revenue is zero when the price is too high ($5 or more) and when the price is $0. Between these two extremes, prices from $1 to $4 generate positive total revenue. Consider what happens when the price drops from $5 to $4. At $4 the first latte is purchased. Total revenue is $4 × 1 = $4. This is also the range where the price elasticity of demand is highly elastic. As a result, lowering the price increases revenue. This continues when the price drops from $4 to $3. Now two lattes are sold so the total revenue continues to rise to $3 × 2 = $6. As we continue to make our calculations, we see that until the price drops below $3, total revenue continues to climb. At the same time, the price elasticity of

TABLE 4.3

The Price Elasticity of Demand and Total Revenues

Price (P) (dollars per skinny latte)	Quantity (Q) (skinny lattes)	Total Revenue P×Q	Percentage change in price	Percentage change in quantity	Elasticity coefficient	Interpretation
$5	0	$0				
			−22	200	−9.1	Highly elastic
4	1	4				
			−29	67	−2.3	Relatively elastic
3	2	6				
			−40	40	−1.0	Unitary
2	3	6				
			−67	29	−0.4	Relatively inelastic
1	4	4				
			−200	22	−0.1	Highly inelastic
0	5	0				

demand remains elastic. From this we conclude that when the price elasticity of demand is elastic, lowering the price will increase total revenue. This relationship can be seen graphically in Figure 4.4.

At a price of $4, one unit is sold and total revenue is $4. When the price is lowered to $3, two units are sold so the total revenue is now $3 × 2 = $6. So, by lowering the price from $4 to $3 the business has generated $2 more in revenue. But to generate this extra revenue, the business has lowered the price from $4 to $3, and therefore given up $1 for each unit it sells. This is represented by the pink-shaded area under the demand curve in Figure 4.5.

When the price drops from $3 to $2, the total revenue stays at $6. This result occurs because demand is unitary, as shown in Figure 4.5. This special condition exists when the percentage price change is exactly offset by an equal percentage change in the quantity demanded. In this situation, revenue remains constant. At $2, three lattes are purchased so the total is $2 × 3, which is the same as it was when $3 was the purchase price. As a result, we can see that total revenues have reached a maximim. Between $3 and $2, the price elasticity of demand is unitary. This finding does not necessarily mean that the firm will operate at the unitary point. Maximizing profit, not revenue, is the ultimate goal of a business, and we have not yet accounted for costs in our calculation of profits.

FIGURE 4.4

The Total Revenue Trade-off When Demand Is Elastic

In the elastic region of the demand curve, lowering the price will increase total revenue. The gains from increased purchases shown in the blue-shaded area are greater than the losses from a lower purchase price, shown in the pink-shaded area.

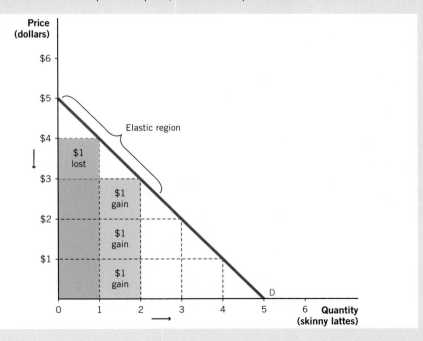

Once we reach a price below unitary demand, we move into the realm of inelastic demand, shown in Figure 4.6. When the price falls to $1, total revenue declines to $4. This result occurs because the price elasiticity of demand is now relatively inelastic, or price insensitive. In other words, latte consumers adding a fourth drink will not gain as much benefit as they did when they purchased the first. Even though the price is declining by $1, price is increasingly unimportant; as you can see by the blue squares, it does not spur a large increase in consumption.

At a price of $2, three units are sold and total revenue is $2 × 3 = $6. When the price falls to $1, four units are sold, so the total revenue is now $4 × 1 = $4. By lowering the price from $2 to $1, the business has lost $2 in extra revenue. This occurs because the business does not generate enough extra revenue from the lower price. Lowering the price from $2 to $1 causes a loss of $3 in existing sales revenue (the pink boxes). At the same time, it generates only $1 in new sales (the blue box).

In this analysis we see that once the demand curve enters the inelastic area, lowering the price decreases total revenue. This is an unambiguously bad thing for a business. The lower price brings in less revenue and requires the business to produce more goods. Since making goods is costly, it does not

FIGURE 4.5

The Total Revenue Trade-off When Demand Is Unitary

When demand is unitary, lowering the price will no longer increase total revenue. The gains from increased purchases, shown in the blue-shaded area, are equal to the losses from a lower purchase price, shown in the pink-shaded area.

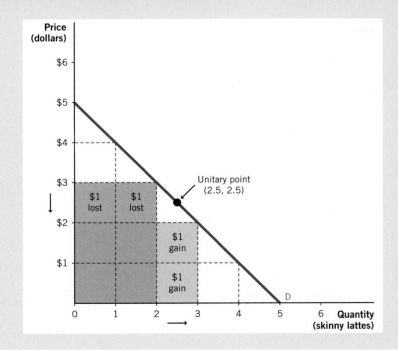

make sense to lower prices into the region where revenues decline. We can be sure that no business will intentionally operate in the inelastic region of the demand curve.

Other Demand Elasticities

We have seen how consumer demand responds to changes in the price of a single good. In this section we will examine how responsive demand is to changes in income and to price changes in other goods.

Income Elasticity

Changes in personal income can have a large effect on consumer spending. The money in your pocket influences not only how much you buy, but also the types of purchases you make. A consumer who is low on money may opt to

FIGURE 4.6

The Total Revenue Trade-off When Demand Is Inelastic
In the inelastic region of the demand curve, lowering the price will decrease total revenue. The gains from increased purchases, shown in the blue-shaded area, are smaller than the losses from a lower purchase price, shown in the pink-shaded area.

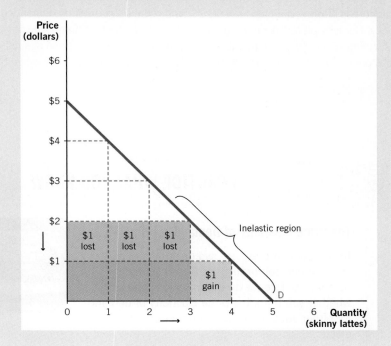

ECONOMICS IN THE MEDIA

Elasticity and Total Revenue

D'oh! The Simpsons and Total Revenue

In the episode "Bart Gets an Elephant," the Simpsons find that their pet elephant, Stampy, is eating them out of house and home. So Bart devises a plan to charge admission for people to see the elephant. He begins by charging $1. However, the revenue collected is not enough to cover Stampy's food bill. When Homer discovers that they are not covering their costs, he raises the cost to see the elephant to $100. However, Homer is not the smartest businessman in the world, and all of the customers who would have paid Bart's $1 admission stay away. We can use our understanding of elasticity to explain why Homer's plan backfires.

Homer's plan is to increase the price. This would work if the demand to see the elephant was inelastic, but it is not. For $100 you could see a concert, attend a major sporting event, or eat out at a very nice restaurant! You'd have to really want to see the elephant to be willing to pay $100. It doesn't help that you can also go to any of the best zoos in the country, and see hundreds of other animals as well, for much less money. Homer's plan is doomed to fail because no one is willing to pay $100. Remember that total revenue = price × quantity purchased. If

The Simpsons cannot afford Stampy. What should they do?

the quantity demanded falls to zero, zero times anything is still zero. So Homer's plan does not generate any revenue.

In contrast, Bart's admission price of $1 brings in $58 in revenue. This is a good start, but not enough to cover Stampy's $300 food bill. Homer actually had the right idea here. Raising the price above $1 would generate more revenue up to a point. Would most of the customers pay $2 to see the elephant? Most likely. $5? Possibly. $10? Maybe. $100? Definitely not. Why not? There is a trade-off dictated by the law of demand. Higher prices will reduce the quantity demanded and vice versa. Therefore, the trick to maximizing total revenue is to balance increases in price against decreases in the quantity purchased.

PRACTICE WHAT YOU KNOW

The Price Elasticity of Demand

In this section there are two questions to give you practice computing the price elasticity of demand. Before we do the math, ask yourself whether you think the price elasticity of demand for either subs or the antibiotic amoxicillin is elastic.

Question: A store manager decides to lower the price of a featured sandwich from $3.00 to $2.00, and finds that sales during the week increase from 240 to 480 units. Is demand elastic?

Is the demand for a sub or amoxicillin more elastic?

Answer: Consumers were flexible and bought significantly more sandwiches in response to the price drop. Let's calculate the price elasticity of demand using Equation 4.2. Recall that

$$E_d = \frac{(Q_2 - Q_1) \div [(Q_1 + Q_2) \div 2]}{(P_2 - P_1) \div [(P_1 + P_2) \div 2]}$$

Plugging in the values from above yields

$$E_d = \frac{(480 - 240) \div [(240 + 480) \div 2}{(\$2 - \$3) \div [(\$2 + \$3) \div 2]} = \frac{240 \div 360}{-\$1 \div \$2.50}$$

Therefore, $E_d = -1.67$.

Whenever the price elasticity of demand is less than –1, demand is considered elastic: the percentage change in the quantity demanded is greater than the percentage change in price. Hopefully this is what you expected. Subs are one option for a meal. There are many other choices. People also enjoy salads, burgers, and chicken. Therefore, we should not be surprised that there is a relatively large percentage increase in sub purchases by price-conscious customers.

Question: A local pharmacy store manager decides to raise the price of a 50-pill prescription of amoxicillin from $8.00 to $10.00. The pharmacy tracks the sales of amoxicillin over the next month and finds that sales decline from 1,500 to 1,480 boxes. Is the price elasticity of demand elastic?

Answer: First let's consider the potential substitutes for amoxicillin. To be sure, you can substitute other drugs, but they might not be as effective. Therefore, most patients prefer to use the drug prescribed by their doctor. Also, in this case, the cost of the drug is relatively small. Finally, your need for amoxicillin is a short-run consideration. You want the medicine now so you will get better! All three of these factors would lead us to believe that the demand for amoxicillin is relatively inelastic. Let's find out if that intuition is confirmed in the data.

The price elasticity of demand using the midpoint method is

$$E_d = \frac{(Q_2 - Q_1) \div [(Q_1 + Q_2) \div 2]}{(P_2 - P_1) \div [(P_1 + P_2) \div 2]}$$

Plugging in the values from the example yields

$$E_d = \frac{(1480 - 1500) \div [(1480 + 1500) \div 2]}{(\$10 - \$8) \div [(\$8 + \$10) \div 2]}$$

Simplifying produces

$$E_d = \frac{-20 \div 1490}{\$2 \div \$9}$$

Therefore, the $E_d = -0.06$. Recall that an E_d near zero indicates that the price elasticity of demand is highly inelastic, which is what we suspected. The price increase does not cause consumption to fall very much. If the store manager had been hoping to bring in a little extra revenue from the sales of amoxicillin, the plan was successful. Before the price increase the business sold 1,500 units at $8.00, so revenues were $12,000. After the price increase, sales decreased to 1,480 units, but the new price is $10.00, so revenues are $14,800. Raising the price of amoxicillin helped the pharmacy make an additional $2,800 in revenue.

buy a cheap generic product, while someone with a little extra cash can afford to upgrade. The grocery store aisle reflects this. Store brands and name products compete for shelf space. Lower-income shoppers can choose the store brand to save money, while more affluent shoppers can choose their favorite cereal without worrying about the purchase price. The **income elasticity of demand** measures how a change in income affects spending. It is calculated by dividing the change in the quantity purchased by the change in personal income:

The **income elasticity of demand** measures how a change in come affects spending.

$$E_I = \frac{\text{percentage change in the quantity consumed}}{\text{percentage change in income}} \qquad (4.3)$$

Ordinarily there is a positive relationship between income and the quantity consumed. When higher levels of income allow the consumer to purchase more, the goods that are purchased are normal goods. Since the demand for normal goods goes up with income, normal goods have a positive income elasticity—a rise in income will cause a rise in the quantity purchased. For instance, if you receive a 20% pay raise and you decide to pay an extra 10% to get HBO on your cable television, the resulting income elasticity is positive, since 10% divided by 20% is 0.5. Whenever the good is normal, the result is a positive income elasticity of demand, and purchases of the good rise as income expands.

Clothing purchases expand with income.

Normal goods fall into two categories: *necessities* and *luxuries*. Goods that people consider to be necessities generally have income elasticities between 0 and 1. Expenditures on items such as milk, clothing, electricity, and gasoline are unavoidable and consumers at any income level must buy them no matter what. Although purchases of necessities will increase as income rises, they do not rise as fast as the increase in income. Therefore, as income increases, spending on necessities will expand at a slower rate than the increase in income.

Rising income allows consumers to enjoy significantly more luxuries. This produces an income elasticity of demand greater than 1. For instance, a family of modest means may travel almost exclusively by car. However, as the family's income rises, they can afford air travel. A relatively small jump in income can cause the family to fly instead of drive.

In Chapter 3 we saw that *inferior goods* are those that people will choose not to purchase when their income goes up. Inferior goods have a negative income elasticity, because as income expands, the demand for the good declines. We see this in Table 4.4 with the example of macaroni and cheese, an inexpensive meal. As a household's income rises, it is able to afford healthier food and also more variety in the meals it enjoys. Consequently, the number of times that mac and cheese is served declines. The decline in consumption indicates that mac and cheese is an inferior good, and this is reflected in the negative sign of the income elasticity.

Air travel is a luxury good.

Cross-Price Elasticity

Now we will look at how a price change in one good can affect the demand for a related good. For instance, if you enjoy pizza, the choice between ordering Domino's and Pizza Hut is influenced by the price of both goods. The **cross-price elasticity of demand** measures the responsiveness of the quantity demanded of one good to a change in the price of another good.

$$E_c = \frac{\text{Percentage change in the quantity demanded of one good}}{\text{Percentage change in the price of another good}} \quad (4.4)$$

The **cross-price elasticity of demand** measures the responsiveness of the quantity demanded of one good to a change in price of another good.

TABLE 4.4

Income Elasticity			
Type of Good	**Subcategory**	**E_I Coefficient**	**Example**
Inferior		$E_I > 0$	Macaroni and Cheese
Normal	Necessity	$0 > E_I > 1$	Milk
Normal	Luxury	$E_I > 1$	Diamond ring

TABLE 4.5		
Cross-Price Elasticity		
Type of Good	E_I Coefficient	Example
Substitutes	$E_C > 0$	Pizza Hut and Domino's
No relationship	$E_C = 0$	A basketball and bedroom slippers
Complements	$E_C < 0$	Turkey and gravy

Consider how two goods are related to one another. If the goods are substitutes, a price rise in one good will cause the quantity demanded of that good to decline. At the same time, since consumers can purchase the substitute good for the same price as before, demand for the substitute good increases. Therefore, a price increase in Domino's pizza is positively related to the demand for Pizza Hut pizza. When the price of Domino's rises, consumers buy more pizza from Pizza Hut.

The opposite is true if the goods are complements. When goods are related to one another, a price increase in one good makes the joint consumption of both goods more expensive. Therefore, the consumption of both goods declines. For instance, if Thanksgiving turkeys are more expensive than usual, consumers will serve less turkey and less gravy. A price increase for turkeys will cause the quantity demanded of both turkey and gravy to decline. This means that the cross-price elasticity of demand is negative.

What if there is no relationship? For example, if the price of basketballs goes up, that probably will not affect the quantity demanded of bedroom slippers. In this case, the cross-price elasticity is neither positive nor negative; it is zero. Table 4.5 lists cross-price elasticity values according to type of good.

To learn how to calculate cross-price elasticity, let's consider an example from the skit "Lazy Sunday" on *Saturday Night Live*. The skit features Chris Parnell and

Have you tried Mr. Pibb and Red Vines together?

Andy Samberg rapping about going to see *The Chronicles of Narnia* and eating cupcakes. In one inspired scene, they describe enjoying the soft drink Mr. Pibb with Red Vines candy and call the combination "crazy delicious." From this we can construct a cross-price elasticity example. Suppose that the price of a two-liter bottle of Mr. Pibb falls from $1.49 to $1.29. In the week immediately preceding the price drop, a local store sells 60 boxes of Red Vines. After the price drop, sales of Red Vines increase to 80 boxes. Calculate the cross-price elasticity of demand for Red Vines when the price of Mr. Pibb falls from $1.49 to $1.29.

The cross-price elasticity of demand using the midpoint method is

$$E_I = \frac{(Q_{A2} - Q_{A1}) \div [(Q_{A1} + Q_{A2}) \div 2]}{(P_{B2} - P_{B1}) \div [(P_{B1} + P_{B2}) \div 2]}$$

Notice that there are now additional subscripts to denote that we are measuring the percentage change in the quantity demanded of good A in response to the percent change in the price of good B.

Plugging in the values from the example yields

$$E_c = \frac{(20) \div [(60 + 80) \div 2]}{(-\$0.20) \div [(\$1.49 + \$1.29) \div 2]}$$

Simplifying produces

$$E_c = \frac{20 \div 70}{-\$0.20 \div \$1.39}$$

Solving for E_c gives us a value of –1.01. Since the result is a negative value, this confirms our intuition that two goods that go well together ("crazy delicious") are complements, since the decrease in the price of Mr. Pibb causes consumers to buy more Red Vines.

ECONOMICS IN THE REAL WORLD

The Wii Rollout and Changes in the Video Game Industry

When Nintendo launched the Wii console in late 2006, it fundamentally changed the gaming industry. The Wii uses motion-sensing technology. Despite relatively poor graphics, it provided a completely different gaming experience from its competitors, Playstation 3 (PS3) and the Xbox 360. Yet the PS3 and Xbox 360 had larger storage capacities and better graphics, in theory making them more attractive to gamers than the Wii.

During the 2006 holiday shopping season the three systems had three distinct price points:

Wii = $249
Xbox = $399
Playstation 3 = $599

Wii and Xbox sales were very strong. As a result, both units were in short supply in stores. However, PS3 sales did not fare as well as Sony had hoped. The

Waiting in line for a Wii.

Wii outsold the PS3 by a more than 4:1 ratio, and the Xbox 360 outsold the PS3 by more than 2:1 during the first half of 2007. More telling, a monthly breakdown of the sales figures across the three platforms shows the deterioration in the PS3 and Xbox 360 sales.

Units Sold in January 2007:

Wii: 460,000
Xbox 360: 249,000
PS3: 244,000

Units Sold in April 2007:

Wii: 360,000 (−22%)
Xbox 360: 174,000 (−30%)
PS3: 82,000 (−66%)

Faced with quickly falling sales, Sony lowered the price of the PS3 console. Sony understood that consumer demand was quite elastic and lowering the price was the only way to retain customers. The lower price stimulated additional interest in the PS3 and helped to increase the number of units sold in the second half of the year. Without a firm grasp of the price elasticity of demand, Sony would not have made this move.

Meanwhile, interest in the Wii continued to be strong. For Nintendo, the market demand was relatively inelastic. Nintendo could have raised the price of its console but chose not to do so. One reason is that Nintendo also makes money by selling peripherals and games. The peripherals and games are strong complements to the console and a higher console price would discourage customers from purchasing the Wii. Since the cross-price elasticity of demand for peripherals and games is highly negative, this strategy makes economic sense. Nintendo had chosen not to do this, in part, because the company wanted to maximize not only the console price, but also the prices of all of the related components. Nintendo's strategy worked. The four top-selling games during 2007 were all associated with the Wii rollout. ✳

PRACTICE WHAT YOU KNOW

Income Elasticity

Question: A college student eats ramen noodles twice a week and earns $300/week working part time. After graduating, the student earns $1,000/week and eats ramen noodles every other week. What is the student's income elasticity?

Yummy, or all you can afford?

Answer: The income elasticity of demand using the midpoint method is

$$E_I = \frac{(Q_2 - Q_1) \div [(Q_1 + Q_2) \div 2]}{(I_2 - I_1) \div [(I_1 + I_2) \div 2]}$$

Plugging in yields

$$E_I = \frac{(0.5 - 2.0) \div [(2.0 + 0.5) \div 2]}{(\$1000 - \$300) \div [(\$300 + \$1000) \div 2]}$$

Simplifying yields

$$E_I = \frac{-1.5 \div 1.25}{\$700 \div \$650}$$

Therefore, the $E_I = -1.1$.

The income elasticity of demand is positive for normal goods and negative when the good is inferior. Therefore, the negative coefficient indicates that ramen noodles are an inferior good over the range of income—between $300 and $1,000, in this example. This result should confirm your intuition. The higher post-graduation income allows the student to substitute away from ramen noodles and towards other meals that provide more enjoyment.

The Price Elasticity of Supply

Producers, like consumers, are sensitive to price changes. However, the determinants of the *price elasticity of supply* are substantially different from the determinants of the price elasticity of demand. The **price elasticity of supply** is a measure of the responsiveness of the quantity supplied to a change in price. In this section we examine how much producers respond to price changes. For instance, if the market price of gasoline increases, how will oil companies respond? The answer depends on the elasticity of supply. Oil must be refined into gasoline. If it is difficult for oil companies to increase their output of gasoline significantly, even if the price increases a lot, the quantity of gasoline supplied will not increase much. In this case we say that the price elasticity of supply is inelastic, or unresponsive. On the other hand, if the price increase is small and suppliers respond by offering significantly more gasoline for sale, the price elasticity of supply is elastic. We would expect to observe this outcome if it was easy for oil to be refined into gasoline.

When supply is not able to respond to a change in price, we say it is inelastic. Think of an oceanfront lot. The amount of land next to the ocean is fixed. If the price of oceanfront property rises, the supply of land cannot adjust to the price increase. In this case, the supply is perfectly inelastic and the elasticity is zero. Recall that a price elasticity coefficient of zero means that supply does not change as price changes.

When the ability of the supplier to make quick adjustments is limited, the elasticity of supply is less than 1. For instance, when a cellular network becomes congested, it takes suppliers a long time to provide additional

The **price elasticity of supply** is a measure of the responsiveness of the quantity supplied to a change in price.

What would it take to own a slice of paradise?

capacity. They have to build new cell towers, which requires the purchase of land and additional construction costs. In contrast, a local hot dog vendor can easily add another cart in relatively short order. As a result, for the hot dog vendor, supply elasticity is elastic with an elasticity coefficient that is greater than 1. Table 4.6 examines the price elasticity of supply. Recall that the law of supply states that there is a direct relationship between the price of the good and the quantity that a firm supplies. As a result, the percentage change in the quantity supplied and the percentage change in price move in the same direction. The E_S coefficient reflects this direct relationship with a positive sign.

Determinants of the Price Elasticity of Supply

When we examined the determinants of the price elasticity of demand, we saw that consumers had to consider the number of substitutes, how expensive the item was compared to their overall budget, and the amount of time they had to make a decision. Time and the adjustment process are also a key element in determining the price elasticity of supply. However, there is also a critical difference: the degree of flexibility that producers have in bringing their product to the market quickly.

The Flexibility of Producers

When a producer can quickly ramp up output, supply tends to be elastic. One way to maintain flexibility is to have spare production capacity. Extra capacity allows producers to quickly meet changing price conditions, so supply is more responsive, or elastic. The ability to store the good is another way to stay flexible. Producers who have stockpiles of their products can respond

TABLE 4.6

A Closer Look at the Price Elasticity of Supply

Elasticity	E_S Coefficient	Example
Perfectly inelastic	$E_S = 0$	Oceanfront land
Relatively inelastic	$0 < E_S < 1$	Cellphone tower
Relatively elastic	$E_S > 1$	Hot dog vendor

more quickly to changes in market conditions. For example, De Beers, the international diamond conglomerate, stores millions of uncut diamonds. As the price of diamonds fluctuates, De Beers is able to quickly change the supply of diamonds it offers to the market. Likewise, hot dog vendors can relocate quickly from one street corner to another or add carts if demand is strong. However, many businesses cannot adapt to changing market conditions quickly. For instance, a golf course cannot easily add holes to meet additional demand. This limits the ability of a golf course owner to adjust quickly and increase the supply of golf as soon as the price changes.

Time and the Adjustment Process

In the immediate run, businesses, just like consumers, are stuck with what they have on hand. For example, a pastry shop that runs out of chocolate glazed donuts cannot bake more instantly. As we move from the immediate run to the short run and a price change persists through time, supply—just like demand—becomes more elastic. A longer time horizon gives a producer additional options to pursue in order to capitalize on price increases. For instance, in the long run a golf resort could add another course or expand its facilities in order to accommodate more customers. The resort may be able to squeeze extra production out of its current facility by staying open longer hours or moving tee times closer together, but those short-run efforts will not match the production potential of adding another course in the long run.

Figure 4.7 shows how the two determinants of supply elasticity are mapped onto the supply curve. In the immediate run the supply curve is

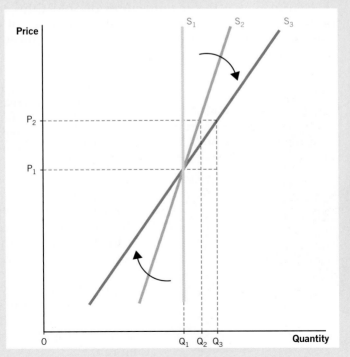

FIGURE 4.7

Elasticity and the Supply Curve

Increased flexibility and more time make supply more elastic. When price rises from P_1 to P_2, producers are unable to expand output immediately and it remains at Q_1. In the short run (S_2), the firm becomes more flexible and output expands to Q_2. Eventually, in the long run (S_3) the firm is able produce even more, and it moves to Q_3 in response to higher prices.

vertical (S_1). A vertical curve tells us that there is no responsiveness when the price changes. As producers gain additional time to make adjustments, the supply curve rotates from S_1, the immediate run, to S_2, the short run, to S_3, the long run. Like the demand curve, the supply curve becomes flatter through time. The only difference is that the supply curve rotates clockwise, whereas, as we saw in Figure 4.2, the demand curve rotates counterclockwise. With both supply and demand, the most important thing to remember is that more time allows for greater adjustment, so the long run is always more elastic.

Calculating the Price Elasticity of Supply

Like the price elasticity of demand, we can calculate the price elasticity of supply. This is useful when a business owner must decide how much to produce at various prices. The elasticity of supply measures how quickly the producer is able to change production in response to changes in price. When the price elasticity of supply is elastic, producers are able to quickly adjust production. If the price elasticity of supply is inelastic, production tends to remain roughly constant, despite large swings in price.

Here is the formula for the price elasticity of supply:

$$E_s = \frac{\text{Percentage change in the quantity supplied}}{\text{Percentage change in the price}} \qquad (4.5)$$

This equation is almost exactly the same as that of the price elasticity of demand. The only difference is that we are measuring the percentage change in the quantity supplied in the numerator.

Consider how the manufacturer of Solo Cups might respond to an increase in demand that causes the market price of the cups to rise. The company's ability to change the amount it produces depends on the flexibility of the manufacturing process and the length of time needed to

ramp up production. Suppose that the price of the cups rises 10%. The company can increase its production 5% immediately, but it will take many months to expand production by 20%. What can we say about the price elasticity of supply? Using Equation 4.5 we can take the percentage change in the quantity supplied immediately (5%) and divide that by the percentage change in price (10%). This gives us an $E_S = 0.5$, which signals that the elasticity of supply is relatively inelastic. However, with time the firm is able to increase the quantity supplied by 20%. If we divide 20% by the percentage change in the price (10%), we get $E_S = 2.0$, which indicates that the price elasticity of supply is relatively elastic in the long run.

PRACTICE WHAT YOU KNOW

Price Elasticity of Supply

Question: Suppose that the price of a barrel of oil increases from $60 to $100. The new output is 2 million barrels a day, and the old output is 1.8 million barrels. What is the price elasticity of supply?

Answer: The price elasticity of supply using the midpoint method is

$$E_d = \frac{(Q_2 - Q_1) \div [(Q_1 + Q_2) \div 2]}{(P_2 - P_1) \div [(P_1 + P_2) \div 2]}$$

Plugging in the values from the example yields

$$E_S = \frac{(.2M) \div [(1.8M + 2.0M) \div 2]}{(\$40) \div [(\$60 + \$100) \div 2]}$$

Oil companies have us over a barrel.

Simplifying yields

$$E_S = \frac{.2M \div 1.9M}{\$40 \div \$80}$$

Therefore, the $E_S = 0.20$.

Recall from our discussion of the law of supply that there is a direct relationship between the price and the quantity supplied. Since the E_S is positive, we see that output rises as price rises. However, the magnitude of the output increase is quite small—this is reflected in the coefficient 0.20. Because oil companies cannot easily change their production process, they have a limited ability to respond quickly to rising prices. That inability is reflected in a coefficient that is relatively close to zero. A zero coefficient would mean that suppliers could not change their output at all. Here suppliers are able to respond, but only in a limited capacity.

Combining Supply and Demand

The interplay between the price elasticity of supply and the price elasticity of demand allows us to explain more fully how the economy operates. With an understanding of elasticity at our disposal, we can provide a much richer and deeper analysis of the world around us. For instance, suppose that we are concerned about what will happen to the price of oil as economic development spurs additional demand in China and India. An examination of the determinants of the price elasticity of supply quickly confirms that oil producers have a limited ability to adjust production in response to rising prices. Oil wells can be uncapped to meet rising demand, but it takes years to bring capacity online. Moreover, storing oil reserves, while possible, is expensive. Therefore, the short-run supply of oil is quite inelastic. Figure 4.8 shows the

PRACTICE WHAT YOU KNOW

Combining Supply and Demand

Is a pumpkin a fruit or a vegetable?

Question: An unusually bad growing season leads to a small pumpkin crop. What will happen to the price of pumpkins as Halloween approaches?

Answer: The demand for pumpkins peaks in October and rapidly falls after Halloween. Purchasing a pumpkin is a short-run decision to buy a unique product that takes up a relatively small share of the consumer's budget. As a result, the price elasticity of demand for pumpkins leading up to Halloween tends to be quite inelastic. At the same time, the small crop causes the entire supply curve to shift left. This causes the market price of pumpkins to rise. Since the demand is relatively inelastic in the short run and the supply of pumpkins is fixed, we expect the price to rise significantly. After Halloween the price of any remaining pumpkins falls, since demand declines dramatically.

FIGURE 4.8

A Demand Shift and the Consequences for Short- and Long-Run Supply

When an increase in demand causes the price of oil to rise from $60 to $90, initially producers are unable to expand output very much—production expands to from Q_1 to Q_2. However, in the long run, as producers expand production, the price will fall back to $80.

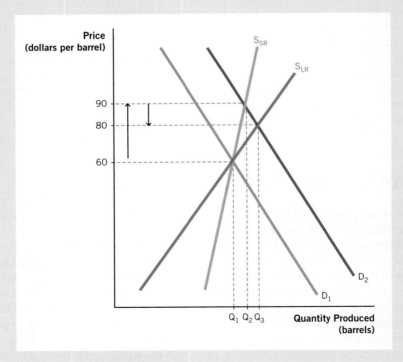

combination of inelastic supply-side production constraints in the short run and the inelastic short-run demand for oil.

An increase in global demand from D_1 to D_2 will create significantly higher prices (from \$60 to \$90) in the short run. This occurs because increasing oil production is difficult in the short run. Therefore, the supply curve (S_{SR}) is relatively inelastic. In the long run, oil producers are able to bring more oil to the market when prices are higher, so the supply curve rotates clockwise (S_{LR}), becoming more elastic, and the market price falls to \$80.

Conclusion

Do producers charge the highest price possible? We can now answer this misconception definitively: no. Producers like higher prices the same way consumers like lower prices, but that does not mean that they will charge the highest price possible. At very high prices we learned that consumer demand is quite elastic. Therefore, a producer who charges too high a price will not sell much. As a result, firms learn that they must lower their price in order to attract more customers.

The ability to determine whether demand and supply are elastic or inelastic also allows economists to calculate the effects of personal, business, and policy decisions. When you combine the concept of elasticity with the supply and demand model from Chapter 3, you get a very powerful tool. As a result, we can now say much more about how the world works than we could before. In subsequent chapters we will employ the understanding of elasticity to refine our models of economic behavior and make our results more realistic.

Price Elasticity of Supply and Demand: Buying Your First Car

When you buy a car, your knowledge of price elasticity can help you negotiate the best possible deal.

Recall that the three determinants of price elasticity of demand are the share of the budget, the number of available substitutes, and the time you have to make a decision.

Let's start with your budget. You should have a budget in mind, but don't tell the salesperson what you are willing to spend; that is a vital piece of personal information you want to keep to yourself. If the salesperson suggests that you look at a model that is too expensive, just say that you are not interested. You might reply, "Buying a car is a stretch for me, I've got to stay within my budget." If the salesperson asks indirectly about your budget by trying to find out if you have a particular monthly payment in mind, tell him that you want to negotiate over the invoice price once you decide on a vehicle. Never negotiate on the sticker price, which is the price you see in the car window, because it includes thousands of dollars in markup. You want to make it clear to the salesperson that the price you pay matters to you—that is, your demand is elastic.

Next, make it clear that you are gathering information and visiting other dealers. That is, make it clear that you have many available substitutes. Even if you really want a Honda, do not voice that desire to the Honda salesperson. Perhaps mention that you are also visiting the Toyota, Hyundai, and Ford showrooms. Compare what you've seen on one lot versus another. Each salesperson you meet should hear that you are seriously considering other options. This indicates to each dealership that your demand is elastic and getting your business will require that they offer you a better price.

Taking your time to decide is also important. Never buy a car the first time you walk onto a lot. If you give the message that you want a car immediately, you are saying that your demand is inelastic. If the dealership thinks that you have no flexibility, they will not give you their best offer. Instead tell the salesperson that you appreciate their help and that you will be deciding over the next few weeks. A good salesperson will know you are serious and ask for your phone number or email and contact you. The salesperson will sweeten the deal if you indicate you are narrowing down your choices and they are in the running. You wait. You win.

Also know that salespeople and dealerships have times when they want to move inventory. In other words, the price elasticity of supply is at work here as well. A good time to buy is when the dealer is trying to move inventory to make room for new models. Prices fall for end-of-the-model-year closeouts. Likewise, many sales promotions and sales bonuses are tied to the end of the month, so salespeople will be more eager to sell at that time. Ask if any internal promotions are going on to move the inventory. The dealership may work harder to get your business if you show up at the right time.

Watch out for shady negotiation practices!

ANSWERING THE BIG QUESTIONS

1. What is the price elasticity of demand and what are its determinants?

✳ The price elasticity of demand is a measure of the responsiveness of quantity demanded to a change in price.

✳ Demand will generally be more elastic if there are many substitutes available, if the item comprises a large share of your budget, or if you have plenty of time to make a decision.

✳ Economists categorize time in three distinct periods: the immediate run, where there is no time to adjust your behavior; the short run, where you can adjust, but only partially; and the long run, where the decision-maker has time to fully adjust.

✳ The price elasticity of demand can be calculated by taking the percentage change in the quantity demanded and dividing it by the percentage change in price. A value of zero indicates that the quantity demanded does not respond to a price change; if the price elasticity is zero, demand is said to be perfectly inelastic. When the price elasticity of demand is between 0 and −1, demand is inelastic. If the price elasticity of demand is less than −1, demand is elastic.

2. How do changes in income and the prices of other goods affect elasticity?

✳ The income elasticity of demand is defined as the change in the quantity purchased divided by the change in personal income. Normal goods have a positive income elasticity. Inferior goods have a negative income elasticity.

✳ The cross-price elasticity of demand measures the responsiveness of the quantity demanded of one good to a change in the price of another good. Positive values for the cross-price elasticity mean that two goods are substitutes, while negative values indicate that the two goods are complements. If the cross-price elasticity is zero, then the two goods are not correlated with one another.

3. What is the price elasticity of supply?

✳ The price elasticity of supply is a measure of the responsiveness of the quantity supplied to a change in price. Supply will generally be more elastic if producers have flexibility in the production process and ample time to adjust production.

✳ The price elasticity of supply is calculated by dividing the percentage change in the quantity supplied by the percentage change in price. A value of zero indicates that the quantity supplied does not respond to a price change; if the price elasticity is zero, supply is said to be perfectly inelastic. When the price elasticity of supply is between 0 and 1, demand is inelastic. If the price elasticity of supply is greater than 1, supply is elastic.

CONCEPTS YOU SHOULD KNOW

Cross-price elasticity (p. 127)   Income elasticity (p. 126)   Price elasticity of supply (p. 131)
Elasticity (p. 106)   Long run (p. 109)   Short run (p. 109)
Immediate run (p. 108)   Price elasticity of demand (p. 107) Total revenue (p. 120)

QUESTIONS FOR REVIEW

1. Define the price elasticity of demand.

2. What are the three determinants of the price elasticity of demand?

3. Give an example of a good that has elastic demand. What is the value of the price elasticity if demand is elastic? Give an example of a good that has an inelastic demand. What is the value of the price elasticity if demand is inelastic?

4. What is the connection between total revenue and the price elasticity of demand? Illustrate this relationship along a demand curve.

5. Explain why slope is different from elasticity.

6. Define the price elasticity of supply.

7. What are the two determinants of the price elasticity of supply?

8. Give an example of a good that has elastic supply. What is the value of the price elasticity if supply is elastic? Give an example of a good that has an inelastic supply. What is the value of the price elasticity if supply is inelastic?

9. Give an example of a normal good. What is the income elasticity of a normal good? Give an example of a luxury good. What is the income elasticity of a luxury good? Give an example of a necessity. What is the income elasticity of a necessity? Give an example of an inferior good. What is the income elasticity of an inferior good?

10. Define the cross-price elasticity of demand. Give an example with negative cross-price elasticity, another with zero cross-price elasticity, and a third with positive cross-price elasticity.

STUDY PROBLEMS

*1. If the government decided to impose a 50% tax on grey t-shirts, would the government generate a large or small increase in revenues? Use elasticity to explain your answer.

2. College logo t-shirts priced at $15 sell at a rate of 25 per week, but when the bookstore marks them down to $10, it finds that it can sell 50 t-shirts per week. What is the price elasticity of demand for the logo t-shirts?

3. Check out the following video: http://www .youtube.com/watch?v=ncZkrO06le8. Do the early shoppers appear to have elastic or inelastic demand on Black Friday?

4. If a 20% increase in price causes a 10% drop in the quantity demanded, is the price elasticity of demand elastic, unitary, or inelastic?

5. Characterize each of the following goods as perfectly elastic, relatively elastic, relatively inelastic, or perfectly inelastic.
   a. A life-saving medication
   b. A copy that costs 11 cents at one copy store, when all of their competitors charge 10 cents per copy
   c. A fast-food restaurant located in the food court of a shopping mall
   d. The water bill you pay

6. A local paintball business receives total revenue of $8,000 a month when they charge $10 per person, and $10,000 in total revenue when they charge $6 per person. Over that range of prices, does the business face elastic, unitary, or inelastic demand?

7. At a price of $200 a cellphone company manufactures 300,000 units. At a price of $150

the company produces 200,000 phones. What is the price elasticity of supply?

8. Do customers who visit convenience stores at 3 A.M. have a price elasticity of demand that is more or less elastic than those who visit at 3 P.M.?

✳ 9. A worker gets a 25% raise. As a result he decides to eat out twice as much as before and cut back on the number of lasagna dinners from once a week to once every other week. Determine the income elasticity of demand for eating out and lasagna.

10. The cross-price elasticity of demand between American Eagle and Hollister is 2.0. What does that tell us about the relationship between these two stores?

11. A local golf course is considering lowering its price in order to increase the revenue coming

in. Under what conditions is the price reduction a good idea?

12. A university notices that in- and out-of-state students seem to respond differently to tuition changes.

Tuition	Quantity Demanded (In-state applicants)	Quantity Demanded (Out-of-state applicants)
$10,000	6,000	12,000
$15,000	5,000	9,000
$20,000	4,000	6,000
$30,000	3,000	3,000

As the price of tuition rises from $15,000 to $20,000, what is the price elasticity of demand for in-state applicants and also for out-of-state applicants?

SOLVED PROBLEMS

1. To answer this question we need to consider the price elasticity of demand. The tax is only on grey t-shirts. That means that t-shirt customers who buy other colors can avoid the tax entirely. Unless you really like to wear grey, you can avoid the tax entirely. This means that the demand for grey t-shirts is relatively elastic. Since not many grey t-shirts will be sold, the government generates a small amount of revenue from the tax.

9. In this question a worker gets a 25% raise, so we can use this information in the denominator when determining the income elasticity of demand. We are not given the percentage change for the meals out, so we need to plug in how often he ate out before (once a week) and the amount he eats out after the raise (twice a week).
Plugging into E_I gives us

$$E_I = \frac{(2 - 1) \div [(1 + 2) \div 2]}{25\%}$$

Simplifying yields

$$E_I = \frac{1 \div 1.5}{25\%}$$

Therefore, the $E_I = 2.67$.

The income elasticity of demand is positive for normal goods. Therefore, eating out is a normal good. This result should confirm your intuition.

Let's see what happens with lasagna once he gets the 25% raise. Now he cuts back on the number of lasagna dinners from once a week to once every other week.

Plugging into E_I gives us

$$E_I = \frac{(.5 - 1) \div [(1 + .5) \div 2]}{25\%}$$

Simplifying yields

$$E_I = \frac{-0.5 \div 0.75}{25\%}$$

Therefore, the $E_I = -2.67$. The income elasticity of demand is negative. Therefore, lasagna is an inferior good. This result should confirm your intuition.

Price Controls

The minimum wage helps people earn a living wage.

You are probably familiar with the minimum wage, which is an example of a *price control*. If you have ever worked for the minimum wage, you

probably think that raising it sounds like a great idea. You may support minimum wage legislation because you believe it will help struggling workers make ends meet. After all, it seems reasonable that firms should compensate workers fairly so that they can earn at least enough to pay for the necessities of life, or what is referred to as a living wage.

Price controls are not a new idea. The first recorded attempt to control prices was 4,000 years ago in ancient Babylon, when King Hammurabi decreed how much corn a farmer could pay for a cow. Similar attempts to control prices occurred in ancient Egypt, Greece, and Rome. Each attempt ended badly. In Egypt, farmers revolted against tight price controls and intrusive inspections, eventually causing the economy to collapse. In Greece, the Athenian government set the price of grain at a very low level. Predictably, the supply of grain dried up. In 301 C.E., the Roman government under Emperor Diocletian prescribed the maximum price of beef, grains, clothing, and many other articles. Almost immediately, markets for these goods disappeared.

History has shown us that price controls generally do not work. Why? Because they disrupt the normal functioning of the market. By the end of this chapter, we hope that you will understand why price controls such as minimum wage laws are rarely the win-win propositions that legislators often claim. To help you understand why price controls lead to disequilibrium in markets, this chapter focuses on the two most common types of price controls: *price ceilings* and *price floors*.

Photo to come

BIG QUESTIONS

* When do price ceilings matter?
* What effects do price ceilings have on economic activity?
* When do price floors matter?
* What effects do price floors have on economic activity?

When Do Price Ceilings Matter?

Price controls
are an attempt to set
prices through government
involvement in the market.

Price controls are an attempt to set, or manipulate, prices through government involvement in the market. In most cases, and certainly in the United States, price controls are enacted to ease perceived burdens on the population. A **price ceiling** creates a legally established maximum price for a good or service. In the next section we will consider what happens when a price ceiling is established. Price ceilings create many unintended effects that policy makers rarely acknowledge.

Price ceilings
are legally established
maximum prices for goods
or services.

Understanding Price Ceilings

Prize cannot be priced higher

To understand how price ceilings work, let's try a simple thought experiment. Suppose that prices are rising because of inflation. The government is concerned that people with low incomes will not be able to afford enough to eat. To help the disadvantaged, legislators pass a law that no one can charge more than $0.50 for a loaf of bread. (Note that this price ceiling is about one-third of the typical price of generic white bread.) Does the new law accomplish its goal? What happens?

The law of supply and demand tells us that if the price drops, consumer demand will increase. At the same time, the quantity supplied will fall because producers are receiving lower profits for their efforts. This twin dynamic of increased consumer demand and reduced quantity will cause a shortage of bread.

On the demand side, consumers will want more bread than is available at the legal price. There will be long lines for bread and many people will not be able to get the bread they want. On the supply side, producers will look for ways to maintain their profits. They will reduce the size of each

Empty shelves

loaf they produce. They can also lower the quality of their product by using cheaper ingredients, and stop making fancier varieties. In addition, *black markets* will develop to help supply meet demand.

Black markets are illegal markets that arise when price controls are in place. For instance, the sale of narcotics and prostitution are illegal in most places. Since demand for these goods and services continues to exist despite the efforts to outlaw them, black markets have developed to match buyers and sellers who wish to circumvent the law. Perhaps the best-known example occurred during Prohibition, which outlawed sales of alcoholic drinks in many countries during the early part of the 20th century. This led to the rise of bootlegging and organized crime syndicates that distributed alcohol to a thirsty public. Prohibition created one of the most well-known black markets, but black markets also happen as the result of price controls. In our bread example, many of those who do not want to wait in line for bread, or who do not succeed in obtaining bread despite waiting in line, will resort to illegal means to obtain it. This means that sellers will go underground and charge higher prices to deliver customers the bread they want.

Table 5.1 summarizes the likely outcome of price controls on bread.

Black markets are illegal markets that arise when price controls are in place.

TABLE 5.1

A Price Ceiling on Bread

Question	Explanation	In Pictures
Will there be more or less bread for sale?	Consumers will want to purchase more since the price is lower, but producers will manufacture less. The net result is a shortage of bread.	Empty shelves
Will the size of a typical loaf change?	Since the price is capped at $.50 per loaf, manufacturers will try to maintain profits by reducing the size of each loaf.	No more giant loaves
Will the quality change?	Since the price is capped, producers will use cheaper ingredients and many expensive brands and varieties will no longer be profitable to produce.	Focaccia bread will disappear.
Will the opportunity cost of finding bread change?	The opportunity cost of finding bread will rise. This means that significant resources will be spent, looking for bread going from store to store to see if a shipment has arrived, and waiting in line for a chance to get it.	Photo to come — Bread lines will become the norm.
Will you have to break the law to buy bread?	Since bread is hard to find, and people still need it, a black market will develop.	Black-market bread dealers will help reduce the shortage.

The Effect of Price Ceilings

Now that we have developed the intuition for how a price ceiling works, we can transfer that knowledge into the supply and demand model for a deeper analysis of how price ceilings affect the market. To explain when price ceilings matter, we will examine two possible outcomes of price ceilings: nonbinding and binding.

Nonbinding price ceilings

The effect of a price ceiling depends on the level at which it is set. When a price ceiling is above the equilibrium price, we say it is *nonbinding*. Figure 5.1 shows a price ceiling of $2.00 a loaf in a market where $2.00 is above the equilibrium price. All prices at, or below, $2.00 (the green area) are legal. Prices above the price ceiling (the red area) are illegal. But since the market equilibrium (e) occurs in the green area, the price ceiling does not influence the market; it is nonbinding. As long as the equilibrium price remains below the price ceiling, price will continue to be regulated by supply and demand. Since there is rarely a compelling political reason to set a price ceiling above the equilibrium price, nonbinding price ceilings are unusual.

Binding price ceilings

When a price ceiling is below the market price, it creates a binding constraint that prevents supply and demand from clearing the market. In Figure 5.2 the price ceiling for bread is set at $0.50 a loaf. Since $0.50 is well below the equilibrium price of $1.00, this creates a binding price ceiling. Notice that at a price of $0.50, Q_D is greater than the Q_S; because the quantity demanded is greater than the quantity supplied, a shortage exists. Shortages typically

If you can touch the ceiling, you can't go any higher. A binding price ceiling stops prices from "rising."

FIGURE 5.1

A Nonbinding Price Ceiling

The price ceiling ($2) is set above the equilibrium price ($1). Since market prices are set by the intersection of supply and demand, as long as the equilibrium price is below the price ceiling, the price ceiling is nonbinding and has no effect.

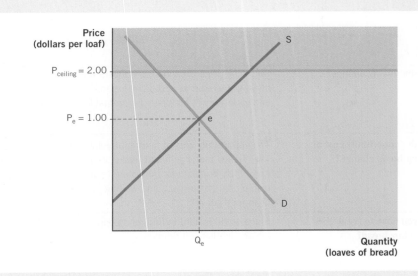

cause prices to rise, but the imposed price ceiling prevents that from happening. A price ceiling of $0.50 allows only the prices in the green area. The market cannot reach the equilibrium point e at $1.00 because it is located above the price ceiling, in the red area. Since the price mechanism is no longer able to ration the good legally, a black market for bread arises at price P $_{black\ market}$ or P_b for short.

The black-market price is also set by supply and demand. Since prices above $0.50 are illegal, sellers are unwilling to produce more than Q_s. Once the price ceiling is in place, producers cannot legally charge prices above the ceiling, so the incentive to produce along the original supply curve vanishes. Since a shortage still exists, an illegal market will form to resolve the shortage. Purchasers can illegally resell what they have just bought for $0.50 for far more than what they just paid. Since the supply of legally produced bread is Q_s, the intersection of the vertical dashed line that reflects Q_s and the demand curve at point e_b establishes the black-market price, P_b, at $2.00 for illegally sold bread. Since the black market price is substantially more than the original equilibrium price of $1.00, illegal suppliers (underground bakers) will also enter the market in order to satisfy demand. As a result, the black-market price eliminates the shortage caused by the price ceiling. However, the price ceiling has created two unintended consequences: a smaller supply of bread is produced (Q_s is less than Q_e), and a higher price exists for those who are forced to purchase bread on the black market.

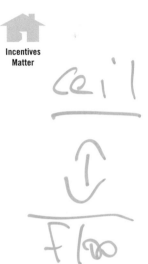

Incentives Matter

Price Ceilings in the Long Run

In the long run, supply and demand become more elastic, or flatter. Recall from Chapter 4 that when consumers have additional time to make choices, they find more ways to avoid high-priced goods and more ways to take

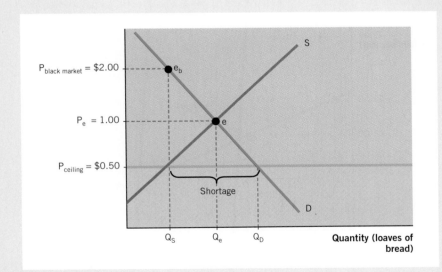

FIGURE 5.2

A Binding Price Ceiling

A binding price ceiling prevents sellers from increasing the price. As a consequence, prices no longer signal relative scarcity. Consumers desire to purchase the product at the price-controlled level and this creates a shortage; many will be unable to obtain the good. As a result, those who are shut out of the market will turn to other means to acquire the good. This establishes a black market for the good at a price of the black market.

advantage of low prices. Additional time also gives producers the opportunity to produce more when prices are high and less when prices are low. In this section, we consider what will happen if a binding price ceiling on bread remains in effect for a long time. We have already observed that when binding price ceilings are in effect in the short run, shortages and black markets develop. Are the long-run implications of price ceilings more or less problematic than the short-run implications? Let's find out by looking at what happens to both supply and demand.

Figure 5.3 shows the result of a price ceiling that remains in place for a long time. Here the supply curve is more elastic than its short-run counterpart in Figure 5.2. The supply curve is flatter because in the long run producers respond by producing less bread and converting their facilities to make similar products that are not subject to price controls—for example, bagels and rolls—that will allow them to earn a reasonable return on their investments. Therefore, in the long run Q_S grows even smaller.

The demand curve is also more elastic in the long run. In the long run more people will attempt to take advantage of the low price ceiling by changing their eating habits to consume more bread. A flatter demand curve means that consumers are more flexible. As a result, Q_D expands and bread is hard to find at $0.50. The shortage will become so acute that consumers will turn to bread substitutes, like bagels and rolls, that are more plentiful because they are not price controlled.

Increased elasticity on the part of both producers and consumers magnifies the unintended consequences we observed in the short run. Therefore, products subject to a price ceiling become progressively harder to find in the long run. A black market will develop. However, in the long run consumers will choose substitutes for expensive black-market bread and demand will go down. In the long run, this will cause somewhat lower black-market prices.

FIGURE 5.3

The Effect of a Binding Price Ceiling in the Long Run

In the long run, increased elasticity on the part of both producers and consumers makes the shortage larger than it was in the short run. Consumers adjust their demand to the lower price and want more bread. Producers adjust their supply and make less of the unprofitable product. As a result, products become progressively harder to find.

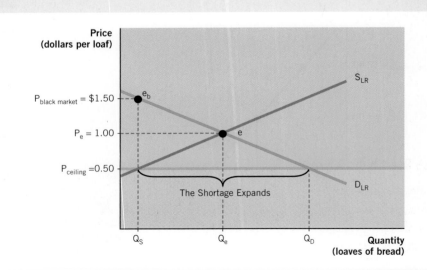

Price Ceilings

Moscow on the Hudson

This 1984 film starring Robin Williams chronicles the differences between living in the United States and the former Soviet Union. In Moscow, we see hundreds of people waiting in line to receive essentials like bread, milk, and shoes. In the Soviet Union production was controlled and prices were not allowed to equalize supply and demand. As a result, shortages were common. Waiting in line served as a rationing mechanism in the absence of price adjustments.

Soviet-era food-rationing coupon

Soviet-era bread line

This film is memorable because of the reactions that Robin Williams has once he immigrates to America. In one inspired scene he walks into a supermarket to buy coffee. He asks the manager where the coffee aisle is located, and when he sees that the aisle is not crowded, he asks the manager where the coffee line is located. The manager responds that there is no coffee line, so he walks down the coffee aisle slowly, naming each variety. We see his joy at being able to buy coffee without waiting and in having so many options to choose from. This nicely showcases the differences between the market system and the controlled economy of the Soviet Union.

PRACTICE WHAT YOU KNOW

Price Ceilings: Concert Tickets

Question: Suppose that fans of Avicii persuade Congress to impose a price ceiling of $25 for every Avicii concert ticket. Would this policy influence the number of people who attend his concerts?

You've got "a good feeling" about this concert.

> **Answer:** The price ceiling prevents supply and demand from reaching the equilibrium price. As a result, at $25 there is a shortage of tickets. Since Avicii controls when and where he tours, he will choose to tour less in the United States and more in countries that do not regulate the ticket prices he can charge. This will make it more difficult for his fans to see him perform live.

What Effects Do Price Ceilings Have on Economic Activity?

We have seen the logical repercussions of a hypothetical price ceiling on bread and the incentives it creates. Now let's use supply and demand analysis to examine two real-world price ceilings: *rent control* and *price gouging laws*.

ECONOMICS IN THE REAL WORLD

Rent Control

Rent control
is a price ceiling that applies to the housing market.

Under **rent control**, a local government caps the price of apartment rentals to keep housing more affordable. While this may be a laudable goal, rent control doesn't work. In fact, it doesn't help poor residents of the city find affordable housing, or gain access to housing at all. In addition, these policies contribute to dangerous living conditions.

Mumbai, India, provides a chilling example of what can happen when rent controls are applied over an extended period of time. In Mumbai, many rent-controlled buildings have become dilapidated. Every monsoon season several of these buildings fall, often with tragic consequences. Since the rent that property owners are permitted charge is so low, they have less income to use for maintenance. Therefore, they cannot afford to maintain the buildings properly and earn a reasonable profit. As a result, rent-control policies have led to the decay of many apartment buildings worldwide.

To understand how a policy can backfire so much, let's look at the history of rent control in New York City. In 1943, in the midst of World War II, the federal government established the Emergency Price Control Act. The act was designed to keep inflation in check during the war when many essential commodities were scarce. After the war the federal government ended price controls, but the state

Many apartment buildings in Mumbai, India, are dilapidated as a result of rent-control laws.

of New York continued rent control. Today there are approximately one million rent-controlled units available in New York City. Rent controls limit the price a landlord can charge a tenant for rent. They also require that the landlord provide certain basic services, but not surprisingly, landlords limit maintenance to a minimum.

Does the presence of so many rent-controlled apartments mean that less affluent households can easily find a cheap place to rent? Hardly. When a rent-controlled unit is vacated, the property is generally no longer subject to rent control. Since most of the rent-controlled apartments are passed from generation to generation to remain in the program, rent control no longer remotely serves its original purpose of helping low-income households. Clearly, the law was never intended to subsidize fancy vacation homes, but that's what it does! This has happened, in part, because some tenants who could afford to live elsewhere choose not to. The subsidized rent that they pay allows them to save enough money to be able to have a second or third place in upstate New York, Florida, or Europe.

The attempt to make housing more affordable in New York City has, ironically, made housing harder to obtain. It has encouraged the building of upscale properties rather than low-income units, and created a set of behaviors among landlords that is inconsistent with the ideals of justice and affordability that rent control was designed address. Figure 5.4 shows why rent control fails. As with any price ceiling, rent control causes a shortage to develop since the demand in the short run (D_{SR}) is greater than the supply in the short run (S_{SR}). Because rent-controlled apartments are vacated slowly, the supply of rent-controlled units contracts in the long run, which causes the supply curve to become more elastic (S_{LR}). Demand also becomes more elastic in the long run (D_{LR}), which causes the quantity demanded for rent-controlled units to rise. The combination of fewer units available to rent and more consumers looking to find rent-controlled units leads to a larger shortage in the long run.

FIGURE 5.4

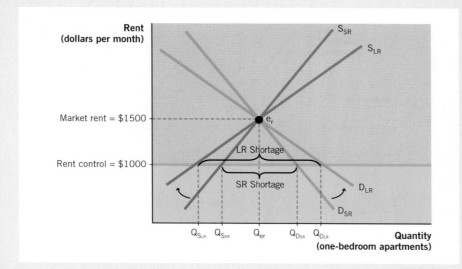

Rent Control in the Short Run and Long Run

Because rent-controlled apartments are vacated slowly, the supply of units contracts in the long run and the supply curve becomes more elastic. Demand also becomes more elastic in the long run, causing the quantity demanded to rise. The combination of fewer units available to rent and more consumers looking to find rent-controlled units leads to a larger shortage in the long run.

Price Gouging

Price gouging laws
make it illegal to profit at
times of national emergency
by excessively raising prices.

Another kind of price control, **price gouging laws**, places a temporary ceiling on the prices that sellers can charge during times of national emergency until markets function normally again. Over thirty states in the United States have laws against price gouging. Like all price controls, price gouging laws have unintended consequences.

Generator: $900 after
hurricane Wilma hit.

The hurricane season of 2005 was arguably the worst in U.S. history. Katrina and Rita plowed through the Gulf of Mexico with devastating effects, especially on Louisiana and Texas. Later that year, Wilma grew into the most powerful hurricane ever recorded in the Atlantic basin. When Wilma hit Fort Myers, Florida, in November, it ended a season for the record books. Florida has one of the strictest price gouging laws in the country. The statute makes it illegal to charge an "excessive" price immediately following a natural disaster. The law is designed to prevent the victims of natural disasters from being exploited in a time of need. But does it work?

Consider David Medina from Miami Beach. Immediately after Wilma hit, he drove to North Carolina, purchased 35 gas-powered generators and returned to Florida, where he sold them from the back of his truck. He charged $900 for large generators, which he had purchased for $529.99, and $600 for small generators, which had cost him $279.99. After selling most of the units, Mr. Medina was arrested for price gouging. Under Florida law his remaining generators were confiscated, and he was fined $1,000 for each sale. In addition, he was charged for selling without a business license. While there is no doubt that Mr. Medina intended to capitalize on the misfortune of others, it is hard to prove that he did any harm. The people who bought from him did so voluntarily.

FIGURE 5.5

Price Gouging

Price gouging laws serve as a non-binding price ceiling during normal times. However, when a natural disaster strikes, price gouging laws go into effect. This shifts the demand curve for generators to the right and causes the new equilibrium price to rise above the legal limit. This creates a shortage. When the emergency is lifted, the market demand returns to normal, and the temporary shortage created by price gouging legislation is eliminated.

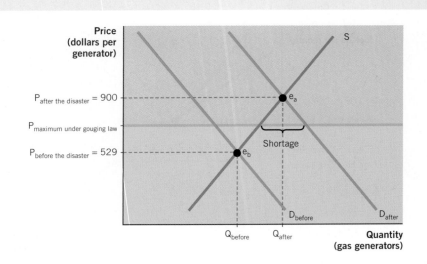

Prices act to ration scarce resources. When the demand for generators or other necessities is high, the price needs to rise to ensure that the available units are distributed to those who value them the most. More important, the ability to charge a higher price provides sellers with an incentive to make more units available. If you limit the ability of the price to change when demand increases, there will be a shortage. Therefore, price gouging legislation means that devastated communities are relying exclusively on the goodwill of others and the slow-moving machinery of government relief efforts. This closes off a third avenue, entrepreneurial activity, as a means to alleviate poor conditions.

Figure 5.5 shows how price gouging laws work and the shortage they create. If the demand for gas generators increases immediately following a disaster, the market price rises from $529 to $900. But since $900 is considered excessive, sales at that price are illegal. This creates a binding price ceiling for as long as a state of emergency is in effect. Whenever a price ceiling is binding, it creates a shortage. You can see this in the difference between quantity demanded and quantity supplied at the price ceiling level mandated by the law. In this case, the normal ability of supply and demand to ration the available generators is short-circuited. Since more people demand generators after the disaster than before it, those who do not get to the store soon enough are out of luck. When the emergency is lifted and the market returns to normal, the temporary shortage created by legislation against price gouging is eliminated. ✳

PRACTICE WHAT YOU KNOW

Price Ceilings: **Student Rental Apartments**

Here is a question that often confuses students.

Question: Imagine a city council decides that the market price for renting apartments is too high and passes a law that establishes a price ceiling of $600 per month. The result of the price ceiling is a shortage. Which of the following is it caused by?

Shabby chic. Would a price ceiling make apartments more affordable for college students?

(a) Both suppliers and demanders. Landlords will cut the supply of apartments and the demand from renters will increase.

(b) The spike in demand from many students who want to rent cheap apartments.

(c) The drop in supply caused by apartment owners pulling their units off the market and converting them into condos for sale.

(d) The price ceiling set by the city council.

Answer: Many students think that markets are to blame when shortages (or surpluses) exist. The first reaction is to find the culpable party—either the supplier or the demander, or both.

Answer (a) is a typical response. Be careful. Supply and demand have not changed—they are exactly the same as they were before the price ceiling was implemented. What has changed is the quantity of apartments supplied at $600. This change in quantity is represented by a movement along the existing supply curve. The same is true for renters. The quantity demanded at $600 is much larger than it was when the price was not controlled. Once again, there is a movement along the demand curve.

The same logic applies to answers (b) and (c). Answer (b) argues that there is a spike in student demand caused by the lower price. Price cannot cause a shift in the demand curve, it only causes a movement along a curve. Likewise, (c) argues that apartment owners supply fewer units for rent. Landlords cannot earn more than $600 per unit, so some apartments will be converted into private residences and offered for sale in order to earn more profit. Since fewer apartments are available at $600, this is represented by a movement along the apartment supply curve.

This brings us to (d). There is only one change in market conditions: the city council passed a new price ceiling law. A binding price ceiling disrupts the ability of the market to reach the equilibrium. Therefore, the change in the price as a result of the price ceiling is to blame for the shortage.

Price floors
are legally established minimum prices for goods or services.

If you're doing a handstand, you need the floor for support. A binding price floor keeps prices from "falling."

When Do Price Floors Matter?

In this section we examine price floors. Like price ceilings, price floors create many unintended effects that policy makers rarely acknowledge. However, unlike price ceilings, price floors result from the political pressure of suppliers to keep prices high. Most consumers prefer lower prices when they go to the store, so the idea of a law that keeps prices high may sound like a bad idea to you. On the other hand, if you are selling a product or service, you might think that legislation that keeps prices high is a very good idea. For instance, many states establish minimum prices for milk. The result is that milk prices are higher than they would be if supply and demand set the price. **Price floors** create a legally established minimum price for a good or service. The minimum wage law is another example of a price floor. In this section we will use follow the same progression we did with price ceilings. We begin with a simple thought experiment. Once we understand how price floors work, we will utilize supply and demand analysis to examine the short- and long-term implications for economic activity.

Understanding Price Floors

To understand how price floors affect the market, let's try a thought experiment. Suppose that a politician suggests we should encourage dairy farmers to produce more milk so that supplies will be plentiful and everyone will get enough calcium. In order to accomplish this, a price floor of $6.00—about twice the price of a typical gallon of fat-free milk—is enacted to make production more attractive to producers. What repercussions should we expect?

First, more milk will be available for sale. We know this because the higher price will increase the quantity that dairies supply. At the same time, because consumers must pay more, the quantity demanded will fall. The result will be a surplus of milk. Since every gallon of milk that is produced and not sold hurts the firm's bottom line, sellers will want to lower their prices enough to get as many sales as possible before the milk goes bad. But the price floor does not allow the market to respond and producers are stuck with milk that goes to waste. Producers will be tempted to offer illegal discounts in order to recoup some of their costs.

What happens next? Since the surplus cannot be resolved through lower prices, the government will try to help equalize supply and demand through other means. This can be accomplished in two basic ways: by restricting the supply of the good or stimulating additional demand. Both of these solutions are problematic. If production is restricted, dairy farmers will not be able to make as much milk as it may be profitable for them to make. Likewise, stimulating additional demand is not as simple as it sounds. In many cases the government purchases surplus agricultural production. This occurs most notably with corn, soybeans, cotton, and rice. Once the government buys the surplus production, it is often sold below cost to developing countries to avoid having the crop go to waste. This has the unintended consequence of making it cheaper for consumers in these disadvantaged nations to buy excess agricultural output from developed countries like the United States than to have local farmers grow the crop. International treaties ban the practice of dumping surplus production, but it continues under the guise of humanitarian aid. This makes little economic sense. Table 5.2 summarizes the result of our price-floor thought experiment using milk.

Got milk? Controlled milk prices prevent many customers from saying yes to that question.

The Effect of Price Floors

We have seen that price floors create unintended consequences. Now we will use the supply and demand model to analyze how price floors affect the market.

Nonbinding price floors

Like price ceilings, price floors can be binding or nonbinding. Figure 5.6 illustrates a nonbinding price floor of $2.00 per gallon on milk. As you can see, at $2.00, the price floor is below the equilibrium price so the price floor is nonbinding. Since the actual market price is above the legally established minimum price, the price floor does not prevent the market from reaching point e. Consequently, the price floor has no impact on the market. As long as the equilibrium remains above the price floor, price is regulated by supply and demand.

Full shelves

TABLE 5.2

A Price Floor on Milk

Question	Explanation	In Pictures
Will the quantity of milk for sale change?	Consumers will purchase less since the price is higher, but producers will manufacture more. The net result is a surplus of milk.	There will be a surplus of milk.
Would producers sell below the price floor?	A surplus of milk would give sellers a strong incentive to undercut the price floor in order to avoid having to discard leftover milk.	Illegal discounts will help to reduce the milk surplus.
Are milk producers better off?	Not if they have trouble selling what they produce.	There will be a lot of spoiled milk.

FIGURE 5.6

A Nonbinding Price Floor

Under a nonbinding price floor, price is regulated by supply and demand. Since the price floor ($2.00) is below the equilibrium price ($3.00), the market will voluntary charge more than the legal minimum. Therefore, the price floor will have no effect on economic activity.

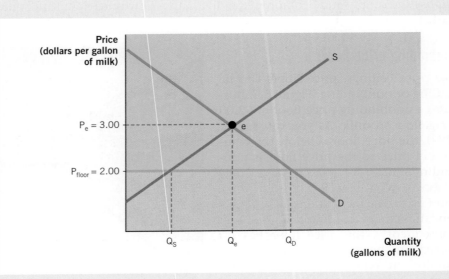

Binding price floors

For a price floor to have an impact on the market, it must be set above the market equilibrium price. In that case, it is known as a binding price floor. With a binding price floor, the quantity supplied will exceed the quantity demanded. Figure 5.7 illustrates a binding price floor in the short run. At $6.00 per gallon, the price floor is above the equilibrium price of $3.00. Market forces always attempt to restore the equilibrium between supply and demand at point e. So we know that there is downward pressure on the price. At a price floor of $6.00 we see that $Q_S > Q_D$. The difference between the quantity demanded and the quantity supplied results in a surplus. Since the price mechanism is no longer effective, sellers find themselves with unwanted inventories of milk. In order to eliminate the surplus of milk, which will spoil unless it is sold, a black market may develop with prices substantially below the legislated price. At a price (P_b) of $2.00, the black market eliminates the surplus that the price floor caused. However, the price floor has created two unintended consequences: a smaller demand for milk ($Q_D < Q_e$), and a black market to eliminate the glut of milk.

Price Floors in the Long Run

Once price-floor legislation is passed, it can be politically difficult to repeal. What happens if a binding price floor on milk stays in effect for a long time? To help answer that question we need to consider elasticity. We have already observed that in the short run binding price ceilings cause shortages, and that black markets follow.

Figure 5.8 shows a price floor for milk that remains in place well past the short run. The long run affords consumers a chance to adopt milk substitutes—for example, products made from soy, rice, or almond that are not subject to the price floor—at lower prices. This added flexibility on the

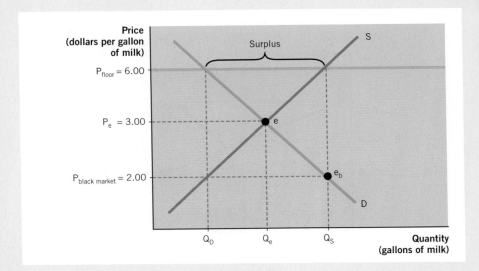

FIGURE 5.7

A Binding Price Floor in the Short Run

A binding price floor creates a surplus. This has two unintended consequences: a smaller demand ($Q_D < Q_e$) than the equilibrium quantity, and a lower black market price to eliminate the glut of the product.

part of consumers makes the long-run demand for milk more elastic in an unregulated market. As a result, the demand curve depicted in Figure 5.8 is more elastic than its short-run counterpart in Figure 5.7. The supply curve also becomes flatter since firms are able to produce more milk by acquiring additional land and production facilities. Therefore, a price floor ($6.00) that is left in place over time causes the supply and demand curves to become more elastic. This magnifies the shortage.

What happens to supply? In the long run, producers are more flexible and therefore supply is more elastic. The pool of potential milk producers rises as other closely related businesses are able to retool their operations to supply more milk. The flatter supply curve in Figure 5.8 reflects this flexibility. As a result, Q_S expands and becomes much larger than it was in Figure 5.7. The increased elasticity on the part of both producers and consumers makes the surplus larger in the long run and the unintended consequences we observed in the short run are magnified.

PRACTICE WHAT YOU KNOW

Price Floors: Fair-Trade Coffee

Fair-trade coffee is sold through organizations that purchase directly from the growers. The coffee is usually sold for a higher price than standard coffee. The goal is to promote more humane working conditions for the coffee pickers and growers. Fair-trade coffee has become more popular but still

FIGURE 5.8

The Effect of a Binding Price Floor in the Long Run

When a price floor is left in place over time, supply and demand each become more elastic. This leads to a larger surplus ($Q_S > Q_D$) in the long run. Since sellers are unable to sell all that they produce at $6.00, a black market develops in order to eliminate the glut of milk.

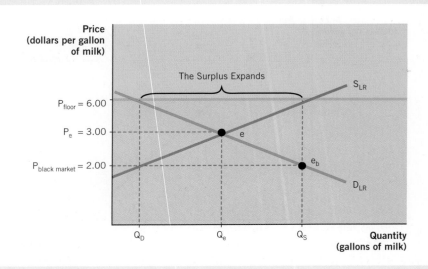

accounts for a small portion of all coffee sales, in large part because fair-trade coffee is substantially more expensive to produce.

Question: Suppose that proponents of fair-trade coffee successfully lobby Congress to impose a price floor of $15 for every pound of coffee that is sold. Will this policy cause more or fewer people to buy fair-trade coffee?

Answer: Fair-trade producers typically sell their product at a higher price than mass-produced coffee brands. Therefore, a $15 price ceiling is binding for brands like Folgers, but nonbinding for premium coffees, which include fair-trade sellers. The price floor will reduce the price disparity between fair-trade coffee and mass-

Would fair-trade coffee producers benefit from a price floor?

produced coffee. To see how this works, consider a fair-trade coffee producer who charges $20 per pound and a mass-produced brand that sells for $10 per pound. A price floor of $15 reduces the difference between the price of fair-trade coffee and the inexpensive coffee brands, which now must sell for $15 instead of $10. This lowers the opportunity cost of choosing fair-trade coffee for the consumer. Therefore, sales of Folgers and other inexpensive brands will decline. As a result, fair-trade producers will benefit indirectly from the price floor.

What Effects Do Price Floors Have on Economic Activity?

We have seen the logical repercussions of a hypothetical price floor on bread and the incentives it creates. Now let's use supply and demand analysis to examine two real-world price floors: *minimum wage laws* and *agricultural price supports*.

The Minimum Wage

The **minimum wage** is the lowest hourly wage rate that firms may legally pay their workers. Minimum wage workers can be skilled or unskilled and experienced or not. The common thread is that these workers, for a variety of reasons, lack better prospects. A minimum wage functions as a price floor. Figure 5.9 shows the effect of a binding minimum wage. Note that the wage, or the cost of labor, on the y-axis ($10.00) is the price that must be paid. However, the market equilibrium wage ($7.00) is below the minimum wage. The minimum wage prevents the market from reaching W_e at e because only the wages in the green shaded area are legal. Since the demand for labor

The minimum wage is the lowest hourly wage rate that firms may legally pay workers.

depends on how much it costs, the minimum wage raises the cost of hiring workers. Therefore, a higher minimum wage will lower the quantity of labor demanded. However, since businesses still need to serve their customers, this means that labor expenses for the firm ordinarily rise in the short run. At the same time, firms will look for ways to substitute additional capital for workers. As a result, a binding minimum wage results in unemployment in the short run since $Q_{S_{SR}} > Q_{D_{SR}}$.

Businesses generally want to keep costs down, so in the long run they will try to reduce the amount they spend on labor. They might replace workers with machinery, shorten hours, offer reduced customer service, or even relocate to countries that do not have minimum wage laws. As we move past the short run, more people will attempt to take advantage of higher minimum wages. Like firms, workers will adjust to the higher minimum wage with the passage of time. Some workers who might have decided to go to school full time or remain retired, or who simply want some extra income, will enter the labor market because the minimum wage is now higher. As a result, minimum wage jobs become progressively harder to find and unemployment is magnified. The irony is that the minimum wage, just like any other price floor, has created two unintended consequences: a smaller demand for workers willing to take low-paying jobs ($Q_{D_{LR}}$ is significantly less than Q_e) and a larger supply of workers $Q_{S_{LR}}$) looking for jobs.

Proponents of minimum wage legislation are aware that it often creates unemployment. To address this problem, they support investment in training, education, and the creation of government jobs programs to provide more work opportunities. While jobs programs increase minimum wage jobs, training and additional education enable workers to acquire skills needed for jobs that pay more than the minimum wage. Economists generally believe that education and training programs have longer-lasting benefits to society as whole since they allow workers to obtain better-paying jobs on a permanent basis.

FIGURE 5.9

Price Floors and a Binding Minimum Wage Market

A binding minimum wage is a price floor above the current equilibrium wage, W_e. At $10, the number of workers willing to supply their labor (S_{SR}) is greater than the demand for workers (D_{SR}). The result is a surplus of workers (which we recognize as unemployment). Since the supply of workers and demand for workers both become more elastic in the long run, unemployment expands ($S_{LR} > D_{LR}$).

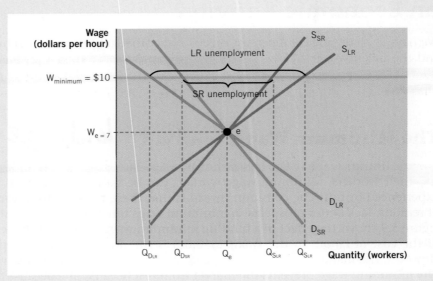

ECONOMICS IN THE REAL WORLD

Wage Laws Squeeze South Africa's Poor

Consider this story that appeared in the *New York Times* in 2010:

NEWCASTLE, South Africa—The sheriff arrived at the factory here to shut it down, part of a national enforcement drive against clothing manufacturers who violate the minimum wage. But women working on the factory floor—the supposed beneficiaries of the crackdown—clambered atop cutting tables and ironing boards to raise anguished cries against it. Thoko Zwane, 43, who has worked in factories since she was 15, lost her job in Newcastle when a Chinese-run factory closed in 2004. More than a third of South Africans are jobless. "Why? Why?" shouted Nokuthula Masango, 25, after the authorities carted away bolts of gaily colored fabric. She made just $36 a week, $21 less than the minimum wage, but needed the meager

Would you work for less than the minimum wage?

pay to help support a large extended family that includes her five unemployed siblings and their children.

The women's spontaneous protest is just one sign of how acute South Africa's long-running unemployment crisis has become. With their own economy saddled with very high unemployment rates, the women feared being out of work more than getting stuck in poorly paid jobs.

In the years since the end of apartheid, the South African economy has grown, but not nearly fast enough to end an intractable unemployment crisis. For over a decade the jobless rate has been among the highest in the world, fueling crime, inequality, and social unrest in the continent's richest nation. The global economic downturn has made the problem much worse, wiping out more than a million jobs. Over a third of South Africa's workforce is now idle. And 16 years after Nelson Mandela led the country to black majority rule, more than half of blacks ages 15 to 34 are without work—triple the level for whites.

"The numbers are mind-boggling," said James Levinsohn, a Yale University economist.[1]

Would you work for less than the minimum wage? ✳

The Minimum Wage Is Often Nonbinding

Most people believe that raising the minimum wage is a simple step that the government can take to increase the standard of living of the working

---

[1] Celia W. Dugger, "Wage Laws Squeeze South Africa's Poor," *New York Times*, Sept. 27, 2010: A1.

The Minimum Wage

30 Days

The (2005) pilot episode of this reality series focused on the minimum wage. Morgan Spurlock and his fiancée spend 30 days in a poor neighborhood of Columbus, Ohio. The couple attempt to survive by earning minimum wage (at that time $5.15 an hour) in order to make ends meet. In addition to making minimum wage, they are required to start off with only one week's minimum wage (about $300) in reserve. In addition, they cannot use credit cards to pay their bills. They experience first-hand the struggles that many minimum wage households face trying to live paycheck to paycheck. *30 Days* makes it painfully clear how difficult it is for anyone to live on a minimum wage for a month, let alone for years.

A quote by Morgan Spurlock sums up what the episode tries to convey, "We don't see the people that surround us. We don't see the people who are struggling to get by that are right next to us. And I have seen how hard the struggle is. I have been here.

Could you make ends meet earning the minimum wage?

And I only did it for a month, and there's people who do this their whole lives."

After watching this episode of *30 Days*, it is hard not to think that raising the minimum wage is a good idea. Unfortunately, the economic reality is that raising the minimum wage does not guarantee that minimum wage earners will make more and also be able keep their jobs.

poor. However, in most places the minimum wage is often nonbinding and therefore has no impact on the market. Adjusting for inflation, the federal minimum wage was highest in 1968, so in real terms minimum wage workers are earning less today than they did almost half a century ago. Why would we have a minimum wage if it is largely nonbinding?

To help us answer this question, consider two nonbinding minimum wage rates ($7 and $9) shown in Figure 5.10. $7 an hour is far below the equilibrium wage of $10, so supply and demand will determine the wage. Suppose that politicians decide to raise the minimum wage to $9. The new minimum wage of $9 remains below the market wage, so there is no impact on the labor market for workers who are willing to accept the minimum wage. Therefore, an increase in the minimum wage from $7 to $9 an hour will not create unemployment. Unemployment occurs only when the minimum wage rises above $10.

Politicians know that most voters have a poor understanding of basic economics. A politician can raise the minimum wage with great fanfare. Voters support the new rate because they do not know that the new minimum wage is likely to be nonbinding; they think that wages will rise. In reality, nothing will change, but the perception of a benevolent action remains. In fact, since its inception in 1938, increases in the minimum wage in the United States have generally trailed the market wage and therefore avoided creating unemployment. As a result, the minimum wage adjusts sporadically upwards every few years but rarely adjusts upward enough to cause the market wage to fall below it. This creates the illusion that the minimum wage is lifting wages. However, it does not cause any of the adverse consequences of a binding minimum wage.

In an effort to raise the minimum wage beyond the national rate, a number of states have enacted higher minimum wage laws. Not surprisingly, some of the states with the highest minimum wage rates, like Washington, Oregon, and California, also have unemployment rates that are among the highest in the country—evidence that binding minimum wage rates can have serious consequences.

ECONOMICS IN THE REAL WORLD

A Sweet Deal, If You Can Get It

Sugar is one of life's small pleasures. Sugar can be extracted and refined from sugar cane and sugar beets. These crops can be grown in a variety of climates around the world. Sugar is both plentiful and cheap. As a result, Americans enjoy a lot of sugar—an average of over 60 pounds of refined sugar per person each year!

We would consume a lot more sugar if it was not subject to price controls. After the War of 1812, struggling sugar cane producers asked the government to pass a tariff that would protect domestic production. Over the years, price supports of all kinds have been used to keep domestic sugar production high. The result is an industry that depends on a high price to survive. Under the current price-support system, the price of U.S. sugar is roughly two to three times the world price. This has led to a bizarre set of outcomes where U.S. farmers grow more sugar than they should and use land that is not well suited to the crop. For instance, sugar cane requires a subtropical climate, but most

FIGURE 5.10

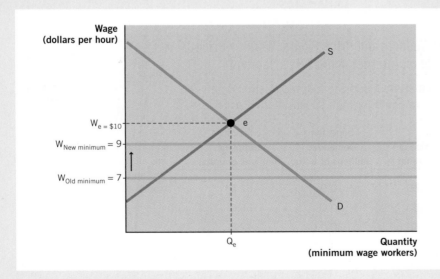

A Nonbinding Minimum Wage

An increase in the minimum wage from $7 to $9 remains nonbinding. Therefore, it will not change the demand for labor or the unemployment rate. If the minimum wage rises above the market wage, additional unemployment occurs.

Sugar is sweet?

Which of these is the real thing? The Coke on the right, with high-fructose corn syrup, was made in the United States; the other, with sugar, was made in Mexico.

of the U.S. crop is grown in Louisiana, in a region that is prone to hurricanes in the summer and killing freezes in the late fall. As a result, many sugar cane crops are completely lost.

Why do farmers persist in growing sugar cane in Louisiana? The answer lies with the political process. Sugar growers have effectively lobbied to keep prices high through tariffs on foreign imports. Since lower prices would put many U.S. growers out of business and cause the loss of many jobs, politicians have given in to their demands.

Meanwhile, the typical consumer of sugar is largely oblivious to the political process that sets the price floor. It has been estimated that the sugar subsidy program costs consumers over one billion dollars a year. To make matters worse, thanks to corn subsidies, high-fructose corn syrup has become a cheap alternative to sugar and is often added to processed foods and soft drinks. In 1980, Coca-Cola replaced sugar with high-fructose corn extract in the United States in order to reduce production costs. However, Coca-Cola continues to use sugar cane in many Latin American countries because it is cheaper. New research shows that high-fructose corn syrup causes a metabolic reaction that makes people more inclined to obesity. Ouch! This is an example of an unintended consequence that few policy makers could have imagined. There is no reason why the United States must produce its own sugar cane. Ironically, sugar is cheaper in Canada primarily because Canada has no sugar growers—and thus no trade restrictions or government support programs. ✳

PRACTICE WHAT YOU KNOW

Price Ceilings and Price Floors: Would a Price Control on Internet Access Be Effective?

A recent study found the following demand and supply schedule for high-speed Internet access:

Price of Internet	Connections Demanded (millions of units)	Connections Supplied (millions of units)
$60	10.0	62.5
50	20.0	55.0
40	30.0	47.5
30	40.0	40.0
20	50.0	32.5
10	60.0	25.0

Four degrees of separation are all that stand between you and the rest of the world.

Question: What is the equilibrium price and quantity of Internet service?

Answer: First, look at the table to see where supply and demand are equal. At a price of $30, consumers purchase 40 million units and producers supply 40 million units. Therefore, the equilibrium price is $30 and the equilibrium quantity is 40 million. At any price above $30 the quantity supplied exceeds the quantity demanded, so there is a surplus. The surplus gives sellers an incentive to cut the price until it

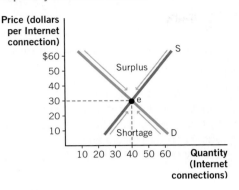

reaches the equilibrium point, e. At any price below $30, the quantity demanded exceeds the quantity supplied, so there is a shortage. The shortage gives sellers an incentive to raise the price until it reaches the equilibrium point, e.

Question: Suppose that providers convince the government that maintaining high-speed access to the Internet is an important piece of technology infrastructure. As a result, Congress approves a price floor at $10 above the equilibrium price to help companies provide Internet service. What is the new market price and how many people are able to connect to the Internet?

Answer: Adding $10 to the market price of $30 gives us a price floor of $40. At $40 consumers demand 30 million connections. Producers provide 47.5 million connections. This is a surplus of 17.5 million units (shown). A price floor means that producers cannot cut the price to increase the quantity that consumers demand. As a result, only 30 million units are sold.

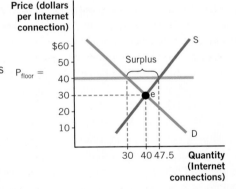

Question: When teachers realize that fewer people are purchasing Internet access, they demand that the price floor be repealed and a price ceiling put in its place. Congress acts immediately to remedy the problem and a new price ceiling is set $10 below the market price. What is the new market price and how many people are able to connect to the Internet?

Answer: Subtracting $10 from the market price of $30 gives us a price ceiling of $20. At $20 consumers demand 50 million connections. However, producers provide only 32.5 million connections. This is a shortage of

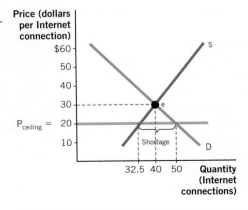

17.5 million units (shown). A price ceiling means that producers cannot raise the price, which will cause an increase in the quantity supplied. As a result, only 32.5 million units are sold.

Question: Which provides the greatest access to the Internet: free markets, price floors, or price ceilings?

Answer: With no government intervention, 40 million connections are sold. Once the price floor is established there are 30 million connections. Under the price ceiling 32.5 million connections exist. Despite legislative efforts to satisfy both producers and consumers of Internet service, the best solution is to allow supply and demand to regulate access to the good.

ECONOMICS FOR LIFE

Price Gouging Disaster Preparedness

Disasters, whether natural or man-made, usually strike quickly and without warning. You and your family may have little or no time to decide what to do next. That's why it is so important to plan for the possibility of disaster and not wait until it happens. Failing to plan is planning to fail. In this box we consider a few simple things you can do now to lessen the impact of a disaster on your personal and financial well-being.

During a disaster, shortages of essential goods and services will be widespread. In the 30 states where price gouging laws are on the books, they prevent merchants from charging unusually high prices. If you live in one of these states, this means that cash alone can't save you. You will have to survive on your own for a time before help arrives and communication channels are restored.

Taking measures to avoid or prepare for a disaster in advance reduces the likelihood of injury, loss of life, and property damage far more than anything you can do after a disaster strikes. An essential part of disaster planning should include financial planning. Let's begin with the basics. Get adequate insurance to protect your family's health, lives, and property; plan for the possibility of job loss or disability by building a cash reserve; and safeguard your financial and legal records. It is also important to set aside extra money in a long-term emergency fund. Nearly all financial experts advise saving enough money to cover your expenses for six months. Most

households never come close to reaching this goal, but do not let that stop you from trying.

Preparing a simple disaster supply kit is also a must. Keep enough water, nonperishable food, sanitation supplies, batteries, medications, and cash on hand to make it for three days. Often the power is out after a disaster, so you cannot count on ATM machines or banks to be open. These measures will help you weather the immediate impact of a disaster.

Finally, many documents are very difficult to replace. Consider investing in a home safe or safe deposit box to ensure that your important records will survive. Place your passports, Social Security cards, copies of drivers' licenses, mortgage and property deeds, car titles, wills, insurance records, and birth and marriage certificates out of harm's way.

Are you ready if disaster strikes?

Conclusion

Does the minimum wage help people earn a living wage? We learned that it is possible to set the minimum wage high enough to guarantee that each worker will earn a living wage. However, the trade-off in setting the minimum wage substantially higher is that it becomes binding and many workers will no longer have jobs. In other words, setting the minimum wage high enough to earn a living wage won't raise every worker out of poverty because many of those workers will no longer have jobs.

The policies presented in this chapter—rent control, price gouging laws, the minimum wage, and agricultural price controls—create unintended consequences. Attempts to control prices should be viewed cautiously. When the price signal is suppressed through a binding price floor or a binding price ceiling, the market's ability to maintain order is diminished, surpluses and shortages develop and expand through time, and obtaining goods and services becomes difficult.

The role of markets in society has many layers and we've only just begun our analysis. In the next chapter we will develop a technique to measure the gains that consumers and producers enjoy in unregulated markets and consider the distortions created by tax policy. Then, in Chapter 7, we will consider two cases—externalities and public goods—in which the unregulated market produces an output that is not socially desirable.

ANSWERING THE BIG QUESTIONS

1. When do price ceilings matter?

* A price ceiling is a legally imposed maximum price. When the price is set below the equilibrium price, the quantity demanded will exceed the quantity supplied. This results in a shortage.

2. What effects do price ceilings have on economic activity?

* Price ceilings create two unintended consequences: a smaller supply of the good (Q_s) and a higher price for those who turn to the black market.

3. When do price floors matter?

* A price floor is a legally imposed minimum price. The minimum wage is an example of a price floor. If the minimum wage is set above the equilibrium wage, a surplus of labor will develop. However, if the minimum wage is nonbinding, it will have no effect on the market wage.

4. What effects do price floors have on economic activity?

* Price floors also lead to many unintended consequences, including surpluses, the creation of black markets, and artificial attempts to bring the market back into balance. For example, proponents of a higher minimum wage are concerned about finding ways to alleviate the resulting surplus of labor, or unemployment.

CONCEPTS YOU SHOULD KNOW

Black market (p. 145)
Minimum wage (p. 159)
Price ceiling (p. 144)

Price control (p. 144)
Price floor (p. 154)

Price gouging laws (p. 152)
Rent control (p. 150)

QUESTIONS FOR REVIEW

1. Does a price ceiling cause a shortage or a surplus? Provide an example to support your answer.

2. Does a price floor cause a shortage or a surplus? Provide an example to support your answer.

3. Will a surplus or shortage caused by a price control become smaller or larger over time?

4. Are price gouging laws an example of a price floor or a price ceiling?

5. What will happen to the market price when a price control is nonbinding?

6. Why do most economists oppose attempts to control prices? Why does the government attempt to control prices anyway, in a number of markets?

STUDY PROBLEMS

1. In the song "Minimum Wage," the punk band Fenix TX comments on the inadequacy of the minimum wage to make ends meet. Using the poverty thresholds provided by the Census Bureau (http://www.census.gov/hhes/www/poverty/data/threshld/index.html), determine whether the federal minimum wage of $7.25 an hour provides enough income for a single full-time worker to escape poverty. (*Note:* the full lyrics for the song can be found by googling the song title and Fenix TX.)

＊ 2. The community you live in decides to enact a rent control of $700 per month on every one-bedroom apartment. Using the following table, determine the market price and equilibrium quantity without rent control. How many one-bedroom apartments will be rented after the rent-control law is passed?

Monthly Rent	Quantity Demanded	Quantity Supplied
$600	700	240
$700	550	320
$800	400	400
$900	250	480
$1,000	100	560

3. Suppose that government places a binding price floor on chocolate. To help support the price floor the government purchases all of the leftover chocolate that consumers do not buy. If the price floor remains in place for a number of years, what do you expect to happen to each of the following:

   a. quantity of chocolate demanded by consumers
   b. quantity of chocolate supplied by producers
   c. quantity of chocolate purchased by the government

4. A group of die-hard sports fans is upset about the high price of tickets to many games. As a result of their lobbying efforts, a new law is passed that caps the maximum ticket price to any sporting event at $50. Will more people be able to attend the games? Will certain teams and events be affected more than others?

5. Many local governments use parking meters on crowded downtown streets. However, the parking spaces along the street are typically hard to find because the metered price is often set below the market price. Explain what happens when local governments set the meter price too low. Why do you think the price is set below the market-clearing price?

6. Local suburban leaders decide to enact a minimum wage. Will the community lose more jobs if the nearby city votes to increase the minimum wage to the same rate?

✳ **7.** Examine the following graph.

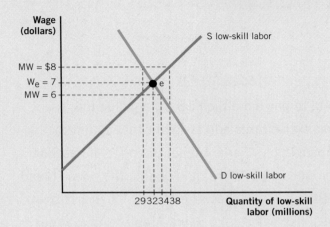

How many laborers will be unemployed when the minimum wage is $8 an hour? How many workers will be unemployed when the minimum wage is $6 an hour?

8. The demand and supply curves that we use can also be represented with equations. Suppose that the demand for low-skilled labor, Q_d, is represented by the following equation, where W is the wage rate:

$$Q_d = 53,000,000 - 3,000,000\,W$$

The supply of low-skilled labor, Q_s, is represented by the equation

$$Q_s = -10,000,000 + 6,000,000\,W$$

a. Find the equilibrium wage. (**Hint:** Set $Q_d = Q_s$ and solve for the wage, W. Then plug the result back into either of the original equations to find Q_e.)

b. Find the equilibrium quantity. (**Hint:** Now plug the value you got in part a back into Q_d or Q_s. You can double-check your answer by plugging the answer from part a into both Q_d and Q_s to see that you get the same result.)

c. What happens if the minimum wage is $8? (**Hint:** Plug W = 10 into both Q_d and Q_s.) Does this cause a surplus or a shortage?

d. What happens if the minimum wage is $6? (**Hint:** Plug W = 10 into both Q_d and Q_s.) Does this cause a surplus or a shortage?

SOLVED PROBLEMS

2. The equilibrium price occurs where the quantity demanded is equal to the quantity supplied. This occurs when $Q_d = Q_s = 800$. When the quantity is 800, the monthly rent is $800. Next the question asks how many one-bedroom apartments will be rented after a rent-control law is passed that limits the rent to $700 a month. When the rent is $700, the quantity supplied is 320 apartments. It is also worth noting that the quantity demanded when the rent is $700 is 550 units, so there is a shortage of 550 − 320 = 230 apartments once the rent-control law goes into effect.

7. How many laborers will be unemployed when the minimum wage is $8 an hour? The quantity demanded is 29M and the quantity supplied is 38M. This results is 38M − 29M = 9M unemployed workers.

How many workers will be unemployed when the minimum wage is $6 an hour? Since $6 an hour is below the market-equilibrium wage of $7, it has no effect. In other words, a $6 minimum wage is nonbinding, and therefore no unemployment is caused.

The Efficiency of Markets and the Costs of Taxation

Raising tax rates always generates more tax revenue.

Most people find it painful to pay more than $3.00 a gallon for gas. In many places, sales and excise taxes add a significant amount to the price that people pay. For example, the price of gasoline throughout Europe is often more than double the prices found in the United States, largely because of much higher gasoline taxes. Other countries, like Venezuela, Saudi Arabia, and Mexico, subsidize the price of gasoline so that their citizens pay less than the market price. In countries where gasoline is subsidized, cars are driven everywhere, mass transportation is largely unavailable, and there is little concern for fuel efficiency. As you might imagine, in countries with high gasoline taxes, consumers drive less, use public transportation more, and tend to purchase fuel-efficient vehicles. How high do gasoline taxes have to rise before large numbers of people significantly cut back on the amount of gas they use? The answer to that question will help us understand the misconception that raising tax rates always generates more tax revenue.

In the previous chapter, we learned about the market distortions that price controls create. We observed that efforts to manipulate market prices cause surpluses and shortages, and lead to black markets. In this chapter we will quantify how markets enhance the welfare of society. We begin with consumer surplus and producer surplus. With these two concepts in mind, we will see that taxation, like price controls, creates widespread distortions in economic behavior by altering the incentives that people face when consuming and producing goods that are taxed.

Photo to come

BIG QUESTIONS

✳ **What are consumer surplus and producer surplus?**

✳ **When is a market efficient?**

✳ **Why do taxes create deadweight loss?**

What Are Consumer Surplus and Producer Surplus?

helps our people on *mih wg*

Welfare economics
is the study of how economic well-being is affected by resource allocation.

Markets create value by bringing together buyers and sellers so that consumers and producers can mutually benefit from trade. **Welfare economics** is the branch of economics that studies how the allocation of resources affects economic well-being. In this section we develop two concepts that will help us measure the value markets create: *consumer surplus* and *producer surplus*. In competitive markets, the equilibrium price is low enough to attract consumers and simultaneously high enough to encourage producers. This balance between demand and supply enhances the welfare of society. That is not to say that society's welfare depends solely on markets. People find satisfaction in many nonmarket settings, including spending time with their families and friends, and doing hobbies and charity work. We will incorporate aspects of personal happiness into our economic model in Chapter 16. For now, let's focus on how markets enhance human welfare.

How much will they pay for an economics textbook?

Consumer Surplus

Willingness to pay
is the maximum price a consumer will pay for a good.

Consider Frank, Beanie, and Mitch, from the well-known 2003 college flick *Old School*. Like students everywhere, each has a maximum price he is willing to pay for an economics textbook. Beanie owns a successful business and the cost of purchasing a textbook does not present a financial hardship. Mitch is a business major who really wants to do well in economics. Frank is not serious about his studies. Table 6.1 shows the maximum value that each student places on the textbook. This value, called the **willingness to pay**, is the upper limit that the student will pay for the book. The willingness to pay is also known as the reservation price. In an auction, or negotiation, the willingness to pay, or reservation price, is the price where the demander decides to walk way.

What is the highest price yall pay.

TABLE 6.1

Willingness to Pay for a New Economics Textbook	
Buyer	**Willingness to Pay**
Beanie	$200
Mitch	150
Frank	100

Consider what happens when the price of the book is $151. If Beanie purchases the book at $151, he pays $49 less than the $200 maximum he was willing to pay. The difference between Beanie's willingness to pay and the amount he actually pays is known as his **consumer surplus**. Beanie values the textbook at $49 more than the purchase price, so buying the book will make him better off.

Consumer surplus is a measure of the benefit that a buyer gains from participating in a market. While Beanie gains $49 in consumer surplus, a price of $151 is more than either Mitch or Frank is willing to pay. Since Mitch is willing to pay only $150, if he purchases the book he will experience a consumer loss of $1. Frank's situation is even clearer. His willingness to pay is $100, so if he buys the book for $151, he will be looking at a consumer loss of $51. Whenever the price is greater than the willingness to pay, the consumer will decide not to buy.

Consumer surplus is the difference between the willingness to pay for a good and the amount that is paid to get it.

Using Demand Curves to Illustrate Consumer Surplus

In the previous section we looked at consumer surplus as an amount. We can also illustrate consumer surplus graphically, with a demand curve. Figure 6.1 shows the demand curve drawn from the data in Table 6.1. Notice that the demand curve looks like a staircase with three steps—one for each additional textbook purchase. Each point on a market demand curve corresponds to one unit sold, so when more consumers are added to the market, the "steps" become narrower and the demand curve becomes smoother.

At any price above $200, none of the students wants to purchase a textbook. This relationship can be seen on the x-axis where the quantity demanded is 0. At any price between $150 and $200, Beanie is the only buyer, so the quantity demanded is 1. At prices between $100 and $150, Beanie and Mitch are each willing to buy the textbook, so the quantity demanded is 2. Finally, if the price is $100 or less, all three students are willing to buy the textbook, so the quantity demanded is 3. As the price falls, the quantity demanded increases.

We can measure the total extent of consumer welfare by examining the area under the demand curve for each of our three consumers, as shown in Figure 6.2. In Figure 6.2a the price is $175 and only Beanie decides to buy. Since his willingness to pay is $200, he is better off by $25; this is his consumer surplus. The green-shaded area under the demand curve and above the price represents the benefit Beanie receives from purchasing a textbook at a price of $175. When the price is lowered to $125, as shown in Figure 6.2b, Mitch also decides to buy a textbook. The total quantity demanded is now 2 textbooks. Mitch's willingness to pay is $150, so his consumer surplus, represented by the pink-shaded area, is $25. However, since Beanie's willingness to pay is $200, his consumer surplus rises from $25 to $75. So a textbook price of $125 raises the total consumer surplus to $100. In other words, lower prices create more consumer surplus in the market.

Producer Surplus

Willingness to sell
is the minimum price a seller will accept to produce a good or service.

Sellers also benefit from market transactions. In this section our three students discover that they are good at economics and decide to go into the tutoring business. They do not want to provide this service for free, but each has a different minimum price, or **willingness to sell.** Table 6.2 shows each tutor's willingness to sell his services.

lowest price they will sell

TABLE 6.2

Willingness to Sell Tutoring Services

Seller	Willingness to Sell
Beanie	$30/hr
Mitch	20/hr
Frank	10/hr

FIGURE 6.1

Demand Curve for an Economics Textbook

The demand curve has a step for each additional textbook purchase. As the price goes down, more students buy the textbook.

Price (dollars per textbook)	Buyers	Quantity Demanded (textbooks)
More than $200	None	0
151 to 200	Beanie	1
101 to 150	Mitch, Beanie	2
Less than 100	Frank, Mitch Beanie	3

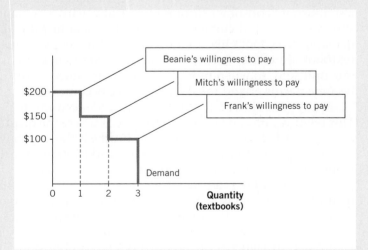

Consider what happens at a tutoring price of $25 an hour. Since Frank is willing to tutor for $10 an hour, every hour that he tutors at $25 an hour earns him $15 more than his willingness to sell. This extra $15 an hour is his *producer surplus*. **Producer surplus** is a measure of the benefit that a seller earns from participating in a market. Mitch is willing to tutor for $20 an hour and earns a $5 producer surplus for every hour he tutors. Finally, Beanie's willingness to tutor, at $30 an hour, is more than the market price of $25. If he tutors, he will have a producer loss of $5 an hour.

How do producers determine their willingness to sell? They must consider two issues: the direct costs of producing the good and the indirect costs, or opportunity costs. Students new to economics often mistakenly assume that the cost of producing an item is the only cost to consider in making the decision to produce. But producers also have opportunity costs. Beanie, Mitch, and Frank each has a unique willingness to sell because they have different opportunity costs. Beanie owns his own business, so for him time spent tutoring is time that he could have been making money elsewhere. Mitch is a business student who might otherwise be studying to get better grades. Frank is neither a businessman nor a serious student, so the $10 he can earn in an hour of tutoring is not taking the place of other earning opportunities or studying more to get better grades.

Producer surplus
is the difference between the willingness to sell a good and the price that the seller receives.

Using Supply Curves to Illustrate Producer Surplus

The supply curve in Figure 6.3 shows the relationship between the price for an hour of tutoring and the quantity of tutors willing to work. As you can see on the supply schedule, at any price less than $10, no one wants to tutor. At

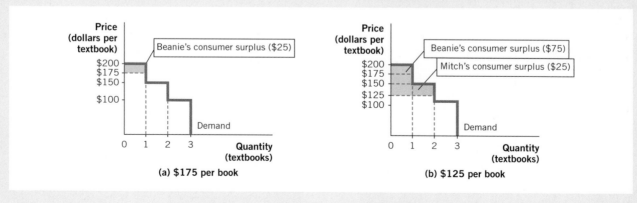

FIGURE 6.2

Determining Consumer Surplus from a Demand Curve
(a) At a price of $175, Beanie is the only buyer, so the quantity demanded is 1. (b) At a price of $125, Beanie and Mitch are each willing to buy the textbook, so the quantity demanded is 2.

prices between $10 and $19 an hour, Frank is the only tutor, so the quantity supplied is 1. Between $20 and $29 an hour, Frank and Mitch are willing to tutor, so the quantity supplied rises to 2. Finally, if the price is $30 or more, all three friends are willing to tutor, so the quantity of tutors supplied is 3. As the price they receive for tutoring rises, the quantity supplied increases.

What do these relationships between price and supply tell us about producer surplus? Let's turn to Figure 6.4. By examining the area above the supply curve we can measure the extent of producer welfare. In Figure 6.4a, the price of an

FIGURE 6.3

Supply Curve for Economics Tutoring

The supply curve has three steps, one for each additional student willing to tutor. Progressively higher prices induce more students to become tutors.

Price (dollars per hour tutoring)	Sellers	Quantity Supplied (tutors)
$30 or more	Frank, Mitch, Beanie	3
20 to 29	Frank, Mitch	2
10 to 19	Frank	1
Less than 10	None	0

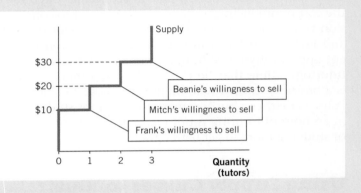

FIGURE 6.4

Determining Producer Surplus from a Supply Curve

(a) The price of an hour of tutoring is $15. At this price, only Frank decides to tutor. (b) The price for tutoring is $25 an hour. At this price, Mitch also decides to tutor.

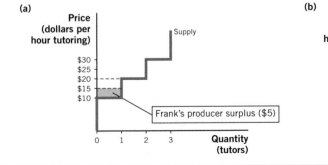

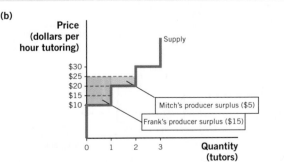

hour of tutoring is $15. At that price, only Frank decides to tutor. Since Frank would be willing to tutor even if the price were as low as $10 an hour, he is $5 better off tutoring. Frank's producer surplus is represented by the pink-shaded area between the supply curve and the price of $15. Since Beanie and Mitch do not tutor when the price is $15, they do not receive any producer surplus. In Figure 6.4b, the price for tutoring is $25 an hour. At this price, Mitch also decides to tutor. Mitch's willingness to tutor is $20, so when the price is $25 an hour, his producer surplus is $5, represented by the blue-shaded area. Since Frank's willingness to tutor is $10, at $25 an hour his producer surplus has risen to $15. By looking at the shaded boxes in Figure 6.4b, we see that an increase in the rates for tutoring raises the combined producer surplus of Frank and Mitch to $20.

PRACTICE WHAT YOU KNOW

Consumer and Producer Surplus: Trendy Fashion

Leah decides to buy a new jacket from D&G for $80. Leah was willing to pay $100. When her friend Becky sees the jacket, she loves it and thinks it is worth $150. So she offers Leah $125 for the jacket and Leah accepts. Leah and Becky are both thrilled with the exchange.

Rachel Bilson wearing a D&G jacket

Question: Determine the total surplus from the original purchase and the additional surplus generated by the resale of the jacket.

Answer: Leah was willing to pay $100 and the jacket cost $80, so she keeps the difference, or $20, as consumer surplus. When Leah resells the jacket to Becky for $125, she earns $25 in producer surplus. At the same time, Becky receives $25 in consumer surplus, since she was willing to pay Leah up to $150 for the jacket, but Leah sells it to her for $125. The resale generates an additional $50 in surplus. Thus, the two exchanges produced $45 in consumer surplus for Leah and $25 in consumer surplus for Becky, for a grand total of $70 in consumer surplus.

When Is a Market Efficient?

We have seen how consumers benefit from lower prices and how producers benefit from higher prices. When we bring together the concepts of consumer and producer surplus, we can build a complete picture of the welfare of buyers and sellers. Adding consumer and producer surplus gives us **total surplus**, also known as **social welfare**, because it measures the welfare of society. Total surplus is the best way we have to measure the benefits that markets create.

Total surplus, also known as **social welfare,** is the sum of consumer and producer surplus.

The buyer and seller each benefit from this exchange.

Figure 6.5 illustrates the relationship between consumer and producer surplus. The demand curve shows that some customers are willing to pay more to get a gallon of milk than others. Likewise, some sellers are willing to sell milk for less than others.

Let's say Alice is willing to pay $7 for milk, but when she gets to the store, she finds that she is able to buy the milk for $4. The difference between the price she is willing to pay, represented by point A, and the price she actually pays, represented by e, is $3 in consumer surplus. This is indicated by the blue arrow that shows the distance from $4 to $7. Alice's friend Betty is willing to pay $5 for milk, but, like Alice, she is able to buy the milk for $4. Therefore she receives $1 in consumer surplus, indicated by the blue arrow that shows the distance from $4 to $5. In fact, all consumers who are willing to pay more than $4 are better off when they purchase the milk at $4. We can show this total area of consumer surplus on the graph as the blue-shaded triangle bordered by the demand curve, the y-axis, and the equilibrium price. At every point in this area, consumers who are willing to pay more than the equilibrium price for milk will be better off.

Producer surplus follows a similar process. Suppose that the Contented Cow is willing to sell milk for $2.50 a gallon, represented by point C. Since the

FIGURE 6.5

Consumer and Producer Surplus for a Gallon of Milk

Consumer surplus is the difference between the willingness to pay along the demand curve and the equilibrium price, P_e. It is illustrated by the blue-shaded triangle. Producer surplus is the difference between the willingness to produce along the supply curve and the equilibrium price. It is illustrated by the red-shaded triangle.

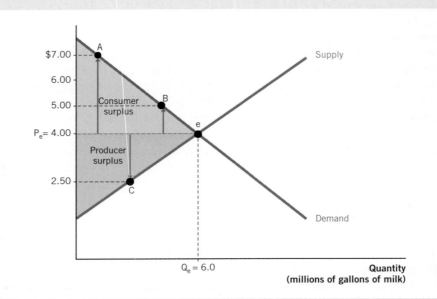

Efficiency

Old School

In the 2003 movie *Old School* Frank tries to give away a bread maker he received as a wedding present. First he offers it to a friend as a housewarming gift. It turns out that this is the friend who originally gave him the bread maker. Ouch. Later in the movie we see him giving the bread maker to a small boy at a birthday party. Both efforts at re-gifting fail miserably.

From an economic perspective, giving the wrong gift makes society poorer. If you spend $50 on a gift and give it to someone who happens to think it is only worth $30, you've lost $20 in value. Whenever you receive a shirt that is the wrong size or style, a fruitcake you won't eat, or something that is worth less to you than what the gift-giver spent on it, an economic inefficiency has occurred. Up until now we have thought of the market as enhancing efficiency by increasing the total surplus in society. But think of the billions of dollars spent on mismatched gifts as a failure to maximize the total surplus involved in exchange. In other words, think of the efficiency of the gift-giving process as less than 100 percent.

Given what we have learned so far about economics, you might be tempted to argue that cash is the best gift you can give. When you give cash it is never the wrong size or color and the recipients can use the money to buy exactly what they want. However, very few people actually give cash (unless it is requested). Considering the advantages of cash, why don't more people give it instead of gifts? One reason is because cash seems impersonal. A second reason is that cash communicates exactly how much the giver spent. To avoid both of these problems, savvy people rarely give cash. Instead, they often buy personalized gifts to communicate how much they care, while making it hard to determine exactly how much they spent.

One way that society overcomes inefficiency in gifting is through disseminating information. For instance, wedding registries provide a convenient way for people who may not know the newlyweds very well to give them what they want. Similarly, prior to holidays many people tell each other what they would like to receive. By purchasing gifts that others want, givers are able to exactly match what would have been purchased if the recipient had received a cash transfer. This eliminates any potential inefficiency. At the same time the giver conveys affection, an essential part of giving. To further reduce some of the potential inefficiencies associated with giving, many large families practice holiday gift exchanges. Another interesting mechanism for eliciting information involves Santa Claus. Children throughout the world send Santa Claus wish lists for Christmas, never realizing that the parents who help write and send the lists are the primary beneficiaries of the revealed preferences. To the economist, providing better information, gift exchanges, and Santa Claus are just a few examples of how society tries to get the most out of the giving process—and that is something to be joyful about!

Frank re-gifts a bread maker.

equilibrium price is $4.00, the business makes $1.50 in producer surplus. This indicated by the red arrow that shows the distance from $4.00 to $2.50. If we think of the supply curve as representing the costs of many different sellers, we can calculate the total producer surplus as the red-shaded triangle bordered by the supply curve, the y-axis, and the equilibrium price. The shaded blue triangle (consumer surplus) and the shaded red triangle (producer surplus) describe the increase in total surplus, or social welfare, created by the production and exchange of the good at the equilibrium price. At the equilibrium quantity of 6 million gallons of milk, output and consumption reach the largest possible combination of producer and consumer surplus. In the region of the graph beyond 6 million units, buyers and sellers will experience a loss.

When an allocation of resources maximizes total surplus, the result is said to be **efficient**. Efficiency occurs at point e when the market is in equilibrium. To think about why the market creates the largest possible total surplus, or social welfare, it is important to recall how the market allocates resources. Consumers who are willing to pay more than the equilibrium price will buy the good, because they enjoy the consumer surplus. Producers who are willing to sell the good for less than the market-equilibrium price will enjoy the producer surplus. In addition, consumers with a low willingness to buy (less than $4) and producers with a high willingness to sell (more than $4) do not participate in the market since they would be made worse off. Therefore, the equilibrium output at point e maximizes the total surplus and is also an efficient allocation of resources.

An outcome is **efficient** when an allocation of resources maximizes total surplus.

The Efficiency-Equity Debate

When economists model behavior, they assume that participants in a market are rational decision-makers. We assume that producers will always operate in the region of the triangle that represents producer surplus and that consumers will always operate in the region of the triangle that represents consumer surplus. We do not, for example, expect Alice to pay more than $7.00 for a gallon of milk or the Contented Cow to sell a gallon of milk for less than $2.50 per gallon. In other words, for the market to work efficiently, voluntary instances of consumer loss must be rare. We assume that self-interest helps to ensure that participants will benefit from exchange.

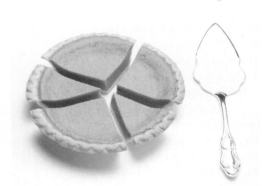

Efficiency only requires that the pie gets eaten. Equity is a question of who gets the biggest share.

However, the fact that both parties benefit from an exchange does not mean that that each benefits equally. Economists are also interested in the distribution of the gains. **Equity** refers to the fairness of how benefits are distributed among the members of a society. In a world where no one cared about equity, only efficiency would matter and no particular division would be preferred. Another way of thinking about fairness versus efficiency is to consider a pie. If our only concern is efficiency, we will simply want to make sure that that none of the pie goes to waste. However, if we care about equity, we also want to make sure that the pie is divided equally among those present, and that no one gets a larger piece.

Equity refers to the fairness of the distribution of benefits within society.

In our first look at consumer and producer surplus, we have assumed that markets produce efficient outcomes. But we know that in the real world this is not always the case. Markets also fail; their efficiency can be compromised

PRACTICE WHAT YOU KNOW

Total Surplus: How Would Lower Income Affect Society's Welfare?

Question: If a fall in consumer income occurs, what will happen to the consumer surplus that customers enjoy at Urban Outfitters? What will happen to the amount of producer surplus that Urban Outfitters receives? Illustrate your answer by shifting the demand curve appropriately and labeling the new and old areas of consumer and producer surplus.

Does less income affect total surplus?

Answer: Since the items sold at Urban Outfitters are normal goods, a fall in income causes the demand curve to shift to the left. The black arrow shows the leftward shift in the figure below. When you compare the area of consumer surplus (in blue) before and after, you can see that it shrinks. The same is true when you compare the area of producer surplus (in red) before and after.

A quick check of the intuition should confirm what the graphs tell us. Since consumers have less income, they buy fewer clothes at Urban Outfitters—so consumer surplus falls. Likewise, since fewer customers buy clothes, Urban Outfitters sells less—so producer surplus falls. This can also be seen in panel (b), since $Q_2 < Q_1$.

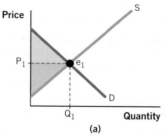

(a)

(a) Before the fall in income

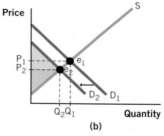

(b)

(b) After the fall in income

in a number of ways. We will discuss market failure in much greater detail in subsequent chapters. For now all you need to know is that failure can occur.

Why Do Taxes Create Deadweight Loss?

Taxes provide many benefits. They also remind us that there is no free lunch; we don't pay the police dispatcher before dialing 911, but society has to collect taxes for the service to exist. Taxes help to pay for many of the things modern society needs—public transportation, schools, police, the court system, and the military, to name just a few. Most of us take these services for

Why do we place excise taxes on cigarettes . . .

. . . and gasoline?

granted, but without taxes it would be hard to find enough funds to pay for them. How much does all of this cost? Three trillion dollars a year!

These taxes incur opportunity costs, since the money could have been used in other ways. In this section we will use consumer and producer surplus to help us understand the effect of taxation on social welfare and market efficiency. Taxes come in many sizes and shapes. Among these are taxes on personal income, payroll, property, corporate profits, sales, and inheritances. This complexity makes it difficult to analyze. Fortunately, we do not have to examine the entire tax code all at once. In this chapter, we will explore the impact that taxes have on social welfare by looking at one of the simplest taxes, the *excise tax*.

Tax Incidence

Excise taxes
focus on a particular good or activity.

Economists want to know how taxes affect the choices that consumers and producers make. When a tax is imposed on an item, do buyers switch to alternative goods that are not taxed? How do producers respond when products they sell are taxed? Since taxes raise prices, they can change how much of a good or service is bought and sold. This is especially clear with **excise taxes**, or taxes levied on one particular good or service. For example, all fifty states levy excise taxes on cigarettes, but the amount assessed varies tremendously. In New York, cigarette taxes are over $4 per pack, while in a handful of tobacco-producing states such as Virginia and North Carolina, the excise tax is less than 50 cents. Excise taxes, such as those on cigarettes, alcohol, and gasoline, account for less than 4 percent of all tax revenues. But because we can isolate changes in consumer behavior that result from taxes on one item, they help us understand the overall effect of a tax.

Incidence
refers to the party who bears the burden of the tax.

In looking at the effect of a tax, economists are also interested in the **incidence** of taxation, which refers to the party who effectively pays the tax through higher prices. To help us understand this idea, consider a $1 tax placed on milk purchases. Each time a consumer buys a gallon of milk, the cash register adds $1 in tax. This means that to purchase the milk, the consumer's willingness pay must be greater than the price of the milk plus the $1 tax.

The result of the $1 tax on milk is shown in Figure 6.6. Because of the tax, the price of milk goes up and the demand curve shifts down. Why does the demand curve shift? Consumers know that they must pay the purchase price and also the tax. The extra cost makes them less likely to buy milk at every price, which causes the entire demand curve to shift down. The intersection of the new demand curve with the existing supply curve creates a new equilibrium price of $3.50, which is $0.50 lower than the original equilibrium price of $4.00. But even though the price is lower, consumers are still worse off. Since they must also pay the $1 tax, the total price rises to $4.50 per gallon.

A similar logic applies to the producer. Since the new equilibrium price after the tax is $0.50 lower than it was before the tax, the producer splits the tax incidence with the buyer. The producer receives $0.50 less and the buyer pays $0.50 more.

The tax on milk purchases also affects the amount sold in the market. Since the after-tax equilibrium price is lower, producers of milk reduce the quantity that they sell to 750 gallons. Therefore, the market for milk is smaller than it was before the tax was placed on the good.

Excise taxes paid by consumers are relatively rare because they are highly visible. If every time you bought milk you were reminded that you had to pay a $1 tax, it would be hard to ignore. As a result, politicians often prefer to place the tax on the seller. The seller will then attempt to fold the tax into

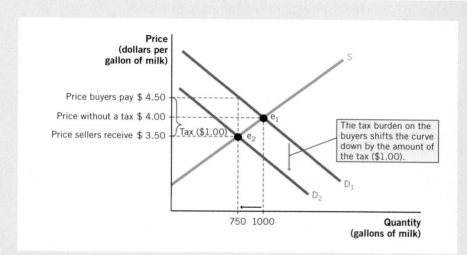

FIGURE 6.6

A Tax on Buyers

After the tax, the new equilibrium price is $3.50, but the buyer must also pay $1.00 in tax to the government. Therefore, despite the fall in price, the buyer still owes $4.50. A similar logic applies to the producer. Since the new equilibrium price after the tax is $0.50 lower, the producer shares the tax incidence equally with the seller in this example. The consumer pays $0.50 more and the seller earns $0.50 less.

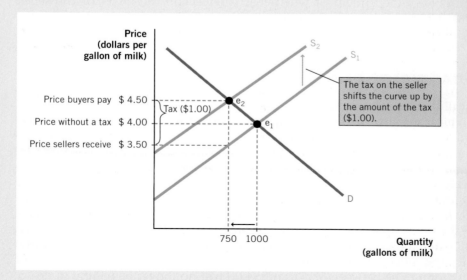

FIGURE 6.7

A Tax on Sellers

After the tax, the new equilibrium price is $4.50, but $1.00 must be paid as tax to the government. Therefore, despite the rise in price, the seller nets only $3.50. A similar logic applies to the consumer. Since the new equilibrium price after the tax is $0.50 higher, the consumer shares the $1.00/gallon tax incidence equally with the seller. The consumer pays $0.50 more and the seller nets $0.50 less.

the sale price and rationally ignorant buyers often forget that the sale price is higher than it otherwise would be if the product was not taxed.

Let's return to the $1 tax on milk. This time the tax is placed on the seller. Figure 6.7 shows the result. First, look at the shift in the supply curve. Why does it shift? The $1/gallon tax on milk lowers the profits that milk producers expect to make, which causes them to produce less milk at every price level. This means that the entire supply curve shifts left in response to the tax that milk producers must pay to the government. The intersection of the new supply curve with the existing demand curve creates a new equilibrium price of $4.50—$0.50 higher than the original equilibrium price of $4.00. This occurs because the seller is able to pass part of the tax increase along to the buyer in the form of a higher price. However, the seller is still worse off. After the tax, the new equilibrium price is $4.50, but $1.00 must be paid as tax to the government. Therefore, despite the rise in price, the seller nets only $3.50, which is $0.50 less than the original equilibrium price.

A similar logic applies to the consumer. Since the new equilibrium price after the tax is $0.50 higher, the consumer shares the $1.00/gallon tax incidence equally with the seller. The consumer pays $0.50 more and the seller nets $0.50 less.

The tax also affects the amount of milk sold in the market. Since the new equilibrium price after the tax is higher, consumers reduce the quantity demanded from 1,000 gallons to 750 gallons.

Have you noticed that the result in Figure 6.7 looks much like that in Figure 6.6? This is because it does not matter whether a tax is levied on the buyer or the seller. The tax places a wedge of $1 between the price that buyers ultimately pay ($4.50) and the net price that sellers ultimately receive ($3.50), regardless of who is actually responsible for paying the tax.

Returning to our milk example, when the tax was levied on sellers, they were responsible for collecting the entire tax ($1/gallon), but they were able to transfer $0.50 of the tax to the consumer by raising the market price to $4.50. Similarly, when the tax was levied on consumers, they were responsible for paying the entire tax, but they were able to transfer $0.50 of the tax to the producer, since the market price fell to $3.50. Therefore, the incidence of a tax is independent of whether it is levied on the buyer or the seller. However, depending on the price elasticity of supply and demand, the tax incidence need not be shared equally, as we will see later.

Deadweight Loss

Deadweight loss is the decrease in economic activity caused by market distortions.

Recall that we measure economic efficiency by looking at total consumer and producer surplus. We have seen that a tax raises the total price consumers pay and lowers the net price producers receive. For this reason, taxes reduce the amount of economic activity. The decrease in economic activity caused by market distortions, such as taxes, is known as **deadweight loss**. In the previous section we observed that the tax on milk caused the amount purchased to decline from 1,000 to 750 gallons, a reduction of 250 gallons sold in the market. In Figure 6.8, the yellow triangle represents the deadweight loss caused by the tax. When the price rises, consumers who would have paid between $4.00 and $4.49 will no longer purchase milk. Likewise, the reduction in the price the seller can charge means that producers who once sold a gallon of milk for a price between $3.51 and $4.00 will no longer be willing to do so.

The combined reductions in consumer and producer surplus equal the dead-weight loss produced by a $1 tax on milk.

In the next sections we will examine how differences in the price elasticity of demand lead to varying amounts of deadweight loss. We will evaluate what happens when the demand curve is perfectly inelastic, somewhat elastic, and perfectly elastic.

Tax Revenue and Deadweight Loss When Demand Is Inelastic

In Chapter 4 we saw that necessary goods and services—for example, water, electricity, and phone service—have highly inelastic demand. These goods and services are often taxed. For example, consider all of the taxes associated with your cell phone bill: sales tax, city tax, county tax, federal excise tax, and annual regulatory fees. In addition, many companies add surcharges, including activation fees, local number portability fees, telephone number pooling charges, emergency 911 service, directory assistance, telecommunications relay service surcharges, and cancellation fees. Of course, there is a way to avoid all of these fees: don't use a cell phone! However, many people feel that cell phones are a necessity. Cell phone providers and government agencies take advantage of the consumer's strongly inelastic demand by tacking on these extra charges.

Hagar the Horrible

FIGURE 6.8

The Deadweight Loss from a Tax

The yellow triangle represents the deadweight loss caused by the tax. When the price rises, some consumers who would have paid between $4.00 and $4.49 no longer purchase milk. Likewise, the reduction in the revenue the seller receives means that producers who once sold a gallon of milk for between $3.51 and $4.00 will no longer be willing to do so.

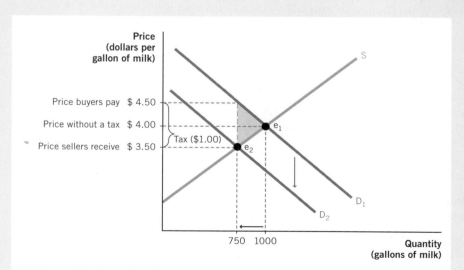

Figure 6.9 shows the result of a tax on products with perfectly inelastic demand, such as phone service—something people need to have no matter what the price. The demand for access to a phone (either a landline or a cell phone) is perfectly inelastic. Recall that whenever demand is perfectly inelastic, the demand curve is vertical. Figure 6.9a shows the market for phone service before the tax. The blue rectangle represents consumer surplus and the red triangle represents the producer surplus. Now imagine that a tax is levied on the seller, as shown in Figure 6.9b. The supply curve shifts from S_1 to S_2. The shift in supply causes the equilibrium to move from e_1 to e_2 and the price to rise from P_1 to P_2. We know that when demand is perfectly inelastic, a price increase does not alter how much consumers purchase. So the quantity demanded remains constant at Q_1 even after the government collects tax revenue equal to the green-shaded area.

There are two reasons the government may favor excise taxes on goods with perfectly (or highly) inelastic demand. First, because these goods do not have substitutes, the tax will not cause consumers to buy less. This means the revenue from the tax will remain steady. Second, since the number of transactions, or Q, remains constant, there is no deadweight loss. As a result, the yellow triangle we observed in Figure 6.8 disappears in Figure 6.9, since the tax does not alter the efficiency of the market. Looking at Figure 6.9 you can see that the same number of transactions exist in (a) and (b). This means that the total surplus, or social welfare, is equal in both panels. You can also see this by comparing the shaded areas in both panels. The sum of the blue-shaded area of consumer surplus and the red-shaded area of producer surplus in (a) is equal to the sum of the consumer surplus, producer surplus, and tax revenue in (b). The green area is subtracted entirely from the blue rectangle, which indicates that the surplus is redistributed from

FIGURE 6.9

A Tax on Products with Perfectly Inelastic Demand

(a) The consumer enjoys the consumer surplus noted in blue and the producer enjoys the surplus noted in red. (b) The incidence, or the burden of taxation, is borne entirely by the consumer. A tax on a good with perfectly inelastic demand, such as phone service, represents a transfer of welfare from consumers of the good to the government, reflected by the reduced size of the blue rectangle in (b) and the creation of the green tax-revenue rectangle between P_1 and P_2.

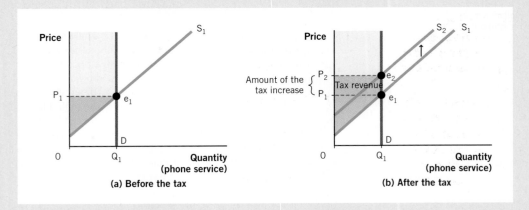

Taxing Inelastic Goals

Taxman by the Beatles

Taxman was inspired by the theme song from the popular 1960s television series *Batman*. The Beatles—and especially George Harrison, who wrote the song—had grown quite bitter about how much money they were paying in taxes. In the beginning of the song, he sings, "Let me tell you how it will be. There's one for you, nineteen for me." This refers to the fact that the British government taxed high-wage earners $19 out of every $20 they earned. Since the Beatles' considerable earnings placed them in the top income tax bracket in the United Kingdom, this made a part of the group's earnings subject to the 95% tax introduced by Harold Wilson's Labour government in 1965. As a consequence, the Beatles became tax exiles living in the United States and other parts of Europe, where tax rates were lower.

The inevitability of paying taxes is a theme that runs throughout the song. The lyrics mention that when you drive a car, the government can tax the "street"; if you try to sit, the government can tax "your seat"; if you are cold, the government can tax "the heat"; and if you decide to take a walk, it can tax

The Beatles were able to avoid high taxes.

your "feet"! The only way to avoid doing and using these things is to leave the country—that's precisely what the Beatles did. All of these examples (streets, seats, heat, and walking) are unavoidable activities, which makes demand highly inelastic. Anytime that is the case, the government is able to collect the tax revenue it desires more easily.

consumers to the government. But society overall enjoys the same total surplus. From this we see that when demand is perfectly inelastic, the incidence, or the burden of taxation, is borne entirely by the consumer. A tax on a good with perfectly inelastic demand represents a transfer of welfare from consumers of the good to the government, reflected by the reduced size of the blue rectangle in (b).

Tax Revenue and Deadweight Loss When Demand Is More Elastic

Now consider a tax on a product with more elastic demand, such as milk, the subject of the earlier discussion on calculating total surplus. The demand for milk is price sensitive but not overly so. This is reflected in a demand curve with a typical slope shown in Figure 6.10. Let's compare the after-tax price, P_2, in Figures 6.9 and 6.10. When demand is perfectly inelastic, as it is in Figure 6.9, the price increase from P_1 to P_2 is absorbed entirely by the consumer. But in Figure 6.10, because demand is more sensitive to price, suppliers must absorb part of the tax, from P_1 to P_3, themselves, and net P_3, which is less than what they received when the good was not taxed. In addition, the total tax revenue generated (the green-shaded area) is not as large in Figure 6.9 as in Figure 6.10, because as the price of the good rises some consumers no longer buy it and the quantity demanded falls from Q_1 to Q_2.

Notice that both consumer surplus, the blue triangle, and producer surplus, the red triangle, are smaller after the tax. Since the price rises after the tax increase (from P_1 to P_2), those consumers with a relatively low willingness to pay for the good are priced out of the market. Likewise, sellers with relatively high costs of production will stop producing the good, since the price they net after paying the tax drops to P_3. The total reduction in economic activity, the change from Q_1 to Q_2, is the deadweight loss, indicated by the yellow triangle.

The incidence of the tax also changes from Figure 6.9 to Figure 6.10. A tax on a good for which demand and supply are each somewhat elastic will cause a transfer of welfare from consumers and producers of the good to the government. At the same time, since the quantity bought and sold in the market declines, it also creates deadweight loss. Another way of seeing this same result is to observe the red- and blue-shaded areas in Figure 6.10a and compare them with the red- and blue-shaded areas in Figure 6.10b. The sum of the consumer surplus and producer surplus in (a) is greater than the sum of the consumer surplus, tax revenue, and producer surplus in (b). Therefore, the total surplus, or efficiency of the market, is smaller. The tax is no longer a pure transfer from consumers to the government, as was the case in Figure 6.9.

Tax Revenue and Deadweight Loss When Demand Is Highly Elastic

We have seen the effect of taxation when demand is inelastic and somewhat elastic. What about when demand is highly elastic? For example, a customer who wishes to buy fresh lettuce at a produce market will find many local

FIGURE 6.10

A Tax on Products with More Elastic Demand

(a) The consumer enjoys the consumer surplus noted in blue and the producer enjoys the surplus noted in red. (b) A tax on a good for which demand and supply are each somewhat elastic will cause a transfer of welfare from consumers and producers to the government. At the same time, it also creates deadweight loss shown in yellow, since the quantity bought and sold in the market declines.

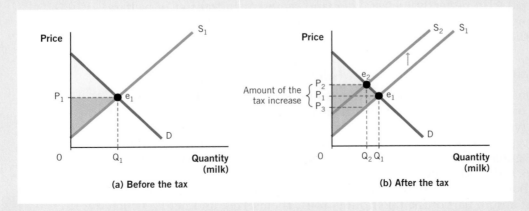

growers charging the same price and many varieties to choose from. If one of the vendors decides to charge $1.00 per pound above the market price, consumers will stop buying from that vendor. Consumers are not willing to pay more when they can get the same product from another grower at a lower price; this is the essence of elastic demand.

Figure 6.11 shows the result of a tax placed on lettuce, a good with highly elastic demand. Unlike milk, where the next-best alternative is to go without, when lettuce is taxed consumers can switch to other greens such as spinach, cabbage, or endive and completely avoid the tax. In this market, consumers are so price sensitive that they are unwilling to accept any price increase. Because sellers are unable to raise the equilibrium price, they bear the entire incidence of the tax. This has two effects. First, producers are less willing to sell the product at all prices. This shifts the supply curve from S_1 to S_2. Since consumer demand is highly elastic, consumers pay the same price as before. However, the tax increase causes the producer to net less, or P_3. Since P_3 is substantially lower than the price before the tax, or P_2, producers offer less for sale after the tax is implemented, as shown in Figure 6.11b in the movement from Q_1 to Q_2. Since Q_2 is a lot smaller than Q_1, there is also more deadweight loss than we observed in Figure 6.10. Therefore, the total surplus, or efficiency of the market, is much smaller than before. Comparing the green-shaded areas of Figures 6.10 and 6.11, you see that the size of the tax revenue continues to shrink. There is an important lesson here for policy makers—tax goods with relatively inelastic demand. Not only will this lessen the deadweight loss of taxation, but it will also generate larger tax revenues for the government.

So far we have varied the elasticity of the demand curve, while holding the elasticity of the supply curve constant. What would happen if we

FIGURE 6.11

A Tax on Products with Highly Elastic Demand

(a) The producer enjoys the surplus noted in red. (b) When consumer demand is highly elastic, consumers pay the same price after the tax as before. But they are worse off because less is produced and sold; the quantity produced moves from Q_1 to Q_2. The result is deadweight loss, as shown by the yellow triangle in (b). The total surplus, or efficiency of the market, is much smaller than before. The size of the tax revenue (in green) is also noticeably smaller in the market with highly elastic demand.

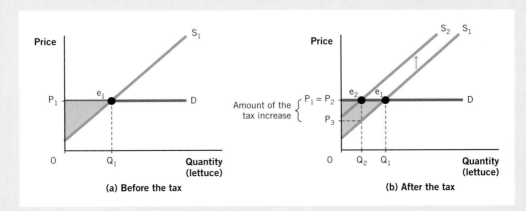

(a) Before the tax

(b) After the tax

Gathering mushrooms is taxing.

did the reverse and varied the elasticity of the supply curve, while keeping the elasticity of the demand curve constant? It turns out that there is a simple method for determining the incidence and deadweight loss. The incidence of a tax is determined by the relative steepness of the demand curve compared to the supply curve. When the demand curve is steeper (more inelastic) than the supply curve, consumers bear more of the incidence of the tax. When the supply curve is steeper (more inelastic) than the demand curve, suppliers bear more of the incidence of the tax. Also, whenever the supply and/or demand curves are relatively steep, dead-weight loss is minimized.

Let's do an example where we consider how the elasticity of demand and elasticity of supply interact. Suppose that a $3.00/pound tax is placed on shiitake mushrooms. Given the information in Figure 6.12, compute the incidence, deadweight loss, and tax revenue from the tax.

Let's start with the incidence of the tax. After the tax is implemented, the market price rises from $7.00 to $8.00. But since sellers must pay $3.00 to the government, they keep only $5.00. Tax incidence measures the share of the tax paid by buyers and sellers, so we need to compare the incidence of the tax paid by each party. Since the market price rises by $1 (from $7 to $8), buyers are paying $1 of the $3 tax, or 1/3. Since the amount the producer keeps falls by $2 (from $7 to $5), sellers are paying $2 of the $3 tax, or 2/3. If you are looking for an intuitive reason why sellers bear more of the incidence, notice that the demand curve is more elastic (flatter) than the supply curve.

FIGURE 6.12

A Realistic Example

A $3.00 tax is placed on mushroom suppliers. This drives the equilibrium price up from e_1 ($7.00) to e_2 ($8.00). Notice that the price only rises by $1.00. This means that the consumer picks up $1.00 of the $3 tax and the producer must pay the remaining $2. Therefore, most of the incidence is borne by the producer. Finally, neither the demand curve nor the supply curve is relatively inelastic, so the amount of deadweight loss is large.

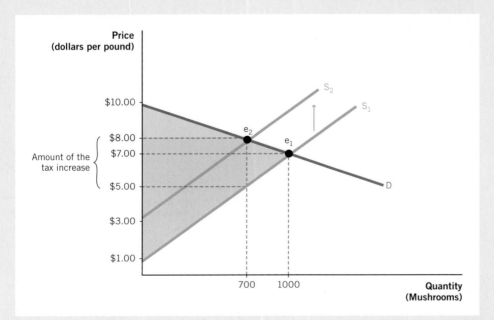

Now let's determine the deadweight loss caused by the tax. The deadweight loss measures the decrease in economic activity caused by the tax. This is represented by the decrease in the total surplus found in the yellow triangle. In order to compute the amount of the deadweight loss, we need to determine the area inside the triangle. The area of a triangle is found by taking

$$\text{The area of a triangle} = 1/2 \times \text{base} \times \text{height} \tag{6.1}$$

The triangle is sitting on its side, so the height of the triangle is $300\,(1000 - 700)$ and the base is $3 ($8 - $5).

$$\text{Deadweight loss} = 1/2 \times (300) \times ($3) = $450 \tag{6.2}$$

Finally, what is the tax revenue generated by the tax? The tax revenue is represented by the green-shaded area. You can calculate the tax revenue by determining the area of the rectangle.

$$\text{Total revenue} = \text{base} \times \text{height} \tag{6.3}$$

The height is the amount of the tax ($3) and the number of units sold after the tax is 700. This gives us $3 \times 700 = $2,100

ECONOMICS IN THE REAL WORLD

The Short-lived Luxury Tax

The Budget Reconciliation Act of 1990 established special luxury taxes on the sale of new aircraft, yachts, automobiles, furs, and jewelry. The act established a 10% surcharge on new purchases as follows: aircraft over $500,000; yachts over $100,000; automobiles over $25,000, and furs and jewelry over $10,000. The taxes were expected to generate approximately two billion dollars a year. However, revenue fell far below expectations and thousands of jobs were lost in each of the affected industries. Within three years the taxes were repealed. Why was the luxury tax such a failure?

The real-life luxury tax was easy to avoid.

When passing the Budget Reconciliation Act, lawmakers failed to consider basic demand elasticity. The purchase of a new aircraft, yacht, car, fur, or jewelry is highly discretionary. Many wealthy consumers decided that they would buy substitute products that fell below the tax threshold or buy a used product and refurbish it. Therefore the demand for these luxury goods turned out to be highly elastic. We have seen that when goods with elastic demand are taxed, tax revenues are small. Moreover, the resulting decrease in purchases was significant. As a result, jobs were lost in the middle of an economic downturn. The combination of low revenues and crippling job losses in these industries was enough to convince Congress to repeal the taxes in 1993.

The failed luxury tax is a reminder that the populist idea of taxing the rich is far more difficult to implement than it appears. In simple terms, it is nearly impossible to tax the toys that the rich enjoy because the wealthy can spend their money in so many different ways. In other words, the rich have options about whether to buy or lease, and many good substitutes to choose from. This means that they can, in many cases, avoid paying excise taxes. ✳

Balancing Deadweight Loss and Tax Revenues

Up to this point we have kept the size of the tax increase constant. This allowed us to examine the impact of the elasticity of demand and supply on deadweight loss and tax revenues. But what happens when the size of a tax is high enough to significantly alter consumer or producer behavior? For instance, in 2002 the Republic of Ireland instituted a tax of 15 euro cents on each plastic bag in order to curb litter and encourage recycling. As a result, consumer use of plastic bags quickly fell by over 90 percent. In this section we will look at how consumers respond to taxes of different sizes and determine the relationship between the size of the tax, the deadweight loss, and tax revenues.

Figure 6.13 shows the market response to a variety of tax increases. The five panels in the figure begin with a reference point, panel (a), where no tax

FIGURE 6.13

Examining Deadweight Loss and Tax Revenues

The panels show that increased taxes result in higher prices. Progressively higher taxes also lead to more deadweight loss, but higher taxes do not always generate more revenue, as evidenced by the reduction in revenue that occurs when tax rates become too large in panels (d) and (e).

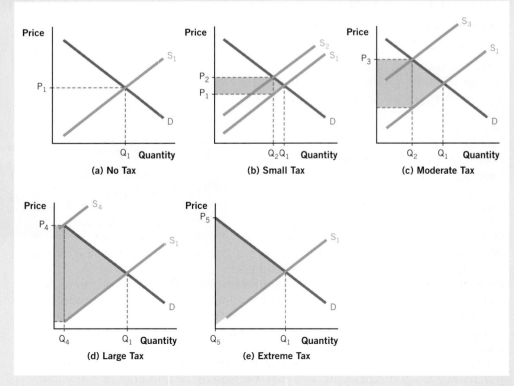

is levied, and progress toward panel (e), where the tax rate becomes so large that it curtails all economic activity.

As taxes rise, so do prices. You can trace this rise from (a), where there is no tax and the price is at P_1, all the way to (e), where the extreme tax causes price to rise above P_5. At the same time, deadweight loss also rises. You can see this by comparing the sizes of the yellow triangles. The trade-off is striking. Without any taxes, deadweight loss does not occur. But as soon as taxes are levied, the market-equilibrium quantity begins to decline, moving from Q_1 to Q_5. As the number of transactions declines, the area of deadweight loss rapidly expands.

When taxes are small, as in Figure 6.13b, the tax revenue (green rectangle) is large relative to the deadweight loss (yellow triangle). However, as we progress through the panels, this process slowly reverses. In (c) the size of the tax revenue remains larger than the deadweight loss. However, in (d) the magnitude of the deadweight loss is far greater than the tax revenue. This means that the size of the tax in (d) is creating a significant cost in terms of economic efficiency. Finally, (e) shows an extreme case where all market activity ceases as a result of the tax. Since nothing is produced and sold, there is no tax revenue.

PRACTICE WHAT YOU KNOW

Deadweight Loss of Taxation: The Politics of Tax Rates

You and two friends are discussing the politics of taxation. One friend, who is fiscally conservative, argues that tax rates are too high. The other friend, who is more progressive, argues that tax rates are too low.

What is the optimal tax rate?

Question: Is it possible that they could both be right?

Answer: Surprisingly, the answer is yes. When taxes rates become extraordinarily high, the amount of deadweight loss dwarfs the amount of tax revenue collected. We observed this in the discussion of the short-lived "luxury tax" above. Fiscal conservatives often note that taxes inhibit economic activity. They advocate lower tax rates and limited government involvement in the market, preferring to minimize the deadweight loss on economic activity (see panel b in Figure 6.13). However, progressives prefer somewhat higher tax rates than fiscal conservatives, since a moderate tax rate (see panel c) generates more tax revenue than a small tax. The additional tax revenues that moderate tax rates create can be used to fund more government services. Therefore, a clear trade-off exists between the size of the public sector and market activity. As much as economists would like to be able to point to an exact tax rate, economics is still a normative endeavor. Depending on how you view the value created by markets versus the value added through government provision, there is ample room for disagreement about the best tax policy.

Excise Taxes Are Almost Impossible to Avoid

The federal government collected $75 billion in excise taxes in 2011. Excise taxes are placed on many different products—making them almost impossible to avoid. They also have the added advantages of being easy to collect, hard for the consumer to detect, and easier to enact politically. You'll find excise taxes placed on many of your everyday household expenses—what you drink, the gasoline you purchase, plane tickets, and much more. Let's add them up.

1. **Gasoline.** 18.3 cents per gallon. This generates $37 billion and helps finance the interstate highway system.

2. **Cigarettes and tobacco.** $1 per pack and up to 40 cents per cigar. This generates $18 billion for the general federal budget.

3. **Air travel.** 7.5% of the base price of the ticket plus $3 per flight segment. This generates $10 billion for the Transportation Security Administration and the Federal Aviation Administration.

4. **Alcohol.** 5 cents per can of beer, 21 cents per bottle of wine, and $2.14 for spirits. This generates $9 billion for the general federal budget.

These four categories account for $74 billion in excise taxes. You could still avoid the taxman with this simple prescription: don't drink, don't travel, and don't smoke. Where does that leave you? Way out in the country somewhere far from civilization. Since you won't be able to travel to a grocery store, you'll need to live off the land, grow your own crops, and hunt or fish.

But there is still one last federal excise tax to go.

5. **Hunting and fishing.** Taxes range from 3 cents for fishing tackle boxes to 11% for archery equipment. This generates $1 billion for fish and wildlife services.

Living off the land and avoiding taxes just got much harder, and that's the whole point. The government taxes products with relatively inelastic demand because most people will still purchase them after the tax is levied. As a result, avoiding taxes isn't practical. The best you can do is reduce your tax burden by altering your lifestyle or what you purchase.[1]

[1]Data from Jill Barshay, "The $240-a-Year Bill You Don't Know You're Paying," *The Fiscal Times*, Sept. 7, 2011.

Excise taxes are everywhere.

Conclusion

Let's return to the misconception we started with: raising tax rates always generates more tax revenue. That's true up to a point. At low and moderate tax rates, increases in the tax rate lead to additional tax revenue. However, when tax rates become too high, tax revenues decline as more consumers and producers find ways to avoid paying the tax.

In the first part of this chapter we learned that society benefits from unregulated markets because they create the largest possible total surplus. However, society also needs the government to provide the infrastructure that the economy relies upon. The tension between economic activity and the amount of government services is reflected in tax rates. The taxation of specific goods and services gives rise to a form of market failure called deadweight loss, which results in the reduction of economic activity. The upshot is that any intervention in the market needs to carry with it a deep understanding of how agents will respond to the incentives created by the legislation. The law of unintended consequences can affect the most well-intentioned tax legislation and, if the process is not thought through, can result in inefficiencies with far-reaching consequences. Of course, this does not mean that taxes are undesirable. Rather, society must balance the need for tax revenues, and the programs those revenues help fund, with the trade-offs this creates in the market.

ANSWERING THE BIG QUESTIONS

1. What are consumer surplus and producer surplus?

* Consumer surplus is a measure of the benefit that a buyer gains from participating in a market. Producer surplus is a measure of the benefit that a seller earns from participating in a market.
* Total surplus is the sum of consumer and producer surplus that exists in a market.

2. When is a market efficient?

* Markets maximize consumer and producer surplus, provide goods and services to buyers who value them most, and reward sellers who can produce goods and services at the lowest cost. As a result, markets create the largest amount of total surplus possible.
* Whenever an allocation of resources maximizes total surplus, the result is said to be efficient. However, economists are also interested in the distribution of the surplus. Equity refers to the fairness of the distribution of the benefits among the members of a society.

3. Why do taxes create deadweight loss?

* Deadweight loss is created because taxes increase the purchase price, and this causes consumers to buy less. Deadweight loss is minimized when a tax is placed on a good or service that has inelastic demand or supply.
* Economists are also concerned about the incidence of taxation. Incidence refers to the party who effectively pays the tax through higher prices, regardless of whom the tax is actually levied on. The incidence is determined by the balance between the elasticity of supply and the elasticity of demand.

CONCEPTS YOU SHOULD KNOW

Consumer surplus (p. 173)
Deadweight loss (p. 184)
Efficient (p. 180)
Equity (p. 180)

Excise taxes (p. 182)
Incidence (p. 182)
Producer surplus (p. 175)
Social welfare (p. 177)

Total surplus (p. 177)
Welfare economics (p. 172)
Willingness to pay (p. 172)
Willingness to sell (p. 174)

QUESTIONS FOR REVIEW

1. Explain how consumer surplus is derived from the difference between the willingness to pay and the market-equilibrium price.

2. Explain how producer surplus is derived from the difference between the willingness to sell and the market-equilibrium price.

3. Why do economists focus on consumer and producer surplus and not on the possibility of consumer and producer loss? Illustrate your answer on a supply and demand graph.

4. How do economists define efficiency?

5. What type of goods should be taxed in order to minimize deadweight loss?

6. Suppose that the government taxes a good that is very elastic. Illustrate what will happen to the consumer surplus, producer surplus, tax revenue, and deadweight loss on a supply and demand graph.

7. What happens to tax revenues as tax rates increase?

STUDY PROBLEMS

1. A college student enjoys eating pizza. Her willingness to pay for each slice is shown in the following table:

Number of Pizza Slices	Willingness to Pay (per slice)
1	$6
2	$5
3	$4
4	$3
5	$2
6	$1
7	$0

a. If pizza slices cost $3, how many servings will she buy? How much consumer surplus does she enjoy?
b. If the price of pizzas falls to $2, how much consumer surplus does she enjoy?

2. A cash-starved town decides to impose a $6 excise tax on t-shirts sold. The following table shows the quantity demanded and the quantity supplied at various prices.

Price of T-shirts	Quantity Demanded	Quantity Supplied
$19	0	60
$16	10	50
$13	20	40
$10	30	30
$ 7	40	20
$ 4	50	10

a. What are the equilibrium quantity demanded and the quantity supplied before the tax is implemented? Determine the consumer and producer surplus before the tax.

b. What are the equilibrium quantity demanded and the quantity supplied after the tax is implemented? Determine the consumer and producer surplus after the tax.
c. How much tax revenue does the town generate from the tax?
d. Compute the deadweight loss created by the tax.

3. Andrew paid $30 to buy a potato cannon, a cylinder that shoots potatoes hundreds of feet. He was willing to pay $45. When Andrew's friend Nick learns that Andrew bought a potato cannon, he asks Andrew if he will sell it for $60 and Andrew agrees. Nick is thrilled, since he would have paid Andrew up to $80 for the cannon. Andrew is also delighted. Determine the total surplus from the original purchase and the additional surplus generated by the resale of the cannon.

4. If the government wishes to raise tax revenue, which of the following items are good candidates for an excise tax?

  a. granola bars
  b. cigarettes
  c. toilet paper
  d. automobile tires
  e. bird feeders

* **5.** If the government wishes to minimize the deadweight loss of taxation, which of the following items are good candidates for an excise tax?

  a. bottled water
  b. prescription drugs
  c. oranges
  d. batteries
  e. luxury cars

6. A new medical study indicates that blueberries help prevent cancer. If the demand for blueberries increases, what will happen to the size of the consumer and producer surplus? Illustrate your answer by shifting the demand curve appropriately and labeling the new and old areas of consumer and producer surplus.

7. Use the following graph to answer questions a–f.

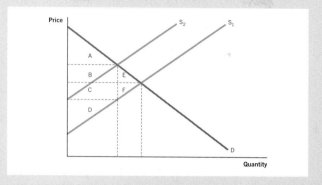

a. What area represents consumer surplus before the tax?
b. What area represents producer surplus before the tax?
c. What area represents consumer surplus after the tax?
d. What area represents producer surplus after the tax?
e. What area represents the tax revenue after the tax?
f. What area represents the deadweight loss after the tax?

8. The cost of many electronic devices has fallen appreciably since they were first introduced. For instance, computers, cell phones, microwaves, and calculators not only provide more functions but they do so at a lower cost. Illustrate the impact of lower production costs on the supply curve. What happens to the size of the consumer and producer surplus? If consumer demand for cell phones is relatively elastic, who is likely to benefit the most from the lower production costs?

9. Suppose that the demand for a concert, Q_D, is represented by the following equation, where P is the price of concert tickets and Q is the number of tickets sold:

$$Q_D = 2500 - 120P.$$

The supply of tickets, Q_S, is represented by the equation:

$$Q_S = 500 + 80P.$$

a. Find the equilibrium price and quantity of tickets sold. (**Hint**: Set $Q_D = Q_S$ and solve for the wage, P, and then plug the result back into either of the original equations to find Q_e.)

b. Carefully graph your result in part a.

c. Calculate the consumer and producer surplus at the equilibrium price and quantity. (**Hint**: Since the areas of consumer and producer surplus are triangles, you will need to use the formula for the area of a triangle [1/2 × (base) × (height)] to solve the problem.)

d. If the government imposes a $5 ticket tax to help fund the building of a new arena, calculate the new equilibrium price, equilibrium quantity, consumer surplus, producer surplus, tax revenue, and deadweight loss created by the tax increase. (**Hint**: The new demand curve is $Q_D = 2500 - 120[P + T]$. Simplifying yields $Q_D = 2500 - 120P - 120T$, and plugging in T = 5 further simplifies the new demand curve to $Q_D = 2500 - 120P - 600$, or $Q_D = 1900 - 120P$.)

10. In this chapter we have focused on the effect that taxes have on social welfare. However, governments also subsidize goods, or make those goods cheaper to buy or sell. How would a $2,000 subsidy on the purchase of new hybrid vehicle impact the consumer surplus and producer surplus in the hybrid market? Use a supply and demand diagram to illustrate your answer. Does the subsidy create dead-weight loss?

* 11. Suppose that a new $5.00 tax is placed on each cell phone. From the information in the following graph, compute the incidence, dead-weight loss, and tax revenue of the tax.

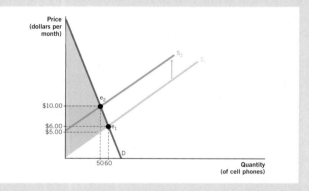

a. What is the incidence of the tax?

b. What is the deadweight loss of the tax?

c. What is the tax revenue generated by the tax?

SOLVED PROBLEMS

5.a. Consumers have many good substitutes available. They can drink tap water, filtered water, or other healthy beverages instead of bottled water. Bottled water is not a good candidate for an excise tax.

b. Taxing prescription drugs will generate significant revenues without reducing sales much, if at all. There is almost no deadweight loss because consumers have few, if any, alternatives. Prescription drugs are a good candidate for an excise tax.

c. Consumers can select many other fruits to replace oranges. The deadweight loss will be quite large. Oranges are not a good candidate for an excise tax.

d. Without batteries many devices won't work. The lack of substitutes makes demand quite inelastic, so the deadweight loss is small. Batteries are an excellent candidate for an excise tax.

e. Wealthy consumers can spend their income in many ways. They do not have to buy luxury vehicles. As a result, the tax will create a large amount of deadweight loss. Luxury cars are a poor candidate for an excise tax.

11.a. After the tax is implemented, the market price rises from $6 to $10, but since sellers must pay $5 to the government, they net only $5. Tax incidence measures the share of the tax paid by buyers and sellers, so we need to compare the proportion of the tax paid by each party. Since the market price rises by $4 (from $6 to $10), buyers are paying $4 of the $5 tax, or 4/5. Since the net price falls by $1 (from $6 to $5), sellers are paying $1 of the $5 tax, or 1/5.

b. The deadweight loss is represented by the decrease in the total surplus found in the yellow triangle. In order to compute the amount of the deadweight loss, we need to determine the area inside the triangle. The area of a triangle is found by taking 1/2 × (base) × (height). The triangle is sitting on its side, so the height of the triangle is 10 (60 − 50) and the base is $5 ($10 − $5). Hence the deadweight loss is 1/2 × (10) × ($5) = $25.

c. The tax revenue is represented by the green-shaded area. You can calculate the tax revenue by taking the amount of the tax ($5) and multiplying it by the number of units sold after the tax (50). This equals $250.

Market Inefficiencies: Externalities and Public Goods

The only acceptable amount of pollution is no pollution.

All or nothing—that's how many people view the issue of how much to protect the environment. Either eliminate all pollution, or leave

businesses alone and let them do what they will.

No one wants to go back to the way it was when businesses were free to dump their waste anywhere. But it is also impractical to eliminate all pollution. If we tried, we would make many businesses so unprofitable that they would simply disappear, and that would damage the economy. Examining the tension between the costs and benefits involved in eliminating pollution will help us explain the misconception that society should eliminate pollution at any cost.

In the preceding chapters, we have seen that markets provide many benefits and that they work because participants pursue their own self-interests. But sometimes markets need a helping hand. Some market exchanges harm innocent bystanders. And others are not efficient because the ownership of property is not clearly defined or actively enforced. To help us understand why markets do not always operate efficiently, this chapter will explore two important concepts: *externalities* and *public goods*.

Photo to come

BIG QUESTIONS

* ✳ **What are externalities and how do they affect markets?**
* ✳ **What are private goods and public goods?**
* ✳ **What are the challenges of providing public goods?**

What Are Externalities and How Do They Affect Markets?

Externalities
are the costs or benefits of a market activity that affect a third party.

We have seen that buyers and sellers benefit from trade. But what about the effects that trade might have on bystanders? **Externalities**, or the effect of economic activity on a third party, can often lead to undesirable consequences. For example, in 2010 an oil well accident in the Gulf of Mexico caused British Petroleum to spill millions of gallons of oil into the water. Even though both BP and its customers benefit from the production of oil, others along the Gulf coast had their lives severely disrupted.

For a market to work as efficiently as possible, two things must happen. First, each participant must be able to evaluate the **internal costs** of participation—the costs that only the individual pays. For example, when we choose to drive somewhere, we typically consider our personal costs—the time it will take to reach our destination, the amount we will pay for gasoline, and what we will pay for routine vehicle maintenance. For a market to work efficiently, the *external costs* must also be paid. **External costs** are costs imposed on people who are not participants in that market. In the case of driving, the congestion and pollution that our cars create are external costs. We define **social costs** as a combination of the internal costs and the external costs of an activity.

Internal costs
are the costs of an activity paid by an individual.

External costs
are the costs of a market activity paid by someone else.

Social costs
are the internal costs plus the external costs of an activity.

In this section we will consider some of the mechanisms that encourage consumers and producers to account for the social costs of their actions.

The Third-Party Problem

An externality exists whenever a private cost, or benefit, diverges from a social cost, or benefit. For example, manufacturers who make vehicles and consumers who purchase them benefit from the transaction, but making vehicles and using them leads to externalities, including air pollution and traffic congestion, that make others worse off. A **third-party problem** occurs when those not directly involved in a market activity experience negative or positive externalities.

The **third-party problem**
occurs when those not directly involved in a market activity nevertheless experience negative or positive externalities.

If a third party is made worse off, the externality is negative. This is what happens when the volume of vehicles on the road causes air pollution. Negative externalities present a challenge to society because it is difficult to make consumers and producers take responsibility for the full costs of their actions. Drivers typically consider only the internal costs of reaching their destination.

Likewise, firms would generally prefer to ignore pollution they create, because addressing the problem would raise their costs. In general, society would benefit if consumers and producers considered both the internal and external costs of their actions. Since this is not a reasonable expectation, we design policies that create incentives for people to limit the amount of pollution they emit.

Washington, D.C., like many communities throughout the United States, has instituted a five-cent tax on every plastic bag a consumer picks up at a store. While five cents may not sound like much of a disincentive, shoppers responded by switching to cloth bags or reusing plastic ones they already had. The use of plastic bags fell from 22.5 million bags per

Taxing plastic bags helps to conserve landfill space.

month in 2009 to just 3 million bags per month in 2010, significantly reducing the amount of plastic waste entering landfills in the process.

Not all externalities are negative. Positive externalities also exist. For instance, education creates a large positive externality for society beyond the benefits to individual students, teachers, and other support staff directly

Incentives Matter

involved. A more knowledgeable workforce benefits employers looking for qualified employees and is more efficient and productive. Because local businesses experience a positive externality from a well-educated local community, they have a stake in the educational process. A good example of the synergy between local business and higher education is the Silicon Valley in California, which is home to many high-tech companies and Stanford University. As early as the late 19th century, Stanford's leaders believed that the university's mission should include fostering the development of self-sufficient local industry. After World War II, Stanford encouraged faculty and graduates to start their own companies. This led to the creation of Hewlett-Packard, Varian Associates, Bell Labs, and Xerox. A generation later, this nexus of high-tech firms also gave birth to leading software and Internet firms like 3Com, Adobe, and Facebook, and—more indirectly—Cisco, Apple, and Google.

Recognizing the benefits that they received, many of the most successful businesses associated with Stanford have donated large sums of money. For instance, the Hewlett Foundation gave $400 million to Stanford's endowment for the humanities and sciences and for undergraduate education—an act of generosity that speaks to the positive externality that Stanford University had on Hewlett-Packard.

Many of the most successful businesses associated with Stanford have made large donations to the university.

When oil refineries are permitted to pollute the environment, they are likely to overproduce.

Correcting for Negative Externalities

In this section, we explore ways to correct for negative externalities. To do this, we use supply and demand analysis to look at how they affect the market. Let's begin with supply and compare the difference between what market forces produce and what is best for society in the case of an oil refinery. A refinery converts crude oil into gasoline. This complex process creates many negative externalities, including releasing pollutants into the air and dumping waste by-products.

Figure 7.1 illustrates the contrast between the market equilibrium and the social optimum in the case of an oil refinery. These costs are indicated on the graph by the supply curve $S_{internal}$, which represents how much the oil refiner will produce if it does not have to pay for the negative consequences of its activity. In this situation, the market equilibrium, e_m, accounts only for the internal costs of production.

When a negative externality exists, the government may be able to restore the social optimum by requiring externality-causing market participants to pay for the cost of their actions. In this case, there are three potential solutions. First, the refiner can be required to install pollution abatement equipment or to change production techniques to reduce emissions and waste products. Second, a tax can be levied as a disincentive to produce. Finally, the government can require that the firm pay for any environmental damage it

FIGURE 7.1

Negative Externalities and Social Optimum

When a firm is required to internalize the external costs of production, the supply curve shifts left and output falls to the socially optimal level, Q_s. The deadweight loss that comes from over-production is eliminated.

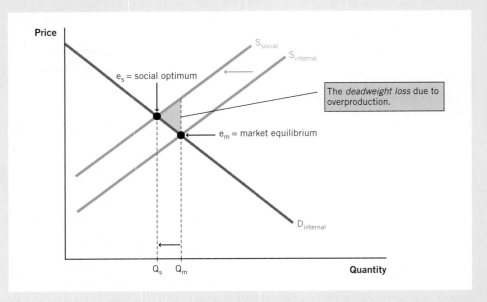

TABLE 7.1

Private and Social Decision Making

Personal Decision	Social Optimum	The Problem	The Solution
Based on internal costs	Social costs = internal costs plus external costs	To get consumers and producers to take responsibility for the externalities they create	Encourage consumers and producers to internalize externalities

creates. Each of these solutions forces the firm to **internalize** the externality, meaning that the firm pays for the externality in some way.

Having to pay the costs of imposing pollution on others reduces the amount of the pollution-causing activity. This result is seen in the shift of the supply curve to S_{social}. The new supply curve reflects a combination of the internal and external costs of producing the good. Since each of the corrective measures requires the refiner to spend money to correct the externality, the willingness to sell the good declines, or shifts left. The result is a social optimum at a lower quantity, Q_S, than at the market equilibrium, Q_m. The trade-off is clear. We can reduce negative externalities by requiring producers to internalize the externality. However, internalizing the externality is not without cost. Since the supply curve shifts left, the quantity produced will be lower. In the real world, there is always a cost.

In addition, when there is an externality, the market equilibrium creates deadweight loss, as shown by the yellow triangle in Figure 7.1. In Chapter 6, we looked at deadweight loss in the context of governmental regulation or taxation. These measures, when imposed on efficient markets, created deadweight loss, or a less than desirable amount of economic activity. In the case of a negative externality, before intervention the market is not efficient because it is not fully capturing the cost of production. Once the firm is required to internalize the external costs of production, output falls to the socially optimal level, Q_S, and the deadweight loss that comes from overproduction is eliminated.

Table 7.1 outlines the basic decision-making process that guides private and social decisions. Private decision-makers consider only their internal costs, but society as a whole experiences both internal and external costs. To align the incentives of private decision-makers with the interests of society, we must find mechanisms that encourage the internalization of externalities.

> An externality is **internalized** when the internal costs (or benefits) take into account the external costs (or benefits) to society.

ECONOMICS IN THE REAL WORLD

Congestion Charges

In 2003 London instituted a congestion charge. Motorists entering the charge zone pay a flat rate of £10 (approximately $16) between 7 a.m. and 6 p.m. Monday through Friday. A computerized scanner automatically bills the driver, so there is no wait at a toll booth. When the charge was first enacted it had an immediate effect. The number of vehicles entering the zone fell by a third, riders on public transportation increased 15%, and bicycle use rose by 30%.

Motorists must pay a flat congestion charge to enter the central business area of London on weekdays.

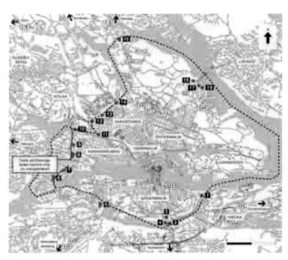

Motorists in Stockholm are charged different amounts depending on when they drive in.

In 2007, Stockholm established a congestion-charge system with a new wrinkle, dynamic pricing. The pricing changes between 6:30 a.m. and 6:30 p.m. During the peak morning and evening commutes, motorists are charged 20 Swedish Krona (approximately $3). At other times the price ratchets down to 15, or even 10 Krona. This pricing scheme encourages motorists to enter the city at nonpeak times.

Because congestion charges become part of a motorist's internal costs, they cause motorists to weigh the costs and benefits of driving into congested areas. In other words, congestion charges internalize externalities. In the case of London, a flat £10 fee encourages motorists to avoid the zone, or find alternative transportation methods. But once you have paid the £10 charge you do not have an incentive to avoid peak flow times. The variable pricing in Stockholm causes motorists to make marginal adjustments in the time they drive. This spreads out the traffic flow.

A major goal of congestion pricing is to avoid traffic-related delays in densely populated areas. The use of a price, or charge, to do this helps to restore the socially optimal level of road usage. ✳

Enhancing Positive Externalities

Positive externalities, such as vaccines, have benefits for third parties. As with negative externalities, we use supply and demand analysis to compare the efficiency of the market with the social optimum. This time we will focus on the demand curve. Consider a person who gets a flu shot. When the vaccine is administered, the recipient is immunized. This creates an internal benefit. But there is also an external benefit: fewer people will catch the flu and

A vaccine offers both individual and social benefits.

become contagious, which helps protect even those who do not get flu shots. Therefore, we can say that vaccines convey a positive externality to the rest of society.

Why do positive externalities exist in the market? Using our example of flu shots, we can see that there is an incentive for people in high-risk groups to get vaccinated for the sake of their own health. In Figure 7.2, we capture this internal benefit in the demand curve labeled $D_{internal}$. However, the market equilibrium, e_m, only accounts for the internal benefits of individuals getting vaccinated. In order to maximize the health benefits for everyone, public health officials need to find a way to encourage as many people as possible to get vaccinated. One way is through school vaccination laws. These laws require that all children entering school provide proof of vaccination against a variety of diseases. The overall effect of child vaccination laws is that more people get vaccinated early in life, which reduces the spread of contagious diseases. This creates a positive externality for society.

Government can also promote the social optimum by encouraging economic activity that helps third parties. For example, it can offer a subsidy, or price break, to encourage more people to get vaccinated. The subsidy acts as a consumption incentive. In fact, governments routinely provide free, or reduced-cost, vaccines to those most at risk from flu and to their caregivers. Since the subsidy allows the consumer to spend less money, the willingness to get the vaccine increases. More people are immunized, a result seen in a shift of the demand curve in Figure 7.2 from $D_{internal}$ to D_{social}. The social demand curve reflects the sum of the internal and social benefits of getting the vaccination. The subsidy encourages consumers to internalize the externality

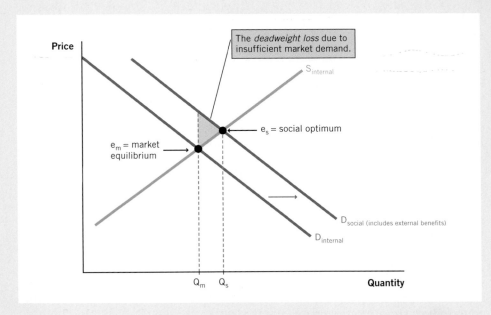

FIGURE 7.2

Positive Externalities and Social Optimum

The subsidy encourages consumers to internalize the externality. As a result, consumption moves from the market equilibrium, Q_m, to a social optimum at a higher quantity, Q_s, and the deadweight loss that comes from insufficient market demand is eliminated.

TABLE 7.2		
A Summary of Externalities		
	Negative	**Positive**
Definition	Costs borne by third parties	Benefits received by third parties
Examples	Oil refining creates air pollution.	Flu shots prevent the spread of disease.
	Traffic congestion causes all motorists to spend more time on the road waiting.	Education creates a more productive workforce and allows citizens to make more informed decisions for the betterment of society.
	Airports create noise pollution.	Restored historic buildings enable people to enjoy the beautiful architectural details.
Corrective measures	Taxes, charges, or regulations	Subsidies or government provision

and, as a result, output moves from the market equilibrium, Q_m to a social optimum at a higher quantity, Q_S.

We have seen that markets do not handle externalities well. With a negative externality, the market produces too much of a good. But in the case of a positive externality, the market does not encourage enough demand. In both cases the market equilibrium creates deadweight loss. When positive externalities are present, the private market is not efficient because it is not fully capturing the social benefits. In other words, the market equilibrium does not maximize the gains for society as a whole. When positive externalities are internalized, the demand curve shifts out and output rises to the socially optimal level, Q_S. The deadweight loss that comes from insufficient market demand, and therefore underproduction, is eliminated.

Table 7.2 provides a summary of the key takeaways about positive and negative externalities and additional examples of each type.

Before moving on, it is worth noting that not all externalities warrant corrective measures. There are times when the size of the externality is negligible and does not justify the cost of increased regulations, charges, taxes, or subsidies that might achieve the social optimum. Since corrective measures also have costs, the presence of externalities does not by itself imply that the government should intervene in the market.

PRACTICE WHAT YOU KNOW

Externalities: A New Theater Is Developed

A developer wants to build a new movie theater in your community. It submits a development proposal to the city council.

Question: What negative externalities might the theater create?

How would a new theater affect your community?

Answer: A successful new theater will create traffic congestion. As a result, planning commissions often insist that developers widen nearby streets, install traffic lights, and create new turning lanes to help traffic flows.

Question: What positive externalities might the theater create?

Answer: Many local businesses indirectly benefit from increased activity in the area of a movie theater. Nearby convenience stores, gas stations, restaurants, and shopping areas all get a boost from the people who attend the movies. Since the demand for these local services rises, businesses in the area will earn more profits and employ more workers.

What Are Private Goods and Public Goods?

The presence of externalities reflects a divide between how markets operate and the social optimum. Why does this happen? The answer is often related to *property rights*. **Property rights** give an owner the ability to exercise control over a resource. When property rights are not clearly defined, resources can be mistreated. For instance, since no one owns the air, firms often feel free to emit pollutants into it.

To understand why firms sometimes overlook the effects of their actions on others, we first need to look more closely at the role of property rights in market efficiency. When property rights are poorly established, or not enforced effectively, it creates the wrong incentives. The difference is apparent when we compare situations where people do have property rights. Private owners have an incentive to keep their property in good repair because they bear the costs of fixing what they own when it breaks. For instance, if you own a personal computer, you will probably protect your investment by treating it with care and dealing with any problems immediately. However, if you access a public computer terminal in a campus lab or library and find that it is not working properly, you will most likely ignore the problem and look for another computer that is working. The difference between solving the problem and ignoring it is crucial to understanding why property rights matter.

Property rights give the owner the ability to exercise control over a resource.

Private Property

Private property
provides an exclusive right
of ownership that allows for
the use and especially the
exchange of property.

One way to minimize externalities is to establish well-defined private property rights. **Private property** provides an exclusive right of ownership that allows for the use, and especially the exchange, of property. This creates incentives to maintain, protect, conserve property, and to listen to the wishes of others. Let's consider each of these four incentives in the context of automobile ownership.

1. *The incentive to maintain.* Car owners have an incentive to maintain the vehicles that they own. This includes routine maintenance, replacement of worn parts, and repairs. These efforts keep the vehicle safe and reliable. In addition, a well-maintained car can be sold for more than one in poor condition.
2. *The incentive to protect.* Owners have an incentive to protect their vehicles from theft or damage. They do this by using alarm systems, locking the doors, and parking in well-lit areas.
3. *The incentive to conserve.* Car owners also have an incentive to extend the usable life of the automobile by limiting how many miles they put on the car each year.
4. *The incentive to trade with others.* Car owners have an incentive to trade with others because they may profit. Suppose someone offers to buy your car for $5,000 and you think it is worth only $3,000. Because you own the car, you can do what you wish with it. If you decline to sell, you will incur an opportunity cost; you will be giving up $5,000 to keep something you value at $3,000. There is no law requiring you to sell your vehicle, so you *could* keep the car—but you probably won't. Why? Because private property gives each owner an incentive to trade for something better in the market.

The incentives to maintain, protect, and conserve help to ensure that private property is kept in good shape. The fourth incentive, to trade with others, helps to ensure that private property is always held by the person with the greatest willingness to pay for it.

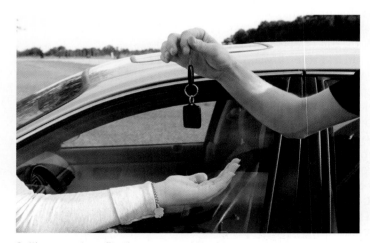
Selling a car benefits the owner and the buyer.

The Coase Theorem

Economist Robert Coase argued that establishing private property rights can also close the gap between internal costs and social costs.

Consider an example involving two adjacent landowners, one who raises cattle and another who grows wheat. Because neither landowner has built a fence, the cattle wander into the neighboring land to eat the wheat. Coase concluded that both parties are equally responsible for solving the problem. He arrived at that conclusion by considering two possible solutions.

The first case supposes that the wheat farmer has the legal right to expect cattle-

The cattle are near the wheat to the same extent . . .

. . . that the wheat is near the cattle.

free fields. In this scenario the cattle rancher is liable for the damage caused to the wheat farmer. If the cattle damage is costly, and the rancher is liable, the rancher will build a fence to keep the cattle in rather than pay for the damage they cause. The fence internalizes the negative externality and forces the rancher to bear the full cost of damage created. If the cost of the damage to the crop is much smaller than the cost of building a fence, the rancher is more likely to compensate the farmer for his losses than build the fence.

What if the wheat farmer does not have the legal right to expect cattle-free fields? In this scenario, the cattle rancher is not liable for any damages his cattle cause to the wheat farmer. If the damage created by cattle wandering into the nearby wheat field is large, and the rancher is not liable, the wheat farmer will build a fence to keep the cattle out. The fence internalizes the negative externality and forces the wheat farmer to bear the full cost of the damage created. If the amount of damage the cattle cause is smaller than the cost of a fence, the farmer may accept occasional damage as the lower cost option.

The **Coase theorem** states that if there are no barriers to negotiations, interested parties will bargain to correct any externalities that exist.

From comparing these two situations, Coase determined that whenever the size of the externality is large enough to justify the expense, the externality gets internalized. As long as the property rights are fully specified, either the cattle rancher or the wheat farmer will build a fence. The fence keeps the cattle away from the wheat, removes the externality, and avoids the destruction of property.

With this in mind, we can now appreciate the **Coase theorem**, which states that if there are no barriers to negotiations, and property rights are fully specified, interested parties will bargain privately to correct any externalities that exist. As a result, the assignment of property rights, under the law, gives each party an incentive to internalize any externalities.

A fence internalizes the externality.

If it is difficult to bargain, because the costs of reaching an agreement are too high, private parties will be unable to internalize the externality among themselves. Therefore, the Coase theorem also suggests that there are times when private solutions to externality problems are not possible. This implies a role for government in solving complex externality issues.

To think about the case for a government role, consider the difference between the example of a rancher and a farmer with adjacent land and a community-wide problem such as pollution. With two landowners, a private solution should be possible because the parties can bargain with each other at a low cost. Pollution is a different story because so many individuals are impacted and the polluting company cannot afford to bargain with each of them. Since bargaining costs are high in the case of pollution, an intermediary, like the government, may be necessary to ensure that externalities are internalized.

Private and Public Goods

When we think of private goods, most of us immediately imagine something that we enjoy, like a slice of pizza or a favorite jacket. When we think of public goods, we think of goods provided by the government like roads, the post office, and the military. The terms "private" and "public" are typically used to imply ownership or production, but that is not how economists categorize private and public goods. To understand the difference between private and public goods, you need to know whether or not a good is *excludable*, *rival*, or both. A good is considered **excludable** if the consumer is required to purchase the good before being able to use it. A good is considered **rival** when it cannot be enjoyed by more than one person at the same time.

Excludable goods
require that the consumer purchase the good before being able to use it.

Rival goods
cannot be enjoyed by more than one person at a time.

Private goods
have two characteristics: they are excludable and rival in consumption.

Public goods
can be jointly consumed by more than one person, and nonpayers are difficult to exclude.

Private Goods

A **private good** is both excludable and rival in consumption. For instance, a slice of pizza is excludable because it must be purchased before you can eat it. Also, a slice of pizza is rival; only one person can eat it. These two characteristics, excludability and rivalry, allow the market to work efficiently in the absence of externalities. Consider a pizza business. The pizzeria bakes pizza pies because it knows it can sell them to consumers. Likewise, consumers are willing to buy pizza because it is a food they enjoy. Since the producer is able to charge a price and the consumer to acquire a rival good, this sets the stage for mutual gains from trade.

Public Goods

Markets have no difficulty producing purely private goods, like pizza, since in order to enjoy private goods you must first purchase them. But when was the last time you paid to see a fireworks display? Many of the nation's best displays of fireworks are viewed by hundreds of thousands of people, and only a small percentage of those people pay an admission price to get a preferred seat. Fireworks displays are a **public good** because they can be jointly consumed by more than one person and, at the same time, it is difficult to exclude

Pizza is a private good.

nonpayers. Since consumers cannot be easily forced to pay, they may desire more of the good than is typically supplied. This leads a market economy to underproduce many public goods.

Public goods are often underproduced because people can get them without paying for them. Consider Joshua Bell, one of the most famous violinists in the world. The day after giving a concert in Boston where patrons paid $100 a ticket, he decided to reprise the performance in a Washington, D.C., subway station and just ask for donations. Any person who passed by could listen to the music—it did not need to be purchased to be enjoyed. In other words, it was nonexcludable and nonrival in consumption. But because it is impossible for a street musician to force bystanders to pay, it is difficult for the musician—even one as good as Joshua Bell—to make a living. Suppose that the musician draws a large crowd and the music creates $500 worth of enjoyment among the audience. At the end of the performance, he receives a loud round of applause and then motions to the donation basket. A number of people come up and donate, but when he counts up the contributions he finds $30—the actual amount Joshua earned while playing in the Metro.

World-renowned violinist Joshua Bell performs incognito in the Washington, D.C., Metro.

Why did Joshua Bell receive $30, when he created many times that amount in value? This phenomenon, known as a **free-rider problem**, exists whenever people receive a benefit they do not need to pay for. A street musician provides a public good and must rely on the generosity of the audience to contribute. If very few people voluntarily contribute, many potential musicians will not find it worthwhile to perform. We tend to see far too few street performances because free-riding lowers the returns. This means that the private equilibrium amount of street performances is undersupplied compared to the social optimum. When payment cannot be linked to use, the efficient quantity is not produced.

A **free-rider problem** exists whenever someone receives a benefit without having to pay for it.

Street performances are just one example of a public good. National defense, lighthouses, street lights, clean air, and open-source software such as Mozilla Firefox are other examples. Let's consider national defense in depth since it is a particularly clear example of a public good subject to a free-rider problem. All citizens value security, but consider the difficulty of trying to organize and provide adequate national defense through private contributions alone. How could you voluntarily coordinate a missile defense system, or get enough people to pay for an aircraft carrier and the personnel to operate it? Society would be underprotected because many people would not voluntarily contribute their fair share of the expense. For this reason, defense expenditures are normally provided by the government and funded by tax revenues. Since most people pay taxes, this almost eliminates the free-rider problem. Most people would agree that government should provide certain public goods for society including, among others, national defense, early-warning sirens for natural disasters, and medical and science-related

Concerned about security? Only the government is capable of providing enough defense.

Photo to come

research to fight pandemics. In each of these cases, public-sector provision helps to eliminate the free-rider problem and restore the socially optimal level of activity.

Club Goods and Common-Resource Goods

There are two additional goods that we have not yet introduced. Since *club* and *common-resource goods* have characteristics of both private and public goods, the line between private provision and public provision is often blurred.

Club goods are nonrival in consumption and excludable. Satellite television is an example of a club good; it is excludable because you must pay in order to receive the signal, yet because more than one customer can receive the signal at the same time, it is nonrival in consumption. Since customers who wish to enjoy club goods can be excluded, markets typically provide these goods. However, once a satellite television network is built, the cost of adding customers is quite low. Firms are motivated to maximize profits, not the number of people they serve, so the market price is higher and the output is lower than what society desires.

Common-resource goods are rival in consumption but nonexcludable. King crab in the Bering Sea off Alaska is an example of a common-resource good. Since any particular crab can be caught by only one boat, the crabs are a rival resource. At the same time, exclusion is not possible because any boat that wishes to brave the elements can catch crab.

We have seen that the market generally works well for private goods. In the case of public goods, however, the market generally needs a hand. In between, club and common-resource goods illustrate the tension between the private and public provision of many goods and services. Table 7.3 highlights each of the four types of goods we have studied.

Club goods
have two characteristics: they are nonrival in consumption and excludable.

Common-resource goods
have two characteristics: they are rival in consumption and nonexcludable.

Satellite television is a club good.

Alaskan king crab is a common-resource good.

TABLE 7.3

The Four Types of Goods

		Consumption		
		Rival		**Nonrival**
Excludable	**Yes**	*Private Goods* pizza, watches, automobiles		*Club Goods* satellite television, education, country clubs
	No	*Common-Resource Goods* Alaskan king crab, sharing a large popcorn at the movies, congested roads, charitable giving		*Public Goods* street performers, defense, tsunami warning systems

PRACTICE WHAT YOU KNOW

Public Goods: Are Parks Public Goods?

Many goods have the characteristics of a public good, but few goods meet the exact definition.

Question: Are parks public goods?

Answer: We tend to think of public parks as meeting the necessary requirements to be a public good. But not so fast. Have you been to

Natural Bridge in Virginia

any of America's top national parks on a peak summer weekend? Parks are subject to congestion, which makes them rival. In addition, most national and state parks require a small admission fee—translation: they are excludable. Therefore, public parks do not meet the exact definition of a public good. Not surprisingly, there are many good examples of private parks that maintain, protect, and conserve the environment alongside their public counterparts. For instance, Natural Bridge (pictured above) is a privately owned and operated park in Virginia that preserves a rare natural arch over a small stream. The East Coast is dotted with private parks that predate the establishment of the national park system.

What Are the Challenges of Providing Public Goods?

Understanding the four types of goods provides a solid foundation for understanding the role of markets and the government in society. In this section we consider some of the special challenges that exist in providing public goods.

Cost-Benefit Analysis

It is relatively easy to measure the cost of supplying a public good. For instance, if a community puts on a Fourth of July celebration, it will have to pay for the fireworks and labor involved in setting up the event. To help make decisions about providing public goods, economists turn to **cost-benefit analysis**, a process used to determine whether the benefits of providing a public good outweigh the costs.

Cost-benefit analysis is a process used to determine whether the benefits of providing a public good outweigh the costs.

Costs are a known quantity. But benefits are difficult to quantify. Since people do not need to pay to see the fireworks, it is hard to determine how much benefit the community receives. If asked, people might misrepresent the social benefit created by the fireworks in two ways. First, some residents who place a high value on the celebration might claim that the fireworks bring more benefit than they actually do, because they want the community to use fireworks in future celebrations. Second, those residents who dislike the crowds and noise might understate the benefit they receive. Since there is no way to know how truthful respondents are to a questionnaire, the actual social benefit of a fireworks show is hard to measure. As a result, there is no way to know the exact amount of consumer and producer surplus created by a public good like fireworks.

Since people do not pay to enjoy public goods, and the government provides them without charging a direct fee, determining the socially optimal amount is typically done through the political system. Generally speaking, elected officials will not get reelected if the populace believes that they have not done a good job with their cost-benefit analyses. However, adept politicians are especially good at securing funding for highly visible projects that benefit their constituents. Unfortunately, this means that many government activities are often designed to manipulate the public. The public is largely unaware of the expenses that are incurred to provide services intended to secure future votes. Therefore the political cost-benefit analysis can be quite different from the ideal set of policies designed to maximize social welfare.

Figuring out the social benefit of a fireworks display is quite difficult.

ECONOMICS IN THE REAL WORLD

Internet Piracy

The digitization of media, and the speed with which it can be transferred across the Internet, has made the protection of property rights very difficult. Many countries do not have strict copyright standards, or fail to enforce them. The result is a black market filled with bootlegged copies of movies, music, and other media.

Since digital "file sharing" is so common, you might not fully understand the harm that is done. Piracy is an illegal form of free-riding. Every song and every movie that is transferred takes away royalties that would have gone to the original artist or the studio. Producing content is expensive, and violations of copyright law cost legitimate businesses the opportunity to make a fair return on their investments. Consumers of content don't often see it this way. Some believe that breaking the copyright encryption is fair game since they "own" the media, or bought it legally, or got it from a friend. The reality is different. One reason copyright law exists is to limit free-riding. When copyrights are fully specified and enforced across international boundaries, content creators are compensated for their efforts. If copyrights are routinely violated, revenues to private businesses will be smaller and the amount of music and movies produced will fall. Free-riders get to listen or watch for nothing and the artists and film studios also get nothing. In the long run, artists will produce less and society will suffer. We will discuss other benefits of copyright law in Chapter 10.

Think about the relationship between artists and the public as reciprocal: each side needs the other. In that sense, the music you buy or the movie you watch is not a true public good, but more of a club good. Copyright laws make the good excludable but nonrival. This means that some people will always have an incentive to violate copyright law, that artists and studios will insist on ever more complicated encryption methods to protect their interests, and that, for the betterment of society as a whole, the government must enforce copyright law to prevent widespread free-riding. ✳

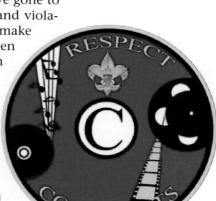

This Boy Scout merit badge signifies a commitment to honoring copyright.

Common Resources and the Tragedy of the Commons

Common resources often give rise to the **tragedy of the commons,** a situation that occurs when a good that is rival in consumption but nonexcludable becomes depleted. The name "tragedy of the commons" refers to a phenomenon Garrett Hardin wrote about in the magazine *Science* in 1968. In the article Hardin described the hypothetical use of a common pasture shared by local herders in pastoral communities. Herders know that intensively grazed land will be depleted and that this is likely to happen to common land. Knowing that the pasture will be depleted creates a strong incentive for individual herders to bring their animals to the pasture as much as possible while the pasture is still green, since every other herder will do the same thing. Each individual herder has the same incentive to overgraze, which quickly makes the pasture unusable. The overgrazing that occurs is a negative externality

Tragedy of the commons occurs when a good that is rival in consumption but nonexcludable becomes depleted.

brought about by poorly designed incentives and the absence of clear private property rights.

Even though the concept of common ownership sounds ideal, it can be a recipe for resource depletion and economic disaster. Why does this occur when property rights are held in common? When common property is damaged, individuals do not have legal recourse. This provides a stark contrast to a system of private property rights where the owner can seek damages in the court system if his property is damaged or destroyed. The same cannot be said for common property, since joint ownership allows any party to use the resource as it sees fit. This creates incentives to use the resource now rather than later and to neglect it. In short, common property leads to abuse and depletion of the resource.

The tragedy of the commons also gives rise to negative externalities. Consider global warming as an example. Evidence points to the connection between the amount of CO_2 being emitted into the atmosphere and the Earth's recent warming. This is a negative externality caused by some but borne jointly by everyone. Since large CO_2 emitters consider only the internal costs of their actions and ignore the social costs, the amount of CO_2 released, and the corresponding increase in global warming, is larger than optimal. The air, a common resource, is being "overused" and degraded.

Incentives Matter

Private property rights give owners an incentive to maintain, protect, conserve, and transfer the property if someone else values it more than the current owner. How are those incentives different under a system of common ownership? Let's examine a real-world example of the tragedy of the commons: the collapse of cod populations off Newfoundland, Canada, in the 1990s. Over the course of three years, cod hauls fell from over 200,000 tons annually to close to zero. Why did the fishing community allow this to happen? Incentives. Let's consider the three incentives associated with common property in the context of the cod industry.

1. *The incentive to neglect.* No one owns the ocean. As a result, specific fishing grounds in international waters cannot be protected. Even fishing grounds within territorial waters are problematic since fish do not adhere to political borders. The fishing grounds in the North Atlantic cannot be maintained the same way you can check the oil in an automobile. The grounds are too large and the population of cod depends on variations in seawater temperature, salinity, and the availability of algae and other smaller fish to eat. The idea that individuals or communities could "maintain" a population of cod in this wild environment is inconceivable.

2. *The incentive to overuse.* Each individual fishing boat would like to maintain a sustainable population of cod so that future harvests are possible. However, conservation on the part of one boat is irrelevant since other boats would catch what it leaves. Since cod are a rival and finite resource, boats have an incentive to harvest as much as they can before another vessel does. With common resources, no one has the direct ability to define how much of a resource can be used. Maintaining economic activity at a socially optimal level would require the coordination of thousands of vested interests, each of whom can gain by free-riding. For instance, if a socially responsible boat (or country) limits its catch in order to protect the species from becoming depleted, this action does

not guarantee that rivals will follow suit. Instead, rivals who disregard the socially optimal behavior stand to benefit by over-fishing what remains.

Since cod are a common resource, the incentives we discussed under a system of private ownership do not apply. With common property, resources are neglected and overused. In other words, if you wanted to design a system that was likely to destroy valuable resources instead of create them, this is it.

Common resources, such as cod, encourage overfishing.

Solutions to the Tragedy of the Commons

Preventing the tragedy of the commons requires planning and coordination. Unfortunately, officials were slow to recognize that there was a problem with Atlantic cod until it was too late to prevent the collapse. Ironically, just as they placed a moratorium on catching northern cod, the collapse of the fish population became an unprecedented disaster for virtually all of Atlantic Canada's fisheries. Cod populations dropped to 1/100th of their former sizes. The collapse of the Atlantic cod and many other species led to the loss of 40,000 jobs and over $300 million annually. The communities in the region relied almost exclusively on fishing and their economies were crippled.

The lesson of the northern cod is a powerful reminder that efforts to avoid the tragedy of the commons must begin before there is a problem. King crab populations off the coast of Alaska have fared much better thanks to proactive management. To prevent the collapse of the king crab population, the state and federal governments enforce several regulations. First, the length of the fishing season is limited. This gives populations time to recover. Second, there are regulations that limit how much fishing boats can catch. Third, to promote sustainable populations, only adult males are harvested. It is illegal to harvest females and young crabs, since these are necessary for repopulation. It is important to note that without government enforcement of these regulations, the tragedy of the commons would result.

Can the misuse of a common resource be foreseen and prevented? If predictions of rapid global warming are correct, our analysis points to a number of solutions to minimize the tragedy of commons. Businesses and individuals can be discouraged from producing emissions through carbon taxes. This policy encourages parties to "internalize the negative externality," since the tax acts as an internal cost that must be considered before creating carbon pollution.

Another solution, known as *cap and trade*, is an approach to emissions reduction that has received much attention lately. The theory

Photo to come

What is the best way to curb global warming?

Cap and trade
is an approach used to curb pollution by creating a system of pollution permits that are traded in an open market.

behind **cap and trade** policy is to create the conditions for carbon producers to internalize the externality by creating markets for tradable emission permits. Under cap and trade, the government sets a *cap*, or limit on the amount of CO_2 that can be emitted. Businesses and individuals are then issued permits to emit a certain amount of carbon each year. Permit owners are allowed to *trade* permits. In other words, companies that produce fewer carbon emissions can sell the permits they do not use. By establishing property rights that control emissions permits, cap and trade causes firms to internalize externalities and to seek out methods that lower emissions. Global warming is an incredibly complex process, but this is one tangible step that minimizes free-riding, creates the incentives for action, and encourages a socially efficient outcome.

Cap and trade is a good idea in theory. However, there are negative consequences to consider as well. Cap and trade presumes that nations can agree on and enforce emissions limits. Such agreements have proven to be difficult to negotiate. Without an international consensus, nations that adopt cap and trade policies will experience higher production costs, while nations that ignore them—and free-ride in the process—stand to benefit. Since cap and trade is ultimately designed to encourage firms to switch to greener sources of energy, the reality is that cap and trade can also be thought of as "cap and tax," since the buying and selling of carbon permits acts as a "tax" on business. An indicator of what cap and trade is likely to cost U.S. consumers can be found by considering what other countries are already experiencing. Britain's Taxpayer Alliance estimates the average family there is paying nearly $1,300 a year in green taxes for carbon-cutting programs. With any policy, there are always costs and benefits to consider.

Tragedy of the Commons

ECONOMICS IN THE MEDIA

Swimming Pools and Water Parks

If you have ever been to a water park or community pool, you know that the staff checks the pH of the water regularly to make sure it is clean. However, in *South Park* (2009) everybody's peeing in Pi Pi's water park, and the resulting pee mix concentration ends up so high that the water turns to pee and causes a flood of biblical proportions that eventually destroys the place.

Why did this happen? Because each person looks at all the water and thinks that it doesn't matter if *they* pee in it. But when *everyone* thinks the same way, the water quality is affected. This leads to the tragedy of the commons, where the overall quality of the water becomes degraded. Pee-ew.

Photo to come

Cartman trying to dodge pee.

ECONOMICS IN THE REAL WORLD

Deforestation in Haiti

Nothing symbolizes the vicious cycle of poverty in Haiti more than the process of deforestation. Haiti was once a lush tropical island covered with pines and broad-leaf trees. Today only about 3 percent of the country has tree cover. A number of factors contributed to this environmental catastrophe: shortsighted logging and agricultural practices, demand for charcoal, rapid population growth, and increased competition for land. Widespread deforestation caused soil erosion, which in turn caused the fertile topsoil layer to wash away. As a result, land that was once lush and productive became desert-like. Eventually nearly all remaining trees were cut down. Not enough food could be produced on this impoverished land, which contributed to widespread poverty.

Haiti, on the left, is deforested. The Dominican Republic, on the right, has maintained its environment.

Haiti is an extreme example of the tragedy of the commons. The tragedy in Haiti is especially striking because Haiti shares the island of Hispaniola with the Dominican Republic. The starkest difference between the two countries is the lush tropical landscape of the Dominican Republic side-by-side with the eroded, deforested Haitian land. In Haiti, the land was a semi-public resource that was overused and abused and therefore subject to the tragedy of the commons. In the Dominican Republic property rights preserved the environment. What does this mean for Haiti? Haiti would not be as poor today if it had relied more on private property rights. ✳

PRACTICE WHAT YOU KNOW

Common Resources: President Obama's Inauguration

Approximately two million people filled the National Mall for President Obama's inauguration.

Inaugural trash

Question: What economic concept explains why the National Mall was trashed after the inauguration?

Answer: Attendees brought snacks to eat and newspapers to read during the long wait. They also bought commemorative programs. So there was a lot of trash. As a public space, the National Mall is subject to the tragedy of the commons. The grass is often trampled and trash is all too common on normal days. No one person can effectively keep the park green and clean. This leads to overuse and littering by many people. When you put two million people in the space, the result becomes much more apparent.

Buying Used Is Good for Your Wallet and for the Environment

Many people waste their hard-earned money buying new. We could do our pocketbooks, and the environment, a favor by opting to buy used instead. The reason many used products are a better value than new products goes back to the premium some customers are willing to pay in order to enjoy that "new" feeling. To avoid the price markup, here are a few suggestions to help save you money and at the same time extend the usable life of a product.

1. **Jewelry**. Would you buy something that immediately depreciates 70%? If you said no, seriously think of avoiding new jewelry. When you buy at a retail store, you'll be lucky to get 1/3 back if you ever need to sell. If you are comfortable with the risk, search Craigslist, or even a local pawn shop. Someone else's need to sell is your gain, and you'll avoid the retail markup. Just be careful if you go the used route and make sure to get an appraisal before buying.

2. **Sports equipment**. Let the enthusiasts buy the latest equipment. When they tire of it and switch to the newest golf clubs or buy a new kayak, swoop in and save big.

3. **Video game consoles and games**. Buy used and you'll pay half or less of what it costs new. The catch is you'll have to wait. But the good news is that you'll never have to pay full retail price only to find out the console or the game is not as good as advertised. Waiting means that you'll have better information about the games that are really worth buying and also pay less. That is a good deal.

4. **Automobiles**. The average new car can lose as much as 20% of its value during the first year. For a $30,000 car, that is $6,000 in depreciation. Let someone else take that hit and buy a used vehicle instead.

5. **Yard equipment**. Before you load up on hand tools at a hardware store, consider buying the equipment used. Many hand tools such as hammers and shovels are designed to last. Used equipment doesn't look as shiny, but it works just as well.

6. **Furniture**. Avoid the retail furniture trap and find deals at garage and estate sales. You can also search online to find individual sellers.

Every time you buy used you help to extend the usable life of a product, which helps maximize the value society gets from its resources. This also illustrates the benefit of private property to help make society richer. Recall that private property has four characteristics. Owners have an incentive to maintain, protect, and conserve the products they own so that they can maximize the trade value when they sell them to others.

Buying used can save you thousands.

Conclusion

Although many people believe that the only acceptable amount of pollution is no pollution, this is a misconception. As with all things, there are trade-offs. When pollution is taxed or regulated, business activity is reduced. If we eliminated pollution entirely, many businesses would cease to operate and the resulting deadweight loss would be enormous. A truly "green" environment without any pollution would leave most people without enough "green" in their wallets. Therefore, attaining zero pollution does not pass a cost-benefit analysis.

In this chapter we have considered two types of market failure: externalities and public goods. When externalities and public goods exist, the market does not provide the socially optimal amount of the good or service. One solution is to encourage businesses to internalize externalities. This can be done through taxes and regulations that force producers to account for the negative externalities that they create. Similarly, subsidies can spur the additional production of activities that generate positive externalities. However, not all externalities require active management from the government. Many externalities are too small to matter and do not justify the costs associated with government regulation or taxation.

Likewise, public goods also present a challenge for the market. Free-riding leads to the underproduction of goods that are nonrival and nonexcludable. Since not enough is produced privately, one solution is to eliminate free-riding by making involvement compulsory through taxation or regulatory requirements. A second problem exists whenever goods are nonexcludable, as is the case with common-resource goods. This condition gives rise to the tragedy of the commons and can lead to the overuse of valuable resources.

ANSWERING THE BIG QUESTIONS

1. What are externalities and how do they affect markets?

* Social costs include the internal costs and the external costs of an activity.
* An externality exists whenever an internal cost, or benefit, diverges from a social cost, or benefit. Third parties experience negative or positive externalities from a market activity.
* When a negative externality exists, government can restore the social optimum by discouraging economic activity that harms third parties. When a positive externality exists, the government can restore the social optimum by encouraging economic activity that benefits third parties.
* An externality is internalized when decision-makers take into account the external effects of their actions.

2. What are private goods and public goods?

* Private property ensures that owners have an incentive to maintain, protect, and conserve their property, and also to trade it to others.
* A public good has two characteristics: it is nonexcludable and nonrival in consumption. This gives rise to the free-rider problem and results in the underproduction of the good in the market.

3. What are the challenges of providing public goods?

* Economists use cost-benefit analysis to determine whether the benefits of providing a type of good outweigh the costs, but benefits can be hard to determine.
* Under a system of common property, the incentive structure causes destruction, neglect, and overuse.

CONCEPTS YOU SHOULD KNOW

Cap and trade (p. 220)
Club good (p. 214)
Coase theorem (p. 211)
Common-resource good
  (p. 214)
Cost-benefit analysis (p. 216)
Excludable goods (p. 212)

External cost (p. 202)
Externalities (p. 202)
Free-rider problem (p. 213)
Internal cost (p. 202)
Internalize (p. 205)
Private good (p. 212)
Private property (p. 210)

Property rights (p. 209)
Public good (p. 212)
Rival goods (p. 212)
Social costs (p. 202)
Third-party problem (p. 202)
Tragedy of the commons,
  (p. 217)

QUESTIONS

1. Does the market overproduce or underproduce when third parties enjoy positive externalities? Show your answer on a supply and demand graph.

2. Can you use the Coase theorem to solve externality problems involving many parties? Explain your reasoning.

3. Describe all of the ways that externalities can be internalized.

4. Does cost-benefit analysis apply to public goods only? If yes, why? If not, name situations in which economists would use cost-benefit analysis.

5. What is the tragedy of the commons? Give an example that is not in the textbook.

6. What are the four incentives of private property? How do those incentives differ from the incentives found in common property?

7. Give an example of a good that is nonrival in consumption and nonexcludable. What do economists call goods that share both of these characteristics?

STUDY PROBLEMS

1. Many cities have noise ordinances that impose stiffer fines and penalties for early-morning and late-evening disturbances. Explain why this is the case.

2. Indicate whether the following activities create a positive or negative externality:
   a. Late-night road construction begins on a new bridge. As a consequence, traffic is rerouted past your house while the construction takes place.
   b. An excavating company is polluting a local stream with acid rock.
   c. A homeowner whose property backs up on a city park enjoys the sound of kids playing soccer.
   d. A student uses her cell phone discretely during class.
   e. You and your friends volunteer to plant wildflowers along the local highway.

3. Indicate whether the following are private goods, club goods, common-resource goods, or public goods:
   a. A bacon double cheeseburger
   b. An NHL hockey game between the Detroit Red Wings and Boston Bruins
   c. A Fourth of July fireworks show
   d. A swimming pool
   e. A vaccination shot for the flu
   f. Street lights

4. Can you think of a reason why making cars safer would create negative externalities?

5. Which of the following activities give rise to the free-rider problem?
   a. Recycling programs
   b. Biking
   c. Studying for an exam
   d. Riding a bus

6. The students at a crowded university have trouble waking up before 10 a.m. and most work jobs after 3 p.m. As a result, there is a great deal of demand for classes between 10 a.m. and 3 p.m., and classes before and after those hours are rarely full. To make matters worse, the university has only a limited amount of classroom space and faculty. This means that not every student can take classes during the most desirable times. Building new classrooms and hiring more faculty are not options. The administration asks for your advice about the best way to solve the problem of demand during the peak class hours. What advice would you give?

7. Two roommates are opposites. One enjoys playing Modern Warfare with his friends all night. The other likes to get to bed early for a full eight hours of sleep. If Coase is right, the roommates have an incentive to solve the noise externality issue themselves. Name at least two solutions that will internalize, or eliminate, the externality.

8. Two companies, Toxic Waste Management and Sludge Industries, both pollute a nearby lake. Each firm dumps 1,000 gallons of goo into the lake every day. As a consequence, the lake has lost its clarity and the fish are dying. The local residents want to see the lake restored. Toxic Waste's production process depends heavily on being able to dump the goo into the lake. It would cost Toxic Waste $10 per gallon to clean up the goo it creates. Sludge can clean up its goo at a cost of $2 per gallon.
   a. If the local government cuts the legal goo emissions in half for each firm, what are the costs to each firm to comply with the law? What is the total cost to both firms in meeting the goo-emissions standard?
   b. Another way of cutting goo emissions in half is to assign each firm tradable pollution permits that allow 500 gallons of goo to be dumped into the lake every day. Will each firm still dump 500 gallons of goo?

9. A study finds that leaf blowers make too much noise, so the government decides to impose a $10 tax on the sale of every unit to correct for the social cost of the noise pollution. Before the corrective tax, Blown Away Manufacturing regularly sold blowers for $100. After the tax is levied, the market price for leaf blowers rises to $105.
   a. Describe the impact of the tax on the number of leaf blowers sold.
   b. What is the socially optimal price?
   c. What is the private market price?
   d. What net price is Blown Away receiving after it pays the tax?

10. In most areas, developers are required to submit environmental impact studies before work can begin on new construction projects. Suppose that a commercial developer wants to build a new shopping center on an environmentally protected piece of property that is home to a three-eyed toad. The shopping complex, if approved by the local planning commission, will cover ten acres. The planning commission wants the construction to go forward since that means additional jobs for the local community, but it also wants to be environmentally responsible. One member of the commission suggests that the developer relocate the toads. She describes the relocation process as follows: "The developer builds the shopping mall and agrees to create ten acres of artificial toad habitat elsewhere." Will this proposed solution make the builder internalize the externality? Explain.

SOLVED PROBLEMS

6. A flat-fee congestion charge is a good start, since this would reduce the quantity demanded between 10 a.m. and 3 p.m., but such a fee is a blunt instrument. Making the congestion charge dynamic (or varying the price by the hour) will encourage students to move outside the window with the most popular class times in order to pay less. For

instance, classes between 11 a.m. and 2 p.m. could have the highest fee. Classes between 10 and 11 a.m. and between 2 and 3 p.m. would be slightly discounted. Classes between 9 and 10 a.m. and between 3 and 4 p.m. would be cheaper still, and those earlier than 9 a.m. and after 4 p.m. would be the cheapest. By altering the price of different class times, the university would be able to offer classes at less popular times and fill them up regularly, thus enabling it to efficiently use its existing resources.

8.a. If the local government cuts the legal goo emissions in half for each firm, Toxic Waste will cut its goo by 500 gallons at a cost of $10 per gallon, for a cost of $5,000. Sludge Industries will cut its goo by 500 gallons; it costs them $2 per gallon, so the cost is $1,000. The total cost to both firms in meeting the goo-emissions standard is $5,000 + $1,000 = $6,000.

b. It costs Toxic $10 per gallon to clean up its goo. It is therefore more efficient for Toxic to buy all 500 permits from Sludge—this allows Toxic to dump an additional 500 gallons in the lake and saves the company $5,000. At the same time, Sludge could not dump any goo in the lake. Since it costs Sludge $2 per gallon to clean up its goo, it will have to pay $1,000. Since Toxic is saving more than it costs Sludge to clean up the goo, the two sides have an incentive to trade the permits. As long as Toxic pays Sludge more than $1,000 but less than $5,000, the two sides have an incentive to trade permits.

Photo to come

The Theory of
THE FIRM

Business Costs and Production

Larger firms have lower costs.

When we think about buying goods at a low cost, bulk purchases come to mind. You can get discounts when you buy paper towels, meat, light bulbs, and many other items in large quantities. What about a seller like Wal-Mart? Wal-Mart is also a buyer. It purchases tens of thousands of products from suppliers and delivers them to its stores through its supply chain. Wal-Mart, the nation's largest retailer, leverages its size to get price breaks on bulk purchases from its suppliers. People commonly believe that this leverage allows larger firms to operate at lower costs. This is often true; large firms also have broader distribution networks, and benefit from specialization and automation compared to their smaller rivals. However, not all industries enjoy lower costs with additional sales the way department stores do. And even Wal-Mart, known for its very low prices, can be undercut by online outlets that have lower costs and, therefore, better prices. This means that larger firms do not always have the lowest cost. More generally, in any industry where transportation and advertising costs are high, smaller localized firms are not always at a disadvantage when it comes to pricing and often have the edge. For instance, in most college towns you will find many pizza shops. There are the national brands (Pizza Hut, Papa John's, Domino's) and then there are the local shops. Often the local pizza shop is the one with the cheapest pizza special, while the name brands charge more. By the end of this chapter you will be able to appreciate the importance of cost and understand why smaller and more nimble firms are sometimes able to undercut the prices of larger companies.

A Wal-Mart distribution center speeds goods to its stores.

We begin the chapter with a rigorous examination of costs, and how costs are related to production. After we understand the basics, we will look at how firms can keep their costs low in the long run by building facilities designed to serve their future customers more efficiently.

BIG QUESTIONS

* **How are profits and losses calculated?**
* **How much should a firm produce?**
* **What costs do firms consider in the short run and long run?**

Profits and **losses** are determined by subtracting total cost from total revenue.

Total revenue is the amount a firm receives from the sale of the goods and services it produces.

How Are Profits and Losses Calculated?

To determine the potential profits of a business, the first step is to look at how much it will cost to run it. Consider a McDonald's restaurant. While you are probably familiar with the products McDonald's sells, you may not know how an individual McDonald's franchise operates. The manager at a McDonald's must decide how many workers to hire and how many to assign to each shift. Other managerial decisions involve the equipment needed and what supplies to have on hand each day—everything from hamburger patties to paper napkins. In fact, behind each purchase a consumer makes at McDonald's there is a complicated symphony of delivery trucks, workers, and managers.

For a company to be profitable, it is not enough to provide products that consumers want. It must simultaneously manage its costs. In this section we will look at how profits and costs are calculated.

The first McDonald's opened in San Bernardino, California, in 1940.

Calculating Profit and Loss

The simplest way to determine **profit** or **loss** is to calculate the difference between expenses and revenues. Losses exist whenever total revenue is less than total cost. The **total revenue** of a business is the amount a firm receives from the sale of the goods and services it produces. In the case of McDonald's, the total revenue is determined by the number of items sold and the prices those items sell for. **Total cost** is the amount that a firm spends in order to produce the goods and services it sells. This is determined by adding the individual costs of the resources used in producing the goods for sale. We can express this relationship as an equation:

$$\text{Profit (or loss)} = \text{total revenue} - \text{total cost} \qquad (8.1)$$

To calculate total revenue, we look at the dollar amount that the business earns over a specific period of time. For instance, suppose that in a given day McDonald's sells 1,000 hamburgers for $1 each, 500 large fries for $2 each, and 100 shakes for $2.50 each. The total revenue is the sum of all of these values, or $2,250. The profit is therefore $2,250 (total revenue) minus the total cost.

Calculating costs, however, is a little more complicated than calculating revenue; it's not simply the cost of making each hamburger, large fries, and shake. Total cost has two parts—one that is visible and one that is largely invisible. In the next section we will see that determining total costs is part art and part science.

Total cost
is the amount a firm spends in order to produce the goods and services it produces.

Explicit Costs and Implicit Costs

Economists break cost into two components: *explicit costs* and *implicit costs*. **Explicit costs** are tangible expenses. To calculate explicit costs, we add every expense incurred to run the business. In the case of a McDonald's franchise, the weekly supply of hamburger patties is an explicit cost; the owner receives a bill from the meat supplier, and has to pay it. **Implicit costs** are the opportunity costs of doing business.

Let's consider an example. Purchasing a McDonald's franchise costs about $1 million; this is an explicit cost. However, there is also a high opportunity cost—the next-best possibility for investing $1 million. That money could have earned interest in the bank, been used to open a different business, or invested in the stock market. Each of these alternatives is an implicit cost.

Implicit costs are hard to calculate and easy to miss. It is difficult to determine how much an investor could have earned from an alternative activity. Is the opportunity cost the 3% interest you might have earned by placing the money in a bank, the 10% you hope to earn in the stock market, or the 15% you might have gained by investing in a different business? We can be sure that there is an opportunity cost for owner-provided capital, but we can never know exactly how much that might be.

In addition to the opportunity cost of capital, implicit costs include the opportunity cost of the owner's labor. Often business owners do not pay themselves a direct salary. However, since they could have been working somewhere else, it is reasonable to consider the fair value of the owner's time—income the owner could have earned by working elsewhere—as part of the business's costs.

To fully account for all the costs of doing business you must calculate the explicit costs, determine the implicit costs, and add them together:

$$\text{Total cost} = \text{explicit costs} + \text{implicit costs} \qquad (8.2)$$

A simple way of thinking about the distinction between explicit costs and implicit costs is to consider someone who wants to build a bookcase. Suppose that John purchases $30 in materials and takes half a day off from work. John

Explicit costs
are tangible out-of-pocket expenses.

Implicit costs
are the opportunity costs of doing business.

TABLE 8.1	
Examples of Explicit and Implicit Costs	
Explicit Costs	**Implicit Costs**
The electricity bill	The labor of an owner who works for the company, but does not draw a salary
Advertising in the local newspaper	The capital invested in the business
Employee wages	The use of the owner's car, computer, or other personal equipment to conduct company business

normally earns $12 an hour. After four hours he completes the bookcase. His explicit costs are $30 but his total cost is much higher. John also gave up 4 hours of work at $12 an hour. His implicit cost is therefore $48. When we add the explicit cost ($30) and implicit cost ($48), we get his total cost ($78).

Table 8.1 shows examples of implicit and explicit costs.

Accounting Profits versus Economic Profits

Now that you know about explicit and implicit costs, we can refine our definition of profit. In fact, there are two types of profits—*accounting profits* and *economic profits*.

A firm's **accounting profits** are calculated by subtracting only the explicit costs from total revenue. Accounting figures permeate company reports, quarterly and annual statements, and the media.

Accounting profits
are calculated by taking total revenues and subtracting the explicit costs.

$$\textbf{Accounting profit} = \text{total revenues} - \text{explicit costs} \qquad (8.3)$$

As you can see, accounting profits do not take into account the implicit costs of doing business. To calculate the full cost of doing business, we need to consider both implicit and explicit costs. **Economic profits** are calculated by subtracting both the explicit and implicit costs of business from total revenue. Economic profits give a more complete assessment of how a firm is doing.

Economic profits
are calculated by taking total revenue minus explicit costs and implicit costs.

$$\textbf{Economic profit} = \text{total revenues} - (\text{explicit costs} + \text{implicit costs}) \qquad (8.4)$$

Simplifying the equation above gives us:

$$\textbf{Economic profit} = \text{accounting profit} - \text{implicit costs} \qquad (8.5)$$

TABLE 8.2	
Historical Rates of Return in Stocks, Bonds, and Savings Accounts	
Financial Instrument	**Historical Average Rate of Return Since 1928 (adjusted for inflation)**
Stocks	7%
Bonds	4%
Savings account at a financial institution	2%

The difference between accounting profits can be misleading. For instance, if a company with $1 billion in assets reports an annual profit of $10 million, we might think it is doing well. After all, wouldn't you be happy to make $10 million in a year? However, that $10 million is only 1% of the $1 billion the company holds in assets. As you can see in Table 8.2, a 1% return is far less than the typical return available in a number of other places, including the stock market, bonds, or a savings account at a financial institution.

If the return on $1 billion in assets is low compared to what an investor can expect to make elsewhere, a firm with a $10 million accounting profit has a negative economic profit. For instance, if the firm had invested the $1 billion in a savings account, it would have earned 2% on $1 billion—$20 million. That would yield an economic profit of:

$$\textbf{Economic profit} = \text{accounting profit} - \text{implicit costs}$$
$$= \$10 \text{ million} - \$20 \text{ million}$$
$$= -\$10 \text{ million}$$

As you can see, economic profits are never misleading. If a business has an economic profit, its revenues are larger than the combination of its explicit and implicit costs. The difficulty in determining economic profits lies in calculating the tangible value of implicit costs.

PRACTICE WHAT YOU KNOW

Accounting versus Economic Profits: Calculating Summer Job Profits

Kyle is a college student who works summers to pay for tuition. Last summer he worked at a fast-food restaurant and earned $2,500. This summer he is working as a painter and will earn $4,000. To do the painting job, Kyle had to purchase $200 of supplies.

How much economic profit do you make from painting?

Question: What is Kyle's accounting profit?

Answer: Accounting profit = total revenues − explicit cost
= $4,000 − $200 = $3,800

Question: If working at the fast-food restaurant was Kyle's next-best alternative, how much economic profit will Kyle earn from painting?

Answer: To calculate economic profit, we need to subtract the explicit and implicit costs from the total revenue. Kyle's total revenue from painting will be $4,000. His explicit costs are $200 for supplies and his implicit cost is $2,500, the salary he would have earned in the fast-food restaurant. So:

Economic profit = total revenues − (explicit cost + implicit cost)
= $4,000 − ($200 + $2,500) = $1,300

Question: Suppose that Kyle can get an internship in an investment banking firm. The internship provides $3,000 and tangible work experience that will help him get a job after graduation. Should Kyle take the painting job or the internship?

Answer: The implicit costs have changed because Kyle now has to consider the $3,000 salary and the increased chance of securing a job upon graduation versus what he can make painting houses. Calculation of economic profit from painting is now:

Economic profit = $4,000 − ($200 + $3,000) = $800

But this number is incomplete. There is also the value of the internship job experience, so the answer is: $800—the value of the job experience. If Kyle wants to work in investment banking after graduation, then this is a no-brainer. He should take the internship—that is, unless some investment banks value painting houses more than work experience!

How Much Should a Firm Produce?

Every business must decide how much to produce. In this section we describe the factors that determine output and how firms use inputs to maximize their production. Since it is possible for a firm to produce too little or too much, we must also consider when a firm should stop production.

The Production Function

Output
is the production the firm creates.

Factors of production
are the inputs used in producing goods and services.

Inputs
are the resources used in the production process.

For a firm to earn an economic profit, it must produce a product, known as its **output**, that consumers want. It must also control its costs. To accomplish this, it must use resources efficiently. There are three primary components of output, known as the **factors of production**: labor, land, and capital. Each of the factors of production is an **input**, or a resource used in the production process, to create the firm's output. Labor consists of the workers, land consists of the geographic location used in production, and capital consists of all the resources that are used by the workers to create the final product. Let's continue using McDonald's as an example. The labor input includes managers, cashiers, cooks, and janitorial staff. The land input includes the land on which the McDonald's building rests. And the capital input includes the building itself, the equipment used, the parking lot, and the signs.

To keep costs down in the production process, a firm needs to find the right mix of these inputs. The **production function** describes the relationship between the inputs a firm uses and the output it creates. As we saw at the beginning of the chapter, the manager of a MacDonald's must make many decisions about inputs. If the man-

McDonald's needs the correct amount of labor to maximize its output.

ager hires too little labor, some land and capital will be underutilized. Likewise, with too many workers and not enough land or capital, some workers will not have enough to keep them busy. For example, suppose that only a single worker shows up at McDonald's one day. This employee will have to do all the cooking, bag up the meals, handle the register, the drive-thru, and the drinks, and clean the tables. This single worker, no matter how productive, will not be able to keep up with demand. Hungry customers will grow tired of waiting and take their business elsewhere—maybe for good!

The **production function** describes the relationship between inputs a firm uses and the output it creates.

When a second worker shows up, the two employees can begin to specialize at what they do well. Recall that specialization and comparative advantage lead to higher levels of output. Therefore, individual workers will be assigned to tasks that match their skills. For example, one worker can take the orders, fill the bags, and get the drinks. The other can work the grill area and drive-thru. When a third worker is added, the specialization process can extend even further. This specialization and division of labor is how McDonald's operates. Production per worker expands as long as additional workers are able to become more specialized and there are enough capital resources to keep each worker occupied.

When only a few workers share capital resources, the resources each worker needs are readily available. What happens when the restaurant is very busy? The manager can hire more staff for the busiest shifts, but the amount of space for cooking, the number of cash registers, drink dispensers, and tables in the seating area are fixed. Because the added employees have less capital to work with, beyond a certain point additional labor will not continue to increase the productivity at the same rate as it did at first. This situation should be familiar to anyone who has gone into a fast-food restaurant at lunchtime. Even though the space behind the counter is filled with busy employees, they can't keep up with the orders. There are only so many meals that can be produced in a short time and in a fixed space; some customers have to wait.

The restaurant must also maintain an adequate supply of materials. If a shipment is late and they run out of hamburger patties, the shortage will impact sales. The manager must therefore be able to decide how many workers to hire for each shift, and manage the inventory of supplies to avoid shortages.

Let's look more closely at the manager's decision about how many workers to hire. On the left side of Figure 8.1, we see what happens when workers

Marginal product

is the change in output divided by the change in input.

are added, one by one. When the manager adds one worker, output goes from 0 meals to 5 meals. Going from one worker to two workers increases total output to 15 meals. This means that a second worker has increased the number of meals produced from 5 to 15, or an increase of 10 meals. This increase in output is known as the **marginal product**, which is the change in output associated with one additional unit of an input. In this case, the change in output, 10 additional meals, divided by the increase in input, one worker, gives us a marginal product of 10 ÷ 1, or 10. Since the table in Figure 8.1 adds one worker at a time, the marginal product is just the increase in output shown in the third column.

Looking down the three columns we see that after the first three workers, the rate of increase in the marginal product becomes slower. The marginal

FIGURE 8.1

The Production Function and Marginal Product

(a) Total output rises rapidly in the green-shaded zone from 0 to 3 workers, rises less rapidly in the yellow zone between 3 and 8 workers, and falls in the red zone after 8 workers. (b) The marginal product of labor rises in the green zone from 0 to 3 workers, falls in the yellow zone from 3 to 8 workers but remains positive, and after 8 workers the marginal product of labor is negative. Notice that the marginal product is zero when total output reaches its maximum at 8 workers. As long as marginal product is positive, total output rises. Once marginal product becomes negative, total output falls.

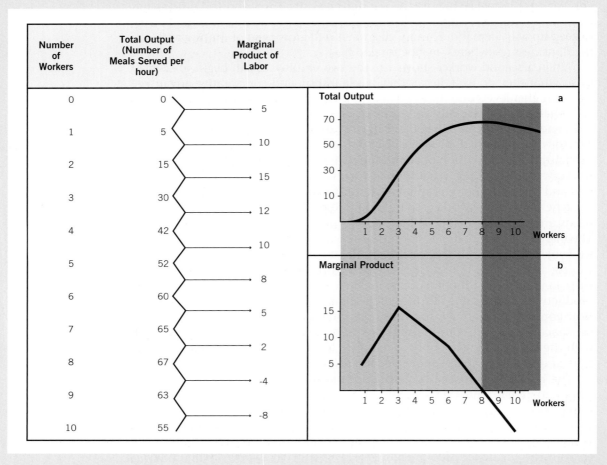

product continues to expand, remaining positive through 8 workers. This occurs because the gains from specialization are slowly declining. By the ninth worker (going from 8 to 9), we see a negative marginal product. Once the cash registers, drive-thru, grill area, and other service stations are fully staffed, there is not much for an extra worker to do. Eventually extra workers get in the way, or distract other workers from completing their tasks.

The graphs on the right side of Figure 8.1 show (a) total output and (b) marginal product. The graph of total output in (a) uses the data in the second column in the table. As the number of workers goes from 0 to 3 on the x-axis, total output rises at an increasing rate from 0 to 30. The slope of the total output curve rises until it reaches 3 workers at the first dashed line. Between 3 workers and the second dashed line at 8 workers, the total output curve continues to rise, though at a slower rate; the slope of the total output curve is still positive but becomes progressively flatter. Finally, once we reach the ninth worker, total output begins to fall and the slope becomes negative.

Diminishing Marginal Product

The marginal product curve in Figure 8.1b explains the shape of the total output curve above it. The marginal productivity of each worker either adds to or subtracts from the overall output of the firm. Marginal product increases from 5 meals served per hour with the first worker to 15 meals per hour with the third worker. From the first worker to the third, each additional worker leads to increased specialization and teamwork. This explains the rapid rise— from 0 to 30 meals—in the total output curve. By the fourth worker, marginal product begins to decline. Looking back to the table, you can see that the fourth worker produces 12 extra meals—3 fewer than the third worker. The point at which successive increases in inputs are associated with a slower rise in output is known as the point of **diminishing marginal product**.

Why does the rate of output slow? Recall that in our example the size of the McDonald's restaurant is fixed in the short run. Because the size of the building, the equipment, and other inputs do not increase, at a certain point, additional workers have less to do, or can even interfere with the productivity of other workers. After all inputs are fully utilized, additional workers cause marginal product to decline, which we see in the fall of the marginal product curve.

What does diminishing marginal product tell us about the firm's labor input decision? Turning again to the two graphs, we see that in the green-shaded area as the number of workers increases from 0 to 3, the marginal product and total output also rise. But when we enter the yellow zone with the fourth worker, we reach the point of diminishing marginal product where the curve starts to decline. Total output continues to rise, though at a slower rate. Finally, in the red zone, which we enter with the ninth worker, total output declines and marginal product is negative. No rational manager would hire more than 8 workers in this scenario, since the total output drops.

A common mistake when considering diminishing marginal product is to assume that a firm should stop production as soon as marginal product starts to fall. This is not true. Diminishing does not mean "negative." There are many times when marginal product is declining but still high. In our example, diminishing marginal product begins with the fourth worker. However, the fourth worker still produces 12 extra meals. If McDonald's can sell those 12 additional meals for more than it pays the fourth worker, the company's profits will rise.

Diminishing marginal product occurs when the marginal product of an input falls as the quantity of the input rises.

Diminishing Marginal Product

A Demonstration of Diminishing Marginal Product

The intuition for how many workers a firm should hire is difficult to grasp unless it is in context. In this short demonstration, groups of student workers are asked to move tennis balls from one bucket to the next. As we might expect, neither the largest nor the smallest group is most productive.

Check out this video on YouTube: http://www.youtube.com/dmateer#p/a/u/2/7m32 KqKBJZE

The tennis ball demonstration shows that although the most profit is earned with 6 workers, diminishing marginal product begins after the fourth worker.

Watch student workers in the production process!

PRACTICE WHAT YOU KNOW

Diminishing Returns: Snow Cone Production

It's a hot day and customers are lined up for snow cones at your small stand. The following table shows your firm's short-run production function for snow cones.

How many workers are too many?

Number of Workers	Total Output of Snow Cones per hour
0	0
1	20
2	50
3	75
4	90
5	100
6	105
7	100
8	90

Question: When does diminishing marginal product begin?

Answer: You have to be careful. Total output is maximized when you have six workers, but diminishing marginal return begins before you hire that many workers. Look at the following table, which includes a third column with marginal product.

Number of Workers	Total Output of Snow Cones per Hour	Marginal Product
0	0	0
1	20	20
2	50	30
3	75	25
4	90	15
5	100	10
6	105	5
7	100	−5
8	90	−10

The marginal product is highest when you hire the second worker. After that, each subsequent worker you hire has a lower marginal product. Diminishing marginal product begins after the second worker.

What Costs Do Firms Consider in the Short Run and Long Run?

Production is one part of the firm's decision-making process. If you have run even a simple business—for example, cutting lawns—you know that it requires decision-making. How many lawns do you want to be responsible for? Should you work on different lawns at the same time or specialize by task, with one person doing all the mowing and the other taking care of the trimming? These are the kinds of production-related questions every firm must address. The other major component of production is cost. Should you invest in a big industrial-size mower? How much gasoline will you need to run your mowers? What does it cost to hire someone to help get the work done? These are some of the cost-related concerns firms have. Each of these may seem like small decisions, but the discovery process that leads to the answers is crucial. Every firm, whether it is just starting out or already well established and profitable, can benefit by assessing how much to produce and how to produce it more efficiently. In addition, production and cost consideration are different in the short run and in the long run. We begin with the short run, because most firms are typically most concerned with making the best short-run decisions, and then extend our analysis to the long run, where planning ahead plays a central role.

Costs in the Short Run

All firms experience some costs that cannot be avoided in the short run. These unavoidable costs—for example, a lease on space or a contract with a supplier—are a large part of short-run costs. In the short run, costs can be *variable* or *fixed*. **Variable costs** change with the rate of output. Let's see what this means for a McDonald's, and further simplify our example by assuming McDonald's produces only Big Macs. In this case, the variable costs include the number of workers the firm hires, the electricity the firm uses, the all-beef patties, special sauce, lettuce, cheese, pickles, onions, and sesame-seed bun needed to create the Big Mac, and the packaging. These items are considered variable costs because you don't need them unless you have customers. The amount of these resources varies with the amount of output you produce.

Fixed costs are unavoidable; they do not vary with output. For instance, no matter how many hamburgers McDonald's sells, the owner costs associated with the building remain the same and the business must pay for them. These fixed costs include rent, insurance, snow plowing, and so on.

Every business must be able to determine how much it costs to provide the products and services it sells. Table 8.3 lists many different ways to measure the costs associated with business decisions. Let's begin with total variable cost (TVC) in column (2) and total fixed cost (TFC) in column (3). Notice that when output is 0, variable cost starts at $0 and rises with production at an uneven rate depending the productivity of labor and the cost of the ingredients that go into making the Big Mac. We attribute this to the simple fact that additional workers and other inputs are needed to create additional output. On the other hand, fixed cost starts at $100, even when output is 0, and remains constant as output rises. As noted above, fixed costs include things such as rent, insurance, and snowplowing. For simplicity we assume that this amount is $100 a day. When we add fixed cost and variable cost together, we get total cost, listed in column (4): TC = TVC + TFC.

Column (5), *average variable cost*, and column (6), *average fixed cost*, allow us to determine the cost of producing a Big Mac by examining the average cost of production. **Average variable cost** (AVC) is the total variable cost divided by the output produced: AVC = TVC ÷ Q. Notice that the average variable cost declines until 60 Big Macs are produced at an average cost of $1.67. This is the lowest average cost. Why should we care about AVC? Total variable costs in column (2) always rise, but the average variable cost falls until 60 Big Macs are produced. The decline in AVC is a powerful signal to the firm to increase its output up to a point.

Average fixed cost (AFC), listed in column (6), is calculated by dividing total fixed cost by the output: AFC = TFC ÷ Q. Since total fixed cost is constant, dividing these costs by the output means that as the output rises, the average fixed cost declines. This means that higher output levels spread the total fixed costs out across more units. As you can see in Table 8.3, average fixed costs are lowest at an output of 100 Big Macs, where:

$$AFC = TFC \div Q$$
$$AFC = \$100 \div \$100$$
$$AFC = \$1$$

What does this tell a business that wants to lower costs? Since costs such as the rent a firm pays cannot be changed, the best way to lower fixed costs is to raise output.

Variable costs
change with the rate of output.

Fixed costs
do not vary with output.

Average variable cost
is determined by dividing total variable costs by the output.

Average fixed cost
is determined by dividing total fixed costs by the output.

TABLE 8.3

Measuring Costs

(1)	(2)	(3)	(4)	(5)	(6)	(7)	(8)
Quantity (Q = Big Macs produced/hour)	Total Variable Cost	Total Fixed Cost	Total Cost	Average Variable Cost	Average Fixed Cost	Average Total Cost	Marginal Cost
Abbreviation:	TVC	TFC	TC	AVC	AFC	ATC	MC
Formula:			TVC + TFC	TVC ÷ Q	TFC ÷ Q	AVC + AFC	ΔTVC ÷ ΔQ
0	$0.00	$100.00	$100.00				
10	30.00	100.00	130.00	$3.00	$10.00	$13.00	$3.00
20	50.00	100.00	150.00	2.50	5.00	7.50	2.00
30	65.00	100.00	165.00	2.17	3.33	5.50	1.50
40	77.00	100.00	177.00	1.93	2.50	4.43	1.20
50	87.00	100.00	187.00	1.74	2.00	3.74	1.00
60	100.00	100.00	200.00	1.67	1.67	3.34	1.30
70	120.00	100.00	220.00	1.71	1.43	3.14	2.00
80	160.00	100.00	260.00	2.00	1.25	3.25	4.00
90	220.00	100.00	320.00	2.44	1.11	3.55	6.00
100	300.00	100.00	400.00	3.00	1.00	4.00	8.00

Average total cost (ATC), shown in column (7), is calculated by adding the AVC and AFC. Let's look at the numbers to get a better understanding of what average total cost tells us. Even though the average variable cost rises after 60 sandwiches are produced, from $1.67 to $1.71, average fixed cost is still falling, from $1.67 to $1.43. The decline in average fixed cost is enough to pull the average total cost down to $3.14. Eventually, increases in variable cost overwhelm the cost savings achieved by spreading fixed cost across more production. We can see this if we compare the average total cost of making 70 Big Macs and 80 Big Macs.

Average total cost is the sum of average variable cost and average fixed cost.

For 70 Big Macs:

$$ATC = AVC + AFC$$
$$ATC = \$1.71 + \$1.43 = \$3.14$$

For 80 Big Macs:

$$ATC = AVC + AFC$$
$$ATC = \$2.00 + \$1.25 = \$3.25$$

At 80 Big Macs the average variable cost rises from $1.71 to $2.00. The average fixed cost falls from $1.43 to $1.25. Therefore, the rise in average variable cost—$0.29—is higher than the fall in average fixed cost—$0.18. This removes the benefit of higher output. Thus, the ideal number of Big Macs to produce is between 70 and 80.

Now that we have walked through the numerical results in Table 8.3, it is time to visualize the cost relationships with graphs. Figure 8.2 shows a graph of total cost curves (a) and the relationship between the marginal cost curve and average cost curves (b).

In panel (a) in Figure 8.2 you can see that although the total cost curve continues to rise, the rate of increase in total cost is not constant. For the first 50 Big Macs the total cost rises at a decreasing rate. This reflects the gains of specialization and comparative advantage that come from adding workers who concentrate on specific tasks. After 50 Big Macs, diminishing marginal product causes the total cost curve to rise at an increasing rate. Since a McDonald's restaurant has a fixed capacity, producing more than 50 Big Macs requires a significantly higher investment in labor, and those workers do not have any additional space to work in—this causes the total cost curve to rise more rapidly at high production levels. The total cost (TC) curve is equal to the sum of the fixed cost and variable cost curves, which are shown in panel (a). Total fixed costs (TFC) are constant, so it is the total variable costs (TVC) that give the TC curve its shape.

But that is not the most important part of the story! A manager at McDonald's can examine total costs. Likewise, the manager can look at the average cost and compare that information to the average cost at other local businesses. But neither the total cost of labor nor the average cost of labor will tell the manager anything about the cost of making additional units.

A manager can make even better decisions about labor by looking at *marginal cost*. The **marginal cost (MC)** is the increase in extra cost that occurs from

Marginal costs
are the increase in cost that occurs from producing additional output.

FIGURE 8.2

The Cost Curves

(a) The total variable cost (TVC) dictates the shape of the total cost (TC) curve. After 50 Big Macs, diminishing marginal product causes the total cost curve to rise at an increasing rate. (b) The marginal cost curve (MC) reaches its minimum before average variable cost (AVC) and average total cost (ATC). Marginals always lead the average either up or down. Average fixed cost, which has no variable component, continues to fall with increased quantity, since total fixed costs are spread across more units. The minimum point of the ATC curve is known as the efficient scale.

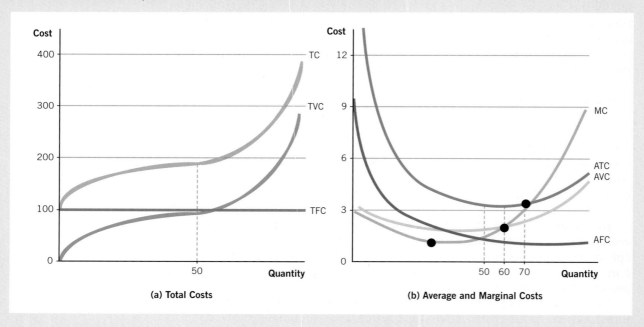

(a) Total Costs

(b) Average and Marginal Costs

producing additional output. For example, in putting together the weekly work schedule the manager has to consider how many workers to hire for each shift. The manager wants to hire additional workers when the cost of hiring them is less than the expected boost in profits. In this situation, it is essential to know the marginal cost, or extra cost, of hiring one more worker. In Table 8.3, marginal cost falls to a minimum of $1.00 when between 40 and 50 Big Macs are produced. Notice that the minimum MC occurs at a lower output level than average variable cost (AVC) and average total cost (ATC) in panel (b) of Figure 8.2. When MC is less than 50 Big Macs, marginal cost is falling because over this range of production, the marginal product of labor is increasing from better teamwork and more specialization. After the fiftieth Big Mac, MC rises. This acts as an early warning indicator that average and total costs will soon follow suit. Why would a manager care about the last few units it produces more than the average cost of producing all the units? Marginal cost tells the manager if making one more unit of output will increase profits or not!

The MC curve reaches its lowest point before the lowest point of the AVC and ATC curves. For this reason, a manager concerned about rising costs would look to the MC curve as an early indicator that average costs will eventually increase as well. Once marginal cost begins to increase, it continues to pull down average variable cost until sales reaches 60 Big Macs. After 60 Big Macs are sold, MC is above AVC and AVC begins to rise as well. However, ATC continues to fall until 70 Big Macs are sold. Why does average total cost fall while MC and AVC are rising? The answer lies in the average fixed cost (AFC) curve shown in Figure 8.2. Since the ATC = AVC + AFC, and AFC always declines as output rises, ATC declines until 70 Big Macs are sold. This is a direct result of the decline in AFC overwhelming the increase in AVC between 60 and 70 Big Macs. Notice that the AVC curve stops declining at 60 Big Macs. Variable costs should initially decline as a result of increased specialization and teamwork. However, at some point the advantages of continued specialization are overtaken by diminishing marginal product and costs begin to rise. The transition from falling costs to rising costs is of particular interest because as long as costs are declining, the firm will be able to lower its costs by increasing its output. Economists refer to the quantity of output that minimizes average total costs as the **efficient scale**.

Businesses pay attention to marginal costs for exactly the same reason college students pay attention to their next exam. When your current grades are higher than your cumulative GPA, the cumulative average rises. Similarly, once the marginal costs in Table 8.3 rise above the average total costs, the average total costs begin to rise as well. We can see this if we compare the average total cost of making 70 Big Macs ($3.14) and 80 Big Macs ($3.25) with the marginal cost ($4.00) of making those extra 10 Big Macs. Since the marginal cost ($4.00) of making Big Macs 71 through 80 is higher than the average total cost at 70 ($3.14), this pulls the average total cost of making 80 Big Macs up (to $3.25).

Marginal costs always lead (or pull) average costs along whether we are considering grades or a firm's costs. The MC eventually rises above the average total cost because of diminishing marginal product. That is, since the firm has to pay a fixed wage, the cost to produce each hamburger increases as each worker decreases in productivity.

There is, however, one "average" curve that the marginal cost does not affect: average fixed costs. Notice that the AFC curve in panel (b) of Figure 8.2 continues to fall even though marginal costs eventually rise. The AFC curve

The **efficient scale** is the output level that minimizes the average total cost.

declines with increased output. Since McDonald's has $100 in fixed costs each day, we can determine the average fixed costs by dividing the total fixed cost ($100) by the number of Big Macs that are sold. When 10 Big Macs are sold, the average fixed cost is $10 per Big Mac, but this value falls to $1 per Big Mac if 100 sandwiches are sold. Since McDonald's is a high-volume business that relies on low costs to compete, being able to produce enough Big Macs to spread out the firm's fixed costs is essential.

Costs in the Short Run

The Office

The Office provides an amusing episode devoted to the discussion of costs. Michael Scott establishes his own paper company to compete with both Staples and his former company, Dunder Mifflin. He out-competes his rivals by keeping his fixed and variable costs low.

In one inspired episode, the Michael Scott Paper Company uses an old church van to deliver paper and the business operates out of a single room. This means the company has very low fixed costs, which allows it to charge unusually low prices. Michael Scott keeps variable costs to a minimum by hiring only essential employees and not paying any benefits, such as health insurance. Despite these efforts, Michael Scott's costs still exceed the price he charges.

As we will discover in the upcoming chapters, firms with lower costs have many advantages in the market. Firms that have lower costs can keep their prices lower to attract additional customers. Cost matters because price matters.

Michael Scott doesn't understand the difference between fixed and variable costs.

Costs in the Long Run

We have seen that in the short run businesses have fixed costs and fixed capacities. In the long run, all costs are variable and can be renegotiated. Firms have more control over their costs in the long run; this allows them to achieve their desired level of production. One way that firms can adjust in the long run is by changing the **scale**, or size, of the production process. If the business is expected to grow, the firm can ramp up production. If the business is faltering, operations can be scaled back. This flexibility allows firms to avoid a situation of diminishing marginal product.

Scale
refers to the size of the production process.

A long-run time horizon allows a business to choose a scale of operation that best suits its needs. For instance, if a local McDonald's is extremely popular, in the short run the manager can only hire more workers or expand its hours to accommodate more customers. However, in the long run all costs are variable; the manager can add drive-thru lanes, increase the number of registers, expand the grill area, and so on.

The absence of fixed factors in the long-run production process means that we cannot explain total costs in the long run the same way we explained short-run costs. Short-run costs are a reflection of diminishing marginal product, whereas long-run costs are a reflection of scale and the cost of providing additional output. One might assume that since diminishing marginal product is no longer relevant in the long run, costs would fall as output expands. However, this is not the case. Depending on the industry and economic conditions, long-run costs can rise, fall, or stay approximately the same.

Three Types of Scale

In this section we describe three different scenarios for the firm in the long run. A firm may experience *economies of scale*, *diseconomies of scale*, or *constant returns to scale*. In the long run, whether costs fall, remain constant, or rise with increasing output will depend on *scale*, or the amount of output a firm desires to produce. Let's consider each of these in turn.

Economies of scale
occur when costs decline as output expands in the long run.

If output expands and costs decline, businesses experience **economies of scale**. National homebuilders, like Toll Brothers, provide a good example of economies of scale. All builders, whether they are local or national, do the same thing—they build houses. Each builder needs lumber, concrete, excavators, electricians, plumbers, roofers, and many more specialized workers. A big company, such as Toll, is able to hire many specialists and also buy the equipment it needs in bulk. This allows Toll to manufacture the same home as a local builder at a much lower cost.

But bigger isn't always better! Sometimes a company grows so large that coordination problems make costs rise. For example, as the scale of an enterprise grows larger, it might require more managers, highly specialized workers, and a coordination process to pull everything together. As the layers of

It is cheaper to build more than one house at a time.

Economies of Scale

Modern Times

Modern Times is regarded as one of the top 100 English-language films of all time. The movie features Charlie Chaplin in his final silent film role. Chaplin, who was a master of slapstick comedy, plays a tramp who finds work on an assembly line in a large factory. The company bosses are ruthless taskmasters. For the production process to remain in sync and maximum efficiency to be achieved, each assembly line worker must complete a small task and pass the product down the line.

The bosses introduce a novel product called the Billows Feeding Machine. The idea is simple: if the lunch break could be shortened, the workers' downtime could be minimized and production increased. Here is the exact transcript from the film,

> "May I take the pleasure of introducing Mr. J. Widdecombe Billows, the inventor of the Billows Feeding Machine, a practical device which automatically feeds your men while at work. Don't stop for lunch: be ahead of your competitor. The Billows Feeding Machine will eliminate the lunch hour, increase your production, and decrease your overhead. Allow us to point out some of the features of this wonderful machine: its beautiful, aerodynamic, streamlined body; its smoothness of action, made silent by our electro-porous metal ball bearings. Let us acquaint you with our automaton soup plate— its compressed-air blower, no breath necessary, no energy required to cool the soup. Notice the revolving plate with the automatic food pusher. Observe our counter-shaft, double-knee-action corn feeder, with its synchro-mesh transmission, which enables you to shift from high to low gear by the mere tip of the tongue. Then there is the hydro-compressed, sterilized mouth wiper: its factors of control insure against spots on the shirt front. These are but a few of the delightful features of the Billows Feeding Machine. Let us demonstrate with one of your workers, for actions speak louder than words. Remember, if you wish to keep ahead of your competitor, you cannot afford to ignore the importance of the Billows Feeding Machine."

Would a feeding machine for workers lower long-run costs?

The company bosses are eager to test the feeding machine. However, things go terribly wrong—in a hilarious way—when they select Chaplin as the human guinea pig. Because the machine does not work as promised, the company decides that the feeding machine is not a practical idea.

Although no firm in the real word is likely to try something like the feeding machine, firms do constantly seek efficiency gains. Of course, not all ideas are practical and sometimes there are not sufficient economies of scale to implement an idea. For instance, the assembly line depicted in *Modern Times* is efficient, but it wouldn't make sense for a company to use this process unless it sells a large volume of bolts. This is analogous to how the automobile industry works. Large manufacturers like Toyota and Ford use assembly lines to create economies of scale, whereas a small specialty shop that produces only a handful of vehicles a year builds each car by hand and fails to enjoy the benefits of economies of scale.

management expand, the coordination process can break down. For this
reason, a larger firm can become less
effective at holding down costs and
the firm experiences **diseconomies of
scale**, or higher average total costs
as output expands. The problem of
diseconomies of scale is especially
relevant in the service sector of the
economy. For example, large regional
hospitals have many layers of bureau-
cracy. These added management costs
and infrastructure expenses can make
medical care more expensive beyond
some point. If you are not convinced,
ask yourself why large cities have many
smaller competing hospitals, rather than
one centralized hospital. The answer
becomes obvious: bigger doesn't always
mean less expensive (or better)!

Doctor du jour or your own physician?

Finally, if the advantages of specialization, mass production, and bulk
purchasing are approximately equal, the long-run costs will remain constant
as the firm expands output. When costs remain constant even as output
expands, we say that the firm has **constant returns to scale**. For example,
large national restaurant chains like Olive Garden compete with local Italian
restaurants. In each case, the local costs to hire workers and build the restaurant are the same. Olive Garden does have a few advantages; for example, it
can afford to advertise on national television and buy food in bulk. But Olive
Garden also has more overhead costs for its many layers of management.
Constant returns to scale in the bigger chain mean that a small local Italian
restaurant will have approximately the same menu costs as its bigger rivals.

Diseconomies of scale
occur when costs rise as output expands in the long run.

Constant returns to scale
occur when costs remain
constant as output expands
in the long run.

Long-Run Cost Curves

Now it is time to illustrate the long-run nature of cost curves. We have seen
that increased output may not always lead to economies of scale. Costs can be
constant, or even rise with output. Figure 8.3 illustrates each of the three possibilities graphically. The long-run average total cost curve (LRATC) is actually
an "envelope" of many short-run average total cost (SRATC) curves. These
short-run average total cost curves are shown as the faint U-shaped dashed
curves drawn in gray. By visualizing what the short-run cost curves would
look like at any given output level, we can trace an envelope around them
to create the LRATC. From this we see that the long-run average total cost
curve is composed of all the short-run cost curves that the firm may choose
to deploy in the long run. In the long run the firm is free to choose any of its
short-run curves, so it always picks the output/cost combination that minimizes costs.

In the long run there are three distinct possibilities: economies of scale,
constant returns to scale, and diseconomies of scale. At first, each LRATC
exhibits economies of scale as a result of increased specialization, the utiliza-
tion of mass production techniques, bulk purchasing power, and increased

The Olive Garden or your local Italian restaurant?

automation. The real question in the long run is whether the cost curve will continue to decline, level off, or rise. In an industry with economies of scale at high output levels—for example, a water company—the cost curve continues to decline and the most efficient output level is always the largest output: the green line in Figure 8.3. In this situation we would expect that only one large firm will come to dominate the industry because larger firms have significant cost advantages. However, in an industry with constant returns to scale—for example, restaurants—the cost curve flattens out: the purple line. Once the curve becomes constant, firms of varying sizes can compete equally with one another because they have the same costs. Finally, in the case of diseconomies of scale—for example, traditional banks—bigger firms have higher costs: the orange line.

FIGURE 8.3

Costs in the Long Run

In the long run there are three distinct possibilities: the long-run average total cost curve can exhibit economies of scale (the green line), constant returns to scale (the purple line), or diseconomies of scale (the orange line).

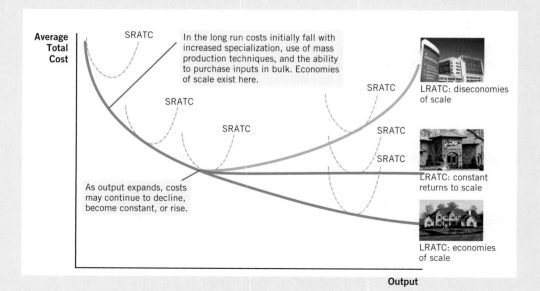

Cost in the Long Run

How Much Does It Cost to Raise a Child?

Raising a child is one of the most rewarding experiences in life, but it can be expensive. According to the U.S. Department of Agriculture, the cost for a middle-income, two-parent family to raise a child from birth to age 18 is more than $250,000—and that does not include college. To determine this number, the government looks at all of the related costs, such as food, clothing, medical care, and entertainment. In addition, the government apportions a share of the costs of the family home and vehicles to any children in the household. To put the cost of raising a child in perspective, the median home value in 2011 was $156,000. Talk about opportunity cost!

What if a family has more than one child? You wouldn't necessarily multiply the cost by two or three because there are economies of scale in raising more children. For example, things can be shared. When there are more kids in a household, the children are more likely to share a bedroom and wear hand-me-downs. Food can also be purchased in bulk without as much waste. As a result, families that have three or more children spend an average of 22% less on each child.

The cost of raising children also forces families to make trade-offs. In many households both parents must work or work longer hours. When one parent steps out of the workforce, the household loses a paycheck. While this may save in expenses associated with working, including expensive clothes, transportation, and childcare, there are also hidden costs. For example, the lack of workplace continuity lowers the stay-at-home parent's future earning power.

Daddy Day Care? Childcare expenses add up.

PRACTICE WHAT YOU KNOW

Marginal Cost: The True Cost of Entering Universal Studios

You and your family travel to Orlando for a week. While there you decide to visit Universal Studios. When you get there you notice that each family member can buy a day pass for $80 or a two-day pass for $90. Your parents are concerned about spending too much, so they decide to calculate

Is one day enough to do it all?

the average cost of a two-day pass to see if it is worth it. The average cost is $90 ÷ 2, or $45 per day. The math is correct, but something you learned in economics tells you that they are not thinking about this the correct way.

Question: What concept can you apply to make the decision more clear?

Answer: Tell them about marginal cost. The first day costs $80, but the marginal cost of going back to the park on the second day is only the extra cost per person, or $90 − $80, which equals $10. They still might not want to spend the extra money, but only spending an extra $10 for the second day makes it an extraordinary value. Someone who does not appreciate economics might think the second day costs an extra $45 since that is the average cost. The average cost is misleading, looking at marginal cost is the best way to think about how to weigh these two options.

Conclusion

Do larger firms have lower costs? Not always. When diseconomies of scale exist, costs will rise with output. This result contradicts the common misconception that bigger firms have lower costs. Simply put, sometimes a leaner firm with less overhead can beat its larger rivals on cost.

Costs are defined in a number of ways, but marginal cost plays the most crucial role in a firm's cost structure. By observing what happens to marginal cost you can understand changes in average cost and total cost. This is why economists place so much emphasis on marginal costs. Going forward, you will find that a solid grasp of marginal analysis will help you understand many of the most important concepts in microeconomics.

You now understand the cost, or supply side, of business decisions. However, to provide a complete picture of how firms operate, we still need to examine how markets work. Costs are only part of the story, and in the next chapter we will take a closer look at profits.

ANSWERING THE BIG QUESTIONS

1. How are profits and losses calculated?

* There are also two types of profits: economic profits and accounting profits. If a business has an economic profit, its revenues are larger than the combination of its explicit and implicit costs.

* Economists break cost into two components: explicit costs, which can be easily calculated, and implicit costs, which are hard to calculate. Since economic profits account for implicit costs, the economic profit is always less than the accounting profit.

2. How much should a firm produce?

✳ In order to maximize production, firms must effectively combine labor and capital in the right quantities.

✳ In any short-run production process there will come a point of diminishing marginal product where additional units of a variable input will no longer produce as much output as before. This occurs because each firm has separate fixed and variable costs.

✳ The marginal cost curve is the key variable in determining the firm's cost structure. The MC curve always leads the ATC and AVC curves.

3. What costs do firms consider in the short run and long run?

✳ With the exception of the AFC curve, which always declines, short-run cost curves are U-shaped. All variable costs initially decline due to increased specialization. At a certain point the advantages of continued specialization give way to diminishing marginal product and the MC, AVC, and ATC curves begin to rise.

✳ Long-run costs are a reflection of scale. Long-run costs can experience diseconomies, economies, or constant returns to scale depending on the industry.

CONCEPTS YOU SHOULD KNOW

Accounting profits (p. 234)
Average fixed costs (p. 242)
Average total costs (p. 243)
Average variable costs (p. 242)
Constant returns to scale (p. 249)
Diminishing marginal
   product (p. 239)
Diseconomies of scale (p. 249)
Economic profits (p. 234)

Economies of scale (p. 247)
Efficient scale (p. 245)
Explicit costs (p. 233)
Factors of production (p. 236)
Fixed costs (p. 242)
Implicit costs (p. 233)
Input (p. 236)
Losses (p. 232)
Marginal cost (p. 244)

Marginal product (p. 238)
Output (p. 236)
Production function (p. 237)
Profits (p. 232)
Scale (p. 247)
Variable costs (p. 242)
Total cost (p. 233)
Total revenue (p. 232)

QUESTIONS FOR REVIEW

1. What is the equation for the profit (or loss) of a firm?

2. Why is economic profit a better measure of profitability than accounting profit? Give an example.

3. What role does diminishing marginal product play in determining the ideal mix of labor and capital a firm should use?

4. Describe what happens to the total product of the firm when marginal product is increasing, decreasing, and negative.

5. Explain why marginal cost is the glue that connects average variable cost and average total cost.

6. Compare the short-run and long-run cost curves. In a few sentences explain their differences.

7. Name examples of industries that illustrate each of the following: economies of scale, constant returns to scale, and diseconomies of scale. Think creatively; do not use the textbook examples.

STUDY PROBLEMS

1. Go to www.lemonadegame.com. This free online game places you in the role of a lemonade seller. Nothing could be simpler, right? Not so fast, my friend! You still need to control costs and ensure you have the right ingredients on hand to be able to sell. You will need to manage your supply of lemons, sugar, ice, and cups. Plus you will also have to set a price and decide how many lemons and how much sugar and ice to put in each glass of lemonade you produce. This is not a trivial process. Play the game. Your challenge is to make $20 in profit over the first five days. (Your business starts with $20, so you need to have $40 in your account by the end of day 5 to meet the challenge. Are you up to it?)

2. The following table shows a short-run production function for laptop computers. Use the data to determine where diminishing product begins.

Input of labor	Total output of laptop computers
0	0
1	40
2	100
3	150
4	180
5	200
6	205
7	200
8	190

3. A pizza business has the cost structure described below. The firm's fixed costs are $25 per day. Calculate the firm's average fixed costs, average variable costs, average total costs, and marginal costs.

Output (pizzas per day)	Total Cost of Output
0	$25
10	75
20	115
30	150
40	175
50	190
60	205
70	225
80	250

✳ **4.** A firm is considering changing its plant size. It runs the numbers and calculates the average cost of production for various plant sizes below. If the firm is currently using plant size C, is the firm experiencing economies, diseconomies, or constant returns to scale?

Plant Size	Average Total Cost
A (smallest)	$10,000
B	9,500
C	9,000
D	8,800
E	8,800
F (largest)	8,900

5. True or false?

a. The AFC curve can never rise.

b. Diminishing marginal product is a long-run constraint that prevents lower costs.

c. The MC curve intersects the AVC and ATC curves at the minimum point along both curves.

d. Accounting profits are smaller than economic profits.

e. Total cost divided by output is equal to marginal cost.

6. Digital media distributed over the Internet often have marginal costs of zero. For instance, you can download music and movies instantly through many providers. Do these products exhibit economies, diseconomies, or constant returns to scale?

7. An airline has a marginal cost per passenger of $30 on a route from Boston to Detroit. At the same time the typical fare charged is $300. The planes that fly the route are usually full, yet the airline claims that it loses money on the route. How is this possible?

8. Many amusement parks offer two-day passes at dramatically discounted prices. If a one-day pass costs $40 but the two-day pass can be purchased for $50, what is the average cost for the two-day pass? What is the marginal cost of the two-day pass?

✳ **9.** Suppose that you own a yard care business. You have your own mower, flatbed truck, and other equipment. You are also the primary employee. Why might you have trouble calculating your profits? (**Hint:** think about the difference between accounting and economic profits.)

10. Use the information provided in the following table to fill in the blanks.

Output	Total fixed cost	Total variable cost	Total cost	Average fixed cost	Average variable cost	Average total cost	Marginal cost
1	$500	$200	___	___	___	___	___
2	___	___	$800	___	___	___	___
3	___	___	$875	___	___	___	___
4	___	___	$925	___	___	___	$25
5	___	___	___	$100	___	___	___
6	___	$450	___	___	___	___	___

SOLVED PROBLEMS

4. The key to solving this problem is recognizing the direction of change in the average total cost. If the firm were to switch to a smaller plant, like B, its average total cost would rise to $9,500. Since the smaller plant cost more, plant C is enjoying economies of scale. When we compare the average total cost of C ($9,000) to D ($8,800), it continues to fall. Since the average total cost is falling from B to D, we know that the firm is experiencing economies of scale.

9. When the owner of a yard care business calculates her costs for the mower, truck, and other expenses, she is computing her explicit costs. Subtracting the explicit costs from her total revenue will give her the accounting profit she has earned. However, she still does not know her economic profits because she has not determined her implicit costs. We know that she is the primary employee, so we also have to add in the opportunity cost of the time she invests in the business. We don't know exactly what she might have earned doing something else, but we can be sure it exists—this is her implicit cost. This is why she may have trouble computing her profits. She might show an accounting profit only to discover that what she thought she made was less than she could have made doing something else. If that is the case, her true economic profits are actually negative.

Firms in a Competitive Market

Firms control the price they charge.

Many people believe that firms set the prices for their products
with little concern for the consumer. However, this is incorrect. The

misconception that firms control the price they charge occurs
because many people believe that the firm is central to the
functioning of the market. However, market forces are much
stronger than individual firms. Under the right conditions, markets
produce high-quality goods at remarkably low prices, to the benefit of
both buyers and sellers. Competition drives the price down, which limits
the ability of the firm to charge as much as it would like.

In this chapter and the next four we will look in more detail at how
markets work, the profits they earn, and how market forces determine
the price that a firm can charge for its product or service. We begin our
sequence on market structure, or how individual markets are interconnected, by looking at the conditions necessary to create a competitive
market. Although few real markets achieve the ideal market structure
described in this chapter, this model provides a benchmark, or starting point, for understanding other market structures. In competitive
markets, firms are at the mercy of market forces which set the price that
is charged throughout the industry.

Our analysis of competitive markets will show that when competition
is widespread firms have little, or no, control over the price that they
can charge and they make little, or no, economic profit. Let's find out
why this is the case.

Individual vendors in flower markets face stiff competition.

THE BIG QUESTIONS

* How do competitive markets work?
* How do firms maximize profits?
* What does the supply curve look like in perfectly competitive markets?

How Do Competitive Markets Work?

Competitive markets exist when there are so many buyers and sellers that each has only a small impact on the market price and output. Recall that in Chapter 3 we used the example of the Pike Place Market, where each fish vendor sells similar products. Because each fish vendor is small relative to the whole market, no single firm can influence the market price. It doesn't matter where you buy salmon because it is the same or very similar at every fish stall. When buyers are willing to purchase a product anywhere, sellers have no control over the price they charge. These two characteristics—similar goods and many participants—create a highly competitive market where the price and quantity sold are determined by the market rather than any one firm.

In competitive markets, buyers can expect to find consistently low prices and a wide availability of the good that they want. Firms that produce goods in competitive markets are known as *price takers*. A **price taker** has no control over the price set by the market. It "takes," that is, accepts, the price determined from the overall supply and demand conditions that regulate the market.

A **price taker** has no control over the price it pays, or receives, in the market.

Competitive markets have another thing in common: new competitors can easily enter the market. If you want to open a copy shop, all you have to do is rent store space and several copy machines. There are no licensing or regulatory obstacles in your way. Likewise, there is very little to stop competitors from leaving the market. If you decide to close, you can lock the doors, return the equipment you rented, and move on to do something else. When barriers to entry into and exit from a marketplace are low, new firms are free to compete with existing businesses, which ensures that prices will be kept low.

Real-life examples of competitive markets usually fall short of perfection. Examples of markets that are almost perfectly competitive, shown in Table 9.1, include the stock market, farmers' markets, online ticket auctions, and currency trading. When markets are almost perfectly competitive, the benefit to society is still extremely large because markets (as we have seen in Chapter 6) create consumer and producer surplus.

TABLE 9.1

Almost Perfect Markets

Example	How It Works	Reality Check

Stock market

Many stocks trade millions of shares a day, and generally the buyers and sellers have access to real-time information about prices. Since most of the traders make up only a small share of the market, they have little ability to influence the market price.

Because of the volume of shares that they control, large institutional investors, like Pacific Investment Management Company (PIMCO), manage billions of dollars in funds. As a result, they are big enough to influence the market price.

Farmers' markets

In farmers' markets, sellers are free to come and go without having to pay a fee. Many buyers are also present. The gathering of numerous buyers and sellers of similar products will cause the market price for similar products to converge to a single price.

Many produce markets do not have enough sellers to achieve a perfectly competitive result. Without more vendors, those who sell better-quality or unique produce can often set their prices higher.

Online ticket auctions

The resale market for tickets to major sporting events and concerts involves many buyers and sellers. The prices for seats in identical sections end up converging quickly to a narrow range.

Some ticket companies and fans get special privileges that enable them to buy and sell blocks of tickets before others can enter the market.

Currency trading

An American dollar is the same everywhere, so currency traders are buying and selling a homogeneous good. Moreover, there are hundreds of thousands of traders around the globe engaged in currency buying and selling on any given day. Since all traders have very good real-time information, currency trades in different parts of the world converge toward the same price.

Currency markets are subject to intervention on the part of governments that might wish to strategically alter the prevailing price of their currency.

ECONOMICS IN THE REAL WORLD

Aalsmeer Flower Auction

The world's largest flower auction takes place in Aalsmeer, a small town in the Netherlands. Each week producers sell over 100 million flowers. Over one-third of all the flowers sold in the world pass through Aalsmeer. Since the Aalsmeer market is populated with thousands of buyers and sellers, it is one of the best examples of a competitive market you will ever find. The supply comes from approximately 6,000 growers worldwide. More than 2,000 buyers attend the auction to purchase flowers.

Aalsmeer uses a Dutch auction to determine the price for each crate of flowers sold. Most people think of an auction as a situation in which two or more individuals try to outbid each other. However, in Aalsmeer that process is reversed. As each crate of flowers goes on sale, the price on a huge board starts at 100 and then goes down until the lot is sold. This special kind of auction was invented here, and it is a very fast way of getting the highest price out of the buyer who wants the lot the most.

Aalsmeer flower auction

At Aalsmeer, individual buyers and sellers are small compared to the overall size of the market. In addition, the flowers from one seller are almost indistinguishable from those of the other sellers. This means that individual buyers and sellers have no control over the price set by the market. ✳

In the next section we will examine the profits that competitive firms make. Profits motivate firms to produce a product, so knowing how a business can make the most profit is central to understanding how competitive markets work.

How Do Firms Maximize Profits?

All firms, whether they are active in a competitive market or not, attempt to maximize profits. Making a profit requires that a firm have a thorough grasp of its costs and its revenues. In the previous chapter we learned about the cost structure of the firm. In this section we examine the firm's revenues. Combining the firm's revenues with its costs allows us to determine how much profit a firm makes.

Profits are the goal of every firm, but they don't always materialize. Sometimes firms experience losses instead of profits, so we also look at whether a firm should shut down or continue to operate in order to minimize its losses. Once we fully understand how the firm's decision-making process

Competitive Markets

The Simpsons

Episode: Mr. Plow
Homer buys a snow plow and goes into the snow removal business. After a few false starts Homer's business, Mr. Plow, becomes a huge success. Every snowy morning he looks out the window and comments about "white gold."

The episode illustrates each of the factors that go into making a competitive market. Businesses providing snow removal all offer the *same* service. Since there are many buyers (homeowners), and many businesses (the "plow people"), the market is competitive.

However, Homer's joy, profits, and notoriety are short-lived. His friend, Barney, buys a bigger plow and joins the ranks of the "plow people." Barney's *entry* into the business shows how easy it is for competitors to enter the market. Homer, who has begun to get lazy and rest on his success, wakes up late

Homer's great idea!

one snowy morning to find all the driveways in the neighborhood already plowed. A nasty battle ensues over customers.

When firms can easily enter the market, any higher-than-usual profits that a firm enjoys in the short run will be dissipated in the long run due to increased competition. As a result, the scene shows an industry that is not just competitive: it is perfectly competitive.

works, we will be able to better understand how the entire market functions. To make this process easier, throughout this section we refer to Mr. Plow to examine the choices every business must make. We'll look at the price Mr. Plow charges and how many driveways he clears, and then we will compare his revenues to his costs in order to determine whether he is maximizing his profit.

The Profit-Maximizing Rule

Let's imagine how much revenue Mr. Plow will make if he charges $10 for each driveway he clears. Table 9.2 shows how much profit he might make if he clears up to 10 driveways. As we learned in Chapter 8, profits (column 4) are determined by taking the total revenue (column 2) minus the total cost (column 3). Mr. Plow's profits start out at −$25 because even if he does not clear any driveways, he incurs a fixed cost for the snowplow. In order to recover the fixed costs, he needs to generate revenue by clearing driveways. As Mr. Plow clears more driveways the losses shown in column 4 gradually contract; he begins to earn a profit by the time he plows 6 driveways.

What does Table 9.2 tell us about Mr. Plow's business? Column 4 shows the profits of Mr. Plow at various output (Q) levels. Profits reach a maximum of $10 in a range of 7–8 driveways. From looking at this table, you might suppose

PRACTICE WHAT YOU KNOW

Price Takers: Mall Food Courts

Are the restaurants in a food court price takers?

Your instructor asks you to find an example of a competitive market nearby. Your friend suggests that you visit the food court at a nearby mall.

Question: Do the restaurants in a food court meet the definition of a price taker?

Answer: Most food courts contain a lot of competition. Customers can choose from burgers, sandwiches, salads, pizza, and much more. Everywhere you turn there is another place to eat and the prices at each place are comparable. Is this enough to make each restaurant a price taker? Not quite. Each restaurant has some market power because it serves different food. This allows the more popular places to charge somewhat more.

While the restaurants in the court are not price takers, the drinks (both fountain drinks and bottled water) that they sell are essentially the same. Any customer who is only interested in getting something to drink has a highly competitive market to choose from.

that the firm can make a production decision based on the data in the profit column. However, firms don't work this way. The total profit (or loss) is typically determined after the fact. For example, Homer may have to fill up with gas at the end of the day, buy new tires for his plow, or purchase liability insur-

TABLE 9.2

Calculating Profit

(1)	(2)	(3)	(4)	(5)	(6)	(7)
Quantity (Q of driveways cleared)	Total Revenue	Total Cost	Profit	Marginal Revenue	Marginal Cost	Change in Profit
Abbreviation: TR	TC		TP	MR	MC	Δ TP
Formula:			TR − TC	Δ TR	Δ TC	MR − MC
0	$0	$25	−$25			
				$10	$9	$1
1	10	34	−24			
				10	7	3
2	20	41	−21			
				10	5	5
3	30	46	−16			
				10	3	7
4	40	49	−9			
				10	2	8
5	50	51	−1			
				10	3	7
6	60	54	6			
				10	6	4
7	70	60	10			
				10 =	**10**	0
8	80	70	10			
				10	25	−15
9	90	95	−5			
				10	50	−40
10	100	145	−45			

ance. His accountant will take his receipts and deduct each of his expenses to determine his profits. All of this takes time. An accurate understanding of Homer's profits may take until the end of the quarter, or even the year, in order to fully account for all the irregular expenses associated with running a business. This means that the information found in the profit column is not available until long after the business decisions have been made. So, in day-to-day operations, the firm needs another way to make production decisions.

The key to determining Mr. Plow's profits comes from understanding the relationship between marginal revenue (column 5) and marginal cost (column 6). The marginal revenue is the change (Δ) in total revenue when the firm produces additional units. So, looking down column 5, we see that for every driveway Mr. Plow clears, he makes $10 in extra revenue. The marginal cost (column 6) is the change (Δ) in total cost when the firm produces additional units. Column 7 calculates the difference between the marginal revenue (column 5) and marginal cost (column 6).

In Chapter 8 we saw that to understand cost structure, a firm focuses on marginal cost. The same is true on the revenue side. To make a good decision on the level of investment, Mr. Plow must use marginal analysis. Looking at column 7, we see that where total profits equal $10, the change in profits, MR − MC, is equal to $0. At output levels below 7, MR − MC is positive, as indicated by the numbers in green. Expanding output to 7 driveways adds to profits. But as Mr. Plow services more driveways, the marginal cost rises dramatically. For instance, Mr. Plow may have to seek driveways that are farther away and thus incur higher transportation costs for those additional customers. Whatever the cause, increased marginal costs (column 6) eventually overtake the constant marginal revenues (column 5).

Recall that we began our discussion by saying that a firm can't wait for the yearly, or even quarterly, profit statements to make production decisions. By examining the marginal impact, shown in column 7, a firm is able to make good day-to-day operational decisions. This means that Mr. Plow has to decide whether or not to clear more driveways. For instance, if he is plowing 4 driveways he may decide to work a little harder the next time it snows and plow 1 more. At 5 driveways his profits increase by $8. Since he enjoys making this extra money, he could expand again from 5 to 6 driveways.

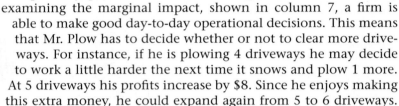

This time he finds that he makes an extra $7. From 6 to 7 driveways he earns $4 more. However, when Mr. Plow expands from 7 to 8 driveways, he discovers that he does not earn any additional profits, and at 9 driveways he loses $15. This would cause him to scale back his efforts to a more profitable level of output.

If you already own a truck, starting your own snow plow business is inexpensive.

Profit maximization occurs when MR = MC.

Marginal thinking helps Mr. Plow discover the production level at which his profits are maximized. **Profit maximization** occurs when a firm expands output until marginal revenue is equal to marginal cost, MR = MC. (This is the point at which 10 = 10 in columns 5 and 6.) The profit-maximizing rule may seem counterintuitive, since at MR = MC—where marginal revenue is equal to the extra cost of production—there is no additional profit. However, according to the MR = MC rule, production should stop at the point where profit opportunities no longer exist. Suppose that Mr. Plow chooses a point where MR > MC. This means that the cost of producing additional units adds more to revenue than to costs, so production should continue. On the other hand, if MR < MC, the cost of producing additional units is more than the additional revenue those units bring in. At that point, production is not profitable. The point at which MR = MC is the exact level of production where no further profitable opportunities exist and losses have not yet occurred. This is the optimal point to stop production. In the case of Mr. Plow, he should stop adding new driveways once he reaches 8.

Deciding How Much to Produce in a Competitive Market

We have observed that a firm in a highly competitive market is a price taker; it has no control over the price set by the market. Since the snow removal companies provide the same service, they must charge the price that is determined from the overall supply and demand conditions that regulate the market.

To help you understand these relationships, we can look at them visually. In Figure 9.1 we use the MR and MC data from Table 9.2 to illustrate the profit calculation. For reference, we also include the average cost curves from Chapter 8. Recall that the marginal cost curve (shown in gold) always crosses the average total cost (ATC) curve and the average variable cost curve at their lowest point. Figure 9.1 highlights the relationship between the marginal cost curve and marginal revenue curve. Since the price Mr. Plow charges is constant at $10, marginal revenue is horizontal. Unlike MR, MC at first decreases and then rises due to diminishing marginal product. Therefore, the firm wishes to expand production as long as MR is greater than MC, and it will stop production at the quantity where MR = MC = $10. When q = 8, MR = MC, and profits are maximized. At quantities beyond 8, the MC curve is above the MR curve; marginal cost is higher than marginal revenue and the firm's profits will fall.

We can use the profit-maximizing rule, MR = MC, to identify the most profitable output in a two-step process:

1. Locate the point at which the firm will maximize its profits: MR = MC.
2. Look for the profit-maximizing output: move down the vertical dashed line to the x-axis at point q. Any quantity greater than, or less than, q would result in lower profits.

Once we know the profit-maximizing quantity, we can determine the average cost of producing q units. From q move up along the dashed line until it intersects with the ATC curve. From that point move horizontally until you come to the y-axis. This tells us the average cost of making 8 units. Since the total cost in Table 9.2 is 70 when 8 driveways are plowed, dividing 70 by 8 gives us 8.75 for the average total cost. We can calculate Mr. Plow's profit rectangle from the figure by calculating the profit as follows:

$$\text{Profit} = (\text{Price} - \text{ATC [along the dashed line at quantity q])} \times q \quad (9.1)$$

This gives us $(10 - 8.75) \times 8 = \$10$, which is the profit we see in Table 9.2. Since the MR is the price, and the price is higher than the average total cost,

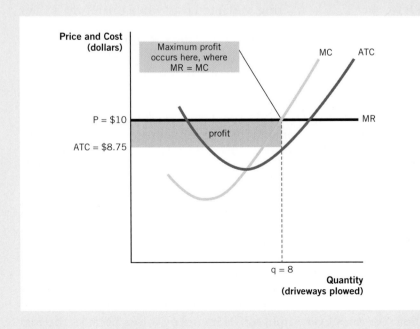

FIGURE 9.1

Profit Maximization

Mr. Plow uses the profit-maximizing rule to locate the point where MR = MC. This determines the ideal output level, q. The firm takes the price from the market; this is shown as the horizontal MR curve at a price = $10. Since the price charged is higher than the average cost curve along the dashed line at quantity q, the firm makes the economic profit shown in green.

the firm makes the profit shown in the green rectangle, which is the visual representation of the profit the firm earns.

The Firm in the Short Run

Deciding how much to produce in order to maximize profits is the goal of every business. However, there are times when it is not possible to make a profit. When revenue is insufficient to cover cost, the firm suffers a loss. The firm must decide whether to operate or temporarily shut down. Successful businesses make this decision all the time. For example, retail stores often close by 9 p.m. because operating overnight would not generate enough revenue to cover the costs of remaining open.

The Ice Cream Float, a cool idea on a hot day at the lake.

Or consider the Ice Cream Float, which crisscrosses Smith Mountain Lake in Virginia during the summer months. You can hear the music announcing its arrival at the public beach from over a mile away. By the time the float arrives, there is usually a long line of eager customers. This is a very profitable business on hot and sunny summer days. However, during the late spring and early fall the float operates on weekends only. Eventually colder weather forces the business to shut down until the crowds return the following season. This shut-down decision is a short-run calculation. If the float were to operate during the winter it would need to pay for employees and fuel. Incurring variable costs when there are so few customers would result in greater total costs than simply dry-docking the boat. When the float is dry-docked over the winter, only the fixed cost of storing the boat remains.

Fortunately there is a simple, intuitive rule that a firm can use to decide whether to operate or shut down: if the firm would lose less by shutting down than by staying open, it should shut down. Recall that costs are broken into two parts—fixed and variable. Fixed costs must be paid whether the business is open or not. Since variable costs are only incurred when the business is open, if it can make enough to cover its variable costs—for example, employee wages and the cost of the electricity needed to run the lighting—it will choose to remain open. Once the variable costs are covered, any extra money goes toward paying the fixed costs.

A business should operate if it can cover its variable costs, and it should shut down if it cannot. Figure 9.2 illustrates the decision using cost curves. As long as the MR curve of the firm is greater than the minimum point on the AVC curve—the blue- and yellow-shaded areas—the firm will choose to operate. Recalling our example of the Ice Cream Float, you can think of the blue-shaded area as the months during the year when the business makes a profit and the yellow-shaded area as the times during the spring and fall when the float operates even though it is incurring a loss because the loss that it experiences would be less than if it shut down. Finally, if the MR curve falls below the AVC curve—the orange-shaded area—the firm should shut down.

To make the shut-down decision more concrete, imagine that the Ice Cream Float's minimum ATC is $2.50 and its minimum AVC is $2.00. During the summer, when many customers are lined up on the dock waiting for it to arrive, it can charge a price higher than $2.50 and earn a substantial profit. However, as the weather cools fewer people want ice cream. The Ice Cream Float still has to crisscross the lake in order to make sales, burning expensive gasoline and paying employees to operate the float. If the Ice Cream Float is to keep its revenues high it needs customers, but cooler weather suppresses demand. If the Ice Cream Float charges $2.25 in the fall, it can make enough to cover its average variable costs of $2.00, but not enough to cover its average total costs of $2.50. Nevertheless, it will operate because it makes enough in the yellow region to pay part of its fixed cost. Finally, it reaches a point where the price drops below $2.00. Now it is no longer able to cover its average variable costs. At this point it shuts down for the winter. It does this since operating when MR is very low causes the firm to incur a larger loss.

Table 9.3 summarizes the conditions for making a profit, operating to minimize loss, and shutting down in the short run.

FIGURE 9.2

When to Operate and When to Shut Down

If the MR curve is above the minimum point on the ATC curve, the Ice Cream Float will make a profit (shown in blue). If the MR curve is below the minimum point on the ATC curve, $2.50, but above the minimum point on the AVC curve, the float will operate at a loss (shown in yellow). If the MR curve is below the minimum point on the AVC curve, $2.00, the float will temporarily shut down (shown in orange).

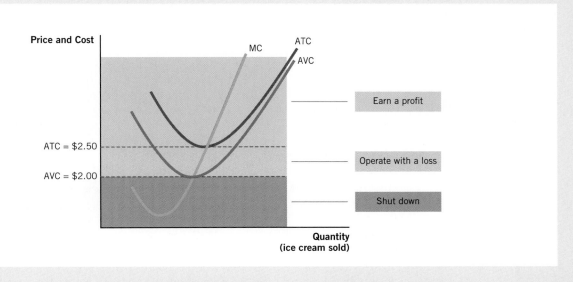

TABLE 9.3		
Profit and Loss in the Short Run		
Condition	In Words	Outcome
P > ATC	The price is greater than the average total cost of production.	The firm makes a profit.
ATC > P > AVC	The average total cost of production is greater than the price the firm charges, but the price is greater than the average variable cost of production.	The firm will operate to minimize loss.
AVC > P	The price is less than the average variable cost of production.	The firm will temporarily shut down.

The Firm's Short-Run Supply Curve

Cost curves provide a detailed picture of the firm's willingness to supply a good or service. We have seen when the MR curve is below the minimum point on the AVC curve, the firm shuts down and production, or output, falls to zero. Another way of stating this is that when revenues are too low, no supply is produced. For example, the Ice Cream Float is dry-docked, so the supply curve does not exist. However, when the firm is operating, it bases its output decisions on the marginal cost. Recall that the firm uses the profit-maximizing rule, or MR = MC, to determine how much to produce. The marginal cost curve is therefore the firm's short-run supply curve as long as the firm is operating.

FIGURE 9.3

The Firm's Short-Run Supply Curve

The supply curve and marginal cost curve are equivalent when the price is above the minimum point on the average variable cost curve. Below that point, the firm will shut down and no supply exists.

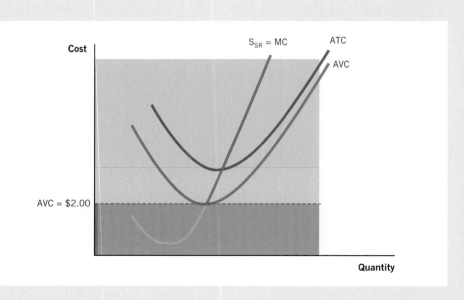

Figure 9.3 shows the Ice Cream Float's short-run supply curve. In the short run diminishing marginal product causes the firm's costs to rise as the quantity produced increases. This is reflected in the shape of the firm's short-run supply curve, shown in red. The supply curve is upward-sloping above the minimum point on the AVC curve. Below the minimum point on the AVC curve, the short-run supply curve becomes vertical at a quantity of zero, indicating that a willingness to supply the good does not exist below a price of $2.00. At prices above $2.00, the firm will offer more for sale as the price increases.

The Firm's Long-Run Supply Curve

In the long run, a firm's output decision is directly tied to profits. Since the firm is flexible in the long run, all costs are variable. As a result, the firm's long-run supply curve exists only when the firm expects to cover its total costs of production, because otherwise the firm would go out of business. Returning to the Ice Cream Float, recall that the boat shuts down over the winter instead of going out of business because demand is low but is expected to return. If for some reason the crowds do not come back, the float would go out of business. Turning to Figure 9.4, we see that at any point below the minimum point, $2.50 on the ATC curve, the float will experience a loss. Since, in the long run, firms are free to enter or exit the market, no firm will willingly produce in the market if the price is less than average total cost (P < ATC). As a result, no supply exists below $2.50. However, if price is greater than cost (P > ATC), the float expects to make a profit and so it will continue to produce.

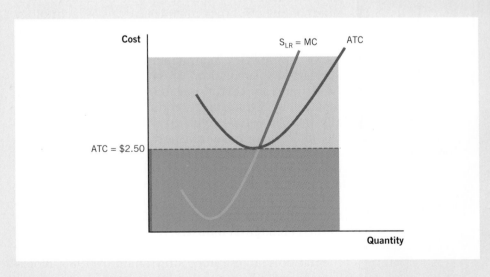

FIGURE 9.4

The Firm's Long-Run Supply Curve

The long-run supply curve and marginal cost curves are equivalent when the price is above the minimum point on the average total cost curve. Below that point, the firm will shut down and no supply exists.

TABLE 9.4		
The Long-Run Shut-Down Criteria		
Condition	**In Words**	**Outcome**
P > ATC	The price is greater than the average total cost of production.	The firm makes a profit.
P < ATC	The price is less than the average total cost of production.	The firm should shut down.

The firm's long-run supply curve, shown in red, is upward sloping above the minimum point on the ATC curve, which is denoted by ATC on the y-axis. The supply curve becomes vertical at a quantity of zero, indicating that a willingness to supply the good does not exist below a price of $2.50. In the long run, a firm that expects price to exceed ATC will continue to operate, since the conditions for making a profit seem favorable. On the other hand, a firm that does not expect price to exceed ATC should cut its losses and exit the industry. Table 9.4 outlines the long-run decision criteria.

BLOCKBUSTER AND THE DYNAMIC NATURE OF CHANGE

Blockbuster's best days are behind them.

What happens if your customers do not return? What if you simply had a bad idea to begin with and the customers never arrived in the first place? When the long-run profit outlook is bleak, the firm is better off shutting down. This is a normal part of the ebb and flow of business. For example, once there were thousands of buggy whip companies. Today, as technology has improved and we no longer rely on horse-drawn carriages, few buggy whip makers remain. However, many companies manufacture automobile parts. Similarly, a succession of technological advances have transformed the music industry. Records were replaced by 8-track tapes, and then cassettes. Eventually the CD will be replaced with better technology. Digital devices make transporting and playing music easy today. However, there was a time when innovation meant playing music on the original Sony Walkman. What was cool in the early 1980s is antiquated today. Any business engaged in distributing music has had to adapt or close. Similar changes are taking place in the video rental industry. Blockbuster was founded in 1982 and experienced explosive growth, becoming the nation's largest video store chain by 1988. Blockbuster's growth was fueled by its large selection and use of a computerized tracking system that made the checkout process faster than the competing video stores. However, by the early 2000s Blockbuster faced stiff competition from online providers like Netflix and in-store dispensers like Redbox. Today, the chain has one-quarter the number of employees it once had and its future is very uncertain.

In addition to changes in technology, other factors such as downturns in the economy, changes in tastes, demographic factors, and migration can all force businesses to close. These examples remind us that the long-run decision to go out of business has nothing to with the short-term profit outlook. ✳

So far we have examined the firm's decision-making process in the short run in the context of revenues versus costs. This allows us to determine the profits each firm makes. We pause to consider *sunk costs*, a special type of cost that all firms, in every industry, must consider when making decisions.

Sunk Costs

Costs that have been incurred as a result of past decisions are known as **sunk costs**. The decision to build a new sports stadium is a good application of the principle of sunk costs. Many professional stadiums have been built in the past few years, even though the stadiums they replaced were built to last much longer. For example, Three Rivers Stadium in Pittsburgh and Veterans Stadium in Philadelphia were built in the early 1970s. They were constructed as multi-use facilities for both football and baseball, each with an expected

Sunk costs
are unrecoverable costs that have been incurred as a result of a past decision.

lifespan of 60 or more years. However, in the early 2000s both were replaced. Each city built a new stadium with features such as luxury boxes and better seats that generate more revenue than the old stadiums did. The additional revenue makes the new stadiums financially attractive even though the old stadiums were still structurally sound. Demolishing a structure that is still in good working order may sound like a waste, but it can be good economics. When the extra benefit of a new stadium is large enough to pay for the cost of imploding the old stadium and constructing a new one, a city will

Stadium implosions are one way to avoid the sunk cost fallacy.

do just that. In fact, since both cities draw significantly more paying spectators with the new stadiums, the decision to replace the older stadiums has made the citizens in Pittsburgh and Philadelphia better off.

Continuing to use an out-of-date facility has an opportunity cost. Thinkers who get trapped in the sunk-cost fallacy might point to the benefits of getting maximum use out of what was built. But good economists learn to ignore sunk costs and focus on marginal value. They compare marginal benefits and marginal costs. If a new stadium, and the revenue it brings in, will create more value than the old stadium, the decision should be made to tear the old one down.

PRACTICE WHAT YOU KNOW

The Profit-Maximizing Rule: Show Me the Money!

Here is a question that often confuses students.

Question: At what point does a firm maximize profits?

(a) where the profit per unit is greatest

(b) where total revenue is maximized

(c) where the total revenue is equal to the total cost

(d) where marginal revenue equals marginal cost

Answer: Each of these answers sounds plausible, so the key is to think about each one in a concrete way. To help do that we will refer back to the Mr. Plow data in Table 9.2.

What is the rule for making the most profit?

(a) Incorrect. Making a large profit per unit sounds great. However, if the firm stops production when the profit per unit is the greatest—$8 in column 7—it will fail to realize the additional profits—$7 and $4 in column 7—that come from continuing to produce until MR = MC.

(b) Incorrect. Recall that total revenue is only half of the profit function, Profit = TR − TC. No matter how much revenue a business brings in, if total costs are more, the firm will experience a loss. Therefore, the firm wishes to maximize profits, not revenue. For example, looking at column 2, we see that at 10 driveways, Mr. Plow earns total revenues of $100. But column 3 tells us that the total cost of plowing 10 driveways is $145. With a total profit of −$45, this level of output would not be a good idea.

(c) Incorrect. If total revenue and total costs are equal, the firm makes no profits.

(d) Correct. Answers (a), (b), and (c) all sound plausible. But a firm maximizes profits where MR = MC, since at this point all profitable opportunities are exhausted. If Mr. Plow clears 7 or 8 driveways, his profit is $10. If he clears 9 driveways his profits fall from $10 to −$5 since the marginal cost of clearing that ninth driveway, $25, is greater than the marginal revenue he earns of $10.

What Does the Supply Curve Look Like in Perfectly Competitive Markets?

We have seen that a firm's willingness to supply a good depends on whether the firm is making a short-run or long-run decision. In the short run, a firm may choose to operate at a loss in order to recover a portion of its fixed costs.

In the long run there are no fixed costs, so a firm is willing to operate only if it expects the price it charges to cover total costs.

However, the supply curve for a single firm represents only a small part of the overall supply of a good provided in a competitive market. We will now turn to market supply and develop the short-run and long-run market supply curves.

The Short-Run Market Supply Curve

A competitive market consists of a large number of identical sellers. Since an individual firm's supply curve is equal to its marginal cost curve, if we add together all of the individual firm supply curves in a market we arrive at the short-run market supply curve. Figure 9.5 shows the short-run market supply curve in a two-firm model consisting of Mr. Plow and the Plow King. At a price of $10, Mr. Plow is willing to clear 8 driveways and the Plow King is willing to clear 20 driveways. When you horizontally sum the output of the two firms, you get a total market supply of 28 driveways, seen in the third graph.

The Long-Run Market Supply Curve

Recall that a competitive market is one in which a large number of buyers seek a product that many sellers produce. Competitive markets are also characterized by easy entry and exit. Existing firms and entrepreneurs decide whether to enter and exit a market based on incentives. When existing firms are enjoying profits, there is an incentive for firms to produce more and for entrepreneurs to enter the market. This leads to an increase in the quantity of the good supplied. Likewise, when existing firms are experiencing losses, there is an incentive for firms to exit the market and the quantity supplied decreases. Entry and exit have the combined effect of regulating how much

FIGURE 9.5

Short-Run Market Supply

The market supply is determined by summing the individual supply of each firm in the market. Although we have only shown this process for two firms, Mr. Plow and Plow King, the process extends to any number of firms that exist in a market.

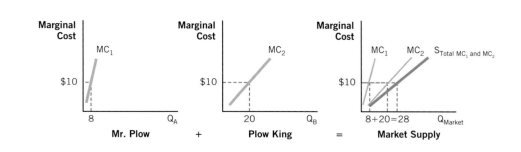

profit a firm can hope to make in the long run. As long as profits exist, the quantity supplied will increase and the price will be driven down. When losses exist, the quantity supplied will decrease and the price will rise. So both profits and losses signal a need for an adjustment in market supply. Therefore, profits and losses act as *signals* for resources to enter or leave an industry. **Signals** convey information about the profitability of various markets.

The only time an adjustment does not take place is when participants in the market make zero economic profit—this is the long-run equilibrium. At that point existing firms and entrepreneurs are not inclined to enter or exit the market; the adjustment process that takes place through price changes ends.

The benefit of a competitive market is that profits guide existing firms and entrepreneurs to produce more goods and services that society values. Losses serve the same valuable function by encouraging firms to exit and move elsewhere. Without profits and losses acting as signals for firms to enter or exit the market, resources will be misallocated and there will be surpluses and shortages of goods.

Figure 9.6 captures how the market supply is determined through entry and exit. The profit-maximizing point of the individual firm in panel (a), MR = MC, is located at the minimum point on the ATC curve. The price (P) that existing firms receive is just enough to cover costs (C), so profits are zero. As a result, new firms have no incentive to enter the market and existing

Signals
convey information about the profitability of various markets.

Incentives Matter

FIGURE 9.6

The Market Supply Curve and Entry and Exit

Entry into the market and exit from it force the long-run price to be equal to the minimum point on the average total cost curve. At all prices above P, firms will earn a profit (the blue-shaded area) and at all prices below P, firms will experience a loss (the orange-shaded area). This means the long-run supply curve must be horizontal at price P. If the price was any higher or lower firms would enter or exit the market, and the market could not be in a long-run equilibrium.

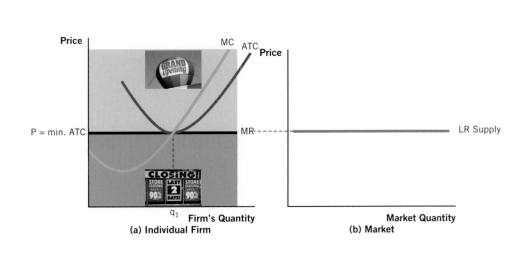

firms have no reason to leave. At all prices above P firms will earn a profit (the blue-shaded area), and at all prices below P firms will experience a loss (the orange-shaded area). This picture is consistent for all markets with free entry and exit; zero economic profit occurs at only one price and that price is the lowest point of the ATC curve.

At this price the supply curve in panel (b) must be a horizontal line at P. If the price was any higher, firms would enter, supply would increase, and this would force the price back down to P. If the price was any lower, firms would exit, supply would decrease, and this would force the price up to P. Since we know that these adjustments will have time to take place in the long run, the long-run supply curve must also be equal to P in order to satisfy the demand that exists at this price.

A Reminder About Economic Profits

Now that you have learned how perfect competition affects business profits in the long run, you may not think that it is a desirable environment for businesses seeking to earn profits. After all, if a firm cannot expect to make an economic profit in the long run, why bother? It's easy to forget the distinction between accounting profits and economic profits. Firms enter a market when they expect to be reasonably compensated for their investment. Firms leave the market when the investment does not yield a satisfactory result. Economic profits are determined by deducting the explicit and implicit costs. Therefore, firms are willing to stay in perfectly competitive markets in the long run when they are breaking even because they are being reasonably compensated for the explicit expenses they have incurred and also for the implicit expenses—like the opportunity costs of other business ventures—that they would expect to make elsewhere.

For example, if Mr. Plow has the following explicit and implicit costs shown in Table 9.5, we can see the distinction between accounting and economic profits more clearly. Mr. Plow has revenues of $25,000 during the year.

If Mr. Plow calls his accountant and asks how much he earned during the year, the accountant adds up all of his explicit costs and subtracts them from his revenues. The account reports back that he earned $25,000 − $10,000, or

TABLE 9.5

Economic Profit and the Entry or Exit Decision

Explicit Costs per Year	
Payment on the loan on his snow plow	$7,000
Gasoline	2,000
Miscellaneous equipment (shovels, salt)	1,000
Implicit Costs	
Forgone salary	$10,000
Opportunity cost of the $50,000 he invested in the snow plow	5,000
Total Cost	$25,000

Photo to come

$15,000 in profits. $15,000 in profit would sound good to a lot of firms, so we would expect many new entrants in the plowing business. Not so fast! We have not accounted for the implicit costs, the money Mr. Plow could have earned working another job instead of plowing, and also the money he invested in the plow that could have been put to work elsewhere. If we add in the explicit costs, we find the economic profit, $25,000 − $10,000 − $15,000 = $0. Zero profit sounds unappealing, but it is not. It means that Mr. Plow covered his forgone salary and also his next-best investment alternative. If you could not make any more money doing something else with your time or your investments, you are in the right place. So Mr. Plow is content to keep on plowing, while others, outside the industry, do not see any profit from entering the industry.

How the Market Adjusts in the Long Run: An Example

We have seen that profits and losses may exist in the short run; in the long run, the best the competitive firm can do is earn zero economic profits. This section looks in more detail at the adjustment process that leads to long-run equilibrium. We begin with the market in long-run equilibrium, shown in Figure 9.7. Panel (a) represents an individual firm operating at the minimum point on its ATC curve. In long-run equilibrium, all firms are operating as efficiently as possible. Since the price is equal to the average cost of production, economic profits for the firm are zero. In panel (b) the SR supply curve and the demand curve intersect along the LR supply curve, so the market is also in equilibrium. If, for instance, the SR supply curve and demand curve happened to intersect above the LR supply curve, the price would be higher than the minimum point on the ATC curve. This would lead to short-run profits and indicate that the market was not in long-run equilibrium. The same is true if the SR supply curve and demand curve happened to intersect below the LR supply curve, since the price would be lower than the minimum point on the ATC curve. This would lead to short-run shortages, thus causing the price to rise, and then once again the market would be in long-run equilibrium.

Entry and Exit

I Love Lucy

This episode finds Ricky Ricardo disillusioned with show business. After some conversation, Ricky and Fred Mertz decide to go into business together and start a diner. Fred and Ethel Mertz have the experience to run the diner, and Ricky plans to use his name and star power to help get the word out about the restaurant, which they name A Little Bit of Cuba.

If you have seen any of the *I Love Lucy* series, you already know that the business venture is destined to fail. Sure enough, the Mertzes get tired of doing all of the hard work—cooking and serving the customers—while Ricky and Lucy Ricardo meet and greet the guests. Things quickly deteriorate and the two couples decide to part ways. The only problem is that they are both part owners, and neither can afford to buy out the other. So they decide to split the diner in half right down the middle!

The result is absurd and hilarious. On one side, guests go to A Little Bit of Cuba. On the other side, the Mertzes set up Big Hunk of America. Since both restaurants use the same facilities and sell the same food, the only way they can differentiate themselves is by lowering the price that they charge. This leads to a hamburger price war to attract customers:

Ethel Mertz: "Three!"
Lucy Ricardo: "Two!"
Ethel Mertz: "One-cent hamburgers."
Fred Mertz: "Ethel, are you out of your mind?" *[Even in the 1950s a penny was not enough to cover the marginal cost of making a hamburger.]*
Ethel Mertz: "Well I thought this could get 'em."
Fred Mertz: "One-cent hamburgers?"

After the exchange, Lucy whispers in a customer's ear and gives him a dollar. He then proceeds

to Big Hunk of America and says, "I'd like 100 hamburgers!"

Fred Mertz replies, "We're all out of hamburgers."

How do the falling prices described here affect the ability of the firms in the market to make a profit?

The exchange is a useful way of visualizing how perfectly competitive markets work. Competition forces the price down, but the process of entry and exit takes time and it is messy. The Ricardos and Mertzes can't make a living selling one-cent hamburgers—one cent is below their marginal cost—so one of the couples will end up exiting. At that point the remaining couple would be able to charge more. If they end up making a profit, that profit will encourage entrepreneurs to enter the business. As the supply of hamburgers expands, the price that can be charged is driven back down. Since we live in a dynamic world, prices are always moving toward the long-run equilibrium.

Now suppose that demand declines, as shown in Figure 9.8. The market demand curve shifts from D_1 to D_2. When demand falls, the equilibrium point moves to point B. The price drops to P_2 and the market output drops to Q_2. The firms in this industry take their price from the market, so the new marginal revenue curve is MR_2 at P_2 in panel (a). Since the firm maximizes profits where $MR_2 = MC$, the firm will produce an output of q_2. When the output is q_2 the firm's costs, C_2, are higher than the price it charges, P_2, so it experiences a loss equal to the orange-shaded area in panel (a). In addition, since the firm's output is lower, it is no longer producing at the minimum point on its ATC curve, so the firm is not as efficient as before.

Firms in a perfectly competitive market can exit the industry easily. Some firms will do so in order to avoid further losses. Figure 9.9 shows that as firms exit, the market supply contracts from S_1 to S_2 and the market equilibrium moves to point C. At point C, the price rises back to P_1. Market output drops to Q3 and the price returns to P_1. The firms that remain in the market no longer experience a short-run loss, since MR_2 returns to MR_1, and costs fall from C_2 to C_1. The end result is that the firm is once again efficient and economic profits return to zero.

FIGURE 9.7

The Market in Equilibrium Before a Decrease in Demand

When a market is in long-run equilibrium, the SR supply curve and SR demand curve intersect along the LR supply curve. When this occurs the price that the firm charges is equal to the minimum point along the average total cost curve. This means that the existing firms in the market earn zero economic profits and there is no incentive for firms to enter or exit the market.

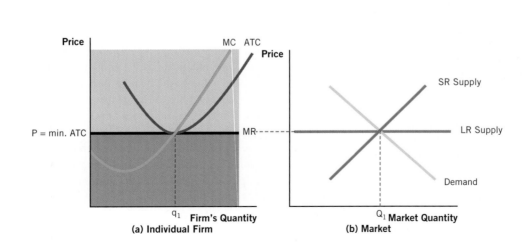

For example, suppose that there is a decline in demand for mangoes due to a false rumor that links the fruit to a salmonella outbreak. The decline in demand causes the price of mangoes to fall. As a consequence, mango producers experience negative economic profits—as seen in Figure 9.8. In response to the negative profits, some mango growers will exit the industry, the mango trees will be sold for firewood, and the land converted to other uses. With fewer mangoes being produced, the supply will contract. Eventually, the smaller supply of mangoes will cause the price of mangoes to rise until a new long-run equilibrium is reached at a much lower level of output, as shown in Figure 9.9.

More on the Long-Run Supply Curve

To keep the previous example as simple as possible, we assumed that the long-run supply curve was horizontal. This is not always the case. There are two reasons why the long-run supply curve may slope upward. First, some resources needed to produce the product may only be available in limited supplies. As firms try to expand production they must bid to acquire those resources and

What does it take to produce more mangoes?

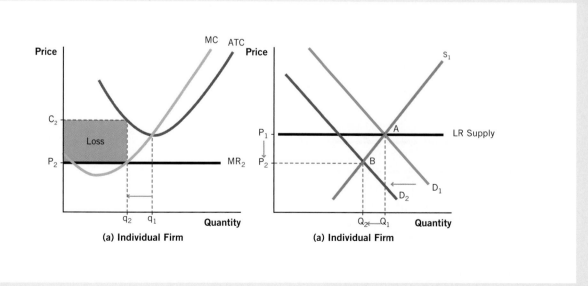

FIGURE 9.8

The Short-Run Adjustment to a Decrease in Demand
A decrease in demand causes the price to fall in the market. Since the firm is a price taker, the price it can charge falls to P_2. The intersection of MR_2 and MC occurs at q_2. At this output level, the firm incurs the short-run loss shown in (a).

this causes the average total cost curve to rise. For instance, a mango grower who wants to plant more trees must acquire more suitable land. Since mangoes grow in tropical areas with warm, wet summers, not all land is perfectly adaptable for growing them. The limited supply of land will cause the price of producing mangoes to rise and this will cause the supply curve to be positively sloped. A second reason the long-run supply curve may be upward sloped is the opportunity cost of the labor used in producing the good. If you want to produce more mangoes you will need more workers to pick the fruit. Hiring extra workers will mean finding people who are both willing and capable. Some workers are better than others at picking mangoes and some workers have higher opportunity costs. As the firm attempts to expand production, it must increase the wage it pays to attract additional help or accept new workers who are not quite as capable. Either way you slice it, this means higher costs, which would be reflected in a rising long-run supply curve. This simply means that higher prices are necessary to induce suppliers to offer more for sale. None of this changes the basic ideas we have discussed throughout this section. The entry and exit of firms ensures that the market supply curve is much more elastic in the long run than the short run.

FIGURE 9.9

The Long-Run Adjustment to a Decrease in Demand

Short-run losses cause some firms to exit the industry. This shifts the market supply curve left in (b) until the price returns to long-run equilibrium at point C. This restores the price to P_1 and shifts the MR curve up in (a) to MR_1. At P_1 the firm is, once again, earning zero economic profits.

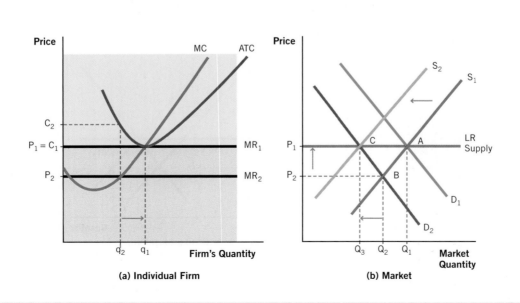

(a) Individual Firm

(b) Market

PRACTICE WHAT YOU KNOW

Long-Run Profits: How Much Can I Expect to Make?

Fill in the blank: In the long run, a firm in a perfectly competitive market earns _____ profits.

(Caution: there may be more than one right answer!)

Calculating profits

(a) positive accounting

(b) zero accounting

(c) positive economic

(d) zero economic

Answers:

(a) **Correct**. Accounting profits only cover the explicit costs of doing business, so they are positive. Accounting profits do not include the implicit costs; once those costs are taken into account the economic profits will be lower. If the implicit costs are exactly equal to the accounting profit, the firm will earn zero economic profits and the long-run equilibrium is reached.

(b) **Incorrect**. If a firm earns zero accounting profits, the implicit costs will make the economic profit negative. When economic profits are negative, firms will exit the market.

(c) **Incorrect**. When a firm earns an economic profit, this sends a signal to firms outside the market to enter. The long-run equilibrium occurs when there is no incentive to enter or exit the market.

(d) **Correct**. This answer only makes sense when you recall that *zero* does not mean *nothing*. Zero economic profits means that the firm can cover its explicit (accounting) and implicit (opportunity) costs. It also means firms inside the market are content to stay and firms outside the market do not see the value of entering. In the long run the only condition that would not signal firms to enter or exit would be zero economic profits.

Conclusion

It is tempting to think that firms control what price they charge. This is not true in competitive markets, where firms are at the mercy of market forces which set the price that is charged throughout the industry. Individual firms have no control over the price because they sell the same products as their competitors. In addition, profits and losses help regulate economic activity

ECONOMICS FOR LIFE

Economics Profits

Tips for Starting Your Own Business

Before you go into business for yourself you need to devise a plan. Over 80 percent of all small businesses are not around after five years because the business was ill conceived or counted on unrealistic sales projections. You don't need a detailed plan as long as it covers these essential points:

Do a cost-benefit analysis and determine how long it will take you to break even. If you don't do this you could run out of money and have to close your doors before you start to make a profit. The break-even point is different from earning an economic profit. Breaking even requires that you cover your explicit expenses with your revenues, or have what is known as a positive cash flow. This is especially important if you enter a perfectly competitive market where long-run profits are not possible. You need to be lean and efficient just to survive.

Keep your start-up costs as low as possible. Consider investing as much of your own money as possible. It can be very tempting to take out loans to cover your start-up costs, but if you expect to start immediately paying back your loans with the profits from your new business, think again. It can take years to become profitable. To lessen this problem you can invest more of your capital into the business to ensure that loans don't sink you. Also, start small and grow your business slowly over time in order to avoid overreaching.

Protect yourself from risk. If you are a sole proprietor you are liable for business debts and judgments and your creditors can come after your personal assets—like your home and savings accounts. To protect yourself against this possibility you can incorporate into what is known as a limited liability

You will need more than a good plan to succeed!

corporation, which helps shield business owners from personal liability.

You need a competitive advantage to attract customers. It could be price, better service, a better product—but it has to be something. Don't expect to be successful unless you can do something better than your rivals!

Hire the right people to help you. Remember what we learned about specialization: embrace it. You don't have to be an expert tax accountant, manager, and marketer. Offload some of these tasks on others who are better at them and focus on doing what you do best. However, once you find the right people to help, treat them well and provide an environment in which they will thrive and give their all.

http://abcnews.go.com/Business/tips-starting-small-business/story?id=14447409#.TzLjrYHZC1h in competitive markets and also promote economic efficiency. Profits reward producers for producing a good valued more highly than the resources used to produce it. This encourages entry into those markets. Likewise, losses penalize producers who operate inefficiently or produce goods that consumers do not want. This encourages exit from the market. The process of entry and exit ensures that resources flow into markets that are undersupplied and away from markets where too many firms exist.

In this chapter we have studied competitive markets to establish a benchmark that will help us understand how other market structures compare to this ideal. In the next few chapters we will explore imperfect markets. These markets provide a significant contrast with the results we have just seen. The closer a market is to meeting the criteria of perfect competition, the better the result for consumers and society in general.

ANSWERING THE BIG QUESTIONS

1. How do competitive markets work?

* The firms in competitive markets sell similar products. Firms are also free to enter and exit the market whenever they wish.
* A price taker has no control over the price it receives in the market.

2. How do firms maximize profits?

* A firm that maximizes profits will expand output until marginal revenue is equal to marginal cost. The profit-maximizing rule is a condition for stopping production at the point where profit opportunities no longer exist.
* The firm should shut down if the price it receives does not cover its average variable costs. Since variable costs are only incurred when operating, if a firm can make enough to cover its variable costs in the short run, it will choose to operate.

3. What does the supply curve look like in perfectly competitive markets?

* Profits and losses act as signals for firms to enter or leave an industry. As a result, perfectly competitive markets drive economic profit to zero in the long run.
* Entry and exit of firms ensure that the market supply curve is much more elastic in the long run than the short run.

CONCEPTS YOU SHOULD KNOW

Price taker (p. 260)   Signals (p. 276)   Sunk cost (p. 273)
Profit-maximizing rule (p. 266)

QUESTIONS

1. What are the necessary conditions for a perfectly competitive market to exist?

2. Describe the three-step process used to identify the profit-maximizing level of output.

3. Under what circumstances will a firm have to decide whether to operate or to shut down?

4. What is the difference between the decision to go out of business and the decision to operate or to shut down?

5. How do profits and losses act as signals that guide producers to use resources to make what society wants most?

6. What are sunk costs? Give an example from your own experience.

7. Why do competitive firms earn zero economic profits in the long run?

STUDY PROBLEMS

1. Using the definition of a price taker as your guide, in the following industries explain why the outcome does not meet the definition.
   a. The pizza delivery business
   b. The home improvement business
   c. Cell phone companies
   d. Cereals

2. A local snow cone business sells snow cones in one size for $3. It has the following cost and output structure per hour:

Output (cones per hour)	Total Cost (per hour)
0	$60
10	90
20	110
30	120
40	125
50	135
60	150
70	175
80	225

   a. Calculate the total revenue for the business at each rate of output.

   b. Calculate the total profit for the business at each rate of output.
   c. Is the business operating in the short run or the long run?
   d. Calculate the profit-maximizing rate of output using the MR = MC rule. (**Hint**: to do this you should first compute the marginal revenue and marginal cost from the table.)

3. Determine whether the following statements are true or false. Explain your answers.
   a. A firm will make a profit when the price it charges exceeds the average variable cost of the chosen output level.
   b. In order to maximize profits in the short run, a firm must minimize its costs.
   c. If economic profits are positive, firms will exit the industry in the short run.
   d. A firm that receives a price greater than its average variable costs but less than its average total costs should shut down.

4. In the following table, fill in the blanks. After you have completed the entire table, determine the profit-maximizing output.

Output	Price	Total Revenue	Marginal Revenue	Total Cost	Marginal Cost	Total Profit
1	$20	___	___	$40	___	-$20
2	___	___	___	50	___	___
3	___	___	___	60	___	___
4	___	___	___	65	5	___
5	___	___	___	85	___	___
6	___	$120	___	120	___	___

5. Use the graph to answer the questions that follow.

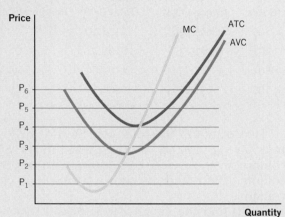

a. At what prices is the firm making economic profit, breaking even, and experiencing an economic loss?

b. At what prices would the firm shut down?

c. At what prices does the firm's short-run supply curve exist? At what prices does the firm's long-run supply curve exist?

✳ **6.** Identify as many errors as you can in the following graph.

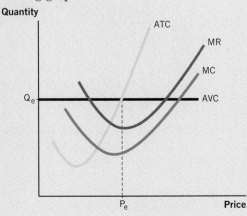

7. A firm is experiencing a loss of $5,000 per year. The firm has fixed costs of $8,000 per year.

  a. Should the firm operate in the short run or shut down?

  b. If the situation persists into the long run, would the firm stay in the industry or go out of business?

  c. Now suppose that the fixed costs are $2,000. How does this change the firm's short-run and long-run decisions?

8. Three students at the same school hear about the success of cookie delivery businesses on college campuses. Each decides to open a local service. The individual supply schedules are shown below.

Delivery Charge	Quantity Supplied		
	Esra	Remzi	Camilo
$1	2	3	6
2	4	6	7
3	6	9	8
4	8	12	9
5	10	15	10
6	12	18	11

  a. Draw the individual supply curves.

  b. Sum the individual supply schedules to compute the short-run industry supply schedule.

  c. Draw the industry supply curve.

9. Do you agree or disagree with the following statement? "A profit-maximizing, perfectly-competitive firm should select the output level at which the difference between the marginal revenue and marginal cost is the greatest." Explain your answer.

10. Barney's snow removal service is a profit-maximizing, competitive firm. Barney clears driveways for $10 each. His total cost each day is $250, and half of his total costs are fixed. If Barney clears 20 driveways a day, should Barney operate or shut down? If this situation persists, will Barney stay in the industry or exit?

✳ **11.** Suppose you are the owner of a firm producing jelly beans. Your production costs are shown in the table. Initially, you produce 100 boxes of jelly beans per time period. Then, a new customer calls and places an order for an additional box of jelly beans, requiring you to increase your output to 101 boxes. She offers you $1.50 for the box. Should you produce it?

JELLY BEAN PRODUCTION

Boxes	Average Cost per Box
100	$1.00
101	$1.01
102	$1.02
103	$1.03

SOLVED PROBLEMS

6. Here is the corrected graph with the errors struck out.

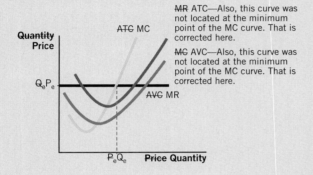

MR ATC—Also, this curve was not located at the minimum point of the MC curve. That is corrected here.

MC AVC—Also, this curve was not located at the minimum point of the MC curve. That is corrected here.

11. This is a problem that requires marginal thinking. We know the profit-maximizing rule, or MR = MC. Here all we need to do is compare the additional costs, or MC, against the additional revenue, or MR, to see if the deal is a good idea. We know that the MR = $1.50, because that is what the customer is offering to pay for another box of jelly beans. Now we need to calculate the marginal cost of producing the additional box.

JELLY BEAN PRODUCTION

Boxes	Average Cost	Total Cost	Marginal Cost
100	$1.00	$100.00	—
101	$1.01	$102.01	$2.01
102	$1.02	$104.04	$2.03
103	$1.03	$106.09	$2.05

First compute the total cost. To do this, we multiply the number of boxes, listed in the first column, by the average cost, shown in the second column. The results are shown in the total cost column.

Next, find the marginal cost. Recall that the marginal cost is the amount that it costs to produce one more unit. So to find the marginal cost of producing one more box, we subtract the total cost of producing 101 boxes from the total cost of producing 100. For 101 boxes, MC = $102.01 – $100.00, or $2.01. Since MR – MC is $1.50 – $2.01, producing the 101st box would create a loss of $0.51. Therefore, at a price of $1.50, the firm should not produce the 101st box.

Understanding Monopoly

Monopolists always make a profit.

In this chapter we will explore another market structure: monopoly. Many people mistakenly believe that monopolists always make a profit.

This is not true. Monopolists enjoy market power for their specific product, but monopolists cannot force consumers to purchase what they are selling. The law of demand regulates how much a monopolist can charge. This means that when a monopolist charges more, people buy less. It also means that if demand is low, a monopolist may experience a loss instead of a profit.

While pure monopolies are unusual, this market structure is important to study because many markets exhibit some form of monopolistic behavior. Microsoft, the National Football League, the United States Postal Service (for first-class mail), and some small-town businesses are all examples of monopoly. In this chapter we explore the conditions that give rise to monopolies and also how monopoly power can erode.

The typical result of monopoly is higher prices and less output than we find in a competitive market. Once we understand the market conditions that give rise to a monopoly, we will look at how governments seek to address the problems that monopolies present.

A small town's sole veterinarian functions as a monopolist.

BIG QUESTIONS

* How are monopolies created?
* How much do monopolies charge and how much do they produce?
* What are the problems with, and solutions for, monopoly?

How Are Monopolies Created?

As we explained in Chapter 3, a monopoly is characterized by a single seller who produces a well-defined product for which there are no good substitutes. Two conditions allow a single seller to become a monopolist. First, the firm must have something unique to sell. Second, it must also have a way to prevent potential competitors from entering the market.

Monopolies occur in many places and for several different reasons. For example, natural gas, water, and electricity are all examples of a monopoly that occurs naturally because of economies of scale. But monopolies can also exist because the government regulates the amount of competition. For example, trash pickup, street vending, taxicab rides, and ferry service are often licensed by local governments. This has the effect of limiting competition and creating **monopoly power**, which measures the ability of firms to set the price for a good.

A monopoly operates in a market with high **barriers to entry**, which are restrictions that make it difficult for new firms to enter a market. High barriers to entry insulate the monopolist from competition. This allows many monopolists to enjoy long-run economic profits. There are two basic ways that this can happen: natural barriers and barriers created by government. Let's look at each.

Monopoly power
measures the ability of firms to set the price for a good.

Barriers to entry
restrict the entry of new firms into a market.

Natural Barriers

Some barriers exist naturally within the market. These include control of resources, problems raising capital, and economies of scale.

Control of Resources

The best way to limit competition is to control a resource that is essential in the production process. This extremely effective barrier to entry is hard to accomplish. If you control a scarce resource, other competitors will not be able to find enough of it to compete. For example, in the early 20th century, the Aluminum Company of America (ALCOA) made a concerted effort to buy bauxite mines around the globe. Within a decade, they owned 90% of the world's bauxite, an essential element in making aluminum. This effort allowed ALCOA to crowd out potential competitors and achieve dominance in the aluminum market.

Problems Raising Capital

Monopolists are usually very big companies that have grown over a long time. Even if you had a wonderful business plan, it is unlikely that a bank or a venture capital company would lend you enough to start a business that could compete effectively with a well-established company. For example, if you wanted to design a new operating system to compete with Microsoft, you would need tens of millions of dollars to fund your start-up. Lenders provide capital for business projects when the chance of success is high. The chance of a new company successfully competing against an entrenched monopoly is not high. Consequently, raising capital to compete against an entrenched monopolist is very difficult.

Economies of Scale

In Chapter 8 we saw that average costs fall as production expands. Low unit costs, and the low prices that follow, give larger firms the ability to drive out rivals. For instance, consider your local electric company. It would be technically possible to run competing sets of wire to every home and business in a community, but the cost of installation and the maintenance of separate lines to deliver electricity would be both prohibitive and impractical. Even if a handful of smaller electric companies could produce electricity at the same cost, each would have to pay to deliver power through its own grid. This would be inefficient.

In an industry that has large economies of scale, production costs per unit continue to fall as the firm expands. Smaller rivals will have much higher average costs that prevent them from competing with a larger company. As a result, firms in the industry naturally tend to combine over time. This leads to the creation of a **natural monopoly**, which occurs when a single large firm has lower costs than any potential competitor.

A **natural monopoly** exists when a single seller experiences lower average total costs than any potential competitor.

Government-Created Barriers

The creation of a monopoly can be intentional or an unintended consequence of a government policy. Government-enforced statutes and regulations, such as laws and regulations covering licenses and patents, limit the scope of competition by creating barriers to entry.

Licensing

In many instances it makes sense to give a single firm the exclusive right to sell a good or service. In order to minimize the existence of negative externalities, governments establish monopolies, or near monopolies, through licensing requirements. For example, in some communities trash collection is licensed to a single company. The rationale usually involves economies of scale, but there are also costs. Since firms cannot collect trash unless they have a government-sponsored

In many communities you don't have any choice about trash collection.

operating license, opportunities to enter the business are limited, which leaves consumers with a one-size-fits-all level of service. This is the opposite of what we'd expect to see in a competitive market, where there would be many varieties of service at different price points.

Licensing also creates an opportunity for corruption. In many parts of the world bribery is a common practice and often determines which companies receive the licenses in the first place.

Patents and Copyright Law

Another area where the government fosters monopoly is through patents and copyrights. When musicians create a new song and copyright their work, they earn royalties over the life of the copyright. The copyright is the government's assurance that no one else can play or sell the work without the artist's permission. Similarly, when a pharmaceutical company creates a new drug, the firm receives a patent that is used to market and sell the drug exclusively, for as long as the patent is in force. By granting patents and copyrights to developers and inventors, the government is creating a monopoly. Patents and copyrights create stronger incentives to find new drugs and make new music than would exist if market forces could immediately copy inventions. The result is that pharmaceutical companies invest heavily in researching

and developing new drugs and musicians devote their time to writing new music. At least in theory, these activities make our society a healthier and culturally richer place. After the patent or copyright expires, rivals can mimic the invention. This opens up the market and provides dual benefits: wider access to the innovation and more sellers—both of which are good for consumers in the long run.

As appealing as the previous paragraph sounds, nothing works quite as well as advertised. Many economists wonder if patents and copyrights are necessary, or have unintended consequences of their own. For instance, illegal file sharing, downloads, and pirated DVDs are common in the music and movie business. At first glance, this appears to be a revenue loss for legitimate companies. But often the companies benefit from the exposure. When a video goes viral on YouTube, the exposure causes many people to buy the original artist's work.

Does Justin Bieber need copyright protection to make money?

Can you say Justin Bieber? He was able to leverage his Internet fame into a successful album launch, concert tours, and appearance fees that might never have occurred if his sound had been tightly controlled by a music studio.

ECONOMICS IN THE REAL WORLD

Merck's Zocor

In 1985 pharmaceutical giant Merck released Zocor, the first statin drug for treating high cholesterol. The company spent millions of dollars developing the drug and bringing it to the market. Zocor is highly effective and has probably saved or extended millions of lives. It was also highly profitable, generating over $4 billion in annual revenues before the patent ran out in

2006. Zocor is now available in an inexpensive generic formulation at a price that is 80–90 percent less than the original patent-protected price.

Would Zocor have been developed without patent protection? Probably not. Merck would have had little incentive to incur the cost of developing a cholesterol treatment if the drug could be immediately copied by other companies. In this case, society benefits because of the two-fold nature of patents. They give firms the incentive to innovate and produce new products. But they also limit the amount of time the patent is in place, thereby guaranteeing that long-run access to the product will be governed by competitive forces. ✳

Though market-created and government-created barriers occur for different reasons, they have the same effect—they create monopolies. In the next section we will examine how the monopolist determines the price it charges and how much to produce. But first, test your understanding of the difference between monopoly and perfect competition with the story of Forrest Gump. Can you detect the flaw in the movie's reasoning?

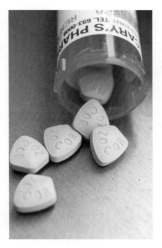

Do you want fries with that?

PRACTICE WHAT YOU KNOW

Monopoly: Can You Spot the Monopolist?

Here are three examples to test your understanding of the conditions necessary to create monopoly power.

Question: Is Lebron James (an NBA superstar) a monopolist?

Answer: Lebron is a uniquely talented basketball player. Because of his physical gifts, he can do things that other players can't do. But that does not mean that there are no substitutes for him around the league. Perhaps more important, his monopoly power is limited because new players are always entering the league and trying to establish themselves as the best.

Monopoly profits!

Question: Is a small-town hairdresser a monopolist?

Answer: For all practical purposes, yes. It sells a unique service with inelastic demand. The nearest competitor is in the next town. This gives the local hairdresser significant monopoly power. At the same time, the size of the town limits potential competitors from entering the market, since the small community may not be able to support two hairdressers.

Question: Is Amazon a monopolist?

Answer: Amazon is the nation's largest bookseller. Amazon's sales dwarf that of its nearest retail rival, Barnes & Noble. But Amazon's market share does not make it a monopolist. Amazon is a lot like Wal-Mart: it relies on low prices to fend off its rivals.

ECONOMICS IN THE MEDIA

Barriers to Entry

Forrest Gump (1994)

Forrest Gump keeps his promise to his deceased friend, Bubba, to go into the shrimping business after leaving the army. He invests $25,000 in an old shrimp boat, but the going is tough—he only catches a handful of shrimp because of the competition for space in the shrimping water. Forrest tries naming his boat for good luck and brings on a first-mate, Lieutenant Dan, who unfortunately is less knowledgeable and resourceful than Forrest. The fledgling enterprise is in a bad way, and eventually Forrest decides to pray for shrimp. Soon after, Forrest's boat, *Jenny*, is caught out in the Gulf of Mexico during a hurricane. Miraculously, the *Jenny* makes it through the storm while the other shrimp boats, all in the harbor, are destroyed.

Forrest recounts the events on a park bench in Savannah:

Forrest: "After that, shrimping was easy. Since people still needed them shrimps for shrimp cocktails and barbecues and all, and we were the *only* boat left standing, Bubba-Gump shrimp's what they got. We got a whole bunch of boats. Twelve *Jennys*, big old warehouse. We even have hats that say "Bubba-Gump" on them. Bubba-Gump Shrimp. A household name."

Man on the bench: "Hold on there, boy. Are you telling me you're the owner of the Bubba-Gump Shrimp Corporation?"

Forrest: "Yes. We got more money than Davy Crockett."

Man on the bench: "Boy, I heard some whoppers in my time, but that tops them all. We were sitting next to a millionaire."

The film suggests that Forrest's good luck—being in the right place at the right time—explains how he became a millionaire. But is this realistic?

If shrimping were easy, everyone would do it.

Remember, Forrest was able to enter the business simply by purchasing a boat. To be sure, he would catch more shrimp in the short run, while the others are docked for repairs. However, once the competitors' boats return, they will catch shrimp and Forrest's short-run profits will disappear. The reason we can be so confident of this result is that shrimping, with low barriers to entry and undifferentiated product, is an industry that closely mirrors a perfectly competitive market. So, when profits exist, new entrants will expand the supply produced and profits will return to the break-even level. Having Forrest become a "millionaire" makes for a good movie, but none of the elements are in place to suggest that he could attain a permanent monopoly. Forrest does not control an essential resource; the other shrimp captains will have little difficulty raising capital to repair their boats, and economies of scale are small.

How Much Do Monopolies Charge and How Much Do They Produce?

Both monopolists and firms in a competitive market seek to earn a profit. However, a monopolist is the sole provider of a product and holds market power. Thus, monopolists are *price makers*. A **price maker** has some control over the price it charges. As you have already learned, a firm in a competitive market is a price taker.

A price maker has some control over the price it charges.

We can see the difference graphically in Figure 10.1. The demand curve for the product of a firm in a competitive market, shown here in panel (a), is horizontal. When individual firms are price takers they have no control over what they charge. In other words, demand is perfectly elastic—or horizontal—because every firm sells the same product. Demand for an individual firm's product exists only at the price determined by the market and each individual firm is such a small part of the market that it can sell its entire output without lowering the price it charges. In contrast, because a monopolist is the only firm in the industry, the demand curve for the monopolist's product, shown in panel (b), is the market demand curve. But the demand curve is downward-sloping, which places a limit on the monopolist's ability to make a profit. The monopolist would like to exploit its market power by charging a high price

FIGURE 10.1

Comparing the Demand Curves of Perfectly Competitive Firms and Monopolists

(a) Firms in a competitive market have a horizontal demand curve. (b) Since the monopolist is the sole provider of the good or service, the demand for its product is the industry demand curve. This is reflected in a downward-sloping demand curve. So while the perfectly competitive firm has no control over the price it charges, the monopolist must search for the price and output combination that maximizes its profits.

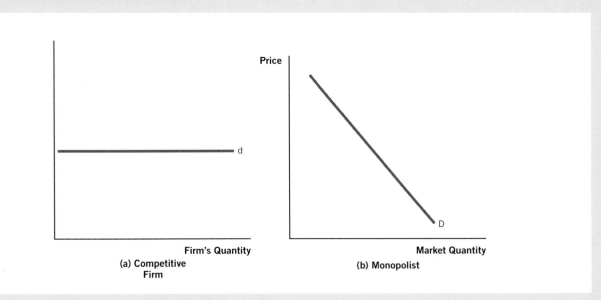

to many customers; the law of demand, which identifies an inverse relationship between price and quantity demanded, dictates otherwise. Unlike the horizontal demand curve of a firm in a competitive market, the downward-sloping demand curve of the monopolist has many price-output combinations. If the monopolist charges a high price, only a few customers will buy the good. If it charges a low price, many customers will buy the good. As a result, monopolists must search for the best possible price-output pair.

The Profit-Maximizing Rule for the Monopolist

The competitive firm can sell all it produces at the existing price. But a monopolist, because of the downward-sloping demand curve, must lower the price to sell more units. To maximize profits, a monopolist can use the profit maximizing rule we developed in Chapter 9: MR = MC. But the monopolist's marginal revenue is computed differently.

Table 10.1 shows the marginal revenue for a cable company that serves a small community. Notice the inverse relationship between output (quantity) and price in columns (1) and (2): as the price goes down, the quantity sold goes up. Total revenue is calculated by multiplying output by price (TR = Q × P). At first total revenue rises as the price falls. Once the price becomes too low ($40), total revenue begins to fall. As a result, the total revenue function in column (3) initially rises to $250,000 before it falls off. The final column, marginal revenue, shows the change in total revenue. Here we see positive

TABLE 10.1

Calculating the Monopolist's Marginal Revenue

(1) Quantity of customers	(2) Price	(3) Total Revenue	(4) Marginal Revenue per 1,000 customers
(Q)	(P)	(TR)	(MR)
Formula:		(Q) × (P)	Δ (TR)
0	$100	$0.00	
1,000	90	90,000	$90,000
2,000	80	160,000	70,000
3,000	70	210,000	50,000
4,000	60	240,000	30,000
5,000	50	250,000	10,000
6,000	40	240,000	−10,000
7,000	30	210,000	−30,000
8,000	20	160,000	−50,000
9,000	10	90,000	−70,000
10,000	0	0.00	−90,000

(though falling) marginal revenue associated with prices above $50. Below $50, marginal revenue becomes negative.

The change in marginal revenue reflects the trade-off that a monopolist encounters in trying to attract additional customers. To gain additional output, the firm must lower its price. But the lower price is available to both new and existing customers. The impact on total revenue therefore depends on how many new customers buy the good because of the lower price.

Figure 10.2 uses the linear demand schedule from Table 10.1 to illustrate the two separate effects that determine marginal revenue. First, there is a *price effect*, which refers to how lower prices affect revenue. If the price drops from $70 to $60, each of the 3,000 existing customers will save $10. The firm would lose $10 × 3,000, or $30,000 in revenue, represented by the yellow-shaded area on the graph. But dropping the price also has an *output effect*, which refers to how lower prices affect the quantity sold. Since 1,000 new customers buy the product when the price is lowered to $60, revenue increases by $60 × 1,000, or $60,000, represented by the green-shaded area. The output effect ($60,000) is greater than the price effect ($30,000). When we subtract the $30,000 in lost revenue (the yellow rectangle) from the $60,000 in revenue gained (the green rectangle), this yields $30,000 in marginal revenue at an output level between 3,000 and 4,000 units. Lost revenues associated with the price effect are always subtracted from the revenue gains created by the output effect. Now let's think of this data at the individual level. Since the firm adds 1,000 new customers, the marginal revenue per customer—$30,000 ÷ 1,000 new customers—is $30. Notice that this is less than the price, $60, that the firm charges. Since there is a price effect whenever the price is lowered, the marginal revenue curve lies below the demand curve.

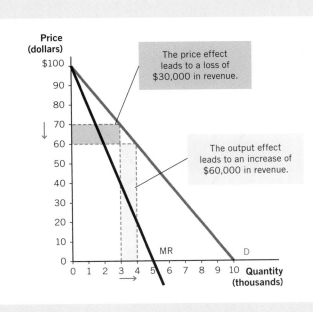

FIGURE 10.2

The Marginal Revenue Curve and the Demand Curve

A price drop creates two effects. (1) Existing customers now pay less—this is known as the price effect. (2) New customers will decide to purchase the good for the first time—this is known as the output effect. The relative size of the two effects, as shown by the light-yellow and light-green rectangles, determines whether or not the firm is able to increase its revenues by lowering its price.

At high price levels—where demand is elastic—the price effect is small relative to the output effect. As the price drops, demand slowly becomes more inelastic. The output effect diminishes and the price effect increases. This means that as the price falls it becomes harder for the firm to acquire enough new customers to make up for the difference in lost revenue. Eventually, the price effect becomes larger than the output effect. When this happens, marginal revenue becomes negative and dips below the x-axis, as shown by the MR curve in Figure 10.2. When the marginal revenue is negative, the firm cannot be profit-maximizing. This puts an upper limit on the amount that the firm will produce. You can see this in Table 10.1; once the price becomes too low, the values of the marginal revenue are negative.

Deciding How Much to Produce

In Chapter 9 we explored the profit-maximizing rule for a firm in a competitive market. This rule also applies to a monopolist: marginal revenue should be set equal to marginal cost. However, there is one big difference: a monopolist does not charge a price equal to marginal revenue.

Figure 10.3 illustrates the profit-maximizing decision-making process. We will use a two-step process to determine the monopolist's profit:

1. Locate the point at which the firm will maximize its profits: MR = MC.
2. Set the price. From the point where MR = MC, determine the profit-maximizing output, q. From q move up along the dashed line until it intersects with the demand curve. From that point move horizontally until you come to the y-axis. This tells us the price (P) the monopolist should charge.

FIGURE 10.3

The Monopolist's Profit Maximization

The firm uses the profit-maximizing rule to locate the point where MR = MC. This determines the ideal output level, q. Since the price (which is determined by the demand curve) is higher than the average cost curve along the dashed line at quantity q, the firm makes the profit shown in green.

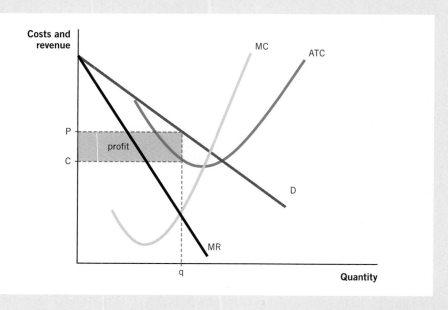

TABLE 10.2

The Major Differences Between a Monopoly and a Competitive Market

Competitive Market	Monopoly
Many firms	One firm
Produces an efficient level of output (since P = MC)	Produces less than the efficient level of output (since P > MC)
Cannot earn long-run economic profits	May earn long-run economic profits
Has no market power (is a price taker)	Has significant market power (is a price maker)

Using this two-step process, we can determine the profit. Locate the average cost, C, of making q units along the dashed line. From that point move horizontally until you come to the y-axis. This tells us the cost of making q units. The difference between the price and the cost multiplied by q tells us the profit (or loss) a firm makes.

Since the price (P) is higher than the average cost (C), the firm makes the profit shown in the green rectangle.

Table 10.2 summarizes the differences between a competitive market and a monopoly. The competitive firm must take the price established in the market. If it does not operate efficiently, it cannot survive. Nor can it make economic profits in the long run. The monopolist operates very differently. Since high barriers to entry limit competition, the monopolist may be able to earn long-run profits by restricting output. It operates inefficiently from society's perspective, and it has significant market power.

ECONOMICS IN THE REAL WORLD

The Broadband Monopoly

Many markets in the United States have only a single high-speed Internet provider. The technology race strongly favors cable over competing DSL. DSL is provided by telephone companies using aging copper wiring, whereas the cable companies have the latest fiber-optic technology. When it comes to truly high-speed Internet access, cable companies benefit from considerable barriers to entry. In many places Comcast owns the Internet and can price accordingly.

The cable monopoly on high-speed Internet access resonates in two ways. First, consumers increasingly need more bandwidth to stream movies, view YouTube, and load media-rich websites. A slow connection can make surfing the Internet a chore. In other words, consumer demand is high and very inelastic. Second, businesses rely on bandwidth to maintain websites

Does Comcast own the Internet in your area?

and provide services to customers. Companies such as Netflix, which delivers streaming content over the Internet, rely on access to a relatively affordable broadband Internet. Therefore businesses also have high demand that is quite inelastic. For this reason, many people argue that relatively inexpensive access to the Internet is crucial if it is to continue to be an engine of economic growth. And without competition, access will continue to be expensive.

Our dependence on the Internet invites a larger question. Where the bandwidth is controlled by only one provider, should the government have a role in providing the infrastructure, or cables, in order to provide more access? This is a concern in metropolitan areas, served by only one high-speed provider, and also in smaller rural communities without high-speed access. For example, Chireno, Texas, has a population of 413 people and remains off the grid. Chireno is not unique. About 45 percent of Texas is in this position and no one expects the rate of high-speed connectivity to change soon because the big cable companies don't see enough profit in connecting low-density areas. Without a fast connection, everything from online banking to social networking and running an Internet-based business is difficult. This makes it harder for small towns to participate in the modern economy. ✳

PRACTICE WHAT YOU KNOW

Monopoly Profits: How Much Do Monopolists Make?

Question: A monopolist always earns _____ economic profits.

a. positive

b. zero

c. negative

d. We cannot be sure about the profits a monopolist makes.

Is there a key profit takeaway?

Answers:

a. Incorrect. The monopolist is a price maker with considerable market power. This usually, but not always, leads to positive economic profits.

b. Incorrect. Zero economic profits exist in competitive markets in the long run. Since barriers to entry protect the monopolist from entry into the market, it is protected from additional competition that would drive profits to zero.

c. Incorrect. Whoa there! Negative profits? There is absolutely no reason to think that would happen. Monopolists sell a unique product, without close substitutes in a market that is insulated from competitive pressures. Time to re-read the first part of this chapter more carefully!

d. Correct. Since a monopolist benefits from barriers that limit the entry of competitors into the industry, we would expect profits. However, this is not guaranteed. Monopolies do not control the demand for the product they sell. Consequently, in the short run the monopolist may experience profits (if demand is high) or losses (if demand is low).

What Are the Problems with, and Solutions for, Monopoly?

Monopolies can make society worse off by restricting output and charging higher prices than competitive markets. This causes monopolies to operate inefficiently, provide less choice, encourage an unhealthy form of competition known as *rent seeking* (see below), and make economic profits that fail to guide resources to their highest-valued use. The occurrence of an inefficient output is known **market failure**. Once we have examined the problems with monopoly, we will turn to the potential solutions for monopoly.

Market failure
Occurs when the output level of the firm is inefficient.

The Problems with Monopoly

Monopolies result in an inefficient level of output, provide less choice to consumers, and encourage firms to lobby for government protection. Let's look at each of these concerns.

Inefficient Output and Price

From an efficiency standpoint, the monopolist charges too much and produces too little. This result can be seen in Figure 10.4, which shows what happens when a competitive market ends up being controlled by a monopoly.

FIGURE 10.4

When a Competitive Industry Becomes a Monopoly

(a) In a competitive industry, the intersection of supply and demand determines the price and quantity. (b) When a monopolist controls an entire industry, the supply curve becomes the monopolist's marginal cost curve. The monopolist uses MR = MC to determine its price and quantity. This means that a monopolist charges a higher price and produces a smaller output than when an entire industry is populated with competitive firms.

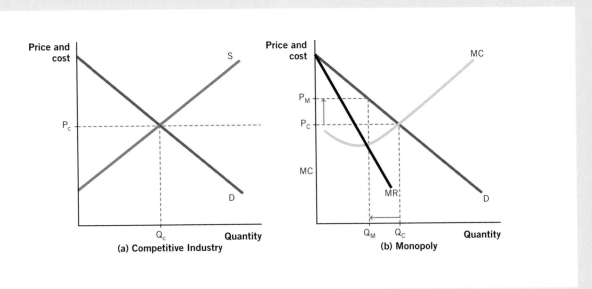

First, imagine a competitive fishing industry in which each individual boat catches a small portion of the fish, as shown in Figure 10.4a. Each firm is a price taker that must charge the market price. In contrast, panel (b) depicts pricing and output decisions for a monopoly fishing industry when it confronts the same cost structure as panel (a). When a single firm controls the entire fishing ground, it is the sole supplier, and to set its price it considers the downward-sloping demand and marginal revenue curves that serve the entire market. Therefore it sets marginal revenue equal to marginal cost. This yields a smaller output ($Q_M < Q_C$) than the competitive industry and a higher price ($P_M > P_C$). The smaller output level is not efficient. In addition, the price the monopolist charges, P_M, is significantly above the marginal cost at the profit-maximizing level of output, which is higher than the price when there are many smaller competing firms.

Figure 10.5 captures the deadweight loss of the monopoly. The monopolist charges too high a price and produces too little of the product, so some consumers who would benefit from a competitive market lose out. Since the demand curve, or the willingness to pay, is greater than the marginal cost between output levels Q_M and Q_C, society would be better off if output was expanded to Q_C. But a profit-maximizing monopolist will limit output to Q_M. The result, a deadweight loss equal to the area of the yellow triangle, is inefficient for society. Consumer surplus is also transferred to the monopolist, as shown in the light-blue rectangle labeled A.

Few Choices

Another problem associated with monopoly is the lack of choice. Have you ever wondered why cable companies offer their services in bundles? You can buy basic, digital, and premium packages, but the one thing you cannot do

FIGURE 10.5

The Deadweight Loss of Monopoly

Since the profit-maximizing monopolist produces an output of QM, an amount that is less than QC, this results in the deadweight loss shown in yellow. The light-blue rectangle is the consumer surplus that is transferred to the monopolist.

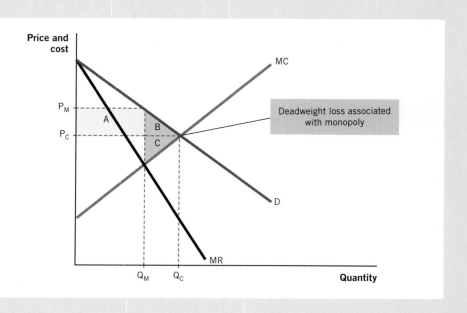

Would you rather watch the Weather Channel . . .   . . . or SportsCenter?

is buy just the cable channels you want. This is because cable companies function like monopolies and monopolies limit consumer choice. Since the monopolist sells a good with few close substitutes, it can leverage its market power to present consumers with product features that benefit the monopolist at the expense of consumer choice. With a monopolist there is only one outlet: if you do not like the design, features, price, or any other aspect of the good provided, you have few other options. For example, in many smaller communities there is only one cable television provider. In a hypothetical competitive market we would expect each company to provide more options to satisfy consumer preferences. For instance, in a competitive market you should be able to find a firm willing to sell only ESPN and the Weather Channel. In a monopoly situation, the cable company forces you to choose between buying a little more cable than you really need or going without cable altogether. Because the cable company has a good deal of market power, it can restrict your options and force you to buy more in order to get what you want. This is profitable for the company but a bad outcome for consumers.

Rent seeking
occurs when resources are used to secure monopoly rights through the political process.

Rent Seeking

The attempt to gain monopoly power encourages **rent seeking**, which is competition among rival firms to secure monopoly profits. Throughout this text we have seen the desirable effects of competition: lower prices, increased efficiency, and enhanced service and quality. Rent seeking is a form of competition that produces an undesirable result. When firms compete to become monopolists, there is one winner, without any of the benefits usually associated with competition. To think about why this is the case, consider the U.S. steel industry. The industry has been in decline for many years, and has lost market share to steel firms in China, Japan and

A former steel plant in Bethlehem, Pennsylvania.

Europe. If a U.S. steel company is losing money because of foreign competition, it can address this situation in two ways. It can modernize by building new facilities and using the latest equipment and techniques, or it can lobby the government to limit imports. The domestic steel industry chose to lobby, and in 2002 the George W. Bush administration imposed tariffs of up to 30% on imported steel. Here is the danger: when lobbying is less expensive than building a new factory, the company will choose to lobby! If politicians give in, and the lobbying succeeds, society is worse off.

Supply and demand tell us that steel prices will rise in the absence of competition. This outcome is inefficient. Also, instead of pushing for legislation that grants market power, the lobbying resources could have been used to produce useful products. As a result, the process of rent seeking benefits the rent seeker and gives little direct benefit to society. Hence, economists view rent seeking as a detrimental form of competition.

ECONOMICS IN THE REAL WORLD

New York City Taxi

In 1932, during the depths of the Great Depression, New York City decided to license taxi cabs. The goal was to standardize fares, operating procedures, and safety requirements. At that time, a taxi cab license, or medallion, was available at no cost. Today, if you find one on the resale market, it costs over $300,000. The medallions are worth so much because the owners often make six-figure incomes from leasing and operating taxis in New York City.

The city did not intend to create an artificial monopoly, but it did. From 1932 until the 1990s the number of medallions, which represents the supply of taxis, was fixed at approximately 12,000. During that same 60-year period, population growth and an increase in tourism raised demand for taxi services. The number of medallions would have had to quadruple to keep up with demand.

In recent years, the city of New York has offered three auctions to introduce more medallions into the market. These auctions have netted the city over 100 million dollars in revenue and raised the number of medallions to slightly more than 13,000. Each of the current medallion holders owns a small part of an artificially created government monopoly. Collectively, the holders of medallions own a monopoly on taxi services worth 13,000 × $300,000, or about $4 billion. Yet demand for the medallions continues to far outpace the supply, and the market price has steadily climbed to an astonishing level.

Imagine what would happen if the city lifted restrictions on the number of medallions and gave them out to any qualified applicant. Applications for licenses would increase, and profits for cab drivers and cab companies would fall until supply roughly equaled demand. Conversely, if taxi cab drivers experienced economic losses, the number of taxis operating would decline until the losses disappeared.

Taxis in Times Square.

Owning and operating a taxi has all the makings of an industry with low barriers to entry. The only reason that medallions are worth so much is the artificially created barrier to entry—this protects medallion holders from competition. Restoring competitive markets would make each of the current medallion holders worse off by reducing the existing barriers to entry into the industry. This would cause the profits that medallion owners earn to fall. Therefore it is not surprising that they seek to keep the number of medallions as small as possible. Since monopolists make profits by charging higher prices than firms in competitive markets, no one who already has a medallion wants the supply to expand. ✳

Solutions to the Problem of Monopoly

We have seen that monopolies fail on many fronts. As a result, public-policy approaches to the problems of monopoly vary. They include harnessing the benefits of competition, reducing trade barriers, and regulating markets.

Harnessing the Benefits of Competition

Eliminating deadweight loss and restoring efficiency can be as simple as promoting competition. From 1913 until 1982 AT&T had a monopoly on the delivery of telephone services. As the years passed it become progressively harder for AT&T to defend its position that having a single provider of phone services was good for consumers. By the early 1980s AT&T was spending over $300 million to fend off antitrust suits from the states, federal government,

The Problems of Monopoly

One-Man Band (2005)

This Pixar short animation from 2005 tells the story of two street musicians trying to compete for the gold coin of a young peasant girl who wants to make a wish in the town square's fountain.

When the short opens there is only one street musician in the plaza. He performs a little bit and almost coaxes the girl to place the coin into his tip basket. Just as she is about to give it to him, another street musician starts playing. Since there is no longer a single performer, a spirited rivalry develops between the two very eager musicians vying to win the little girl's attention and money.

This clever story illustrates monopoly and competition in a number of compelling ways. The first street musician plays only half-heartedly in the beginning, when he does not face any competition. Lack of

A little competition goes a long way to reduce monopoly.

choice is one of the major criticisms of monopoly. The second musician's arrival completely changes the dynamic, inspiring a spirited competition for the gold coin. The "one-man band" is not really a monopolist; he is providing a service that has many good substitutes and lacks the ability to keep imitators from entering the market.

and many private firms. The end of the AT&T monopoly came in 1982, when enormous pressure from the government led the company to split into eight smaller companies. Suddenly AT&T had to compete to survive. Because customers could now choose to switch, the newly competitive phone market forced each of the phone companies to expand the services it offered—and sometimes even lower prices—to avoid losing customers. For example, rates on long-distance calls, which were quite high before the break-up, plummeted.

From this example, we see that the government can help limit monopoly outcomes and restore a competitive balance. This is often done through antitrust legislation. Antitrust laws are designed to prevent monopoly practices and promote competition. The government has exercised control over monopoly practices since the passage of the Sherman Act in 1890 and the task falls to the Department of Justice. The scope of these regulations will be explored at greater length in Chapter 13.

Reducing Trade Barriers

Countries use tariffs, which are taxes on imported goods, as a trade barrier to prevent competition and protect domestic business. However, any barrier—tariffs, quotas or prohibitions—limits the gains from trade. For a monopolist, trade barriers prevent rivals from entering their territory. For example, imagine that Florida could place a tariff on California oranges. For every California orange sold in Florida, the seller would have to pay a fee. Florida orange producers might like this because it would limit competition from California. California growers would cry foul and reciprocate with a tariff on Florida oranges. Growers in both states would be happy, but consumers would be harmed. For example, if a damaging freeze in Florida depleted the crop, Florida consumers would have to pay more than the demand-driven price for imported oranges from California. If, on the other hand, Florida had a bumper crop, the tariff would keep prices artificially high and much of the extra harvest would go to waste.

The United States has achieved tremendous growth by limiting the ability of individual states to place import and export restrictions on goods and services. The Constitution reads, "No State shall, without the consent of Congress, lay any imposts or duties on imports or exports." Rarely have so few words been more profound. With this simple law in place, states must compete on equal terms.

Reducing trade barriers creates more competition, reduces the influence of monopoly, and promotes the efficient use of resources. Prior to 1994, private air carriers comprised less than 0.5% of the air traffic in India. In 1994, Indian airspace was opened to allow private airlines to operate scheduled service. This forced state-owned Air India to become more competitive. These changes in Indian aviation policies have raised the share of private airline operators in domestic passenger carriage to over 70% in 2012. Two private companies, Jet Airways and IndiGo, are now the largest

Since 1994, reduced barriers to competition have transformed the Indian airline industry.

carriers in India, while Air India—which once controlled the market—has slipped to third place.

Regulating Markets

In the case of a natural monopoly, it is not practical to harness the benefits of competition. Consider the economies of scale that utility companies experience. Breaking up a company that provides natural gas, water, or electricity would result in higher production costs. For instance, a second water company would have to build infrastructure to each residence or business in a community. Having redundant water lines with only a fraction of the customers would make the delivery of water more expensive. This means that the final price to the consumer, even with competition, would be higher. Therefore, keeping the monopoly intact is the best option. In this situation, policy makers may attempt to create a more efficient outcome and maximize the welfare of society by regulating the prices that the monopolist charges. Theoretically this is a straightforward process—as we will see below. However, the reality is that few regulators are experts in the fields of electricity, natural gas, water, and other regulated industries, so they often lack sufficient knowledge to make the regulations work as designed.

When a natural monopoly exists, the government may choose to use the marginal-cost pricing rule to generate the greatest welfare for society. This is done by setting P = MC. Since the price is determined along the demand curve, setting P = MC guarantees that the good will be produced as long as the willingness to pay exceeds the additional cost of production. Figure 10.6 shows the difference in pricing and profits for a regulated and unregulated natural monopoly.

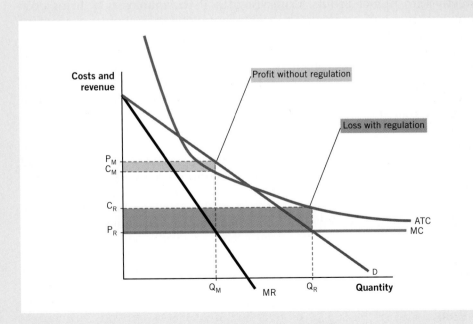

FIGURE 10.6

The Regulatory Solution for Natural Monopoly

An unregulated monopolist uses the profit-maximizing rule, MR = MC, and earns a small profit, shown in the green rectangle. If the monopolist is regulated using the marginal cost pricing rule, P = MC, it will experience the loss shown in the orange rectangle.

To maximize profits, an unregulated monopolist sets MR = MC and produces Q_M at a price of P_M. Since P_M is greater than the average cost of producing Q_M units, or C_M, the monopolist earns the profit shown in the green rectangle. If the firm is regulated and the price is set at marginal cost, regulators can set P = MC and the output expands to Q_R. In this example, since the cost of production is subject to economies of scale, the cost falls from C_M to C_R. This is a large improvement in efficiency. The regulated price, P_R, is lower than the monopolist's price, P_M, and production increases. As a result, consumers are better off. But what happens to the monopoly? It loses profits in the amount of the orange rectangle. This occurs since the average costs under the marginal-cost pricing solution, C_R, are higher than the price charged by regulators, P_R. This outcome is problematic, since a firm that suffers losses will go out of business. That outcome is not desirable from society's standpoint, since the consumers of the product will be left without it. There are three possible solutions. First, to make up for the losses incurred at the higher output level, C_R, the government could subsidize the monopolist. Second, the regulated price could be set so that P = ATC at Q_R and the monopoly breaks even. Third, the government could own and operate the business in lieu of the private firm. This, however, has its own challenges, as we will explore in the next section.

Government Failure

From a practical standpoint there is little difference between a privately owned firm that is regulated by the government and a firm that the government owns. Since neither has a profit motive, the incentives that drive unregulated private businesses to operate efficiently, innovate, and compete for new customers are lacking. Firms with a profit motive have an incentive to minimize the costs of production, since lower costs translate directly into higher profits. Consequently, if the managers of firms do a poor job they will be fired. The same cannot be said about government managers, or bureaucrats. Government employees are rarely let go, regardless of performance. As a result, the government oversight and management of monopolies is problematic because there are no incentives to keep costs in check.

Incentives

Consequently, the marginal-cost pricing rule is not as effective as it first seems. Regulated firms and government-owned businesses do not have the same incentives to keep costs down. Without the correct incentives in place we would expect to see cost inefficiencies develop.

Public policy has the ability to mitigate the power of monopolies, and therefore help to swing the balance of economic power away from the firm and back toward the consumer. But this outcome is not guaranteed. While monopolies are not as efficient as firms in competitive markets, this is not always the relevant comparison group. The question we need to ask is how the inefficiency of monopoly compares with the inefficiencies associated with government involvement in the market. Since good economists learn to assess the benefits as well as the costs, when the costs of government involvement are greater than the efficiency gains that can be realized, the best solution to the problem of monopoly might be to do nothing.

PRACTICE WHAT YOU KNOW

Problems with Monopoly: Coffee Consolidation

A community has many competing coffee shops.

Question: Use the market demand curve to illustrate the consumer and producer surplus created by a competitive market.

Answer:

When companies compete, consumers win.

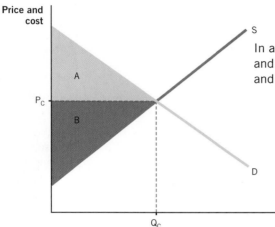

In a competitive market, supply and demand determine the price and quantity.

Question: Now imagine that all of the independent coffee shops are combined under one fictional franchise, known as Harbucks. Create a new graph that illustrates the consumer surplus, producer surplus, and deadweight loss created by establishing a monopoly in the market.

Answer:

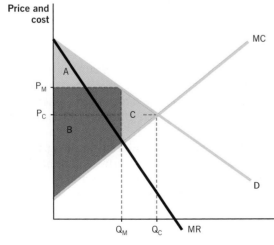

In this figure we see that the consumer surplus, A, has shrunk; the producer surplus, B, has increased; and the higher price charged by Harbucks creates deadweight loss equal to C. Allowing a market to be captured by a monopolist is bad for consumers and inefficient for society.

ECONOMICS FOR LIFE

Playing Monopoly ® Like an Economist

Monopoly is the ultimate zero-sum game. You profit only by taking from other players. The assets of its world are fixed in number. The best player drives others into bankruptcy and is declared the winner after gaining control of the entire board.

Here is some "friendly" advice on how to play the game. Monopoly is built on trade. You are unlikely to acquire a monopoly by landing on the color-groups you need. You will need to trade properties in order to acquire the missing properties you need. Since everyone knows this, acquiring the last property to complete a color-group is nearly impossible. Your competitors will never willingly hand you a monopoly unless they get something of great value in return. Don't wait to trade until it is obvious what you need. Instead, try to acquire as many properties as you can to gain trading leverage as the game unfolds. Always pick up available properties if no other player owns one of the same color-group; purchase properties that will give you two or three of the same group; or purchase a property if it blocks someone else from completing a set.

Think about probability. The mathematicians have determined that Illinois Avenue is the property most likely to be landed on. B&O is the best railroad to own. Know the odds and you stand a better chance of winning. This is just like doing market research

before you buy. Being informed matters in Monopoly and business.

When you get a monopoly, develop it quickly. Build as many houses as you can. That's sound advice in the board game and in life. Monopoly power is fleeting—you must capitalize on your advantages as soon as possible.

Finally, if you gain the upper hand and have a chance to bankrupt a player from the game—do it. Luck plays a key role in Monopoly as it does in life. Although it may sound harsh, eliminating a competitor moves you one step closer to winning the game.

The decisions you make while playing Monopoly are all about cost-benefit analysis.

Conclusion

It is tempting to believe that monopolies must earn a profit, but that is a misconception. The monopolist controls the supply, not the demand, so monopolies occasionally suffer losses despite the advantages they enjoy. Still, many monopolists do make profits, though profits, by themselves, don't make monopolies undesirable.

In this chapter, we examined the monopoly model and, along the way, compared the result under monopoly with the competitive model that we developed in the previous chapter. While competitive markets generally bring about welfare-enhancing outcomes for society, monopolies often do the opposite. Since monopolists do not produce an efficient outcome, government often seeks to limit monopoly outcomes and promote competitive markets.

Competitive markets and monopoly are market structures at opposite extremes. We rarely encounter the conditions necessary for either a pure monopoly or for a perfectly competitive market. Most economic activity takes place between these two alternatives. In the upcoming chapters we will examine monopolistic competition and oligopoly, two markets that comprise the bulk of the economy. Fortunately, if you understand the market structures at the extremes, understanding the middle ground is straightforward. As a result, one way to think of how firms operate is to imagine a broad spectrum of industries, from those that are highly competitive to those where competition is nonexistent. As we move forward, we will deploy the same tools we have used to examine monopoly to understand monopolistic competition and oligopoly.

ANSWERING THE BIG QUESTIONS

1. How are monopolies created?

* Monopoly is a market structure characterized by a single seller who produces a well-defined product with few good substitutes.
* Monopolies operate in a market with high barriers to entry, the chief source of market power.

2. How much do monopolies charge and how much do they produce?

* Monopolists are price makers who may earn long-run profits.
* Like perfectly competitive firms, a monopoly tries to maximize its profits. To do so it uses the profit-maximizing rule, or MR = MC, to select the optimal quantity.

3. What are the problems with, and solutions for, monopoly?

* From an efficiency standpoint, the monopolist charges too much and produces too little. Since the output of the monopolist is smaller than would exist in a competitive market, monopolies lead to deadweight loss.
* Government grants of monopoly power encourage rent seeking.
* There are four potential solutions to the problem of monopoly. First, the government may break up firms that gain too much market power in order to restore a competitive market. Second, government can promote open markets by reducing trade barriers. Third, the government can regulate a monopolist's ability to charge excessive prices. Finally, there are circumstances in which it is better to leave the monopolist alone.

CONCEPTS YOU SHOULD KNOW

Barriers to entry (p. 292)
Market failure (p. 303)

Monopoly power (p. 292)
Natural monopoly (p. 293)

Price maker (p. 297)
Rent seeking (p. 305)

QUESTIONS

1. Describe the difference between a monopoly and a natural monopoly.

2. What are barriers to entry and why are they crucial to the creation of potential long-run monopoly profits? Give an example of a barrier that can lead to monopoly.

3. Explain why a monopoly is a price maker, but a perfectly competitive firm is a price taker.

4. Why is a monopolist's marginal revenue curve less than the price of the good it sells?

5. What is the monopolist's rule for determining the profit-maximizing output? What three steps will the monopolist follow to maximize profits?

6. Why does a monopolist operate inefficiently? Draw a demand curve, marginal revenue curve, and marginal cost curve to illustrate the deadweight loss from monopoly.

7. Why is it difficult to regulate a natural monopoly?

STUDY PROBLEMS

1. In the figure below, identify the price the monopolist will charge and the output the monopolist will produce. How does the monopolist's decision compare to the efficient price and output?

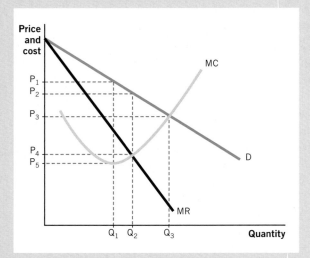

2. Which of the following could be considered a monopoly?

a. Your local water company
b. Boeing, a manufacturer of airplanes
c. Brad Pitt (an actor)
d. Wal-Mart
e. The only gas station along a 100-mile stretch of road

3. A monopolist has the following fixed and variable costs:

Price	Quantity	Fixed Cost	Variable Cost
$10	0	$8	$0
9	1	8	5
8	2	8	8
7	3	8	10
6	4	8	11
5	5	8	13
4	6	8	16
3	7	8	20
2	8	8	25

At what level of output will the monopolist maximize profits?

4. The year is 2278, and the starship *Enterprise* is running low on dilithium crystals, which are used to regulate the matter-antimatter reactions to propel the ship across the universe. Without the crystals, space-time travel is not possible. If there is only one known source of dilithium crystals, are the necessary conditions met to establish a monopoly? If the crystals are government-owned or -regulated, what price should the government set for the crystals?

* 5. If demand falls, what is likely to happen to price, output, and the economic profits of a monopolist?

* 6. A new musical group called *The Incentives* cuts a debut album. Their record company determines a number of price points for their first single, "The Big Idea."

Price	Downloads
$2.99	25,000
$1.99	50,000
$1.49	75,000
$0.99	100,000
$0.49	150,000

The record company can produce the song with fixed costs of $10,000 and no variable cost.

a. Determine the total revenue at each price. What is the marginal revenue as the price is dropped from one level to the next?
b. What price would maximize the record company's profits? How much would the company make?

c. If you were the agent for *The Incentives*, what signing fee would you request from the record company? Explain your answer.

7. Recalling what you have learned about elasticity, what can you say about the connection between the price the monopolist chooses to charge and whether or not demand is elastic, unitary, or inelastic at that price? (**Hint:** examine the marginal revenue curve of a monopolist. Since marginal revenue becomes negative at low prices, this implies that a portion of the demand curve cannot possibly be chosen.)

8. A small community is served by five independent gas stations. Gasoline is a highly competitive market. Use the market demand curve to illustrate the consumer and producer surplus created by the market. Now imagine that the five independent gas stations are all combined under one franchise. Create a new graph that illustrates the consumer surplus, producer surplus, and deadweight loss after the creation of monopoly in the market.

9. The local community bus service charges $2.00 for a one-way fare. The city council is thinking of raising the fare to $2.50 to generate 25 percent more revenue. The council has asked for your advice as a student of economics. In your analysis, be sure to break down the impact of the price increase into the price effect and also the output effect. Explain why the city council's estimate of the revenue increase is likely to be overstated. Use a diagram to illustrate your answer.

10. Suppose that a monopolist's marginal cost curve shifts upward. What is likely to happen to the price the monopolist charges, the quantity it produces, and the profit it makes? Use a diagram to illustrate your answer.

SOLVED PROBLEMS

5. There is a two-part answer here. The first graph shows a monopolist making a profit:

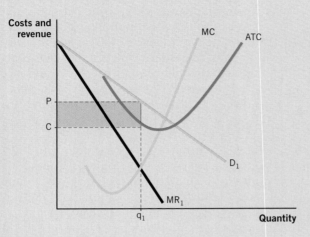

Now let's show what happens if demand falls:

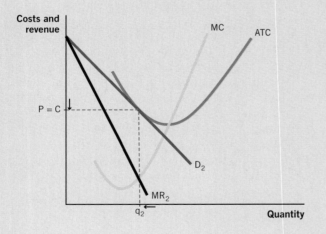

Lower demand causes the profit to disappear, the price to fall and the quantity sold to decline.

6.a.

Price	Downloads	Total Revenue	Marginal Revenue
$2.99	25,000	$74,750	$74,750
$1.99	50,000	99,500	24,750
$1.49	75,000	111,750	12,250
$0.99	100,000	99,000	−12,750
$0.49	150,000	73,500	−25,500

b. Since marginal costs are $0, the firm maximizes its profits at $1.49. The company makes $111,750 − $10,000, or $101,750.

c. The company makes $101,750 from production, so the agent could request any signing fee up to that amount. Since determining a fee is a negotiation and both sides have to gain from trade, we'd expect the agent to argue for a number close to $100,000 and for the firm to argue for a much smaller fee.

Price Discrimination

Charging different prices to different people is unfair and harmful.
Have you ever wondered why out-of-state students pay more for the
same education than in-state students, as happens at many public universities? Or why private colleges have high sticker prices and
then offer tuition discounts to some students, but not others?
Maybe you have noticed that many clubs let women in without a cover charge, but require men to pay. And why do theaters charge
more for adults and less for children when everyone sees the same
movie? In each of these examples, some customers pay more and others
end up paying less. Is this unfair and harmful? Not really. When a firm
can charge more than one price, markets work more efficiently.

In this chapter we examine many real-life pricing situations and how
businesses can make additional profits if they are able to charge more
than one price to different groups of customers. The study of *price discrimination* adds a layer of complexity to the simple models of perfect
competition and monopoly. A thorough understanding of how price
discrimination works will be especially useful as we complete our study
of market structure with monopolistic competition and oligopoly in the
next two chapters.

Why do some clubs offer "no cover" charge to ladies, but not to men?

* What is price discrimination?
* How is price discrimination practiced?

What Is Price Discrimination?

Price discrimination
exists when a firm sells the
same good at more than one
price to different groups of
customers.

Price discrimination exists when a firm sells the same good at more than one price to different groups of customers. The difference in price is not related to differences in cost. Although "price discrimination" sounds like it should be illegal, in fact it is beneficial to both sellers and buyers. When a firm can charge more than one price, markets work more efficiently. Also, some consumers are able to buy the product at a lower price than would otherwise exist. Of course, firms are not in business to provide goods at low prices; they want to make a profit. Price discrimination allows firms to make more money by partitioning their customers into at least two groups; customers who get a discount and others who pay more.

We have seen that in competitive markets firms are price takers. If a competitive firm attempts to charge a higher price, its customers will buy elsewhere. To practice price discrimination, a firm must be a price maker. Therefore a firm must have some market power before it can charge more than one price. Both monopolies and non-monopoly companies use price discrimination to earn higher profits. Common examples of price discrimination include movie theater tickets, restaurant menus, college tuition, airline reservations, discounts on academic software, and coupons.

Conditions of Price Discrimination

For price discrimination to take place, two conditions must be met. First, the firm must be able to distinguish groups of buyers with different price elasticities of demand. Second, the firm must be able to prevent resale of the product or service. Let's look at each in turn.

Distinguishing Groups of Buyers

In order to price-discriminate, the firm must be able to distinguish groups of buyers with different price elasticities of demand. Firms can generate additional revenues by charging more to customers with inelastic demand and less to customers with elastic demand. For instance, many restaurants offer lower prices, known as "blue-plate specials," to people who eat dinner earlier. Who are these customers? Many, such as retirees and families with children, are on a limited budget. These early diners have less demand and also demand that is more elastic; they will eat out only if the price is low enough.

Blue-plate specials work for restaurants by separating customers into two groups: one that is price-sensitive and another that is willing to pay full price. This allows the restaurant to serve more customers and generate additional revenue.

Preventing Resale

For price discrimination to be a viable strategy, a firm must also be able to prevent resale of the product or service. In some cases preventing resale is easy. Airlines require that electronic tickets match the passenger's government-issued photo ID. This prevents a passenger who received a discounted fare from reselling it to another passenger who is willing to pay more. This process works well for airlines and allows them to charge more to groups of flyers with more inelastic demand. It also works well for restaurants offering blue-plate specials, since the restaurant can easily distinguish between customers who arrive in time for the specials and those who arrive later.

Perfect Price Discrimination

A business that practices price discrimination would prefer to differentiate every customer by selling the same good at a price unique to that customer— a situation known as **perfect price discrimination**. To achieve this, a business would have to know exactly what any particular customer would be willing to pay and charge exactly that price. Many jewelry stores and automobile dealerships attempt to practice perfect price discrimination by posting high sticker prices and then bargaining with the customer to reach a deal. When you enter a jewelry store or a vehicle showroom, the salesperson tries to determine the highest price you are willing to pay, known as the *reservation price*. The salesperson bargains with you until that price is met.

Perfect price discrimination exists when a firm sells the same good at a unique price to every customer.

In practice, perfect price discrimination is hard to implement. To see why, let's look at a hypothetical example. Consider two small airlines, Flat Earth Air and Discriminating Fliers. Each airline has a monopoly on the route it flies, and they each face the same market demand curves and marginal costs. The costs of running a flight—fuel, pilots, flight attendants, ground crew, and so on—are about the same no matter how many passengers are on board. Both firms fly the same airplane and it seats 200 passengers. So the marginal cost of adding one passenger—the extra weight and the cost of a can of soda or two—is very small. What happens if one of the airlines uses price discrimination but the other does not?

In Figure 11.1 Flat Earth Air charges the same price to every flyer, while Discriminating Fliers uses two different price structures for its customers. To keep our example easy to work with, the marginal cost is set at $100, shown as a horizontal line.

Flat Earth sets its price, using the profit-maximizing rule, MR = MC. It charges $300 for every seat and serves 100 customers. Since the marginal cost is $100, every passenger who gets on the plane creates $200 in marginal revenue. The net revenue, represented by the green rectangle in the graph, is $200 × 100, or $20,000. At 100 passengers, this airline has done everything it can to maximize profits at a single price. At the same time, there are plenty of unsold seats in the plane that holds 150 passengers. Those unfilled seats represent a lost opportunity to earn additional revenue. As a result, airlines typically try to fill the plane by discounting the price of some seats.

In contrast, Discriminating Fliers decides to experiment with two prices. It charges $400 for midweek flights or last-minute bookings, and it charges $200 for weekend flights and to customers who book in advance. Let's look at the reasoning behind these two prices.

Since the firm faces a downward-sloping demand curve, the airline cannot sell every seat on the airplane at the higher price. So it saves a number of seats, in this case 50, for last-minute bookings to capture customers with less flexibility who are willing to pay $400. These are travelers with inelastic demand, such as people who travel for business. The airline offers the rest of the seats at a low price, in this case $200, to capture customers with more elastic demand. The difficulty for the airline is to make sure that the people willing to pay $400 do not purchase the $200 seats. To do this it makes the low fare available to customers who book far in advance, because these customers are typically more flexible and shop for the best deal. It is common for a business person who needs to visit a client to make arrangements just days before the meeting, which precludes purchasing a $200 ticket available only to customers who reserve their seats many weeks in advance. The customers who book early fill seats that would otherwise be empty if the airline

FIGURE 11.1

One Price versus Price Discrimination

(a) A firm that charges a single price uses MR = MC to earn a profit. (b) When a firm is able to price-discriminate, it takes in more revenue than a firm that charges a single price. By charging two prices, the discriminating firm is able to increase its revenue by charging some customers more and charging other customers less, as shown in blue. The increase in revenue is partly offset by the loss of revenue from existing customers who receive a lower price, as shown in orange.

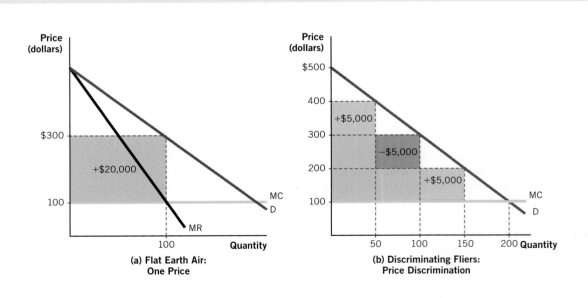

(a) Flat Earth Air:
One Price

(b) Discriminating Fliers:
Price Discrimination

had only charged one price, as Flat Earth does. We can see this by comparing the total number of passengers under the two strategies. Discriminating Fliers, with its two-price strategy, serves 150 passengers. Flat Earth's single price brings in 100 passengers.

The net effect of price discrimination is apparent in the shaded areas in the two panels in Figure 11.1b. By charging two prices, Discriminating Fliers generates more net revenue. The high price, $400, generates additional revenue equal to the upper blue rectangle—$5,000—from passengers who must pay more than the $300 charged by Flat Earth. Discriminating Fliers also gains additional revenue with its low price of $200. The less expensive tickets attract

Airlines offer lower fares if you are willing to take the red-eye.

those with more elastic demand, such as college students, vacationers, and retirees. This generates $5,000, as shown by the lower blue rectangle.

Some customers would have paid Discriminating Fliers more if the airline had charged a single price. The group of customers willing to pay $300 is able to acquire tickets on Discriminating Fliers for $200. This is reflected by the orange rectangle, which represents lost revenues equal to $5,000. The $10,000 in revenue represented by the blue rectangles more than offsets the $5,000 in lost revenue represented by the orange rectangle. The airline that price-discriminates generates a net revenue of $25,000 in panel (b). The airline that charges a single price generates a net revenue of $20,000 in panel (a).

In reality, airlines often charge many prices. You can find higher prices for travel on Friday and midday flights. If your stay includes a Saturday night, or you choose a red-eye flight, your prices will be lower. Airlines also change prices from day to day and even hour to hour. All of these efforts are designed to price-discriminate on multiple fronts.

Since passengers cannot resell their tickets and many plans cannot be changed easily, airlines can effectively price-discriminate. In fact, if an airline could charge unique prices for every passenger booking a flight, it would transform the entire area under the demand curve and above the marginal cost curve into more revenue.

Photo to come

The Welfare Effects of Price Discrimination

Price discrimination is profitable for the companies that are able to do it. But it also increases the welfare of society. How can companies make more profit and benefit consumers? Because a price discriminator charges a high price to some and a low price to others, more consumers are able to buy the good.

To make this point clearer, let's imagine an airline, Perfect Flights, that is able to perfectly price-discriminate. Perfect Flights charges each passenger a price exactly equal to what the passenger is willing to pay. As a result, some customers pay more and some customers pay less than they would under a single-price system. This is shown in Figure 11.2, where a profit-maximizing firm charges $300. At this price the firm captures the net revenue in the lower blue rectangle, c. However, Perfect Flights charges each passenger a price based on that passenger's willingness to pay. Therefore, it is able to earn significantly more net revenue. By charging higher prices to those willing to pay more than $300 ($P_{high}$), the firm is able to capture additional net revenues in the upper blue triangle, a. Likewise, by charging lower prices to those not willing to pay $300 ($P_{low}$), the firm is able to capture additional net revenues in triangle c. The end result is that Perfect Flights is making more money and serving more customers.

By charging a different fare to every customer, Perfect Flights is also able to increase the number of tickets sold to 200. This creates two results worth noting. First, in the long run, a perfectly competitive firm would charge a price just equal to marginal cost. In the case of Perfect Flights, the last customer who gets on the plane will be charged an extraordinarily low price of $100—the price you might find in a competitive market. Second, this outcome also mirrors the result of a government-regulated monopolist who uses

FIGURE 11.2

Perfect Price Discrimination

If the firm charges one price, the most it can earn is the net revenue in the green rectangle. However, if a firm is able to perfectly price-discriminate, it can pick up the additional revenue represented by the blue triangles.

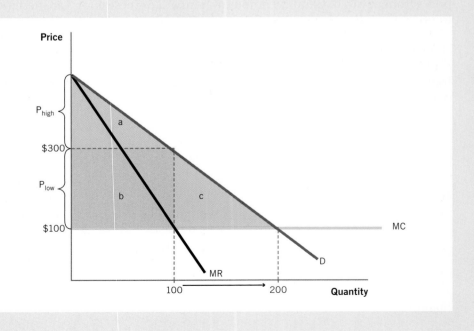

the marginal-cost pricing rule, P = MC, to curtail monopoly profits. Perfect Flights is therefore achieving the efficiency noted in a competitive market while also producing the output a regulated monopolist would choose. This provides the firm with the opportunity to convert the area consisting of the two blue triangles into more revenue. This process maximizes the quantity sold. The efficiency of the market is improved and the firm generates more revenue.

Comparing Perfect Price Discrimination with Perfect Competition and Monopoly

To understand the welfare effects of perfect price discrimination, we can compare the consumer and producer surplus in three scenarios: a competitive market, a monopolist that charges a single price, and perfect price discrimination. The results are shown in Table 11.1 and they are derived by examining Figure 11.2.

In a "perfectly" competitive market there are no barriers to entry and no firm has market power. In the long run, the price will be equal to the marginal cost. In our example of airline ticket prices, the price is driven down to $100. At this price, 200 tickets are sold. The entire area above the marginal cost curve (a + b + c) is consumer surplus, since the willingness to pay—as determined along the demand curve—is greater than the price that is charged. Because ticket price is the same as the marginal cost, the producer surplus is zero. Also, since every customer who is willing to pay $100 or more can find a ticket, there is no deadweight loss. Under perfect competition, the market structure clearly favors consumers.

A monopoly holds substantial market power, so the firm sets a price using the profit maximizing rule, MR = MC, without having to worry about competition driving the price down to marginal cost. The monopolist's profit-maximizing price, or $300 in Figure 11.2, is higher than the price, $100, under perfect competition. This higher price reduces the amount of consumer surplus to triangle a and creates a producer surplus equal to rectangle b. In addition, because the number of tickets sold falls to 100, there is now deadweight loss equal to triangle c. Economic activity associated with triangle c no longer exists and the total welfare of society is now limited to (a + b). From this we see that monopoly causes a partial transfer of consumer surplus to producers and a reduction in total welfare for society.

TABLE 11.1

The Welfare Effects of Perfect Price Discrimination

	Perfect Competition	A Monopolist that Charges a Single Price	Perfect Price Discrimination
Consumer Surplus	a + b + c	a	0
Producer Surplus	0	b	a + b + c
Deadweight Loss	0	c	0
Total Welfare	a + b + c	a + b	a + b + c

Perfect Price Discrimination

Legally Blonde (2001)

Reese Witherspoon stars as Elle Woods, a sun-washed sorority girl who defies expectations.

Believing that her boyfriend is about to propose to her, Elle and two of her friends go shopping to find the perfect dress to wear for the occasion. They enter an exclusive boutique and start trying on dresses.

The saleswoman comments to another associate, "There's nothing I love more than a dumb blonde with daddy's plastic." She grabs a dress off the clearance sale rack and removes the "half price" tag. Approaching Elle, she says, "Did you see this one? We just got it in yesterday." Elle fingers the dress, then the price tag, and looks at the saleswoman with excitement.

> **ELLE:** "Is this a low-viscosity rayon?"
> **SALESWOMAN:** "Uh, yes—of course."
> **ELLE:** "With half-loop top-stitching on the hem?"
> **SALESWOMAN** (smiling a lie): "Absolutely. It's one of a kind."

Elle hands the dress back to her, no longer pretending to be excited.

> **ELLE:** "It's impossible to use a half-loop topstitch on low-viscosity rayon. It would snag the fabric. And you didn't just get this in, because I remember it from the June *Vogue* a year ago, so if you're trying to sell it to me at full price, you picked the wrong girl."

How much would you pay to look good on the night your boyfriend proposes?

The saleswoman slinks off, embarrassed.

The scene is a wonderful example of an attempt at price discrimination gone wrong. Unbeknownst to the saleswoman, Elle is majoring in fashion merchandising in college and knows more about fashion than she does. Her poor effort to cheat Elle fails miserably.

What makes the scene powerful is the use of stereotypes. When merchants attempt to price-discriminate, they are looking for clues to help them decide whether the buyer is willing to pay full price or needs an incentive, or discount, in order to make a purchase. In this case, Elle's outward appearance makes it look like she is an uninformed buyer, with highly inelastic demand. Consequently, the saleswoman's strategy backfires.

A firm that can conduct perfect price discrimination is able to charge each customer a price exactly equal to the price the customer is willing to pay. This allows the firm to convert the entire area of consumer surplus that existed under perfect competition into producer surplus (a + b + c). For the firm to be able to capture the entire area of available consumer surplus, it must be willing to lower some prices all the way down to marginal cost. The number of tickets sold returns to 200, the market is once again efficient, and deadweight loss disappears. Perfect price discrimination transfers the gains from trade from consumers to producers, but it also creates maximum efficiency. Note that this gives us a better understanding of what economists mean when they use the word "perfect" in connection with a market. It can mean that consumer surplus is maximized, as it is under perfect competition, or that producer surplus is maximized, as it is under perfect price discrimination. It does not specify an outcome from a particular perspective, but rather describes any market process that produces no deadweight loss. If society's total welfare is maximized, economists do not distinguish whether the benefits accrue to consumers or producers.

ECONOMICS IN THE REAL WORLD

Outlet Malls—Build It and They Will Come

Have you ever noticed that outlet malls along major roadways are often a considerable distance from major population centers? Moreover, every item at an outlet mall can be found closer to home. The same clothes, shoes, and kitchenware are available nearby.

Logic tells us that it would be more convenient to shop locally and forget the time and hassle of getting to an outlet center. But that is not how many shoppers feel.

Discount shopping is a big deal. How big? Here are a few statistics. Potomac Mills, 30 miles south of Washington, D.C., is Virginia's most popular attraction, with nearly 17 million visitors a year. That figure rivals the number of annual visitors to Disney World's Magic Kingdom. Potomac Mills is not unique. Two adjacent outlet malls in San Marcos, Texas, attract over 6 million visitors a year, many more than the number that visit the Alamo. In Pigeon Forge, Tennessee, over ten million shoppers go to the outlets annually, more than the number of visitors to nearby Great Smoky Mountains National Park.

Outlet shopping is an example of price discrimination at work. Traditional malls are usually found in urban settings and offer a wide variety

How far would you drive to visit an outlet mall?

of choices, but not necessarily low prices. If you want convenience, the local shopping mall is right around the corner. But if you want a bargain, shopping at a traditional mall is not the best place to go.

What makes outlets so attractive to many shoppers are discounts. Bargain hunters have much more elastic demand than their traditional mall-shopping counterparts who desire convenience. Moreover, the difference in the price elasticity of demand between these two groups means that traditional malls can more easily charge full price, while outlets must discount their merchandise in order to attract customers. This gives merchants a chance to price-discriminate based on location—which is another way of separating your customers into two groups and preventing resale at the same time. Retailers are therefore able to earn additional profits through price discrimination, while consumers who are price-sensitive can find lower prices at outlets.

It is worth noting that the convenience of being able to find discounts online threatens not only the traditional malls but also the sales of outlets. When savvy shoppers can click to find the best deal, will they continue to drive to the outlets? ✳

PRACTICE WHAT YOU KNOW

Price Discrimination: Taking Economics to New Heights

Consider the table below, which shows seven potential customers, each interested in taking a 30-minute helicopter ride. The helicopter has room for eight people, including the pilot. The marginal cost of taking on additional passengers is $10.

How much would you pay to fly in a helicopter?

Customer	Maximum Willingness to Pay	Age
Amelia	$80	66
Orville	70	34
Wilbur	40	17
Neil	50	16
Charles	60	9
Chuck	100	49
Buzz	20	9

Question: If the company can charge only one price, what should it be?

Answer: First create an ordered array of the customers, from those willing to pay the most to those willing to pay the least.

Customer	Maximum Willingness to Pay	Price	TR	MR
Chuck	$100	$100	$100	$90
Amelia	80	80	160	60
Orville	70	70	210	50
Charles	60	60	240	30
Neil	50	50	250	10
Wilbur	40	40	240	−10
Buzz	20	20	140	−100

If the price the firm charges is $100, only Chuck will take the flight. When the firm drops the price to $80, Chuck and Amelia both buy tickets, so the total revenue is $80 × 2, or $160. Successively lower prices result in higher total revenue for the first five customers. Since the marginal cost is $10, the firm will benefit from lowering its price as long as the increase in marginal revenue is greater than, or equal to, the marginal cost. When the price is $50, five customers get on the helicopter, for a total of $250 in revenue. Adding the fifth passenger brings in exactly $10 in marginal revenue, so this is the best possible single price to charge. Since each of the five passengers has a marginal cost of $10, the company makes $250 − (5 × $10), or $200 in profit.

Question: If the company could charge two prices, what should they be and who would pay them?

Answer: First, arrange the customers in two distinct groups: adults and children.

Adult Customers	Willingness to Pay	Age	Price	TR	MR
Chuck	$100	49	$90	$90	$90
Amelia	80	66	80	160	60
Orville	70	34	70	210	50

Young Customers	Willingness to Pay	Age	Price	TR	MR
Charles	60	9	60	$60	60
Neil	50	16	50	100	40
Wilbur	40	17	40	120	20
Buzz	20	9	20	80	−40

As you can see, two separate prices emerge. For adults, total revenue is maximized at a price of $70. For children, total revenue is maximized at $40. The company should charge $70 to the adult customers, which brings in $70 × 3, or $210 in total revenue. The company should charge $40 for each child under 18, which brings in $40 × 3, or $120. Note that if the company lowered the price of a child's ticket to $20 in order to entice Buzz to buy a ticket, it would earn $20 × 4, or $80, a lower total revenue.

Price discrimination earns the company $210 + $120 − (6 × $10), or $270 in profit. This is a $70 improvement over charging a single price. In addition, six passengers are now able to get on the helicopter instead of only five under the single-price model.

How Is Price Discrimination Practiced?

Price discrimination is one of the most interesting topics in economics because each example is slightly different. In this section we take a closer look at real-world examples of price discrimination at movie theaters and on college campuses. As you will see, price discrimination takes many forms, some that are easy to describe and others that are more nuanced.

Price Discrimination at the Movies

Have you ever gone to the movies early so you can pay less for tickets? Movie theaters price-discriminate based on the time of day, age, and whether or not you buy snacks. Let's examine each of these pricing techniques to see if they are effective.

Pricing Based on the Time of the Show

Why are matinees priced less than evening shows? To encourage customers to take advantage of movies during the afternoon, theaters discount ticket prices for matinees. This makes sense because customers who can attend matinees (retirees, people on vacation, and those who do not work during the day) either have less demand or are more flexible, or price elastic. Work and school limit the options for many potential customers. As a result, theaters discount matinee prices to encourage moviegoers who have elastic demand and are willing to watch at a less crowded time. Movie theaters are also willing to discount the price of matinee shows since they pay to rent films on a weekly basis— so it is in their interest to show a film as many times as possible. Since the variable cost of being open during the day is essentially limited to paying a few employees the minimum

Moviegoers who attend matinees have more elastic demand.

wage, the theater can make additional profits even with a relatively small audience. On weekends, matinees also provide a discount to families that want to see a movie together—adding yet another layer of price discrimination.

Theaters charge two different prices based on show time because they can easily distinguish between high-demand customers and price-sensitive customers who have the flexibility to watch a matinee by offering reduced admission. Those with higher demand or less flexible schedules must pay higher show prices to go in the evening.

Pricing Based on Age

Why are there different prices for children, seniors, and everyone else? This is a complex question. Income does not fully explain the discounts that the young and old receive. Movie attendance is highest among 13- to 24-year-olds

Seniors enjoy discounted tickets because they are less likely to go to the movies, not because of low purchasing power.

and declines thereafter with age. Given the strong demand among teenagers, it is not surprising that "child" discounts are phased out at most theaters by age 12. But did you know that most "senior" discounts begin before 65? In some places a senior discount can be secured starting at age 50. People in their fifties tend to be at the peak of their earning power, so discounting ticket prices would seem to be a bad move. However, since interest in going to the movies declines with age, the "senior" discount provides an incentive to a population that might not otherwise go to a movie theater. As we have seen, age-based price discrimination does not always work perfectly. Theaters do not usually ask for proof of age and it may be hard to tell the difference between a child who is just under 12 and one who is over 12. However, the process of price discrimination works well enough to make age a useful revenue-generating tool.

Concession Pricing

Have you ever wondered why it is so expensive to purchase snacks at the movie theater? The concession area is another way movie theaters practice price discrimination. To understand this, we need to think of two groups of customers: those who want to eat while they watch movies and those who do not. By limiting outside food and drink, movie theaters push people with inelastic demand for snacks to buy from the concession area. Of course, that does not stop some customers with elastic demand from sneaking food into the theater. But as long as some moviegoers are willing to buy concession fare at exorbitant prices, the theater will generate more revenue. Movie theaters cannot prevent smuggling, and they don't have to. All they really want to do is separate their customers into two groups: a

If you have ever smuggled food into a movie theater, it is because your demand for movie theater concessions is elastic.

price-inelastic group of concession-area snackers and a price-elastic group of nonsnackers and smugglers who fill up the remaining empty seats in the theaters. This is very similar to the problem we examined with airlines. Empty seats represent lost revenue, so it makes sense to try to price-discriminate through a combination of high and low prices.

Price Discrimination on Campus

Colleges and universities are experts at price discrimination. Look at tuition. Some students pay the full sticker price, while others enjoy a free ride. Some students receive the in-state rate, while out-of-state students pay substantially more. And once you get to campus, discounts for students are everywhere. In this section, we look the many ways that colleges and universities differentiate among their students.

Tuition

Price discrimination begins before you ever set foot on campus, with the Free Application for Federal Student Aid (known as the FAFSA) that most families complete. The form determines eligibility for federal aid. Families that qualify are eligible for grants and low-interest loans. This has the effect of lowering the tuition cost for low- and medium-income families. Therefore, the FAFSA application allows colleges to separate the applicants into two groups based on income. Since many colleges also use the FAFSA to determine eligibility for their own institutional grants of aid, the FAFSA makes it possible for colleges to precisely target grants and loans to the students who need the most help in order to attend.

Many state institutions of higher education have a two-tiered pricing structure. In-state students get a discount on the tuition and out-of-state students pay a much higher rate. Part of the difference in the tuition rates is explained by state subsidies intended to make in-state institutions more affordable for residents. In-state students pay less because their parents have been paying taxes to the state, often for many years, and the state then uses those tax dollars to support its system. This creates two separate groups of customers with distinctly different elasticities of demand. Students choose an out-of-state college or university because they like what that

Colleges and universities use the FAFSA to determine your eligibility for student loans, grants and scholarships.

institution has to offer more than institutions in their home state. It might be that a particular major or program is more highly rated, or simply that they prefer the location of the out-of-state school. Whatever the reason, they are willing to pay more for the out-of-state school. Therefore, out-of-state students have a much more inelastic demand. Colleges know this and price their tuition accordingly. Conversely, in-state students often view the opportunity to attend a nearby college as the most economical decision. Since price is a big factor in choosing an in-state institution, it is not surprising that in-state demand is more elastic.

Selective private colleges also play the price discrimination game by advertising annual tuition and room and board fees that exceed $50,000. With price discrimination, the "sticker" price is often discounted. Depending on how much the college wants to encourage a student to attend, it can discount the tuition all the way to zero. This enables selective private colleges to price-discriminate by offering scholarships based on financial need, while also guaranteeing placements for the children of wealthy alums and others willing and able to pay the full sticker price.

Student Discounts

The edge of campus is a great place to look for price discrimination. Local bars, eateries, and shops all want college students to step off campus, so student discounts are the norm. Why do establishments do this? Think about the average college student. Price matters. Local merchants in search of college customers can provide student discounts without lowering their prices across the board. This allows them to charge more to their regular clients, while providing the necessary discounts to get college students to make the trek off campus.

Price discrimination also occurs on campus. Students typically receive discounts for many campus events like concerts and sporting events. Since students generally have elastic demand, price discrimination gives greater student access to on-campus events than if a single price was charged.

Resort or college? Sky-high tuition and room and board are one way to help pay for a beautiful campus.

ECONOMICS IN THE REAL WORLD

Groupon

Groupon is an organization that negotiates sizable discounts (typically 50% or more) with local businesses. It then sends the deals it finds to local subscribers through email, a Facebook post, or Twitter. If enough subscribers decide

ECONOMICS IN THE MEDIA

Price Discrimination

Extreme Couponing (2011)

Most of us use coupons from time to time, when it is convenient. *Extreme Couponing* showcases the lives of a small number of shoppers who plan their trips to the store with military precision. They clip coupons, scout out the stores that offer the best coupon deals, and buy products in enormous quantities to save money.

While these couponers often get groceries for practically nothing and appear to beat the system, they go to a lot of trouble to secure a "deal." Some dive in dumpsters to get the discarded Sunday news-paper coupon sections. Others keep food stashes that take up most of the space in their homes. They use spreadsheets, folders, and calculators to deter-mine how to save as much as possible. The returns are typically hundreds of dollars in savings each time they visit the store.

However, as good economists we know that get-ting a really good deal on something doesn't make it "free." The amount of time it takes to be an extreme couponer is staggering. It is the equivalent of a part-time job. Clearly the participants do not fully account for the time they spend on couponing. Saving $200

Would you dumpster-dive to get coupons?

at the store sounds great unless it takes you 20 hours to do so; that's only $10 an hour. If many of the people on the show did the math, they might find that they could earn substantially more by putting their organizational skills to use in the workforce. It is this very reason that causes many households not to clip very many coupons in the first place. Time is money.

If enough people sign up, they each get a discount.

they like the deal, Groupon sends—for a fee—a discount coupon to everyone who signed up. The Groupon subscriber gets a deal and the business gets addi-tional customers. Both parties win: sub-scribers score a deal on something they might not otherwise have purchased, and businesses generate additional rev-enue through price discrimination.

Does Groupon price-discriminate perfectly? No. Some people who might have been willing to pay full price will occasionally score a discount. But on balance, since Groupon operates in many major cities, there are many resi-dents who want to try something new. In addition, Groupon users tend to be more price-sensitive than nonusers.

Because Groupon requires some effort, not everyone will bother to become a subscriber, sign up for coupons, and remember to use them. This is imperfect price discrimination, but it is still good business. ✳

PRACTICE WHAT YOU KNOW

Price Discrimination in Practice: Everyday Examples

Question: Test your understanding by thinking about the examples below and then read the descriptions to find out if you were right.

(a) Retail coupons. Programs such as discount coupons, rebates, and frequent-buyer plans help firms differentiate between the affluent and the price-conscious. Is this price discrimination?

(b) Using Priceline to make hotel reservations. "Naming your price" on Priceline is a form of haggling that allows users to get hotel rooms at a discount. Hotels negotiate with Priceline to fill unused rooms while still advertising the full price on their websites, Expedia, and other travel services. Is this price discrimination?

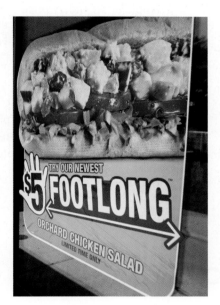

Price discrimination or not?

(c) $5 footlong subs at Subway. Customers who buy a $5 footlong get more sub at a substantially lower price per inch than customers who choose the 6-inch sub. Is this price discrimination?

(d) The Dollar Menu at McDonald's. Customers who order off the Dollar Menu get a variety of smaller menu items for $1. Is this price discrimination?

(e) Discounts for early shoppers on Black Friday. Customers who line up in the early-morning hours after Thanksgiving gets first dibs on a limited quantity of reduced items at many retailers. Is this price discrimination?

Answers:

(a) Retail coupons. Well-to-do customers generally will not bother with the hassle of clipping, sending in, and keeping track of the coupons. However, customers with lower incomes will take the time to get the discount. Since affluent customers generally value their time more than the small amount of savings that a discount offers, they are far less likely to take the trouble to cut a coupon or search for a deal. This allows coupons, rebates, and frequent-buyer programs to do a good job of price discriminating.

(b) Using Priceline to make hotel reservations. Priceline allows hotels to divide their customers into two groups: those who don't want to be bothered with haggling, and those who value the savings enough to justify the time spent negotiating. This is a good example of price discrimination.

(c) $5 footlong subs at Subway. The $5 price is available to anyone who enters the store at any time of the day. Therefore, the $5 footlong is catchy marketing, but it does not strictly meet the definition of price discrimination. However, to get the deal you must buy a 12-inch sub. This is an example of secondary price discrimination—that is, the price per unit varies with the quantity sold. So even though anyone could conceivably get the deal, only those with big appetites will choose a footlong. Those with smaller appetites are stuck paying $3.50 for a 6-inch sub—which is not nearly as good a price.

(d) The Dollar Menu at McDonald's. Anyone can buy off the Dollar Menu at any time. Since McDonald's does not force you to buy a large serving in order to get the deal, this is not price discrimination.

(e) Discounts for early shoppers on Black Friday. The discounts are time-sensitive. Shoppers who arrive before the deadline get a lower price, customers who arrive after do not. This is a clear-cut example of price discrimination.

Conclusion

Discriminating against anyone, for any reason, sounds awful, but that misconception does not apply to price discrimination. Charging different prices to different groups of customers results in more economic activity and is more efficient. Under price discrimination, many consumers pay lower prices than they would if a firm charged a single price. This has the effect of increasing social welfare, reducing deadweight loss, and creating a more efficient outcome. Perfect price discrimination occurs when the firm is able to charge a different price to every customer. The result is a socially efficient outcome in which most of the gains from exchange accrue to producers.

Price discrimination also helps us understand how many markets actually function, since instances of highly competitive markets and monopoly are rare.

Avoiding Grocery Store Tactics

Throughout this chapter we have considered the shopping experience in the context of price discrimination. Here we focus on how each grocery store is set up to manipulate the buyer into spending more. Grocery stores generate sensory overload, from the smell of the bread in the bakery, to the cut flowers and fresh produce, to the eat-in restaurants and coffee bars, and the tens of thousands of items to purchase. You need to be on your game. Here is some advice to help you save a few dollars.

Grocery stores want to route you through the store. Have you ever wondered why the produce is where it is? Or why the stuff you really need is at the back of the store? The grocery store has set things up to entice you to purchase more than you really need. Suppose that you are there to pick up a gallon of milk. In most stores the refrigerated section is in the back, so that you have plenty of opportunities to impulsively grab something else that looks good.

Popular items are placed at eye-level. Supermarkets make more profits from *manufacturers* than from consumers. Manufacturers pay "slotting fees" to have their products placed in desirable locations. The product you want may be on a higher or lower shelf—it pays to look up and down.

Beware of sales. Stores know that shoppers gravitate to markdowns and sales. The problem is that many shoppers are not very diligent in determining if the sale is any good. Don't buy something simply because it is "on sale" and located at the end of the aisle. This is one way that groceries make extra money and you end up buying stuff you don't really need.

Find the loss leaders. To drive traffic to the store, groceries compete by offering a few fantastic promotions. Sometimes the sale items are priced so low that the store is actually losing money by selling them. The store's management is counting on making up the difference when you buy other items

Grocery stores try to tempt you to buy more than you need.

throughout the store. The deal you get on one item should not cause you to let down your guard on the other purchases you make.

Beware of coupons! Coupons aren't always the best deal either. Stores know which manufacturer coupons customers have. Those products are rarely reduced. If you have to pay full price in order to use a coupon, is it really a good deal? Consider store brands or other brands of the same item before you use a coupon.

Store brands. Generally the store brands will be cheaper than the name brands. The store brand is often exactly the same product as the name brand—it is just repackaged at the manufacturing plant and sold for less. You can save a lot of money by using store brands.

Finally, get a smaller shopping cart. When your cart fills up, most shoppers instinctively ration the remaining space and become far more selective about what they pick up.

If you are aware of the tactics that grocery stores deploy, you will start beating them at their own game.

ANSWERING THE BIG QUESTIONS

1. What is price discrimination?

* A firm must have some market power before it can charge more than one price.

* Price discrimination occurs when firms have downward-sloping demand curves, can identify different groups of customers with varying price elasticities of demand, and have the ability to prevent resale among their customers.

2. How is price discrimination practiced?

* Under price discrimination some consumers pay a higher price and others are given a discount. Price discrimination is profitable for the firm, reduces deadweight loss, and helps to restore a higher output level.

CONCEPTS YOU SHOULD KNOW

Perfect price discrimination (p.321)

Price discrimination (p. 320)

QUESTIONS

1. What two challenges must a firm overcome to effectively price-discriminate?
2. Why does price discrimination improve the efficiency of the market?
3. Why is preventing resale a key to successful price discrimination?

4. If perfect price discrimination reduces consumer surplus to zero, how is it possible that this leads to the most socially desirable level of output?

STUDY PROBLEMS

1. Seven potential customers are interested in seeing a movie. Since the marginal cost of admitting additional customers is zero, the movie theater maximizes its profits by maximizing its revenue.

Customer	Maximum Willingness to Pay	Age
Allison	$8	66
Becky	11	34
Charlie	6	45
David	7	16
Erin	6	9
Franco	10	28
Grace	9	14

   a. What price would the theater charge if it could only charge one price?
   b. If the theater could charge two prices, what two prices would it choose? Which customers would pay the higher price and which would pay the lower price?

2. Identify whether each of following is an example of price discrimination. Explain your answers.
   a. A cell phone carrier offers unlimited calling on the weekends for all of its customers.
   b. Tickets to the student section for all basketball games are $5.
   c. A restaurant offers a 20% discount for customers who order dinner between 4 and 6 p.m.
   d. A music store has a half-price sale on last year's guitars.
   e. A well-respected golf instructor charges each customer a fee just under the customer's maximum willingness to pay for lessons.

3. At many amusement parks, customers who enter the park after 4 p.m. receive a steep discount on the price they pay. Explain how this practice is a form of price discrimination.

4. Name three products for which impatience on the part of the consumer allows the firm to price-discriminate.

＊ 5. Prescription drug prices in the United States are often three to four times higher than in Canada, the United Kingdom, and India. Today, pharmacies in these countries fill millions of low-cost prescriptions through the mail to U.S. citizens. Given that the pharmaceutical industry cannot prevent the resale of these drugs, are the industry's efforts to price-discriminate useless?

＊ 6. Metropolitan Opera tickets are the most expensive on Saturday night. There are often a very limited number of "student rush" tickets.

A lucky student can wind up paying $20 for a $250 seat if the student is willing to go to Lincoln Center at noon and stand in line for 2 hours. But there is no guarantee that the rush tickets won't sell out before the student gets to the front of the line. Why do student rush tickets exist? How does the opera company benefit from this practice? Why are students, and not other groups of customers, willing to wait in line to get the discounted tickets?

SOLVED PROBLEMS

5. Buying prescription drugs outside the United States is increasingly common. Since the pharmaceutical companies charge three to four times more for domestic drugs than they do in most other countries, it would seem that drug industry's efforts to price-discriminate aren't working, but that is not true. Not everyone fills their prescriptions from foreign sources—only a small fraction of U.S. customers go to that much effort. Since most U.S. citizens still purchase the more expensive drugs here, the pharmaceutical companies are benefitting from price discrimination, even though some are able to navigate around their efforts.

6. The Met hopes to sell all of its $250 tickets, but not every show sells out and some tickets are made available at the last minute. The student rush tickets benefit both the opera company and the students. The company can fill last-minute seats and the students, who have elastic demand and a low income, get a steep discount. The Met is able to perfectly price-discriminate, since the rush tickets require a student ID. Other groups of operagoers are therefore unable to buy the rush tickets, effectively separating the customer base into two groups: students and nonstudents. Students make ideal rush customers because they are more willing to wait in line for last-minute tickets than other groups because their time is worth less. Some opera companies also open up the rush tickets to seniors, another group that can be easily identified and has the time to wait in line.

CHAPTER

12 | Monopolistic Competition and Advertising

Advertising increases the price of products without adding value for the consumer.

If you drive down a busy street you will find many competing businesses, often right next to each other. For example, in most places

MIS CONCEPTION
a consumer in search of a quick bite has many choices, and new fast-food restaurants appear all the time. These competing firms advertise heavily. The temptation is to see advertising as driving up the price of a product, without any benefit to the consumer. However, this misconception doesn't account for why firms advertise. In markets where competitors sell slightly differentiated products, advertising allows firms to inform their customers about new products and services; costs rise, but consumers also gain information to help them make a purchase decision.

In this chapter we look at *monopolistic competition,* a widespread market structure that has features of both competitive markets and monopoly. We will also explore the benefits and disadvantages of advertising, which is prevalent in markets with monopolistic competition.

Want something to eat quickly? There are many choices.

BIG QUESTIONS

* What is monopolistic competition?
* What are the differences among monopolistic competition, competitive markets, and monopoly?
* Why is advertising prevalent in monopolistic competition?

What Is Monopolistic Competition?

Some consumers prefer the fries at McDonald's, while others may crave a salad at Panera Bread, or the chicken at KFC. Each fast-food establishment has a unique set of menu items. The different products in fast-food restaurants give each seller a small degree of market power. This combination of market power and competition is typical of the market structure known as *monopolistic competition*. A **monopolistically competitive** market is characterized by free entry, many different firms, and *product differentiation*. **Product differentiation** is the process firms use to make a product more attractive to potential customers. Firms use product differentiation to contrast their product's unique qualities with competing products. The differences, which we will examine in detail, can be minor and involve subtle changes in packaging, quality, availability, and promotion.

How does monopolistic competition compare to other market structures we have studied? As Table 12.1 shows, monopolistic competition shares certain features with both perfect competition and monopoly.

We have seen that firms in competitive markets do not have any market power. As a result, buyers can expect to find consistently low prices and wide availability. And we have seen that monopolies charge more and restrict availability. In markets that are monopolistically competitive, firms sell differentiated products. This gives the monopolistic competitor some market power, though not as much as a monopolist, who controls the entire market. Monopolistically competitive firms have a small amount of market power that enables them to search for the price that is most profitable.

To understand how monopolistic competition works, we will begin with a closer look at product differentiation.

Monopolistic competition is characterized by free entry, many different firms, and product differentiation.

Product differentiation is the process that firms use to make a product more attractive to potential customers.

TABLE 12.1

Perfect Competition, Monopolistic Competition, and Monopoly		
Perfect Competition	**Monopolistic Competition**	**Monopoly**
Many sellers	Many sellers	One seller
Similar products	Differentiated products	A unique product without close substitutes
Free entry and exit	Free entry and exit	Barriers to entry and exit

Product Differentiation

We have seen that monopolistically competitive firms create some market power through product differentiation. Differentiation can occur in a variety of ways including style, location, and quality.

Style or Type

A trip to a mall is a great way to see product differentiation first hand. You will find many clothing stores, each offering a unique array of styles and types of clothing. Some stores, such as Abercrombie and Fitch, carry styles that attract younger customers. Others, such as Ann Taylor, appeal to older shoppers. Clothing stores can also vary by the type of clothing they sell, specializing in things such as business clothing, plus sizes, or sportswear. Each store is hoping to attract a specific type of customer.

When you're ready for lunch at the mall you can go to the food court, where you will find many different places to eat with an almost endless variety of choices. Where you decide to eat is a matter of your preferences and the price you are willing to pay. Like most consumers, you will select the place that gives you the best combination of choice and value. This makes it possible for a wide range of food vendors to compete side by side with other rivals who provide many good substitutes.

Taco Bell provides a low-quality Mexican fast-food option.

Location

Many businesses attract customers because of their convenient location. Gasoline stations, dry cleaners, barber shops, and car washes provide products and services that customers tend to choose by convenience of location rather than price. When consumers prefer to save time and to avoid the inconvenience of shopping for a better deal, a firm with the more convenient location will have some pricing power. As a result, producers who sell very similar products can create some market power by locating their businesses along routes to and from work, or in areas where customers frequently travel.

Quality

Firms also compete on quality. For instance, if you want Mexican food, you can go to Taco Bell, which is inexpensive and cooks food in advance. On the other hand, at Baja Fresh the food is freshly prepared and, as a result, more expensive. This form of product differentiation ends up serving consumers quite well. Budget-conscious consumers can feast at Taco Bell, while those with a taste for

Baja Fresh provides a high-quality Mexican fast-food option.

higher-quality Mexican food and a higher budget have Baja Fresh as another option. Even though the two chains sell Mexican food, they have carved up the market for Mexican food into two distinct segments and do not directly compete with each other.

PRACTICE WHAT YOU KNOW

Product Differentiation: Would You Recognize a Monopolistic Competitor?

Question: Which of the following are monopolistic competitors?

a. A local apple farm that grows Red Delicious apples
b. Hollister, an apparel store
c. Your local water company

Answers:

a. Since Red Delicious apples are widely available at the grocery store, this local apple farm does not have a differentiated product to sell. In addition, it has many competitors who grow exactly the same variety of apples. This apple farm is part of a competitive market.

b. Hollister has a slightly different mix of clothes than competitors Abercrombie and Fitch and American Eagle. This gives the brand some pric-

Is Hollister a monopolistic competitor?

ing power. Hollister is a good example of a monopolistically competitive firm.

c. Because water is essential and people cannot easily do without it, the local water company has significant monopoly power. It doesn't hurt either that purifying and distributing water are subject to economies of scale. Your local water company is definitely a monopolist.

What Are the Differences Among Monopolistic Competition, Perfect Competition, and Monopoly?

Monopolistic competition occupies a place between competitive markets, which produce low prices and an efficient output, and monopoly, which produces high prices and an inefficient output. To help you decide whether monopolistic competition is desirable or not, we consider the outcomes that individual firms are able to achieve when facing monopolistic competition in the short run and in the long run. Once you understand how monopolistic competition works, we will be able to compare the long-run equilibrium result with that of competitive markets, and then determine if monopolistic competition is desirable from society's standpoint.

Monopolistic Competition in the Short Run and Long Run

A monopolistically competitive firm sells a differentiated product; this gives it some market power. We see this in the shape of the demand curve for the monopolistic competitor, which is downward-sloping. Like a monopolist, the monopolistic competitor uses the profit-maximizing rule, MR = MC, and locates the corresponding point on its demand curve to determine the best price to charge and quantity to produce. Whether the firm is able to earn profits, experiences a loss, or breaks even is a function of entry and exit from the market. Recall that entry and exit do not take place in the short run. However, in the long run firms are free to enter an industry when they see a potential for profits, or leave if they are making losses. Therefore, entry and exit regulate how much profit a firm can make in the long run. Suppose you own a Hardee's fast-food restaurant in Asheville, North Carolina. Your business is doing well and making a profit. Then one day a Five Guys opens up across the street. Some of your customers will try Five Guys and switch, while others still prefer your fare. Your profits will take a hit. Whether or not you stay in business depends on how much you are losing. To understand how a business owner would make this decision, we now turn to the short-run and long-run implication of monopolistic competition.

Monopolistic Competition in the Short Run

Figure 12.1 depicts a firm, like Hardee's, in a monopolistically competitive environment. In 12.1a, the firm makes a profit. Figure 12.1b shows the same firm incurring a loss after a new competitor, like Five Guys, opens nearby. In each case the firm uses the profit-maximizing rule to determine the best price to charge by locating the point where marginal revenue equals marginal cost. This establishes the profit-maximizing output along the vertical dashed line. The firm determines the price to charge by locating the intersection of the demand curve with the vertical dashed line.

In Figure 12.1a we see that because price is greater than cost (P > C), the firm makes a short-run economic profit. The situation in Figure 12.1b is different. Because P < C, the firm experiences a short-run economic loss. What accounts for the difference? Since we are considering the same firm, the marginal cost (MC) and average total cost (ATC) curves are identical in both panels. The only functional difference is the location of the demand (D) and marginal revenue (MR) curves. The demand in panel (a) is high enough for the firm to make a profit. In panel (b), however, there is not enough demand; perhaps too many customers have switched to the new Five Guys. So even though the monopolistic competitor has some market power, if demand is too low the firm may not be able to price its product high enough to make a profit.

Monopolistic Competition in the Long Run

In the long run, when firms can easily enter and exit a market, competition will drive economic profits to zero. This dynamic should be familiar to you from our previous discussions of competitive markets. If a firm is making an economic profit, it attracts new entrants to the business. The larger supply of competing firms means that the demand for an individual firm's product will contract. Eventually, as more firms enter the market, it will no longer be possible for existing firms to make an economic profit. A reverse process unfolds in the case of a market that is experiencing a loss. Some firms will exit the industry. Consumers will have fewer options to choose from, and the remaining firms will experience an increase in demand. Eventually, demand will increase to the point where firms will no longer experience a loss.

Figure 12.2 shows the market after the long-run adjustment process takes place. Price, P, is just equal to the average total cost of production, C, at the profit-maximizing rate of output, Q_{max}. At this point firms are earning zero economic profits, as noted by P = C along the vertical axis; the market reaches a long-run equilibrium where there is no reason for firms to enter or exit the industry. Note that the demand curve is drawn just *tangent* to the average total cost curve. If demand was any larger, the result would look like Figure 12.1a and firms would experience economic profits. Conversely, if demand was any lower, the result would look like Figure 12.1b and firms would experience economic losses. Where entry and exit exist, profits and losses are not possible in the long run. In this way monopolistic competition resembles perfectly competitive markets.

Returning to our example, of Hardee's, the firm's success will attract attention and encourage rivals, like Five Guys, to enter the market. As a result, the short-run profits that Hardee's enjoys will erode. As long as profits exist in

FIGURE 12.1

The Monopolistically Competitive Firm in the Short Run

In this graphic we look at how a single monopolistic firm may make a profit or incur a loss depending on the demand conditions it faces. Notice that the marginal cost (MC) and average total cost (ATC) curves are identical in both panels, since we are considering the same firm. The only functional difference is the location of the demand (D) and marginal revenue (MR) curves. The demand in (a) is high enough for the firm to make a profit. In (b), however, there is not enough demand, so the firm experiences a loss.

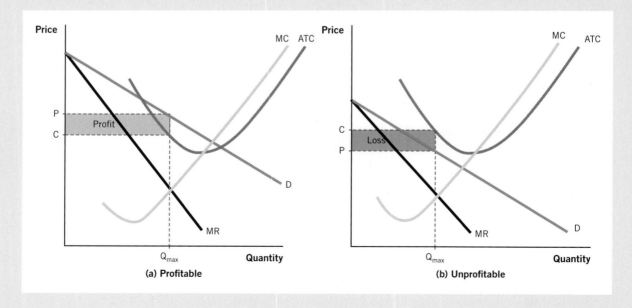

the short run, this will encourage other competitors to enter, while short-run losses will encourage some existing firms to close. The dynamic nature of competition guarantees that long-run profits are not possible.

Monopolistic Competition and Competitive Markets

We have seen that monopolistic competition and competitive markets are similar; both market structures drive profits to zero in the long run. But monopolistic competitors enjoy some market power, which is a crucial difference. In this section we will compare pricing and output decisions in these two market structures. Then we will look at issues of scale and output.

The Relationship Among Price, Marginal Cost, and Long-Run Average Cost

Monopolistically competitive firms have some market power. This allows firms to charge slightly more than firms in competitive markets. Figure 12.3 compares the long-run equilibrium in monopolistic competition and perfect competition. Turning first to the firm in a market characterized

Photo to come

Designer Jean-Paul Gaultier created the look of Evian—but it is still just water inside!

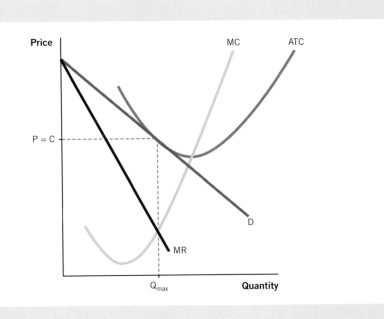

FIGURE 12.2

The Monopolistically Competitive Firm in the Long Run

Entry and exit cause short-run profits and losses to disappear in the long run. This means that the price charged, P, must be equal to the average total cost, C, of production. At this point firms are earning zero economic profits, as noted by P = C along the vertical axis; the market reaches a long-run equilibrium where there is no reason for firms to enter or exit the industry.

Markup
is the difference between
the price the firm charges
and the marginal cost of
production.

by monopolistic competition, notice that the price, P, is greater than the marginal cost, MC, of making one more unit. The difference between P and MC is known as the **markup**, which is shown in Figure 12.3a. A markup is possible when a firm enjoys some market power and sells a differentiated product. Products such as bottled water, cosmetics, prescription medicines, eyeglass frames, brand-name clothing, restaurant drinks, and greeting cards all have hefty markups. Let's focus on bottled water. In most cases, it costs pennies to produce bottled water, but good luck trying to find it for less than $1; there is a lot of markup on every bottle! Firms are able to differentiate their product by marketing their water as the "purest" or "cleanest." Other companies use special packaging. While the marketing of bottled water is unquestionably a successful business strategy, the markup means that consumers are paying more. You can observe this result in Figure 12.3a, where the price in monopolistic competition is higher than the price in perfect competition, shown in Figure 12.3b.

Next, look at the ATC curves in both panels. Since a monopolistic competitor has a downward-sloping demand curve, the point of tangency between the demand curve and the ATC curve occurs at different points. As a result, the point where P = C is higher for the monopolistic firm. Panel (b) shows the demand curve just tangent to the ATC curve at its lowest point under perfect competition. Consequently, monopolistic competition produces higher prices

FIGURE 12.3

The Long-Run Equilibrium in Monopolistic Competition and Competitive Markets

There are two primary differences between the long-run equilibrium in monopolistic competition (a) and a competitive market (b). First, monopolistic competition produces markup, since P is greater than MC. In a competitive market, P = MC. Second, the output in monopolistic competition is smaller than the efficient scale. In a perfectly competitive market, the firm's output is equal to the most efficient scale.

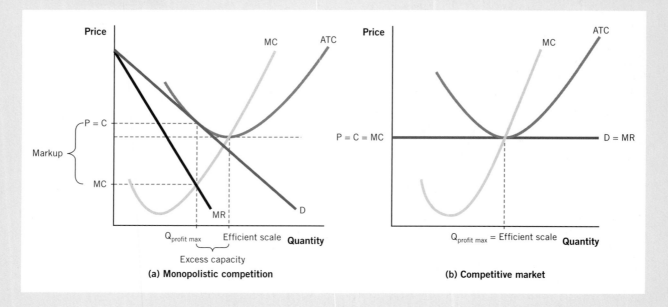

(a) Monopolistic competition

(b) Competitive market

than competitive markets. If this result seems odd to you, recall that entry and exit do not ensure the lowest possible price, only that the price is equal to the average total cost of production. Under perfect competition, where the demand curve is horizontal, the price is always the lowest possible cost of production. This is not the case for monopolistic competition.

Scale and Output

When a firm produces at an output level smaller than the output level needed to minimize average total costs, we say it has **excess capacity**. Turning back to Figure 12.3a, we see excess capacity in the difference between $Q_{\text{profit max}}$ and the efficient scale.

Excess capacity occurs when a firm produces an output that is smaller than the output level needed to minimize average total costs.

This result differs from what we see in Figure 12.3b for a competitive market. Under perfect competition, the profit-maximizing output is equal to the most efficient scale of operation. This result is guaranteed because each firm sells an identical product and must therefore set its price equal to the minimum point on the average total cost curve. If, for instance, a corn farmer tried to sell a harvest for more than the prevailing market price, the farmer would not find any takers. In contrast, the monopolistic competitor in the food court has market power because some customers prefer its product. This allows food court vendors to charge more than the lowest average total cost. Therefore, under monopolistic competition, the profit-maximizing output is less than the minimum efficient scale. Monopolistically competitive firms have the capacity to produce more at a lower cost. However, if they produced more they would have to lower the price. Because a lower price decreases the marginal revenue the firm receives, it is more profitable for the monopolistic competitor to operate with excess capacity.

Monopolistic Competition, Inefficiency, and Social Welfare

Monopolistic competition produces a higher price and lower output than a competitive market. Recall that we looked at efficiency as a way to determine whether or not the decisions of a firm are consistent with an output level that is beneficial to society. Does monopolistic competition display efficiency?

In Figure 12.3a we observed that a monopolistic competitor has costs that are slightly above the lowest possible cost. So the average total costs of a monopolistically competitive firm are higher than those of a firm in a competitive market. This result is not efficient. To achieve efficiency, the firm could lower the price it charges to what we would find in competitive markets. However, since a monopolistic competitor's goal is to make a profit, there is no incentive for this to happen. Every monopolistic competitor has a downward-sloping demand curve, so the demand curve cannot be tangent to the average total cost, as seen in the first panel of Figure 12.3.

Markup is a second source of inefficiency. We have seen that for the monopolistically competitive firm at the profit-maximizing output level, $P > MC$ by an amount equal to the markup. The price reflects the consumer's willingness to pay, and this amount exceeds the marginal cost of production. A reduced markup would benefit consumers by lowering the price and decreasing the spread between the price and the marginal cost. If the firm did away with the markup entirely and set P = MC, the output level would benefit the greatest number of consumers. However, this result is not practical. At the point where the greatest efficiency is achieved, the demand curve is below the average total cost curve and the firm will be losing money. It is unreasonable to expect a profit-seeking firm to pursue a pricing strategy that benefits its customers at the expense of its own profits.

What if the government intervened on behalf of the consumer? Increased efficiency could be achieved through government regulation. The government regulates monopolists to reduce market power and restore social welfare. Couldn't the government do the same in monopolistically competitive markets? Yes and no! It is certainly possible, but not desirable. Monopolistically competitive firms have a limited amount of market power, so they are not able to make long-run economic profits like monopolists. In addition, regulating the prices that firms in a monopolistically competitive market can charge would put many of them out of business. Bear in mind we are talking about firms in markets like the fast-food industry. Doing away with a significant percentage of these firms would mean fewer places to grab a quick bite. The remaining restaurants would be more efficient, but with fewer restaurants, the tradeoff for consumers would be less convenience and fewer choices.

Regulating monopolistic competition through marginal cost pricing, or setting P = MC, would also create a host of problems like those we discussed for monopoly. A good proportion of the economy consists of monopolistically competitive firms—so the scale of the regulatory effort would be enormous. And since implementing marginal cost pricing would result in widespread losses, the government would need to find a way to subsidize the regulated firms to keep them in business. Since the only way to pay for these subsidies would be through higher taxes, the inefficiencies present in monopolistic competition do not warrant government action.

Varying Degrees of Product Differentiation

We have seen that products sold under monopolistic competition are more differentiated than those sold under perfect competition and less differentiated than those sold under monopoly. At one end of these two extremes we have a perfect competitor who sells identical products, has no market power, and faces a perfectly elastic demand curve. At the other end we have a monopolist who sells a unique product without good substitutes and a steep downward-sloping demand curve indicative of strongly inelastic demand. What about the firm operating under monopolistic competition?

Figure 12.4 illustrates two monopolistic competitors with varying degrees of product differentiation. Firm A enjoys significant differentiation. This occurs when the firm has an especially attractive location, style, type, or quality of product that is in high demand among consumers and is not easily replicated by competitors. H&M, Urban Outfitters, and Abercrombie and Fitch are good examples. Consumers have strong brand loyalty for the clothes these firms sell and so the demand curve is more inelastic. The relatively steep slope of the demand curve means that the point of tangency between the demand curve and the average total cost curve occurs at a high price. This produces a large amount of excess capacity. Firm B sells a product that is only slightly different from its competitors'. Here we can think of T.J. Maxx, Ross, and

Marshall's—three companies that primarily sell discounted clothes. In this case, consumers have only weak preferences for a particular firm and consumer demand is elastic. The relatively flat nature of the demand curve means that the point of tangency between demand and average total cost occurs at a relatively low cost. This produces a small amount of excess capacity.

Monopolisitic competition creates substantial product variety and greater selection and choice, all of which are beneficial to consumers. Therefore, any policy efforts that attempt to reduce inefficiency by lowering the prices that monopolistically competitive firms can charge will have the unintended consequence of limiting the product variety in the market. That sounds like a small price to pay for increased efficiency. But not so fast! Imagine a world without any product differentiation in clothes.

Would you want to dress like this every day? Product variety is something consumers are willing to pay for.

FIGURE 12.4

Product Differentiation, Excess Capacity, and Efficiency

Firm A enjoys more product differentiation. As a result, it has more excess capacity and is less efficient. Firm B sells a product that is only slightly different from its competitors. In this case, consumers have only weak preferences about which firm they prefer and consumer demand is elastic. This produces a small amount of excess capacity and a more efficient result.

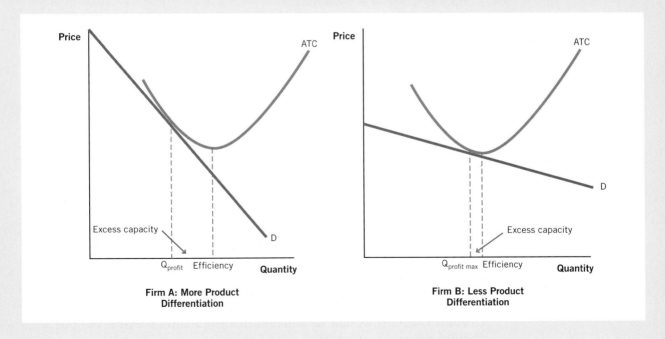

PRACTICE WHAT YOU KNOW

Markup: Punch Pizza versus Pizza Hut

Question: Punch Pizza is a small upscale chain in Minnesota that uses wood-fired ovens. Pizza Hut is a large national chain. Would one have more markup on each pizza?

Punch Pizza uses wood-fired ovens.

Answer: If you ask people in the Twin Cities about their favorite pizza, you will find a cultlike following for Punch Pizza. That loyalty translates into inelastic demand. Punch Pizza claims to make the best Neapolitan pie. Fans of this style of pizza gravitate to Punch Pizza for the unique texture and flavor. Pizza Hut competes in the middle of the pizza market and has crafted a pizza taste that appeals to a broader set of customers. Pizza Hut's customers have many other places that serve a similar product, and are therefore much more price-sensitive. The marginal cost of making pizza at both places consists of the dough, toppings and wages for labor. At Pizza Hut pizza assembly is streamlined for efficiency. Punch Pizza is more labor-intensive, but the marginal cost is still relatively low. The prices at Punch Pizza are much higher than at Pizza Hut. As a result, the markup, or the difference between the price that is charged and the marginal cost of production, is greater at Punch Pizza than at Pizza Hut.

Part of the reason why fashions go in and out of style is the desire among consumers to express their individuality. Therefore, consumers are willing to pay a little more for product variety in order not to look exactly like everyone else.

Why Is Advertising Prevalent in Monopolistic Competition?

Advertising is a familiar fact of daily life. It is also a means by which companies compete and, therefore, a cost of doing business in many industries. In the United States, advertising expenditures account for approximately 2 percent of all economic output annually. Worldwide, advertising expenses are a little less—about 1 percent of global economic activity. While the percentages are small in relative terms, in absolute terms worldwide advertising costs are over half a trillion dollars each year. Is this money well spent? Or is it a counterproductive arms race that increases cost without adding value for the consumer? In this section we will find that the answer is a little of both. Let's start by seeing who advertises.

Advertising: Super Bowl Commercials

The be-all of advertising spots is the televised Super Bowl. Because commercial time costs $3 million for a 30-second spot, examining the companies that choose to advertise provides a useful barometer of economic activity. In 2011, three of the most recalled commercials were by Anheuser-Busch, Doritos, and Volkswagen. They joined the usual suspects, Coca-Cola and Pepsi (soft drinks), Bridgestone (tires), Universal (motion pictures), and BMW, Audi, Toyota, Chevrolet, Kia, and Hyundai (autos), in buying advertising time. Super Bowl ads highlight sectors of the economy that are thriving. In addition, firms that advertise during the Super Bowl build brand recognition, which helps to differentiate their product from the competition.

"Ladies, look at me, now look at your man, now back to me."—Old Spice guy

Why Firms Advertise

No matter the company or slogan, the goal of advertising is to drive additional demand for the product being sold. Advertising campaigns use a variety of techniques to stimulate demand. In each instance, advertising is designed to highlight an important piece of information about the product. Table 12.2 shows how this process works. For instance, the Federal Express slogan, *"When it absolutely, positively has to be there overnight,"* conveys reliability and punctual service. Some customers who use FedEx are willing to pay a premium for overnight delivery because FedEx has differentiated itself from its competitors—UPS, DHL, and (especially) the United States Postal Service.

A successful advertising campaign will change the demand curve in two dimensions; it will shift the demand curve to the right and alter its shape. Turning to Figure 12.5, we see this change. First, the demand curve shifts right in response to the additional demand created by the adverting. Second, the demand curve becomes more inelastic, or vertical. This happens because advertising has highlighted features that make the product attractive to specific customers who are now more likely to want it. Since demand is more inelastic after advertising, the firm increases its market power and can increase the price it charges.

TABLE 12.2

Advertising and Demand

Company / Product	Advertising Slogan	How It Increases Demand
Quaker / Life cereal	*He likes it! Hey, Mikey!*	The slogan attempts to convince parents that children will like Life cereal, making it a healthy choice that their children will eat.
John Deere / tractors	*Nothing runs like a Deere.*	The emphasis on quality and performance appeals to buyers who desire a high-quality tractor.
Frito-Lay / Lay's potato chips	*Betcha can't eat just one.*	The message that one potato chip is not enough to satisfy your craving appeals to chip buyers who choose between taste or lower-priced generics.
Energizer / batteries	*He keeps going and going and going.*	The campaign focuses attention on longevity in order to justify the higher prices that top-quality batteries cost.
Federal Express / delivery service	*When it absolutely, positively has to be there overnight*	Reliability and timeliness are crucial attributes of overnight delivery.
Visa / credit card	*It's everywhere you want to be.*	Acceptance and usability are two of the major reasons for carrying a credit card.
Avis / rental cars	*We're number two; we try harder.*	The emphasis on service encourages people to use the company.

In addition to increasing demand, advertising conveys information that consumers may find helpful in matching their preferences. It tells us about the price of the goods offered, the location of products, and the introduction of new products. Firms also use advertising as a competitive mechanism to underprice each other. Finally, an advertising campaign signals quality. Firms that run expensive advertising campaigns are making a significant investment in their product. It is highly unlikely that a firm would spend a great deal on advertising if it did not think the process would yield a positive return. So, a rational consumer can infer that firms spending a great deal on advertising are likely to have a higher-quality product than a competitor who does not advertise.

Advertising in Different Markets

Many firms engage in advertising, but not all market structures find advertising equally productive. In our continuum from competitive markets to monopoly, markets that function under monopolistic competition invest the most in advertising.

Advertising in Competitive Markets

Competitive firms sell nearly identical products at an identical price. This means that advertising dollars raise a firm's costs without directly influencing its sales. Advertising for a good that is undifferentiated functions like a public good for the industry as a whole: the benefits flow to every firm in the market

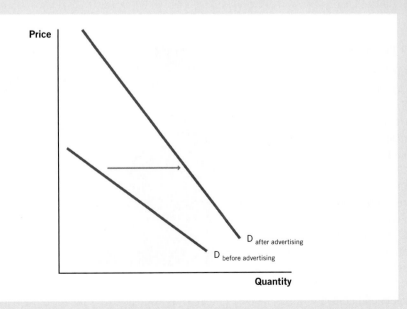

FIGURE 12.5

Advertising and the Demand Curve

A successful advertising campaign increases demand. Advertising also makes the demand curve more inelastic by informing consumers about differences that they care about. After advertising, consumers desire the good more intensely, which makes the demand curve for the firm's product more vertical.

Photo to come

through increased market demand for the product. However, each firm sells essentially the same good, so consumers can find the product at many competing locations at the same price. An individual firm that advertises in this market is at a competitive disadvantage because it will have higher costs that it cannot pass on to the consumer.

This does not mean that we never see advertising in competitive markets. Although individual firms do not benefit from advertising, competitive industries can. For example, you have probably heard the slogan "Beef—it's what's for dinner." The campaign, which began in 1992, is recognized by over 80 percent of Americans and has been widely credited with increasing the demand for beef products. The campaign was funded by the National Cattlemen's Beef Association, an organization that puts millions of dollars a year into advertising. In fact, industry-wide marketing campaigns such as "It's not just for breakfast anymore" by the Florida Orange Juice Growers

Advertising

E.T.: The Extra-Terrestrial (1982)

E.T. contains one of the most famous examples of product placement. In the movie, a boy leaves a trail of candy to bring E.T. closer to him. Originally, the filmmakers offered Hershey's the chance to have M&Ms used in the movie. Hershey's said no thanks. The filmmakers instead approached Mars, the manufacturers of Reese's Pieces—at that time a rival product of M&Ms that was not terribly successful. When *E.T.* became a blockbuster, the demand for Reese's Pieces suddenly tripled and firmly established the product in the minds of many Americans. How much did Mars pay? $1 million—not bad considering how successful Reese's Pieces have become. This is a great example of how firms must think beyond their advertising budgets and consider the strategic repercussions that may occur when market share is

Hungry for something to eat?

lost to a rival. Hershey's failed to protect its position in the market.

Association, or "Got milk?" by the National Milk Processor Board, generally indicate that competitive firms have joined forces to advertise in an effort to increase demand.

Advertising Under Monopolistic Competition

Advertising is widespread in monopolistic competition because firms have differentiated products. This is easy to observe if we look at the behavior of pizza companies. Television commercials by national chains such as Domino's, Pizza Hut, Papa John's, and Little Caesar's are widespread, as are flyers and advertisements for local pizza places. Since each pizza is slightly different, advertising increases the demand for the firm's product. In short, the gains from advertising go directly to the firm spending the money. This creates a strong incentive to advertise to gain new customers or to keep customers from switching to other products. Since each firm feels the same way, advertising becomes the norm among monopolistically competitive firms.

Monopoly

The monopolist sells a unique product without close substitutes. The fact that consumers have few good alternatives when deciding to buy the good makes the monopolist less likely to advertise than a monopolistic competitor. When consumer choice is limited, the firm does not have to advertise to get business. In addition, the competitive aspect is missing, so there is no need to advertise to prevent consumers from switching to the products sold by rivals. However, that does not mean that the monopolist never advertises.

   The monopolist may wish to advertise to inform the consumer about its product and stimulate demand. This strategy can be beneficial to the firm as long as the gains from advertising are enough to cover the cost. For example, DeBeers, the giant diamond cartel, controls most of the world's supply of rough-cut diamonds. The company does not need to advertise to fend off competitors, but it advertises nevertheless because it is interested in creating more demand for diamonds. DeBeers authored the famous "A diamond is forever" campaign and, more recently, has developed an entirely new marketing campaign that suggests women should purchase a "right-hand ring" for themselves.

The Negative Effects of Advertising

We have seen the benefits of advertising, but there are also drawbacks. Two of the most significant are that advertising raises costs and can be deceitful.

Advertising and Costs

Advertising costs are reflected in the average total cost curve of the firm. Figure 12.6 shows the paradox of advertising for most firms. When a firm advertises, it hopes to increase demand for the product and sell more units, say from point 1 at q_1 to point 2 at the higher quantity, q_2. If the firm can sell enough additional

Pearl ear studs are a nice gift, but they are even better when they come in the . . .

units, it will enjoy economies of scale and the cost will fall from C_1 to C_2. This return on the advertising investment looks like a good business decision.

However, the reality of advertising is much more complex. In monopolistic competition each firm is competing with many other firms selling somewhat different products. Rival firms will respond with advertising of their own. This dynamic makes advertising the norm in monopolistic competition. Each firm engages in competitive advertising to win new customers and keep the old ones. As a result, the impact on each individual firm's demand largely cancels out. This result is shown in the movement from point 1 to point 3. Costs rise from C_1 to C_3, but demand may remain at q_1. The net result is that advertising creates higher costs. In this case we can think of advertising as causing a negative *business-stealing externality* where no individual firm is able to easily gain market share but feels compelled to advertise to protect its customer base.

We have seen that advertising raises costs for the producer. It also raises prices for consumers. Consumers who consistently favor a particular brand of a product have more inelastic demand than consumers who are willing to switch from one product to another. Therefore brand loyalty often means higher prices. Let's look at an example.

FIGURE 12.6

Advertising Increases Cost

By advertising, the firm hopes to increase demand from point 1 to point 2. In this scenario, the increase in demand from q_1 to q_2 is large enough to create economies of scale even though advertising causes the average total cost curve to rise. Since monopolistically competitive firms each advertise, the advertising efforts often cancel each other out. This raises the average total costs without increasing demand much, so the firm may move from point 1 to point 3 instead.

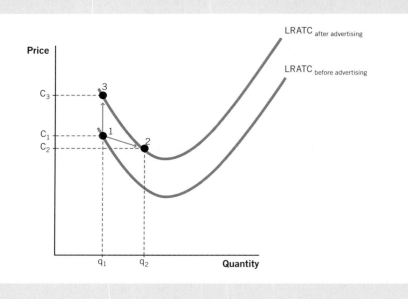

Suppose that you buy all of your jewelry at Tiffany's. One day you enter the store to pick up pearl ear studs. You can get a small pair of pearl studs at Tiffany's and pay $300. But it turns out that you can get studs of the same size, quality, and origin (freshwater) at Pearl World for $43, and find them online at Amazon for $19. There are no identifying marks on the jewelry that would enable you, or a seasoned jeweler, to tell the ear studs apart! Why would you buy the ear studs at Tiffany's when you can purchase the same item for far less elsewhere? The answer, it turns out, is that buying ear studs is a lot like consuming many other goods. Name recognition matters. So does perception and brand loyalty. Many jewelry buyers

. . . blue box.

also take cues from the storefront, how the staff dresses, and how the jewelry is packaged. $300 is a lot of money for the Tiffany blue box. Consumers believe that the jewelry at Tiffany's is better, when all that Tiffany's is doing is charging more markup.

Truth in Advertising

Finally, many advertising campaigns are not informative—they are designed to produce a psychological response. When a slogan moves you to buy or act in a particular way, it crosses the line from beneficial to manipulative and advertising produces a negative externality. Because advertising can be such a powerful way to reach customers, there is a temptation to lie about a product. To prevent firms from spreading misinformation about their products, the Federal Trade Commission (FTC) regulates advertising and promotes economic efficiency. At the FTC, the Division of Advertising Practices protects consumers by enforcing truth-in-advertising laws. While the FTC does not have enough resources to be able to track down every violation, they do pay particular attention to claims involving food, non-prescription drugs, dietary supplements, alcohol, and tobacco. Unsubstantiated claims are particularly prevalent on the Internet, and they tend to target vulnerable populations seeking quick fixes to a variety of medical conditions.

Of course, even with regulatory oversight, consumers must still be vigilant. At best, the FTC can remove products from the market and levy fines against companies that make unsubstantiated claims. However, the damage is often already done. The Latin phrase *caveat emptor*, or "buyer beware," sums up the dangers of false information.

ECONOMICS IN THE REAL WORLD

The Federal Trade Commission versus Kevin Trudeau

Channel flippers will surely recognize Kevin Trudeau. He has been a staple of infomercials for over a decade. Trudeau has a formula: he writes books about simple cures for complex medical conditions. He is an engaging, smooth talker. The infomercial is usually a "conversation" between Trudeau and a good-looking woman who seems really excited to learn more about the product. Unfortunately, Trudeau's claims are often unsubstantiated.

Do you trust this guy?

In 2009 a federal judge ordered Trudeau to pay more than $37 million for misrepresenting the content of his book *The Weight Loss Cure "They" Don't Want You to Know About* and banned him from appearing in infomercials for three years. This is not the first time Kevin Trudeau has been taken to task by the FTC. The FTC first filed a lawsuit against Trudeau in 1998, charging him with making false and misleading claims in infomercials for products he claimed could cause significant weight loss, cure drug addictions, and improve memory.

More recently Trudeau has been offering his products for "free." Customers who call in receive a copy of one of his books and one issue of a monthly newsletter at no charge. However, consumers who fail to cancel the newsletter incur the monthly charge of $9.95 on their credit card. While there is nothing illegal about the 30-day free trial period and many other firms use this tactic, it has sparked additional outrage. ✳

PRACTICE WHAT YOU KNOW

Advertising: Brands versus Generics

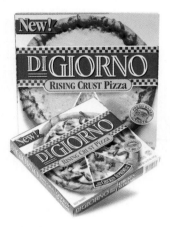

DiGiorno or . . .   . . . generic?

Why do some frozen pizzas cost more than others, when brands that offer similar quality are only a few feet away? To answer that question, consider the following three questions:

Question: Create a graph showing the price and the markup for DiGiorno.

Answer:

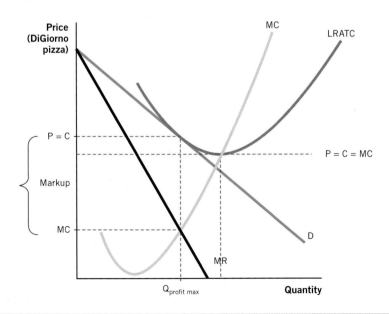

Question: In a separate graph, show the price and output for the generic pizza.

Answer:

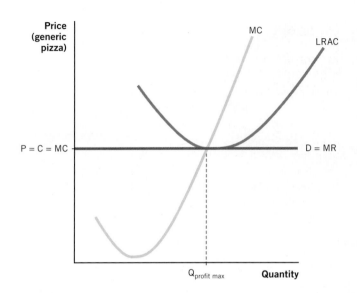

Question: Does DiGiorno or a generic brand have a stronger incentive to maintain strict quality control in the production process? Why?

Answer: DiGiorno has a catchy slogan: "It's not delivery. It's DiGiorno!" This tries to position the product as being just as good as a freshly delivered pizza. Some customers who buy frozen pizzas will opt for DiGiorno over comparable generics since they are familiar with the company's advertising claim about its quality. Therefore, DiGiorno has a strong incentive to make sure that the product delivers as advertised. Since generic, or store-bought, brands are purchased based mostly on price, the customer generally does not have high expectations about the quality.

Conclusion

We began this chapter with the misconception that advertising increases the price of goods and services without adding value for the consumer. Advertising does cost money, but that does not mean it is harmful. Firms willingly spend on advertising because it can increase demand, create brand loyalty, and provide consumers with useful information about differences in products. Monopolistic competitors advertise and mark up their products like monopolists, but, like firms in a competitive market, they cannot earn long-run profits. While economic profits are possible in the short run for all three,

Product Differentiation: Would You Buy a Franchise?

Franchises are valuable in markets where product differentiation matters. McDonald's, Panera Bread, and KFC each has a different take on serving fast food. But what does it mean to own a franchise? Franchises are sold to individual owners, who operate subject to the terms of their agreement with the parent company. For instance, purchasing a McDonald's franchise, which can cost as much as $2 million, requires the individual restaurant owner to charge certain prices and offer menu items selected by the parent corporation. As a result, customers who prefer a certain type and quality of food know that the dining experience at each McDonald's will be similar. Most franchises also come with noncompete clauses that guarantee that another franchise will not open nearby. This gives the franchise owner the exclusive right to sell a differentiated product in a given area.

Suppose that you want to start a restaurant. Why would you, or anyone else, be willing to pay upwards of $2 million just for the right to sell food? For that amount, you could open your own restaurant in which you could create a custom menu and interior, create your own marketing plan, and locate anywhere you pleased. For example, Golden Corral and Buffalo Wild Wings are two restaurants with high franchising fees that exceed $1 million. Golden Corral is the largest buffet-style restaurant in the country, and Buffalo Wild Wings is one of the top locations to watch sporting events. You might think that it would

How much do different franchises cost?

make more sense to avoid the franchising costs by opening your own buffet or setting up a bank of big-screen TVs. However, failures in the restaurant industry are high. With a franchise, the customer knows what to expect.

Franchise owners are assured of visibility and a ready supply of customers. Purchasing a franchise means that more potential customers will notice your restaurant, and that drives up revenues. Is that worth $2 million? Yes, in some cases. Suppose that you'll do $1 million in annual sales as part of a franchise, but only $.5 million on your own. That half-million difference over 20 years means $10 million more in revenue, a healthy chunk of which will turn into profits. This is the magic of franchising.

---

only the monopolist, who has significant barriers to entry, can earn economic profits in the long run. Entry and exit cause long-run profits to equal zero in competitive and monopolistically competitive firms.

Monopolistic competitors are price makers who fail to achieve the most efficient welfare-maximizing output for society. But this does not tell the entire story. Monopolistic competitors do not have as much market power or create as much excess capacity or markup as monopolists. Consequently, the monopolistic competitor lacks the ability to exploit consumers. The result is not "perfect," but widespread competition generally serves consumers and society well.

In the next chapter we continue our exploration of market structure with *oligopoly*, which produces results that are much closer to monopoly than monopolistic competition.

ANSWERING THE BIG QUESTIONS

1. What is monopolistic competition?

* Monopolistic competition is a market characterized by free entry and many firms selling differentiated products.
* Differentiation of products takes on three forms: differentiation by style or type, location, and quality.

2. What are the differences among monopolistic competition, competitive markets, and monopoly?

* Monopolistic competitors, like monopolists, are price makers who have downward-sloping demand curves. Whenever the demand curve is downward-sloping, the firm is able to mark up the price above marginal cost. This leads to excess capacity and an inefficient level of output.
* In the long run, barriers to entry allow a monopoly to earn an economic profit. This is not the case for monopolistic competition or competitive markets.

3. Why is advertising prevalent in monopolistic competition?

* Advertising performs useful functions. It conveys information about the price of the goods offered for sale, the location of products, and new products. It also signals quality differences. However, advertising also encourages brand loyalty, which makes it harder for businesses to successfully enter the market. Advertising can be manipulative and misleading.

CONCEPTS YOU SHOULD KNOW

Excess capacity (p. 351)   Monopolistic competition   Product differentiation (p. 344)
Markup (p. 350)   (p. 344)

QUESTIONS

1. Why is product differentiation necessary for monopolistic competition? What are three types of product differentiation?

2. How is monopolistic competition like competitive markets? How is monopolistic competition like monopoly?

3. Why do monopolistically competitive firms produce less than those operating at the most efficient scale of production?

4. Draw a graph that shows a monopolistic competitor making an economic profit in the short run and a graph that shows a monopolistic competitor making an economic profit in the long run.

5. Monopolistic competition produces a result that is inefficient. Does this mean that monopolistically competitive markets should be regulated? Discuss.

6. Draw a typical demand curve for competitive markets, monopolistic competition and monopoly. Which of these demand curves is the most inelastic? Why?

7. How does advertising benefit society? In what ways can advertising be harmful?

STUDY PROBLEMS

＊1. At your high school reunion, a friend describes his plan to take a break from his florist shop and sail around the world. He says that if he continues to make the same economic profit for the next five years, he will be able to afford to take the trip. Do you think the high school friend will be able to achieve his dream in five years? What do you expect to happen to his firm's profits in the long run?

2. Which of the following could be considered a monopolistic competitor?
   a. Local corn farmers
   b. The Tennessee Valley Authority, a large electricity producer
   c. Pizza delivery
   d. Grocery stores
   e. Kate Spade, fashion designer

3. Which of the following produces the same outcome in monopolistic competition and perfect competition in the long run?
   a. The markup the firm charges
   b. The price the firm charges to consumers
   c. The firm's excess capacity

   d. The average total cost of production
   e. The amount of advertising
   f. The firm's profit
   g. The efficiency of the market structure

4. Under perfect competition, price is equal to marginal cost in the long run. Explain why this is not true for monopolistic competition.

5. Econoburgers, a fast-food restaurant in a crowded local market, has reached a long-run equilibrium.
   a. Draw a diagram showing demand, marginal revenue, average total cost, and marginal cost curves for Econoburgers.
   b. How much profit is Econoburgers making?
   c. Suppose that the government decides to regulate burger production to make it more efficient. Explain what would happen to the price of Econoburgers and the firm's output.

＊6. Consider two different companies. The first manufactures cardboard and the second sells books. Which firm is more likely to advertise?

7. In the diagram below, identify the demand curve consistent with a monopolistic competitor making zero long-run economic profit. Explain why you have chosen that demand curve and why the other two demand curves are not consistent with monopolistic competition.

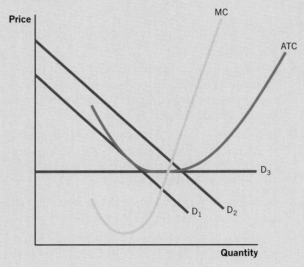

8. Titleist has an advertising slogan, "The #1 ball in golf." Consumers can also buy generic golf balls. The manufacturers of generic golf balls do not engage in any advertising. Assume that the average total cost of producing Titleist and generic golf balls is the same.

   a. Create a graph showing the price and the markup for Titleist.

   b. In a separate graph show the price and output for the generic firms.

   c. Which company has a stronger incentive to maintain strict quality control in the production process? Why?

SOLVED PROBLEMS

1. The florist business is monopolistically competitive. This means that firms are free to enter and exit at any time. Firms will enter because your friend's shop is making an economic profit. As new florist shops decide to open, the added competition will drive prices down, causing your friend's profits to fall. In the long run this means that he will not be able to make an economic profit. He will only earn enough to cover his opportunity costs, or what is known as a fair return on his investment. That is not to say that he won't be able to save enough to sail around the world, but it won't happen as fast as he would like because other firms will crowd in on his success and limit his profits going forward.

6. The cardboard firm manufactures a product that is a component used mostly by other firms that need to package final products for sale. As a result, any efforts at advertising will only raise costs without increasing the demand for cardboard. This contrasts with the bookseller. Bookstores advertise to attract consumers to the store. More traffic means that more books and the other items sold in the store are purchased. The bookstore has some monopoly power and markup. In this case it pays to advertise. A cardboard manufacturing firm sells exactly the same product as the other cardboard producer,s so it has no monopoly power and advertising expenses will only make its cost higher than its rivals'.

CHAPTER 13 | Oligopoly and Strategic Behavior

Cell phone companies are highly competitive.

If you have a cell phone, chances are that you receive service from one of four major cell phone carriers in the United States: AT&T, Verizon,

Sprint, or T-Mobile. Together these firms control 85 percent of all cellular service. In some respects this market is very competitive. Cell phone companies advertise intensely, and they offer a variety of phones and voice and data plans. There are differences in network coverage and in the number of applications you can access. But despite outward appearances, the cell phone companies are not a good example of a competitive, or even monopolistically competitive, market. How can we explain this misconception? An important reason is the expense it takes to build and maintain a cellular network. The largest cell phone companies have invested billions of dollars in infrastructure. Therefore, the cost of entry is very high. And as we learned in Chapter 10, barriers to entry are a key feature of monopolies.

The cell phone industry has features of both monopolistic competition and monopoly; competition is fierce but smaller firms and potential entrants into the market find it difficult to enter and compete. This mixture of characteristics represents another form of market structure—*oligopoly*. In this chapter we will examine oligopoly by comparing it to other market structures that are already familiar to you. We will then look at some of the strategic behaviors that firms in an oligopoly employ; this will lead us into a fascinating subject known as game theory.

Lots of advertising and regular promotions lead most people to view cell phone companies as highly competitive firms—is that true?

BIG QUESTIONS

* What is oligopoly?
* How does game theory explain strategic behavior?
* How do government policies affect oligopoly behavior?
* What are network externalities?

What Is Oligopoly?

Oligopoly
exists when a small number of firms sell a product in a market with high barriers to entry.

Oligopoly exists when a small number of firms sell a product in a market with significant barriers to entry. An oligopolist is like a monopolistic competitor in that it typically sells a differentiated product. But, like pure monopolists, oligopolists enjoy significant barriers to entry. Table 13.1 compares the differences and similarities among these three market structures.

We have seen that firms in monopolistically competitive markets usually have a limited amount of market power. As a result, buyers often find low prices and wide availability. In contrast, an oligopoly sells in a market with significant barriers to entry and fewer rivals. This gives the oligopolist more market power than a firm operating under monopolistic competition. However, since an oligopolistic market has more than one seller, no single oligopoly has as much market power as a monopoly.

Our study of oligopoly begins with a look at how we measure market power in an industry. We will then work through a simplified model of oligopoly to explore the choices that oligopolists make.

Measuring the Concentration of Industries

In markets with only a few sellers, industry output is highly concentrated among a few large firms. Economists use *concentration ratios* as a measure of the oligopoly power present in an industry. The most common measure, known as the four-firm concentration ratio, measures the sales of the four

TABLE 13.1

Comparing Monopolistic Competition, Oligopoly, and Monopoly		
Monopolistic Competition	Oligopoly	Monopoly
Many sellers	A few sellers	One seller
Differentiated product	Typically differentiated product	Unique product without close substitutes
Free entry and exit	Significant barriers to entry	Significant barriers to entry

TABLE 13.2

Highly Concentrated Industries in the United States

Industry	Concentration Ratio of the Four Largest Firms (percent)	Top Firms
Search engines	98.5	Google, Yahoo, Microsoft
Wireless telecommunications	94.7	Verizon, AT&T, Sprint Nextel, T-Mobile
Satellite TV providers	94.5	DIRECTV, Dish Network
Soda production	93.7	Coca-Cola, Pepsi, Dr. Pepper Snapple
Sanitary paper products	92.7	Kimberly-Clark, Procter & Gamble, Georgia-Pacific
Lighting and bulb manufacturing	91.9	General Electric, Philips, Siemens
Tire manufacturing	91.3	Goodyear, Michelin, Cooper, Bridgestone
Major household appliances	90.0	Whirlpool, Electrolux, General Electric, LG
Automobile manufacturing	87.0	General Motors, Toyota, Ford, Daimler-Chrysler

Source: Highly Concentrated: Companies That Dominate Their Industries, www.ibisworld.com. Special Report, February 2012.

largest firms in an industry as a percentage of that industry's total sales. Table 13.2 lists the four-firm concentration ratios for highly concentrated industries in the United States. This ratio is determined by taking the output of the four largest firms in an industry and dividing that output by the total production in the entire industry.

In highly concentrated industries like search engines, cell phones, soda production, and tire manufacturing, the market share held by the four largest firms approaches 100 percent. At the bottom of our list of most concentrated industries is domestic automobile manufacturing. General Motors, Daimler-Chrysler, Ford, and Toyota (which has eight manufacturing plants in the United States) domi-

Competition from foreign car companies keeps the market power of the U.S.-based automobile companies in check.

nate the domestic automobile industry. These large firms have significant market power. However, when evaluating market power in an industry, it is important to be aware of international activity. In several industries, including automobile and tire manufacturing, intense global competition keeps the market power of U.S. companies in check. For instance, manufacturers that produce automobiles also must compete globally against cars that are produced elsewhere. This means that vehicles produced by Honda, Nissan,

Volkswagen, Kia, and Volvo, just to name a few companies, limit the market power of domestic producers. As a result, the concentration ratio is a rough gauge of oligopoly power—not an absolute measure.

Collusion and Cartels in a Simple Duopoly Example

In this section we explore the two conflicting tendencies found in oligopoly. Oligopolists would like to act like monopolists but often end up competing like monopolistic competitors. To help us understand oligopolistic behavior, we will start with a simplified example: an industry consisting of only two firms, known as a *duopoly*. Duopolies are rare in national and international markets, but not that uncommon in small, local markets. For example, in many small communities, the number of cell phone carriers is limited. Imagine a small town where only two providers have cell phone towers. Both towers were built to service all of the customers in the town, so each carrier has substantial excess capacity when the customers are divided between the two carriers. Also, since there is extra capacity on each network, the marginal cost of adding additional customers is zero.

Table 13.3 shows the community's demand for cell phones. Since the prices and quantities listed in the first two columns are inversely related, the data are consistent with a downward-sloping demand curve.

TABLE 13.3

The Demand Schedule for Cell Phones

(1) Price/Month (P)	(2) Number of Customers (Q)	(3) Total Revenue (TR)
Formula:		(P) × (Q)
$180	0	$0
165	100	16,500
150	200	30,000
135	300	40,500
120	400	48,000
105	500	52,500
90	600	54,000
75	700	52,500
60	800	48,000
45	900	40,500
30	1,000	30,000
15	1,100	16,500
0	1,200	0

Column (3) calculates the total revenue from columns (1) and (2). With Table 13.3 as our guide we will examine the output in this market under three scenarios: competition, monopoly, and duopoly.

Duopoly sits between the two extremes. Competition still exists, but it is not as extensive as you would see in competitive markets, which ruthlessly drive the price down to cost. Nor does the result always mirror that of monopoly, where competitive pressures are completely absent. In an oligopoly, a small number of firms feel competitive pressures and also enjoy some of the advantages of monopoly.

Recall that competitive markets drive prices down to the point where marginal revenue is equal to the marginal cost. So, if the market is highly competitive and the marginal cost is zero, we would expect the final price of cell phone service to be zero and the quantity supplied to be 1,200 customers—the number of people who live in the small town. At this point anyone who desired cell phone service would be able to receive it without cost. Since efficiency exists when the output is maximized, and everyone who lives in the community would have cell phone service, the result would be socially efficient. However it is unrealistic to expect this outcome. Firms are in business to make money—they will not provide something for nothing.

At the other extreme of the market structure continuum, since a monopoly faces no competition, price decisions do not depend on the activity of other firms. A monopoly can search for the price that allows it to make the most profit. Looking at Table 13.3, we see that total revenue peaks at $54,000. At this point, the price is $90 per month and 600 customers sign up for cell phone service. The total revenue is the monopolist's profit since the marginal cost is zero. Notice that the monopolist's price, $90, is more than the marginal cost of $0. In this case, the monopolist's marginal revenue is $1,500. The marginal revenue is determined by looking at column (3) and observing that total revenue rises from $52,500 to $54,000—an increase of $1,500. Since the firm serves 100 customers, the marginal revenue is $15 per customer. When the price is lowered to $75, marginal revenue is –$1,500, since total revenue falls from $54,000 to $52,500. Dividing –$1,500 by 100 yields a marginal revenue of –$15 per customer. The monopolist will maximize profit where MC = MR = 0, and the point closest to this in Table 13.3 with discrete data is where P = $90. Compared to a competitive market, the monopoly price is higher and quantity sold is lower. This represents a loss of efficiency.

In a duopoly, the two firms can decide to cooperate, though this is illegal in the United States, as we will discuss shortly. If the duopolists cooperate, we say that they *collude*. **Collusion** is an agreement among rival firms that specifies the price each firm charges and the quantity it produces. The firms that collude can act like a single monopolist to maximize their profits. In this case, the monopoly would maximize its profit by charging $90 and selling to 600 customers. If the duopolists divide the market equally they will each have 300 customers who pay $90, for a total of $27,000 in profit.

When two or more firms act in unison, economists refer to them as a **cartel**. In the United States, **antitrust laws** prohibit collusion. However, even if collusion were legal, it would probably fail more often than not. Imagine that two cell phone companies, AT-Phone and Horizon, have formed a cartel and agreed that each will serve 300 customers at a price of $90 per month per customer. But AT-Phone and Horizon can each make more profit by cheating while the rival company keeps the agreement. Suppose that AT-Phone believes

Collusion
is an agreement among rival firms that specifies the price each firm charges and the quantity it produces.

A cartel
is a group of rival firms that engage in collusion.

Antitrust laws
attempt to prevent oligopolies from behaving like monopolies.

Horizon will continue to serve 300 customers per their collusive agreement, and AT-Phone lowers its price to $75. Looking at Table 13.3 we see that at this price, total market demand rises to 700 customers. So AT-Phone will be able to serve 400 customers and its profit will be 400 × $75, or $30,000. This is an improvement of $3,000 over what AT-Phone made when the market price was $90 and the customers were equally divided.

How would Horizon react? Horizon would certainly not sit on the sidelines and do nothing while AT-Phone increases market share and profits. Horizon would decide that it should also cover 400 customers. For both firms to provide cell phone coverage to 400 customers, the market price would fall to $60. At this price level each firm earns $24,000 in profit, which is $3,000 less than when they served only 600 customers.

From what we know about competitive markets, we might expect the competition between the two to cause a price war in which prices eventually fall to zero. But this is not the case. The duopolist will try to gain more market share and then wait to see its competitor's response. Once the market participants understand that a competitor is likely to match their movements, they will stop trying to increase production and end up at the second-best option. For example, if AT-Phone is serving 400 customers and Horizon decides to service 500 customers, the price of cell phone service will fall to $45. Horizon will make $45 × 500 customers, or $22,500. This is $1,500 less than what the company would have earned if it simply matched its rival's price at $60. As a result, duopolists are unlikely to participate in an all-out price war and the result of their competition is more efficient than a monopoly. In the end, each firm will supply 400 customers, for a total of 800 customers—or 200 more than the monopolist would supply.

From this example we see that a market with a small number of sellers is characterized by **mutual interdependence**; the actions of one firm have an impact on the price and output of its competitors. As a result, a firm's market share is determined by the products it offers, the price it charges, and the actions of its rivals.

Mutual interdependence is a market situation where the actions of one firm have an impact on the price and output of its competitors.

TABLE 13.4

Outcomes Under Competition, Duopoly, and Monopoly

	Competitive Markets	Duopoly	Monopoly
Price	$0	$60	$90
Output	1,200	800	600
Socially Efficient?	Yes	No	No
Explanation	Since the marginal cost of providing cell phone service is zero, the price is eventually driven to zero. Since firms are in business to make a profit, it is unrealistic to expect this result.	Since each firm is mutually interdependent, it adopts a strategy based on the actions of its rival. This leads both firms to charge $60 and service 400 customers.	The monopolist is free to choose the profit-maximizing output. In the cell phone example it maximizes its total revenue. As a result, the monopolist charges $90 and services 600 customers.

Table 13.4 summarizes the different results under competition, duopoly, and monopoly, using our cell phone example.

ECONOMICS IN THE REAL WORLD

OPEC

The best known cartel is the Organization of the Petroleum Exporting Countries, or OPEC, a group of oil-exporting countries that have a large influence on the world crude oil price and output of petroleum. In order to maintain relatively high oil prices, each of the member nations colludes to limit the overall supply of oil. While OPEC's activities are legal under international law, collusion is illegal under United States antitrust law.

OPEC controls almost 80 percent of the world's known oil reserves and accounts for almost half of the world's crude production. This gives the 12 member nations of OPEC a significant ability to control the price of oil. OPEC's production is dominated by Saudi Arabia, which accounts for approximately 40 percent of OPEC's reserves and production. As is the case within any organization, conflict inevitably arises. In the 50 years that OPEC has existed, there have been oil embargoes, oil gluts, production disputes, and periods of falling prices. As a result, OPEC has been far from perfect in consistently maintaining high prices. In addition, OPEC is careful to keep the price of oil below the cost of alternative energy options. Despite the limitations on OPEC's pricing power, the evidence suggests that OPEC has effectively acted as a cartel during the periods when it adopted output rationing in order to maintain price. ✳

What would oil prices be like if there was no OPEC?

Oligopolists want to emulate the monopoly outcome, but the push to compete with their rivals makes it difficult to maintain a cartel. As a result, most firms in oligopoly fall short of fully maximizing profits. But they do not compete to the same degree as firms in competitive markets either. Therefore, when a market is an oligopoly, output is likely to be higher than monopoly and lower than perfect competition. As you would expect, the amount of output affects the prices. The higher output than a monopoly makes oligopoly prices generally lower than monopoly prices, and lower output than a competitive market makes oligopoly prices higher than those found in competitive markets.

The Nash Equilibrium

As we have discussed in earlier chapters, the market price is the price at which the quantity of a product or service demanded is equal to the quantity supplied. At this price, the market is in equilibrium. In oligopoly, the process

Nash Equilibrium

A Brilliant Madness (2002)

A Brilliant Madness is the story of a mathematical genius, John Nash, whose career was cut short by a descent into madness. At the age of 30, Nash began claiming that aliens were communicating with him. Nash spent the next three decades fighting paranoid schizophrenia. Before this time, while he was a graduate student at Princeton, Nash wrote a proof about non-cooperative equilibrium. The proof established the Nash equilibrium and became a foundation of modern economic theory. In 1994 Nash was awarded a Nobel Prize in Economics. The documentary features interviews with John Nash, his wife Alicia, his friends and colleagues, and experts in both game theory and mental illness.

A Brilliant Madness conveys the essentials about Nash without taking liberties with the facts, as Ron Howard did in his 2001 film *A Beautiful Mind,* based on the life of Nash. If you watch *A Brilliant Madness* and then watch the famous bar scene in *A Beautiful Mind* you should be able to catch the error Ron Howard made in describing how the Nash equilibrium works!

Modern microeconomics was revolutionized by a mathematician.

A Nash equilibrium occurs when a decision-maker has nothing to gain by changing its own strategy without collusion.

that leads to equilibrium may take on a special form referred to as the *Nash equilibrium,* named for mathematician John Nash.

The **Nash equilibrium** occurs when an economic decision-maker has nothing to gain by changing strategy unless it can collude. The phone example we just explored was an example of a Nash equilibrium. The best strategy for AT-Phone and Horizon is to increase their output to 400 customers each. When both firms reach that level of output, neither has an incentive to change. Bear in mind that the rivals can do better if they collude. Under collusion, each rival serves 300 customers and their combined profits rise. However, as we saw, if one rival is willing to break the cartel, it will make more profit if it services 400 customers ($30,000) while the other firm continues to serve only 300 ($22,500). The firms continue to challenge each other until they reach a combined output level of 800 customers. At this point the market reaches Nash equilibrium and neither firm has a reason to change its short-term profit-maximizing strategy.

Oligopoly with More than Two Firms

We have seen how firms behave in a duopoly. What happens when more firms enter the market? The addition of a third firm complicates efforts to maintain a cartel and increases the possibility of a more competitive result.

We can see this interaction in the cell phone market. The four major companies are not all equal. AT&T and Verizon are significantly larger than Sprint Nextel and T-Mobile. If AT&T and Verizon were the only two providers, the market might have very little competition. However, the smaller Sprint Nextel and T-Mobile play a crucial role in changing the market dynamic. Even though Sprint Nextel and T-Mobile have significantly less market share, they still have developed extensive cellular networks in order to compete. Since Sprint Nextel and T-Mobile have networks with smaller subscriber bases and significant excess capacity, they both aggressively compete on price. As a result, in many respects the entire cell phone industry functions competitively.

To see why this is the case, consider what the addition of a third firm will do to price and output in the market. When a firm enters the market there are two effects to consider, price and output. For example, if a third firm builds a cell phone tower, it will increase the overall capacity to provide cell phone service. As we observed in the duopoly example, if the total number of cell phone contracts sold (the supply) increases, firms must charge a lower price. This is known as the **price effect**, which occurs when the price is affected by the entrance of a rival firm in the market. But since the marginal cost of providing cell phone service is essentially zero, the price that each firm charges is substantially higher than the marginal cost of adding a new customer to the network. When the firm sells an additional unit, it generates additional profits for the firm. This is known as the **output effect**, which occurs when the entrance of a rival firm in the market affects the amount produced.

The price effect and output effect make it difficult to maintain a cartel when there are more than two firms. Generally, as the number of firms grows, each individual firm becomes less concerned about its impact on the overall price level, because any price above marginal cost creates a profit. Therefore, individual firms are more willing to lower prices since this creates a large output effect for the individual firm and only a small price effect in the market.

Of course, not all firms are the same size. This means that smaller and larger firms in an oligopolistic market react differently to the price and output effects. Increased output at smaller firms will have a negligible impact on overall prices because small firms represent only a tiny fraction of the market supply. This is not true for firms with a large market share—decisions at these firms will have a substantial impact on price and output because the overall amount supplied in the market will change appreciably. In other words, in an oligopoly, the decisions of one firm directly affect other firms.

A **price effect** occurs when the price is affected by the entrance of a rival firm in the market.

An **output effect** occurs when the entrance of a rival firm in the market affects the amount produced.

PRACTICE WHAT YOU KNOW

Oligopoly: Can You Recognize the Oligopolist?

Are airlines a good example of an oligopolist?

Question: Which firm is the oligopolist?

a. This firm is in retail. It is one of the largest and most popular clothing stores in the country. It also competes with many rivals and there is intense price competition.

b. The firm is in the airline industry. It is not the largest carrier but significant barriers to entry allow it to serve a number of very profitable routes.

c. This firm is a restaurant in a small, isolated community. It is the only local eatery. People drive from miles away to eat there.

Answer: Firm A sells clothing, a product with many competing brands and outlets. The competition is intense and this means that the firm has little market power. As a result firm A is in a monopolistically competitive market. B has market power on a number of routes it flies. Since barriers to entry often prevent new carriers from being able to get gate space, even smaller airlines are oligopolists. Firm C is a monopolist. It is the only place to eat out in the isolated community and no other restaurant is nearby.

How Does Game Theory Explain Strategic Behavior?

Decision-making under oligopoly can be complex. Recall that with the Nash equilibrium, participants make decisions based on the behavior of others around them. This is an example of a branch of mathematics known as

game theory, which economists use to understand how individual firms make decisions. In particular, the techniques of game theory can help us determine what level of cooperation is most likely. A game consists of a set of players, a set of strategies available to those players, and a specification of the payoffs for each combination of strategies. The game is usually represented by a payoff matrix which shows the players, strategies, and payoffs. It is presumed that each player acts simultaneously or without knowing the actions of the other.

In this section we will learn about the prisoner's dilemma, an example from game theory that will help us understand how dominant strategies often frame short-run decisions. We will use the idea of the dominant strategy to explain why oligopolists often choose to advertise. Finally, we will come full circle and argue that the dominant strategy in a game may be overcome in the long run through repeated interactions.

Game theory
is a branch of mathematics that economists use to analyze the strategic behavior of decision-makers.

Strategic Behavior and the Dominant Strategy

We have seen that in oligopoly there is mutual interdependence. A rival's business choices affect the earnings that the other rivals can expect to make. In order to learn a little more about the decisions firms make, we will look at a fundamental problem in game theory known as the *prisoner's dilemma*. The prisoner's dilemma takes its name from a famous scenario devised by pioneer game theorist Al Tucker soon after World War II.

The scenario goes like this: there are two prisoners who are being interrogated separately about a crime they both participated in, and each is offered a plea bargain to cooperate with the authorities by testifying against the other. If both suspects refuse to cooperate with the authorities, neither can be convicted of a more serious crime, though they will have to spend some time in jail. But the police have offered full immunity if one cooperates and the other does not. This means that each suspect has an incentive to betray the other. When decision-makers face incentives that make it difficult to achieve mutually beneficial outcomes, we say they are in a **prisoner's dilemma**. This situation makes the payoff for cooperating with the authorities more attractive than keeping quiet. We can understand why this is so by looking at Figure 13.1, a payoff matrix, that shows the possible outcomes in a prisoner's dilemma situation. Starting with the first box in the upper-left-hand corner, we see that if

Incentives Matter

The **prisoner's dilemma**
occurs when decision-makers face incentives that make it difficult to achieve mutually beneficial outcomes.

	Tony Montana	
	Confess	Keep quiet
Manny Ribera — Confess	10 years in jail / 10 years in jail	25 years in jail / goes free
Manny Ribera — Keep quiet	goes free / 25 years in jail	1 year in jail / 1 year in jail

FIGURE 13.1

The Prisoner's Dilemma

The two suspects know that if they both keep quiet they will spend only one year in jail. The prisoner's dilemma occurs because the decision to confess results in less time in jail for the one who confesses if the other does not confess. However, this outcome means both are likely to confess and get 10 years.

both suspects testify against each other, they each get 10 years in jail. If one suspect testifies while his partner remains quiet—the upper-right and lower-left boxes—he goes free and his partner gets 25 years in jail. If both keep quiet—the result in the lower-right-hand corner—they each get off with one year in jail. This result is better than the outcome in which both prisoners testify.

Since each suspect is interrogated separately, the decision about what to tell the police cannot be made cooperatively; each prisoner faces a dilemma. The interrogation process makes it a non-cooperative "game" and changes the incentives that each party faces.

Under these circumstances, what will our suspects choose? Let's begin with the outcomes for Tony. Suppose that he testifies. If Manny also testifies, Tony will get 10 years in jail (the upper-left box). If Manny keeps quiet, Tony will go free (the lower-left box). Now suppose that Tony decides to keep quiet. If Manny testifies, Tony can expect 25 years in jail (the upper-right box). If Manny keeps quiet, Tony will get 1 year in jail (the lower-right box). No matter what choice Manny makes, Tony is always better off choosing to testify. If his partner testifies and he testifies, he gets 10 years in jail as opposed to 25 if he keeps quiet. If his partner keeps quiet and he testifies, Tony goes free, as opposed to spending a year in jail if he also keeps quiet. A similar analysis applies to the outcomes for Manny.

When a particular strategy produces a better outcome for a person regardless of strategies others choose, we say it is a **dominant strategy**. We can see this at work in the case of our two suspects. They know that if they both keep quiet they will spend one year in jail. The dilemma occurs because both suspects are more likely to testify and get 10 years in jail. This choice is obvious for two reasons. First, neither suspect can monitor the actions of the other suspect after they are separated. Second, once each suspect understands that his partner will save jail time if he testifies, he realizes that the incentives are not in favor of keeping quiet.

The dominant strategy in our example is a Nash equilibrium. Recall that a Nash equilibrium occurs when economic decision-makers choose the best possible strategy after taking into account the decisions of others. If each suspect reasons that the other will testify, the best response is also to testify. Each suspect may wish that he and his partner can coordinate their actions and agree to keep quiet. However, without the possibility of coordination, neither has an incentive to withhold the testimony. So they think strategically, and decide to testify.

A **dominant strategy** exists when a particular strategy produces the best outcome for a player regardless of the strategies deployed by the other.

Incentives
Matter

Duopoly and the Prisoner's Dilemma

The prisoner's dilemma example suggests that cooperation can be difficult to achieve. To get a better sense of the incentives that oligopolists face when trying to collude, we will use game theory to evaluate the outcome of our cell phone duopoly example.

Recall that our duopolists, AT-Phone and Horizon, produced an output of 800 customers, an amount that was lower than would occur under perfect competition (1,200) but more than monopoly (600). Figure 13.2 puts the information from Table 13.3 into a payoff matrix and highlights the profit that AT-Phone and Horizon could earn at various production levels.

Looking at the bottom two boxes, we see that at high production, Horizon can earn either $30,000 or $24,000, depending on what AT-Phone does.

ECONOMICS IN THE MEDIA

Prisoner's Dilemma

Murder by Numbers (2002)

There is an especially compelling example of the prisoner's dilemma at work in *Murder by Numbers*. In this scene, the district attorney's office decides to interrogate two murder suspects. Without a confession they don't have enough evidence and the two murderers are likely to go free. Each is confronted with the prisoner's dilemma by being placed in a separate room and threatened with the death penalty. In order to get the confession, the detective tells one of the suspects, "Just think of it as a game. Whoever talks first is the winner." The detective goes on to tell one of the suspects that his partner in the other room is "rolling over" (even though the partner is not actually talking) and that he is going to get a lighter sentence because he is cooperating. This places

Would you rat on your partner in crime?

added pressure on the suspect, since once you think your partner is talking, the rational choice is to begin talking as well.

At a low production level, it could earn either $27,000 or $22,500. The same reasoning is true for AT-Phone. Now look at the right-hand column and you will see that AT-Phone can earn either $30,000 or $24,000, depending on what Horizon does. At a low production level, it could earn either $27,000 or $22,500. So, once again, the high production levels dominate. The two companies always have an incentive to service more customers because this strategy makes the most profit if its competitor also chooses to expand production. A high level of production leads to a Nash equilibrium; both firms make $24,000. If the companies operate as a cartel they can be more profitable, with both earning $27,000. Therefore, the Nash equilibrium is their second-best outcome.

FIGURE 13.2

		AT-Phone	
		Low production: 300 customers	High production: 400 customers
Horizon	Low production: 300 customers	$27,000 profit / $27,000 profit	$30,000 profit / $22,500 profit
	High production: 400 customers	$22,500 profit / $30,000 profit	$24,000 profit / $24,000 profit

The Prisoner's Dilemma in Duopoly

Each company has a dominant strategy to service more customers because it makes the most profit even if its competitor also expands production. A high level of production leads to a Nash equilibrium where both firms make $24,000.

Advertising and Game Theory

We have seen that oligopolists function like monopolistic competitors in that they sell differentiated products. We know that advertising is commonplace in markets with a differentiated product. In the case of an oligopoly, mutual interdependence means that advertising can create an "arms race" among firms looking to gain customers. This may lead to exploding advertising budgets and little, or no, net gain of customers. Therefore, oligopolists have an incentive to scale back their advertising, but only if the other rivals also agree to scale back. Like all cooperative action among competitors, this is easier said than done.

Figure 13.3 highlights the advertising choices of Coca-Cola and Pepsi, two fierce rivals in the soft drink industry. Together Coca-Cola and Pepsi account for 75 percent of the soft drink market, with Coca-Cola the slightly larger of the two firms. Both companies are known for their advertising campaigns, which cost hundreds of millions of dollars. To determine if they gain anything by spending so much on advertising, let's look at the dominant strategy. In the absence of cooperation, each firm will choose to advertise, because the payoffs under advertising ($100 M or $150 M) exceed those of not advertising ($75 M or $125 M). When this happens, each firm generates a profit of $100 M. This is a second-best outcome compared to the $125 M profit each could earn if neither firm advertises. The dilemma is that each firm needs to advertise to market its product and retain its customer base, but most advertising expenditures end up cancelling each other out and costing the companies millions of dollars.

ECONOMICS IN THE REAL WORLD

The Cold War

The idea that companies benefit from spending less on advertising has an analog in warfare. Countries benefit from a "peace dividend" whenever war ends. There is no better example of this than the Cold War between the Soviet Union and the United States that began in the 1950s. When the Cold War ended in the late 1980s, both countries had amassed thousands of nuclear warheads in an effort to deter aggression.

This buildup put enormous economic pressure on each country to keep up with the other. During the height of the Cold War each country found itself in a prisoner's dilemma in which spending more in an arms race was the dominant

FIGURE 13.3

The Prisoner's Dilemma and Advertising

The two companies each have a dominant strategy to advertise. We can see this by observing that Coca-Cola and Pepsi Co. each make $25 M more by choosing to advertise. As a result they both end up in the upper-left box earning $100 M when they could have each made $125 M in the lower-right box if they had agreed not to advertise.

		Coca-Cola	
		Advertises	Does not advertise
Pepsi Co.	Advertises	$100 M / $100 M	$75 M / $150 M
	Does not advertise	$150 M / $75 M	$125 M / $125 M

strategy. When the Soviet Union dissolved, the United States was able to spend less money on deterrence. In the post-Cold War world of the 1990s the U.S. military budget fell from 6.5 to 3.5 percent of Gross Domestic Product (GDP) as the nation reaped a peace dividend. Of course, the prisoner's dilemma cannot account for all military spending, and following the terrorist attacks of 2001 military spending increased again to near 5 percent of GDP. ✳

The cold war created a prisoner's dilemma for the United States and Soviet Union.

Escaping the Prisoner's Dilemma in the Long Run

We have seen how game theory can be a useful tool for understanding strategic decision-making in non-cooperative environments. When you examine the prisoner's dilemma, or the Nash equilibrium, the solution represents an outcome that yields the largest gain in the short run. However, many decisions are not made this way. The dominant strategy does not consider the possible long-run benefits of cooperation.

Game theorist Robert Axelrod decided to examine the choices that participants make in a long-run setting. He ran a sophisticated computer simulation in which he invited scholars to submit strategies for securing points in a prisoner's dilemma tournament over many rounds. All the submissions were collected and paired, and the results were scored. After each simulation, he eliminated the weakest strategy and re-ran the tournament with the remaining strategies. This evolutionary approach continued until the best strategy remained. Among all strategies, including those that were solely cooperative or uncooperative, *tit-for-tat* dominated. **Tit-for-tat** is a long-run strategy that creates cooperation among participants by following the opponent's most

Tit-for-tat
is a long-run strategy designed to create cooperation among participants, by mimicking the decision your opponent made in the previous round.

Photo to come

Prisoner's Dilemma

The Dark Knight (2008)

In what is arguably the greatest superhero movie of all time, the Joker (played by the late Heath Ledger) always seems to be one step ahead of the law. The strategic interactions between the police and the conniving villain are an illustration of game theory in action.

Near the end of movie, the Joker rigs two full passenger ferries to explode at midnight and tells the passengers that if they try to escape, the bomb will detonate earlier. To complicate matters, one of the ferries is filled with civilian passengers and includes a number of children, while the other ferry is transporting prisoners. Each ferry is given the chance to save itself by hitting a detonator button attached to the other ferry.

The Joker's plan sets up a prisoner's dilemma between the two boats and an ethical experiment. Are the lives of those on the civilian boat worth more than those of the prisoners? The Joker's intention is to have one of the ferries blow up the other, and thereby create chaos in Gotham City.

In the payoff matrix, the dominant strategy is to detonate the other boat. Failing to detonate the other boat results in death—either your ferry blows up at midnight, or the other boat detonates you first. In this scenario, the only chance of survival is if your ferry detonates the other ferry first. As the scene unfolds and the tension builds, the passengers on both boats realize their plight and wrestle with the consequences of their decisions. Gradually, everyone becomes aware that the dominant strategy is to detonate the other boat. What is interesting is how the civilians and prisoners handle this information.

What actually happens? Each boat decides that they would rather be detonated than willingly participate in the Joker's experiment. Watching the scene as a game theorist will give you a new appreciation for the film.

		Prisoner ferry	
		Detonate other boat	Do not detonate other boat
Civilian ferry	Detonate other boat	Cannot simultaneously happen / Cannot simultaneously happen	Dead / Survive
	Do not detonate other boat	Survive / Dead	Dead / Dead

recent decision with repayment in kind. As the name implies, a tit-for-tat strategy is one in which you do whatever your opponent does. If your opponent breaks the agreement, you break the agreement, too. If the opponent behaves properly, then you behave properly, too.

Since the joint payoffs for cooperation are high in a prisoner's dilemma, tit-for-tat begins by cooperating. In subsequent rounds, the tit-for-tat strategy mimics whatever the other player did in the previous round. The genius behind tit-for-tat is that it changes the incentives and encourages cooperation. Turning back to our example in Figure 13.3, suppose that Coca-Cola and Pepsi want to save on advertising expenses. The companies expect to have repeated interactions so they both know from past experience that any effort to start a new advertising campaign will be immediately countered by the other firm. Since the companies react to each other's moves in kind, this means that any effort to exploit the dominant strategy of advertising will ultimately fail. This dynamic can alter the incentives that the firms face in the long run and lead to mutually beneficial behavior.

Incentives Matter

Tit-for-tat makes it less desirable to advertise by eliminating the long-run benefits. Advertising is still a dominant strategy in the short run because the payoffs with advertising ($100 M or $150 M) exceed those of not advertising ($75 M or $125 M). In the short run, the firm that advertises could earn $25 M extra but in every subsequent round—if the rival responds in kind—the firm should expect profits of $100 M because its rival will also be advertising. As a result, there is a large long-run opportunity cost for not cooperating. If one firm stops advertising and the other follows suit, they will each find themselves making $125 M in the long run. Why hasn't this happened? Coke and Pepsi don't trust each other enough to earn the $25 M dividend that comes from an advertising truce.

The prisoner's dilemma nicely captures why cooperation is so difficult in the short run. But most interactions in life occur over the long run. Scam artists and sketchy companies take advantage of short-run opportunities that cannot last because relationships in the long run—with businesses and with people—involve mutual trust. Cooperation is the default because you know that the other side is invested in the relationship. Under these circumstances, the tit-for-tat strategy is successfully employed.

A Caution About Game Theory

Game theory is a decision-making tool, but not all games have dominant strategies that make player decisions easy to predict. Perhaps the best example is the game known as "Rock, Paper, Scissors." This simple game has no dominant strategy. Paper beats rock (because the paper will cover the rock) and rock beats scissors (because the rock will break the scissors), but scissors beats paper (because the scissors will cut the paper). The preferred choice is strictly a function of what the other player selects. Many situations in life, and business, are more like Rock, Paper, Scissors than the prisoner's dilemma. Winning at business in the long run often occurs because you are one step ahead of the competition, not because you deploy a strategy that attempts to take advantage of a short-run opportunity.

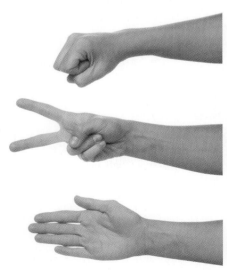

Rock, Paper, Scissors is a game without a dominant strategy.

To help you think about this, consider two friends who enjoy playing racquetball together. Both players are of equal ability, so each point comes down to whether the players guess correctly about the direction the other player will hit. Take a look at Figure 13.4. The success of Joey and Rachel depends on how well each guesses where the other will hit.

In this competition neither Rachel nor Joey has a dominant strategy that guarantees success. Sometimes Joey wins when hitting right, other times he loses the point. Sometimes Rachel wins when she guesses left, other times she loses. Each player will only guess correctly half the time. Since we cannot say what each player will do from one point to another there is no Nash equilibrium. Any of the four outcomes are equally likely on successive points and there is no way to predict how the next point will be played. In other words, don't expect every game to include a prisoner's dilemma and produce a Nash equilibrium. Game theory, like real life, has many different possible outcomes.

PRACTICE WHAT YOU KNOW

Dominant Strategy: To Advertise or Not, That Is the Question!

Question: University Subs and Savory Sandwiches are the only two sub shops in a small college town. If neither runs a special promotion, both are able to keep their prices high and earn $10,000 a month. However, when both run promotions, their profits fall to $1,000. Finally, if one sub shop runs a promotion and the other does not, the

How much should a firm charge for this sandwich?

shop that runs the promotion earns a profit of $15,000 and the other loses $5,000. What is the dominant strategy for University Subs? Is there a Nash equilibrium in this example?

FIGURE 13.4

No Dominant Strategy Exists

Neither Rachel nor Joey has a dominant strategy that guarantees winning the point. Any of the four outcomes are equally likely on successive points, and there is no way to predict how the next point will be played. As a result, there is no Nash equilibrium here.

		Rachel	
		Guesses to the left	Guesses to the right
Joey	Hits to the left	Rachel wins the point / Joey loses the point	Rachel loses the point / Joey wins the point
	Hits to the right	Rachel loses the point / Joey wins the point	Rachel wins the point / Joey loses the point

	University Subs	
	Runs a 2–for–1 promotion	Keep price high
Savory Sandwiches — Runs a 2–for–1 promotion	Makes $1,000 / Makes $1,000	Loses $5,000 / Makes $15,000
Savory Sandwiches — Keep price high	Makes $15,000 / Loses $5,000	Makes $10,000 / Makes $10,000

Answer:

If University Subs runs the "2 for 1" promotion, it will make either $1,000 or $15,000, depending on its rival's actions. If University Subs keeps the price high, it will make either –$5,000 or $10,000, depending on what Savory Sandwiches does. So, the dominant strategy will be to run the special, since it guarantees a profit of at least $1,000. Savory Sandwiches has the same dominant strategy and the same payoffs. Therefore both companies will run the promotion and each will make $1,000. Neither firm has a reason to switch to the high-price strategy since it would lose $5,000 if the other company runs the 2-for-1 promotion. The Nash equilibrium occurs when both companies run the promotion.

How Do Government Policies Affect Oligopoly Behavior?

When oligopolists in an industry are able to form a cooperative alliance, they function like a monopoly. Competition disappears, which is clearly bad for society. One way to improve the social welfare of society is to restore competition and limit monopoly practices through policy legislation.

Antitrust Policy

Efforts to curtail the adverse consequences of oligopolistic cooperation began with the **Sherman Antitrust Act** of 1890. This was the first federal law to place limits on cartels and monopolies. The Sherman Act was created in response to the increase in the concentration ratios in many leading U.S. industries, including steel, railroads, mining, textiles, and oil. Prior to the passage of the Sherman Act, firms were free to pursue contracts that created mutually beneficial outcomes. Once the act took effect, certain cooperative actions became criminal. Section 2 of the Sherman Act reads, "Every person who shall monopolize, or attempt to monopolize, or combine or conspire with any other person or persons, to monopolize any part of the trade or commerce among the several States, or with foreign nations, shall be deemed guilty of a felony."

The **Sherman Antitrust Act** is the first federal law limiting cartels and monopolies.

The **Clayton Act**
targets corporate behaviors
that reduce competition.

The **Clayton Act** of 1914 was enacted to further prevent the abuse of corporate power. Large corporations had been vilified during the presidential election of 1912 and the Sherman Act was largely seen as ineffective in curbing monopoly power. To shore up antitrust policy, the Clayton Act added to the list of activities that were deemed socially detrimental, including:

1. *Price discrimination* if it lessens competition or creates monopoly
2. *Exclusive dealings* that restrict the ability of the buyer to deal with competitors
3. *Tying arrangements* that require the buyer to buy an additional product in order to buy the first
4. *Mergers and acquisitions* that lessen competition, or situations where a person serves as a director on more than one board in the same industry

As the Clayton Act makes clear, there are many ways to reduce competition.

Over the past hundred years, lawmakers have continued to refine antitrust policy. Additional legislation, and court interpretations of existing antitrust law, have made it difficult to determine whether or not a company has violated the law. The U.S. Justice Department is charged with oversight, but it often lacks the resources to be able to fully investigate every case. Antitrust law is complex and cases are hard to prosecute, but these laws are essential to maintain a competitive business environment. Without effective restraints on excessive market power, firms would organize into cartels more often, or find ways to restrict competition. Table 13.5 briefly describes the most influential antitrust cases in United States history.

Predatory pricing
occurs when firms deliberately set their prices below average variable costs with the intent of driving rivals from the market.

Predatory Pricing

While firms have a strong incentive to cooperate in order to keep prices high, they also want to keep potential rivals out of the market. The practice of setting prices deliberately below average variable costs is known as **predatory pricing**. The firm suffers a short-run loss in order to prevent rivals from entering the market or to drive rival firms out of business in the long run. Once the rivals are gone, the firm should be able to act like a monopolist without the need to form a cartel.

Predatory pricing is illegal, but it is difficult to prosecute. Neither the court system nor economists have a simple rule that they follow to determine when a firm steps over the line. Predatory pricing can look and feel like spirited competition. Moreover, the concern with predatory pricing is not the competitive aspect or lower prices, but the affect on the market when all rivals fail. To prove that predatory pricing occurred, the courts need evidence that prices were increased significantly after the rivals failed. Wal-Mart is often cited as an example of a firm that engages in predatory pricing because its low prices effectively drive

Though Wal-Mart keeps its prices low, there is little evidence that it engages in predatory pricing.

TABLE 13.5

Influential Antitrust Cases in U.S. History

Case	Year	Description
Standard Oil	1906	Standard Oil was founded in 1870. By 1897 the company had driven the price down to 6 cents a gallon, which put many of its competitors out of business. Standard Oil became the largest company in the world. In 1906, the U.S. government filed suit against Standard Oil for violating the Sherman Antitrust Act. Three years later the company was found guilty and forced to break up into 34 independent companies.
ALCOA	1937	The Aluminum Company of America (ALCOA), founded in 1907, maintained its position as the only producer of aluminum in the United States for many years. To keep that position, the company acquired exclusive rights to all U.S. sources of bauxite, the base material from which aluminum is refined. It then acquired land rights to build and own hydroelectric facilities in both the United States and Canada. By owning both the base materials and the only sites where refinement could take place, ALCOA effectively barred other firms from entering the U.S. aluminum market. In 1937 the Department of Justice filed suit against ALCOA. Seven years later, the court ruled that ALCOA had taken measures to restrict trade and functioned as a monopoly. ALCOA was not divested because two rivals, Keiser and Reynolds, emerged soon after.
AT&T	1974	In 1974, the U.S. Attorney General filed suit against AT&T for violating antitrust laws. The case took seven years before a settlement was reached to split the company into seven new companies, each serving a different region of the United States. However, five of the seven have since merged together to become AT&T Incorporated, which is now one of the largest companies in the world.
Microsoft	1995	When Internet Explorer was introduced in 1995, Microsoft insisted that it was a feature rather than a new Windows product. The U.S. Department of Justice did not agree and filed suit against Microsoft for illegally discouraging competition to protect its software monopoly. After a series of court decisions and appeals, a settlement ordered Microsoft to share application programming interfaces with third-party companies.

many smaller companies out of business. However, there is no evidence that Wal-Mart has ever systematically raised prices after a rival fails. Therefore, Wal-Mart's price strategy does not meet the legal standard for predatory pricing. Similarly, Microsoft came under intense scrutiny in the 1990s for giving away its browser, Internet Explorer, in order to undercut Netscape, which also ended up giving away its browser. Microsoft understood that the key to its long-term success was the dominance of the Windows platform. Giving away Internet Explorer enabled Microsoft to gain over 80 percent of the browser market and also enabled it to keep its leadership with the Windows operating system. Eventually, Microsoft was prosecuted by the government, but not for predatory pricing, which could not be proved because Microsoft never significantly raised the price of Internet Explorer. Instead, Microsoft was prosecuted for tying the purchase of Internet Explorer to the Windows operating system in order to restrict competition. The Microsoft case lasted over four years and it ended in a settlement that placed restrictions on the firm's business practices.

PRACTICE WHAT YOU KNOW

Predatory Pricing: Price Wars

You've undoubtedly encountered a price war at some point. It could be two gas stations, clothing outlets, or restaurants that are charging prices that seem to be unbelievably low.

Predatory pricing? Check out the two competing signs above!

Question: Is a "price war" between two adjacent pizza restaurants evidence of predatory pricing?

Answer: One essential element for proving predatory pricing is that there must be evidence of the intent to raise prices after others are driven out of business. That is a problem in this example. Suppose one of the pizza places closes. The remaining firm can now raise its price substantially. But barriers to entry in the restaurant industry are low in most metropolitan areas, so any efforts to maintain high prices for long will fail. Customers will vote with their feet and wallets by choosing another pizza place a little further away that offers a better value. Or, a new competitor will sense that the victor is vulnerable because of the high prices and open nearby. Either way, the market is competitive, so any market power created by driving out one rival is fleeting.

The aggressive price war is probably just promotional pricing to protect market share. Firms often price some items below their variable costs to attract customers. These firms hope to make up the difference and then some with high profit margins on other items, such as beverages and side dishes.

What Are Network Externalities?

We end the chapter by considering a special kind of externality that often occurs in oligopoly. A **network externality** exists when the number of customers who purchase or use a good influences the quantity demanded. This means that firms with many customers often find it easier to attract new customers, and also to keep their customers from switching to other rivals. For example, the sheer size of Facebook makes it a better place to do social networking than MySpace. As a result, Facebook will be able to grow its business even if MySpace, Google+, or another rival builds a social networking site with better features. The first firm to enter the market is often the one that ends up dominating the industry.

A **network externality** exists when the number of customers who purchase a good influences the quantity demanded.

Most examples of network externalities involve the introduction of new technologies. For instance, some technologies need to reach a critical mass before consumers can effectively use it. Today everyone seems to have a cell phone. However, when cell phones were introduced in the United States in 1983 the coverage was quite limited. The first users of these phones could not surf the Internet, roam, text, or use many of the applications we enjoy today. Moreover, the phones were large and bulky. How did we get from 1983 to today? As additional people bought cell phones, networks expanded and manufacturers and telephone companies responded by building more cell towers and offering better phones. The expansion of networks brought more users and new adopters benefited from an ever-expanding customer base.

Users of the first generation cell phone, the Motorola DynaTAC 8000X, created a positive network externality for future users.

Other technologies have gone through similar transformations. The Internet, fax machines, and Blu-ray disks all depend on the number of users. If you were the only person on the Internet, or the only person with the ability to send and receive a fax, your technical capacity would have little value. Likewise, the owner of a Blu-ray machine depends on the willingness of movie studios to create content in that format. In a world with ever-changing technology, first adopters pave the way for the next generation of users.

Positive network externalities are also generated by the **bandwagon effect**, which arises when a buyer's preference for a product increases as the number of people buying it increases. Fads of all sorts fall into this category. North Face jackets, oversized handbags, Uggs, and Bluetooth headsets are in today, but how long that remains true is anyone's guess.

The **bandwagon effect** arises when a buyer's preference for a product increases as the number of people buying it increases.

In addition to the advantages of forming a larger network, firms also find that many of their customers face significant **switching costs** if they leave. For instance, the transition from listening to music on CDs to using digital music files involved a substantial switching cost for many users. Today, there are switching costs among the many digital music options. Once a consumer has established a library of MP3s, or uses iTunes, the switching costs of trans-

Switching costs are the costs incurred when a consumer changes from one supplier to another.

ferring the music from one format to another creates a significant barrier to change. When consumers face switching costs, the demand for the existing product becomes more inelastic. As a result, oligopolists leverage not only the number of customers they maintain in their network but they also try to make switching to another network more difficult. There is no better example of the costs of switching than cell phone providers. First, contract termination fees apply to many cell phone agreements if the contract is broken. Second, many providers do not charge for calls inside the network, or among a circle of friends. This means that if you switch and your friends do not, you will end up using more minutes on a rival network. These two tactics create high switching costs for many cell phone customers. To reduce switching costs, the Federal Communications Commission in 2003 began requiring that phone companies allow customers to take their cell phone numbers with them when the change to a different provider. This change in the law has reduced the costs of switching from one provider to another and made the cell phone market more competitive.

Oligopolists are keenly aware of the power of network externalities. As new markets develop, the first firm into the industry often gains a large customer

PRACTICE WHAT YOU KNOW

Examples of Network Externalities

Question: In which of these examples are network externalities important?

a. College alumni

b. Netflix

c. A local bakery that sells fresh bread

Does Netflix benefit from network externalities?

Answers:

a. Institutions that have more alumni are able to raise funds more easily so the size of the alumni network matters. The number of alumni also matters when graduates look for jobs, since alumni are often inclined to hire employees who went to the same school. For example, Penn State University has the nation's largest alumni base. This means that each graduate from PSU benefits from network externalities.

b. Netflix's size allows it to offer a vast array of DVDs and downloads. If it was smaller, Netflix would be unable to make as many obscure titles available. This means that Netflix customers benefit from network externalities by having more DVDs to choose from.

 The local bakery is a small company. If the bakery attracts more customers, each customer will have to compete harder to get fresh bread. Since the supply of bread is limited, additional customers create congestion, and network externalities do not exist.

Why Waiting Is Generally a Good Idea

If you are like a lot of people when you hear of something new, and cool, you check it out. There is no harm in doing that. But what happens when you decide to purchase the latest gadget or join a new website? You've made an investment of money or time. The fruitfulness of that investment often depends on how many other people do that same thing.

Suppose you were one of the first people to get a 3D television—the first purchasers paid well over $5,000 for the new technology. What exactly could they watch? The amount of 3D programming to start was tiny. You have a very expensive TV that you could rarely use to watch 3D because the content was playing catch-up. Those that waited could buy a 3D unit with greater clarity at a lower price and more content would be available to watch. That's a win-win-win for procrastinators. The early adopter gets penalized for paving the way.

The same is true with many social media sites. Waiting for a website to gain traction will save you from setting up a profile and investing your time and effort only to find out that other people are not nearly as excited about the features as you are. You end wasting a lot of time, and because other online users never show up, you don't get the benefits that come from network externalities. If you wait until a platform is already established then you can be fairly confident that your return on investment will be rewarded. This is certainly true with Facebook, Twitter, and LinkedIn—all of which have come to dominate segments of the social media market.

Google glasses? Should you buy the newest gadget when it comes out?

Network externalities are also important on dating sites. Just consider the overwhelming number of choices you have in this market: match.com, Zoosk, eHarmony, OurTime, chemistry.com, and many other sites. You could sign up for dozens of dating sites or simply choose the largest site, match.com, because it offers you the biggest database. Since dating sites charge members fees, waiting and seeing which sites are more popular is one way to use network externalities to improve your odds of success.

base. When there are positive network externalities, the customer base allows the firm to grow quickly. In addition, consumers are often more comfortable purchasing from an established firm. These two factors favor the formation of large firms and make it difficult for smaller competitors to gain customers. As a result, the presence of significant positive network externalities causes small firms to be driven out of business or forces them to merge with larger competitors.

Conclusion

The misconception is that cell phone companies compete like firms in competitive markets or monopolistically competitive markets do. The reality is that cell phone companies are oligopolists. Firms in oligopoly markets can compete or collude to create monopoly conditions. The result is often hard to predict. In many cases the presence of a dominant short-run strategy causes firms to compete on price and advertising even though this results in lower economic profits. In contrast, the potential success of a tit-for-tat strategy suggests that oligopolistic firms are capable of cooperating in order to jointly maximize their long-run profits. Whether oligopoly mirrors the result found in monopolistic competition or monopoly matters a great deal since society's welfare is higher when more competition is present. Since oligopoly is not a market structure with a predictable outcome, each oligopolistic industry must be examined on a case-by-case basis by examining data and utilizing game theory. This makes the study of oligopoly one of the most fascinating parts of the theory of the firm.

In the next section of the book we examine how resource markets work. Each firm needs access to resources such as land, labor, and capital to produce goods and services. As a result, understanding how resource markets work will deepen our grasp of the theory of the firm. We will pay special attention to the labor market going forward since the labor market determines the job prospects of workers and the amount of income inequality within society.

ANSWERING THE BIG QUESTIONS

1. What is oligopoly?

* Oligopoly exists when a small number of firms sell a differentiated product in a market with significant barriers to entry. An oligopolist is like a monopolistic competitor in that it sells differentiated products. It is also like a monopolist in that it enjoys significant barriers to entry. The small number of sellers in oligopoly leads to mutual interdependence.

* Oligopolists have a tendency to collude and to form cartels in hope of achieving monopoly-like profits.

* Oligopolistic markets are socially inefficient since price and marginal cost are not equal. The result under oligopoly will fall somewhere between the competitive and monopoly outcomes.

2. How does game theory explain strategic behavior?

* Game theory helps determine when cooperation among oligopolists is most likely. In many cases, cooperation fails to materialize because decision-makers have dominant strategies that lead them to be uncooperative. This can cause firms to compete with price, advertising, or

research and development when they could potentially earn more profit by curtailing these activities.

* A dominant strategy ignores the possible long-run benefits of cooperation and focuses solely on the short-run gains. Whenever repeated interaction exists, decision-makers fare better under tit-for-tat, an approach that maximizes the long-run profit.

3. How do government policies affect oligopoly behavior?

* Antitrust law is complex, and cases are hard to prosecute. Nevertheless, these laws are essential in providing firms an incentive to compete rather than collude.

4. What are network externalities?

* A network externality exists when the number of customers who purchase a good or use it influences the quantity demanded. The presence of significant positive network externalities can cause small firms to be driven out of business.

CONCEPTS YOU SHOULD KNOW

Antitrust laws (p. 375)
Bandwagon effect (p. 393)
Cartel (p. 375)
Clayton Act (p. 390)
Collusion (p. 375)
Dominant strategy (p. 382)

Game theory (p. 381)
Mutual interdependence (p. 376)
Nash equilibrium (p. 378)
Network externality (p. 393)
Oligopoly (p. 372)
Output effect (p. 379)

Predatory pricing (p. 390)
Price effect (p. 379)
Prisoner's dilemma (p. 381)
Sherman Antitrust Act (p. 389)
Switching costs (p. 393)
Tit-for-tat (p. 385)

QUESTIONS

1. Compare the price and output under oligopoly to that of monopoly and monopolistic competition.

2. How does the addition of another firm affect the ability of an oligopolistic industry to form an effective cartel?

3. What is predatory pricing?

4. How is game theory relevant to oligopoly? Does it help explain monopoly?

5. What does the prisoner's dilemma indicate about the longevity of collusive agreements?

6. What is a Nash equilibrium? How does it differ from a dominant strategy?

7. What practices do antitrust laws prohibit?

8. What are network externalities? Describe why network externalities matter to an oligopolist.

STUDY PROBLEMS

1. Some places limit the number of hours that alcohol can be sold on Sunday. Is it possible that this sales restriction could help liquor stores? Use game theory to construct your answer. **Hint:** even without restrictions on the hours of operation, individual stores could still choose to limit Sunday sales if they wanted to.

2. Which of the following markets are oligopolistic?
   a. passenger airlines
   b. cereal
   c. fast food
   d. wheat
   e. golf equipment
   f. the college bookstore on your campus

3. At many local concerts the crowd will stand for some songs and sit for others. You are a fan of the concerts but you are not a fan of having to stand, you prefer to stay seated throughout the concert. What would be your "tit-for-tat" strategy to try to encourage other concertgoers to change their behavior?

4. After teaching a class on game theory your instructor announces that if every student skips the last question on the next exam, everyone will receive full credit for that question. However, if one or more students answer the last question, all responses will be graded and those who skipped the question will get a "zero." Will the entire class skip the last question?

5. For which of the following are network externalities important?
   a. gas stations
   b. American Association of Retired Persons (AARP)
   c. eHarmony, an Internet dating site

6. Your economics instructor is at it again (see question 4). This time you have to do

a two-student project. Assume that you and your partner are both interested in maximizing your grade but you are both very busy and get more happiness if you can get a good grade with less work.

	Your partner	
	Work hard	**Work less hard**
Work hard	Grade = A, but you had to work 10 hours. Happiness = 7/10.	Grade = A, and you only worked 5 hours. Happiness = 9/10.
You	Grade = A, but you had to work 10 hours. Happiness = 7/10.	Grade = A, but you had to work 15 hours. Happiness = 4/10.
Work less hard	Grade = A, but you had to work 15 hours. Happiness = 4/10.	Grade = B, but you only worked 5 hours. Happiness = 6/10.
	Grade = A, and you only worked 5 hours. Happiness = 9/10.	Grade = B, but you only worked 5 hours. Happiness = 6/10.

a. What is your dominant strategy? Explain.
b. What is your partner's dominant strategy? Explain.
c. What is the Nash equilibrium? Explain.
d. If you and your partner are required to work together on a number of projects throughout the semester how might this change the outcome you predicted in parts a, b, and c?

7. Suppose that the marginal cost of mining gold is constant at $300 per ounce and the demand schedule is as follows:

Price	Quantity
$1,000	1,000
900	2,000
800	3,000
700	4,000
600	5,000
500	6,000
400	7,000

a. If the number of suppliers is large, what would be the price and quantity?
b. If there is only one supplier, what would be the price and quantity?
c. If there are only two suppliers and they decide to form a cartel, what would be the price and quantity?

d. Suppose that one of the two cartel members in part (c) decides to increase its production by 1,000 ounces while the other member keeps its production constant. What will happen to the profits of both firms?

8. Trade agreements encourage countries to curtail tariffs so that goods are able to flow across international boundaries without restrictions. Using the following payoffs, determine the best policies for China and the United States in this example.

	China	
	Low tariffs	**High tariffs**
Low tariffs	China gains $50 billion	China gains $100 billion
United States	U.S. gains $50 billion	U.S. gains $10 billion
High tariffs	China gains $10 billion	China gains $25 billion
	U.S. gains $100 billion	U.S. gains $25 billion

a. What is the dominant strategy for the United States?
b. What is the dominant strategy for China?
c. What is the Nash equilibrium for these two countries?
d. Suppose that the United States and China decide to enter into a trade agreement that simultaneously lowers trade barriers. Is this a good idea?

9. A small town has only one pizza place, The Pizza Factory. A small competitor, Perfect Pies, is thinking about entering the market. The profits of these two firms depends on whether Perfect Pies enters the market and whether The Pizza Factory—as a price leader—decides to set a high or low price. Use the payoffs below to answer the questions that follow.

	Perfect Pies	
	Enter	**Stay out**
High price	Perfect Pies makes $10,000	Perfect Pies makes $0
The Pizza Factory	The Pizza Factory makes $20,000	The Pizza Factory makes $50,000
Low price	Perfect Pies loses $10,000	Perfect Pies makes $0
	The Pizza Factory makes $10,000	The Pizza Factory makes $25,000

a. What is the dominant strategy of The Pizza Factory?

b. What is the dominant strategy of Perfect Pies?

c. What is the Nash equilibrium?

d. The combined profit for both firms is highest when The Pizza Factory sets a high price and Perfect Pies stays out. If Perfect Pies enters the market how will this affect the profits of the Pizza Factory? Would The Pizza Factory be willing to pay Perfect Pies not to enter the market? Explain.

SOLVED PROBLEMS

3. Since standing at a concert imposes a negative externality on those who like to sit, the behavior is non-cooperative by nature. When one person, or a group of people, stand up, it forces those who would prefer to sit to have to stand up as well to see the performance. When this happens repeatedly it diminishes the enjoyment of those who like to sit—especially when others nearby dance, sway, scream, and raise their arms. A concert typically consists of two sets of music with 20–25 songs played over the course of a few hours. As a result, your behavior has the potential to influence the behavior of those nearby. Think of this as a game where you utilize tit-for-tat, or your behavior mimics what the standers did when the next song is played. Eventually they will get the message that standing imposes a cost on the sitters. Once they understand this they remain seated, you can sit down as well and everyone can see the performance.

8. a. The dominant strategy for the United States is to impose high tariffs, because it always earns more from that strategy than if it had low tariffs no matter what policy China decides to pursue.

b. The dominant strategy for China is to impose high tariffs, because it always earns more from that strategy than if it had low tariffs no matter what policy the United States pursues.

c. The Nash equilibrium for both countries is to levy high tariffs. Each country will earn $25 B.

d. China and the United States would each benefit from cooperatively lowering tariffs. In that case, both countries would each earn $50 B.

Two Alternative Theories of Pricing Behavior

Two alternative theories argue that oligopolists will form long-lasting cartels. These are the kinked demand curve and price leadership.

The Kinked Demand Curve

Imagine that a group of oligopolists has established an output level and price designed to maximize economic profit. The **kinked demand curve** theory states that oligopolists have a greater tendency to respond aggressively to the price cuts of rivals but will largely ignore price increases. When a rival raises prices, the other firms all stand to benefit by holding their prices steady to capture those customers who do not want to pay more. In this scenario, the firm that raises its price will see a relatively large drop in sales. However, if any of the rivals attempts to lower the price, the price decrease will be immediately matched by the other firms in the industry. The price match policy means that the firm that lowers its price does not pick up very many new customers. In practice, since a price drop by one firm will be met immediately

The **kinked demand curve theory** states that oligopolists have a greater tendency to respond aggressively to price cuts but will largely ignore price increases.

FIGURE 13A.1

The Kinked Demand Curve

At prices above P*, demand is relatively elastic. At prices below P*, demand is relatively inelastic. This creates a kink in the demand curve that causes the marginal revenue curve to become discontinuous. As a result, small changes in marginal cost do not cause firms to change their pricing and output. Therefore, firms are generally slow to adjust to changes in cost.

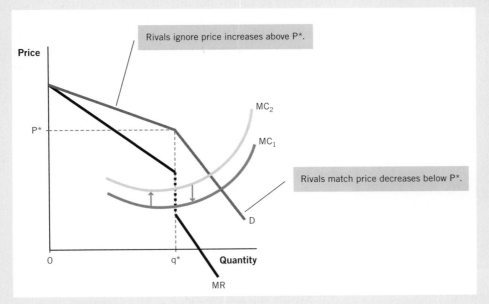

Rivals ignore price increases above P*.

Rivals match price decreases below P*.

by a price drop from all the competitors, no one firm is able to pick up very many new customers. This is the case at any price below the agreed-to price.

The behavior of the firms creates a demand curve that is more elastic (or flatter) at prices above the cartel price and more inelastic (or steeper) at prices below the cartel price. The junction of the elastic and inelastic segments on the demand curve creates a "kink" that can be seen in Figure 13A.1.

This illustration begins with each of the firms in the industry charging P* and producing q*. Since demand is more elastic above P* and less elastic below P*, the marginal revenue curve is discontinuous. The gap is illustrated by the dashed black vertical line. The presence of the gap in marginal revenue means that more than one marginal cost curve intersects marginal revenue at output level q*. This can be seen by looking at MC_1 and MC_2. As a consequence, small changes in marginal cost, like those shown in Figure 13A.1, will not cause the firms to deviate from the established price, P*, and quantity, q*.

Price leadership
occurs when a dominant firm in an industry sets the price that maximizes profits and the smaller firms in an industry follow.

Price Leadership

The kinked demand curve explains why firms generally keep the same price, but it cannot explain how prices change. The theory of price leadership provides some insight.

In many industries, smaller firms may take a cue from the decisions of the price leader. **Price leadership** generally occurs when a single firm, known as the price leader, produces a large share of the total output in the industry. The price leader sets the price and output level that maximizes its profits. Smaller firms then set their prices to match the price leader. Since the impact on price is small to begin with, it makes sense that smaller rivals tend to follow the price leader.

Price leadership is not illegal since it does not involve collusion. Rather, it relies on an understanding that an effort to fight changes implemented by the price leader will lead to increased price competition and lower profits for every firm in the industry. Since the firms act in accordance with each other, this practice is commonly known as *tacit collusion*.

One well-known example of price leadership is pricing patterns in the airline industry. On almost any route with multiple-carrier options, a price search for flights will reveal almost identical prices on basic economy-class flights. This happens even though the firms do not collude to set a profit-maximizing price. Rather, when one firm sets a fare, the other carriers feel compelled to match it. Airlines are very good at matching low prices, just like the model predicts. They are much less successful in implementing across-the-board fare increases since the leader is sticking its neck out trusting that the other firms will follow suit.

The airline industry is often cited as a market where price leadership is at work behind the scenes.

CONCEPTS YOU SHOULD KNOW

Kinked demand curve (p. 401)   Price leadership (p. 402)

STUDY PROBLEMS

1. A parking garage charges $10 a day. Whenever the garage tries to raise its price, the other parking garages in the area keep their prices constant and it loses customers to the cheaper garages. However, when the parking garage lowers its price, the other garages almost always match the price reduction. Which type of oligopoly behavior best explains this situation? If the parking garage business has marginal costs that generally vary only a small amount, should the garage change the price it charges when its marginal costs change a little?

2. Most large banks charge the same or nearly the same prime interest rate. Banks avoid changing the rate, and try to do it only when market conditions require an adjustment. When that happens, one of the major banks announces a change in its rate and other banks quickly follow suit. Is this an example of price leadership or the kinked demand curve? Explain.

Photo to come

Labor Markets and
EARNINGS

The Demand and Supply of Resources

Think of your favorite restaurant. Inside you will find managers, cooks, bussers, wait staff, hosts, and bartenders. Some of these workers earn a little, and others earn a lot. We have seen that profit-maximizing firms must decide how much to produce. For production to be successful, firms must combine the right amounts of labor and capital in order to maximize output while simultaneously holding costs down. In this chapter, we will use the forces of supply and demand to help us understand the role the labor market plays in the U.S. economy. We will then extend the lessons learned about labor into the markets for land and capital.

Since labor often comprises the largest share of the costs of production, we will begin with an examination of the labor market. This approach will also allow us to extend our understanding of the labor market and tackle income inequality, employment discrimination, and poverty in the next chapter.

Learning Objectives:

- To understand how the demand for resources is derived.
- To understand how the demand and supply of labor determine the equilibrium wage.
- To understand how outsourcing works.
- To appreciate how the value of the marginal product that each resource creates determines its value in the production process.

The Factors of Production

Wages and salaries account for two-thirds of all the income generated by the U.S. economy. The remaining one-third goes to the owners of land and capital. Together labor, land, and capital make up the **factors of production**, or the inputs used in producing goods and services.

Factors of production are the inputs used in producing goods and services.

Like land and capital, labor is an input that is used to produce goods and services. For instance, let's imagine that Sophia wants to open a Mexican restaurant named Tequila Mockingbird. She will need a waitstaff, cooks, employees to bus tables, and managers to coordinate everyone else; these are labor inputs. She also needs a physical location—this is the land input. Finally, she needs a building in which to operate, along with ovens, seating, and registers to collect payment; these are capital inputs.

Photo to come

Derived demand
is the demand for an input used in the production process.

Of course, Sophia's restaurant won't need any inputs if there is no demand for the food she plans to sell. As a result, the demand for each of the factors of production (land, labor, and capital) is said to be a **derived demand** that stems from the firm's efforts to supply a good in another market. Sophia secures the land, builds a building, and hires employees because she expects there to be demand for the food her restaurant makes and serves. Sophia is so sure that will happen that she is willing to spend a lot of money up front to build and staff the restaurant, even before one customer sets foot in the door. This is another example of the ubiquity of opportunity cost; Sophia could do other things with her money besides opening a restaurant.

Derived demand is not limited to the demand for restaurant help. For example, owners of iPads buy the device because of its functionality. This causes Apple to demand the resources used to make the iPad. The switches, glass, memory, battery and other parts have little value in isolation, but when they are combined they are transformed into a device that many people find very useful. Therefore, when economists speak of derived demand, they are differentiating between the demand for the final good and service and the demand for the resources used to make those final goods.

- What are the three factors of production?
- What is derived demand?

The Demand for Labor

As a student you are probably hoping that one day your education will translate into practical skills that employers will seek. One consideration you are keeping in mind as you choose your major is how much workers in different occupations have the potential to earn. Have you ever wondered why there is so much variety in levels of salary and wages? For instance, economists generally earn more than elementary school teachers but less than engineers. Workers on night shifts earn more than those who do the same job during the day. And professional athletes and actors, whose jobs are not essential, earn much more than janitors, construction workers, and nurses. In one respect the explanation is surprisingly obvious. The twin forces of supply and demand regulate the labor market in much the same way they determine the prices of goods and services sold in the marketplace.

To help understand why some people get paid more than others, we will explore the output of each worker. The value that each worker creates for the firm is highly correlated with the demand for labor. Then we will examine the factors that influence labor demand in order to develop a more complete understanding of how the labor market works.

The Marginal Product of Labor

To gain a concrete appreciation for how labor demand is determined, let's look at the restaurant business—a market that is highly competitive.

In Chapter 8 we saw that firms determine how many workers to hire by comparing the output of labor with the wages it must pay. We will apply this

TABLE 14.1

Deciding How Many Laborers to Hire

(1) Labor (number of workers)	(2) Output (daily meals produced)	(3) Marginal Product of Labor	(4) Value of the Marginal Product of Labor	(5) Wage (daily)	(6) Marginal Profit
Formula:		Δ (2)	P × (3)		(4) – (5)
0	0				
		50	$500	$100	$400
1	50				
		40	400	100	300
2	90				
		30	300	100	200
3	120				
		20	200	100	100
4	140				
		10	100	100	0
5	150				
		0	0	100	–100
6	150				

analysis of production to the labor market in the restaurant business. Table 14.1 should look familiar to you; it highlights the key determinants of the labor hiring process.

Let's work our way through the table. Column (1) lists the number of laborers. Column (2) reports the daily numbers of meals that can be produced with differing numbers of workers. Column (3) is the **marginal product of labor,** or the change in output associated with hiring one additional worker. For instance, when the firm decides to hire four workers instead of three, output expands to 140 meals from 120, an increase of 20 meals. Therefore, 20 meals is the marginal product of labor for the fourth worker. Note that the values in column (3) decline as additional workers are hired. Recall that when each successive worker adds less value, this is known as diminishing marginal product.

The **marginal product of labor** is the change in output associated with hiring one additional worker.

Marginal Thinking

We can use the marginal product of labor to determine how much value each worker creates for the firm. When we multiply the marginal product of labor in column (3) by the price the firm charges its customers, $10 per meal, this gives us the **value of the marginal product** in column (4). This new measure tells us how much value each worker creates for the firm and it places an upper limit on the amount the company is willing to pay each worker. When the firm compares the gain shown in column (4) with the wage that must be paid to achieve that gain, shown in column (5), it can determine whether the extra labor is profitable. The hiring decision can be seen as a straightforward cost-benefit analysis: wage (5) is subtracted from the value of the marginal product (4) to determine the marginal profit (6) of each worker.

The **value of the marginal product** is the marginal product of an input multiplied by the price of the output it produces.

The green numbers in Table 14.1 show where marginal profit is positive—for the first four workers. After that, marginal profit is zero for the fifth worker, shown in black, and negative for the sixth, shown in red. The firm is better off hiring four workers, it would be indifferent about hiring the fifth since the marginal cost of hiring that employee is equal to the marginal benefit, and it would not hire the sixth worker.

Figure 14.1 plots the value of the marginal product (VMP) from Table 14.1. Look at the curve: what do you see? Did you think of a demand curve? The VMP is the firm's willingness to pay for each laborer; in other words, it is the firm's labor demand curve.

The VMP curve slopes downward due to diminishing marginal product—which we see in column (3) of Table 14.1. As long as the value of the marginal product is higher than the market wage, shown as $100 a day, the firm will hire more workers. For example, when the firm hires the first cook, the VMP is $500. This amount easily exceeds the market wage of hiring an extra worker and creates a marginal profit of $400. We illustrate this additional profit with the longest green arrow under the demand curve and above the market wage. Additional profits of $300, $200, and $100 are created by the second, third, and fourth cooks, each represented by progressively smaller green arrows. As the value of the marginal product declines, there will be a point at which hiring additional workers will cause profits to fall. As a result, whenever the value of the marginal product is less than the market wage, the firm will not hire additional workers. Therefore, labor demand is contingent upon the value of the marginal product that is produced, and the value of the marginal product is equivalent to the firm's labor demand curve. Since the VMP curve allows us to see how many workers the firm would hire at each wage, the VMP curve is the demand for labor curve.

FIGURE 14.1

The Value of the Marginal Product

The firm will hire workers as long as the value of the marginal product is greater than the wage it must pay. The value of the marginal product is the firm's labor demand curve. When the value of the marginal product is higher than the market wage, the firm will hire more laborers. However, since labor is subject to diminishing marginal product, eventually the value created by hiring additional labor falls below the market wage.

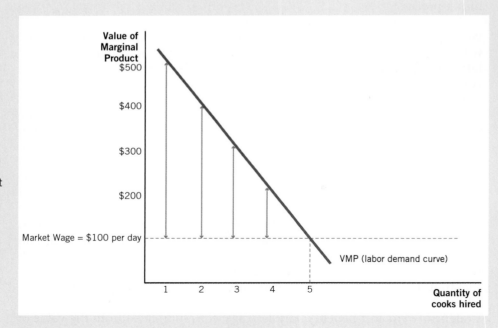

Changes in the Demand for Labor

We know that customers desire food and that restaurants like Tequila Mockingbird hire cooks to satisfy their customers. Figure 14.2 illustrates the relationship between the demand for restaurant meals and the demand for restaurant cooks. Notice that the demand for labor is downward sloping; this tells us that at high wages Tequila Mockingbird will use fewer cooks, and at lower wages it will hire more cooks. This is illustrated by the orange arrow that moves along the original demand curve. Recall from Chapter 3 that this relationship is known as a change in the quantity demanded. In addition, the demand for cooks depends on, or is derived from, the number of customers who place orders. So changes in the restaurant business as a whole can influence the number of cooks that the restaurant hires. For example, if the number of customers increases, the demand for cooks will increase, or shift to D_{+1}. Likewise, if the number of customers decreases, the demand for cooks will decrease, or shift to the left to D_{-1}.

Two primary factors shift labor demand: a change in demand for the product that the firm produces, and a change in the cost of producing that product. Changes in cost can be positive—for example, a new technology; or negative—for example, an increase in the cost of a needed raw material.

Changes in Demand for the Product the Firm Produces

A restaurant's demand for workers to provide meals is derived from the firm's desire to make a profit. Because the firm is primarily interested in profits, it only hires workers when the value of the marginal product of labor is higher than the cost of hiring labor. Consider Tequila Mockingbird. If a rival Mexican restaurant closes down, many of those customers will switch to Sophia's

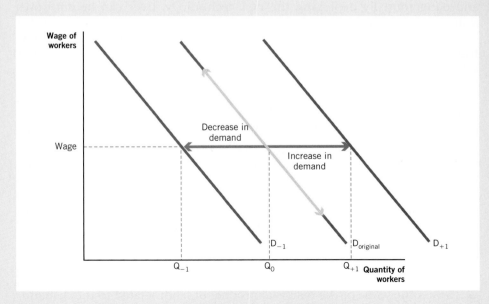

FIGURE 14.2

The Labor Demand Curve

When the wages of workers change, the quantity of workers demanded, shown by the orange arrow moving along the demand curve, also changes. Changes that shift the entire labor demand curve, shown by the gray arrows, include changes in the demand for the product that the firm produces, in labor productivity, or innovation.

restaurant. Tequila Mockingbird will need to fix more meals and this will cause the entire demand curve for cooks, bussers, and waitstaff to shift out to D_{+1}.

Changes in Technology and Productivity

Technology can act as a substitute for workers. For example, microwave ovens make it easier and quicker to prepare meals. Microwave ovens allow the firm to prepare the same number of meals with fewer workers. Or consider the growing trend of using conveyor belts to help prepare or serve meals. As we see with these examples, changes in technology can lower the demand for workers.

In the short run, this may seem like a bad outcome for the workers, and for society in general. For example, in the forestry business, as timber companies invest in new harvesting technology they are able to replace traditional logging jobs with more efficient equipment. In the short run, every harvester operator employed at a higher wage displaces perhaps ten traditional lumberjacks, who must find employment elsewhere. Those adjustments are painful for the workers involved, and they often have difficulty finding jobs that pay as well as the job that was eliminated.

However, in the long run society benefits. The decline in demand for lumberjacks means fewer jobs in the timber industry, but the new equipment is safer and needs trained operators. Skilled operators can fell more trees in a shorter time than traditional lumberjacks, and with less risk of injury. As a result, harvester operators have a safer job at a higher marginal product of labor and can command higher wages. Moreover, harvester equipment frees up nine workers to produce other goods and services that society values.

If we insisted on using traditional methods to fell trees, we could employ more lumberjacks; but the process of cutting wood would remain expensive and dangerous. By deploying the new technology, trees can be cut down faster and more safely. Overall production rises because while one worker harvests trees, nine others are able to move into related fields, or to do something entirely different. With the use of new technology, one person can now safely produce the same amount that formerly required ten men to risk their lives.

This is how economic development works through time. The most successful countries have moved from simple, low-income economies with a high proportion of jobs in manual labor, to modern, high-income economies by utilizing more capital in the production process to raise the VMP of each worker. At the same time, the quality of life is improved since workers in modern economies earn more and have safer jobs.

To summarize, if labor becomes more productive, the VMP curve shifts to the right, driving up both wages and employment. There is the potential for substitution as well, causing the demand for traditional labor to fall. This is what has happened to traditional lumberjack jobs, leading to a decrease in the wages of those workers.

- What two factors shift the demand curve for labor?
- How is the value of the marginal product of labor related to the demand for labor?

The Supply of Labor

In this section we examine the connection between the wage rate and the number of workers willing to supply their services to employers. Since workers also value leisure, the supply curve is not always directly related to the wage rate. At high wage levels, workers may choose to cut back the number of hours they work. In addition, we will look at the factors that influence the labor supply including the changing composition of the workforce, migration, and immigration.

The Labor-Leisure Trade-off

People work because they need to earn a living. While it is certainly true that many workers enjoy their jobs, this does not mean they would work for nothing. In other words, while many people experience satisfaction in the work they perform, most of us have other interests, obligations, and goals. As a result, the supply of labor depends both on the wage that is offered and how individuals want to use their time. This is known as the *labor-leisure trade-off*.

Individuals must work to meet their basic needs. Once those needs are met, a worker might be more inclined to use his time in leisure. Would higher wages induce an employee to give up leisure and work more hours? Both yes and no!

At higher wage rates workers may be willing to work more hours, or substitute labor for leisure. This is known as the *substitution effect*. One way to think about this is to note that higher wages make leisure time more expensive

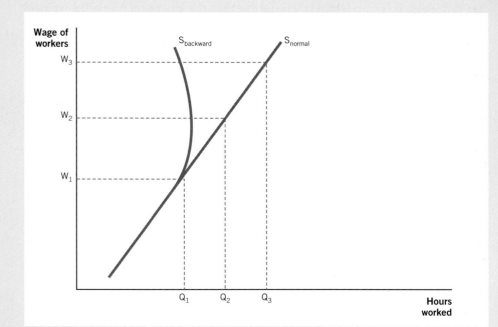

FIGURE 14.3

The Labor Supply Curve
At high wage levels the income effect may become larger than the substitution effect and cause the labor supply curve to bend backwards. The backward-bending supply curve exists when additional leisure time becomes more valuable than additional income.

because the opportunity cost of enjoying more leisure means giving up more income. For instance, suppose that Emeril is a short-order cook at Tequila Mockingbird. He works 40 hours at $10 an hour and can also work four hours overtime at the same wage. If Emeril decides to put in the overtime, he ends up working 44 hours and earns $440. In that case, Emeril substitutes more labor for less leisure.

But at higher wage rates other workers may work fewer hours, or substitute leisure for labor. This is known as the *income effect*. Leisure is a normal good, so as income rises, some workers may use the added income they have earned to demand more leisure. As a consequence, at high income levels the income effect may overwhelm the substitution effect and the supply curve bends backwards. For example, suppose that Rachael chooses to work overtime for $10 an hour. Her total pay, like Emeril's, will be $10 × 44, or $440. If the wage rises to $11, she may continue to work the overtime at a higher wage. However, if she does not work overtime, she will earn as much as she was earning before the wage increase ($11 × 40 = $440) and she might choose to discontinue the overtime. In this case, Rachael enjoys more leisure.

Figure 14.3 shows what can happen to the labor supply curve at high wage levels. When the supply of labor responds directly to wage increases, the wage rises from W_1 to W_3, and the number of hours worked increases from Q_1 to Q_3, along S_{normal}. However, at high wage rates workers might experience diminishing marginal utility from additional income and find that they value increased leisure time more than increased income. In this situation, workers may choose to work less. This causes the normal supply curve to bend backwards beyond W_2, creating what is known as a **backward-bending labor supply curve.** The shape of the curve reflects the decision to work fewer hours as the wage goes up. Since most workers do not reach wage level W_2, we will draw the supply curve as upward sloping throughout the chapter. Nevertheless, it is important to recognize that the direct relationship we normally observe does not always hold.

A **backward-bending labor supply curve** occurs when workers value additional leisure more than additional income.

Changes in the Supply of Labor

If we hold the wage rate constant, there are a number of additional factors that determine the supply of labor. Immigration, migration, demographic shifts in society, and job characteristics and opportunities all play important roles in determining the number of workers willing to perform various jobs. In this section we will look beyond the wage rate to other forces that govern the supply of labor.

Turning to Figure 14.4, the orange arrow along $S_{original}$ shows that more workers will supply labor when the wage is higher. But what will cause a shift in the supply curve? There are three primary factors that affect the supply curve: other employment opportunities, the changing composition of the workforce, and migration and immigration.

Other Employment Opportunities

The supply of workers for one job depends on the employment opportunities and prevailing wage in related labor markets. Let's consider the supply of labor at Sophia's restaurant. Notice that the supply curve for labor in

Figure 14.4 is upward sloping; this tells us that if Tequila Mockingbird offers higher wages, more table clearers will be willing to work there. This situation is illustrated by the orange arrow that moves along the original supply curve. In addition, the supply of table clearers also depends on a number of non-wage factors. Since table clearers are generally young and largely unskilled, the number of laborers willing to work is influenced by the prevailing wages in similar jobs. For instance, if the wages of baggers at local grocery stores increase, some of the table clearers will decide to bag instead. This decreases the supply of table clearers and causes a leftward shift to S_{-1}. If the wages of baggers were to fall, the supply of table clearers would increase, or shift to the right to S_{+1}. As a consequence, differences in wages across jobs that require comparable labor skills can have a marked effect on the number of workers willing to supply their labor.

The Changing Composition of the Workforce

In the period from 1980 to 2000, the rate of participation of women in the labor force outside the home increased almost 15 percent in developed countries. Among that group, to name a few examples, the United States raised its female labor force participation rate from 60 to 72 percent, Switzerland from 54 to 69 percent, and New Zealand from 45 to 67 percent. Since male participation rates were down only slightly over the same period, overall there are many more employees in the workforce today and the supply of workers in many occupations has expanded significantly.

Migration and Immigration

Demographic factors also play a crucial role in the supply of labor available. In 2008, over one million people from foreign countries entered the

FIGURE 14.4

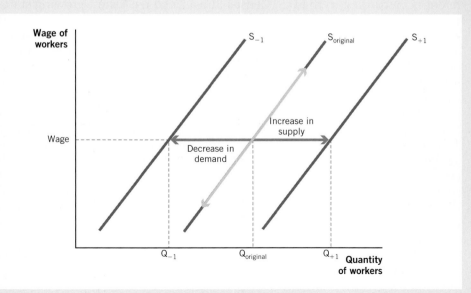

The Labor Supply Curve
A change in the quantity supplied occurs when the wages of workers change. This causes a movement along the supply curve $S_{original}$, shown by the orange arrow. Changes in the supply of labor, shown by the gray arrows, can occur due to immigration, migration, demographic shifts in society, and other employment opportunities.

Immigration

A Day Without a Mexican (2004)

This offbeat film asks a simple question: What would happen to California if all of the Latinos in the state suddenly disappeared? The answer: the state economy would come to a halt.

The loss of Latino workers would have a dramatic impact in the labor market. The film makes fun of affluent Californians who must do without low-cost workers to help take care of their yards and homes. It also showcases a farm owner whose produce is ready to be picked without any migrant workers to do the job.

In addition, the film adeptly points out that migrants from Mexico add a tremendous amount of value to the local economy through their purchases as well as their labor. In one inspired scene, the movie depicts a television commercial for a "disappearance sale" put on by a local business after it realizes that most of its regular customers are gone.

In *A Day Without a Mexican* we see both sides of the labor relationship at work. Demand and supply are inseparably linked and the disappearance of all of the Mexican workers creates a series of voids that requires serious adjustments for the economy.

United States through legal channels and have been given permission to seek employment. This remarkable influx adds significantly to the labor supply. There are now close to 40 million legal immigrants. In addition, illegal immigrants comprise another 15 to 20 million workers. Taken together, legal and illegal immigration has a significant impact on the available supply of workers.

Internal migration factors are also relevant. Although the U.S. population grows at an annual rate of approximately 3 percent, we see large regional differences. According to the U.S. Census Bureau, the ten fastest-growing states were all located in the south or west, with some states adding as much as 4 percent to their population in a single year. Southern and western states accounted for 84 percent of the nation's population growth from 2000 to 2010, with Nevada, Utah, North Carolina, Idaho, and Texas all adding at least 20 percent to their populations. Even the statewide data can hide significant localized changes. A number of counties experienced 50 percent or more population growth over that same span. The biggest population winner was Kendall County, Illinois, a far-flung suburb of Chicago, which grew nearly 100 percent between censuses. The county has been transitioning from an agricultural area to a bedroom community—albeit one far from the main job center. Most of the fastest-growing counties are, like Kendall, relatively distant suburbs in major metropolitan areas. These are areas where new homes can be purchased at comparatively reasonable prices. Large population influxes create significant regional changes in the demand for labor and also the supply of people looking for work.

Now that we have studied the forces that determine the supply of labor, we can combine this information with the demand for labor to study the labor market.

- What effect causes a backward-bending labor supply curve?
- What three factors shift the labor supply curve?

Determinants of Demand and Supply in the Labor Market

In earlier chapters we have seen how markets reconcile the forces of demand and supply by means of a price. Now that we have looked at the forces that govern demand and supply in the labor market, we are ready to see how the equilibrium wage is established. We will then be able to examine the labor market in greater detail and identify what causes shortages and surpluses of labor, why outsourcing occurs, and what happens when there is a single buyer. The goal of this section is to provide a rich set of examples that will help you become comfortable using demand and supply curves to explain how the labor market operates.

How Does the Market for Labor Reach Equilibrium?

You can think about wages as the price at which workers are willing to "rent" their time to an employer. Turning to Figure 14.5, we see that at wages above equilibrium ($W_{equilibrium}$), the supply of workers willing to rent their time exceeds the demand for that time. This causes a surplus of available workers. The surplus, in turn, places downward pressure on wages. As wages drop, fewer workers are willing to rent their time to employers. When wages drop to the equilibrium wage, the surplus of workers is eliminated. A similar process guides the labor market toward equilibrium from low wages. At wages below the equilibrium, demand for labor exceeds the available supply. The shortage forces firms to offer higher wages in order to attract workers. Wages rise until the shortage is eliminated at the equilibrium wage.

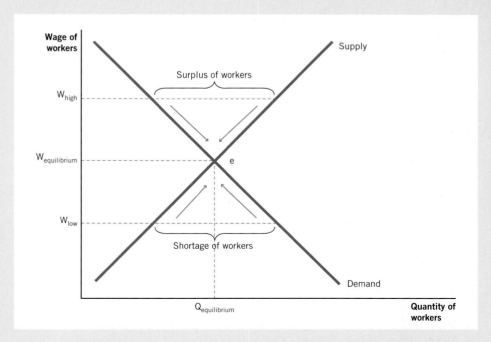

FIGURE 14.5

Equilibrium in the Labor Market

At high wages a surplus of workers exists. This drives the wage rate down until the supply of workers and the demand for workers reach the equilibrium. At low wages a shortage occurs. A shortage forces the wage rate up until the equilibrium wage is reached and the shortage disappears.

ECONOMICS IN THE REAL WORLD

Where Are the Nurses?

In the United States, there is a shortage of nurses. Nursing is a stressful job, with long hours and years of required training. The shortage of nurses will not disappear overnight; in fact, there are reports that it will grow to close to one million by 2020, making nursing the number 1 job in the country in terms of growth prospects. As baby boomers age, the demand for nursing care is expected to rise. At the same time, the existing pool of nurses is rapidly aging and nearing retirement. All of this points to the acute nature of the shortage. However, we can be confident that the shortage of nurses will eventually disappear. When there is a shortage, there is always upward pressure on wages. Rising wages also signal to potential nurses that their services are in high demand and that wages will continue to rise, leading to a surge in applications to nursing schools and also causing some practicing nurses to postpone their retirements. Since the training process takes two or more years to complete, the nursing shortage will persist for a few years until the quantity of nurses supplied to the market increases. As more newly trained nurses enter the market, the shortage will disappear. ✳

Change and Equilibrium in the Labor Market

Now that we have seen how labor markets find an equilibrium, let's see what happens when the demand or supply changes. Figure 14.6 contains two graphs; panel (a) shows a shift in labor demand and panel (b) shows a shift in

FIGURE 14.6

Shifting the Labor Market Equilibrium

In panel (a) the demand for nurses increases. This creates a shortage of workers, which leads to a higher equilibrium wage (e_2) and quantity of nurses employed (q_2) than before. In panel (b) the supply of nurses increases. This leads to a surplus of workers and causes the equilibrium wage to fall (e_2) and the number of nurses employed to rise (q_2).

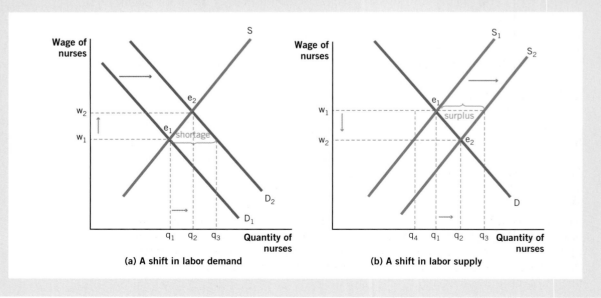

(a) A shift in labor demand

(b) A shift in labor supply

labor supply. In both cases the equilibrium wage and the equilibrium quantity of workers employed adjust accordingly.

Let's start with a shift in labor demand, shown in panel (a). Imagine that demand for medical care increases due to an aging population and that, as a result, the demand for nurses increases and the demand curve shifts from D_1 to D_2. This creates a shortage of workers. The shortage of workers places upward pressure on wages, which increase from w_1 to w_2. As wages rise, nursing becomes more attractive; additional people go into nursing and existing nurses decide to work longer hours or postpone retirement. The number of nurses employed rises from q_1 to q_2. Eventually, the wage settles at e_2 and the number of workers employed ends up at q_2.

Turning to panel (b), we see what happens when the supply of nurses increases. As additional nurses are certified the overall supply shifts from S_1 to S_2. A surplus of workers at w_1 places downward pressure on wages. Eventually, the market wage settles at w_2, at the new equilibrium point e_2, and the number of workers employed ends up at q_2.

Outsourcing

Why would a firm hire someone from outside if it has a qualified employee nearby? This practice, known as *outsourcing,* has gotten a lot of attention in recent years. In this section we explain what outsourcing is, how it works, why companies engage in it, and how it affects the labor market for workers.

The **outsourcing of labor** is the shifting of jobs from within a firm to an outside company. Usually, the outside company is overseas, where the cost of labor is cheaper. For example, in the publishing industry, typesetting and page makeup, also known as composition, are often done overseas to take advantage of cheaper labor. The outsourcing of labor in the publishing industry has been made possible by advances in information technology. The Internet eliminates shipping delays and costs that were once a large part of the business. This allows a qualified worker to set type and lay out book pages anywhere in the world. Even twenty years ago, completing those tasks would have required a laborer to work inside the firm with cumbersome equipment and printed pages. Sometimes, outsourcing occurs when firms relocate within the country to capitalize on cheaper labor or low-cost resources. For example, when General Motors introduced its Saturn division in 1985, it built an entirely new production facility in Tennessee, where wages were substantially lower than in other GM plants.

The ability to outsource means the pool of workers expands. But whether that expansion is driven by outsourcing, which is an external factor, or by increases in the domestic supply of workers, those who are already employed find they earn less and unemployment in that occupation rises. To understand why, let's turn once more to Figure 14.6b. If you think of S_1 as the supply of domestic workers, when the wage falls to w_2, the supply of domestic workers along S_1 is q_4. S_2 represents the total supply of workers and includes both domestic workers and foreign workers. Therefore, foreign workers make up the rest of the labor pool, or the difference between q_4 and q_2. The result is that domestic labor ends up receiving lower wages (w_2) and also experiences declining employment (q_4).

Outsourcing of labor
is the shifting of jobs from within the firm to an outside company.

PRACTICE WHAT YOU KNOW

Explain how labor is affected by these events.

(1) A company builds a new facility that doubles its workspace and equipment.

Answer: The company that builds the new facility has probably experienced additional demand for the product it is selling. Therefore, the company needs additional employees to staff the facility, causing a positive shift in the demand curve. When the demand for labor rises, wages increase and so does the number of people employed.

(2) A company decides to outsource 100 jobs from a facility in Indiana to Indonesia.

Answer: This situation requires two changes. First, there is a decrease in demand for labor in Indiana that results in lower wages and fewer workers being hired. At the same time, there is an increase in demand for labor in Indonesia that results in higher wages and more workers being hired.

ECONOMICS IN THE REAL WORLD

Pregnancy Becomes Latest Job Outsourced to India

ANAND, India—The small clinic at Kaival Hospital matches infertile couples with local women, cares for the women during pregnancy and delivery, and counsels them afterward. Anand's surrogate mothers, pioneers in the growing field of outsourced pregnancies, have given birth to roughly 40 babies.

More than 50 women in this city are now pregnant with the children of couples from the United States, Taiwan, Britain and beyond. The women earn more than many would make in 15 years. But the program raises a host of uncomfortable questions that touch on morals and modern science, exploitation and globalization, and that most natural of desires: to have a family.

Dr. Nayna Patel, the woman behind Anand's baby boom, defends her work as meaningful for everyone involved. "There is this one woman who desperately needs a baby and cannot have her own child without the help of a surrogate. And at the other end there is this woman who badly wants to help her (own) family," Patel said. "If this female wants to help the other one . . . why not allow that? . . . It's not for any bad cause. They're helping one another to have a new life in this world."

Experts say commercial surrogacy—or what has been called "wombs for rent"—is growing in India. While no reliable numbers track such pregnancies nationwide, doctors work with surrogates in virtually every major city. The women are impregnated in-vitro with the egg and sperm of couples unable to conceive on their own.

Commercial surrogacy has been legal in India since 2002, as it is in many other countries, including the United States. But India is the leader in making it a viable industry rather than a rare fertility treatment. Experts say it could take off for the same reasons outsourcing in other industries has been successful: a wide labor pool working for relatively low rates.

Critics say the couples are exploiting poor women in India—a country with an alarmingly high maternal death rate—by hiring them at a cut-rate cost to undergo the hardship, pain and risks of labor. "It raises the factor of baby farms in developing countries," said Dr. John Lantos of the Center for Practical Bioethics in Kansas City, Mo. "It comes down to questions of voluntariness and risk."

Ritu Sodhi, a furniture importer from Los Angeles who was born in India, spent $200,000 trying to get pregnant through in-vitro fertilization, and was considering spending another $80,000 to hire a surrogate mother in the United States. Then, on the Internet, Sodhi found Patel's clinic. After spending about $20,000—more than many couples because it took the surrogate mother several cycles to conceive—Sodhi and her husband are now back home with their 4-month-old baby, Neel. They plan to return to Anand for a second child.

"Even if it cost $1 million, the joy that they had delivered to me is so much more than any money that I have given them," said Sodhi. "They're godsends to deliver something so special."

Patel's center is believed to be unique in offering one-stop service. Other clinics may request that the couple bring in their own surrogate, often a family member or friend, and some place classified ads. But in Anand the couple just provides the egg and sperm and the clinic does the rest, drawing from a waiting list of tested and ready surrogates.

Young women are flocking to the clinic to sign up for the list. Suman Dodia, a pregnant, baby-faced 26-year-old, said she will buy a house with the $4,500 she receives from the British couple whose child she's carrying. It would have taken her 15 years to earn that on her maid's monthly salary of $25.

The surrogate mothers and the parents sign a contract that promises the couple will cover all medical expenses in addition to the woman's payment, and the surrogate mother will hand over the baby after birth. The couples fly to Anand for the in-vitro fertilization and again for the birth. Most couples end up paying the clinic less than $10,000 for the entire procedure, including fertilization, the fee to the mother and medical expenses.

Counseling is a major part of the process and Patel tells the women to think of the pregnancy as "someone's child comes to stay at your place for nine months."

Kailas Gheewala, 25, said she doesn't think of the pregnancy as her own. "The fetus is theirs, so I'm not sad to give it back," said Gheewala, who plans to save the $6,250 she's earning for her two daughters' education. "The child will go to the U.S. and lead a better life and I'll be happy."

But if commercial surrogacy keeps growing, some fear it could change from a medical necessity for infertile women to a convenience for the rich. "You can picture the wealthy couples of the West deciding that pregnancy is just not worth the trouble anymore and the whole industry will be farmed out," said Lantos.

For now, the surrogate mothers in Anand seem as pleased with the arrangement as the new parents. "I know this isn't mine," said Jagrudi Sharma, 34, pointing to her belly. "But I'm giving happiness to another couple. And it's great for me."[1] ✳

---

1. Source: Associated Press, Dec. 31, 2007.

The Global Implications of Outsourcing

What happens when foreign countries outsource their production to the United States? For example, many cars from the German manufacturer Mercedes-Benz are now being built in Alabama. If you were an assembly-line worker in Germany who had spent a lifetime making Mercedes, how would you feel if your job was being outsourced to North America? You would be upset. You would feel like the American technician who lost a job to someone in India, or the software writer who was replaced by a worker in China. Outsourcing always produces a job winner and a job loser. In the case of foreign outsourcing to the United States, employment in this country rises. The Mercedes-Benz plant in Alabama employs more than 3,000 workers. Those jobs were transferred to the United States because the company felt that that could be more profitable if it hired American workers and made the vehicles in the United States rather than constructing them in Germany and transporting them across the ocean.

Figure 14.7 shows how outsourcing by foreign firms helps increase U.S. labor demand. In panel (a) we see the job loss and lower wages felt in Germany when jobs are outsourced to the United States. This occurs because the demand for labor in Germany falls from D_1 to D_2 and the wages drops to w_2 and employment declines to q_2. Panel (b) illustrates the corresponding increase in demand for U.S. labor in Alabama. Demand shifts from D_1 to D_2 and the wage rises to w_2 and employment rises to q_2.

Since each nation will experience outsourcing flows out of and into the country, one cannot say anything definitive about the overall impact of outsourcing

FIGURE 14.7

Shifting the Labor Market Equilibrium

Outsourcing creates more demand in one market at the expense of the other. In panel (a) the demand for German labor declines from D_1 to D_2, leading to lower wages and less employment. Panel (b) shows the increase in the demand for labor from D_1 to D_2 in Alabama. This leads to higher wages and more employment.

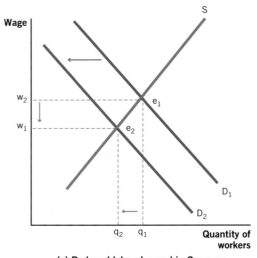

(a) Reduced labor demand in Germany

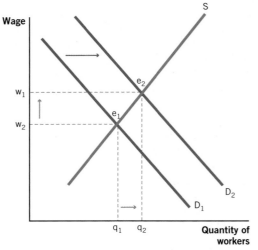

(b) Increased labor demand in Alabama

Outsourcing

Outsourced (2006)

After his entire department is outsourced, an American novelty-products salesman from Seattle heads to India to train his replacement.

The most interesting scenes in this charming movie occur in the call center. The Indian workers speak fluent English, but lack American manners and sensibilities, so they often come across awkwardly. In one memorable phone call, an American caller becomes irate when he learns that the product he is ordering was not made in the United States. He gives the voice on the other end an earful about the loss of jobs in America. However, the call center supervisor devises a clever tactic to convince the disgruntled customer to buy the product despite his objections. She points out that there is a manufacturer in the United States that also makes the same product, and she asks if the caller would be interested in purchasing the product. He says yes and she gives him a new—much higher—price. He pauses and after some thought indicates that he would rather buy the foreign-made product.

on labor in the short run. However, workers who lose high-paying jobs toward the end of their working lives are not likely to find a job that pays as well.

Outsourcing in the Long Run

Although we see mixed results for outsourcing in the short run, in the long run, outsourcing benefits domestic consumers and producers. Outsourcing is a key component in international trade. We have seen that trade creates value. When companies and even countries specialize, they become more efficient. The efficiency gains, or cost savings, help producers expand production. In the absence of trade barriers, lower costs benefit consumers in domestic and international markets through lower prices, and the outsourcing of jobs provides the income for foreign workers to be able to purchase domestic imports. Therefore, the mutually interdependent nature of international trade makes everyone better off.

In the long run, outsourcing also benefits workers. Recall that labor demand is a derived demand and that firms hire more labor when workers have higher marginal revenue products. Since outsourcing moves jobs where the marginal product per dollar is cheaper, the net effect of outsourcing is to increase the overall productivity of workers everywhere. As a result, the marginal revenue product rises throughout the economy and this directly translates into higher wages for workers. Essentially, outsourcing reallocates jobs toward more-productive workers, independent of where those workers may reside. As we learned earlier in this chapter, whenever the marginal product of labor increases, demand for labor increases as well. Therefore, outsourcing increases the demand for labor in the long run.

Monopsony

We have looked at supply, demand, and equilibrium in the labor maket. Until this point we have assumed that the market for labor is competitive. But that is not always the case. Sometimes the labor market has only a few buyers

Monopsony
is a situation where there is
only one buyer.

or sellers who are able to capture market power. One extreme form of market power is **monopsony**, which occurs when a single buyer exists. Like a monopolist, a monopsonist has a great deal of market power. As a consequence, the output in the labor market will favor a monopsony.

In Chapter 10 we examined how a monopolist behaves. Compared to a firm in a competitive market, the monopolist charges a higher price for the product it sells. A monopsonist in the labor market is also able to leverage its market power; it does so by paying its workers less. Isolated college towns serve as a good example. Workers who wish to live in college towns often find that they must either work for the college or leave the town in order to find suitable work elsewhere. Since a college in an isolated small town is the chief provider of jobs, that employer is said to have a monopsony in the labor market. This means that the college can use its market power to hire workers at low wage levels.

 ECONOMICS IN THE REAL WORLD

Pay and Performance in Major League Baseball

Gerald Scully was the first sports economist. In his seminal article "Pay and Performance in Major League Baseball," published in 1974 in the *American Economic Review,* Scully used economic analysis to determine the value of the marginal product that each player produced during the season. Scully's work was important because, at the time, each player had a condition in his contract, known as the reserve clause, which meant that that the player belonged to the team for his entire career, unless he was traded or released.

If a player was unhappy with his contract, his only option was to withdraw from playing. Since most of the best players could not earn nearly as much in their next most productive job, the teams knew that the players would stay for the wage that the team was willing to pay. Therefore, under the reserve clause, each team was a monopsonist. The teams used their market power to suppress wages and increase their profits.

Scully's work changed everything. He used two baseball metrics—slugging percentage for hitters, and the strikeout-to-walk ratio for pitchers—to evaluate the performance of the players and then estimate how much player performance affected winning. He then examined the correlation between winning and revenues. From this he was able to estimate how many dollars of revenue each player generated for his team. The results were stunning. The top players of the era earned about $100,000 per season but generated nearly $1,000,000 in revenue for their teams, or approximately 9 times more than they were being paid. However, since each player was tied to a particular team through the reserve clause, no matter how good the player was he lacked the leverage to bargain for higher wages.

Scully's work played a key role in court decisions affecting two players, Andy Messersmith and Dave McNally, whose cases led to the repeal of the reserve clause in 1975. The reserve clause was struck down because the practice was deemed anticompetitive. Today, because players have gained limited free agency, salaries have steadily increased. Top professional baseball players can earn over $30 million a year, and the average salary is slightly more than $3 million. ✳

- What will happen to the wage rate if a shortage of labor exists?
- How does the outsourcing of labor affect the wage rate and number of workers that are hired?
- How is monopsony different from monopoly?

PRACTICE WHAT YOU KNOW

Labor Supply and Demand: Why Do Some Workers Make More Than Others?

While most workers generally spend 35–40 hours a week at work, what they earn while working varies dramatically. In this box we ask a number of simple questions in order to illustrate why some workers make more than others.

Question: Why do economists generally earn more than elementary education teachers but less than engineers?

Answer: Supply is the key. There are fewer qualified economists and engineers than there are teachers who are certified to teach elementary education. Therefore, the equilibrium wage in economics and engineering is higher than it is for teachers. It's also important to note that demand factors may also be part of the explanation. The value of marginal product of engineers is likely to be higher than the value of marginal product of economists, and the value of marginal product of economists is generally higher than that of most teachers.

Question: Why do workers who toil the night shift earn more than those who do the same job during the day?

Answer: Again, supply is the key. There are fewer workers willing to work at night, so the wage necessary to attract labor to perform the job must be higher.

Question: Why do professional athletes and actors make so much when what they do is hardly essential?

Answer: Now demand takes over. The paying public is willing, even eager, to spend a large amount of income on entertainment. Thus, demand for entertainment is high. On the supply end of the equation, the number of individuals who capture the imagination of the paying public is small. Those who do capture the imagination of the public are paid handsomely to do so. The value of the marginal product that they create is incredibly high and this allows them to earn huge incomes.

Question: Why do janitors, construction workers, and nurses—who do essential jobs—earn salaries that are a tiny fraction of what celebrities earn?

Answer: Demand again. The value of the marginal product created in these jobs is low, so employers are unable to pay high wages.

Land and Capital

In addition to labor, firms need land and capital to produce goods and services. In this section we complete our analysis of the resource market by considering how land and capital enter into the production process. Returning to the restaurant Tequila Mockingbird for a moment, we know that the restaurant hires labor to make meals, but to do their jobs, workers need equipment, tables, chairs, cash registers, and a kitchen. Without a physical location and a host of capital resources, labor would be irrelevant.

The Market for Land

Like the demand for labor, the demand for land is determined by the value of the marginal product that it creates. However, unlike the supply of labor, the supply of land is fixed. We can think of the supply of land as not responsive to prices, or perfectly inelastic.

In Figure 14.8, the vertical supply curve reflects the inelastic supply. The price of land is determined by the intersection of supply and demand. Notice the label on the y-axis, which reflects the price of land as the rental price necessary to use it, not the price necessary to purchase it. When evaluating a firm's economic situation, we do not count the entire purchase price of the land it needs. Because the land is only occupied for a period of time, counting the entire cost would be an overstatement. For example, imagine you have a new car. You drive the car for a year and put 15,000 miles on it. But if you want to determine the operating cost for one year of service, you would not count the entire purchase price. The true cost of operating the vehicle considers the wear and tear along with operating expenses such as gasoline, maintenance, and service visits. A similar process is used to calculate the cost

Supply and Demand in the Market for Land

Since the supply of land is fixed, the price it commands depends on demand. If demand increases from D_1 to D_2, the price will rise from P_1 to P_2.

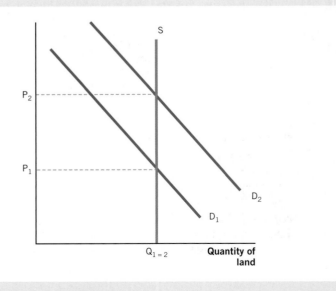

of a firm's use of land. Firms count the rent they could have earned if they had rented the land to a tenant for the year. This captures the opportunity cost of using the land.

Since the supply of land is fixed, changes in demand determine the rental price. When demand is low—say, at D_1—the rental price received, P_1, is also low. When demand is high—say, at D_2—the rental price of land is high, at P_2. Apartment rentals near college campuses provide a clear example of the conditions under which the demand for land is high. Since students and faculty want to live near campus, the demand for land is often much higher there than even a few blocks away. Like labor, the demand for land is derived from the demand for the products that it is used to produce. In this case, the demand for apartments, homes, and retail space near campus is very high. The high demand drives up the rental price of land closer to campus because the marginal product of land is higher.

When economists talk about an **economic rent**, they mean the difference between what a factor of production earns and what it could earn in the next-best alternative. Economic rent is different from rent seeking. Recall that rent seeking occurs when firms compete to try to attain a monopoly position. "Rents" here refer to the ability of investors to beat their opportunity cost. For instance, in the case of housing near college campuses, a small studio apartment will often command a much higher rent than a similar apartment located 10 miles away. This occurs because the rent near campus must be high enough to compensate the owners for using their land for an apartment instead of other ways that might also be profitable in the area—for example, for a single residence, a business, or even a parking lot. Once you move 10 miles further out, the number of people interested in using the land for these purposes declines. More generally, in areas where many people would like to live or work, rental prices are often very high. There are many places in the United States with high rental prices, but none compares with Hong Kong, where an average two-bedroom apartment rents for almost $7,000 a month. That staggering amount makes most apartment rental prices in the United States seem downright inexpensive. While not as high as Hong Kong, owners of property in Moscow, Tokyo, London, and New York all receive more economic rent on properties than those who own similar two-bedroom apartments in Peoria, Idaho Falls, Scranton, or Chattanooga. The ability to earn a substantial economic rent comes back to opportunity costs—since there are so many other uses of property in densely populated areas, rents are correspondingly higher.

Economic rent is the difference between what a factor of production earns and its next-best alternative.

The Market for Capital

Capital, or the equipment and materials needed to produce goods, is a necessary factor of production. In this section we will look at the role that capital plays in the production process.

The demand for capital is determined by the value of the marginal product that it creates. Like land and labor, the demand for capital is a derived demand—the firm requires capital only if the product it produces is in demand. The demand for capital is also downward sloping; this reflects the fact that the value of the marginal product associated with its use declines as the amount used rises. The accompanying box provides an example to help you put these ideas to use.

PRACTICE WHAT YOU KNOW

The Marginal Product of Capital versus Labor

Suppose that Tequila Mockingbird is considering the purchase of a new industrial dishwasher. It cleans faster, uses less labor and less water, but it costs $10,000. Should the restaurant make the capital expenditure, or would it be better off saving the money and incurring higher operating costs?

To help you decide what TM should do, consider the following costs. The dishwasher has a usable life of five years before it will need to be replaced. The dishwasher saves the restaurant $300 a year in water and it saves TM 10 hours of labor each week.

Question: Should TM purchase the new dishwasher?

Answer: This is the kind of question every business wrestles with on a regular basis. The answer is very straightforward. It turns out that a firm should invest in new capital when the value of marginal product it creates per dollar spent is greater than the value of the marginal product per dollar spent on the next-best alternative. In other words, invest in the new capital when the bang per buck exceeds that of labor or other investments.

The total cost of the dishwasher is $10,000, but the savings are larger. The water saved is $300 for each year, or $1,500. Plus the restaurant saves an additional 520 hours of labor each year. If TM pays its dishwashers $8 an hour, the annual labor costs savings are $4,160. The total savings over five years is $22,300. This makes the investment in the dishwasher the better choice!

When to Use More Labor, Land, or Capital

A firm must evaluate whether hiring additional labor, utilizing more land, or deploying more capital is the best use of its resources. In order to do this, firms compare the value of the marginal product per dollar spent across the three factors of production.

Let's consider an example. Suppose a company pays its employees $15 per hour, the rental rate of land is $5,000 an acre per year, and the rental rate of capital is $1,000 per year. The manager of the firm determines that the value of the marginal product of labor is $450, the value of the marginal product of an acre of land is $125,000, and the value of the marginal product of capital is $40,000. Is the firm using the right mix of resources? To answer the question, turn to Table 14.2. Here we compare the ratios of the value of the marginal product of each factor of production to the cost of attaining that value. This gives us the revenue per dollar spent for each resource.

Looking at these results, we see that the revenue per dollar spent for capital is the value of 40 created by the ratio of the value of marginal product of

TABLE 14.2

Determining the Revenue per Dollar Spent for Each Resource

Factor of Production	Value of the Marginal Product ($)	Wage or Rental Price ($)	Revenue per Dollar Spent ($)
Notation/Formula	(1)	(2)	(1) ÷ (2) = (3)
Labor	450	15	450 ÷ 15 = 30
Land	125,000	5,000	125,000 ÷ 5,000 = 25
Capital	40,000	1,000	40,000 ÷ 1,000 = 40

capital to the rental price of capital in column (3). When we compare this value for capital, it tells us that the firm is earning more revenue per dollar spent from using capital than it is from using labor ($30) or land ($25). Therefore the firm would benefit from using capital more intensively. In order to bring the three benefit-cost ratios into alignment, the firm must invest in more capital, such as new machinery, better equipment, and computers. This in turn will increase the productively of its workers as well, since they will have better capital to work with. At the same time, if land is not as productive, some of it can be sold. If the firm does this the VMP of capital in column (1) will fall due to diminishing returns. As a result, the benefit-cost ratio of utilizing additional capital will drop from 40 in column (3) to a number that is more in line with labor and land. Similarly, the firm is using land ($25) too intensively. Using less land will raise the value of the marginal product it produces and increase the revenue per dollar spent for land in column (3). By using less land and more capital, and also by tweaking the use of labor, the firm will eventually be able to bring the value created by all three factors to a point where the revenue per dollar spent is equal for each of the factors. At this point, the firm will be utilizing its resources efficiently.

The markets for land, labor, and capital are connected. The amount of labor a firm uses is not only a function of the marginal product of labor; it also depends on the marginal product of land and capital. Therefore, a change in the supply of one factor will alter the returns of all factors. For instance, falling wages will induce firms to hire more labor, and simultaneously use less capital to produce goods. Capital itself is not any more, or less, productive. Rather, lower wages reduce the demand for capital. In this situation, the demand curve for capital would shift left, lowering the rental price of capital and also the quantity of capital deployed.

ECONOMICS IN THE REAL WORLD

The Impact of the Financial Crisis on Land, Labor, and Capital

The financial crisis of 2008 resulted in the loss of 40 percent of all global wealth. By most measures, 10 trillion dollars of wealth was destroyed in just over a few months. The results can be seen in the land, labor, and capital markets. Since demand in the factor markets is derived from the demand in the market for final goods and services, it is not surprising that the underlying factor markets felt the impact of the crisis. Unemployment in the United States rose from under 6 percent to over 10 percent due to the fall in demand for labor. Home prices and land values plummeted over 30 percent from the peak in 2007. Finally, the cost of acquiring, or renting, capital fell toward historic lows.

Since the demand for each factor is interconnected, it is not surprising that the crisis touched more than just the financial markets. Our understanding of the factor markets teaches us that workers and land owners alike were vulnerable to systemic changes in the capital markets. As a result, the pain has been shared by Main Street and Wall Street. ✳

- How is the supply curve of land different from the supply of labor and capital?
- What are economic rents?
- If a factor of production has a very high value of the marginal product, should the firm use more or less of it?

Conclusion

Throughout this chapter we have learned that the compensation for factor inputs depends on the interaction between demand and supply. Resource demand is derived from the demand for the final product a firm produces, and resource supply depends on the other opportunities and compensation levels that exist in the market. As a result, the equilibrium prices and outputs in the land, labor, and capital markets reflect, in large part, the tensions between the opposing forces of demand and supply.

In the next chapter we will look at income and poverty. As you will soon discover, there are many factors beyond the demand for and supply of workers that explain why some laborers make more than others. For instance, wages also depend on the amount of human capital required in order to be hired, location, lifestyle choices, union membership, and the riskiness of the profession. Adding these elements in the next chapter will allow us to deepen our understanding of why workers earn what they do.

Summary

- The demand for each factor of production is a derived demand that stems from a firm's desire to supply a good in another market.
- Labor demand is contingent upon the value of the marginal product that is produced, and the value of the marginal product is equivalent to the firm's labor demand curve. The supply of labor depends on the wage rate that is offered, and also on each person's goals and other opportunities. At high wage levels the income effect may become larger than the substitution effect and cause the supply curve to bend backwards.

- Labor markets reconcile the forces of demand and supply into a wage signal that conveys information to both sides of the market. At wages above the equilibrium, the supply of workers exceeds the demand for labor. This results in a surplus of available workers that places downward pressure on wages until they reach the equilibrium wage, where the surplus is eliminated. At wages below the equilibrium, the demand for labor exceeds the available supply of workers and a shortage develops. The shortage forces firms to offer higher wages in order to attract workers. Wages rise until they reach the equilibrium wage, at which point the shortage is eliminated.

- There is no definitive result for outsourcing of labor in the short run. In the long run, outsourcing moves jobs to workers who are more productive, and thus increases the overall productivity of workers everywhere. The marginal revenue product rises throughout the economy, which translates into higher wages for workers.

- A monopsony is a market with only a single buyer. A monopsonist in the labor market is able to leverage its market power by paying its workers less.

- An economic rent is the difference between what a factor of production earns, and what it could earn in the next-best alternative. Highly paid celebrities and professional athletes often generate rents far in excess of their next-best option.

- The firm must consider how best to combine land, labor, and capital.

CONCEPTS YOU SHOULD KNOW

Backward-bending labor supply
  curve (p. 414)
Derived demand (p. 408)
Economic rent (p. 427)

Factors of production (p. 406)
Marginal product of labor
  (p. 409)
Monopsony (p. 424)

Outsourcing of labor (p. 419)
Value of the marginal product
  (p. 409)

QUESTIONS

1. Why is the demand for factor inputs a derived demand?

2. What rule does the firm use when deciding to hire an additional worker?

3. What can cause the labor supply curve to bend backwards?

4. If wages are below the equilibrium level, what would cause wages to rise?

5. What are the two labor demand shifters? What are the three labor supply shifters?

6. What would happen to the wages of movie stars if all of the major film studios merged into a single firm, creating a monopsony for film actors?

7. If workers become more productive, what will happen to the demand for labor, the wages of labor, and the number of workers employed?

STUDY PROBLEMS

1. Would a burrito restaurant hire an additional worker for $10 an hour if that worker could produce an extra 30 burritos and each burrito adds $0.60 in revenues?

2. Illustrate each of the following changes using a separate supply and demand curve. Diagram the new equilibrium point and note how the wage and quantity of workers employed changes.
   a. There is a sudden migration out of an area.
   b. Laborers are willing to work more hours.
   c. Fewer workers are willing to work the night shift.
   d. A company discovers a new production technique that makes its workers more productive.
   e. The demand for California wines suddenly increases.

3. Pam's Pretzels has a production function shown in Table 14.3. It costs Pam's Pretzels $80 per day per worker. Each pretzel sells for $3.

Quantity of Labor	Quantity of Pretzels
0	0
1	100
2	180
3	240
4	280
5	320
6	340
7	340
8	320

   a. Compute the marginal product and the value of the marginal product that each worker creates.
   b. How many workers should Pam hire?

4. Jimi owns a music school that specializes in teaching guitar. Jimi has a very limited supply of rooms for his instructors to use for

lessons. As a result, each successive instructor adds less to Jimi's output of lessons. Table 14.4 lists Jimi's production function. Guitar lessons cost $25 per hour.

Quantity of Labor	Quantity of Lessons (hours)
0	0
1	10
2	17
3	23
4	28
5	32
6	35
7	37
8	38

a. Construct Jimi's labor demand schedule at each of the following daily wage rates for instructors ($75, $100, $125, $150, $175, $200).
b. Suppose that Jimi is able raise the cost of guitar lessons to $35. What does his new labor demand schedule look like at the daily wage rates in part a?

5. Maria is a hostess at a local restaurant. When she was paid $8 an hour she worked 35 hours per week. When her wage increased to $10 per hour, she decided to work 40 hours. However, when her wage increased again to $12 per hour, she decided to cut back to 37 hours a week. Draw Maria's supply curve. How would you explain Maria's actions to someone unfamiliar with economics?

6. How does outsourcing affect wages and employment in the short run and the long run?

7. Suppose that the current wage rate is $20 per hour, the rental rate of land is $10,000 an acre, and the rental rate of capital $2,500. The manager of a firm determines that the value of the marginal product of labor is

$400, the value of the marginal product of an acre of land is $200,000, and the value of the marginal product of capital is $4,000. Is the firm maximizing profit?

8. Farmers in Utopia experience perfect weather the entire growing season, and as a result their crop is double its normal size. How will this bumper crop affect the following?
a. The price of the crop
b. The marginal product of workers helping to harvest the crop
c. The demand for the workers who help harvest the crop

9. What will happen to the equilibrium wage of the crop harvesters in Dystopia if the price of the crop falls by 50 percent and the marginal product of workers increases by 25 percent?

10. In an effort to create a health care safety net, the government requires employers to provide health care coverage to all employees. What impact will this increased coverage have in the following labor markets?
a. The demand for doctors
b. The demand for medical equipment
c. The supply of hospital beds

11. A football team is trying to decide which of two running backs (A or B) to sign to a one-year contract.

Predicted Stats	Player A	Player B
Touchdowns	7	10
Yards gained	1,200	1,000
Fumbles	4	5

The team has done a statistical analysis to determine the value of each touchdown, yard gained, and fumble to the team's revenue. Each touchdown is worth an extra $250,000, each yard gained is worth $1,500, and each fumble costs $75,000. Player A costs $3 million and Player B costs $2.5 million. Based on their predicted statistics in the table given, which player should the team sign?

Income, Inequality, and Poverty

Why do large differences in income exist? How can you position yourself to earn more? These are two questions that might go hand in hand for any student of introductory economics. In the last chapter we learned that two primary factors govern wage income: productivity and the forces of supply and demand. You may be an outstanding babysitter or short-order cook, but because there are many other workers who can easily replace you, neither occupation will ever pay much more than minimum wage. On the other hand, even an average neurosurgeon can expect to be paid very well, since few individuals are able to perform neurosurgery. In addition, society values neurosurgeons more than babysitters because they are saving lives. If you wish to make a sizable income, it is not enough to be good at something; that "something" needs to be an occupation that society values highly. What matters are your skills, what you produce, and the supply of workers in your occupation.

In this chapter we will continue our exploration of labor by looking at income and inequality in labor markets, including the characteristics of successful wage earners and the impediments the poor face in trying to escape poverty. Examining those at the top and the bottom of the income ladder will help us understand the many forces that determine income. In addition, we will look at the topic of poverty, which is brought on by many factors, including low worker productivity, insufficient education, cyclical downturns in the economy, employment discrimination, and bad luck.

Learning Objectives:

- To understand the nonmonetary determinants of wages.
- To learn how discrimination influences income, employment, and markets.
- To appreciate that some degree of income inequality is desirable.
- To understand how economists look at poverty and its solutions.

The Determinants of Wages

The reasons that some workers get paid more than others are complex. Part of the explanation involves *compensating differentials*—differences in the nature of the job undertaken—that cause workers in some locations or occupations to earn more or accept less. Pay discrimination is another reason some people earn more than others. There are also several unusual determinants of wages, including winner-take-all contests and the role of workers' physical attractiveness.

Photo to come

The Nonmonetary Determinants of Wages

Jobs that may seem to be the same often have characteristics that make them more or less desirable than they first appear. Similarly, no two workers are exactly alike. These differences in jobs and workers affect the supply and demand of labor. In this section we will examine the impact of nonmonetary differences, including location, stress, working conditions, prestige, and danger.

Compensating Differentials

Some jobs are more unpleasant, risky, stressful, inconvenient, or monotonous than others. If the characteristics of the job make it unattractive, firms must offer more to attract workers. For instance roofing, logging, and deep-sea fishing are some of the most dangerous occupations in the world. Workers who do these jobs must be compensated with higher wages to offset the higher risk of injury. A **compensating differential** is the difference in income that employers must offer so workers choose a particular job over other jobs they could perform. If a job's characteristics make it unattractive, the compensating wage differential must be positive. On the other hand, some jobs are highly desirable. For example, restaurant critics sample a lot of great food, radio DJs spend the day playing their favorite music, and video game testers try beta versions before they are released. Some jobs are simply more fun, exciting, prestigious, or stimulating than others. In these cases, the compensating differential is negative and the firm will offer lower wages. Being a newspaper reporter or a radio DJ are jobs that are known to be low-paying. Video game testing is so desirable that most people who do it are not paid at all.

*A **compensating differential** is the extra income that a worker must be paid to perform a job.*

Education and Human Capital

Many complex jobs require substantial education, training, and industry experience. Qualifying to receive the specialized education required for certain occupations—for example, getting into medical school—is often very difficult. Only a limited number of students are able to pursue these degrees. In addition, education is expensive, both in terms of tuition and also the opportunity cost of forgone income.

The skills that workers acquire on the job and through education are collectively known as **human capital**. Unlike other forms of capital, investments in human capital accrue to the employee. As a result, workers who have high human capital can shop those skills among competing firms. Engineering, medicine, and other occupations that require extensive education and training pay high wages in part because the human capital needed to do the job is high. On the other hand, ushers, baggers, sales associates, and other low-skill workers earn less because the human capital required to do those jobs is quite low; it is easy to find replacements.

Human capital is the skill that workers acquire through training and education.

Table 15.1 shows the relationship between education and pay. Each step up the education ladder produces a significant jump in earnings. Workers who earn advanced degrees have higher marginal products, but they have also invested heavily in education. This works both ways. The higher marginal product of workers who have earned at least a bachelor's degree helps to create high demand for their skills. In addition, the time required to

TABLE 15.1

The Relationship between Education and Pay

Education Level	Median Annual Earnings in 2008 (persons age 25 and over)
Doctoral degree	$80,860
Master's degree	63,856
Bachelor's degree	50,856
Associate degree	38,272
Some college, no degree	33,540
High school degree	30,732
High school dropout	22,152

Source: Bureau of Labor Statistics, Current Population Survey, March 6, 2009.

complete advanced degrees limits the supply of workers with high marginal products. Taken together, the firm's demand for workers with high marginal products and the limited supply of such workers causes earnings to escalate. Higher wages represent a compensating differential that rewards additional education.

ECONOMICS IN THE REAL WORLD

Does Education Pay?

An alternative perspective on the value of education argues that the returns to increased education are not the education received but largely the product of *signaling*. According to this idea, a degree is not evidence of a set of skills that makes a worker more productive. Rather, earning degrees and attending more prominent institutions is a signal—or a sign—to employers of the potential employee's quality.

It is possible to test the importance of signaling by looking at the returns to earning a college degree, controlling for institutional quality. At many elite institutions the four-year price tag has reached extraordinary levels. What type of return do graduates of highly selective institutions make on their sizable investments? And are those returns the result of a rigorous education or a function of the institution's reputation? This is difficult to determine because the students who attend more selective institutions would be more likely to have higher earnings potential regardless of where they attend college. These students enter college as high achievers, a trait that carries forward into the workplace, wherever they decide to go to school.

Economists Stacy Dale and Alan Krueger used data to examine the financial outcomes for over 6,000 students who were accepted or rejected by a comparable set of colleges. They found that twenty years after graduation, students who had been accepted at more selective colleges but decided to attend a less selective college earned approximately the same income as their counterparts from more selective colleges.

Although Table 15.1 shows that additional education pays, the reason is not simply an increase in human capital. There is also a "signal" that employers can interpret about unobservable qualities. For instance, Harvard graduates presumably learn a great deal in their time at school, but they were also highly motivated and successful even before they went to college. Part of the increase in income attributable to completing college is a function of a set of unobservable traits that the student already possessed independent of the school or the degree. ✳

Location and Lifestyle

For most people, sipping margaritas in Key West, Florida, sounds more appealing than living in Eureka, Nevada, along the most isolated stretch of road in the continental United States. Likewise, being able to see a show, visit a museum, or go to a Yankees game in New York City provides a different lifestyle from what you'd find living in Dodge City, Kansas. Some places are generally considered more desirable to live in than others. So how does location affect wages? Where the climate is more pleasant, all other things being equal, people are willing to accept lower wages, since the nonmonetary benefits of being able to enjoy the weather act as a compensating differential. Similarly, jobs in metropolitan areas, where the cost of living is significantly higher than other places, pay higher wages as a compensating differential. This helps employees afford a quality of life similar to what they would enjoy if they worked in less expensive areas.

Choice of lifestyle is also a major factor in determining wage differences. Some workers are not particularly concerned with maximizing their income—they care more about working for a cause. This is true for many employees of nonprofits or religious organizations, or even people who take care of loved ones. Others follow a dream of being a musician, writer, or actor. And still others are guided by a passion such as skiing in the winter or surfing in the summer. Many workers view their pay as less important than doing something they are passionate about. For these workers, lower pay functions as a compensating differential.

Unions

A union
is a group of workers that bargains collectively for better wages and benefits.

A strike
is a work stoppage designed to aid a union's bargaining position.

A **union** is a group of workers that bargains collectively for better wages and benefits. Unions are able to increase wages by creating significant market power over the supply of labor available to a firm. The ability of a union to achieve higher wages depends on a credible threat of a work stoppage, known as a **strike**. In effect, unions are able to raise wages because they represent labor, and labor is a key factor input in the production process. Since firms cannot do without labor, an effective union can use the threat of a strike to negotiate higher wages for its workers. By law, not all unions are allowed to go on strike; transit workers, teachers, law enforcement, and workers in other essential services are often prohibited from striking. If workers and employees in one of these industries reach an impasse in wage and benefit negotiations, the employee union is required to submit to the decision of an impartial third party, a process known as *binding arbitration*. The television show *Judge Judy* is an example of binding arbitration in action: two parties with a small-claims grievance agree in advance to accept the verdict of Judith Sheindlin, a noted family court judge.

The effect of unions in the United States has changed since the early days of unionization in the late 1800s Early studies of the union wage premium found wages to be as much as 30 percent higher for workers who were unionized. At the height of unionization, approximately sixty years ago, 1 in 3 jobs was unionized. Today about 1 in 8 workers is a member of union and the union wage premium has narrowed to between 6 and 15 percent. The demise of many unions coincides with the transition of the U.S. economy from a manufacturing base to a greater emphasis on the service sector, which by its nature is less centralized.

While union membership in the private sector has steadily declined, membership in the public sector has increased and stands at almost 40 percent. This asymmetry is explained by competitive pressure. In the private sector, higher union labor costs encourage firms to substitute more capital and use more technology in the production process. Higher union labor costs also encourage firms to relocate production to places that have large pools of nonunion labor. These competitive pressures limit how successful unions are at organizing and maintaining membership, and the wage premium they can secure. However, in the government sector competition is largely absent. Federal, state and local governments can pay employees according to union scale, without having to worry about cost-containment. As a result, unions are common among public-school teachers, police, fire, and sanitation workers.

Efficiency Wages

When it comes to paying wages, one approach stands out as unique. Ordinarily we think of wages being determined in the labor market at the intersection of supply and demand. When the labor market is in equilibrium, the wage guarantees that every qualified worker is able to find employment. However, some firms willingly pay more than the equilibrium wage. **Efficiency wages** exist when an employer pays its workers more than the equilibrium wage. Why would a business do that? Surprisingly, the answer is to make *more* profit. That hardly seems possible when a firm that uses efficiency wages pays its workers more than its competitors. But think again. Above-equilibrium wages help to reduce slacking, decrease turnover, and increase productivity. If the gains in overall productivity are higher than the increased cost, the result is greater profits.

Efficiency wages are wages higher than equilibrium wages, offered to increase worker productivity.

Automaker Henry Ford used efficiency wages in an effort to create more productivity on the Model T assembly line. In 1914, Ford decided to more than double the pay of assembly line workers to $5.00 a day—an increase that his competitors did not match. He also decreased the work day from nine to eight hours. Ford's primary goal was to reduce worker turnover, which was frequent because of the monotonous nature of assembly work; by making the job so lucrative, he figured that most workers would not quit so quickly. He was right. The daily turnover rate plummeted from over 10 percent per day to less than 1 percent. As word of the high wages spread, workers flocked to Detroit. The day after the wage increase was announced, over 10,000 eager job seekers lined up outside Ford's Highland Park plant. From this crowd, Ford was able to hire the most productive employees. The productivity increase per worker was more than enough to offset the wage increase. In addition, reducing the length of each shift allowed Ford to add an extra shift, which also increased productivity.

We have seen that the wages that workers earn are influenced by compensating differentials, differences in human capital, location and lifestyle, union membership, and the presence of efficiency wages. Table 15.2 summarizes these nonmonetary determinants of income differences.

Wage Discrimination

Wage discrimination occurs when workers of the same ability are not paid the same as others because of their race, ethnic origin, sex, age, religion, or some other group characteristic. Most economic studies of wage discrimination indicate that discrimination today accounts for only small wage differences—3 to 5 percent. However, less than forty years ago it was a serious problem. Economists and policy makers continue to study the issue, to understand its effect in the past and to help address any remaining discrimination. Most of us would like to believe that employers no longer pay men more than women for doing the same job. However, wage discrimination does still exist. In 2009, President Obama signed the Lilly Ledbetter Fair Pay Act, which gives victims of wage discrimination more time to file a complaint with the government. This act is named after a former employee of Goodyear who sued the company in 2007. The courts determined that she was paid 15–40 percent less than her male counterparts. That a major U.S. corporation

TABLE 15.2

The Key Nonmonetary Determinants of Wages

Determinant	Impact on Wages
Compensating differentials	Some workers are eager to have jobs that are more fun, exciting, prestigious, or stimulating than others. As a result, they are willing to accept lower wages.
Human capital	Many jobs require substantial education, training, and experience. As a result, workers who acquire additional amounts of human capital are able to earn higher wages.
Location and lifestyle	When the location is desirable, the compensating wage will be lower. Similarly, when employment is for a highly valued cause, wage is less important. In both situations, the compensating wage will be lower.
Unions	Since firms cannot do without labor, unions can threaten a strike to negotiate higher wages.
Efficiency wages	The firm pays above-equilibrium wages to help reduce slacking, decrease turnover, and increase productivity.

was violating the Equal Pay Act of 1963 almost 50 years after it was passed is a poignant reminder that wage discrimination is still with us.

Determining discrimination is no longer so simple, or obvious, as it once was. Table 15.3 presents median earnings in the United States by age, race, experience, and location. Looking at the data, we see that large earnings differences exist across many groups in society. You might be tempted to conclude that this reflects employer discrimination. However, most of the differences in earnings can be explained by compensating differentials and differences in human capital. For example, women have fewer years of work experience, women work fewer hours per year, women are less likely to work a full-time schedule, and women leave the labor force for longer periods of time. The result of these differences is that in general men earn more than women.

Although female workers earn 23 percent less than their male counterparts, much of this gap can be explained by compensating differentials. The types of jobs that women and men typically work are different. Men are more likely to work outdoors. The higher wages offered for jobs such as road work and construction reflects, in part, a compensating differential for exposure to extreme temperatures, bad weather, and danger. Because women spend more time out of the workforce—the result of pregnancy and child rearing—their work history tends to have more interruptions. These factors—the jobs that men and women undertake, experience, and employment history—explain most of the female-male wage gap. However, the gender gap is shrinking. In 2009 more women than men in the United States received doctoral degrees. The number of women at every level of academia has been rising for decades. Women now hold a nearly 3-to-2 majority in undergraduate and graduate education. Over time this educational advantage will help offset some of the other compensating differentials that have kept the wages of men higher than women.

TABLE 15.3

Median Annual Earnings by Group

Group	Median Earnings in 2008	Percentage Difference within Each Group
Males	$46,376	–
Females	35,745	−23%
White	$52,312	–
Black	34,218	−35
Asian	65,637	26
Hispanic	37,913	−27
Early-career workers (25–34)	$51,400	−19
Midcareer workers (35–54)	63,652	–
Late-career workers (55–64)	57,265	−10
Inside a metropolitan area	$51,853	–
Outside a metropolitan area	40,785	−19

Source: U.S. Census Bureau, Current Population Survey, 2008 and 2009 Annual Social and Economic Supplements.

Similarly, wide gaps in earnings data by race can largely be explained by differences in human capital. Asians often have much higher education levels than whites, who in turn, often have much higher education levels than blacks and Hispanics. Much of the difference in educational attainment is directly related to cultural values; some groups place more emphasis on formal education than others. We would expect the wage disparities among groups to decrease as these cultural differences become less pronounced.

The earnings gap between midcareer workers and others can also be explained by differences in human capital. Workers who are just starting out have limited experience. As workers age they acquire on-the-job training and experience that make them more productive and increase the amount they are paid. For older workers, the gains from increased experience are eventually offset by diminishing returns. Workers nearing retirement are less likely to keep up with advances in technology or learn new approaches. Consequently, wages peak when workers are in their fifties and slowly fall thereafter. This wage pattern, known as the **life cycle**, refers to the predictable effect that age has on earnings over the course of a person's working life.

As we noted earlier in the chapter, location is also a source of wage differentials. Workers who live outside metropolitan areas make, on average, 19 percent less than their counterparts who live in cities. This gap arises because the cost of living is much higher in metropolitan areas.

Clearly, broad measures of the differences in earnings do not provide evidence of wage discrimination. Since no employer will admit to discriminating, researchers can only infer the amount of discrimination after first correcting for observable differences from compensating differentials and differences in human capital. The unobservable differences that remain are presumed to be discrimination. Because the unobserved differences are small, estimates generally put discrimination at less than 5 percent of wage differences.

The **life cycle** refers to the predictable effect that age has on earnings.

ECONOMICS IN THE REAL WORLD

Beauty Pays: The Effects of Beauty on Earnings

In research that spans the labor market from the law profession to college teaching, and in countries as different as the United States and China, beauty matters. How much? Beautiful people make as much as 10 percent more than persons of average looks, while those whose looks are considered significantly below average can expect their earnings to be as much as 25 percent below normal.

The influence of beauty on wages can be viewed of two ways. First, you can think of beauty as a marketable trait that has a value in many professions. Actors, fashion models, waiters, and litigators all rely upon their appearance to make a living, so it is not surprising to find that beauty is correlated with wages. If beautiful people are more productive (because of their beauty), then attractiveness/beauty is simply a measure of the value of the marginal product that they create. In other words, being beautiful is a compensating differential, or a form of human capital that the worker possesses.

However, there is a second interpretation—discrimination. If employers prefer "beautiful" people as employees, then part of the earnings increase associated with beauty could reflect that preference. In addition, the success of workers who are more beautiful could also reflect the preferences of customers who prefer to work with more attractive people.

Since it is impossible to determine whether the beauty premium is a compensating differential or the result of overt discrimination, we can only acknowledge the possibility that the truth, in many cases, is a little bit of both. ✳

Occupational Crowding: How Discrimination Affects Wages

Discrimination is not as overt or widespread as it was a few generations ago. Today, doors that were once closed are now open, and this has helped equalize wages among qualified workers. Still, the impact of wage discrimination continues to be felt. In many jobs *occupational crowding* continues to suppress wages for women. **Occupational crowding** is the phenomenon of relegating a group of workers to a narrow range of jobs in the economy. To understand how occupational crowding works, let's begin by imagining a community named Utopia with only two types of jobs: a small number in engineering and a large number in secretarial services. Furthermore, everyone is equally proficient at both occupations and everyone in the community is indifferent to working either job. Under these assumptions we would expect the wages for engineers and secretaries to be the same.

Now imagine that not everyone in Utopia has the same set of opportunities. Suppose that we roll back the clock to an age when women in Utopia were not allowed to be engineers. Women who wanted to work could only find employment as secretaries. Furthermore, let's imagine that the number of jobs as engineers was relatively small compared to the number of jobs as secretaries. In Figure 15.1, women are crowded into secretarial jobs, which increases the supply of secretaries, shown in (a), to S_2. Because employment in engineering is restricted to men, the supply of engineers, shown in (b), decreases to S_2.

Occupational crowding is the crowding of a group of workers into a small number of jobs.

FIGURE 15.1

How Occupational Crowding Affects Wages
(a) If workers are crowded into secretarial jobs, the supply of secretaries will expand from S_1 to S_2. The result is lower wages in secretarial positions. (b) At the same time, the absence of workers in engineering means that the supply contracts from S_1 to S_2 and wages for engineers rise.

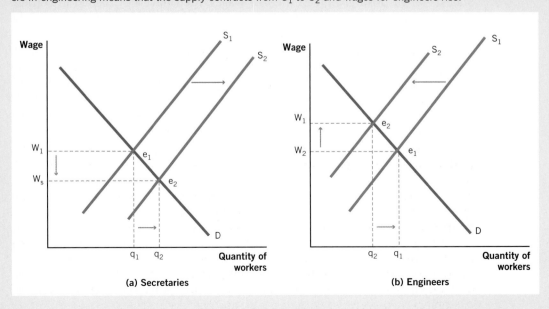

(a) Secretaries

(b) Engineers

TABLE 15.4	
Where the Men Aren't	
Job	Percent Female
Kindergarten teachers	98
Dental hygienists	98
Secretaries	98
Child care workers	97
Nurses	93
Bank tellers	87
Librarians	86
Legal assistants	84
Telephone operators	83

Source: Department of Labor, Bureau of Labor Statistics.

The result of occupational crowding is that workers who have limited opportunities (women in this example) find themselves competing with each other for a small number of jobs. Wages fall to W_S in secretarial jobs and rise to W_E for engineers. Since only men can work in engineering, they are paid more than their similarly qualified female counterparts who are crowded into secretarial positions and earn less. Furthermore, since women who want to work can only receive a low wage as a secretary, many will stay home and produce nonmarket services, like child rearing, with a higher value to them than the wages they can earn as secretaries.

Of course, in the real world women are not restricted to engineering. However, many of the lower-paying jobs in our society are dominated by women. Table 15.4 shows a number of female-dominated occupations in the United States. Not surprisingly, given the low wages, men have not rushed into these jobs. However, because women have not exited them to the extent one might expect, wages have remained low. Rigidity in changing occupations, social customs, and personal preferences all help to explain why this is the case. The same forces are at work in traditionally male-dominated jobs, where men have enjoyed higher wages due to a lack of female employees. Engineers, auto mechanics, airline pilots—to name a few—are careers that have begun to admit women in large numbers over the last twenty years. As the supply of workers expands, the net effect will be to lower wages in traditionally male-dominated jobs.

Winner-Take-All

In 1930, baseball legend Babe Ruth demanded and received a salary of $80,000, approximately $1 million in today's dollars, from the New York Yankees. Babe Ruth earned a lot more than the other baseball players of his era. When told that President Herbert Hoover earned less than he was asking for, Ruth famously said, "I had a better year than he did." In fact, the annual salary of the president of the United States is far less than that of top professional athletes, movie stars, and even many corporate chief executive officers

Occupational Crowding

Anchorman: The Legend of Ron Burgundy (2004)

This film is about the television news industry in the early days of female anchors—the 1970s! Stations were diversifying their broadcast teams and beginning to add women and minorities to previously all-white male lineups.

Veronica Corningstone, a new anchor, introduces herself: "Hello, everyone. I just want you all to know that I look forward to contributing to this news station's already sterling reputation."

The added competition for air time does not sit well with Ron Burgundy and his male colleagues.

"I mean, come on, Ed! Don't get me wrong. I love the ladies. They rev my engine, but they don't belong in the newsroom! It is anchorman, not anchor lady! And that is a scientific fact!"

Veronica overhears the conversation, and after leaving the office she begins a monologue:

"Here we go again. Every station it's the same. Women ask me how I put up with it. Well, the truth is, I don't really have a choice. This is definitely a man's world. But while they're laughing and carrying on, I'm chasing down leads and practicing my nonregional diction. Because the only way to win is to be the best."

The movie, and more specifically the scene described above, points to the difficulties in breaking into new labor markets in which entrenched interests stand in the way. Veronica Corningstone felt that she had to be the "best," a not-so-subtle reference to the discrimination she was facing. She had to be better than the existing male anchors to get the job. Ron and his friends viewed Veronica as a threat because she, and others like her, increased the pool of qualified applicants, thereby lowering the wages throughout the industry and also making it harder for male anchors to find positions.

(CEOs). Why does the most important job in the world pay less than jobs with far less value to society? Part of the answer is compensating differentials. Being the president makes you the most powerful person in the world, so compensation is only a small part of the benefits of holding the office. The other part of the answer has to do with the way labor markets function. Pay at the top of most professions is subject to a form of competition known as **winner-take-all**, which exists when extremely small differences in ability lead to sizable differences in compensation. This compensation structure has been common in professional sports and in the entertainment industry for many years, but it can also be found the legal profession, medicine, journalism, investment banking, fashion design, and corporate management.

In a winner-take-all market, being a little bit better than your rivals can be worth a tremendous amount. For example, in 2007 baseball player Alex Rodriguez received a ten-year contract worth $275 million, or $27.5 million a year. As good as Rodriguez is, he is not ten times better than an average major league baseball player, who makes almost $3 million. Nor is he a thousand times better than a typical minor league player, who earns a few thousand dollars a month. In fact, it is hard to tell the difference between a baseball game played by major and minor leaguers. Minor league pitchers throw just about as hard, the players run almost as fast, and the fielding is almost as good. Yet major league players make hundreds of times more. Winner-take-all has

Winner-take-all
exists when extremely small differences in ability lead to sizable differences in compensation.

also found its way into corporate America. Exploding CEO pay is a relatively recent phenomenon in U.S. history, growing from an average of 35 times the salary of the average American worker in 1975 to 150 times by 1990. According to some estimates, CEO salaries today are more than 500 times greater than that of the average worker.

Paying so much to a relatively small set of workers may sound unfair, but the prospect of much higher pay or bonuses motivates many ambitious employees to exert maximum effort. If we look beyond how much some get paid, we can see that winner-take-all creates incentives that encourage supremely talented workers to maximize their abilities.

- What are three examples of a compensating differential?
- Why is wage discrimination difficult to prove?
- What is the difference between a compensating differential and winner-take-all?

Inequality of Income

Income inequality exists when some workers earn more than others. Compensating differentials, discrimination, corruption, and differences in the marginal product of labor all lead to inequality of income. Would it surprise you to learn that we shouldn't want everyone to have the same income? Income inequality is a fact of life in a market economy. In this section we first examine why income inequality exists. Once we understand the factors that lead to income inequality, we examine how it is measured. Income inequality is difficult to measure and is also easily misinterpreted, so we spend considerable time explaining how observed income inequality statistics are constructed and what they mean. We end by discussing income mobility, a trait in many developed nations that lessens the impact of income inequality of the life cycle.

The Factors That Lead to Income Inequality

To help you understand the nature of income inequality, we begin with a simple question: "What would it take to equalize wages?"

For all workers to get the same wages, three conditions would have to be met. First, every worker would have the same skills, ability, and productivity. Every job would be equally attractive. Finally, all workers would be perfectly mobile. In other words, perfect equality of income would require that workers be clones who perform the same job. Be glad we don't live in a world like that! In the real world, some people work harder and are more productive. Some people, like aid workers, missionaries, teachers, and even ski bums, choose to earn less. What makes us unique—our traits, our desires, and our differences—is also part of what leads to income inequality.

Income inequality is perfectly consistent with the forces that govern a market economy. Each society must determine how much inequality it is able it tolerate and understand the unintended consequences of reducing income inequality. If society's income structure is too equal, the incentive to work hard is diminished—many of us will slack off, or free-ride on the efforts of others.

There are also institutional impediments that can lead to greater income inequality. Some societies value the rule of law more than others. In the next section we look at how corruption contributes to income inequality.

The Role of Corruption in Income Inequality

All economic systems require trust in order to exact gains from trade. However, many less developed countries suffer from widespread corruption. Corruption can play a large role in income inequality. In societies where corruption is common, working hard or being innovative is not enough; getting ahead often requires bribing officials to obtain business permits or to ward off competitors. In some places, people cannot be sure their assets are safe from government seizure or criminals, and investors are therefore less likely to develop a business. Political systems that are subject to bribery and other forms of corruption allow dishonest people to benefit at the expense of the poor. As a result, when corruption is common, people learn that short-run gains can be achieved through manipulation and dishonesty rather than investing in long-term projects based on sound cost-benefit analysis. Recognizing the damage caused by corruption has led people to fight back. For example, 5th Pillar, an independent organization, has developed zero rupee notes in India where corruption is rampant. The note is a way for persons who are asked for a bribe to indicate that they are not willing to participate. Presenting a zero rupee note lets the other person know that you refuse to give or take any money for services required by law or to give or take money for an illegal activity. Since the 5th Pillar reports attempted bribery to the authorities, persons brave enough to use them know that they are not alone in fighting corruption.

Corruption drives out legitimate business opportunities and magnifies income inequality. In the next section we look at how economists measure income inequality.

Measuring Inequality

In order to understand when income inequality is a serious concern or simply exists as part of the normal functioning of the market, we begin with an examination of income inequality in the United States. Economists look at the distribution of household income in the United States by quintiles, or five equal groups, ranging from the poorest fifth of households to the top fifth. Figure 15.2 shows the most recent data available, for the year 2008.

The poorest 20 percent of households earn just 3.4 percent of all income earned in the United States. The next quintile, the second fifth, earns 8.6 percent of income. This means that 40 percent of U.S. households account for only 12 percent of earned income. The middle quintile earns 14.7 percent, the second-highest quintile 23.3 percent, and the top quintile earns 50.0 percent. The figure shows the wide disparity between the percent of total U.S. income earned by the poorest households (3.4 percent) and the households in the top quintile (50.0 percent). If we divide the percent of income earned by households in the top fifth by the percent of income earned by households in the bottom fifth, we get about 14.5. Looking at the numbers this way, we can say that households in the top fifth have approximately 14.5 times the income of those in the bottom fifth. That number, viewed in isolation, makes the amount of income inequality in the United States look large.

To provide some perspective, Table 15.5 compares the income inequality in various countries from around the world. The countries above the middle line are more developed and those below are less developed.

As you can see, the United States has an income inequality ratio that is high compared to other highly developed nations, but relatively low compared to less developed nations. In general, highly developed nations have lower degrees of income inequality. This occurs because more developed countries have less poverty, so those at the bottom of the income ladder earn more than the poor in other countries.

Understanding Observed Inequality

Translating income inequality into a number, as we've done with the income quintiles, can mask the true nature of income inequality. In this section we step back and consider what income inequality ratios can, and cannot, tell us.

Since the inequality ratio measures the success of the top earners against the bottom earners, if the bottom group is doing relatively well, the inequality ratio will be smaller. This explains why many highly developed countries have ratios under 10. However, the United States has an inequality ratio that is close to 16. What is driving the difference? The United States has many highly successful workers and poverty rates that are similar to those found in other highly developed countries. According to the Organization for Economic Cooperation and Development (OECD), the average poverty rate is 26.4 percent among highly developed nations. By comparison, the

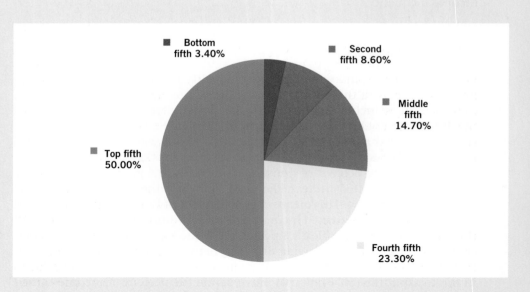

FIGURE 15.2

The Distribution of Income in the United States by Quintile

This pie chart shows the income earned by each quintile. The top fifth makes 50 percent of all income, an amount equal to the combined income of the four remaining quintiles. Income declines across the quintiles, falling to 3.4 percent in the lowest fifth.
Source: U.S. Bureau of the Census, *Income, Poverty, and Health Insurance Coverage in the United States, 2008*. Available at www.census.gov.

Bottom fifth 3.40%

Second fifth 8.60%

Middle fifth 14.70%

Top fifth 50.00%

Fourth fifth 23.30%

TABLE 15.5

Inequality in Selected Countries

Country	Inequality Ratio (of the richest 10% to the poorest 10%)
Japan	4.5
Germany	6.9
Canada	9.4
United Kingdom	13.8
United States	15.9
Mexico	21.0
Brazil	40.6
Bolivia	93.9
Namibia	106.6

Source: United Nations Development Programme, *Human Development Report 2009*, Table M. Available at http://hdr.undp.org.

United States has a poverty rate of 26.3 percent, and Japan and the United Kingdom, two countries with markedly lower inequality ratios, have poverty rates of 26.9 and 26.3 percent, respectively. (The OECD defines poverty differently than the U.S. government. The OECD poverty rate is defined as the percentage of people living on less than half of the median household income.) Given that the poverty rate in the United States is not unusually large, we cannot explain the higher inequality ratio by pointing to the percentage of poor people. Rather, it is the relative success of the top income earners in the United States compared with other highly developed countries that causes the markedly higher inequality ratio. This means that the inequality ratios in Japan and United Kingdom are deceptively low.

High levels of income inequality also occur when the poorest are *really* poor. There are many successful people in Mexico, Brazil, Bolivia, and Namibia. The problem in these countries is that the success of some people is benchmarked against the extreme poverty of many. Therefore, high inequality ratios are a telltale sign of a serious poverty problem. For example, suppose that the poorest quintile of the population in Bolivia has an average income of $500, while those in the top quintile earn $47,000. The income inequality ratio is 47,000 ÷ 500 ≈ 94.0. By comparison, consider Canada. If the poorest quintile of the population in Canada has an average income of $5,000, while those in the top quintile earn $47,000, the income inequality ratio is 47,000 ÷ 5,000 = 9.4. In both countries the top quintile is doing equally well, but it is the widespread poverty problem in Bolivia that produces the alarming income inequality ratio. A high income inequality ratio can exist if people at the bottom earn very little or if the income of high wage earners is much greater than the income of others. The key point to remember is that while income inequality ratios give us some idea about the amount of inequality in a society, a single number cannot fully reflect the sources of the underlying differences in income.

Difficulties in Measuring Inequality

In-kind transfers
are transfers (mostly to the poor) in the form of goods or services instead of cash.

Not only can income inequality numbers be misinterpreted, they are often unreliable. Because inequality data reflects income before taxes, it does not reflect disposable income, which is the portion of income that people actually have to spend. Nor does the data account for **in-kind transfers**—goods and services given to the poor instead of cash. Examples of in-kind services include government housing and the Subsidized Nutrition Assistance Program that provides food supplements to 35 million low-income citizens in the United States. In addition, the data does not account for unreported or illegally obtained income. Because less developed countries generally have larger underground economies, their income data is even less reliable.

In addition to these problems, many economists note that using only income data does not capture the value created from goods and services produced in the household. For example, if you mow your own lawn or grow your own vegetables, those activities have a positive value that is not expressed in income data. In less developed countries, many households engage in very few market transactions and produce a large portion of their own goods and services. If we do not count these, a comparison of data with other countries will overstate the amount of inequality present in the less developed countries. Finally, the number of workers per household and the median age of each worker differs from country to country. When households contain more workers or those workers are, on average, older and therefore more experienced, comparing inequality across countries is less likely to be accurate.

Individually, none of these shortcomings poses a serious measurement issue from year to year. However, if you try to measure differences in income across generations, the changes are enough to invalidate the *ceteris paribus* condition that allows us to assume outside factors are held constant. In short, comparing inequality data from this year with last year is generally fine, but comparing inequality data today with fifty years ago is largely meaningless. For instance, we might note that income inequality in the United States increased slightly from 2011 to 2012. However, since this is just a single data point we must be cautious about interpreting it as a trend. To eliminate that problem, we can extend the time frame from 1962 to 2012. That data shows an unmistakable upward trend in income inequality, but *ceteris paribus* is also violated; the last fifty years have seen dramatic shifts in tax rates, a surge in in-kind transfers, lower birthrates, and an aging population. Decomposing the impact of these changes on income inequality is a complex task. As a result, a good economist tries to make relevant comparisons, but only by comparing similar countries over a relatively short period of time without significant social changes.

Finally, the standard calculations and models that we have looked at assume that the income distribution is a direct reflection of a society's welfare. However, we must be very careful not to infer too much about how well people are living based on their income alone. In Chapter 16 we will see that income is only one factor that determines human happiness and well-being. People also value leisure time, nonwage benefits, a sense of community, safety from crime, and social networks. As a result, income analysis does not offer a complete picture of human welfare.

PRACTICE WHAT YOU KNOW

Consider two communities, Alpha and Omega. Alpha has ten residents, five who earn $90,000, and five who earn $30,000. Omega also has ten residents; five earn $250,000 and the other five earn $50,000.

Calculate the degree of inequality in each community.

Answer: To answer this question we must use quintile analysis. Since there are ten residents in Alpha, the top two earners represent the top quintile and the lowest two earners represent the bottom quintile. Therefore, the degree of inequality using quintile analysis is $90,000 ÷ $30,000, or 3. In Omega, the top two earners represent the top quintile and lowest two earners represent the bottom quintile. Therefore, the degree of inequality is $250,000 ÷ $50,000, or 5.

Question: Which community has the more unequal distribution of income?

Answer: Omega has the more unequal distribution of income since the quintile analysis yields 5, versus 3 for Alpha.

Question: Can you think of a reason why someone might prefer to live in Omega?

Each rich citizen of Omega earns more than each rich citizen in Alpha and each poor citizen earns more than each poor citizen of Alpha. Sure, there is more inequality in Omega, but there is also more income across the entire income distribution. So depending on your preferences, you could prefer Omega if the absolute amount of income is what matters more to you, or Alpha if relative equality is what you value more.

Income Mobility

We have seen that income inequality statistics can be misleading and that they can also be unreliable. In this section we focus on the ability of workers to move up or down the economic ladder. When workers have a realistic chance of moving up the economic ladder, each person has an incentive to work harder and invest in human capital. **Income mobility** is the ability of workers to move up or down the economic ladder over time. Think of it this way: if today's poor must remain poor tomorrow and twenty years from now, income inequality remains high. However, if someone in the lowest income category can expect to experience enough economic success to move to a higher income quintile, being poor is a temporary condition. Why does this matter? Economic mobility reduces inequality over long periods of time.

Table 15.6 reports income mobility in the United States over a ten-year period, 1996–2005, among taxpayers over the age of 25. The dynamic nature of the U.S. economy is captured by income mobility data. This result can be seen by examining the values on the main diagonal, in red. These represent the percentage of earners in each quintile who remained there ten years later. Note that the percentage of people who stayed in a particular quintile is

Income mobility
is the ability of workers to move up or down the economic ladder over time.

TABLE 15.6					
Income Mobility in the United States					
1996 Income Quintile	**2005 INCOME QUINTILE**				
	Lowest	**Second**	**Middle**	**Fourth**	**Highest**
Lowest	42.4	23.7	10.8	6.9	3.6
Second	17.0	37.1	21.9	10.6	5.6
Middle	7.1	23.4	34.1	23.0	8.7
Fourth	4.1	11.0	24.2	38.1	20.8
Highest	2.6	4.7	9.0	21.5	61.4

Source: *Income Mobility in the U.S. from 1996 to 2005*, U.S. Department of the Treasury, November 13, 2007.

smallest in the middle (34.1) and largest at the extremes (42.4 and 61.4). In other words, people in the middle quintile have the greatest mobility.

Those in the highest quintile experience the least mobility, though you won't hear people at the top of the economic ladder complain about remaining well to do. A lack of mobility is a problem in the lowest quintile, where 42.4 percent remained after almost ten years. The remainder, or 57.6 percent, advanced at least one quintile. This data shows that mobility, even among those in the lowest quintile, is the norm.

The idea of mobility allows us to separate those at the bottom of the economic ladder into two groups: (1) the *marginal poor*, or people who are poor at a particular point in time but have the skills necessary to advance up the ladder, and (2) the *long-term poor*, or people who lack the skills to advance to the next quintile. The differences in income mobility among the marginal poor and long-term poor provide a helpful way of understanding how mobility affects poverty.

For the marginal poor, low earnings are the exception. Since most young workers expect to make higher incomes as they get older, many are willing to borrow in order to make a big purchase—for example, a car or a home. Conversely, middle-aged workers know that retirement will be possible only if they save now for the future. As a result, workers in their fifties have much higher savings rates than young workers and also higher savings rates than workers who are already retired. Upon reaching retirement, earnings fall, but if the worker has saved enough, retirement need not be a period of low consumption. The life-cycle theory argues that the changes in borrowing and savings patterns over one's life smooth out the spending pattern.

When we examine how people actually live in societies with substantial mobility, the cursory glance at the annual income inequality data creates a false impression about the spending patterns of the rich and poor. This occurs because the young, who have lower incomes, are spending more than you might expect by borrowing; the middle-aged, who have relative high incomes, spend less than you might expect because they are saving for retirement; and the elderly, who have lower incomes, spend more than you might expect because they are drawing down their retirement savings. The result for many people is that low incomes do not necessarily equate with a low standard of living.

In the next section, we turn our attention to the long-term poor who do not have the skills to escape the lowest quintile. People in this group live their entire lives near or below the poverty threshold.

- Is income equality desirable?
- What is the life cycle?
- How does income mobility lessen income inequality?

Poverty

The United States does not have a wealth problem, but it does have a poverty problem. According to the Census Bureau, close to 15 percent of all households are below the poverty threshold. To help us understand the issues we will begin with the poverty statistics. Then, once we understand the scope of the problem, we will examine policy solutions.

The Poverty Rate

For the last fifty years the U.S. Bureau of the Census has been tracking the **poverty rate**, or the percentage of the population whose income is below the *poverty threshold*. The **poverty threshold** is the income level below which a person or family is considered impoverished. The specific threshold is set at approximately three times the amount of income required to afford a nutritionally balanced diet. To keep up with inflation, the poverty threshold is adjusted each year for changes in the level of prices. However, an individual family's threshold is calculated to include only the money income earned by family members in the household. It does not include in-kind transfers, nor is the data adjusted for differences in the cost of living in the family's specific geographic area. For these reasons, poverty thresholds are a crude yardstick. Figure 15.3 shows the poverty rate for households in the United States from 1959 to 2010.

The **poverty rate** is the percentage of the population whose income is below the poverty threshold.

The **poverty threshold** is the income level below which a person or family is considered impoverished.

FIGURE 15.3

The Poverty Rate for Households

Poverty rates for households remained in a small range from the late 1960s through 2008. Since then the poverty rate has spiked due to the Great Recession.
Source: U.S. Bureau of the Census.

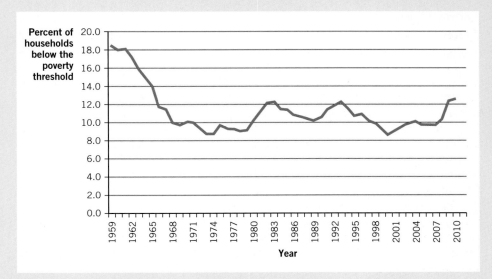

In 1964, Congress passed the Economic Opportunity Act and a number of other measures designed to fight poverty. Despite those initiatives, the rate of poverty today is slightly higher than it was 40 years ago. This result is surprising, since the economy's output has roughly doubled in that time. One would have hoped that the progress of the economy would have been felt by those at the bottom of the economic ladder, as well as at the top. Unfortunately, the stagnant poverty rate suggests that the gains from economic growth over that time span have accrued to households in the middle and upper quintiles, rather than the poor. Poverty has remained persistent, in part, because many low-income workers lack the necessary skills to earn living wages. This is not something that can be easily solved by public-sector job initiatives—it will require a long-run investment in education programs targeted at the poor and retraining programs designed to help structurally unemployed workers attain jobs in growing segments of the economy.

Table 15.7 illustrates that the incidence of poverty is felt disproportionately by the young, women, and minorities. When you combine at-risk groups—for example, minority women—the poverty rates can approach 50 percent.

In the next section we look at how public policy can address the issue of poverty. As Table 15.7 shows, poverty is a wide-ranging and multifaceted problem. Therefore, constructing policies that are targeted at specific groups will be more effective.

TABLE 15.7

The Poverty Rate for Various Groups

Group	Poverty Rate (percent)
Age:	
Children (under 18)	19.0
Adults (18–64)	11.7
Elderly (65 or older)	9.7
Race:	
White	8.6
Asian	11.8
Hispanic	23.2
Black	24.7
Type of household:	
Married couple	5.5
Male head only	13.3
Female head only	28.7

Source: U.S. Bureau of the Census, 2008.

Poverty Policy

In this section we outline a number of policies designed to address the problem of poverty. Each policy comes with costs and benefits. As a result, efforts to help the poor must be thought through carefully. Policies do not always distinguish between the truly needy and those who can help themselves. Therefore, in order to help the poor, we encounter two conflicting motivations: we want to give generously, but we also want the poor to become self-sufficient and eventually contribute to society. Almost everyone agrees that both goals are vital. Unfortunately, achieving both simultaneously has proven to be almost impossible.

Welfare

"Welfare" is not a government program but a term that describes a series of initiatives designed to help the poor by supplementing their income. Welfare can come in a variety of forms, such as monetary payments, subsidies and vouchers, health services, or housing. Welfare is provided by the government and other private and public organizations. It is intended to help the unemployed, those with illnesses or disabilities that prevent them from working, the elderly, veterans, and households with dependent children. An individual's eligibility for welfare is often limited to a set amount of time and is available only as long as the recipient's income remains below the eligibility cutoff. Some examples of welfare programs include: Temporary Assistance for Needy Families (TANF), which provides financial support to families with dependent children; the Supplemental Security Income (SSI) program, which provides financial support to those who are unable to work; and the Subsidized Nutrition Assistance Program (SNAP), which gives financial assistance to those who need help to purchase basic foods.

In-Kind Transfers

In addition to financial assistance, the poor also receive direct assistance in the form of goods and services. Local community food banks, housing shelters, and private charities like Habitat for Humanity and Toys for Tots each provide in-kind benefits to the poor. The government also gives out food stamps and provides health care to the poor through Medicaid.

The idea behind in-kind transfers is that they protect recipients from the possibility of making poor decisions if they are given cash. Recipients may choose to use cash transfers to feed drug or alcohol addictions, gamble, or spend their funds frivolously on vacations, expensive clothes, or fancy meals. None of these decisions will alleviate the future need for food, clothing, and shelter. To curtail the "poor" decisions made by recipients when they receive cash transfers, in-kind transfers can be targeted at essential services.

The Earned Income Tax Credit (EITC)

The Earned Income Tax Credit (EITC) is a refundable tax credit designed to encourage low-income workers to work more. At very low income levels the EITC offers an incentive to work by supplementing earned income with a tax credit that can reduce the amount of taxes owed by as much as $6,000 a year.

The amount is determined, in part, by the number of dependent children in the household and the family's location. Once a family reaches an income level above its earnings threshold, the EITC is phased out and workers gradually lose the tax credit benefits that they had been receiving. In many welfare and in-kind transfer programs, the qualifying income is a specific cutoff point: you are either eligible or not. However, the EITC is gradually reduced, which means that workers do not encounter a sizable disincentive to work as the program is phased out.

The EITC helps over 20 million families, making it the largest poverty-fighting program in the United States. EITC payments are sufficient to lift more than five million households out of poverty. In addition, the EITC creates stronger work incentives than found under traditional welfare and in-kind transfer programs.

A **negative income tax** is a credit paid to poor households out of taxes received from middle- and upper-income households.

The EITC is a form of *negative income tax*. A **negative income tax** is a tax credit paid to poor households out of taxes collected from middle- and upper-income taxpayers. For example, suppose that a household's tax liability is computed based on the following formula:

$$\text{Taxes owed} = (.25 \text{ of your income}) - \$10{,}000$$

Table 15.8 shows taxes that would be owed using this formula at various income levels.

At any income below $40,000, the government pays a credit. People with incomes above $40,000 owe taxes. Although taxes in the real world are far more complex, economists have long admired the simple elegance of the negative income tax, and this is essentially how the EITC, with a few extra wrinkles, works in practice.

The Minimum Wage

The minimum wage is often viewed as an antipoverty measure. However, we learned in Chapter 5 that the minimum wage cannot create jobs or guarantee higher pay. Despite rhetoric that trumpets the minimum wage as a potential cure to poverty, in reality low-skill workers lack productivity. Predictably, firms respond to higher minimum wages by hiring fewer workers and utilizing more capital-intensive production processes. Since the minimum wage does not guarantee employment, it only offers hope for a slightly higher wage

TABLE 15.8

How the Negative Income Tax Works

Income	Calculation	Tax Owed/Credit
$80,000	($80,000 × .25) − $10,000	$10,000
$60,000	($60,000 × .25) − $10,000	$5,000
$40,000	($40,000 × .25) − $10,000	$0
$20,000	($20,000 × .25) − $10,000	−$5,000
$0	($0 × .25) − $10,000	−$10,000

if employers continue to hire the same number of low-skill workers as before. The real problem remains: some workers lack skills, motivation, or both, and cannot improve their earning ability by means of a minimum wage law.

Problems with Traditional Aid

Many welfare programs create work disincentives. A serious incentive problem arises when we examine the combined effects of welfare and in-kind transfer programs. Many benefits are severely reduced, or curtailed altogether, once certain income thresholds are reached. This leads low-income workers to consciously work less in order to maintain eligibility for government assistance.

To see why this matters, consider a family of five with a combined income of $20,000 a year. Suppose that the family qualifies for additional public assistance that amounts to another $10,000 in benefits. The family's combined income from employment and benefits is $30,000. What happens if another family member gets a part-time job and income from wages rises from $20,000 to $30,000? Under the current law, $30,000 disqualifies the family from receiving most of the financial assistance it had been receiving. As a result, their benefits fall from $10,000 to $2,000 per year. The family nets $32,000 in total. The person who secured employment may feel that this isn't worth it. The family earned an additional $10,000 but lost $8,000 in "welfare" benefits. Since they are only able to raise their net income by $2,000, they have effectively returned $8,000. The loss of benefits feels like an 80 percent tax, which creates a large disincentive to work.

This is a basic dilemma in creating poverty-reducing programs; programs that provide substantial benefits discourage participation in the workforce because once the recipient starts to work, he no longer qualifies for the benefits and loses them. Among the three options we have discussed so far, the EITC does the best job of addressing the work incentive problem by phasing out assistance to the poor at a gradual rate.

While few dispute that welfare program programs are well intentioned, many economists are concerned about the unintended consequences that welfare programs create. A society that establishes a generous welfare package for the poor will find that it faces a *Samaritan's dilemma*. A **Samaritan's dilemma** occurs when an act of charity creates disincentives for recipients to take care of themselves. President Bill Clinton addressed this concern in 1996 when he vowed "to end welfare as we know it." As part of the TANF program, Clinton changed the payout structure for federal assistance and encouraged states to require employment searches as a condition for aid. In addition, the TANF program imposed a five-year maximum for the time a recipient could receive benefits. This changed welfare from an entitlement under the law into a temporary safety-net program, thereby reducing the Samaritan's dilemma.

Samaritan's dilemma
occurs when an act of charity causes the recipient not to work hard on their own to try to escape poverty.

ECONOMICS IN THE REAL WORLD

Muhammad Yunus and the Grameen Bank

One economist, Muhammad Yunus, stands alone. In 2006, he received the Nobel Peace Prize for his work helping poor families in Bangladesh. What did Yunus do to win that honor? He founded the Grameen Bank, which was instrumental in creating a new type of loan that has extended more than $8 billion to the poor in an effort to eliminate extreme poverty.

The Grameen Bank gives out very small loans, known as *microcredit*, to the poor of Bangladesh who are unable to qualify for conventional loans from traditional lenders. The loans are provided without collateral and repayment is based on an honor system. By conventional standards that sounds preposterous, but it works! The Grameen Bank reports a 99 percent repayment rate, and according to one survey, over 50 percent of the families of Grameen borrowers have crossed the poverty line.

It all started with less than $50. In 1974, Yunus, who was trained as an economist in the United States, returned to Bangladesh and lent a total of $27 to 42 villagers who made bamboo furniture. The loans, which were all paid back, allowed them to cut out the middlemen and purchase their own raw materials. A few years later Yunus won government approval to open the Grameen Bank, named for the Bengali word for "rural."

Yunus had a truly innovative idea. In order to receive a loan, applicants must belong to a five-member group. Once the first two members begin to pay back their loans, the others can get theirs. While there is no group responsibility for returning the loans, the Grameen Bank believes it creates a sense of social responsibility, ensuring that all members will pay back their loans. More important, Yunus made a bet that people would honor their commitments, and he was proven right. With just a few dollars, Yunus changed the perception about how to best fight poverty in the third world—how remarkable is that! ✳

ECONOMICS IN THE REAL WORLD

Dress for Success

The mission of Dress for Success is to promote the economic independence of disadvantaged women by providing professional attire, a network of support, and the career development tools to help women thrive in work and in life.

Founded in 1997, Dress for Success is an international not-for-profit organization. Each Dress for Success client receives one suit when she has a job interview. When she finds work, she can return for a second suit or separates. Dress for Success has served more half a million women around the world.

While the organization is best known for providing suits to women, it is primarily concerned with employment retention. Remaining employed and building a rewarding career is essential if more women are to become self-sufficient. ✳

- Name four policies designed to fight poverty.
- What is the Samaritan's dilemma and how does it affect poverty policy?

Conclusion

Income inequality, a measure of the disparity between the rich and the poor, is often misunderstood. As we have seen, income inequality in itself is neither good nor bad. However, if incomes are too equal, the incentive to work hard is reduced; if incomes are too unequal, it can lead to political and economic unrest. As a consequence, decision-makers must design policies that strike a balance between these opposing forces in order to create the right incentives for economic growth.

Since the long-term poor are perpetually below the poverty threshold, welfare policies must also differentiate between those who are temporarily impoverished and those who need more long-term assistance. The EITC program gives the marginal poor incentives to escape poverty, while welfare and other in-kind transfers create a safety net for those who need more assistance. The challenge for policy makers is designing aid programs so that they provide a safety net for the long-term poor while creating disincentives for the marginal poor to remain on welfare. Since some degree of income inequality is inevitable, policies that reduce inequality too much will result in decreased work incentives.

Summary

- Nonmonetary determinants of earnings include compensating differentials, human capital, location, lifestyle, unions, and efficiency wages.
- Economic studies of wage discrimination have found that the amount of discrimination is relatively small—accounting for 3 to 5 percent of wage differences.
- Despite recent gains, women still earn significantly less than men. The wage gap can be partially explained by occupational crowding. As long as supply imbalances remain in traditional male and female jobs, significant wage differences will continue exist.
- Some amount of income inequality is to be expected in a market economy. Income inequality is measured by using quintile analysis.
- Economic mobility reduces inequality over long periods of time. Due to the life cycle, we see that distinct borrowing and saving patterns over one's life smooth out the spending pattern. Therefore, in societies with substantial mobility the annual income inequality data overstates the amount of inequality.
- The poverty rate in the United States has been stagnant for the last 40 years, despite many efforts (welfare, in-kind transfers, and the EITC) designed to reduce it.

CONCEPTS YOU SHOULD KNOW

Compensating differentials
  (p. 436)
Efficiency wages (p. 439)
Human capital (p. 436)
Income mobility (p. 451)
In-kind transfers (p. 450)

Life cycle (p. 442)
Negative income tax (p. 456)
Occupational crowding (p. 443)
Poverty rate (p. 453)
Poverty threshold (p. 453)

Samaritan's dilemma (p. 457)
Strike (p. 438)
Union (p. 438)
Wage discrimination (p. 440)
Winner-take-all (p. 445)

QUESTIONS

1. Why do garbage collectors make more than furniture movers?

2. What are efficiency wages? Why are some employers willing to pay them?

3. Why is it difficult to determine the amount of wage discrimination in the workplace?

4. Discuss some of the reasons that working women make, on average, 77 percent as much as full-time working men.

5. How does the degree of income inequality in the United States compare to that in similarly developed countries? How does U.S. income inequality compare with that in less developed nations?

6. Why do high rates of income mobility mitigate income inequality?

7. Which antipoverty program (welfare, in-kind transfers, or the Earned Income Tax Credit) creates the strongest incentive to work? Why?

STUDY PROBLEMS

1. Suppose that a wealthy friend asks your advice on how to reduce income inequality. Your friend wants to know if it would be better to give $100 million to poor people who will never attend college, or $100 million in financial aid to students who could not otherwise afford to attend college. What advice would you give?

2. What effect would doubling the minimum wage have on income inequality? Explain your answer.

3. Suppose that society restricted the economic opportunities of right-handed persons to jobs in construction, while left-handed persons could work any job.
   a. Would the wages in construction be higher or lower than in other jobs?
   b. Would left-handed workers make more or less than righties?
   c. Now suppose that right-handers are allowed to work any job they like. What effect will

   this change have on the wages of right- and left-handers over time?

4. Internships are considered a vital stepping-stone to full-time employment after college, but not all internship positions are paid. Why do some students take unpaid internships when they could be working summer jobs and earning an income? Include a discussion of human capital in your answer.

5. Consider two communities. In Middletown, two families earn $40,000, six families earn $50,000, and two earn $60,000. In Polarity, four families earn $10,000, two earn $50,000, and four earn $90,000. Which community has the most unequal distribution of income?

6. Look at the following mobility table. Do you think the mobility it shows would be desirable? Explain your answer.

INCOME QUINTILE	INCOME QUINTILE FIVE YEARS LATER				
	Lowest	Second	Middle	Fourth	Highest
Lowest	**0.0**	10.0	20.0	30.0	40.0
Second	10.0	**0.0**	10.0	20.0	60.0
Middle	40.0	10.0	**0.0**	10.0	40.0
Fourth	60.0	20.0	10.0	**0.0**	10.0
Highest	40.0	30.0	20.0	10.0	**0.0**

7. The government is considering three possible welfare programs:
   a. Give everyone $10,000.
   b. Give everyone $20,000 minus the recipient's income.
   c. Give everyone two times their income, where the maximum they can receive in benefits is capped at $10,000.

Which program does the most to help the poor? Describe the work incentives under each program.

8. The United States has attracted many highly productive immigrants who work in fields like education, health, and technology. How do these immigrants affect the income inequality in this country? Is this type of immigration good or bad for the United States? What impact is this type of immigration having on the countries that are losing some of their best workers?

9. Suppose that a company has ten employees. It agrees to pay each worker based on productivity. The output of the workers is 10, 14, 15, 16, 18, 19, 21, 23, 25, and 30 units. However, some of the workers complain that they are making less than the other workers, so they appeal to management to help reduce the income inequality. As a result, the company decides to pay each of the workers the same salary. However, the next time the company measures the output of each worker they find 6, 7, 7, 8, 10, 10, 11, 11, 12, and 12 units are produced. Why did this happen? Would you recommend that the company continue the new compensation system?

Photo to come

Special Topics in
MICROECONOMICS

The more money you have, the happier you'll be.

Imagine it is a hot afternoon and you decide to make a quick stop at a convenience store for a cold drink. While you are in the store you decide

to get a snack as well. Brownies are your favorite, but apple pie is on sale and you choose that instead. You may not think about these purchases very carefully, but they involve several trade-offs, including the time you could use to do something else and the money that could have been spent on something else.

If brownies are your favorite dessert, why do you sometimes choose to eat a slice of apple pie? Why do many people pay thousands of dollars for diamond jewelry, when it is not essential for life, and yet pay only pennies for water? These are the kinds of questions we must answer if we are to understand how people make personal buying decisions. We also address the misperception that money can buy happiness. More money is better, right? Not so fast! There are two important issues to consider: the satisfaction that you receive from the choices you make and the constraints of a limited budget.

In this chapter we will use our understanding of income constraints, price, and personal satisfaction to determine which economic choices bring the greatest benefits.

Photo to come

BIG QUESTIONS

＊ **How do economists model consumer satisfaction?**

＊ **How do consumers optimize their decisions?**

＊ **What is the diamond-water paradox?**

Modeling Consumer Satisfaction

Utility
measures the satisfaction that consumers enjoy from the consumption of goods and services.

Utility is a measure of the relative levels of satisfaction consumers enjoy from the consumption of goods and services. Utility theory seeks to measure contentment, or satisfaction. To understand why people buy the goods and services they do, we need to recognize that some products produce more utility than others and that everyone receives different levels of satisfaction from the same good or service; utility varies from individual to individual. To quantify this idea of relative satisfaction, economists measure utility with a unit they refer to as a "util."

There is tremendous value in modeling decisions this way. When we understand utility we can explain what people are likely to purchase. This process is similar to the models we used to describe the decisions of the firm or how the labor market works. We expect the firm to maximize profits, the laborer to accept the best offer, and the consumer to find the combination of goods that gives the most utility. For example, a brownie lover may get 25 utils from her favorite dessert, but someone who is less susceptible to the pleasures of warm, gooey chocolate may rate the same brownie at 10 utils. However, even this is not a completely accurate measurement of relative utility. Who can say whether one person's 25 is more than another person's 10? Even if you and a friend agree that you received 10 utils from eating the brownie, you cannot say that you both received the same amount of happiness; each has a unique personal scale. However, the level of enjoyment one receives can be internally consistent. For example, if you rate a brownie 25 utils and a slice of apple pie 15 utils, we know that you like brownies more than apple pie.

Utility, or what most of us think of as happiness, is a balance between economic and personal factors. Even though there is an inherent problem with equating money and happiness, this has not stopped researchers from exploring the connection.

ECONOMICS IN THE REAL WORLD

Happiness Index

Since 2006, the Organization for Economic Co-Operation and Development (OECD) has compiled a happiness index that includes social variables alongside economic data for 34 highly developed countries. Which country topped the list? Denmark came in first, followed closely by Finland and then the Netherlands.

What makes Northern Europeans so happy? It's not the weather—it is often cold and grey in Scandinavia. The OECD used data from a Gallup poll conducted in over 100 countries. The Gallup poll asked six questions about how people felt on a scale of 0–100. The average score for each of the countries was 62.4 out of 100.

While it was clear that income matters some, it did not matter as much as you would think. For instance, Norway had the highest per capita income at $98,822 and it ranked ninth. But New Zealand, with a per capita income of $30,556, ranked ahead of Norway. Just as important as money were family and social and community networks. In China, workers average almost 50 hours a week on the job, or about 15 hours more than in many more-developed countries. Not surprisingly, China checked in with an abysmal score of 14.8 in the survey. A typical Chinese worker has a per capita income of $3,600, and they work awfully hard to earn it. Long hours on the job, along with low levels of personal freedom, contribute to the miserable Chinese happiness score. By the way, the United States scored well in the rankings, finishing a respectable twelfth, with an average score of 74 out of 100. ✳

In the next section we explore the connection between total and marginal utility. This connection will help us understand why more money does not necessarily bring more happiness.

Total and Marginal Utility

Thinking about choices that consumers make can help us understand how to increase total utility. Consider the person who really likes brownies. In this case, the **marginal utility** is the extra satisfaction enjoyed from consuming one more. In Figure 16.1 we see that the first brownie brings 25 utils. Eating additional brownies increases total utility until it reaches 75 utils after eating five brownies.

Looking at the graph in Figure 16.1a reveals that while the total utility (the blue curve) rises until it reaches 75, the rate of increase slowly falls from 25 utils for the first brownie down to five additional utils for the fifth. The marginal utility values from the table are graphed on panel b, which shows that marginal utility declines steadily as consumption rises.

The relationship between total utility and marginal utility can be seen by observing the dashed line that connects panels a and b. Since the marginal utility becomes negative after five brownies are consumed the total utility eventually falls. To the left of the dotted line, the marginal utility is positive in panel b and the total utility is rising in panel a. Conversely, to the right of the dashed line the marginal utility is negative and total utility is falling.

When marginal utility becomes negative, it means that the consumer is tired of eating brownies. At that point the brownies are no longer adding to the consumer's utility and a rational consumer will stop eating them. Even with brownies, too much of a good thing is undesirable.

Marginal utility is the additional satisfaction derived from consuming one more unit of a good or service.

Diminishing Marginal Utility

As you can see in Figure 16.1b, the satisfaction that a consumer derives from consuming a good or service declines with each additional unit consumed. Consider what happens when you participate in a favorite activity for an

Diminishing marginal utility occurs when marginal utility declines as consumption increases.

hour and then decide do something else. **Diminishing marginal utility** occurs when marginal utility declines as consumption increases. The concept of diminishing marginal utility is so universal that it is one of the most widely held ideas in all of economics.

In rare cases, marginal utility can rise—but only temporarily. Consider running. Many people choose to run for recreation because it is both healthy and pleasurable. Often the first mile is difficult as the runner's body gets warmed up. Thereafter, running is easier—for a while. No matter how good you are at distance running, eventually the extra miles become more exhausting and less satisfying, and you stop. This does not mean that running is not healthy or pleasurable—far from it! But it does mean that more running after you have already pushed your limit brings less utility. Your own intuition should confirm this. If increasing marginal utility was possible, you would find that with every passing second you would enjoy what you were doing more and never want to stop. Since we do not observe this behavior among rational consumers, we can be highly confident that diminishing marginal utility has tremendous explanatory power.

FIGURE 16.1

Total and Marginal Utility

The relationship between total utility and marginal utility can be seen by observing the dashed line that connects a and b. Since the marginal utility becomes negative after five brownies are consumed, the total utility eventually falls. To the left of the dashed line, the marginal utility is positive in panel b and the total utility is rising in panel a. Conversely, to the right of the dashed line the marginal utility is negative and total utility is falling.

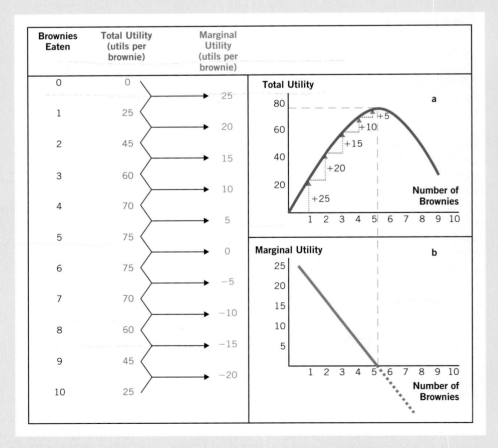

Table 16.1 highlights how diminishing marginal utility can be used to explain a number of interesting real-world situations.

TABLE 16.1

Examples of Diminishing Marginal Utility

Example	Explanation Using Diminishing Marginal Utility
Discounts on two-day passes to amusement parks	The excitement on the first day is palpable—running to rides, waiting in line, and experiencing the thrill for the first time. But by the second day people are not as enthusiastic, so the price must be lower to entice customers to return.
Discounts on season tickets	Over the course of any season there are games and concerts that are highly anticipated and others that are less talked about. In order to get someone to buy the entire season package, the total price must be discounted.
All-you-can-eat buffet	Buffets offer the promise of unlimited food, but the average diner has a limited capacity. Eating more eventually leads to negative marginal utility. Restaurants rely on diminishing utility to regulate how much customers eat.
Unlimited night and weekend minutes on cell phone plans	Cell phone companies rely on the diminishing marginal utility of conversation. Customers grow tired of talking and eventually decide to do something else. Because of unused capacity at night and on the weekends, the cell phone companies offer "unlimited" plans since they know that consumers will not stay on the phone indefinitely.
Newspaper vending machines	A second copy of the same paper is rarely something a person wants, so most people do not steal an extra copy from a vending machine. Since the value of the second paper is close to zero, a rational person will leave it in the machine. (Sunday papers with money-saving coupons are a possible exception.)
Nathan's Famous hot dog eating contest	Most people enjoy eating a hot dog or two at a picnic or tailgate, but Nathan's hot dog eating contest is very difficult to watch.

PRACTICE WHAT YOU KNOW

Diminishing Marginal Utility

Question: A friend confides to you that a third friend has gradually lost interest in watching *Gossip Girl* with her and has begun saying she's too busy. How would you advise your friend to handle the situation?

Answer: Tell your friend about diminishing marginal utility! Even the best television show runs its course. Plot lines become less interesting and the characters more predictable. Then suggest to your friend that they mix it up and do something different together. If that doesn't work, it may not be *Gossip Girl* that is the problem—it may be that your friend's friend has grown tired of her.

Optimizing Consumption Decisions

Maximizing utility requires that consumers get the most satisfaction out of every dollar they spend, or what is more commonly called "getting the biggest bang for your buck." When this is accomplished we say that the consumer has optimized. However, this is easier said than done. Over the course of the year each of us will make thousands of purchases of different amounts. Our budgets are generally not unlimited and we try to spend in a way that allows us to meet both our short-run and long-run needs. The combination of goods and services that maximizes the level of satisfaction that is possible with our income is the consumer optimum. In this section we examine the decision process that leads to the consumer optimum. We will start with two goods and then generalize those findings across a consumer's entire budget.

The **consumer optimum** is the combination of goods and services that maximizes utility for a given income.

How Consumers Decide What to Buy

Let's begin by imagining a world with only two goods: Pepsi and pizza. This will help us to focus on the opportunity cost of purchasing Pepsi instead of pizza or pizza instead of Pepsi.

Pepsi is available for $1 a can and each pizza slice costs $2. Suppose that you have $10 to spend. How much of each good should you buy in order to maximize your satisfaction? Before we can answer that question we need a rule for making decisions. To reach the optimum you must allocate your income by choosing goods that give you the most utility per dollar spent. By attempting to get the biggest bang for your buck, you will end up optimizing your choices. This relationship, shown below, helps quantify this decision. So, if you get more for your money purchasing Pepsi than pizza, you should buy Pepsi, and vice versa.

$$\frac{MU_{Pepsi}}{Price_{Pepsi}} \quad \textbf{Which is larger?} \quad \frac{MU_{pizza}}{Price_{pizza}} \qquad (16.1)$$

If we divide the marginal utility (MU) of a good by its price, we get the utility per dollar spent. Since you wish to optimize your utility, a direct comparison of the marginal utility per dollar spent on Pepsi versus pizza gives you a road map to consumer satisfaction. Table 16.2 shows the marginal utility for each can of Pepsi (column 2) and the marginal utility for each slice of pizza (column 5).

To decide what to consume first, look at column 3, which lists the marginal utility per dollar spent for Pepsi, and column 6, which lists the marginal utility per dollar spent for pizza. Now it's time to make your first spending decision—whether to drink a Pepsi or eat a slice of pizza. Since the marginal utility per dollar spent for the first slice of pizza, 10.0, is higher than the marginal utility for the first can of Pepsi, 9.0, you order a slice of pizza, which costs $2. You have $8 left.

After eating the first slice of pizza, you can choose between a second slice of pizza, which brings 8.0 utils per dollar spent, and the first can of Pepsi,

TABLE 16.2

The Consumer Optimum with Pepsi and Pizza

(1)	(2)	(3)	(4)	(5)	(6)
Pepsi Consumed (cans)	Marginal Utility (MU Pepsi)	MU Pepsi / Price Pepsi (Pepsi $1/can)	Pizza Consumed (slices)	Marginal Utility (MU pizza)	MU Pizza / Price Pizza (pizza $2/slice)
1	9	9/1 = 9.0	1	20	20/2 = 10.0
2	8	8/1 = 8.0	2	16	16/2 = 8.0
3	7	7/1 = 7.0	3	12	**12/2 = 6.0**
4	6	**6/1 = 6.0**	4	8	8/2 = 4.0
5	5	5/1 = 5.0	5	4	4/2 = 2.0
6	4	4/1 = 4.0	6	0	0/2 = 0.0
7	3	3/1 = 3.0	7	−4	−4/2 = −2.0
8	2	2/1 = 2.0	8	−8	−8/2 = −4.0
9	1	1/1 = 1.0	9	−12	−12/2 = −6.0
10	0	0/1 = 0.0	10	−16	−16/2 = −8.0

which brings 9.0 utils per dollar spent. This time you order a Pepsi, which costs $1. You have $7 left.

Now you can choose between a second slice of pizza, 8.0 utils per dollar spent, and the second can of Pepsi, also 8.0 utils per dollar spent. Since the two choices each bring the same amount of utility per dollar spent and you have enough money to afford both, we'll assume you would probably purchase both at the same time. This costs another $3, which leaves you with $4.

Your next choice is between the third slice of pizza at 6.0 utils per dollar spent and the third can of Pepsi at 7.0 utils per dollar spent. Pepsi is the better value, so you buy that. This leaves you with $3 for your final choice, between the third slice of pizza, at 6.0 utils per dollar spent, and the fourth can of Pepsi, also 6.0 utils per dollars spent. Since you have exactly $3 left, and the items are of equal utility, you end your purchases by buying both.

Let's see how well you have done. Looking at column 2 we calculate that the four Pepsis you consumed yielded a total utility of (9 + 8 + 7 + 6) = 30 utils. Looking at column 5, we see that three slices of pizza yielded a total utility of (20 + 16 + 12) = 48 utils. Adding the two together (30 + 48) gives 78 total utils of satisfaction. This is the most utility you can afford with $10. To see why, look at Table 16.3, which reports the maximum utility for every affordable combination of Pepsi and pizza.

The optimum combination of Pepsi and pizza is highlighted in red. This is the result we found by comparing the marginal utilities per dollar spent in Table 16.2. Notice that Table 16.3 confirms that this process results in the highest total utility. All other affordable combinations of Pepsi and pizza produce less utility. Table 16.3 also illustrates diminishing marginal utility. If you select either pizza or Pepsi exclusively, you will have a much lower total utility— 60 with pizza and 45 with Pepsi. In addition, the preferred outcome of 4 Pepsis

TABLE 16.3	
The Maximum Utility from Different Combinations of Pepsi and Pizza	
Affordable Combination of Pizza and Pepsi	**Total Utility**
5 pizza slices (20 + 16 + 12 + 8 + 4)	60 utils
2 Pepsis (9 + 8) and 4 pizza slices (20 + 16 + 12 + 8)	73 utils
4 Pepsis (9 + 8 + 7 + 6) and 3 pizza slices (20 + 16 + 12)	**78 utils**
6 Pepsis (9 + 8 + 7 + 6 + 5 + 4) and 2 pizza slices (20 + 16)	75 utils
8 Pepsis (9 + 8 + 7 + 6 + 5 + 4 + 3 + 2) and 1 pizza slice (20)	64 utils
10 Pepsis (9 + 8 + 7 + 6 + 5 + 4 + 3 + 2 + 1 + 0)	45 utils

and 3 slices of pizza corresponds to a modest amount of each good—this avoids the utility reduction associated with excessive consumption.

By thinking at the margin about which good provides the highest marginal utility, you also maximize your total utility. Of course, we rarely think this way! But consumers make choices like this all the time. Instead of adding up utils, we think, "That isn't worth it" or "That's a steal." Consumer choice is not so much a conscious calculation as an instinct to seek the most satisfaction. Next we ramp up our analysis by generalizing the two-good example.

Marginal Thinking

Marginal Thinking with More Than Two Goods

The idea of measuring utility makes our instinctive sense more explicit and allows us to solve simple optimization problems. For instance, when you travel you instinctively make choices about which route to take in order to save time. The decision to turn left or right when you come to a stop sign is a marginal decision—one route will be better than the other. If you consistently make the best choices about which way to turn, you will arrive at your destination faster. This is why economists focus first on marginal decision making.

In reality, life is more complex than the simple two-good model; when you have $10 to spend, you have many goods to choose from. Since we buy many items at all kinds of prices over the course of a year, the consumer must juggle hundreds (or thousands) of purchases so that we enjoy roughly the same utility per dollar spent. Consumer equilibrium captures this idea by comparing the utility gained with the price paid for every item the consumer buys. This means that a consumer's income is balanced so that the ratio of the marginal utility per dollar spent on every item, from good A to good Z, is equal. In mathematical terms:

$$\text{MU}_A \div \text{Price}_A = \text{MU}_B \div \text{Price}_B = \ldots = \text{MU}_Z \div \text{Price}_Z \quad (16.2)$$

Recall our example of pizza and Pepsi: you reached an optimum when you purchased 4 Pepsis and 3 slices of pizza. At that point, the marginal utility per dollar spent for Pepsi and pizza was equal:

$$MU_{pizza}(12 \text{ utils}) \div \$2 = MU_{Pepsi}(6 \text{ utils}) \div \$1 \qquad (16.3)$$

In the earlier example the price of a slice pizza (\$2) and a can of Pepsi (\$1) was held constant. But suppose that the price of pizza drops to \$1.50. This causes the ratio of $MU_{pizza} \div Price_{pizza}$ to change from $12 \div 2$, or 6 utils per dollar, to $12 \div 1.5$, or 8 utils per dollar. The lower price for pizza increases the quantity of pizza that the consumer will buy:

$$MU_{pizza}(12 \text{ utils}) \div \$1.50 > MU_{Pepsi}(6 \text{ utils}) \div \$1 \qquad (16.4)$$

As a result, lower prices increase the marginal utility per dollar spent and cause consumers to buy more of a good. Higher prices have the opposite effect, by lowering the marginal utility per dollar spent. If that sounds an awful lot like the law of demand—it is! We have just restated the law of demand in terms of marginal utility.

We know that according to the law of demand, the quantity demanded falls when the price rises, and the quantity demanded rises when the price falls, all other things being equal. If we think of consumer desire for a particular product as demand, it makes sense to find a connection between the prices that consumers pay, the quantity that they buy, and the marginal utility they receive. In the next section we explore the relationship between changes in price and changes in the consumer optimum.

Price Changes and the Consumer Optimum

When a price changes, there are two effects. Because the marginal utility per dollar spent is now higher, consumers substitute the product that has become relatively cheaper, a behavior known as the **substitution effect**. At the same time, a price change can also change the purchasing power of income, which is known as the **real-income effect**.

Let's go back to our Pepsi and pizza example to separate these two effects. A lower price for pizza makes it more affordable. If a slice of pizza costs \$2.00, a consumer with a budget of \$10 can afford 5 slices. If the price drops to \$1.50 per slice, the consumer can afford six slices and still have \$1 left over.

When the price of a slice of pizza is \$2.00, your optimum is 3 slices of pizza and 4 Pepsis. If we drop the price of a slice of pizza to \$1.50, you save \$0.50 per slice. Since you are purchasing 3 slices, you save \$1.50. The \$1.50 you save is enough to buy another slice. Looking back at column 5 in Table 16.2, we see that the fourth slice of pizza brings an additional 8 utils. Alternatively, you could use the \$1.50 you saved on pizza to buy a fifth can of Pepsi—which has a marginal utility of 5—and still have \$0.50 left over.

The **substitution effect** occurs when a consumer buys more of a good as a result of a relative price change.

The **real-income effect** occurs when there is a change in purchasing power as a result of a change in the price of a good.

The lower price of pizza may cause you to eat more pizza because it has become relatively cheaper. This is a demonstration of the substitution effect. In addition, as a result of the real-income effect you also have more purchasing power, which you can use to buy other items, like more Pepsi.

The real-income effect and substitution effect always exist. However, the real-income effect only matters when prices change enough to cause a measurable effect on the purchasing power of your income. For example, suppose that a 10 percent price reduction in peanut butter cups occurs. Will there be a substitution effect, a real-income effect, or both? The secret to answering this question is to consider how much money is saved. Most candy bars cost less than a dollar, so a 10 percent reduction in price is less than ten cents. The lower price will encourage some consumers to switch to peanut butter cups—a substitution effect that can be observed through increased purchases of peanut butter cups. However, the income effect is negligible. You have saved less than ten cents. The money saved could be deployed to purchase other goods—but very few things cost so little and the enhanced purchasing power is effectively zero.

PRACTICE WHAT YOU KNOW

Consumer Optimism

Question: Suppose your favorite magazine, *The Economist*, costs $6 per issue and *People* magazine costs $4 per issue. If you receive 20 utils when you read *People*, how many additional utils would you need to get from reading *The Economist* to cause you to spend the extra $2 it costs to purchase it?

Answer: We need to equate the MU per dollar spent for both magazines and solve for the missing variable, the utility from *The Economist*.

$$MU_{The\ Economist}\ (X\ utils) \div \$6 = MU_{People}\ (20\ utils) \div 4$$

$$X \div \$6 = 20 \div \$4$$

$$X = \$120 \div \$4$$

$$X = 30$$

When the $MU_{The\ Economist}$ is equal to 30 utils, you are indifferent between purchasing the two magazines. Since the question asked how many additional utils are needed to consider purchasing *The Economist*, we subtract the utils from *People*, or 20, to get the difference, which is 30 – 20, or 10 utils.

The Diamond-Water Paradox

Now that you understand the connection between prices and utility, we can tackle one of the most interesting puzzles in economics, the diamond-water paradox. First described by Adam Smith in 1776, the diamond-water paradox explains why water, which is essential to life, is inexpensive, while diamonds, which do not sustain life, are expensive. Many people of Smith's era found the paradox perplexing. Today, we can use consumer choice theory to answer the question.

Essentially, the diamond-water paradox unfairly compares the amount of marginal utility a person receives from a small quantity of something rare, the diamond, with the marginal utility from a small amount of additional water after already consuming a large amount.

We know that marginal utility is captured in the law of demand, and therefore by the price. For example, when the price of a diamond increases, the quantity demanded declines. Moreover, total utility is determined by the amount of consumer surplus enjoyed from a transaction. We learned that consumer surplus is the area under the demand curve and above the price, or the gains from trade a consumer enjoys. Therefore, if the price of a diamond rises, consumers enjoy less surplus from buying them.

Figure 16.2 contrasts the demand and supply equilibrium in both the market for water and the market for diamonds. Notice that the consumer surplus

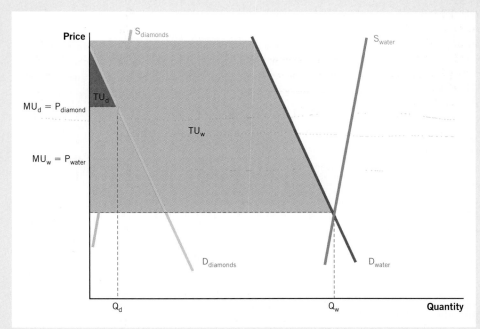

FIGURE 16.2

The Diamond-Water Paradox

The diamond-water paradox exists because people fail to recognize that demand and supply are equally important in determining the value a good creates in society. The demand for water is large while the demand for diamonds is small. If we look at the amount of consumer surplus, we observe that the pink area (TU_w) is much larger than the gray area (TU_d), because water is essential for life. As a result, water creates significantly more total utility than diamonds. However, since water is abundant in most places, the price, P_{water}, is low. On the other hand, diamonds are rare and the price is high, $P_{diamond}$.

is the triangular area highlighted in pink for water and gray for diamonds. The pink area (TU_w) is much larger than the gray area (TU_d) because water is essential for life. Therefore, water creates significantly more total utility than diamonds. However, in most places in the United States water is very plentiful, so we take additional units of it for granted. In fact, it is so plentiful that if someone offered you a gallon of water right now, you would probably hesitate to take it. But what if someone offered you a gallon-sized bucket of diamonds? You bet you would take that! Therefore, it should not surprise you that something which is quite plentiful, water, would yield less marginal utility than diamonds ($MU_w < MU_d$).

Let's consider how we use water. We bathe in it, cook with it, and drink it. Each of those uses has high value—so the marginal utility of water is high. But we also use it to water our lawns and fill our fish tanks. Those uses are not nearly as essential—so the marginal utility of water for these uses is much lower. The reason we use water in both essential and nonessential ways is that the price of water is relatively cheap, so low-value uses, like filling fish tanks, bring enough utility to justify the cost. Since water is abundant in most places, the price, P_{water}, is low. On the other hand, diamonds are rare and the price, $P_{diamond}$, is high. The cost of attaining a diamond means that a consumer must get a great deal of marginal utility from a purchase of diamonds to justify the expense. This explains why diamonds are given as gifts for special occasions.

The Diamond-Water Paradox

ECONOMICS IN THE MEDIA

Super Size Me (2004)

What would happen if you ate all your meals at McDonald's for an entire month—without ever working out? *Super Size Me*, a 2004 documentary by Morgan Spurlock, endeavored to find out. It is the absurd nature of Spurlock's adventure that drags us in. No one would *actually* eat every meal at the same restaurant for a month because diminishing marginal utility would cause the utility from the meals to plunge.

Why does Spurlock take aim at McDonald's, and more generally the fast-food industry? The answer lies in the business model that many fast-food restaurants follow. These restaurants provide filling food at a low cost, a combination that encourages consumers to eat more than they would if the price was higher. Since eating a lot of food results in diminishing marginal utility, often the last bite of a sandwich, or fries, or the last gulp of a 32-ounce drink brings very little additional utility, so it is not uncommon to discard the excess, since the MU of completing the

meal would become negative. We will leave aside the fact that fast food is often unhealthy for the diner.

This provides quite a contrast with fine dining. At fancy establishments, the portions are smaller by design. A five-course meal is meant to be savored and the experience trumps price. What makes someone willing to pay significantly more when dining out? Upscale restaurants are creating high MU by making every bite mouthwatering. They do not want to diminish the marginal value through overeating.

To summarize, McDonald's is a lot like water in the paradox we discussed. McDonald's restaurants are everywhere, serving close to 50 million customers a day, so the total value the chain creates is quite high, despite the fact that the MU of an individual meal is quite low. Upscale restaurants are a lot like the diamonds we discussed—they are uncommon and the number of customers they serve is small; thus the total value they create is low by comparison, but the MU of an individual meal is quite high.

PRACTICE WHAT YOU KNOW

Question: Every guy wears underwear, but comparatively few guys wear ties. Can you explain why ties are so much more expensive than underwear if the demand for underwear is so much greater than the demand for ties?

Answer: Demand is only half of the market. Far fewer ties are produced than underwear. The supply of ties also plays a role in determining the price. In addition, ties are a fashion statement. This makes ties luxury goods, whereas underwear is a necessity. As a result, ties are a lot like diamonds (small overall market but high prices) and underwear is a lot like water (much larger overall market and lower prices). There is nothing inherently paradoxical about ties being more expensive than underwear. The fact that ties generally cost more does not mean that ties are more valuable to society—it only means that people get more marginal utility from purchasing the "perfect" tie as opposed to finding the "perfect" underwear.

In Figure 16.2 you can see that the price of water is low because the supply is abundant. At the same time, the price of a diamonds is high because the supply of diamonds is low. If water were as rare as diamonds, there is no doubt that the price of water would exceed the price of diamonds. Fortunately for all of us, that is not the case!

Conclusion

Does more money make people much happier? The answer is no. More money enables people to buy more stuff, but because of diminishing marginal utility the increases in happiness from being able to buy more goods, or higher-quality goods, become progressively smaller with rising income. So we could say that more money makes people somewhat happier—and that's partly true. But it seems more appropriate to add that the relationship between quality of life and money is not direct. More money sometimes leads to more utility; at other times, more money means more problems.

As we have seen in this chapter, prices play a key role in determining utility. Since consumers face a budget constraint and wish to maximize their utility, the prices they pay determine their marginal utility per dollar spent. When the marginal utility per dollar spent is compared across many goods, this helps us to understand the consumption patterns of individuals. Diminishing marginal utility also helps describe consumer choice. Since marginal utility declines with additional consumption, consumers do not exclusively purchase their favorite products; instead, they diversify their choices in order to gain more utility. In addition, changes in prices create two separate effects, one on income and a separate substitution effect that determines the composition of the bundle of goods that are purchased.

Real Budget Constraints for College Graduates

It is the day you have been waiting for. You are a college graduate, with a shiny new degree ready for framing. You even have a job! You will probably want to buy a car to go with your new life. Now that you're on your own financially, you will need health insurance and a place to call your own. And once you have your place, you'll want to fill it with the latest cool stuff, like a large-screen TV.

But, as much as you might want all of these things right away, you'll probably have to wait awhile. Why? Constraints. For example, nearly six out of ten college graduates have educational debt and those debts delay purchases. In fact, 38 percent of college graduates must postpone buying their first home, and 14 percent put off getting married in order to rein in their college debt. Even if you are lucky enough to be debt-free upon graduation, your income does not travel as far you might imagine. Taxes, insurance, utilities, lodging, basic food purchases, and transportation costs are additional constraints that can severely curtail disposable income.

On average first-time homebuyers spend 3.5 times their annual income on a first home. So a recent graduate making $60,000 could probably get a mortgage of $210,000. That mortgage requires a $1,300 monthly payment. Throw in home insurance and property taxes and you have a $1,700 monthly commitment—or $20,000 a year. And don't forget the cost of heat, electricity, water, and maintenance. Likewise, a new car with a monthly payment of $500 and insurance, gas, and maintenance costs to keep it running adds another few hundred dollars a month to your bills.

According to a recent Bureau of Labor Statistics Consumer Expenditure Survey, a typical household that earned $63,000 paid approximately $12,000 in taxes, leaving a disposable income of $51,000. Our recent college graduate will find that after taxes, housing and transportation expenditures, surprisingly little remains. Where does the rest of the money go? Figure on spending another $6,000 in food (eating out and eating at home), $2,000 on clothing, $3,000 on health care, and another $5,000 in saving for retirement.

So what's left after you are fed, clothed, and sheltered and have taken care of your other basic needs? The typical household spends 1.3 percent on personal-care products and services, another 2.0 percent on continued education, 2.5 percent on miscellaneous goods and services, and contributes 3.4 percent to charity. This leaves 5.0 percent, or $3,000 of their income, for entertainment and vacations. Welcome to the real world, where budget constraints and financial trade-offs are a fact of life. There is a reason why people say that college is the best four years of your life!

Source: Bureau of Labor Statistics, Consumer Expenditures Survey 2010. Available at http://www.bls.gov/news.release/cesan.toc.htm.

In the next chapter we question how much consumers use consumer choice theory to make their decisions. An alternative approach, known as behavioral economics, argues that decision-makers are much less rational about the choices they make.

In the appendix that follows this chapter we refine consumer theory using indifference curves, a somewhat more complicated approach. If this subject fascinates you, please read the appendix to get a glimpse into how economists model consumer choice in greater detail.

ANSWERING THE BIG QUESTIONS

1. How do economists model consumer satisfaction?

✳ Economists model consumer decisions by examining utility, which is a measure of the satisfaction that consumers enjoy from the consumption of goods and services.

✳ An important property of utility is the fact that it diminishes with additional consumption. This limits the amount of any particular good or service that a person will consume.

2. How do consumers optimize their decisions?

✳ The consumer optimum is the combination of goods and services that maximizes the level of satisfaction from a given income. This occurs when a consumer balances income, so that the ratio of the marginal utility per dollar spent on every item in the budget is equal.

✳ Changes in price have two distinct effects on consumer behavior. If the price falls, the marginal utility per dollar spent will be higher. As a result, consumers will substitute toward the product that has become relatively cheaper. This is known as a substitution effect. If the lower price also results in substantial savings, it causes an increase in purchasing power known as the real-income effect.

3. What is the diamond-water paradox?

✳ The diamond-water paradox explains why water, which is essential to life, is inexpensive, while diamonds, which do not sustain life, are expensive. Many people of Adam Smith's era (the eighteenth century) found the paradox perplexing. The diamond-water paradox can be solved by recognizing that the supply of water is abundant and therefore its price is low. At the same time, the price of a diamonds is high because the supply of diamonds is low. If water were as rare as diamonds, there is no doubt that the price of water would exceed the price of diamonds.

CONCEPTS YOU SHOULD KNOW

Consumer optimum (p. 470)
Diminishing marginal
  utility (p. 468)

Marginal utility (p. 467)
Real-income effect (p. 473)

Substitution effect (p. 473)
Utility (p. 466)

QUESTIONS FOR REVIEW

1. After watching a movie your friend and you both indicate that you liked it. Does this mean that each of you received the same amount of utility?

2. What is the relationship between total utility and marginal utility?

3. How is diminishing marginal utility reflected in the law of demand?

4. What does it imply when we say that the marginal utility per dollar spent is equal for two goods?

STUDY PROBLEMS

1. A local pizza restaurant charges full price for the first pizza, but a second pizza is 50 percent off. Using marginal utility, explain the restaurant's pricing strategy.

2. Suppose that the price of trail mix is $4 per pound and the price of cashews is $6 per pound. If you get 30 utils from the last pound of cashews you consume, how many utils would you have to get from the last pound of trail mix to be in consumer equilibrium?

3. Complete the missing cells in the table below:

Number of Cookies	Total Utility of Cookies	Marginal Utility of Cookies	Number of Pretzels	Total Utility of Pretzels	Marginal Utility of Pretzels
0	0		0	0	
		25			___
1	___		1	10	
		15			___
2	___		2	18	
		10			___
3	___		3	24	
		5			4
4	___		4	___	
		___			2
5	55		5	___	
		___			0
6	50		6	___	

4. Use the table in problem 3. Suppose that you have an $8 budget and that cookies and pretzels (in problem 3 above) cost $1 each. What is the consumer optimum?

5. Use the table in problem 3. What is the consumer equilibrium if the price of cookies rises to $1.50 and the price of pretzels remains at $1?

6. You are considering dining at Cici's, an all-you-can-eat pizza chain, or buying pizza by the slice at a local pizzeria for $2 per slice. At which restaurant are you likely to experience the most marginal utility from the last slice you eat?

7. In consumer equilibrium a person buys four cups of coffee at $2 a cup and two $2 muffins each day. Suppose that the price of coffee rises to $3, what do we expect to happen to the number of coffee cups and muffins consumed?

8. How do dollar stores survive when *none* of the items sold bring a high amount of total utility to the consumer?

9. Imagine that the total utility from consuming five tacos is 10, 16, 19, 20, and 17 utils, respectively. When does marginal utility begin to diminish?

10. You and your friends are considering vacationing in Cabo San Lucas or Cancun for spring break. When you first checked the cost of your hotel and flights, the total price was $1,000 to both destinations. However, a sale has lowered the total cost of going to Cancun to $800. Does this create a substitution effect, a real-income effect, or both?

16A Indifference Curve Analysis

There is much more to economic analysis than the simple supply and demand model can capture. Chapter 16 looked at the question of how consumers can get the biggest bang for their buck. Here we explore the question in more detail, using the tool of indifference curve analysis. The purpose of this appendix is to get you thinking about the connections between price changes and consumption decisions at a deeper level.

Learning Objectives:

- To understand how indifference curves are used to model consumer choice.
- To understand the properties that indifference curves possess.
- To understand how indifference curves can be used to separate the substitution effect from the real-income effect.

Indifference Curves

In this section we introduce indifference curves, a tool economists use to describe the trade-offs that exist when making consumer decisions.

An **indifference curve** represents the various combinations of two goods that yield the same satisfaction, or utility. The simplest way to think about indifference curves is to envision a topographical map, where each line represents a specific elevation. When you look at a topographical map you see ridges, mountains, valleys, and the subtle flow of the land. An indifference curve conveys the same complex set of information about personal satisfaction. Indifference curves visually lead upward to a top called the **maximization point,** or the point where utility is maximized.

Returning to our example of pizza and Pepsi, recall that you had $10 to spend and only two items to purchase, Pepsi at $1 a can and pizza at $2 a slice. Like all consumers you will optimize your utility by maximizing the marginal utility per dollar spent and, as a result, you select 4 Pepsis and 3 slices of pizza. But what happens if you don't have a budget? If you are free to spend as much you would like, how much pizza and Pepsi would you want?

Economic "Goods" and "Bads"

Are Pepsi and pizza always economic goods? This may seem like a curious question, but think about your own consumption habits. Would you keep eating something after you were full? Would you continue to eat even if your stomach ached? At some point we all stop eating and drinking. In this sense, economic

An **indifference curve** represents the various combinations of two goods that yield the same satisfaction, or utility.

A **maximization point** is the combination of two goods that yields most utility.

Indifference Curves / 483

goods, like Pepsi and pizza, are "good" only up to a point. Once you are full, the utility from attaining another unit of the good becomes negative—a "bad."

Each indifference curve represents lines of equal satisfaction. For simplicity, Figure 16A.1 shows the indifference curve as circles around the point of maximum satisfaction. The closer the indifference curve is to the maximization point, the higher the consumer's level of satisfaction.

Indifference curves are best seen as approaching the maximization point from all directions (like climbing up a mountain on four different sides). In any hike, some paths are better than others. The figure details four separate ways to reach the maximization point. However, only one of the paths makes any sense. In quadrants II, III, and IV, either pizza or Pepsi is a bad, or both are. Since the consumer must pay to acquire pizza and Pepsi, and at least one of them is reducing their utility, their satisfaction will increase by purchasing less of the bad. In other words, why would anyone willingly pay in order to feel worse? Quadrants II, III, and IV are highlighted in pink because people are unlikely to choose an option that makes them feel bad. That leaves quadrant I as the preferred path to the highest utility. In quadrant I, increasing amounts of pizza and Pepsi produce more utility.

The Budget Constraint

Figure 16A.1 illustrates the choices of a consumer with an unlimited budget and no opportunity costs. However, in real life money spent on Pepsi and pizza is money that cannot be spent elsewhere. We need to account for a person's budget and the cost of acquiring each good. The amount you have to spend is known as the **budget constraint**, or the set of consumption bundles

The **budget constraint** is the set of consumption bundles that represent the maximum amount the consumer can afford.

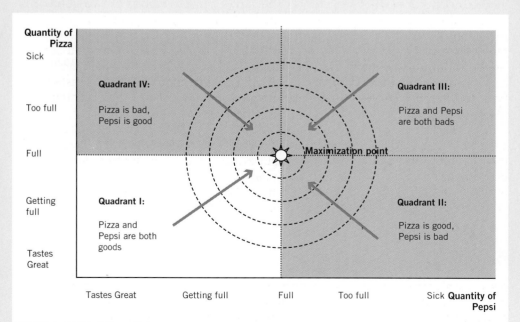

Indifference Curves

The maximization point indicates where a consumer attains the most utility. In quadrant I both Pepsi and pizza are goods, so attaining more of each will cause utility to rise toward the maximization point. In quadrants II, III, and IV, either pizza or Pepsi is a bad, or both are, since the consumer must pay to acquire pizza and Pepsi, and at least one of the items is reducing the consumer's utility. As a result, the most affordable path to the maximization point is quadrant I.

that represent the maximum amount a consumer can afford. If you have $10 to spend on pizza ($2/slice) and Pepsi ($1/can), you could choose to purchase ten cans and forgo pizza. You could purchase five slices of pizza and do without Pepsi. Or you can choose a number of different combinations of pizza and Pepsi, as we saw in Chapter 16. The budget constraint in Figure 16A.2 maps out the affordable combinations of pizza and Pepsi.

There are many different affordable combinations of the two goods. Let's take the pairs along the budget constraint first. If you spend your entire $10 on Pepsi, the combination of coordinates would be the point (10,0). If you spend everything on pizza, the coordinates would be at (0,5). These two points are the extreme outcomes. By connecting these two points with a line—the budget constraint—we can see the many combinations that would fully exhaust $10. As a consumer, your goal is to pick the combination that maximizes your satisfaction, subject to your budget constraint. One possibility would be spend the $10 on four slices of pizza and three cans of Pepsi (4,3), which happens to be the utility maximizing point we discovered in the chapter.

What about the points located below and above the budget constraint? For example, at the point (2,2) you are spending $6—$2 on Pepsi and $4 on pizza. You still have $4 to spend on more of either good. Since both goods are desirable, spending the leftover income will increase satisfaction. So the combination (2,2) represents a failure to maximize utility. On the other side of the budget constraint, we find the point (10,5). This combination, which would cost $20 to attain, represents a lack of income. Since you only have $10, you cannot afford that combination. From this you can see that the budget constraint is a limiting set of choices, or a constraint imposed by scarcity.

In the next section we examine the indifference curve in greater detail. Once we fully understand the properties that characterize indifference curves, we can join them with the budget constraint to better describe how consumers make choices.

FIGURE 16A.2

The Budget Constraint

The budget constraint line shows the set of affordable combinations of Pepsi and pizza with a budget of $10. Any point inside the budget constraint—for example, (2,2)—is also affordable. Points beyond the budget constraint—for example, (10,5)—are not affordable.

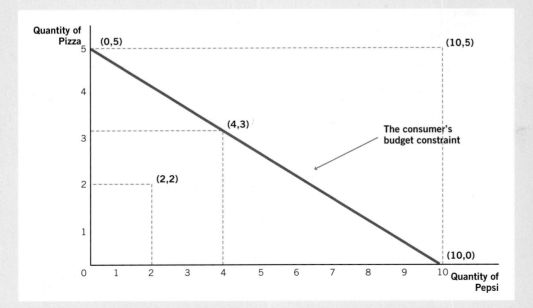

Properties of Indifference Curves

Several assumptions about indifference curves are useful to keep in mind. The properties that follow help to ensure that our model is logically consistent.

Nonsatiation

A rational consumer will only operate in quadrant I in Figure 16A.1. Within that quadrant the higher indifference curves—those nearer the utility maximization point—are preferred to the lower ones (nearer the origin). Also, nonsatiation, or the idea that consumers cannot get too much of a good thing, requires that indifference curves are bowed inward with respect to the origin. This convex shape eliminates any outcome in quadrants II through IV, by requiring that goods be good, not bad.

Figure 16A.3 shows an indifference curve that reflects the trade-off between two goods. Since the indifference curve is bowed in, the **marginal rate of substitution**, or the rate at which a consumer is willing to trade one good for another, varies. This is reflected in the slope of the indifference curve in Figure 16A.3. Points A and B are both on the same indifference curve, so the consumer finds the combinations (1,5) and (2,3) equally attractive. Between points A and B, the consumer must receive two slices of pizza to compensate for the loss of a can of Pepsi. We can see this in the figure by observing that the consumer buys only two cans of Pepsi and three slices of pizza at (2,3). Since Pepsi is a relatively scarce commodity, giving up one Pepsi requires that they receive back two slices of pizza to reach the point (1,5). Therefore, the marginal rate of substitution (MRS) is 2 to −1, or −2. However,

The **marginal rate of substitution** is the rate at which a consumer is willing to trade one good for another.

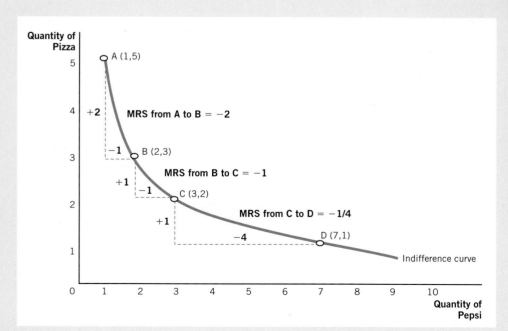

FIGURE 16A.3

The Marginal Rate of Substitution

The marginal rate of substitution along an indifference curve varies. This is reflected in the slope of the indifference curve. Since Pepsi and pizza are both subject to diminishing marginal utility, it takes more of the plentiful good to keep the consumer indifferent when giving up another good that is in short supply.

if we examine the same indifference curve between points C and D we see that the consumer is also indifferent between the combination (3,2) and (7,1). However, this time the consumer is willing to give up four cans of Pepsi to get one more slice of pizza, so the MRS is −1 to 4, −1/4. Why is there such a big difference between (3,2) and (7,1) compared to (2,3) and (1,5)? At (7,1) the consumer has a lot of Pepsi and very little pizza to enjoy it with. As a result, the marginal utility of the second pizza is so high that it is worth four Pepsis! We can see the change in the marginal rate of substitution visually; since the slope between A and B is steeper than it is between C and D. What explains why Pepsi is more valuable between A and B? The consumer starts with only two cans. Pizza is more valuable between C and D because the consumer starts with only two slices of pizza. Since Pepsi and pizza are both subject to diminishing marginal utility, it takes more of the plentiful good to keep the consumer indifferent when giving up another good that is in short supply.

Thickness of Indifference Curves

Another property of indifference curves is that they cannot be thick. If indifference curves could be thick, then it would be possible to draw two points inside a thick indifference curve where one of the two points was preferred to the other. Therefore, a consumer cannot be indifferent between those points. This can be seen in Figure 16A.4. Points A, B, and C are all located on the same indifference curve. However, points B and C are both strictly preferred to point A. Point B has one extra slice of pizza and point C has two extra cans of Pepsi than point A. Since nonsatiation is assumed, more pizza and Pepsi add to the consumer's utility, and the consumer cannot be indifferent among these three points.

FIGURE 16A.4

Indifference Curves Cannot Be Thick

If indifference curves could be thick, it would be possible to draw two points inside the curve in a way that indicates one of the two points was preferred to the other. Point B has one extra slice of pizza and point C has two extra cans of Pepsi than point A. Therefore, the consumer cannot be indifferent among these three points and the indifference curves cannot be thick.

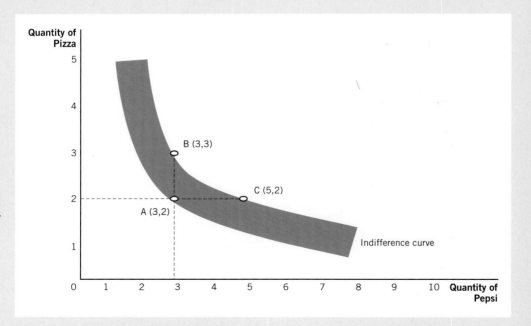

Intersection of Indifference Curves

Indifference curves, by their very nature, cannot intersect. To understand why, let's look at a hypothetical case. Figure 16A.5 shows two indifference curves crossing at point A. Points A and B are located along IC_1, so we know that those two points bring the consumer the same utility. Points A and C are located along IC_2, so those two points also result in the same utility for the consumer. Therefore, the utility at point A equals the utility at point B, and the utility at point A also equals the utility at point C. This means that the utility at point B should also equal the utility at point C, but that cannot be true. Point B is located at (1,3) and point C at (2,4). Since (2,4) strictly dominates (1,3), point C is preferred to point B. Therefore, indifference curves cannot cross without violating the assumption that consumers are rational utility maximizers.

We have seen that indifference curves have three properties: they are convex with respect to the origin, they cannot be thick, and they cannot cross. These properties guarantee that they take on the general shape in quadrant I of Figure 16A.1.

Extreme Preferences: Perfect Substitutes and Complements

Ordinarily indifference curves are convex, and bow inward toward the origin. However, there are two exceptions: *perfect substitutes* and *perfect complements*. These are found on either side of the standard-shaped, convex indifference curve.

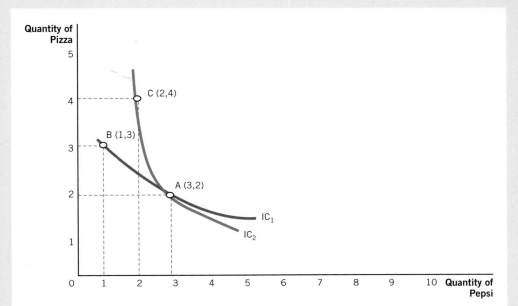

FIGURE 16A.5

Indifference Curves Cannot Cross

The utility at point B should equal the utility at point C, but that cannot be true even though the utility at point B is equal to the utility at point A (along IC_1) and the utility at point C is equal to the utility at point A (along IC_2). Point B is located at (1,3) and point C is located at (2,4). Since (2,4) strictly dominates (1,3), point C is preferred to point B.

A perfect substitute
exists when a consumer
is completely indifferent
between two goods, resulting
in straight-line indifference
curves.

A **perfect substitute** exists when a consumer is completely indifferent between two goods. Suppose that you cannot taste any difference between Aquafina and Evian bottled water. You would be indifferent between one additional bottle of Aquafina or one additional bottle of Evian. Turning to Figure 16A.6a, you can see that the indifference curves for these two goods are straight parallel lines with a marginal rate of substitution, or slope, of -1 everywhere along the curve. The slope of an indifference curve of perfect substitutes need not always be -1; it can be any constant rate. Since perfect substitutes have a marginal rate of substitution with a constant rate, they are drawn as straight lines.

A perfect complement
exists when a consumer is
interested in consuming two
goods in fixed proportions,
resulting in right-angle indifference curves.

A **perfect complement** exists when a consumer is interested in consuming two goods in fixed proportions. Shoes are an excellent example. We buy shoes in pairs because the left or right shoe is not valuable by itself; you need both shoes to be able to walk comfortably. This explains why shoes are not sold individually. An extra left or right shoe has no marginal value to the consumer, so the indifference curves end up being right angles. For instance, left and right shoes are needed in a 1:1 ratio. Let's look at indifference curve IC_1 in panel b. This indifference curve forms a right angle at the point (1,1) where the person has one left and one right shoe. Now notice that the points (1,2) and (2,1) are also on IC_1. Since an extra left or right shoe does not add utility, the points (1,2), (1,1) and (2,1) are all connected. Perfect complements can also occur in combinations other than 1:1. For instance, an ordinary chair needs four legs for each seat. In that case the indifference curve is still a right angle, but additional chair legs do not enhance the consumer's utility unless they come in groups of four.

FIGURE 16A.6

Perfect Substitutes and Complements

(a) Since perfect substitutes have a marginal rate of substitution with a constant rate, they are drawn as straight lines. (b) Perfect complements are drawn as right angles. A typical indifference curve which reflects the trade-off between two goods that are not perfect substitutes or complements has a marginal rate of substitution that falls between these two extremes.

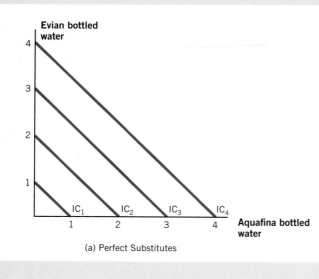

(a) Perfect Substitutes

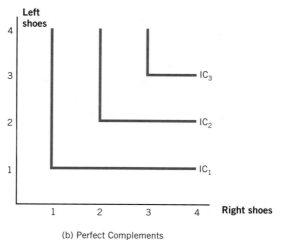

(b) Perfect Complements

Illustrating the Consumer Equilibrium Using Indifference Curves

Figure 16A.7 shows the relationship between indifference curves and the budget constraint. As the indifference curves move higher, the consumer moves progressively closer to the maximization point. At some point the consumer will run out of money. Therefore, the area bounded by the budget constraint (in orange) represents the set of possible choices. The highest indifference curve that can be attained within the set of possible choices is IC_3, where the budget constraint is just tangent to IC_3. Even though all of the points on IC_4 are more desirable than those on IC_3, the consumer lacks the purchasing power to reach that level of satisfaction. Moreover, the point (4,3) is now clearly the preferred choice among the set of possible decisions. Other choices that are also affordable—for example, the combination (2,4)—fall on a lower indifference curve. Progressively higher indifference curves bring the consumer closer to the maximization point. Since their budget constraint limits what they can afford, the tangency of the budget constraint with the highest indifference curve represents the highest affordable level of satisfaction.

Using Indifference Curves to Illustrate the Income and Substitution Effects

The power of indifference curve analysis is its ability to display how price changes affect consumption choices. Part of the intuition behind the analysis involves understanding when the substitution effect is likely to dominate the real-income effect and vice versa.

FIGURE 16A.7

Consumer Equilibrium
Progressively higher indifference curves bring a consumer closer to the maximization point. Since the budget constraint limits what the consumer can afford, the tangency of the budget constraint with the highest indifference curve represents the highest level of affordable satisfaction. In this case, point (4,3) represents the consumer's preferred combination of Pepsi and pizza.

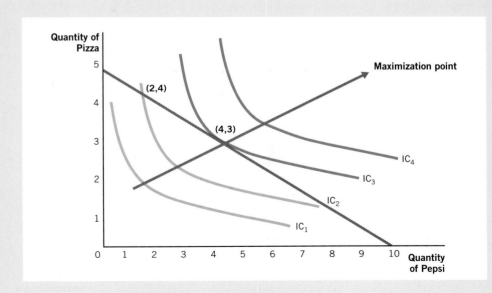

In our example you have only $10, so when the price of Pepsi increases from $1 to $2 a can, it represents a financial burden that significantly lowers your real purchasing power. However, we can easily think of cases where a change in the price of Pepsi wouldn't matter. Suppose you are a typical American household with a median income of $50,000 annually. While out shopping you observe that a local Toyota car dealer is offering 10 percent off new cars and a nearby grocery store is selling Pepsi at a 10 percent discount. Since the percentage saved on each product is the same, the substitution effect will be of an equal magnitude; more people will buy Toyotas instead of Hondas and more people will buy Pepsi instead of Coca-Cola. However, the real-income effects are quite different. Saving 10 percent on the price of a new car could easily amount to a savings of $3,000 or more. Saving 10 percent on a two-liter bottle of Pepsi will only save a couple of dimes. In the case of the new car there is a substantial real-income effect, while the amount you save on the Pepsi is almost immaterial.

Changes in prices can have two distinct effects. The first is a substitution effect, where changes in prices will cause the consumer to substitute toward a good that becomes relatively less expensive. In our example, suppose that the price of Pepsi rises to $2 a can. This rise in the price of Pepsi reduces the marginal utility per dollar of consuming Pepsi. As a result, you would probably buy fewer Pepsis and use the remaining income to purchase more pizza. In effect, you substitute the relatively less expensive good (pizza) for the relatively more expensive good (Pepsi).

However, this is not the only effect at work. The change in the product price alters the purchasing power of your income. A change in purchasing power creates a real-income effect. In this case, your $10 will not go as far as it used to. In Figure 16A.8 we can see that the inward rotation of the budget constraint along the x-axis from BC_1 to BC_2 is a result of the rise in the price of Pepsi. At $2 a can you can no longer afford to buy ten cans; the most you can purchase is five. Therefore, the budget constraint moves inward along

FIGURE 16A.8

How a Change in Price Rotates the Budget Constraint

The inward rotation of the budget constraint along the x-axis from BC_1 to BC_2 is a result of the rise in the price of Pepsi. At $2 a can, you can no longer afford to buy ten cans; the most you can purchase is five. Therefore, the budget constraint moves inward along the x-axis to five units while remaining constant along the y-axis (since the price of pizza did not change).

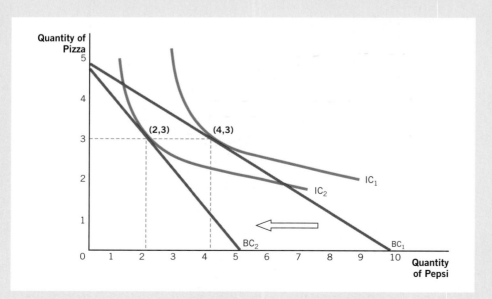

the x-axis to five units while remaining constant along the y-axis (since the price of pizza did not change). As a result, the combination (4,3) is no longer affordable. This produces a new consumer equilibrium at (2,3) along IC_2. The end result is predictable: a rise in the price of Pepsi causes you to purchase less Pepsi and results in a lower level of satisfaction at IC_2 than at your former point on IC_3, which is no longer possible.

Separating the Substitution Effect from the Real-Income Effect

Sometimes the substitution effect and real-income effect reinforce each other and sometimes they work against each other. In this section we will separate the substitution effect from the real-income effect.

Breaking down the movement from IC_3 to IC_2 into the separate real-income effect and substitution effect allows us to see how each effect impacts the consumer's choice. Imagine that you were given just enough money to attain IC_2 in Figure 16A.9, with the original prices of pizza and Pepsi intact. The budget constraint will now be parallel to BC_1 but just tangent to IC_2. The change from BC_1 to BC_{RI} separates the real-income effect from the substitution effect. Since the slope of the new budget constraint, BC_{RI}, is less steep than BC_2, the point of tangency between BC_{RI} and IC_2, A, is lower. Furthermore, since the slopes of BC_{RI} and BC_1 are equal, we can think of the movement from (4,3) to point A as a function of the real-income effect alone. This occurs because we have kept the slope of the budget constraint

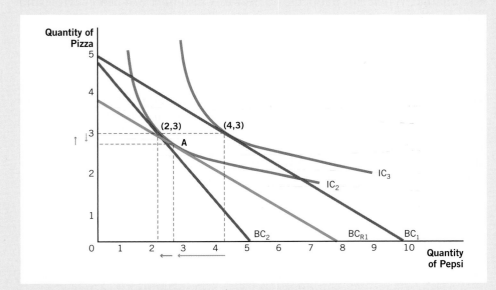

FIGURE 16A.9

Decomposing the Substitution from the Real-income Effect

Breaking down the movement from IC_3 to IC_2 into the separate real-income effect and substitution effect allows us to see how each effect impacts the consumer's choice. The real-income effect causes the budget constraint to shift to BC_{RI} and the loss of purchasing power lowers the consumption of both Pepsi and pizza, as noted by the green arrows. At the same time, the substitution effect reduces the amount of Pepsi consumed and increases the consumption of pizza, as noted by the orange arrows.

constant. The slope is constant, which reflects the fact that the consumer has less money to spend, while the prices of Pepsi and pizza are held constant. The subsequent movement along IC_2 from point A to (2,3) results from the substitution effect exclusively, and it occurs because the price of Pepsi is now more expensive. This result causes BC_2 to become steeper.

Beginning with the real-income effect, we see that the impact of a loss of purchasing power is to lower consumption of both Pepsi and pizza. Notice the green arrows in Figure 16A.9. At the same time, the substitution effect reduces the amount of Pepsi consumed and increases the consumption of pizza. Now observe the orange arrows in the figure. Since Pepsi is now relatively more expensive, you reallocate consumption toward pizza. Consumption of Pepsi falls dramatically while the consumption of pizza remains constant. More generally, whenever the price of a good increases (as Pepsi does in this example), this will lead to a reduction in the amount consumed, since both the real-income and substitution effects (as represented by the orange and green arrows along the x-axis) move in the same direction. However, since the real-income effect and substitution effect move in opposite directions with respect to the good whose price has not changed (pizza), the result is ambiguous for pizza and any change in consumption depends on which effect, the substitution effect or real-income effect, is greater.

In our example, when the price of Pepsi rose to $2 a can it produced a large real-income effect (the green arrow along the x-axis). Prior to the price increase you were spending $4 out of your $10 budget on Pepsi, so Pepsi expenditures represented 40 percent of your budget. When the price doubled, it was like finding out that your rent just doubled from $800 a month to $1,600 a month! Since Pepsi is a big component of your budget, a doubling of its price leads to a sizable real-income effect. This is not always the case; the price of a candy bar can double and the typical household will barely notice this change. When this happens, the real-income effect will be negligible and the substitution effect will tend to dominate.

Conclusion

Economists use indifference curve analysis to gain additional insights into consumer behavior. This analysis extends the basic understanding found in supply and demand by pressing utility theory. Because indifference curves are lines of equal utility, we can impose a budget constraint in order to describe the bundle of goods that maximizes utility. This framework allows us to illustrate the effect of price changes and budget constraints on the decisions that consumers make.

Summary

- The point of maximum consumer satisfaction is found at the point of tangency between an indifference curve and the budget constraint.
- Indifference curves share three properties: they are convex with respect to the origin (nonsatiation), they cannot be thick, and they cannot cross.
- Indifference curves can be used to separate the substitution effect from the real-income effect.

CONCEPTS YOU SHOULD KNOW

Budget constraint (p. 483)　　Marginal rate of substitution, (p. 485)　Perfect complement (p. 488)
Indifference curve (p. 482)　　Maximization point (p. 482)　　　　Perfect substitute (p. 488)

QUESTIONS FOR REVIEW

1. If your budget constraint increases, what generally happens to the amount of utility you experience?

2. If your budget constraint increases, is it possible for your utility to fall?

3. What is the difference between an economic "good" and an economic "bad"?

4. Describes what happens to your budget constraint if the price of one item in your budget becomes less expensive. Show this on a graph.

5. A friend mentions to you that the campus coffee shop offers a 10 percent discount each Thursday morning before 10 a.m. Is this more likely to cause a significant substitution or real-income effect?

STUDY PROBLEMS

1. Kate has $20. Fish sandwiches cost $5 and a cup of espresso costs $4. Draw her budget constraint. If espresso goes on sale for $2 a cup, what does her new budget constraint look like?

2. When you head home for dinner your mother always sets her table with one spoon, two forks, and one knife. Draw her indifference curve for forks and knives.

3. Frank's indifference curves for movies and bowling look like this:

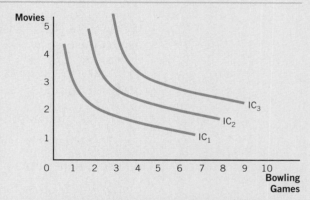

Each game of bowling costs $4 and each movie cost $8. If Frank has $24 to spend, how many times will he go bowling and to the movies?

Behavioral Economics and Risk Taking

People always make rational decisions.

In this textbook we have proceeded as if every person was *Homo eco-nomicus*, or a rationally self-interested decision-maker. *Homo eco-nomicus* is acutely aware of opportunities in the environment

and strives to maximize the benefits received from each course of action while minimizing the costs. We have assumed that decision-making is rational; individuals attempt to maximize util-ity and firms attempt to maximize profits. We don't want to leave you with this misperception. The standard economic model of behavior is a tool that is used to explain many human activities, but human decision-making is far more complex than the decisions we have modeled so far. This is the reason for this chapter. We want you to step back and consider what you have learned and ask yourself the following question: do people and firms always follow their narrow self-interest, or are they motivated by other factors as well?

As human beings, we laugh and cry. Sometimes we seek revenge and at other times, forgiveness. We can be impulsive and shortsighted, and fail to see the benefits of pursuing long-run gains. Each of these behav-iors is real, although they do not fit squarely within our economic mod-els. To fold the broadest possible set of human behavior into economic analysis, we must turn to psychology for help. Economics seeks to develop models with a high degree of explanatory power. In this chapter we will expand our understanding of decision-making with insights from the field of *behavioral economics*, which will allow us to capture a wider range of human motivations than the rational agent model alone.

Photo to come

BIG QUESTIONS

* How can economists explain irrational behavior?
* What is the role of risk in decision-making?
* Can economic theory explain why some people feel crime pays?

Behavioral Economics and Nonrational Behavior

The study of psychology, like economics, endeavors to understand the choices that people make. One key difference is that psychologists do not assume people behave in a fully rational way. As a result, psychologists have a much broader toolbox at their disposal to describe human behavior. **Behavioral economics** is the field of economics that studies how human psychology influences the decision-making process. Behavioral economists draw upon insights from experimental psychology to explore how people behave in economic settings.

Until relatively recently, economists have dismissed, or assumed away, many human behaviors that do not fit their models. For example, traditional economic theory has nothing to say about buying something on impulse. Because it assumed that people make optimal decisions like robots, economic theorists did not try to explain why people might make an impulse purchase. Behavioral economists, however, recognize behaviors that contradict the standard assumptions about rationality. They employ the idea of **bounded rationality**, which argues that although decision-makers want an acceptable outcome, they are neither capable of performing the problem-solving that traditional theory assumes, nor inclined to do so.

Bounded rationality, or limited reasoning, can be explained in three ways. First, the information that is used to make the decision may be limited or incomplete. Second, the human brain has a limited capacity to process information. Third, there is often a limited amount of time to make a decision. These bounds prevent the decision-maker from reaching the results predicted under perfect rationality.

The world is large and complex; no one has the capacity to understand everything or an unlimited amount of time in which to make decisions. These two factors limit the accuracy of economic models that assume we make fully rational decisions. For example, suppose you find yourself at the mall shopping with friends. You enter a store and begin browsing the sale rack. You find a T-shirt you like at a good price. But you were not planning to buy a T-shirt. Do you make the purchase or not? The decision to buy depends on whether you believe that the value is high enough to justify the expense. But there is one problem: because this is an impulsive decision, you have a limited

Behavioral economics is the field of economics that studies how human psychology influences the decision-making process.

Bounded rationality argues that economic agents are only capable of making limited strategic decisions.

amount of information. In a fully rational world, you would check out alternatives in other stores and on the Internet and then make the decision to purchase the T-shirt only after you were satisfied that it was the best possible choice. This is what our rational models predict. However, in reality you walk into a store, you see something you like on the sale rack, and you make the purchase using partial information. Whenever we end up making decisions without perfect information, the decision reflects bounded rationality.

We will begin our discussion of behavioral economics by looking at a number of behaviors that do not fit the standard assumptions of fully rational behavior. These include misperceptions of probability theory, issues concerning question design, and the role of fairness in making decisions. The goal in this section is to recognize and understand many of the behaviors that lead to contradictions between what economic models predict and what people actually do.

Misperceptions of Probabilities

Economic models that assume rationality in decision-making do not account for the way people perceive the probability of unlikely events. Low-probability events are often over-anticipated and high-probability events are often under-anticipated. To see why this is the case, we will consider a number of familiar examples.

Games of Chance

Playing games of chance—for example, a lottery or slot machines—is generally a losing proposition. Yet even with great odds against winning, millions of people spend money to play games of chance. How can we explain this behavior?

For some people, the remote chance of winning a lottery offers hope that they will be able to purchase something they need but cannot afford, or even to escape from poverty. In many cases people have incomplete information about the probabilities and prize structures. Most gamblers do not calculate the exact odds of winning. Lottery agencies typically highlight winners, as if the game has a positive expected value, which gets people excited about playing. Imagine how sobering it would be if every headline trumpeting the newest lottery millionaire was followed by all the names of people made poorer by playing and losing. In fact, almost all games of chance have negative expected values for the gambler, meaning that players are not likely to make money while playing.

Players often have the irrational belief that they have control over the outcome. They are sure that playing certain numbers or patterns—for example, birthdays, anniversaries, or lucky numbers—will bring success. Many players also feel they must stick with their favorite numbers to avoid regret; everyone has heard stories about players who changed from their lucky pattern only to watch it win.

Some gaming behaviors are rational. For example, when the expected value of the gamble is positive, it makes sense to play. If a friend wants to wager $10 on the flip of a coin and promises you $25 if you guess right, the expected value is half of $25, or $12.50. Since $12.50 is greater than the $10 you are wagering, we say that the gamble has a positive expected value. Gambles can also make sense when you have very little to lose or no other options. Some people find the thrill of gambling enjoyable whether they win or lose. However, most gambling behaviors do not have rational motivations.

The Difficulties in Assessing Probabilities

In our discussion of games of chance, we saw that people who gamble do not usually evaluate probabilities in a rational way. But this intuitive, non-rational decision-making also happens in everyday life. For example, on a per-mile basis airplane travel is approximately ten times safer than traveling in an automobile. However, millions of people who refuse to fly because they are afraid of a crash do not hesitate to get into a car. Driving seems to create a false sense of control over one's surroundings.

The television game show *Let's Make a Deal* provides a well-known example of the difficulties in assessing probabilities accurately. At the end of the show the host, Monty Hall, asks a contestant to choose one of three curtains. Behind each curtain is one of three possible prizes: a car, a nice but less expensive item, or a worthless joke item. Suppose that you pick curtain 3. The host, who knows what is behind the curtains, opens a different one, say number 1, which has a pen filled with chickens—the joke prize. He then offers you the opportunity to switch your choice to curtain 2. According to probability theory, what is the right thing to do? Most contestants stay with their original choice. They figure that they have a 50/50 chance of winning the car. But the probability of winning with your original choice remains 1/3, since the chance that you guessed correct the first time remains unchanged. But the chance that one of the other curtains contains the car is 2/3. Therefore, when presented with the opportunity to switch, the contestant should take it. Few do. Almost all contestants think that each of the two remaining unopened curtains has an equal probability of holding the car, so they decide not to switch for fear of regretting their decision.

The difficulty of recognizing the true underlying probabilities, combined with an irrational fear of regret, leads to many poor decisions. Understanding these tendencies helps economists better evaluate why some decisions are difficult to get right.

Seeing Patterns Where None Exist

The **gambler's fallacy** is the belief that recent outcomes are unlikely to be repeated and outcomes that have not occurred recently are due to happen.

Two fallacies, or false ways of thinking, help explain how people make decisions. The first is the **gambler's fallacy**, which is the belief that outcomes that have not occurred in the recent past are more likely to occur soon, and that more recent outcomes are unlikely to be repeated in the near future. Studies examining state lotteries find that bets on recent winning numbers decline. Because the selection of winning numbers is made randomly, just like flipping coins, the probability that a certain number will be a winner in one week is not related to whether the number came up in the previous week. In other words, someone who uses the gambler's fallacy believes that if too many "heads" have occurred in a row, "tails" is more likely to occur next. The gambler's fallacy reflects a failure to understand how uncorrelated—that is, statistically independent—random sequences behave through time.

The second fallacy is the opposite of the first. The **hot hand fallacy** is the belief that random sequences exhibit a positive correlation. The classic study in this area examined perceptions about the game of basketball. Most sports enthusiasts believe that a player who has scored several points in a row—one with a "hot hand"—is more likely to score a basket with his next shot than he might be at another time. However, the study found no positive correlation between success in one shot and success in the next shot.

The **hot hand fallacy** is the belief that random sequences exhibit a positive correlation.

ECONOMICS IN THE REAL WORLD

How Behavioral Economics Helps to Explain Stock Price Volatility

We have all heard the expression "Buy low, sell high," but how exactly does that work? For every trader who makes a great call by selling when the market tops, there is another trader who buys in at the top, only to see the market tumble.

Let's examine some of the traps people fall into when they invest in the stock market.

In a fully rational world, the gambler's fallacy and hot hand fallacy would not exist. However, in our world people are prone to seeing patterns in data even when there are none. Consider the stock market. Investors often believe that the rise and fall of the stock market is driven by specific events and by underlying metrics such as profitability, market share, and return on investment. But in fact, investors often react with a herd mentality by rushing into stocks that are doing well and selling off stocks when a discernable downward trend is in place. Similarly, there are times when investors believe the stock market has run up or down too fast and they expect it to change soon.

The fact that investors are not entirely rational makes it possible to profit from the miscalculations of others. Day traders buy and sell stocks over very short time periods, often a matter of minutes. They exploit short-lived information lags in the market, where some investors learn of an important event before others. In addition, the market has had historically good months (December) and bad months (September and October). Predictable fluctuations that exist for a few minutes, or across months, should not be possible if the market is always accurately valued. Likewise, many speculators believe it can be profitable to keep track of market volatility, buying into the market when it is low and selling after the market price runs up. This is evidence that some segments of the market are driven by investor psychology instead of metrics that measure valuation. It has even been noted that there is a small correlation between the weather outside and how the stock market moves on a particular day. The market is more likely to move higher on sunny days on Wall Street than when the weather is cloudy! ✳

Consistency in Decision-Making

If people were entirely rational, they would always be consistent in how they respond and make decisions. For instance, if you prefer rock over country music, your preference should remain the same no matter how people phrase a question about what you like. Suppose a questionnaire begins by highlighting

Misperceptions of Probabilities

π (1998)

This psychological thriller from 1998 tries to make sense out of chaos. The title refers to the mathematical constant π (pi). In the film, Max Cohen is using his supercomputer to find predictable patterns within the stock market. What makes the film especially interesting are the three assumptions that rule Max's life:

1. Mathematics is the language of nature.
2. Everything around us can be represented and understood from numbers.
3. If you graph the numbers in any system, patterns emerge.

Based on these assumptions, Max attempts to identify a mathematical pattern that will predict the behavior of the stock market. As Max gets closer to uncovering the answer, he is pursued by two parties, a Wall Street firm that wishes to use Max's discovery to manipulate the market, and a religious person who believes that the pattern is a code sent from God.

If the world can be reduced to a set of predictable patterns, then the idea of rational human beings driven to maximize their utility and firms that seek to maximize their profits is a very powerful approach. If, however, the state of nature is more akin to chaos, and filled with all sorts of unpredictable behaviors, then the predictive power of the economic approach is reduced. π illustrates the basic human desire to seek out patterns where none exist and to try to find order in chaos.

the success of Lady Antebellum and this causes you to recall one of the band's songs. This causes you to respond more favorably to the country music section of the questionnaire. How a question is asked should not alter our responses, but research has shown that it does. Likewise, rational decision-making also requires the ability to take the long run into account; if the returns are large enough, people should be willing to sacrifice current enjoyment for future benefits. Yet many of us make shortsighted decisions when stepping back and planning for the future would benefit us in the long run. In this section we examine a variety of decision-making mistakes, including *framing effects*, *priming effects*, *status quo bias*, and *intertemporal decision-making*.

Framing and Priming Effects

Framing effects occur when people change their answer (or action) depending on how the question is asked.

We have seen a number of ways in which economic models do not entirely account for the behavior of real people. One common mistake people make is known as the **framing effect**, which occurs when an answer depends on how a question is asked or a decision is influenced by the way alternatives are presented. Consider an employer-sponsored retirement plan. Companies can either ask employees if they want to join or they can use an automatic enrollment system and ask employees to let them know if they do not wish to participate. Studies have shown that workers who are asked if they want to join tend to participate in company retirement plans—known as 401(k) plans for the tax advantages they create—at a much lower rate than those who are automatically enrolled and must say they want to opt out. Surely a rational economic decision-maker would determine whether to participate based on the plan itself, not on how the decision to participate is presented. However, people are rarely that rational! Another decision-making pitfall, known as the **priming effect**, occurs when the order of questions influences the answers. For example, consider two groups of college students. The first group is asked, "How happy are you?" followed by, "How many dates have you had in the last year?" A second group is asked, "How many dates have you had in the last year?" followed by "How happy are you?" They are asked the same two questions, but in reverse order. In the second group, students who had gone out on more dates reported being much happier than similar students in the first group! In other words, because they were reminded of the number of dates first, those who had more dates believed they were happier.

The order in which questions are asked shouldn't matter, but it does. You have probably experienced both of these effects on exams. Poorly designed exams lead many students to give the wrong answer when they know the correct answer, whereas exams created with an understanding of framing and priming effects produce unbiased measures of student understanding.

Priming effects occur when the ordering of the questions that are asked influences the answers.

Status Quo Bias

When people want to maintain their current lifestyle, they may exhibit what is known as the **status quo bias**. This leads decision-makers to try to protect what they have, even when an objective evaluation of their circumstances suggests that a change would be beneficial. In behavioral economics the status quo bias is often accompanied by **loss aversion**, which exists when a person places more value on avoiding losses than attempting to realize gains. Loss aversion causes people to behave conservatively. The cost of this behavior is missed opportunities that could enhance welfare. For example, a loss-averse individual would maintain a savings account with a low yield instead of actively shopping for better rates elsewhere. This person would lose the potential benefits from higher returns on savings. Status quo bias also explains why new products have trouble gaining traction; many potential customers prefer to buy their favorite brand, even if something new might bring them more utility. One of the greatest marketing failures of the twentieth century can be explained by status quo bias. In 1985 Coca-Cola introduced "new Coke" by altering the secret formula it had used for one hundred years. The backlash eventually caused Coca-Cola to reintroduce the original formula as "Coca-Cola Classic."

Status quo bias is the desire among individuals to maintain the lifestyle associated with their income level.

Loss aversion exists when individuals place more weight on avoiding losses than attempting to realize gains.

ECONOMICS IN THE REAL WORLD

Are You an Organ Donor?

More than 25,000 organ transplants take place every year in the United States, with a vast majority coming from deceased donors. Demand greatly exceeds supply. Over 100,000 people are currently on various organ donation waiting lists. The vast majority of Americans are aware of the need, and 90% of all Americans say they support donation. But only 30% know the essential steps to take to be a donor.

There are two main donor systems: individuals can "opt in," meaning that anyone who has not given consent is not a donor, or they can "opt out," meaning that anyone who has not refused is considered a donor. Opt-out systems generally result in higher rates of consent for donation. This is not universally true, since some countries have other public policies in place and cultural factors can influence the donation rate.

In the United States, donors are required to "opt in." Since opting in generally produces fewer donors than opting out, many states have sought to raise donation awareness by allowing consent to be noted on the individual driver's licenses. In Europe, many countries have opt-out systems, where consent is presumed. The difference is crucial, since many people who would be willing to donate organs never get around to completing the necessary steps to opt in. In countries like France and Poland, where people must opt out, over 90 percent of their citizens indicate their presumed consent. As a result, opting out creates organ donation rates that are significantly higher than in countries where people must opt in.

According to traditional economic analysis, opting in or opting out should not matter—the results should be the same. The fact that we find strong evidence to the contrary is a compelling illustration of the insights that behavioral economics has to offer. ✳

Intertemporal Decision-Making

Intertemporal decisions occur across time. Consider two ways you might prepare for an exam. You could study two hours a week for the next three weeks or wait and spent eight hours studying the night before the exam. Both produce the same grade. If you're like most people, you will choose to cram the night before. In effect, you study more (8 hours versus 6 hours) at the last moment when some advance preparation would have lowered the overall amount of time you needed to study.

Planning to do something over a period of time requires the ability to value the present and the future consistently. For instance, many people, despite their best intentions, do not end up saving enough for retirement. The temptation to spend today ends up overwhelming the willpower to save for tomorrow. This is why people use commitment mechanisms such as company pension plans. In a perfectly rational world a person would not need outside assistance to save enough for retirement. In the real world, workers depend on 401(k) plans and other work-sponsored retirement programs to deduct funds from their paychecks before they are able to spend them. It may seem odd that people would need an outside agency to help them do something that is in their own long-term interest, but as long as their intertemporal decisions, or decisions made over a period of time, are likely to be inconsistent, the additional commitment helps them to achieve their long-run objectives.

Fairness

Some behaviors, like intertemporal decision-making, are the result of misperceptions. Others—for example, the pursuit of fairness—explain why people often evaluate the desirability of an outcome based on the distribution of goods and services throughout society, instead of their own gains and losses.

Fairness plays an important role in society, yet it is absent from economic models. For example, fairness is one of the key drivers in determining tax rate structure for income taxes. Proponents of fairness believe that the rich should pay higher tax rates on their income than the poor, a tax structure known as progressive taxation. Likewise, some people object to the high pay of chief executive officers or the high profits of some corporations because they believe there should be an upper limit to what constitutes fair compensation.

While fairness is not normally modeled in economics, behavioral economists have developed experiments to determine the role of fairness in personal decisions. The **ultimatum game** is an economic experiment in which two players decide how to divide a pot of money. The game shows how fairness enters into the rational decision-making process. In the game, Player 1 is given a sum of money and asked to propose a way of splitting it with Player 2. Player 2 can either accept or reject the proposal. If Player 2 accepts, the sum is split according to the proposal. However, if Player 2 rejects the proposal, neither player gets anything. The game is played only once, so the first player does not have to worry about reciprocity.

Consider an ultimatum game that asks Player 1 to divide $1,000. Player 1 must decide whether or not to make a fair proposal. The decision tree in Figure 17.1 highlights four possible outcomes.

Traditional economic theory presumes that both players are fully rational and wish to maximize their income. Player 1 should therefore maximize his gains by offering the minimum, $1, to Player 2. The reasoning is that Player 2 values $1 more than nothing and so will accept the proposal, leaving Player 1 with $999. But real people are not always economic maximizers; fairness matters. Most of the time Player 2 would find such an unfair division infuriating and reject it.

Player 1 knows that Player 2 will definitely accept an offer of $500; this division of the money is exactly equal and therefore fair. This means that the probability of a 50/50 agreement is 100 percent. On the other hand, the probability of Player 2 accepting an offer of $1 is close to 0. Offering increasing amounts from $1 to $500 will continue to raise the probability of an acceptance until it reaches 100 percent at $500.

Player 2's role is simpler: the only decision is whether to accept or reject the proposal. Player 2 desires a fair distribution but has no direct control over

The **ultimatum game** is an economic experiment where two players decide how to divide a sum of money.

FIGURE 17.1

The Decision Tree for the Ultimatum Game

The decision tree for the ultimatum game has four branches. If Player 1 makes a fair proposal, Player 2 will accept the distribution and both players earn $500. However, if Player 1 makes an unfair proposal, Player 2 may reject the distribution even though it means receiving nothing.

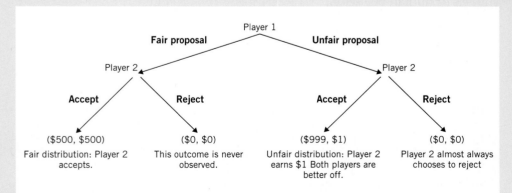

Player 1

Fair proposal   Unfair proposal

Player 2   Player 2

Accept   Reject   Accept   Reject

($500, $500)   ($0, $0)   ($999, $1)   ($0, $0)

Fair distribution: Player 2 accepts. | This outcome is never observed. | Unfair distribution: Player 2 earns $1 Both players are better off. | Player 2 almost always chooses to reject

PRACTICE WHAT YOU KNOW

Gambler's and Hot Hand Fallacies: Patterns on Exams

Question: In the following situation, identify whether the gambler's or hot hand fallacy is at work.

Your instructor is very conscientious and always makes sure that exam answers are randomly distributed. However, you notice that the first five answers on the multiple-choice section are each "C." Unsure what this pattern means, you consider the next question, but because you do not know the answer, you are forced to guess. For the next question you choose to avoid "C' because you believe that "C" cannot happen six times in a row.

Answer: The gambler's fallacy argues that recent events are less likely to be repeated again in the near future. So this student believes in the gambler's fallacy. If her behavior was different, and she believed in the hot hand fallacy, she would mark the next answer "C" because the hot hand fallacy is the belief that random sequences exhibit a positive correlation.

the division. To punish Player 1 for being unfair, Player 2 must reject the proposal altogether. The cost of penalizing Player 1 for unfairness is a complete loss of any prize. So while Player 2 may not like any given proposal, rejecting it would cause a personal loss. Player 2 might therefore accept a number of unfair proposals because he would rather get something than nothing.

Each of the ideas presented in this section, including misperceptions of probability, inconsistency in decision-making, and fairness, represents a departure from the traditional economic model of rational maximization. In the next section we focus on risk taking. As you will soon learn, not everyone evaluates risk in the same way. This has led economists to reconsider their models of human behavior.

Risk-Taking Behavior

In this section we examine the role that risk plays in decision-making. The standard economic model of consumer choice assumes that people are risk neutral. As we will soon learn, people's risk tolerances vary widely and are subject to change. We begin with a phenomenon known as *preference reversal*. We then consider how negative surprises can cause people to take more risk, which is explained by *prospect theory*. The unifying theme is that risk-taking behavior is not nearly as simple, or predictable, as economists once believed.

Preference Reversals

Economists assume that individuals make predictable, repeatable decisions that can be modeled. However, as you already know, trying to predict human behavior is not so easy. One of the first economists to recognize the insufficiency of the rational model of human behavior was Maurice Allais, the recipient of the 1988 Nobel Prize in Economics. Allais noticed that people's tolerance for risk appeared to change in different situations. This did not agree with the standard economic model, which assumes that an individual's risk tolerance is constant. People who are **risk averse** prefer a sure thing over a gamble with a higher expected value. People who are **risk neutral** choose the outcome with the highest expected value. **Risk takers** prefer gambles with lower expected values, but potentially higher winnings, over a sure thing. Allais developed a means of assessing risk behavior by presenting the set of choices depicted in Table 17.1. Individuals were asked to choose their preferred options among gambles A or B and then again among gambles C or D.

Economic science predicts that people will choose two predictable sets of choices, A and D or B and C. Let's see why.

1. *Risk Averse:* People who select gamble A over gamble B take the sure thing. If asked to choose between C and D, we would expect them to try to maximize their chances of winning something by selecting D, since it has the higher probability of winning.
2. *Risk Neutral:* Gamble B has a higher expected value than gamble A. We know that gamble A always pays $1 million. Gamble B's expected value is $5M × 0.10 + $1M × 0.89, which equals $1.39M, so a risk-neutral player will select gamble B. Likewise, gamble C has a higher expected value than D. Gamble C has an expected value of $5M × 0.10, or $0.5M. Gamble D's expected value is $1M × 0.11, or $0.11M. Therefore, a risk-neutral player will choose gambles B and C in order to maximize their potential winnings from the game.

While we would expect people to be consistent in their choices, Allais found that approximately 30 percent of the population selected a contrasting

Risk-averse
people value a sure thing over another gamble with a higher expected value.

Risk-neutral
people choose the highest expected value regardless of the risk.

Risk takers
prefer gambles with lower expected values, but potentially higher winnings, over a sure thing.

TABLE 17.1

The Allais Paradox

CHOOSE GAMBLE A OR B	
Gamble A	**Gamble B**
No gamble—receive $1 million in cash	A lottery ticket that pays $5 million 10% of the time, $1 million 89% of the time, and nothing 1% of the time
CHOOSE GAMBLE C OR D	
Gamble C	**Gamble D**
A lottery ticket that gives you $5 million 10% of the time	A lottery ticket that gives you $1 million 11% of the time

set of pairs of gambles, A and C. A is the sure thing; C, though it has the higher expected value, carries more risk. This is what is known as a *preference reversal*. A **preference reversal** occurs when risk tolerance is not consistent. Allais argued that a person's risk tolerance depends on financial circumstances. Someone who prefers A over B prefers the certainty of a large financial prize—the guarantee of $1 million over the uncertainty of the larger prize. Choosing A could be seen as similar to purchasing insurance; you pay a fee, known as a premium, in order to protect your winnings. In this case, you forfeit the chance to win $5 million. In contrast, gambles C and D offer small chances of success, and therefore the choice is more like playing the lottery. People who play games of chance are more likely to participate in games with large prizes, such as Powerball, because the winnings will measurably improve their lives. As the study showed, people care about how much they might win and also how much they stand to lose. This distinction causes people to choose gambles A and C. By establishing that many people behave this way, Allais reshaped how traditional economists viewed risk-taking behavior.

It turns out that preference reversals are more common than economists once believed. For example, approximately 80 percent of all income tax filers expect to get a refund because they overpaid the previous year. This is odd, since there is an opportunity cost of waiting to get money back from the government when it didn't need to be paid in the first place. Employees could simply have asked their employers to withhold less and enjoyed their money sooner. Individuals who choose to wait to receive their money later are said to have a negative time preference. In most circumstances, people have positive time preferences, or prefer to have what they want sooner rather than later. So what do these taxpayers do when they learn the amount of their refund? In many cases, they pay tax preparers extra money to have their refunds electronically sent to their bank accounts sooner! Traditional economic analysis is unable to explain this behavior, but armed with Allais's insights we now see this behavior as a preference reversal.

A similar process is at work with our next example of risk-taking behavior, prospect theory.

Prospect Theory

The television game show *Deal or No Deal* provides an opportunity for economists to examine the risk choices that contestants make in a high-stakes setting. *Deal or No Deal* has created particular excitement among researchers who study game shows because it involves no skill whatsoever. Taking skill out of the equation makes it easier to analyze the strategy choices of the contestants. Other TV game shows, like *Jeopardy!* and *Who Wants to Be a Millionaire?*, require skill to win prizes. Highly skilled players may have different risk tolerances than their less-skilled counterparts. As a result, part of the beauty of studying *Deal or No Deal* is that the outcome is a pure exercise in probability theory.

For those unfamiliar with *Deal or No Deal*, here is how the show works: 26 models each hold a briefcase that contains a sum of money varying from one cent to $1 million. The contestant picks one briefcase as her own and then begins to open the other 25 one at a time, slowly revealing a little more about what her own case might hold. Suspense builds and the contestant's chance of a big payoff grows when small sums are eliminated and the $1 million case and other valuable cases remain unopened. As cases are eliminated, a "banker" periodically calls the host to offer the contestant a "deal" in exchange for quitting the game.

At the start of the game, the expected value of the chosen briefcase is determined as follows:

$$EV_{briefcase} = \$.01 \times (1/26) + \$1 \times (1/26) + \$5 \times (1/26)$$
$$+ \ldots + \$1M \times (1/26) \tag{17.1}$$

This value computes to approximately $131,000. As the game progresses and cases are opened, the bank offers a settlement based on whether the expected value of the briefcase has increased or decreased.

Some contestants behave as the traditional model of risk behavior predicts: they maximize the expected value of the briefcase while remaining risk neutral. Since contestants who are risk neutral don't make for exciting television, the "bank" typically offers a "deal" that is far less than the expected value of the remaining cases throughout the early part of the game. This encourages contestants to play longer and the excitement and tension have a chance to build. But not all contestants do what the traditional model expects them to do. For example, some contestants take more risks if they suffer setbacks early in the game, such as opening the $1 million briefcase. This behavior is consistent with *prospect theory* from psychology. **Prospect theory**, articulated by Daniel Kahneman and Amos Tversky, suggests that individuals place more emphasis on gains than losses. This implies that people evaluate the risks that lead to gains separately from the risks that lead to losses. This result is useful because it tells us why some investors try to make up for the losses they have experienced by taking more chances later instead of seeking to maximize the utility they receive from money under a rigid calculation of expected value. Armed with this knowledge, we can explain a wider range of human reactions. For instance, some people routinely set their clocks forward in order to guarantee that they will arrive on time so as to avoid the large utility loss associated with being late. As a result, they often arrive five minutes early, whereas standard economic theory presumes that a rational person would never try to fool themselves.

Prospect theory
argues that individuals place more emphasis on gains than losses.

PRACTICE WHAT YOU KNOW

Risk Aversion: Risk-Taking Behavior

In the following situations, determine whether the choice is evidence of risk aversion or risk taking.

1. You have a choice between selecting heads or tails. If your guess is correct, you earn $2,000. But you earn nothing if you are incorrect. Alternatively, you can simply take $750 without the gamble. You decide to take the $750.

> **ANSWER:** The expected value of a 50/50 outcome worth $2,000 is $1,000. Therefore, the decision to take the sure thing, which is $250 less, is evidence of risk aversion.
>
> **2. You have a choice between predicting the roll of a six-sided die, with a $3,000 prize for a correct answer, or taking a sure $750. You decide to roll the die.**
>
> **ANSWER:** The expected value of the roll of the die is 1/6 × $3,000, or $500. Therefore, the sure thing has an expected value that is $250 more. By rolling the die you are taking the option with the lowest expected value and also the most risk. This indicates that you are a risk taker.

A Case Study: The Economics of Crime

We have seen that people don't always behave as economists expect. In this section we apply the ideas of behavioral economics to the economics of crime. We will also draw on what we already know about incentives and utility theory. So although criminals may lack a social conscience, with a little economics we can better understand their actions.

Speeding

Most of us speed; some a little bit, others a lot! We know that slowing down decreases the incidence of injury and death. Does this mean that the quest to save time by speeding is an irrational behavior? To answer that question we need to understand the incentives that govern how fast we drive.

Driving faster saves time. But time saved accumulates at a decreasing rate. This relationship can be seen in Figure 17.2. For example, suppose you are traveling at 5 miles per hour from Richmond to Washington, D.C., a distance of 100 miles. At this rate, the trip would take 20 hours. If you drive 10 mph, the trip will take 10 hours, or half the time. However, a 5 mph increase in speed will not save you very much time if you are already traveling at a much faster rate. For example, if you change from 50 to 55 mph, you will save comparatively little time. Traveling 100 miles at 50 mph takes 2 hours, whereas increasing to 55 mph reduces the travel time to 1 hour and 49 minutes, for a savings of 11 minutes. Therefore, the marginal benefit from driving 1 mph faster goes down as the speed goes up.

The benefits of driving faster are only half the equation. We must also consider the costs. Most vehicles are designed to operate efficiently between 40 and 60 mph. Driving too slowly increases the cost of operation, since fuel efficiency begins to decline. Driving too fast has the same effect. In addition, errors in judgment and decreased reaction time that happen at higher speeds are associated with accidents involving more significant injuries and damage. For instance, the Transportation Research Board found that the difference between a crash on a 55 mph limit road and a crash on a 65 mph limit road means a 28 percent increase in the likelihood that the accident will be fatal.

Driving at speeds beyond the posted limit also risks the cost of a speeding ticket. The faster you go, the greater your probability of getting a ticket.

Clearly, driving at lower speeds is safer and less expensive. Once we approach a comfortable speed we begin to look at the speedometer and focus on maintaining the speed. We can think of the speed we maintain as a personal equilibrium. At higher speeds, the costs are likely to exceed the benefits and at lower speeds the opposite is true. Each of us tries to find a speed that balances the marginal benefits (saved time) with the marginal costs (potential tickets, accidents, operating expenses).

As Figure 17.2 illustrates, the equilibrium speed may or may not correspond with the posted speed limit. One can easily imagine an interstate highway where the speed at which marginal benefit and marginal cost are equal (MB = MC) happens to be at a speed slightly over 70 mph. Typical drivers settle on a speed near this point on the open highway because at that speed they experience equilibrium.

We can use this framework to describe the behaviors of different sets of drivers. The elderly tend to drive slower than others. An older person is not likely to recover as quickly from a crash. Also, reaction time is a fraction slower in the elderly. The costs of driving faster are therefore higher than for a younger person. Seniors are also likely to have lower opportunity costs. People who are retired place a lower value on their time and are usually less likely to hurry. The next time you pass an elderly driver who happens to be going slower than the speed limit, remember that you and the other driver are experiencing different personal equilibriums.

Running a Red Light

Running a red light is less common than speeding. However, there are times when you may be tempted not to wait for the light to change. For example, imagine pulling up to a deserted intersection after midnight. The red light

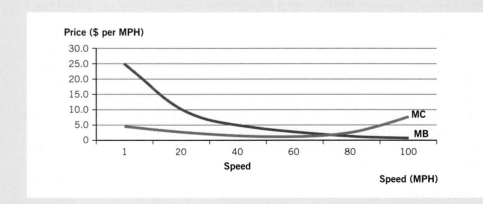

FIGURE 17.2

The Marginal Costs and Marginal Benefits of Speeding

The marginal benefits from driving faster, in terms of time saved, decline as shown by the MB curve. However, as speeds increase the marginal cost curve starts to rise. This leads the marginal cost curve to eventually cross the marginal benefits curve. At the point where the MC and MB are equal, the driver reaches a personal equilibrium that determines her optimal speed.

seems to take an eternity to change. If you check both ways and see no one around, it may reasonable to assume that no one will get hurt. This is one of the reasons many stoplights blink late at night; the blinking signal transforms the stoplight into a caution signal or a stop sign, thereby allowing the driver to save time when it is safe to go.

But what if the intersection is clear and another car is approaching from about 500 meters away? You could proceed through the intersection without interrupting the flow of traffic coming from the other direction. Would you do it? Would it harm anyone? The decision to run the red light becomes increasingly less safe as the flow of traffic increases.

At this point you might be wondering why society has speed limits and stop lights. These limits on our behavior serve as commitment mechanisms that encourage most people to act responsibly. In other words, traffic laws promote intertemporal decision-making; instead of everyone rushing around trying to get where they are going as fast as possible, well-designed traffic laws combined with adequate enforcement and penalties act to curb aggressive driving. Behavioral economics tells us of the need for "limits," whereas a strict analysis of the economics of speeding and red lights sends the jarring message that breaking traffic laws can be rational behavior.

Vehicle Theft

We can use the subject of theft to see how behavioral economics explains risk taking. Over 1 million vehicles are stolen each year in the United States, making motor vehicle theft one of the most common crimes. According to the National Insurance Crime Bureau, in 2011 the most commonly stolen car in the United States was the 1994 Honda Accord. Other vehicles to make the top-ten list include the 1995 Honda Civic, 1991 Toyota Camry, and 2004 Dodge Ram Explorer. What do these vehicles have in common? These vehicles escape notice. When was the last time you stopped to watch a 1994 Honda Accord? The 1999 Chevrolet pickup, 1997 Ford F150 pickup, 2000 Dodge Caravan, 1994 Acura Integra, 2002 Ford Explorer, and 1999 Ford Taurus round out the top-ten list. Criminals often avoid detection by stripping stolen vehicles for parts. Because the vehicles on the list were all cars that sold well in their time, there is a large demand for replacement parts. This suggests that the perpetrators of crimes involving motor vehicles consider what type of automobile to steal and make a rational judgment about what crime will have the best payoff. It also explains why criminals don't steal more expensive vehicles. Parts from a Mercedes, Jaguar, or BMW would be worth more. However, luxury vehicles are more noticeable and easier to trace. The rational criminal knows that it will be more difficult to resell the stolen parts.

Generally, a rational criminal is aware of the chances of being caught, prosecuted, and imprisoned, and even the possibility of being paroled early. Therefore, criminals avoid activities that will create greater scrutiny. However, not all automobile thefts are rational. Economists can't explain every theft, in part because some criminals steal cars for far less calculating reasons, such as joyrides by thrill seekers.

ECONOMICS IN THE REAL WORLD

Why Are There Cold Openings at the Box Office?

Economists Alexander L. Brown, Colin F. Camerer, and Dan Lovallo studied 856 widely released movies and found that cold openings, or movies withheld from critics before their release, produced a significant increase (15 percent) in domestic box-office revenue. Most movie openings are accompanied by a marketing campaign to increase consumer demand. As a consequence, cold openings provide a natural field setting to test how rational moviegoers are. Their results are consistent with the hypothesis that some moviegoers do not infer low quality from a cold opening, as they should. Movie studios generally make a film available for review if the screenings are expected to generate any positive buzz. Also, access to movie reviews provides moviegoers with one measure of a film's quality. So a rational moviegoer should infer that if a movie studio releases a film without reviews, it is signaling that the movie is not very good—the studio didn't want to risk negative reviews, so it didn't preview the movie at all. This makes the success of cold openings surprising.

The authors have shown that movies that were cold-opened earned more than other prescreened movies after they controlled for a number of characteristics. Importantly, they also found that films that were cold-opened did not fare better than expected once they reached foreign film or video rental markets. In both of those cases, movie reviews are widely available, so any advantage from cold-opening a film would have dissipated. The disappearance of the advantage in rental and overseas markets is consistent with the hypothesis that the premium is due to some moviegoers failing to realize that no advance review is a poor signal about quality. The fact that moviegoer ratings from the Internet Movie Database (www.imdb.com) are lower for movies that were cold-opened also suggests that in the absence of any information moviegoers overestimated the expected quality.

Over time, distributers have learned that there is a certain amount of moviegoer naiveté, especially among teenagers. Distributors have overcome their initial reluctance and cold-opened more movies in recent years.

These findings provide another example that contradicts the notion of the fully rational consumer. Evidently, the best movie distribution strategy does not depend entirely upon generating positive movie reviews, despite what traditional economic models would lead us to believe. ✳

PRACTICE WHAT YOU KNOW

Economics of Crime: How Fast Would You Drive?

Question: Imagine that you are a lawyer who travels the same road to work each weekday. But there is a problem: once every two weeks the cops set up a speed trap. You never know when this will happen—it occurs randomly. You can travel the speed limit of 35 mph and avoid a $25 ticket, or you can travel at 45 mph, get to work five minutes faster, and pay the ticket. If your time is worth $50 per hour, what speed should you travel?

Answer: We need to determine if enough time is saved to warrant driving faster. If you drive 45 mph, you will save five minutes on nine of the ten mornings—or 45 minutes over two weeks. Since 45 minutes is 3/4 of an hour, you are able to bill your clients for an extra $37.50. This is enough extra money to offset the $25 ticket. Zoom, zoom!

ECONOMICS FOR LIFE

Economics of Crime: How to Guard Yourself Against Crime

Suppose that a recent crime wave has hit your community and you are scared about your family's security. Determined to make your house safe, you consider many options: an alarm system, bars on your windows, deadbolts for your doors, better lighting around your house, and a guard dog. Which of these solutions will protect you from a rational criminal at the lowest cost? All of these solutions provide a measure of protection, but only one solution provides deterrence at a low cost. If you trim away the shrubs and install flood lights,

criminals know they can be seen approaching your home. Since criminals look for the easiest target to rob, they will find a house that is easy to break into without detection. A few hundred dollars spent on better lighting will dramatically lower your chances of be robbed. However, there is an even better answer. A rational criminal may not know what is inside your house, so a couple of prominently displayed "beware of dog" signs would discourage the robber for less than $10 and save you money in the process!

Conclusion

The material presented in this chapter is designed to challenge what you have learned about economic theory. It also represents a departure from the previous 16 chapters. Behavioral economics questions the traditional economics model, but it does not merely question—it invites a deeper understanding of human behavior by treating rationality as the basis for many but not all decisions. Behavioral economics helps to dispel the misperception that economics is based solely on rational decision-making. Armed with the insights from behavioral economics, we can answer questions that span a wider range of behaviors. We have seen this in the examples in this chapter that include the "opt-in" or "opt-out" debate, the economics of crime, risk taking, question design, and the status quo bias. These ideas do not fit squarely into traditional economic analysis, and that is OK. You have learned enough at this point to question the assumptions we have made throughout this book. In the next chapter, on health care and insurance, we will apply all of the tools we have acquired so far to examine one of the most important sectors of the economy.

ANSWERING THE BIG QUESTIONS

1. How can economists explain irrational behavior?

* In this chapter we have learned that bounded rationality, prospect theory, misperceptions of probabilities, the status quo bias, intertemporal decision-making, fairness, and many other ideas help to frame how choices are made.

* Folding the behavioral approach into the standard model makes our predictions about human behavior less precise but much richer at the same time.

2. What is the role of risk in decision-making?

* In the traditional economic model, risk tolerances are assumed to be constant. If you were a risk taker by nature, you'd respond that way in any circumstance. Likewise, if you did not like to take chances, you'd avoid risk.

* Allais proved that many people have inconsistent risk preferences, or what are known as preference reversals. Moreover, he showed that just because some people's preferences were not constant, this does not necessarily mean that their decisions are irrational.

* Prospect theory shows that some participants are willing to take on additional risk in order to try to recover losses that are caused by negative shocks.

3. Can economic theory explain why some people feel crime pays?

* Most crimes are intentional and therefore predictable. Our standard economic model works well. People speed, jaywalk, and even steal because of incentives. Knowing what those incentives are, and how to shape them, allows society to rein in those who are tempted to break the law.

* An understanding of intertemporal decision-making, and the misperception that getting caught is a low-probability event, helps explain why some criminals continue to break the law despite odds that indicate that getting away with it over the long run is a losing proposition.

CONCEPTS YOU SHOULD KNOW

Behavioral economics (p. 496)
Bounded rationality (p. 496)
Framing effects (p. 500)
Gambler's fallacy (p. 498)
Hot hand fallacy (p. 499)

Loss aversion (p. 501)
Preference reversal (p. 506)
Priming effects (p. 501)
Prospect theory (p. 507)
Risk averse (p. 505)

Risk neutral (p. 505)
Risk taker (p. 505)
Status quo bias (p. 501)
Ultimatum game (p. 503)

QUESTIONS FOR REVIEW

1. What is bounded rationality? How is this idea relevant to economic modeling?

2. What are the hot hand fallacy and the gambler's fallacy? Give an example of each.

3. How can constrained choice improve the decisions that people make?

4. How does the status quo bias reduce the potential utility that consumers enjoy?

5. Economists use the ultimatum game to test fairness. What result does economic theory predict?

6. What is prospect theory? Have you ever suffered a setback early in a process (for example, seeking a job or applying for college) that caused you to alter your behavior later on?

7. Is criminal activity a rational or irrational activity? Defend your answer.

STUDY PROBLEMS

1. You have a choice between taking two jobs. The first job pays $50,000 annually. The second job has a base pay of $40,000, with a 30 percent chance that you will receive an annual bonus of $25,000. You decide to take the $50,000 job. Can we tell if you are risk averse or a risk taker?

2. Suppose that Danny Ocean decides to play roulette, one of the most popular casino games. Roulette is attractive to gamblers because the house's advantage is small (less than 5 percent). If Danny Ocean plays roulette and wins big, is this evidence that Danny Ocean is risk averse or a risk taker? Explain.

3. Many voters go to the polls every four years to cast their ballots for president. The common refrain among those who voted is that their vote "counts' and that voting is important. A skeptical economist points out that with over 100 million ballots cast, the probability that your vote will be decisive is close to zero.

What idea, discussed in this chapter, explains why so many people actually vote?

4. Your instructor is very conscientious and always makes sure that exam answers are randomly distributed. However, you notice that the first five answers on the true/false section are "true." Unsure what this pattern means, you consider the next question. However, you do not know the answer. What answer you would give if you believed in the gambler's fallacy? What answer would you give if you believed in the hot hand fallacy?

5. Suppose that a university wishes to maximize the response rate for teaching evaluations. The administration develops an easy-to-use online evaluation system that can be completed by each student at the end of the semester. However, very few students bother to complete the survey. The registrar's office suggests that the online teaching evaluations be linked to course scheduling. When students access the course-scheduling

system, they will be redirected to the teaching evaluations. Under this plan each student could opt out and go directly to the course-scheduling system. Do you think this plan will work to raise the response rate on the teaching evaluations? What would traditional economic theory predict? What would behavioral economics predict?

6. Ray likes his hamburgers with American cheese, lettuce, and ketchup. Whenever he places an order for a burger he automatically orders these three toppings. What type of behavior is Ray exhibiting? What does traditional utility theory say about Ray's preferences? What would a behavioral economist say?

7. Many people give to charity and leave tips. What prediction does utility theory make

about each of these activities? (**Hint:** think of the person's narrow self-interest.) What concept from behavioral economics explains this behavior?

8. Given a choice of an extra $1,000 or a gamble with the same expected value, a person prefers the $1,000. But given a choice of a loss of $1,000 or a gamble with the same expected value, the same person prefers the gamble. How would a behavioral economist describe this decision?

9. Suppose that you own a used car with high mileage, a rusted outer body, and engine parts that are almost completely worthless on the resale market. Should you buy a steering-wheel locking device to prevent theft?

The Economics of Information, Insurance, and Health Care

* What makes health care different from other industries?
* Why does asymmetric information make it difficult to administer health care?
* How do demand and supply contribute to high medical costs?

We have come a long way in our exploration of microeconomics. In this chapter we will apply our economic tool kit to one particular industry—health care. The goal of this chapter is not to sway your opinion but to provide you with a simple set of tools to help focus your thinking about how medical care can best serve individuals and society as a whole. We will also dispel the misperception that the health care debate is about universal health care versus private medical care.

Health care is big business. Together, the education and automobile sectors represent about 10 percent of America's economic output, or gross domestic product. But health care alone accounts for 15.8 percent of GDP. That's one out of every six dollars spent annually in the United States—more than 2 trillion dollars, or $7,000 for every citizen. However you slice it, that is a lot of money!

We begin this chapter with an overview of the health care system. Unless you have been seriously ill, have helped to care for someone with an acute medical condition, or have paid someone's medical bills, it is unlikely that you have first-hand knowledge of how the health care system functions. We will look at how health care is delivered, who pays, and what makes the provision of medical care unlike any other sector of the economy. Then we will use supply and demand analysis to look at how the medical market functions. One of the unusual aspects of medical care is the role that information plays in the incentive structure for patients and providers. Finally, we will examine a number of case studies to pull all of this information together so you can decide for yourself where you stand on one of the most important issues of the twenty-first century.

Photo to come

Health Care Overview

At the start of the twentieth century, the average life expectancy in the United States was slightly less than 50 years. Now, life expectancy is close to 80 years—a longevity gain that would have been unthinkable a few generations ago. Let's go back in time to examine the way medical care was delivered and some of the advances that have improved the human condition.

At the beginning of the 20th century, infectious diseases were the most common cause of death in this country. Typhoid, diphtheria, gangrene, gastritis, smallpox, and tuberculosis were major killers. Today, because of antibiotics, they have either been completely eradicated or are extremely uncommon. Moreover, the state of medical knowledge 100 years ago was so dismal that a cure was often far worse than the condition it was supposed to treat. For instance, tobacco was recommended for the treatment of bronchitis and asthma, and leeches were used to fight laryngitis. Throughout the first half of the 20th century a trip to the doctor was expensive, painful, and rarely produced positive results.

Since 1950, advances in cellular biology and discoveries in biochemistry have led to a better understanding of the disease process and more precise diagnostic tests. Discoveries in biomedical engineering have led to the widespread use of imaging techniques like ultrasound, computerized axial tomography (CAT scans), and nuclear magnetic resonance imaging (MRI), which have replaced the medical practices of the past and made medical care safer, gentler, and more effective. In addition, pharmaceutical companies have developed a number of "miracle" drugs for fighting many conditions, including high blood pressure, leukemia, and bad cholesterol, thereby limiting the need for more invasive treatments.

In this section we examine how much is spent on health care, where the money goes, and the key players in the industry. The goal is to give you a sense of how the sector functions. Then we will turn our attention to supply and demand.

Health Care Expenditures

We have noted that health expenditures in the United States are 15.8 percent of GDP. As you can see in Table 18.1, this is quite a bit higher than in other developed nations. France spends only 11 percent of GDP on health care, Canada 10 percent, Italy 9 percent, and Japan slightly more than 8 percent.

The United States spends significantly more on health care than any other country but has a life expectancy that is between two and four years lower than most developed countries. How can that be? Increased health care expenditures are making people healthier, happier (since they feel better), and more productive—this is true for all of the countries in Table 18.1. However, longevity in the United States lags behind that in many peer countries. One explanation is natural variation in longevity as a function of environmental factors, genetics, and lifestyle choices. Even if these factors help to explain why the United States has a lower life expectancy, they do not explain why the United States spends roughly 50 percent more than most developed nations to achieve approximately the same results.

TABLE 18.1

Health Care Facts in Selected OECD Countries

Region	Country	Total Expenditure on Health (percent of GDP)	Per Capita Expenditure on Health (in U.S. dollars)	Life Expectancy at Birth, Total Population
North America				
	Mexico	5.8	777	74.8
	Canada	10.0	3,696	80.7
	U.S.	15.8	6,933	78.1
Europe				
	France	11.0	3,423	80.7
	Germany	10.5	3,464	79.8
	Italy	9.0	2,673	81.4
	Norway	8.6	4,507	80.5
	Spain	8.4	2,466	81.1
	U.K.	8.5	2,885	79.5
Asia Pacific				
	Australia	8.8	3,167	81.1
	Japan	8.1	2,581	82.4

Source: Organization for Economic Co-Operation and Development, http://stats.oecd.org. Data is for 2006.

Why is health care taking up so much of our budget? There are a number of reasons. Health insurance plays a contributing role. When private insurance covers most treatment costs, many patients agree to additional tests or medical visits. Doctors are more willing to order tests that might not be necessary if they know the patient isn't paying directly. Medicare and Medicaid, the two government-sponsored forms of health insurance, add to the overall demand for medical services by providing medical coverage to the elderly and poor. As we learned earlier, any time there is more demand for services the market price rises in response. Another reason is the number of uninsured—close to 50 million in the United States. When the uninsured need immediate medical treatment, they often seek care from emergency rooms and clinics. This raises costs in two ways. First, emergency care is extraordinarily expensive. Second, waiting until one has an acute condition that requires immediate attention often requires more treatment than preventive care or an early diagnosis. For example, an insured person who develops an acute cough with fever is likely to see a physician. If the patient has bronchitis, a few days of medicine and rest will be all it takes to feel better. However, an uninsured person who develops bronchitis is less likely to seek medical help and risks the possibility of a worsening condition, such as pneumonia, which can be difficult and costly to treat. Medical demand is quite inelastic, so when competition is absent, hospitals and other providers can charge what they want and patients will pay. In addition, health care costs are high because people are not usually proactive about their health. Many health problems could be dramatically reduced and costs contained if people curbed habits such as cigarette use, excessive alcohol consumption, and overeating and got more exercise. Finally, heroic end-of-life efforts are extraordinarily expensive. These efforts may extend life for a few months, days, or hours and come at a steep price. In most cases the benefits to society are not worth the costs.

Diminishing Returns

In the United States, it has become the norm to spare no expense in efforts to extend life for even a few days. However, providing more medical care is subject to diminishing returns. This is shown in Figure 18.1. The health production function initially rises rapidly when small amounts of health care are provided, but the benefits of additional care have progressively smaller marginal effects on longevity, general health, and the quality of life as it relates to health. This is seen by looking at points A and B. At point A, only a small amount of medical care is provided, but this has a large impact on health. The slope at point A represents the marginal product of medical care. However, by the time we reach point B, the marginal product of medical care is much lower, indicating that diminishing returns have set in.

As a result, higher medical care expenditures, beyond some point, are unlikely to measurably improve longevity and quality of life. This is because many other factors, such as disease, genetics, and lifestyle, also play a key role in determining health, quality of life, and longevity. In addition, advances in medical care have made many conditions treatable and saved billions of dollars in the process. But advances in medical care have also extended life for those with terminal conditions, and this is very costly. As we move out along the medical production function, extending life becomes progressively

FIGURE 18.1

Health Production Function

The marginal product of medical care, indicated by the slope of the health production function, is higher at point A than point B.

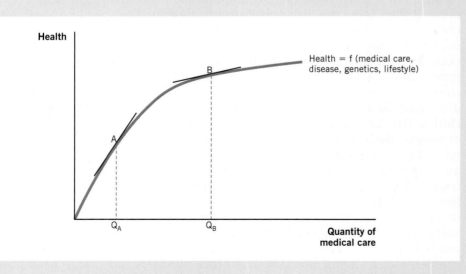

more difficult, so it is not surprising that medical costs have risen appreciably. Society has two questions to answer. First, what is the optimal mix of expenditures on medical care? Second, could we get more from each dollar spent by reallocating funding away from heroic efforts to extend life toward prevention and medical research?

Figure 18.2 shows where the typical health dollar goes. Hospital care, physicians, and clinics account for half of all medical expenses. After that, prescription drugs, dental care, home health care, continuing care, and nursing homes each represent smaller parts of health care expenditures. Medical care has become much more efficient. Medical records are increasingly computerized and many procedures that required days of hospitalization a generation ago can now be done on an outpatient basis. The implication is that reducing medical costs through efficiency gains is ongoing, and yet costs continue to rise. There are many reasons for high costs. In the next section we examine the incentives that patients, providers, and insurance companies face when making medical decisions and how the incentives structure contributes to escalating costs.

Who's Who in Health Care

Health care consumption is different from that of most goods and services. Health care services have consumers and producers. But because of intermediaries, such as insurance companies, the two rarely interact directly. This creates a unique set of incentives and creates distortions in the standard supply and demand analysis. It is important to understand how medical care is delivered and paid for, and the incentives that patients, medical providers, and insurers face when making decisions.

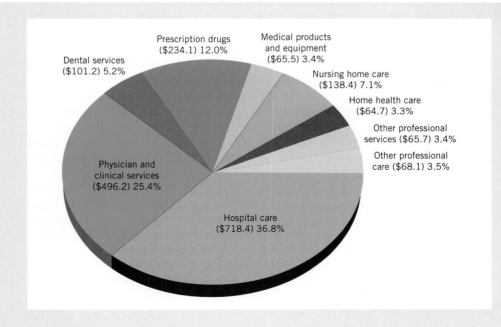

Prescription drugs
($234.1) 12.0%

Medical products
and equipment
($65.5) 3.4%

Dental services
($101.2) 5.2%

Nursing home care
($138.4) 7.1%

Home health care
($64.7) 3.3%

Other professional
services ($65.7) 3.4%

Other professional
care ($68.1) 3.5%

Physician and
clinical services
($496.2) 25.4%

Hospital care
($718.4) 36.8%

FIGURE 18.2

The Nation's Health Dollar

Hospital care, physicians, and clinics make up over half of all personal health care expenditures, which totaled $1.9523 trillion in 2008. *Source:* National Health Expenditures, June 2010, Centers for Medicare and Medicaid Services. (Dollar amounts shown in chart are in billions.)

Consumers

The two biggest consumers of medical care are patients and the government. Patients demand medical care when they are ill, and to prevent illness. The federal government runs Medicare, a program that provides medical assistance to the elderly, and Medicaid, a program that provides medical assistance to the poor. Medicare and Medicaid are social insurance programs that each serve over 40 million enrollees. The two programs account for approximately one-third of all medical spending in the United States, and represent about 20 percent of all U.S. government expenditures.

Producers

The medical care industry employs millions of workers, including doctors, nurses, psychologists, and technicians. There are also over 500,000 medical facilities in this country, including small medical offices, large regional hospitals, nursing homes, and pharmacies and stores that supply medical equipment. In addition, pharmaceutical companies generate over $300 billion in sales in the United States.

Intermediaries

A unique feature of the medical industry is the presence of intermediaries. These intermediaries, such as insurance companies, cover certain medical expenses in exchange for a set monthly fee, known as a premium. Unlike most markets, the consumers of medical care and the producers of medical care products and services typically work through insurance companies. Medical insurance allows consumers to budget their expenses and limit what they will have to pay in the event of a serious condition.

Insurance companies use the premiums they receive from their customers to pay medical suppliers. You may not need an appendectomy this year, but a predictable number of insured customers will. Using statistical techniques, an insurance company with millions of customers can accurately predict how many of its patients will visit the doctor and require hospitalization and other services. This allows the insurance company to estimate its costs in advance. Because it can estimate its costs, an insurance company can charge an amount that allows it to make a profit. The same process is at work for medical malpractice, or negligent treatment. By looking at the number of malpractice cases for each type of medical procedure each year, insurers know the probability that a particular doctor will face a malpractice claim and can incorporate this known probability into the fee they charge for malpractice insurance.

Many people receive medical care through *health maintenance organizations*, or HMOs, another example of an intermediary. HMOs provide managed care for their patients by assigning their customers a primary care physician who oversees their medical care. The HMO then monitors the primary care provider to ensure that unnecessary care is not prescribed. This process helps to contain costs, but it is also points to the inherent conflict that exists between consumers, producers, and intermediaries. Consumers want every treatment to be covered, producers don't want to be sued for malpractice, and the insurance company wants to make a profit. As a result, it is difficult to insure unlimited medical care at a reasonable cost.

PRACTICE WHAT YOU KNOW

Health Care Overview: Getting the Most out of the Health Care Dollar

Question: You suggest to your father that he get a physical, but he is reluctant to go since he feels fine. He points out that the physical would take a couple of hours and costs a $10 co-pay. How could you convince your father that getting the physical will benefit not only him but also the rest of the family and society?

Answer: Begin by pointing out that many conditions are easily cured when detected early. Not only might your father avoid getting seriously ill, but the cost of treating any condition that the doctor finds is lower when caught sooner. This benefits him directly, since any out-of-pocket expenses he would incur will be less. It also creates a positive externality for society, since preventive care lowers the overall amount spent on medical care. Since medical insurance premiums are determined by insurance companies, the premiums that are paid will be higher if many people do not seek preventive care. In that sense, your father's reluctance to have routine medical exams imposes a negative externality on the rest of society.

Asymmetric Information

We have seen that incentives play an important role in how medical care is delivered. Another important element is the information available to participants. Imbalances in information, known as **asymmetric information**, exist whenever one party knows more than the other. Asymmetric information takes on two forms: *adverse selection* and the *principal-agent problem*.

Asymmetric information exists whenever one party has more information than the other.

Adverse Selection

Most of us know very little about medicine. We know when we don't feel well and we want to feel better, so we seek medical attention. Because we know very little about the service we are buying, we are a poor judge of quality. How can you know your provider is qualified, or better than the alternative? **Adverse selection** exists when one party has information about some aspect of product quality that the other party does not have. As a result, the party with the limited information should be concerned that the other party will misrepresent information to gain an advantage. When one side knows more than the other, the only way to avoid an adverse outcome is to gather better information. For example, many patients seek a second opinion from another doctor before making a decision about a major medical procedure. People ask friends and acquaintances to recommend doctors. In recent times, people have turned more and more to the Internet to read evaluations of doctors and hospitals.

Adverse selection exists when one party has access to some aspect of product quality that the other party does not have.

The term *adverse selection* also refers to the situation in which buyers are more likely to seek insurance if they have a higher risk of needing it. However, an insurance company will not make any profit if every client requires expensive medical care. For this reason, insurance companies must manage the risk they face. Consider the case of a man who has a chronic illness but has changed jobs and must purchase new insurance. The insurance company doesn't know anything about this new customer and wants to avoid selling an inexpensive policy to someone who is likely to require costly medical care. The insurance company has to gather additional information about the applicant. The insurance company can require a medical exam and delay eligibility for full benefits until it can determine that the client has no pre-existing health conditions. As a result, the process of gathering information about the applicant is crucial in minimizing the risk associated with adverse selection.

New laws complicate matters for the insurance companies. For example, the Health Insurance Portability and Accountability Act (HIPAA), which was passed in 1996, makes it illegal for insurance companies to deny coverage of pre-existing conditions. This makes it harder for insurance companies to keep premiums affordable. Few people believe that unhealthy individuals should be denied medical insurance. However, if insurance companies want to stay in business, they have to price their policies based on risk. As a result, unhealthy people pay higher premiums than healthy people. This process is similar to how automobile insurance works, where drivers with poor records pay substantially higher premiums, and safer drivers pay substantially lower prices.

More important, markets do not work well when adverse selection exists. Some insurance applicants who are good risks will be denied insurance and others who are bad risks will receive it. This curtails the gains from trade that characterize most market interactions between buyers and sellers.

The Principal-Agent Problem

The **principal-agent problem** arises when an agent does not complete a task to the principal's liking.

Patients generally trust doctors to make good treatment decisions based on medical welfare. Unfortunately, in our current medical system *the principle-agent problem* means this is not always the case. A **principal-agent problem** arises when a principal, in this case a patient, entrusts an agent, in this case the physician or hospital, to complete a task and the agent does not do so in a satisfactory way. For example, in a medical setting the principal-agent problem exists whenever patients cannot directly observe how their interests are being managed by medical providers and insurers. The lack of oversight on the part of patients gives their agents, the physicians and insurance companies, some freedom to pursue other objectives that do not directly benefit patients. In the case of medicine, doctors and hospitals may order more tests, procedures, or visits to specialists than are medically necessary. The physician or the hospital may be more concerned about profits or about avoiding medical malpractice lawsuits than about the patient's health and well-being. At the same time, insurance companies may desire to economize on treatment costs in order to maximize the bottom line. In both cases, the patient's desire for the best medical care is at odds with the objectives of the agents carrying out the care.

Moral Hazard

The Simpsons: King-Sized Homer

A new corporate fitness policy is intended to encourage the power plant workers to become healthier. Morning exercises are instituted and the employees are whipped into shape. Homer hates working out, so he decides to gain a large amount of weight in order to claim disability and work at home. In order to qualify he must weigh at least 300 pounds. This means that Homer must go on an eating binge. Of course, his behavior is not what the designers of the new fitness policy had in mind. This amusing episode is a wonderful example of moral hazard and shows how well-intentioned policies are often abused.

The principal-agent problem creates **moral hazard**, which occurs when a party that is protected from risk behaves differently from how it would behave if it were fully exposed to the risk. Moral hazard does not necessary entail behavior that is "immoral" or "unethical." But it does imply that some people will change their behavior because their risk exposure is reduced and the "it's insured" mentality sets in. This can lead to a number of inefficient outcomes. Patients visit the doctor more often. Employees on a salary take longer breaks. Financial firms assume that the government won't let them fail and therefore accept more risk. In each of these examples there is a moral hazard problem that can be lessened by restructuring the incentives. For the patient, a higher co-payment—the amount paid out of pocket in addition to insurance coverage—will discourage unnecessary doctor visits. To give workers an incentive to use their time productively, a company might tie a portion of the employee's salary to performance. Large financial institutions could be split into smaller companies that would not cause undue harm to the economy if they failed.

To solve a moral hazard problem in medical care you have to fix the incentive structure. This explains why many insurance companies encourage preventive care; it lowers medical costs. It also explains why insurance companies impose payment limits on preventable conditions such as gum disease and tooth decay.

Moral hazard
occurs when a party that is protected from risk behaves differently from how it would behave if it were fully exposed to the risk.

The Demand and Supply of Health Care

Now that we have a basic understanding of how the health care industry functions and the key players in the industry, it is time to examine how demand and supply operate in the market for health care. On the demand side we consider what makes health care demand stubbornly inelastic. Health care, when

PRACTICE WHAT YOU KNOW

Asymmetric Information

For each of the following situations, determine whether adverse selection, the principal-agent problem, or moral hazard is at work.

1. You decide to use an online dating site, but you are not entirely sure the posted picture of your date is accurate.

Answer: This is adverse selection. The person you are interested in knows more about himself than you. He can, and probably would, post a picture of himself that is flattering. When you finally meet you are likely to be disappointed.

2. You hire a substitute babysitter and agree to pay $40 up front. Later you find out that the sitter spent more time on the phone than watching your child.

Answer: Since you paid up front for a one-time job, the babysitter has very little incentive to watch your child as well as your regular sitter, who expects repeat business and a tip. The poor outcome is a result of moral hazard.

3. You hire a college student to feed your cats and change the litter twice a day while you are on vacation. However, the student only visits your house every other day.

Answer: This is a principal-agent problem. Since you are out of town, there is no way to tell how often the student goes to your house. The student knows that the cats are largely self-sufficient and you won't be able to tell how often he visited your home.

you need it, is not about the price—it is about getting care you need. When you consider this fact and the presence of third-party payments, or payments made by insurance companies, you can begin to understand why medical expenses have risen so rapidly. On the supply side, medical licensing requirements help to explain why the supply of medical services is limited. The combination of strong demand and limited supply pushes up prices for medical services.

Health Care Demand

Health care is usually a necessity, without many good alternatives. This explains why the demand for health care is typically inelastic. For example, doing without a heart transplant, when you need one, isn't an option. In fact, health care has an average price elasticity coefficient of −0.17. This means that a 1 percent increase in the price of health care will lead to a 0.17 percent reduction in health care expenditures. Recall that the closer the elasticity coefficient is to 0, the more inelastic is demand, so the demand for medical care is quite inelastic. (For a refresher on elasticity, see Chapter 4.)

But there are situations in which health care expenditures can be reduced. For example, otherwise healthy people with minor colds and other viruses

Inelastic Demand

John Q (2002)

John Q follows John Quincy Archibald's quest to help his son receive a heart transplant. His son suddenly collapses while playing baseball and is rushed to the emergency room. Doctors inform John Q that his son's only hope is a transplant. Since the child will die without the transplant, John Q's demand for this surgery is perfectly inelastic. Unfortunately, due to an involuntary work reduction at his job, John Q's insurance won't cover his son's transplant. The tagline of the film is: "Give a father no options and you leave him no choice." This nicely summarizes the dilemma that many without insurance face. However, this does not stop the uninsured from demanding medical care when a condition is life-threatening. This is problematic on two fronts. First, when those without insurance turn to the emergency room as their only source of medical care, their medical conditions are treated in the most expensive manner possible. Second, hospitals transfer the cost of treating the uninsured by raising the prices of the other services that they provide. As a result, society picks up the tab for the uninsured indirectly through higher insurance premiums.

No one likes to see a child die because his family lacks health insurance. After exploring every available financial option, John Q takes matters into his own hands and holds the emergency room staff hostage until the hospital agrees to do the transplant. Of course, this sensationalizes the problem, but it also makes a very powerful point about the costs and benefits of life-saving care.

can use home remedies, including drinking fluids and resting. So the price elasticity of demand also depends on the severity of the medical need and the sense of urgency involved in treatment. Urgent needs have the most inelastic demand. As the time horizon expands from the short run to the long run, the demand for health care becomes progressively more elastic. Nonemergency long-term treatments have the greatest price elasticity. For instance, a significant portion of the adult population postpones routine dental visits, despite the obvious benefits. When a tooth goes bad, people are more likely to choose extractions, which are less expensive, though less attractive, than root canals and crowns.

In recent years demand for health care has grown increasingly inelastic. As people live longer, demand rises for expensive medical goods and services like nursing homes, hearing aids, replacements joints, and so on. In an aging population, certain illnesses and conditions, such as cancer and Alzheimer's disease, become more common. In addition, new technologies have made it possible to treat medical conditions that were previously incurable. While these medical advances have improved the quality of life for many, they drive up demand for more advanced medical procedures, equipment, and specialty drugs.

Third-Party Participation

People who are risk averse generally choose to purchase insurance because it protects them against the possibility of extreme financial hardship in the case of illness or other medical problems. But when people have insurance it may distort their idea of costs and change their behavior. For example, if an insurance policy requires the patient to pay nothing or very little to see the doctor, the patient may wind up seeing the doctor more than necessary.

Consider how this affects two patients. Ebenezer Scrooge does not have insurance and therefore must pay the full cost of medical care out of pocket. Bob Cratchit has an insurance policy that requires a small co-payment for medical care. Figure 18.3 illustrates the difference between how Scrooge and Cratchit might react. Let's suppose that they both get sick five times during the year. Scrooge, because he pays the full cost of seeking treatment, will only go to the doctor's office three times. He ends up paying $300. Bob Cratchit pays $10 per visit, so he will go to the doctor's office five times for a total of $50. The rest of the cost for Bob, $90 per visit, is picked up by the insurance company.

The overall impact on health costs is large. Since each visit costs $100, total health care costs are only $300 when self-insured, but increase to $500 with coverage—a $200 increase in total health care costs. Since insurance companies are paying 90 percent of the cost, the consumer has little reason not to seek medical attention, even for minor problems that will respond to home treatment. The two extra visits per year illustrate a change in consumer behavior as a result of the lower co-payment. This is one reason why insurance costs are so high.

Health Care Supply

While consumers worry about the price they pay, producers are concerned about profits. As much as we might like to think that medical providers care only about our health, they are providing a service for which they expect

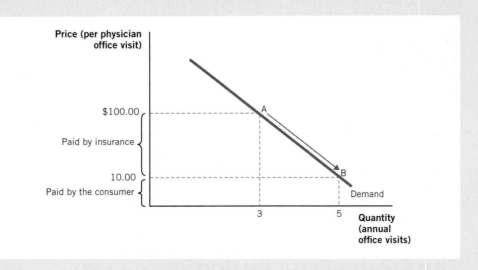

FIGURE 18.3

Price and the Quantity Demanded of Medical Care Services

Without insurance, the consumer bears the entire cost of an office visit, or $100. At this amount the consumer might think twice about whether the medical care is truly necessary. As a result of these costs, the consumer makes 3 office visits per year, represented by point A. However, when the consumer has insurance and is charged only a $10 co-payment per visit, the marginal price drops and the quantity demanded increases. Physician visits rise to 5 per year, represented by point B.

to be paid. Those in the business of health care do care about the bottom line. Therefore, it is more accurate to think of health providers like any other producers: when the price rises, they are willing to supply additional health care. Producers of medical care such as physicians and hospitals also enjoy significant market power. In this section we look at how licensing requirements limit the supply of health care providers and the effect this has on the market.

Becoming a skilled medical provider is a lengthy process that requires extensive training, education, and certification. Physicians must secure licenses from a medical board before they can practice, and nurses must become registered. Restrictions associated with entering the medical profession limit the supply of workers. This is captured in Figure 18.4, which illustrates how entry barriers limit the number of physicians and nurses and the impact that this has on the wages they receive.

Barriers to entry in the medical profession restrict the supply of physicians and nurses. The subsequent decrease in the supply of medical workers (from q_1 to q_2) causes the wages of these workers to increase to w_2. Because other workers in the industry, such as physician assistants, technicians, and nurse assistants, do not benefit as much from barriers to entry, their wages are not as high.

In addition, many medical facilities do not face direct competition. Many smaller communities have only one hospital. Familiarity, the need for immediate care, and convenience make the nearest hospital the default option for most patients. Since economies of scale are important in the provision of medical care, even large metropolitan areas tend to have only a few large hospitals rather than many smaller competitors. As the population base expands, larger hospitals can afford to offer a wider set of services than smaller hospitals.

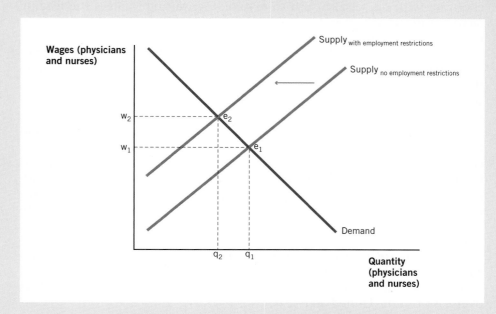

FIGURE 18.4

Barriers to Entry Limit the Supply of Medical Workers

Restrictions associated with entering the medical profession limit the supply of workers. This causes a decrease in the supply of medical workers from q_1 to q_2, and an increase in wages from w_1 to w_2.

For instance, pediatric care units, oncology centers, organ transplants, and a host of other services require that the hospital develop a particular expertise. The availability of specialized care is, of course, a good thing. However, as hospitals become larger and more highly specialized, competitive pressures subside and they are able to charge higher prices.

The market power of suppliers is held in check to some extent by insurance companies, Medicare, and Medicaid. Also, some services are not reimbursed by insurance. The insurance companies push back against medical charges by limiting the amount they reimburse, and Medicare and Medicaid also place strict limits on the billable amounts for certain treatments. Elective medical services, such as Lasik surgery, are not reimbursed and are more subject to competition. Lasik surgery fees have been falling due to intense competition and consumer demand that is quite elastic. Still, overall medical costs have continued to rise faster than inflation.

 ## ECONOMICS IN THE REAL WORLD

Economics in the Real World: Medical Tourism

Medical tourism has grown explosively over the last twenty years as the quality of medical care has improved rapidly around the globe and international travel has become more convenient. Today it is possible to have cardiac surgery done in India, your hip replaced in Egypt, and a face-lift performed in Rio de Janeiro. Supply and demand help explain the rapid growth of medical tourism. There are two reasons why persons seek medical care abroad: costs and wait times.

Medical care costs as much as 90 percent less in a developing country than in the United States. Second, long wait times exist for certain procedures in countries with universal health care. Avoiding waiting times is the leading factor for medical tourism from the United Kingdom and Canada, whereas in the United States the main reason for traveling are the cheaper prices found abroad. Many procedures performed abroad cost a fraction of the price in developed countries. A liver transplant in the United States can cost more than $250,000, but it costs less than $100,000 in Taiwan. Elective surgeries such as Lasik and face-lifts are also available at a fraction of the cost in the United States.

Some insurance plans do not cover orthopedic surgery, making knee and hip replacement surgery prohibitively expensive in the United States. In other cases, such as cosmetic surgery, the procedure is entirely elective. This has led to the creation of medical "safaris" where patients go to South Africa or South America for cosmetic surgery, stay at luxurious accommodations, and take in the savannah or rainforests while recuperating. The patient returns to the United States after a couple of weeks looking refreshed and younger, with no one the wiser.

Medical tourists also travel because they do not want to wait. In Canada the wait times for hip replacements can exceed six months. Canadian patients with the means can get the operation performed in a matter of weeks overseas or in the United States. ✳

PRACTICE WHAT YOU KNOW

Demand for Health Care: How Would Universal Health Care Alter the Demand for Medical Care?

Question: Suppose that the United States scraps its current health care system and all citizens are 100 percent covered for all medical care with no co-payments or deductibles. How would the new system affect the demand for medical care? Illustrate your answer on a graph.

Answer: Without any co-payment or deductibles, the patient's out-of-pocket expense is zero. Society would pick up the tab through taxes. As a result, the quantity demanded by the patient increases from point A to point B.

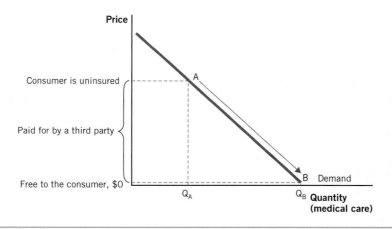

Case Studies in Health Care Economics

In this section we apply what we've learned to two important health care issues. First, we look at the universal health care debate by comparing the health care systems in the United States and Canada. Then we examine the shortage of human organs available for transplant.

Single-Payer versus Private Health Care

Rationing is fact of life because we live in a world of scarcity. The simplest way of thinking about the health care issue is to understand how different rationing mechanisms are used in medical care. In the United States the primary rationing mechanism is the ability to pay. One consequence of using prices to ration medical care is that close to 50 million U.S. citizens forgo some medical care because they lack insurance or the means to pay for care on their own. In Canada, no citizen lacks the means to pay because medical care is paid for by taxes. This does not mean that medical care is unlimited. In Canada rationing occurs through wait times, fewer doctors, and limited availability of certain drugs. As in almost all things economic, there is a trade-off. No medical system will create the perfect set of incentives. In the United States, a large majority of its citizens has the means to pay for medical care, access to some of the best medical facilities in the world, and relatively short wait times. However, this same system marginalizes the health care that the poorest members of society receive.

In Canada each citizen is treated equally, but access to immediate medical treatment is more restricted. We have seen that Canada spends far less than the United States per capita ($3,596 versus $6,933). How does Canada provide medical care to every citizen at approximately half the price? The government sets the rates that are paid to medical providers. Physicians are not permitted to have private practices. In an effort to eliminate outside competition and to prevent wages from rising with the market, physician salaries are capped. In addition, hospitals receive grants from the government to cover the costs of providing care. This system, where there is only a single payer, makes the government the single buyer of most medical care. Under Canada's Health Act, government funding is required for medically necessary care, but only if it is delivered in hospitals or by physicians. This means that the Canadian government funds about 70 percent of all medical expenses, with the remaining 30 percent of costs related to prescription medications, long-term care, physical therapy, and dental care. In these areas private insurance operates much the same way it does in the United States.

A single buyer, as we have previously learned, is a monopsony. The Canadian government uses the leverage it has as a monopsonist to set compensation levels for physicians below the competitive market wage rate, and provides grants to hospitals for the services they provide. Predictably, these cost-containment measures have an influence on physician flows. Medical schools in the United States produce a relatively constant number of new physicians each year, but the supply is not enough to keep up with the demand for physicians in the United States. U.S. demand exceeds the supply by approximately 30 percent annually. As a result, physicians flow into the United States each year, and one of the major suppliers is Canada. Since Canada caps physician compensation, physicians in Canada are 20 times more likely to emigrate to the United States than their U.S. counterparts are to emigrate to Canada.

Patients seeking medical care in Canada are also far more likely to seek additional care in the United States than U.S. citizens are to seek care in Canada. This result may strike you as odd. After all, Canada has national health care and health services are covered under the Canadian Health Act. However, there is a difference between access and availability. Canada keeps a tight control over medical costs, and that means that people with conditions that are not life-threatening often require extended waits. Ironically, closely related services that are not regulated, such as veterinarian visits, provide pet owners access to medical care without waiting. For example, dogs in Canada have no trouble getting MRIs and chemotherapy quickly.

ECONOMICS IN THE REAL WORLD

Health Care Lessons from France

In 2000 the World Health Organization ranked every country's health care system. France came in first. The United States finished 37th out of 191 nations. When the WHO study was questioned, researchers in London decided to control for longevity and tried to determine how effective each system was at preventing deaths with good medical care. In the second study, done in 2008, researchers looked at health care in 19 industrialized nations. France, again, finished first. The United States was last.

What separates the United States from France? Not as much as you might think. The French balk at any notion that they have socialized health care. France, like the United States, relies on both private insurance and government insurance. Also, just like in America, people generally get their private insurance through their employer. Both health care systems value choice and patients can choose preferred providers and specialists. What is different is that the French government secures most of the medical funding through income and payroll taxes. Roughly 70 percent of medical charges are paid for by the government, with the remaining 30 percent covered by private insurance. 99.9 percent of French people hold private insurance as opposed to 85 percent of Americans.

Another difference between the French and American systems is how coverage works for the sickest patients. In France, the most serious conditions are 100 percent covered. In the United States, patient out-of-pocket expenses for the most serious conditions often require supplemental insurance, and experimental procedures and drugs are rarely covered. As a result, the French report that they are quite satisfied with their health care system, while similar surveys in the United States find a much more mixed reaction, with roughly half the population happy and the other half concerned.

Of course, none of this comes cheap. In France, the average person pays slightly over 20 percent of their income to support the national health care system. Since French firms must pick up a large chunk of the health care tab, they are more reluctant to hire workers. In the United States, workers do not pay as much in taxes, but they do pay more for medical care than the French when you add in the costs of private insurance and higher out-of-pocket expenses. The lower overall costs of providing medical care in France can be traced to the government controlling how much hospitals and providers receive in compensation. In other words, the French do a better job of using monopsony power to control costs. Despite the use of monopsony power, health care costs in France have risen rapidly and this has led to cuts in services in order to help keep the system solvent.[1] ✳

---

1. Source: Joseph Shapiro, National Public Radio, July 11, 2008. Available at http://www.npr.org/templates/story/story.php?storyId=92419273.

The Human Organ Shortage

Many altruistic people donate their blood each year to help save the lives of tens of thousands of people. Their generosity makes transplants and surgeries possible. Unfortunately, the same cannot be said for organ donations. The demand for replacement organs exceeds the supply made available each year, resulting in thousands of deaths. Many of these deaths would be preventable if people were allowed to sell organs. However, the National Organ Transplant Act of 1984 makes it illegal. Restrictions do not cover the entire body. People can sell platelets, sperm, and ova. In those markets prices determine who donates. With blood, kidneys, livers, and lungs, the donors are not paid. This has created two unintended consequences. First, many people die unnecessarily. In the United States, close to 5,000 patients on transplant waiting lists die each year. Second, demand for human organs has created a billion-dollar-a-year black market.

Let's consider the market for kidneys. Figure 18.5 examines how the supply and demand for human kidneys work. Almost everyone has two kidneys and life can continue almost normally with only one healthy kidney. There are risks associated with donation, including complications from the surgery, recovery, and no longer having a backup kidney. However, since there are 300 million "spare" kidneys in the United States, there is a large pool of potential donors who are good matches for recipients waiting for a transplant.

Since kidneys cannot be legally bought and sold, the supply curve does not respond to price. As a result, the supply curve becomes a vertical line at

FIGURE 18.5

The Supply and Demand for Human Organs

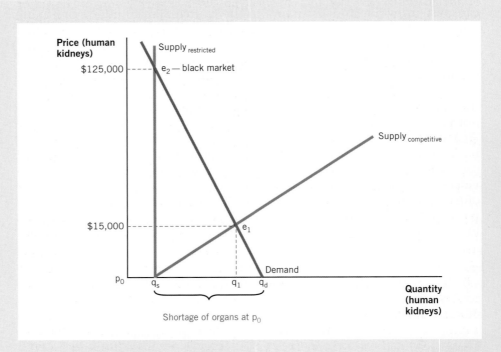

point q_s. Notice that the quantity of kidneys supplied is not zero. Many people donate kidneys to friends and family members in need. Others agree to enter into exchange programs where they donate a kidney to someone they don't know in exchange for someone else agreeing to donate a kidney to a friend or family member. Exchange programs help to provide better matches so that the kidney transplant is less likely to be rejected by the recipient. And a few altruistic persons donate their kidneys to complete strangers. Nevertheless, the quantity supplied still falls short of quantity demanded, since $q_d > q_s$ at a price of p_0.

Markets would normally reconcile a shortage by increasing prices. An equilibrium market price of $15,000 is shown. Economists have estimated that this would be the market price if the sale of kidneys were legal in the United States. Since the sale of kidneys is illegal, the shortage illustrated in Figure 18.5 exists. Over 3,000 people die each year in this country waiting for a kidney transplant. Many others experience a lower quality of life while waiting to receive a kidney. Because patients waiting for human organs will eventually die without a transplant, a black market for kidney transplants exists outside the United States. However, the price—which is typically $100,000 or more—requires doctors, hospitals, staff, and patients to circumvent the law. As a consequence, the black market price is much higher than it would be if a competitive market existed.

ECONOMICS IN THE REAL WORLD

Selling Ova to Pay for College

Young, bright American women with college loans and credit card debt can pay off their debts by donating their ova. The process is relatively simple. The donor is paid to travel to a fertility clinic where an operation is performed to remove pairs of ova, which are then placed inside the womb of an infertile couple. With luck the procedure works. The donor receives between $5,000 and $15,000, depending on her track record as a donor. Those whose ova have been successfully implanted and lead to the birth of a healthy child are in high demand.

Despite the success of ova donations, concerns about equity and ethics have made the sale of many vital organs illegal. In its simplest form, why should the affluent, who can afford to pay for organ transplants live, while the poor, who also need organ transplants, die? That hardly seems fair. Unfortunately, altruism alone has not supplied enough organs to meet demand, leading to a shortage of many vital organs. Since we continue to experiences shortages of human organs, the supply of organs must be rationed. Whether the rationing takes place through markets, waiting in line, or some other mechanism is really a matter of efficiency. As a result, using markets, in some form, may be one way to prevent avoidable deaths. However, the ethical considerations are considerable. For example, if organs can be bought and sold, what would prevent coercion from being used to force people to sell their organs? Of course, the ethical dilemma goes away if viable artificial organs can be created. Medical science is on track to solve the organ shortage. In the meantime, if you are uncomfortable with markets determining the price, remember that relying solely on altruism is not enough. If we really want to increase the supply of organs, we need to try incentives. Some proposals include allowing people to receive tax deductions, college

The Black Market for Organs

Law & Order: Special Victims Unit

In one inspired episode of *SVU* the officers try to track down a sleazy kidney dealer. What makes the episode compelling is the tension between doing what the law requires—stopping an illegal kidney transplant in the middle of surgery—and subsequently wrestling with watching the patient suffer as a result. In addition, the officers interview the dealer, the physician, patients on kidney waiting lists, and an administrator of the national kidney wait list. Their opinions, which run a wide gamut, allow the viewer to experience all of the emotions and arguments for and against the purchase of kidneys. Each character tugs on your emotions in a different way. The sleazy dealer

proudly proclaims that he was making his customers happy and that the officers wouldn't be so judgmental if one of their family members needed a kidney. The physician who does the transplant explains that he is not making money but saving lives. The patients all know where they can get an illegal kidney, but most accept their fate within the current system. The administrator of the wait list notes that "they have enough trouble getting people to volunteer as it is. What would happen if donors learned that we had made an exception and approved the transplant of an illegally purchased kidney?" By the end of the episode we see that the economic and ethical dimensions of the issue are not straightforward.

PRACTICE WHAT YOU KNOW

Human Organ Shortage: Liver Transplants

Question: Most liver transplants are done using cadaveric organs. However, liver organ transplants are also possible using live donors. Donating part of a live liver is major surgery that lasts between 4 and 12 hours. The complication rate for the donor is small, but the recovery time is typically 2–3 months. Not surprisingly, a shortage of live livers for transplant still exists. What solutions can you think of that would cause more people to agree to donate part of their liver to help save the life of someone else?

Answer: One answer would be to repeal the National Organ Transplant Act. This would create a market for livers and set a price that would eliminate the shortage. There are also ways to incentivize donations by allowing donors to claim a tax deduction equal to the value of the liver donated, or receive scholarships for themselves or members of their family.

Life Insurance: Getting the Right Life Insurance for You

Life insurance protects your family in the event of your death. Most people try to buy enough life insurance to make sure that their family will be able to manage financially without them. Typically, this means that they buy enough insurance to pay off the mortgage on the house they own, set up a fund so their children will be able to attend college, and provide a reserve fund for other expenses.

Buying the right life insurance is usually presented as a choice between term insurance and whole-life insurance. Don't be fooled. You should buy term insurance. We'll tell you why in a bit, but first let's review the differences between these two types of policies.

A term policy includes only life insurance. A whole-life policy combines a term policy with an investment component. The term policy provides a fixed benefit upon the death of the insured. A term policy is in force for a specific term that may range up to 30 years, after which the policy expires. A whole-life policy buys you a specific amount of coverage that does not expire and combines this insurance with an investment component. Whole-life policies are typically sold as investment vehicles that you can tap into if you need to borrow cash later in life. This may sound appealing, but it is a bad investment. Commission rates and fees are very high. If you want to invest your money, you can find stock and bond funds on your own with far lower fees and, correspondingly, much higher rates of return.

Premiums for term insurance are low for anyone in good health before age 50. Beyond 50, term premiums rise quickly as the rate of death for any given age rises. By the time someone reaches age 65, term insurance is very expensive.

The real value of term insurance can be seen by making a direct comparison. Suppose you are a 30-year-old in great health. You can purchase a $1 million policy for a 20-year term for under $1,000 annually, or a $1 million whole-life policy for $10,000 a year. If you invest the $9,000 difference, your investment will grow faster than it would as part of a whole-life policy. After 20 years you will have over $450,000, assuming an 8 percent return. Your whole-life policy at the end of 20 years is only worth $325,000. You have an extra $125,000 saved up. If you are also doing the right things like paying down your mortgage and saving for college, there will come a point where you need less insurance. In a sense, you become self-insured. Term insurance is the cheapest bridge to that point. Whole-life forces you to save; for some people, that commitment mechanism may be worth pursuing. For others, term insurance is the path to greater long-term wealth.

scholarships, or even guaranteed health care in exchange for donating an organ. All of these suggestions reduce the ethical dilemma while still harnessing the power of incentives to save lives.

Conclusion

Our primary focus in this chapter has been on behavioral changes at the micro level. However, health care straddles the boundary between microeconomic analysis, which focuses on individual behavior, and macroeconomics, where society's overarching concern is how best to spend so large an amount of money. Collectively, how individual participants (from patients to medical providers, insurance companies, and the government) deal with different health care issues affects how well our overall health care system functions. Supply and demand work just fine in outlining the incentives that participants face when considering health care options. What complicates the analysis, and makes it a multifaceted exercise, is the impact third parties have on the incentives that patients face. Moreover, health decisions are an unavoidable part of each of our lives. Medical expenditures account for one out of every six dollars spent in the United States. Therefore, fundamental changes to the health care system will have a large impact—or macro effect—on our economy.

ANSWERING THE BIG QUESTIONS

1. What makes health care different from other industries?

✳The widespread use of insurance alters the incentives that consumers and producers face when making health care decisions. Consumers pay premiums up front and much smaller deductibles and co-payments when seeking medical care. Producers receive the bulk of their revenue from intermediaries such as insurance companies. The result is a system where consumers demand more medical care because they are insured and many providers have an incentive to order additional tests or procedures that may not be absolutely necessary.

2. Why does asymmetric information make it difficult to administer health care?

✳Adverse selection, or insuring at-risk patients, complicates how medical insurance is structured. Since insurance companies do not want to take on customers with pre-existing conditions, they typically limit the amount of care new customers are eligible for to avoid the incentive for patients with known risks (to them) from buying insurance only when needed. Likewise, insurance companies try to structure their plans to align the incentives of patients to seek care only when they need it. This can be done by establishing deductibles and co-payments that are high enough to discourage unnecessary trips to the doctor or seeking additional procedures. To solve a moral hazard problem you have to fix the incentive structure. This explains why many insurance companies encourage preventive care; it lowers medical costs. It also explains why insurance companies impose payment limits on preventable conditions.

✳Inelastic demand for many medical services, combined with third-party payments that significantly lower the out-of-pocket expenses to consumers, give rise to a serious moral hazard problem where patients demand more medical care than is medically advisable. As a consequence of how health care is structured and the moral hazard it creates, the United States devotes a far larger share of its national output to health care than is optimal.

3. How do demand and supply contribute to high medical costs?

*Inelastic demand and third-party payments help explain why medical expenses have risen so rapidly, while licensing helps explain why the supply of medical services is limited. The combination of third-party payments and inelastic demand for medical care increases the quantity of medical care demanded, since both of these factors result in increased expenditures. As we have learned previously, more demand means higher prices. In addition, licensing requirements limit the supply of health care providers. This provides a supply-side explanation leading to increased medical expenditures. In addition, hospital charges are rarely subject to competitive pressures. In many smaller communities, there is only one local hospital, clinic, or specialist nearby. This gives providers market power which they can use in setting prices.

CONCEPTS YOU SHOULD KNOW

Adverse selection (p. 523)   Moral hazard (p. 525)   Principal-agent problem (p. 524)
Asymmetric information (p. 523)

QUESTIONS FOR REVIEW

1. What is asymmetric information? Why does it matter for medical care?

2. Give one example each of adverse selection, moral hazard, and the principal-agent problem.

3. For each of the examples you gave in question 2, discuss a solution that lessens the asymmetric information problem.

4. Describe why the marginal product of medical care declines as medical expenditures rise.

5. What are two primary reasons why health care demand has increased dramatically over the last twenty years?

6. What is a supply-related reason that leads to high medical care costs?

7. What are the two primary ways that health care is rationed?

STUDY PROBLEMS

1. Suppose that a medical specialist charges $300 per consultation. If your insurance charges you a $25 deductible, what is the marginal cost of your consultation? Suppose that a second patient has a different policy that requires a 25 percent co-insurance but no deductible. What is the second patient's marginal cost of the consultation? Which patient is more likely to see the specialist?

2. Newer automobiles have many safety features, including antilock brakes, side air bags, traction control, and rear backup sensors, to help prevent accidents. Do these safety features lead the drivers of newer vehicles to drive more safely? In your answer, consider how an increased number of safety features affects the problem of moral hazard.

3. A customer wants a new medical insurance policy. Even though the customer has a good health history, the insurance company requires a medical exam before coverage can be extended. Why would the insurance company insist on a medical exam?

4. Describe whether the following medical services have elastic or inelastic demand.
   a. An annual physical for someone between the ages of 20 and 35
   b. An MRI used to detect cancer
   c. Removing a noncancerous mole on your back
   d. Seeing a physician when your child has a 104-degree temperature

5. Most people have two working kidneys. Humans need only one working kidney to survive. If the sale of kidneys were legalized, what would happen to the price and the number of kidneys sold in the market? Would a shortage of kidneys continue to exist?

6. An isolated community has one hospital. The next-closest hospital is two hours away. Given what you have learned about monopoly, what prices would you expect the hospital to charge? How much care do you expect it to provide? Compare the prices and amount of care provided to those provided by a comparably sized hospital in a major metropolitan area where competition is prevalent.

7. One insurance plan costs $100 a month and has a $50 co-payment for all services. Another insurance plan costs $50 a month and requires patients to pay 15 percent co-insurance. A customer is trying to decide which plan to purchase. Which plan would the customer select with an anticipated $200 a month in medical bills? What about $600 a month in medical bills? Set up an equation to determine the monthly amount of medical expenses where the consumer would be indifferent between the two plans.

8. For each of the following situations, determine whether adverse selection, moral hazard, or the principal-agent problem is at work.
   a. You decide to buy a scalped ticket before a concert, but you are not entirely sure the ticket is legal.
   b. A contractor takes a long time to finish the construction work he promised after you gave him his final payment.
   c. You hire a neighborhood teenager to mow your grass once a week over the summer while you are traveling. The teenager mows your grass every three weeks instead.

CREDITS

CHAPTER 1

5 John Lund/Stephanie Roeser/Getty Images; 6 Phang Kim Shan | Dreamstime.com; 7 top Nguyen Thai | Dreamstime.com; 7 bottom Visions of America, LLC / Alamy; 8 Corbis Premium RF / Alamy; 9 Haywiremedia | Dreamstime.com; 12 Paramount / The Kobal Collection; 13 Linqong | Dreamstime.com; 14 Joe Robbins/Getty Images; 15 top Yusputra | Dreamstime.com; 15 bottom Stromcarlson / Wikimedia; 16 Jacqueline Larma / AP Photo; 17 Stockbyte/ Getty Images; 18 Courtesy of Dirk Mateer; 19 Seanyu | Dreamstime.com; 20 Andres Rodriguez | Dreamstime.com

CHAPTER 2

27 Archive Holdings Inc. /The Image Bank/Getty Images; 29 top M.L. Watts/Wikimedia; 29 bottom Nikolai Sorokin | Dreamstime.com; 30 Paul Springett / Alamy; 36 Lou-Foto / Alamy; 42 Dreamworks / Album/Newscom; 43 top UK History / Alamy; 43 bottom Philcold | Dreamstime.com; 44 left Teraberb | Dreamstime.com; 44 right Yuri Arcurs | Dreamstime.com; 47 top Globe Photos/ZUMAPRESS/ Newscom; 47 bottom Monkeybusi . . . | Dreamstime.com; 48 © Boeing

CHAPTER 3

67 AP Photo/The Day, Sean D. Elliot; 68 All Canada Photos / Alamy; 69 top Getty Images/First Light; 69 bottom Peter Horree / Alamy; 70 William Perry | Dreamstime.com; 71 Maren Caruso/Photodisc/Getty Images; 75 Edith Layland | Dreamstime.com; 76 Sean Gallup/Getty Images; 76 Bookworm Classics / Alamy; 76 sselimaksan / iStockphoto .com; 77 John DeFeo/iStockphoto.com; 79 Polygram/ Warner/Silver Pictures / The Kobal Collection/ James Bridges; 80 left Radius Images / Alamy; 80 right Showface | Dreamstime.com; 84 Lucian Coman | Dreamstime.com; 85 AP Photo/Ted S. Warren; 88 Stockbyte/Getty Images;

91 Crankshaft © 2005 King Features 93 AP Photo / IBM, Ho; 96 Hugoht / Dreamstime.com; 97 R. Gino Santa Maria | Dreamstime.com;

CHAPTER 4

106 © Columbia Pictures/courtesy Everett Collection; 107 Allstar Picture Library / Alamy 108 top Blaircwh | Dreamstime.com; 108 bottom Cobalt88 | Dreamstime .com; 109 top Evan-Amos /Wikimedia Commons; 109 bottom Seanyu | Dreamstime.com; 110 (table) Wisconsinart | Dreamstime.com; 110 (table) Oleksiy Mark | Dreamstime.com; 110 (table) David Lee / Alamy; 110 (table) IFCAR / Wikimedia Commons; 111 © 20th Century Fox Film Corp. All rights reserved. Courtesy: Everett Collection; 114 Mathew Hayward | Dreamstime.com; 116 left Rick Rhay/iStockphoto.com; 116 right Johnfoto | Dreamstime.com; 117 Wikimedia Commons; 118 (table 4.2) Mathew Hayward | Dreamstime.com; 118 (table 4.2) Johnfoto | Dreamstime.com; 118 (table 4.2) Wikimedia Commons; 118 (table 4.2) Rick Rhay/iStockphoto.com; 124 top © 20th Century Fox. All rights reserved/courtesy Everett Collection; 124 bottom Barbara Helgason | Dreamstime.com; 125 Geoffrey Kidd / Alamy; 126 Eliza Snow/iStockphoto.com; 127 Aleksandar Mijatovic | Dreamstime.com; 127 (table 4.4) Steven von Niederhausern / iStockphoto.com; 127 (table 4.4) Ragoarts | Dreamstime .com; 127 (table 4.4) Svetlana Foote | Dreamstime.com; 128 (table 4.5)Steve Shepard/iStockphoto.com; 128 (table 4.5) Robert Convery / Alamy; 128 (table 4.5) Chaoss | Dreamstime .com; 128 (table 4.5) Ljupco Smokovski | Dreamstime.com; 128 (table 4.5) Olga Lyubkina/iStockphoto.com; 128 (table 4.5) Daniel R. Burch/iStockphoto.com; 128 http://www.flickr.com/photos/turkeypants/135934601/ sizes/m/in/photostream/ 130 top Jack Guez/AFP/Getty Images; 130 bottom Daniel Bendjy/iStockphoto.com; 132 Yuri Arcurs | Dreamstime.com; 132 (table 4.6) Yuri Arcurs | Dreamstime.com; 132 (table 4.6) Ildar Sagdejev/Wikimedia; 132 (table 4.6) Julie Feinstein | Dreamstime.com; 134 George Peters/iStockphoto.com; 135 PSL Images / Alamy; 136 Rich Legg/iStockphoto.com; 138 Jeffry W. Myers/Corbis

CHAPTER 5

143 The Gallery Collection/Corbis; 144 Chhobi | Dreamstime.com; 145 (table 5.1) Chhobi | Dreamstime .com; 145 (table 5.1) AP Photo; 145 (table 5.1) Inga Nielsen | Dreamstime.com; 145 (table 5.1) Justin Sullivan/Getty

Courtesy of Everett Collection / Everett Collection; **334 bottom** Scott Olson/Getty Images; **335** Tripplaar Kristoffer/SIPA/Newscom; **337** AP Photo/Charles Agel

343 ZUMA Press/Newscom; **345 top** iStockphoto; **345 bottom** Emile Wamsteker/Bloomberg via Getty Images; **346** Geraint Lewis / Alamy; **353** Monkey Business Images | Dreamstime.com; **354** Serafino Mozzo/iStockphoto; **355** Robin Platzer/ Twin Images/LFI/Photoshot/Newscom; **356a** credit TK **356b** Anthony Seebaran/iStockphoto; **356c** Stanley Marquardt / Alamy; **356d** AP Photo/Tom Gannam; **356e** Lynn Watson | Dreamstime.com; **356f** Carlos Gawronski/iStockphoto; **356g** David Paul Morris/ Bloomberg via Getty Images; **358** Universal / The Kobal Collection; **360** Atm2003 | Dreamstime.com; **361** Pedro Antonio Salaverría Calahorra | Dreamstime.com; **362** RW3

WENN Photos/Newscom; **363 left** Bob Fila and James F. Quinn, KRT/Newscom; **363 right** Michael Neelon(misc) / Alamy; **365** Johnny Rockets/PRNewsFoto/AP Photo

371 Stephen Krow/iStockphoto; **373** iStockphoto; **377** Jack Sullivan / Alamy; **378** Reuters/Corbis; **380** Icholakov | Dreamstime.com; **383** Murder By Numbers, Ryan Gosling, 2002, © Warner Brothers/courtesy Everett Collection; **385 top** AP Photo/ Sergey Ponomarev; **386** The Dark Knight, Heath Ledger as The Joker, 2008. © Warner Bros./ Courtesy Everett Collection; **387** Nickilford/iStockphoto; **388** TheCrimsonMonkey/iStockphoto; **390** Scott Olson/ Getty Images; **392** Richard Levine / Alamy; **393** Tim Boyle/ Bloomberg/Getty Images; **394** Brandon Alms | Dreamstime .com; **395** Google/ZUMA Press/Newscom; **402** Stephen Strathdee/i-Stockphoto.com